T0301007

ROUTLEDGE LIBRARY EDITIONS: TRADE UNIONS

Volume 3

THE RAILWAYMEN

THE RAILWAYMEN

Volume 2:
The Beeching Era and After
The History of the National
Union of Railwaymen

PHILIP S. BAGWELL

Routledge
Taylor & Francis Group

LONDON AND NEW YORK

First published in 1982 by George Allen & Unwin Ltd.

This edition first published in 2023
by Routledge
4 Park Square, Milton Park, Abingdon, Oxon OX14 4RN

and by Routledge
605 Third Avenue, New York, NY 10158

Routledge is an imprint of the Taylor & Francis Group, an informa business

British Library Cataloguing in Publication Data
A catalogue record for this book is available from the British Library

ISBN: 978-1-032-37553-3 (Set)
ISBN: 978-1-032-41080-7 (Volume 3) (hbk)
ISBN: 978-1-032-41108-8 (Volume 3) (pbk)
ISBN: 978-1-003-35616-5 (Volume 3) (ebk)

DOI: 10.4324/9781003356165

Publisher's Note
The publisher has gone to great lengths to ensure the quality of this reprint but points out that some imperfections in the original copies may be apparent.

Disclaimer
The publisher has made every effort to trace copyright holders and would welcome correspondence from those they have been unable to trace.

THE RAILWAYMEN

Volume 2: The Beeching Era and After

The History of the National Union of Railwaymen

BY

PHILIP S. BAGWELL

London
GEORGE ALLEN & UNWIN
Boston   Sydney

George Allen & Unwin (Publishers) Ltd,
40 Museum Street, London WC1A 1LU, UK

George Allen & Unwin (Publishers) Ltd,
Park Lane. Hemel Hempstead, Herts HP2 4TE. UK

Allen & Unwin Inc.,
9 Winchester Terrace. Winchester, Mass 01890. USA

George Allen & Unwin Australia Pty Ltd,
8 Napier Street. North Sydney, NSW 2060, Australia

First published in 1982

British Library Cataloguing in Publication Data

Bagwell, Philip S.
    The railwaymen.
Vol. 2: The Beeching era and after
1. National Union of Railwaymen – History
I. Title
331.88′11′3850941   HD6668.R3
ISBN 0–04–331084–2

Library of Congress Cataloging in Publication Data

Bagwell, Philip Sidney.
    The railwaymen.
Vol. 2 has subtitle: The Beeching era and after.
Includes bibliographies and index.
1. National Union of Railwaymen. I. Title.
HD6668.R3B3   331.88′11385′0941   65–2331
ISBN 0–04–331084–2 (v. 2)   AACR1

Set in 10 on 11 point Times by Grove Graphics. Tring
and printed in Great Britain
by Mackays of Chatham

CONTENTS

LIST OF ILLUSTRATIONS

LIST OF ILLUSTRATIONS

FOREWORD

In this second volume of Dr Bagwell's survey of the history of the NUR, covering the period since publication of the first volume in 1963, the story of a struggle is recorded. The vastly important role of the union within the general Labour movement comes out clearly because the NUR has been always in the forefront of protection of workers' rights as well as fighting to strengthen the political influence of the unions in British politics.

In the transport industry, especially in the railway sector, we have persistently and often expensively fought to maintain the vital part publicly owned transport resources play in the life of the nation's industry and people.

The campaigning, negotiating, urging and acting function of our union has had to be carried through without pause. And since Dr Bagwell completed his work, around the middle of 1980, we have been faced with crisis on all fronts – industrial, legal, political and within the union.

Recession in the economy, miserly support of the railways from government, pressures to cut and reduce and the still-strong bias towards private road transport and all its related parts have accumulated to present us with very great problems. Our union has continued its pressure directly with government Ministers, through the NUR-sponsored group of MPs and strongly through the various media, including the press, radio and television, to stress the urgent need for financial support to be increased. Joint approaches with the British Railways Board have been made to the government.

Despite this the Conservative government has continued with its doctrinaire approach to transport in two Acts of Parliament. This has been in line with its actions concerning other nationalised industries. We have countered this by creating a tripartite alliance with the steelworkers and the miners to defend our industries and to lean on the government to give us financial support. Government Ministers have paid lip-service to the arguments we put forward, but persisted with their policies. The National Freight Corporation has been denationalised. Our members in National Carriers have by this action had their whole futures put at risk. Fortunately, an alternative plan has been put forward to retain the NFC as a viable company based on shareholding by the workers in the undertaking.

The 1981 Transport Act contained clauses to introduce private

capital into the four major subsidiary companies of the BRB –
British Transport Hotels, Sealink UK Limited, Hovercraft and
the BR Property Board – as well as removing effective control of
the British Transport Docks Board.

The NUR has thousands of members in these undertakings and
through this political dogmatism of the government our members'
jobs, pay and conditions have been made subject to the characteristic uncertainties of private sector management. And more interference is foreshadowed in the 1981 Act which gives sweeping
powers to government not only to determine the character and
pace of the transfer of these businesses to the private sector but
also to compel the privatisation of other sectors of BRB activity;
British Rail Engineering Limited is in that category.

We condemned these regressive measures, and sponsored MPs
in Parliament resisted them line-by-line. In the end the government brought in the guillotine to get through the legislation. The
future of publicly owned transport has been put in serious
jeopardy with inescapable consequences for our members.

We have not given in by any means and have continued our
campaigning in by supporting TUC rallies of protest and taking
a leading part in the large-scale transport lobby of Parliament on
6 April 1981.

Inside and outside Parliament we have propagated the case for
an expansion of electrification and for a start to be made on the
Channel Tunnel. The final report of the joint BRB – Department
of Transport Working Party on main line electrification, published at the end of 1980, concluded that there should be a substantial programme of main line electrification and that it would
be 'worthwhile' as an investment. In mid-June 1981 the government approved in principle a limited programme of further electrification. The House of Commons transport committee, in February 1981, supported a single-track railway tunnel Channel Link.
These developments have vindicated the NUR's confidence in
the future of the railway system. But doubt remains on the question of adequate financial support to maintain the system and to
provide for the massive investment required.

Since the 1980 pay settlement attempts have been made to
force the union to accept productivity conditions to help to
generate investment funds from inside the industry; that is, to
place an intolerable burden on the staff to submit to economies
which would result in the loss of jobs. We have said we will not
trade jobs. Our consistent aim has been to discuss the whole
question of productivity, including changes in working practices,
but only on the condition that the basic pay of the staff is raised

sufficiently to reduce excessive overtime and rest day working. Coupled with that is the demand for a shorter working week and longer holidays. We have sought to establish common ground with our colleagues in ASLEF and the TSSA. We have gone further and proposed a formal federation of the three unions in line with our AGM policy decision of 1972. With the aid of TUC, the NUR and ASLEF have now agreed a federal structure with the object of creating one union.

In the meantime, the 1981 pay claim was pursued through the machinery to the point of a hearing before the Railway Staff National Tribunal. At this hearing I urged an immediate substantial increase in basic rates for all BRB staff; an early restoration of the value of the 1975 settlement; the abolition of the Railman's rate of pay; and that the BRB should immediately return to the formula for calculating the London Allowance agreed in 1974. I pointed out that 'many railwaymen are on rates of pay which scarcely allow them to earn more than they would get if they were unemployed; and many more are caught up in the poverty trap'. I also stated that 'the NUR and its members are tired of BR's posturing in the role of "good employer" while hiding behind the industry's financial position in order to avoid fulfilling their commitment to better pay and conditions. Their attitude is breeding a growing feeling of resentment and frustration amongst my members as they see their living standards falling and they are determined in the current pay round to fight to achieve a settlement which they consider just.

Since May 1979 we have suffered severe onslaughts by the Conservative government. Yet despite the unpopularity of the government it was a source of disappointment that we found the Labour Party – the only alternative to the Conservatives – divided on the question of reforms in the party's structure and constitution, including the method of electing the leadership. The 1980 Labour Party annual conference was a frustrating one for the union where these important matters were concerned. The NUR submissions to the Labour Party's commission of inquiry were widely circulated in our leaflet *Towards a New Compact for Labour*. We supported radical changes in the party's policy-making procedures aimed at permitting a far more democratic and responsible consideration of party policy than previously was the case. We called for changes in the composition of the NEC of the party, designed to include proper representation of both rank-and-file activists and the Parliamentary Labour Party. Unfortunately, the commission declined to take up the challenge of these proposals. The conference also approved mandatory reselection of MPs and failed to come to a clear decision on the method of electing the Party Leader. There was a narrow majority for an electoral college arrangement for the Leader's election. But conference reached no agreement on the detailed allocation of votes between the three main elements in the party's structure – trade unions, constituency parties and the Parliamentary Labour Party. On a trade union initiative, supported by the NUR, it was finally resolved that a special conference should be held in the early part of 1981 to determine the party's policy on this issue. The special rules revision conference was held on 24 January. Although the period between the two conferences was supposed to allow the movement to deliberate on the matter, the NUR was the only affiliated union to consult the membership through a special general meeting, which took place just before the Wembley Conference.

The NUR policy before the SGM was firmly in favour of the continued election of the leadership by the Parliamentary Labour Party. We considered that Labour MPs were best placed to make the judgement on the personal as well as political qualities of the leadership candidates. We sent three options to branches, before the SGM, for branch amendments if they so wished. The other options, apart from election by the PLP, were an electoral college and the balloting of individual Labour Party members. The SGM, after thorough debate, decided on an electoral college, with the PLP having 50 per cent of the votes and affiliated organisations, mainly trade unions, and the CLPs with 25 per cent each. It was also agreed that voting should be by postal ballot. That became the NUR policy to be conveyed to the Wembley Conference. At that conference, the decision was in favour of an electoral college in which affiliated organisations would hold 40 per cent of the votes and the PLP and the constituency parties would each cast 30 per cent of the votes.

The unsatisfactory decision did not end the debate. Following the Wembley Conference, the Parliamentary Labour Party reaffirmed its commitment to an electoral college formula along the lines supported by the SGM of our union. So unity eluded the movement and the divisions continued. Following the resignation of James Callaghan as Party Leader, in the autumn of 1980, Michael Foot was elected Leader and Denis Healey Deputy Leader. The local government elections in May 1981 resulted in large-scale gains for Labour, particularly in the industrial areas of England and Wales, showing the deep antagonism that had built up against the Conservative government.

At the time of bringing this Foreword to a close, the movement is split and our political power is a blunted instrument – because some in the party seem to care more for their own personal interests than those of the party and the country.

SIDNEY WEIGHELL

July 1981

INTRODUCTION

Volume 1 of *The Railwaymen* told the story of the Amalgamated
Society of Railway Servants (1871–1913) and its successor the
National Union of Railwaymen up to the time of the Guillebaud
Report on railway pay in 1960. Volume 2 carries the story forward
until 1980. The reader may question why a second volume,
covering only twenty years of history, should be needed when the
first volume recorded events in a span of years at least four times
as great. The two decades under review, in fact, witnessed an
unprecedented proliferation of private car ownership and of road
freight haulage which brought about a sharp decline in rail traffic.
The railway industry responded to this challenge by a drastic
slimming down of its services and manpower, and by the adoption
of new technologies such as the high-speed train and the application
of electronics to signalling, communications and freight movement.
The impact of these innovations on the NUR was far-reaching. It is
arguable that in the last twenty years more fundamental changes
took place in the organisation of the union and in its role in British
transport than had occurred in the half-century before Dr Beeching
became Chairman of the British Transport Commission in 1961.

It is hoped, therefore, that this book will serve as a case study
of how an old-established trade union adapted itself to serve the
workforce in a completely transformed industry. The transition
from a labour-intensive to a much more capital-intensive railway
industry affected the composition of the NUR's membership. The
rundown in manpower was less severe in London Transport, in
hotel restaurant car and buffet services, in the bus industry and in
British Transport Docks, than it was in British Rail, so that in
1980 those members who were employed in organisations other
than British Rail formed a larger proportion of total NUR membership than they had done in 1960. For these reasons the account of
the union's work for these members has been given more
prominence in this volume than was the case with its predecessor.

Although, in the main, this account is confined to happenings
of the last twenty years, where new developments, such as the
establishment of the union shop, are considered, it has been thought
worthwhile to examine their origins in earlier years. The ASRS/
NUR has played a larger role than any other British trade union
in influencing legislation on industrial relations. In Volume 1 it
was shown how the union's confrontation with the courts in the

Taff Vale and Osborne cases served as preludes to the introduction of the Trade Disputes Act 1906 and the Trade Union Act 1913. In this volume the story of how the NUR helped to destroy the credibility of the Industrial Relations Act 1971 is told in Chapter 7. During 1899–1901 the ASRS played a leading part in establishing the Labour Party. In the later 1970s – as related in Chapter 12 – the NUR made a significant contribution to the discussion on the revision of the party's constitution.

Running a railway is a team job; writing a railway trade union history likewise involves the co-operation of many people. One name appears on the title page; but the work would not have been completed without the help unstintingly given by a large number of persons. Sidney Weighell, the General Secretary, in several interviews, gave me the benefit of his experience, while leaving me completely free to make my own interpretation of events. I am also grateful for help received from Russell Tuck, Senior Assistant General Secretary, and Frank Cannon and Charles Turnock, Assistant General Secretaries, who gave generously of their time in recalling past events and in reading through parts of the typescript. Lord Greene of Harrow Weald was most helpful in throwing new light on events in the Beeching era and after. Three NUR presidents, Dave Bowman, Alun Rees and Tom Ham, made me better informed on locomotive and workshop problems. Arnold Edmondson placed his unrivalled knowledge of the pay and efficiency discussions at my disposal. Three divisional officers, Roy Trench, Brian Arundel and Andy Dodds, willingly spared the time to answer my many questions. Numerous members of the executive committee and branch officers were interviewed by me, or wrote to me, and thereby gave me a clearer insight into grass-roots opinion. Their help in different ways is acknowledged in the footnotes. I would like to thank Jack Hyland for explaining problems about BT Hotels and catering and George Doherty for giving me the benefit of his expert knowledge on railway accidents. Ron Lewis, MP and Peter Snape, MP put me wise on the activities of the NUR parliamentary group, and I am much indebted to Keith Hill for explaining the nature of his work as Political Liaison Officer. To Frank Moxley, editor of *Transport Review*, I am grateful for his contribution, in Chapter 13, on the NUR's educational activities as well as for the many conversations we have had. Bill Little, who has served as secretary to two General Secretaries, helped to make the past come to life by recalling personal anecdotes. The research staff at Unity House, and especially Mike Evans and Laurie Harries, should find life a little easier now that my task is finished. Though I plagued them with many questions and requests for documents, help was always generously given. Tom Millman and Colin Sheehan of the Publicity Department helped me to find suitable illustrations. Albert Dudley answered innumerable questions on the union's organisation. Dennis Hambly led a dusty life searching for box files in the labyrinth of shelves in the basement. Were I to attempt to name everyone at Unity House who gave me assistance this Introduction would become unduly long. It has been a pleasure to work in an atmosphere of co-operation and friendliness.

I would like to thank Barbara Roweth and Margaret Morris of the Polytechnic of Central London for reading through parts of the typescript and for helping me with the preparation of diagrams. Mick Hamer provided me with valuable information about the early days of Transport 2000 and Professor Christopher Foster explained aspects of the Transport Act of 1968. I am very grateful to Sir Peter Parker for encouraging members of the British Railways Board and their staff at Rail House to provide me with information on the board's standpoint on a number of issues including compulsory trade union membership. I am particularly indebted to David Bowick, J. W. Wickes and D. F. Rugman and their assistants for detailed answers to questions. I am pleased to acknowledge the help given by Dr M. Bonavia and Mr D. Robertson in making clear the early problems of the British Transport Commission. Dr David Rubinstein spared the time from a very busy academic life to read through the entire manuscript and saved me from many pitfalls; I am most grateful. My friend, Jim Forge, also read through the entire script and made helpful suggestions; I wish to thank him, too, for his three maps which will, I am sure, make the text more intelligible. I would like to thank George Ottley for helping with suggestions for the illustrations, and Michael Holdsworth and Cecily Blackley for their help in seeing the book through the press. My acceptance of the task of writing this book was made easier in the knowledge that Irene Ellis, who had the stamina to type out the chapters of Volume 1, was again available. Any author would be lucky to have the services of such a meticulous and skilful typist. I alone accept responsibility for any inaccuracies that remain in the text. Finally, I want to thank my wife, Rosemary, who put up with my being immersed in books and papers instead of being more involved in the work of the family and the home.

ACKNOWLEDGEMENTS FOR ILLUSTRATIONS

Thanks are due to British Rail for permission to reproduce Plates 3, 4, 5, 6 (a), 7, 8, 10 11 (b), 12 and 13, to OPC Ltd for Plates 14 and 15, to the BBC Hulton Picture Library for Plates 2 and 11 (a), and to the British Library for Plate 6 (b).

GLOSSARY

———◆———

AA	Automobile Association
ACAS	Advisory Conciliation and Arbitration Service
ASLEF	Associated Society of Locomotive Engineers and Firemen
ASRS	Amalgamated Society of Railway Servants
AUEW	Amalgamated Union of Engineering Workers
BR	British Railways
BRB	British Railways Board
BRJCC	British Railways Joint Consultative Council
BRS	British Road Services
BTC	British Transport Commission
BTDB	British Transport Docks Board
BTH	British Transport Hotels
CIR	Commission on Industrial Relations
CONGOT	Conciliation Grades other than trainmen
CSEU	Confederation of Shipbuilding and Engineering Unions
DC	District Council
DOE	Department of the Environment
EEC	European Economic Community
FL	Freightliner Ltd
GWR	Great Western Railway
ILO	International Labour Organisation
ITWF	International Transport Workers' Federation
LDC	Local Departmental Committee
LNWR	London and North Western Railway
LT	London Transport
LTE	London Transport Executive
MR	Midland Railway
NALGO	National and Local Government Officers' Association
NBC	National Bus Company
NCOI	National Council of the Omnibus Industry
NUGMW	National Union of General and Municipal Workers
NUM	National Union of Mineworkers
NUR	National Union of Railwaymen
NUS	National Union of Seamen
OMO	One-man operation
PIB	Prices and Incomes Board
RE	Railway Executive
RNC	Railway Negotiating Committee
RSJC	Railway Staff Joint Council
RSNC	Railway Staff National Council
RSNT	Railway Staff National Tribunal
SC	Sectional Council
TGWU	Transport and General Workers' Union

TSSA   Transport Salaried Staffs' Association
UPSS   United Pointsmen's and Signalmen's Society
URS   Union of Railway Signalmen

Conciliation grades: those railway workers of the traffic grades whose
conditions of service were determined by the first Railway Conciliation
Boards after 1907. The salaried, supervisory and workshop staffs were
excluded from the jurisdiction of these boards.

CHAPTER 1

BRITISH TRANSPORT
DEVELOPMENTS SINCE 1945

I

FROM 1 January 1948, when the British Transport Commission began business under the Transport Act of the preceding year, the membership of the NUR was recruited almost exclusively from those working in publicly owned transport undertakings or their ancillary establishments. The prosperity of public transport was therefore a primary concern for the union as, indeed, it was for the nation. It is, thus, appropriate to begin this book by recalling the outstanding developments in British transport in the postwar years. These events provided the backcloth against which the union's officers struggled to secure improvements in the working conditions and financial rewards of the membership.

In the thirty-five years following the conclusion of the Second World War the character of British transport underwent radical change. In the first years of peace the railways were responsible for a greater quantity of freight haulage, measured in ton miles, than were the road hauliers. The first reliable postwar survey was conducted in 1952, when it was found that the railways were responsible for 43 per cent of the ton mileage carried compared with the roads' 37 per cent, the balance being mainly carried by coastal shipping.[1] It is highly probable that the proportion of rail-borne freight was larger in the late 1940s than it was in 1952, since in the first seven years of peace road hauliers were in a better position to expand their capital and their activities than were the railways. In the immediate postwar years most travellers who did not walk or cycle all the way to their destinations used public transport. In 1951 journeys by train, bus, tram and trolley-bus reached the enormous total of 71,000 million miles.[2] As late as 1953 traffic counts conducted by the Ministry of Transport revealed that, of passenger miles travelled other than by foot or bicycle, only 36 per cent were by private car, moped, or motor cycle, compared with 43·3 per cent by bus, tram, or trolleybus, and 20·6 per cent by rail.[3] This was the situation three years *after* the ending of petrol rationing in May 1950. In the second half of the 1940s, when the private use of petrol was severely restricted, the proportion of journey miles travelled by means of public transport must have been substantially greater.

In 1978, by contrast, private road transport was dominant. It was responsible for 76·7 per cent of all freight movements, measured in ton miles, whereas the railways' share had fallen to only 15·5 per cent, the balance being carried by coastal shipping and inland waterways. At the same time private-sector motor transport accounted for 81 per cent of all passenger miles travelled, with buses and coaches taking only 11 per cent and rail a mere 7 per cent. It was not that the total number of passenger miles travelled by train fell so dramatically – it declined from 24,000 million miles in 1953 to 19,066 million in 1978 – it was rather that there was an exceptionally steep increase in private car passenger mileage, which rose by nearly six times during 1953–78 to a total of 242,000 million.[4]

Lest it be suggested that the British experience of a general decline in rail traffic was common to that of all advanced industrial nations, it needs to be pointed out that, comparing sixty national railway systems over the period 1938–74, British railways were almost unique in carrying a smaller ton mileage of freight at the end of the period than at its beginning. Only the Argentine could match this depressing record. Over the same years the increase in rail freight traffic in the USA was 3·2 times, in the USSR 17 times, and in Japan 24 times.[5] In 1977, when only 15·8 per cent of the total ton mileage of freight carried in Great Britain went by rail, the comparable figure for West Germany was 27 per cent (despite the availability of cheap water transport on the Rhine and other principal inland waterways) and for France 37 per cent.[6] Nor was it the case that the British experience of declining rail passenger traffic – at least until the later 1970s when it revived – was in any way typical of most other countries. Passenger train miles travelled on Austrian, Belgian, Czechoslovak, Danish, French, German Democratic Republic, West German, Hungarian, Irish, Italian, Japanese, Netherlands, Portuguese, Spanish, Swiss and USSR railways all increased in the period 1963–77. In Europe only Finland, Sweden and Norway had, like Britain, declining passenger traffics.[7]

The consequences of these important changes in the pattern of British transport were serious for those employed in the public transport industry. There were the depressing effects on morale of working in a declining industry. The decreasing commercial viability of public transport undertakings made it certain that the task of union negotiators, striving to secure a decent standard of living for the workforce, would be an uphill one. The three-and-a-half decades following the nationalisation of some of the principal means of transport in 1947 were punctuated by frequent crises in which management found it difficult, because of financial restraints, to meet the legitimate claims of labour.

II

How did it happen that Great Britain fell behind other countries in the importance given to public transport by rail and road? A variety of explanations may be offered. In Britain, as was supremely the case in the USA, the assumption went virtually unchallenged that supplies of cheap oil fuel would continue to be available for the foreseeable future. In 1974 the Shah of Iran said that, in the twenty-two years 1947–69, buoyed by the apparently inexhaustible supply of cheap and abundant oil from Middle East wells, the industrialised world took off like a runaway horse with the bit between its teeth. It was now that the belief took hold that the cycle of boom and depression had been conquered'.[8] It was in these years that it was widely considered axiomatic that the automobile would largely displace the railway as the principal means of transport and that there was no reason to become too alarmed at this 'inevitable' development. However, there was an important difference of emphasis between prevalent opinion in Britain and in the countries of continental Europe. The other European countries had a longer and more firmly established tradition of public ownership of transport undertakings, which were regarded as providing the essential infrastructure for prosperous economic development. There was little difference of opinion between the main political parties in this important area of public policy. There was, therefore, much less hesitation about giving railway and bus undertakings, whether national or municipal, the financial support needed if they were to meet successfully the challenge of the private motorist and road haulier. In Britain, on the other hand, transport policy was a political shuttlecock. Labour administrations in 1945–51, 1964–70 and 1974–9 favoured public ownership of transport undertakings, though they vacillated between emphasis on the need for commercial viability and the importance of offering an adequate public service. The Conservative governments of the intervening years generally sought to reduce the role of public transport and to encourage the growth of privately owned road transport of all kinds.

Figure 1.1 *Annual central government support for railways per head of population*

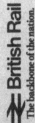

Source: **Statistical Office of the European Community, June 1977 (reproduced by kind permission of British Railways Board)**

These differences of emphasis between policy in Britain and the European continent were reflected in the financial support given to state railway systems. The British Railways Board cleverly spotlighted the relative impoverishment its railways experienced, by comparison with other European systems in 1977, in a full-page advertisement in *The Times,* reproduced in Figure 1.1. In June 1977 the EEC produced comparable figures, showing how much taxpayer support was received by each of the nine Common Market countries. British Rail's subsidy amounting to 59 per cent of gross traffic receipts was less than the French railways' subsidy of 63 per cent and far below the West German railways' 104 per cent and the Italian railways' 182 per cent.[9] Support as a percentage of Gross Domestic Product is shown in Figure 1.2. The lack of firm commitment at Westminster to a policy of strong and sustained support for public transport was perhaps the most decisive reason for the declining volume of freight and passenger business on British railways and the publicly owned bus and coach undertakings.

Figure 1.2 *Government support for railways and railway performance*

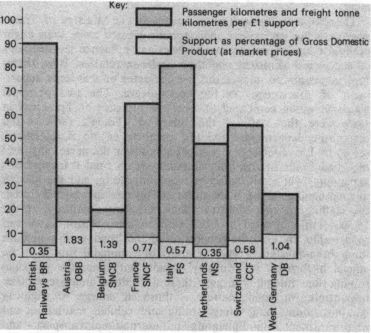

Source: British Railways Board. *Facts and Figures* (2nd edn), p. 38

Transport questions have generally received low priority in Britain in Parliament and Cabinet. An appointment as Minister of Transport has often been seen as providing an ambitious, capable younger politician with a stepping-stone from which shortly to advance to some more important office of state. Between 1947 and 1979 there were no less than fifteen different Ministers of Transport. The combined effect of transport policy being a political shuttlecock, with the fact that Ministers held office for brief periods of time, has been to bring about frequent changes in direction in transport policy. In January 1968 Sir Stanley Raymond, Chairman of the British Railways Board, declared that in his twenty-one years' service in public transport at least half his time had been devoted to 'organisation, reorganisation, acquisition, denationalisation, centralisation and decentralisation', responding to the volatile winds of political change.[10] Had he still been in office ten years later, he might have conceded some improvement in the stability of direction; but his observations provide a sad commentary on the twenty years following nationalisation. He and his colleagues had all too little time to follow their real vocation of transport management.

The frequent changes in leadership at the Ministry of Transport gave the permanent civil servants greater scope than might otherwise have been the case to brief and influence the decisions of successive Ministers and their under-secretaries. It is, therefore, necessary to understand the character of this large department of government in the postwar era. The two principal elements which combined to form the Ministry of Transport in 1919 were the staff of the Board of Trade's railway and mercantile departments and the members of the Road Board, set up by Lloyd George in 1909 to administer the pertol duty and the road fund. In the following sixty years road transport was expanding, while rail transport was contracting, and the growth in road haulage and private motor car ownership was reflected in the staffing of the Ministry. Thus, the large majority of the 15,500 staff employed in 1958 were concerned with roads and road traffic. In 1970 the proportion of the 'road' staff was more than three-quarters.[11] The hierarchy of command shown in the official history of the Ministry reveals that under the principal sub-division 'Inland Transport' there were three under-secretaries responsible for road matters – those in charge of highway administration· road safety, traffic and vehicle regulation and road transport: inland planning and international transport – and only one other under-secretary, who combined responsibility for railways with that for inland waterways.[12] Judged by the balance of its staffing, and by the fact that the road divisions were the initiating and policy-creating ones, while the one railway and inland waterway division maintained the established traditions of safety regulations, and so on, but had less power to initiate policy, it would have been less misleading if this department of government had been called the Ministry of Roads and Motorised Transport.

The Ministry of Transport, whether as a unit of government in its own right, or as a part of the Department of the Environment, has always had strong ties with the road transport industry, whose personnel often possessed the technical knowledge and the operational research findings that the government department found useful. There was a frequent recruiting of staff from the industry into the Ministry which was often regarded by critics (whether rightly or wrongly) as the mouthpiece of the road lobby. Pressure on Ministers to comply with the demands of the road lobby was often intense. One of those who felt those pressures was Barbara Castle, who became Minister of Transport in December 1965. Recalling her experience over seven years later she confessed:

When I took over as Minister of Transport the most vociferous lobby in the country was that represented by road interests. The propaganda and pressure groups led by the British Road Federation said that we must concentrate all our resources on building the first 1,000 miles of motorway. The environment lobby had barely been born, and when I tried to suggest there were other considerations that we should bear in mind I had an uphill task because about the whole of public opinion and the then opposition were against me.[13]

For a few days in the autumn of 1978 the curtain was drawn aside to reveal the continuing influence of road haulage interests within the Ministry of Transport. A memorandum, dated 16 October 1978, and signed by Mr J. Peeler, Under-Secretary, Freight Directorate, was leaked to the press to the embarrassment of its author and of Mr William Rodgers, Secretary of State for Transport. It concerned an impending inquiry into the question of whether or not maximum lorry weight should be raised from the current maximum of 32 tons to 38 or 40 tons. To the under-secretary the purpose of the ostensibly independent and impartial inquiry was 'presentational' (of the department's view) rather than 'fact-finding', which would be 'heavily subsidiary'. The 'main end of the inquiry', as seen by Mr Peeler, was 'the establishment in the public mind of a clear and overwhelming case on balance for heavier lorry weights'. Mr Rodgers subsequently assured the *Guardian* that, although he considered it was altogether proper for top members of the civil service to express their own views, the ultimate policy decision was his alone.[14] All the same, the disclosure did reveal the community of interest between the Road Haulage Association and leading civil servants in the Ministry of Transport.

An important reason for the influence of the road lobby in the department and in Parliament was its command over large sums of money which could be directed to influencing opinion. To maintain an effective parliamentary lobby substantial financial backing is essential. The British Road Federation through its wealthy affiliates, such as the Society of Motor Manufacturers and Traders, the Freight Transport Association and the Road Haulage Association, possessed such resources. Its income in 1972 was £115,000, sufficient to enable it to ply all MPs and other influential persons with its literature, including the cleverly designed pocket-sized folder *Fact: Road Transport in Britain,* and to pay for the services of a parliamentary agent, Roger Sewill, a director of the Road Haulage Association, who was assiduous in his attendance on MPs. The British Road Federation and the Society of Motor Manufacturers and Traders for many years had the services of Lt Commander Christopher Powell, the author of a classic paper on public relations and Parliament. By contrast the environmentalists were in no position to match these resources and their influence on policy-making was minimal.[15]

There were indications that even HM Customs had come under the spell of road interests to the detriment of the railways. It gave priority to road, rather than rail, vehicles when clearing goods for export. Kurt Gescheidle, the West German Transport Minister, in a letter to his British counterpart, William Rodgers, in October 1977, pointed out that over the years 1970–5 road freight traffic between Britain and Germany increased by 932 per cent, while rail freight traffic declined by 49 per cent. He attributed the fall in the rail freight volume partly to the fact that British Customs took between four and five days to clear railway wagons compared with the few hours taken to examine and clear the contents of lorries.[16]

Private motorists have no special affection for heavy lorries. It would have been folly for the British Road Federation to have courted their support for a campaign to boost road haulage as against carriage by the unobtrusive railways. But car owners did favour the construction of more motorways, dual carriageways and urban bypasses. This preference was exploited by the Auto-mobile Association, one of the British Road Federation's affiliates, when it launched its new magazine, Drive, in the spring of 1967. Commending the new journal to the Association's members, Mr A. C. Durie, the Director General, wrote:

Motoring . . . is the life blood of the nation's economy and perhaps the most significant explanation for the great advance in living standards in the last decade . . .
   All these are reasons why the AA is speaking out strongly against any attempt from any quarter to thrust inferior, incon-venient and inflexible mass transport on a society which is so obviously determined to use the superior, flexible, transport of the motor car.
   This magazine, posted free to 3,750,000 AA members each quarter, will be in itself a powerful weapon to influence trans-port policy, car design and town planning and to create a positive attitude to the problem of accommodating the motor vehicle for the betterment of the community.

The same writer, five issues later, warned readers of the 'sinister threat to prohibit the driver using his car in the centres of towns and cities'. Such proposals reflected 'dangerous thinking'. If they were adopted people would be 'compelled to travel to work, to shop, to seek entertainment, by public transport – forced to use an outmoded system they have so plainly rejected'.[17]
   A further reason for the decreasing role of public transport in the British economy was the failure of successive governments to invest sufficient funds in the nation's railway system. For the greater part of two decades after nationalisation in 1948 the railways were saddled with the consequences of excessive com-pensation paid to the former railway shareholders. In the debate on the Transport Bill in the House of Commons in December 1946, Hugh Dalton, the Chancellor of the Exchequer, was accused by the Conservative opposition of being niggardly in the compensation proposed. However, the terms offered were based on a stock market valuation made before investors fully realised the damage which would be inflicted on railway revenues by the growth of road haulage competition. They also reflected a degree of optimism resulting from the large, though forced, transfer of

traffic from road to rail during the war.[18] It soon became apparent that the 3 per cent British Transport stock, offered when the going gilt-edged security rate was 2·5 per cent, was a remarkably good bargain for the investor. Between 1948, when the British Transport Commission started business, and 1962, when it was dissolved, the debt was a millstone round the neck of the railways whose capital constituted a large majority of the Commission's assets. Not until the passing of the Transport Acts of 1962 and 1968 was the greater part of this debt written off.

In the intervening two decades there took place investment of a very different character in areas most likely to damage the railways' interests. The sudden ending of American Lease Lend on 21 August 1945 and the necessity, by the terms of loans from Washington, to establish the full convertibility of the pound in September 1947 obliged the Attlee government to bend all its efforts to achieve a 50 per cent growth in exports by 1950 in order to balance payments. Great successes were gained in the export of motor vehicles. A large part of the investment in the immediate postwar period went into the motor industry. There was a rapid expansion of domestic sales as well as exports. The number of motor vehicles in Britain rose from 3 million in 1946 to nearly 4·5 million in 1950.[19] In the 1950s the British Road Federation's plea that Britain's roads were antiquated gained a more attentive hearing, especially after the appointment of Ernest Marples as Minister of Transport on 14 October 1959. The extent to which investment was concentrated in road-building rather than on railways in those years is revealed in a chart included in the final report of the British Transport Commission in 1962 and reproduced here as Figure 1.3.

In the 1970s, with recurring balance of payments difficulties, an IMF lifeline in 1975 and drastic reductions in public expenditure designed to curb inflation in 1978 and 1979, investment in British Rail was still on a meagre scale by comparison with that of many other European countries. Thus in 1976 British Railways allocated only £194·4 million at the same time as the Belgian National Railways, with only a quarter of the network of BR, invested £281 million and the French SNCFF invested an impressive £525 million.[20]

The smaller scale of financial support for public transport from central or regional government in Britain than was often the case abroad meant that British Rail, London Transport, the National Bus Company, and other public transport undertakings, felt obliged to raise the level of their charges. Despite the sharp increase in oil prices since 1973, the cost of travel by rail, bus

Figure 1.3 *Road and rail transport: investment expenditure, 1952–61*

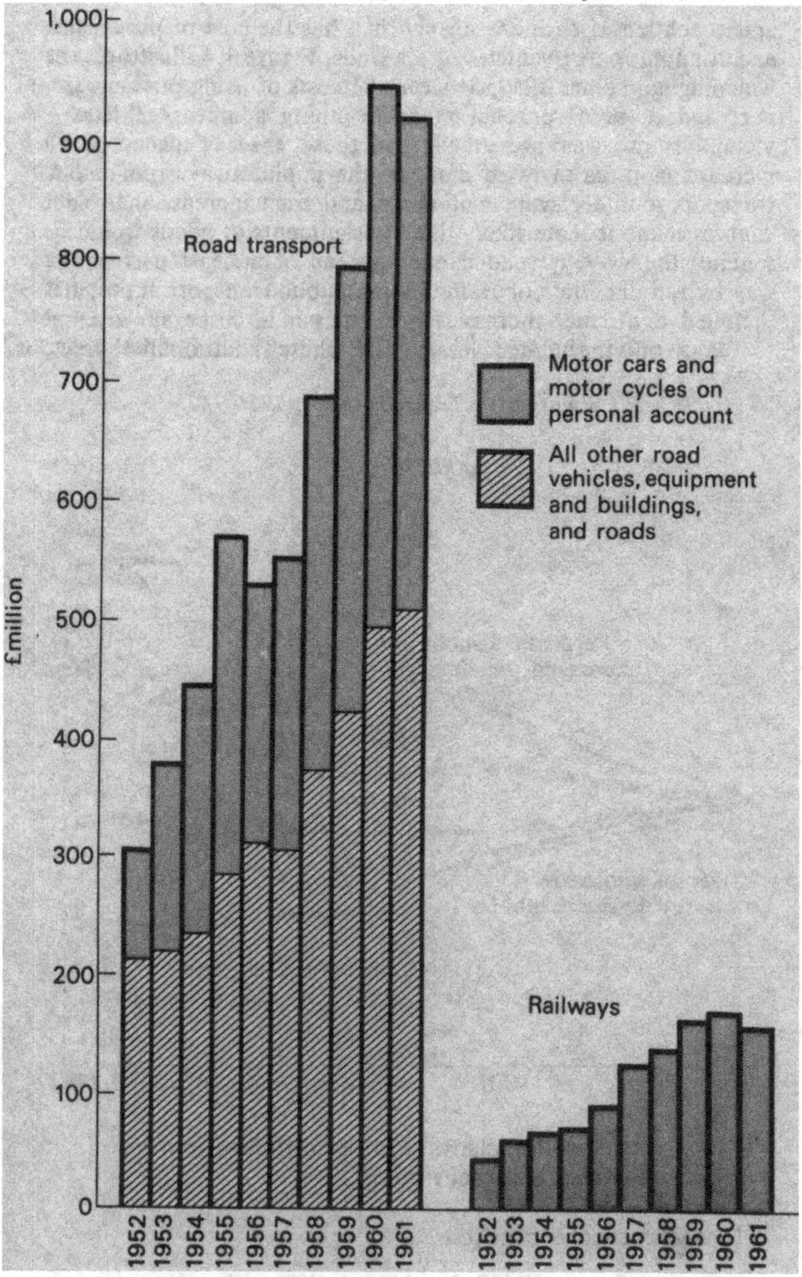

Source: British Transport Commission, *Annual Report and Accounts*, 1962

and coach has risen more steeply than has the cost of purchasing and running motor vehicles of all kinds. Figure 1.4 illustrates the widening gap, since 1950, between the costs of using public transport and those of purchasing and running a motor vehicle. A vicious spiral was present during those three decades. Each increase in fares diverted more of the public away from public transport to the private motor car, and each increase in freight charges made it more likely that consignments of goods would be sent all the way by road haulier instead of at least part of the way by rail. The loss of traffic by the public transport authorities then led to further increases in charges in a desperate attempt to stave off threatened losses. But these additional charges,

Figure 1.4   *Transport costs, 1951–77*

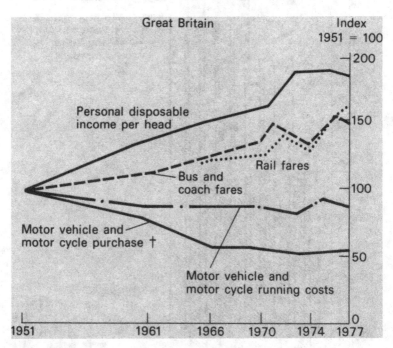

* Real changes in the relative costs of different forms of transport and of personal income

† New and second-hand

Source: HMSO, Social Trends (1980 edn), p. 31

though providing a temporary financial respite, frightened off yet more customers – since their private road transport costs had risen less steeply – and before many months had passed there was a renewed financial crisis within public transport. Between March 1974 and May 1975 British Rail and London Transport fares rose by 115 per cent.[21] The social consequences were serious. Thousands of commuters ceased to travel by rail or travelled by this means less frequently and stopped buying season tickets. On the Brighton–London service the number of season-ticket holders fell from 2,980 in 1961 to 1,769 in 1975, while at Chelmsford, on the Eastern Region, the drop was from 8,037 to 7,001 over the same period of time.[22] When fare increases of between 10 and 17·5 per cent were announced by British Rail on 17 February 1976, Sidney Weighell, General Secretary of the NUR, said 'We cannot be a party to a policy which will lead to line closures and cuts in services as more people desert the railways. In effect we are being asked to dig our own graves.'[23] But this proposal that British Rail should cut all fares by 10 per cent for an experimental period was not adopted by management.

III

The shrinking role of public transport in British economic and social life in the second half of the twentieth century can partly be explained by the shortcomings of transport legislation. Both the main political parties proclaimed their belief in transport co-ordination in which each means of transport carries out the function for which it is best suited – but whereas the Labour Party believed that this objective could only be achieved by public ownership of all the principal forms of transport, the Conservative view was that the surest way to its attainment was by giving maximum freedom to allow market forces to operate. The Transport Act of 1947 was the closest expression to the Labour ideal, while that of 1953 reflected Tory philosophies.

Even before 1914 railway trade unions were committed to a policy of public ownership of the nation's railways. In the case of the predecessor of the NUR, the ASRS, it was as early as October 1894 that the AGM passed a resolution in favour of the nationalisation of the industry. At that time the main reasons for advocating the change of ownership were the need to humanise working conditions, enhance the earnings of the staff and eliminate the waste which was seen as inherent in a system of competition. Since the railways enjoyed a virtual monopoly, at least of long-distance transport, the words 'co-ordination' and 'integration' did not arise in the discussions of transport policy. By the 1930s, however, the emphasis had changed. The four main line railway companies' profits were being undermined through the motor vehicle's encroachment into short-distance passenger and goods transport. It was realised that to ensure tolerable working conditions for employees in road as well as rail transport, public ownership of all major transport undertakings was needed. A resolution adopted by the Labour Party Conference, in 1932, proposed the nationalisation of all the principal means of transport and the creation of a National Transport Board whose members would be appointed by the Minister of Transport and given the task of co-ordinating the different transport services into an integrated whole.[24] By co-ordination was meant the dovetailing of one transport service into another as in the case when the local bus service is timed to link with the arrival and departure of trains from the nearest railway station. By integration was meant the welding together under unified direction and control of the principal means of transport.

In support of the party's policy of unified public ownership it was pointed out that the Parliamentary Select Committee on Transport in 1918 had recommended nationalisation as a precondition of co-ordination and that the Royal Commission on Transport, though not specifically advocating state ownership in its report of 1930, did state that 'It appears to us that without unification – however it may be accomplished – no attempt to bring about co-ordination would be successful.'[25]

The General Election manifesto, *Let Us Face the Future,* on which Labour came to power in August 1945, included a section 'Public ownership of inland transport', in which it was stated:

Co-ordination of transport services by rail, road, air and canal cannot be achieved without unification. And unification without public ownership means a steady struggle with sectional interests or the enthronement of a private monopoly, which would be a menace to the rest of industry.

However, there was very little detailed planning of transport policies either within the Labour Party, or the trade unions, before Clement Attlee took office as Prime Minister in August 1945. During the war the Railway Clerks' Association, for a fee of £400, employed the young Harold Wilson, at that time still a don at Oxford, to write a report on the future organisation of transport. It influenced that union's subsequent keen advocacy of an integrated transport policy under public ownership, but it was never published.[26] Perhaps the most valuable document was the TUC's *The Public Operation of Transport,* approved by the Blackpool Congress in September 1945.

The Labour government's Transport Bill was introduced in the House of Commons by Alfred Barnes, the Minister of Transport, on 16 December 1946. It was enacted on 6 August 1947 and came into operation on 1 January 1948. Although ostensibly Barnes's Act, it embodied the ideas of Herbert Morrison, Lord President of the Council, who had been Minister of Transport in MacDonald's Labour Cabinet of 1929–31. Morrison's Bill for London Transport had failed to reach the statute book before the Labour government broke up in August 1931; but it was taken over by the National government and became the London Passenger Transport Act in 1933. London Transport was thereafter to be administered by the London Passenger Transport Board, an independent body but under public control. This was the pattern of management of nationalised industries which Herbert Morrison favoured.

The Transport Act 1947 established the British Transport Commission to which all railways (including their steamships, hotels and all other ancilliary undertakings), canals, all privately owned railway wagons and some road haulage and road passenger concerns were transferred on 1 January 1948. Separate Executives for Railways, London Transport, Docks and Inland Waterways, Hotels and Road Transport (from June 1949 split into Road Haulage and Road Passenger Executives) were established under the direction of the Commission, but with their members nominated by the Minister, not by the Chairman of the BTC. The task of the Commission, in the words of the Act, was 'to provide or secure the provision of an efficient, adequate, economical and properly integrated system of public inland transport and port facilities'. The powers formerly possessed by the Railway Rates Tribunal were transferred to a Transport Tribunal, set up under the Act, whose approval was required before any changes could be made in freight charges and passenger fares. On the other hand the Commission was under obligation to levy such fares, rates, tolls, dues and other charges as were needed to cover its costs 'taking one year with another'. The nineteenth-century legislation, obliging railways to be common carriers, that is, to undertake the transport of all goods handed in at railway stations and sidings, irrespective of its immediate profitability, and forbidding them from giving undue preference to one class of customer as against another, remained unrepealed. These

obligations were a millstone round the neck of the Railway
Executive in its endeavours to compete with the road hauliers.

The Act differed in some important respects from the Bill
(which had to run the gauntlet of sustained opposition lasting
over seven months). Few measures have been so keenly contested
both within and outside Parliament; over 800 amendments were
moved in the Commons and over 200 in the Lords. The Road
Haulage Association pulled out all the stops in an endeavour
either to destroy or, failing that, to mutilate, the Bill. It dispatched thousands of letters to its constituent bodies and to likely
sympathisers. The advice given was:

> On the morning of the 17th December, without fail, send a
> telegram to your Member ... Conservative, Liberal or Socialist,
> condemning the Bill. .... You should remember that all Con-
> servative MPs are on our side and word your telegram more
> politely to them than to the supporters of the Government.[27]

The opposition was most fiercely directed against the proposal
contained in the Bill to limit to forty miles the range of operation
of holders of 'C' licence commercial vehicles, that is, those
vehicles used only for carrying their owners' goods, as distinct
from professional hauliers' vans and lorries. Mr Barnes was
vulnerable on this issue. He was a Labour/Co-operative Party
MP and well aware that both wholesale and retail co-operative
societies had shown 'a distinct lack of enthusiasm' for this part of
the Bill.[28] Under the pressure of the road lobby and of his own
co-operative movement he decided to remove from the Bill all
restraint on the movement of 'C' licence vehicles. However, he
was not alone on the Labour benches in hesitating about limiting
the range of operations of traders' vans. In one of the last prewar
Commons debates on transport policy, held on 17 November
1937, Mr F. C. Watkins, seconding a Labour motion in favour
of nationalisation, reassured Conservative and Liberal members
that Labour did not want 'public ownership of bakers' carts or
undertakers' hearses'. This prompted Mr H. Holdsworth, the
traditionalist Manchester-school, Liberal MP for Bradford, South,
to make the prophetic comment:

> What do they mean when they talk of the unification of this
> industry? If they do not mean to take over all private goods
> vehicles will it not destroy the other part of their suggested
> bargain?[29]

Mr Barnes never had any intention of 'taking over' bakers' carts or undertakers' hearses; but the original intention had been to restrict the range of 'C' licence vehicles to forty miles from their base in the hope that, for longer-distance road transport, traders would find it worth while to use the comprehensive network of road haulage service to be provided by the vehicles of the Road Haulage Executive, in the same way as an earlier generation had used the network of rail services for longer-distance movements. His surrender on the 'C' licence question undermined the chances of success of the whole Transport Act. In 1947 the number of 'C' licence vehicles was more than double that of all other commercial vehicles ('A', 'A contact' and 'B' licensed vehicles), and it was rapidly increasing. As Mr Holdsworth had foretold, a decision not to control in any way the movement of this type of vehicle greatly reduced the chances of establishing a co-ordinated transport system in Britain.

A further weakness of the Act lay in the inadequate powers given to the British Transport Commission as distinct from those accorded the separate executives, particularly the Railway Executive. Herbert Morrison still harboured a resentment against the former National government for destroying aspects of his plan for the control of London Transport. In his 1930 Bill the members of the proposed London Passenger Transport Board were to be appointed by the Minister of Transport; in the Act of 1933 Mr Pybus had substituted appointment by a board of trustees rather than by the Minister. Thus when it came to a discussion on whether the members of the five executives should be chosen by the chairman of the Commission or by the Minister of Transport, Morrison, as chairman of the Socialisation of Industry Committee, strongly favoured ministerial appointments. His views found expression in the Act. In his Commons speech on the second reading of the Bill Alfred Barnes endeavoured to dispel any fears that, because the members of the five executives would not owe their appointment to the chairman of the Commission, they would be as powerful as the Commission itself. He claimed that because the whole of the property would be vested in the commission, which would also have control over the direction of the national transport finances and power to delegate management functions, he had 'completely safeguarded the authority and adequacy of the commission'.[30] It proved otherwise.

The man appointed by the Minister to be the first chairman of the commission was Cyril Hurcomb (later Sir Cyril Hurcomb and Lord Hurcomb), who, when employed in the Ministry of War

Transport in 1942, circulated a plan for a public control board with supervision and control over separate executives representing railways and the other principal forms of transport. He was keen to integrate the various rail, road, canal interests into a 'transport' interest. To foster the growth of a transport outlook, he made arrangements that members of the Road Transport Executive (from June 1949 split into the Road Haulage and Road Passenger Executives) should be accommodated, with the Railway Executive, at 222 Marylebone Road. One restaurant was to serve the members of both rail and road executives and their staff. By these means, it was hoped men whose careers had been devoted to one specific form of transport would be reoriented to a national transport approach. The chairman's hopes were frustrated: railwaymen used one part of the restaurant, and road transport men another.[31]

Though this was symptomatic, more serious was the aloofness of the Railway Executive from the BTC. It tried to avoid the commission's exercising too great a control over 'railway' policy. It was under obligation to send copies of the minutes of its proceedings to the BTC, but it asserted its independence by issuing 'a second set of Minutes entitled *Memoranda of Decisions at Meeting*, which were issued on coloured paper and reserved for internal circulation'.[32]

The differences of approach were most starkly shown on locomotive policy. Within four months of the vesting date (1 January 1948) Sir Cyril Hurcomb wrote to the chairman of the Railway Executive advising the appointment of a committee (which would include a representative of BTC) to investigate, as a matter of some urgency, the respective merits of diesel and electric locomotives. The Railway Executive, preoccupied with building up its stock of steam locomotives, was in no hurry to act. It delayed the appointment of the committee for eight months, failed to include in it a representative of the BTC and came up with its report only in 1951.

Even if there had been the fullest co-operation between the BTC and the various executives a wide area of transport policy would still have been beyond the Commission's control. Decisions on the allocation of investment between road construction and railway modernisation rested with the Treasury Ministers, whose substantial preference for road construction is shown in Figure 1.3. The Chancellor of the Exchequer was responsible for determining the level of taxation of commercial road vehicles and private cars. The licensing of commercial motor vehicles was still the responsibility of the traffic commissioners.

What was remarkable was the degree of success achieved by the BTC despite the damaging blow of the exclusion from any control of the 'C' licence operators, the sometimes divided loyalties of the members of the executives and, above all, the scarcity of funds available for investment. Early in 1949 the BTC proposed that by 1952 railway investment should be 43 per cent higher than it had been in 1948. Due to restrictions imposed by the government, it fell by one-fifth. The railways' proportion of British capital investment fell from 4·4 per cent in 1948 to 3·3 per cent in 1951.[33] Nevertheless, in 1952 with 40,000 fewer staff, 1,500 fewer locomotives and 100,000 fewer wagons than in 1948 the railway carried 12 million tons more merchandise than in 1948 and 19 million tons more than in 1938. In 1952 the ton miles carried per engine hour worked were the highest achieved to that date and were 11 per cent better than in 1948 and 31 per cent better than in 1938.[34]

In the first six years of the life of the BTC, that is, between 1948 and 1953, a working surplus was achieved, and in 1951–3 inclusive an overall surplus was earned after making deductions for central charges, the principal element of which was interest on British Transport Stock issued at the time of nationalisation. The outstanding reason for this favourable financial position was the increasing profitability of British Road Services, the BTC's road haulage undertaking. During 1948–53 BRS earned surpluses amounting to £15·1 million. It is also noteworthy that following the early teething-troubles, associated with the building up of a nationwide network of road haulage services, the profitability of BRS was steadily increasing. The success of the road transport undertaking was the keystone of the arch of the BTC's finances. The whole edifice depended on its contribution to the balance of the whole.[35]

A period of ten years was needed to enable the BTC to achieve an appreciable degree of transport integration and co-ordination. During the first five years of its existence the various executives were integrating their own major segments of the transport industry. Thus, the BRS was engaged in welding together hundreds of large and small road haulage businesses into a national undertaking. The second stage should have been the co-ordination of the various means of transport under the direction of the BTC, in such a way that each form of transport performed the role for which it was best suited.

IV

Before this second stage of reorganisation could be carried out the Conservatives' General Election victory on 25 October 1951 ushered in a complete change of direction in transport policy. In its election manifesto the party had promised that: 'Publicly owned rail and road transport will be re-organised into regional groups of workable size. Private road hauliers will be given the chance to return to business, and private lorries will no longer be crippled by the 25 mile limit.' The government White Paper, *Transport Policy* (Cmnd 8538), which followed in May 1952, maintained that co-ordination under the BTC comprised not much more than 'working arrangements between separate transport entities' and that integration, even if achieved, would result in 'a huge unwieldy machine'. It was, therefore, necessary to decentralise the operation of both rail and road services. *The Economist* was not impressed. It complained that the document contained 'no study of any serious issues of transport'.[36] The EC of the NUR considered it 'unfortunate that political spite, and a complete lack of community interest should cause the Conservative government to propose legislation which in the ultimate will be detrimental to transport services as a whole and railways in particular'.[37] There is evidence to support a later NUR EC judgement of the Transport Bill, that it 'bore all the marks of haste, lack of fundamental thinking and back bench pressure to secure a victory for free enterprise in road haulage'.[38] When it was pointed out that the original Bill proposed to sell off most of the vehicles of BRS to private interests and to remove all restraints on the operation of 'A' and 'B' licensed vehicles, namely, those plying for hire, while at the same time retaining the railways' 'obligation to carry' and the restraints on their charging, the palpable one-sidedness of the proposed legislation became uncomfortably apparent. The Bill was then substantially modified to release British Railways from the 'obligation to carry' and to confer greater freedom in charging policy.

There were two main features of the Transport Act which became law on 6 May 1953. First, the Road Haulage Disposal Board was set up to sell from the BRS stock of 42,000 vehicles, transport units of between one and fifty vehicles to private buyers. The original plan was that the BTC would be allowed to retain only 4,200 vehicles, but under the Transport (Disposal of Road Haulage Property) Act of 2 August 1956 the process was stopped before its completion and the BTC was allowed to retain over 10,000 vehicles. Secondly, the BTC was required, within twelve months of the passing of the Act, to submit a scheme for the reorganisation of the railways, the abolition of the Railway Executive and the setting up of regional railway boards. The BTC's plans were printed in a government White Paper, *Railways Reorganisation Scheme* (Cmnd 9191), in July 1954. Of the five executives established in 1948 only the London Transport Executive survived:

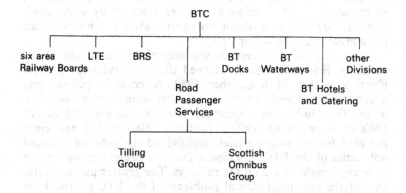

The Act, which may be considered the least justified and most harmful of any piece of transport legislation of the twentieth century, finally destroyed any chances of transport co-ordination achieved by a unified system of public ownership. The break up of BRS as an integrated national undertaking, the great enlargement of the private sector in road haulage and the removal of all limitations on the range of operation of 'A' and 'B' licensed vehicles, disintegrated the structure set up in 1948 and made it virtually impossible for either British Railways or the BTC to be run at a profit.

The editor of *Modern Transport,* writing at the time when the proposals for denationalisation saw the light of day, considered that these clauses in the Bill were 'purely destructive and wholly unjustified by the progress made' over the previous five years.[39] Three years after the passing of the Act, G. W. Quick Smith, a member of the board of management of BRS, had difficulty in finding words to describe 'the upheaval of the past few years in the road haulage industry', since: 'The gigantic task of acquiring 4000 road haulage undertakings in four short years (1948–51) was followed, after a two-year interim period of legislation, by the colossal operation involved in disposing 20,000 vehicles in small lots in 1953–56.'[40] There was a case for some devolution of authority in railway management. The BTC itself was contemplating some gradually applied changes in this direction. But the disruption caused by the rapid reorganisation provided for under the 1953 Act created a great upheaval and diverted railway management from its all-important task of modernisation. Lord Missenden, formerly General Manager of the Southern Railway until his appointment as first chairman of the Railway Executive, considered it 'folly to throw away by hasty action . . . the lasting economies achieved by unification'. Another 'internal convulsion' so shortly after the previous one put a great strain on senior staff.[41]

Major structural change in the administration of the public sector of British transport followed the Conservatives' General Election victory of 8 October 1959. A crisis in railway pay negotiations confronted the new Ministry soon after it had taken office. The Guillebaud Committee recommendation of 2 March 1960 of increases of ten per cent for salaried staff and eight per cent for the wages grades, highlighted the growing financial difficulties of the BTC, principally due to a decline in the volume of heavy freight traffic on the railways. The greater public awareness of the growing financial problems of the BTC provided the newly appointed Minister of Transport, Ernest Marples, with the opportunity to complete the work of its dismemberment.

In place of the BTC, which it abolished, the Transport Act 1962, provided for the creation of four new public authorities; the British Railways Board; the London Transport Board; the British Transport Docks Board and the British Waterways Board, all of whose members were to be appointed by the Minister of Transport. For the management of the road passenger and road freight (including the BRS) undertakings, Thomas Cook & Sons Ltd and other concerns previously the responsibility of the BTC, there was established a Transport Holding Company the members of whose board were also to be appointed by the Minister. The British Railways Board was to have charge of the management of the hotels. Decentralisation was carried a stage further than in 1953, in that the six regional railway boards were to prepare separate accounts.[42] The production of these six separate sets of figures was a colossal time-wasting irrelevance, because 43 per cent of all railway traffic at the time crossed the boundaries of the regions. The BTC's view was that to ascertain the costs and the receipts of particular streams of traffic was a meaningful and ascertainable exercise, but that to try and find the profit and loss of traffic in a geographical area was much more difficult.[43]

In his aim of making competition the key to efficient transport operation Mr Marples was consistent, in that under section 43(3) of the Act all boards, except the London Transport Board, were given complete freedom to adjust their fares and freight rates as they saw fit. All boards, without exception, were given powers to use any surplus land for commercial development and to construct and operate pipelines for commercial gain. The Minister was inconsistent, in that under section 13 none of the boards had the power to manufacture or repair equipment to order from private or public customers at home or abroad. Early in 1964 the Railways Board appealed to the Minister to remove this ban, but he refused to change his ruling.[44] This obduracy had damaging effects on employment in the railway workshops. As diesel and electric locomotives replaced the steam variety under the Railway Modernisation Plan of 1955, the proportion of BR locomotives built in railway workshops declined. In 1957 it was 75 per cent; by 1962 it was down to 39 per cent. Thus there was plenty of spare capacity and spare manpower, though re-equipment and retraining would have been needed to meet the demands of modern equipment. Not surprisingly, in the Beeching era, severe redundancy was first experienced in the railway workshops.

The Minister was aware that he would be criticised for abolishing the BTC, whose task had been to achieve an efficient, economical and properly integrated system of public transport. With the Commission's guiding hand removed, who was to be responsible for securing national interests in transport policy? Section 55 of the Act established a Nationalised Transport Advisory Council; but this was no real substitute for the Commission, since it had advisory powers only. Henceforward it was Mr Marples, the Minister of Transport, and Dr R. Beeching, Chairman of the BTC in its closing months and Chairman of the British Railways Board from 1 January 1963 (when the new Act came into operation), who directed the new transport policy. At Margate on 2 July 1962 the AGM of the NUR was unanimous in deprecating the new transport legislation, since it represented a decision 'that the sole criterion in the future was to be profitability'; that all unprofitable services were to be eliminated and all questions of social necessity ignored.[45]

The passing of the Transport Act in 1962 must be seen alongside Dr Beeching's remit to restructure the railway system with the object of achieving its commercial solvency. The NUR's response to his *The Reshaping of British Railways* published in March 1963, is discussed in Chapter 4 of this book· but some of the salient features of the report are worth outlining here. The

findings were based on a railway traffic survey made in 1961 and
the limited aim was to discover which passenger and freight
services were financially profitable and which were not. The
report revealed that one-third of the route mileage of the railways
carried only 1 per cent of the total passenger miles and only
1.5 per cent of the freight ton miles (pp. 62–4); that a mere 118
stations, out of 2,067 dealing with freight, carried 52 per cent of
the traffic (pp. 72–3); that on half the route miles traffic density
was so low that it scarcely sufficed to cover the basic costs of
maintaining the route in service without any allowance for
operating costs, and that on the other half there was enough
traffic to cover route costs more than six times (p. 10). As much
as £131 million of the total losses of £172 million were accounted
for in 1961 by stopping passenger trains and general merchandise
traffic.

Dr Beeching's remedy was to abandon 5,000 route miles of
railway (out of a 1961 total of 18,214), to close more than one-
third of the passenger stations and to reduce the number of
stations receiving coal from over 5,000 to 'a few hundred'. Many
thousand of the 862,000 small-capacity wagons would be broken
up to be replaced by a much smaller number of large-capacity
steel ones fitted with vacuum brakes. For freight traffic there
would have to be a concentration on 'liner' and merry-go-round
trains, carrying large consignments for relatively long distances.
Passenger traffic would need to be concentrated on the fast inter-
city routes.

Dr Beeching produced a further report *The Development of
the Major Trunk Routes* before his resignation at the end of May
1965. Improvements in track signalling and services on 7,500 of
the surviving 16,000 route miles of railway, with special attention
given to improvements in the most-used 3,000 miles, would enable
concentrations of heavy traffic in both passengers and freight to
be conveyed speedily and profitably. On 16 February 1965 he told
a press conference that, given the full implementation of the
proposals recommended in his two reports, British railways could
be run at 'a good profit'.[46] By the end of 1967 many of the
Beeching Plan changes had been carried out: 5,000 route miles
of railway had been closed to traffic, 84 per cent of the planned
passenger train withdrawals and 72 per cent of the station closures
had been effected. The number of freight wagons had been
reduced by 478,523 to a total of 458,475.

On 2 July 1963 the AGM of the NUR held at Scarborough
found three main reasons for the condemnation of the Marples/
Beeching policies. They were

(a) that they led to unplanned and uncontrolled transport and a perpetuation of the chaotic condition in the industry;
(b) that railways had been dealt with in isolation without regard to road and other forms of transport;
(c) that no account had been taken of social need or industrial development.

One of the principal criticisms which can be made of the Beeching Plan is that it was based on an analysis of railway operation in isolation from any consideration of other forms of transport. No calculations were made of the additional costs which would have to be borne by road transport as a result of the curtailment of rail services. The report demonstrated that substantial parts of the rail system were not covering the costs of their maintenance. But the same could be said of many roads. Because the owners of the heaviest lorries were not paying and, at the time of writing, still do not pay, in licence duties and fuel taxes the full cost of the damage their vehicles inflict on the roads, buildings and bridges, their charges to their customers are artificially low. In the debate on the Beeching Plan in the Commons Jeremy Thorpe warned that if Mr Marples was to follow the recommendations in the report and to 'decide railway policy in isolation from transport problems generally', it would be 'like a judge making up his mind on the evidence of one expert witness'.[47]

Sensitive to these criticisms, in October 1963, Mr Marples appointed a small committee under the chairmanship of Lord Geddes, a shipowner, to investigate the commercial road vehicle licensing system. Its report, which did not become available until June 1965, found from checks in a sample of 15,000 lorries, 'a shocking state of affairs', with many instances of gross and unsafe overloading of vehicles, widespread evasion of the statutory limitation of drivers' hours and 'vehicles which were capable of doing a great deal of harm to life, limb, and property'.[48] In the meantime, however, a substantial part of the Beeching Plan – at least in its negative aspects of station and line closures – had been carried out. Nearly 2,000 route miles of railway were closed in the time between the appearance of the Beeching and the Geddes reports.[49]

The modernisation aspects of the Beeching Plan led to substantial improvements in the efficiency of operation of the railways. The 127 express trains that each day in 1969 averaged over 75 m.p.h. exceeded in number those averaging 60 m.p.h. in 1939. Concentration of freight in train loads led to a 15 per cent reduction in the charge for the movement of cement and a 43 per cent reduction in charges for carrying oil products. But despite these improvements in productivity and drastic curtailment of 'unremunerative' services, the financial objective of the Beeching Plan was not achieved. In 1967 and 1968 the overall deficits on railway operation were greater than those of 1963 and 1964.[50] It is true that there were small operating surpluses in 1969 and 1970 and it is virtually certain that, in default of the Beeching changes, the general trend to accounting deficits would have been aggravated; but it was the staff who bore much of the burden of these years. Heavy redundancies destroyed the careers of thousands of men and women and the continuing financial difficulties made it all the harder for the trade unions to wring any improvements in pay and working conditions from an otherwise generally sympathetic management.

V

The Labour Party's General Election manifesto in October 1964 promised that, if returned to power, Labour would 'draw up a national plan for transport covering the national network of road, rail and canal communications, properly co-ordinated with air, coastal shipping and port services'. The new regional authorities would be asked to draw up transport plans for their own areas, and while these were being prepared, major rail closures would be halted. It was not until 1966, when Barbara Castle had replaced Tom Fraser and a further General Election had given the Labour Party a substantial working majority in Parliament, that it proved possible to give closer attention to the fulfilment of these promises.

The Transport Act 1968 was the longest piece of legislation in British history covering this area of policy. Its introduction was preceded by the publication of a record number of White Papers outlining the government's intentions – *Transport Policy* (Cmnd 3057), 27 July 1966; *British Waterways* (Cmnd 3401), 7 September 1967; *Railway Policy* (Cmnd 3439), 6 November 1967; *Transport of Freight* (Cmnd 3470), 16 November 1967; *Public Transport and Traffic* (Cmnd 3481), 5 December 1967; and *Transport in London* (Cmnd 3686), 2 July 1968. Before her Bill was published, but after she had determined the broad outlines of its contents, the Minister engaged in separate discussions with members of the General Council of the TUC and with the leaders of the railway trade unions.

It was recognised that the publicly owned sector of freight haulage, whether by rail or road, was losing ground to the private hauliers and that, from the socialist viewpoint, new measures were required to bring about its revival. The instrument created to effect this change was the National Freight Corporation which, through two newly created subsidiaries, Freightliner Ltd and National Carriers Ltd, would be responsible for the movement of all freight in the public sector. The Corporation was to take over not only the assets of British Road Services, but also the British Rail Sundries and collection and delivery services, and the subsidiary companies under the control of the Transport Holding Company. British Rail would still provide the haulage services for goods which were rail-borne. The Minister's approach to the problem of integration of freight traffic was paradoxical, in that 'separate nationalised corporations were created to handle parts of an operation that had formerly been dealt with by a single body, namely rail carriage with road collection and delivery at each end'. Christopher Foster, who was Barbara Castle's Director General of Economic Planning and her principal adviser during her tenure at the Ministry of Transport, said that the Minister's view was that British Rail's marketing of its freight services left much to be desired, and that if freight haulage was made the responsibility of a separate organisation, there would be a more effective campaign to get freight haulage back into the public sector.[51]

In the course of 1966 Mrs Castle experienced delays in establishing the Freightliner system through British Rail, when NUR members at the Stratford rail terminal in East London, standing out for a policy of 'Railway work for railwaymen', had struck work in an attempt to prevent private hauliers, particularly Tartan Arrow, being allowed into the new Freightliners terminal. There were long delays in bringing in the new service until a compromise was reached, reserving bay 10 of the terminal for British Rail's haulage vehicles. This frustrating experience may have helped to persuade the Minister to set up an organisation, independent of British Rail, for the movement of freight.

In important discussions which took place at St Christopher House, Southwark Street, London, between the leaders of the railway trade unions and Barbara Castle on 8 June 1966, Mr Bothwell, of the TSSA, expressed concern that, under the proposed new arrangements, most of the freight traffic would be sent by road rather than by rail:

Mr Bothwell – You say the Corporation is to acquire the assets

of the subsidiaries of the Transport Holding Company and of
British Road Services. They would then have enough for the
road services, but for rail they would not have the track,
signalling or power and they would have to employ the Railway
Board as an agent. I am very much afraid that having on hand
all the assets necessary they would be inclined to use the road
facilities and only as a secondary consideration use the rail.

Mrs Castle – The terms of reference of the freight corporation
are to get traffic on to rail as far as possible where it can be
done. This is one of the purposes of the freight corporation.

Mr Bothwell – I am afraid that it is not quite satisfactory to
me. There are, as is well known, the practical difficulties of
how this is going to work. If the traffic is offered they will
determine whether it is to be taken by road or rail. If they say
it is to be sent by rail the question arises how they will fit in
with the passenger authorities who are working separately.
They are independent and it is bristling with difficulties.

Mrs Castle – That is why it is important to take over the
appropriate assets.

Mr Bothwell – These are useless unless you have track and
engines.

Mrs Castle – Yes, but is it important to British Rail to have its
track and signalling used.

Sidney Greene, General Secretary of the NUR, also put some
very pertinent questions to the Minister. He asked: 'Will the
railways have any say in what traffic goes by the railway?' He
pointed out that on the road side the new Corporation would
'have the propulsion', whereas on the rail side they would not.[52]

Despite the union leaders' serious and well-informed criticisms,
Barbara Castle, in characteristically determined fashion, stuck
to her plan to set up the National Freight Corporation with its
widespread powers of freight carriage. Certainly, she included
in the Bill three safeguards intended to ensure that railways
secured the kind of freight traffic they were best suited to carry.
Under clause (a)(ii) of section 1 of the Act the National Freight
Corporation was under obligation to secure that goods were
carried by rail wherever such carriage was 'efficient and
economic'. Under section 6 there was to be a Freight Integration
Council, which would have among its tasks the duty of ensuring
that railways gained a fair share of the traffic. Section 72 provided
for quantitative licensing of vehicles of over six tons' laden
weight. In cases where the consignment of goods was to be
carried for distances of 100 miles and over, authority for trans-

port by road would not be given where there was a suitable rail alternative. None of these safeguards proved effective. The quantitative licensing provisions were never put into effect. Strong Road Haulage Association lobbying and Conservative Party opposition in the Commons led to a postponement of the operative date for this part of the Act for two years, during which time the Wilson government was defeated in the general election of June 1970 and the Heath Conservative administration, pledged to repeal this part of the Transport Act, came into office. The Freight Integration Council, on which British Rail, as well as the National Freight Corporation, was represented, being only an advisory body – Barbara Castle said it was to have 'real influence rather than real power' – soon faded out of existence, having neither real influence nor real power. As for the third safeguard, that the NFC was to see that freight was carried by rail when such carriage was 'efficient and economic', the apprehension of the union leaders was proved wholly justified in the event. In succeeding years when complaints were made that, under the NFC, more and more freight was being directed by road the Corporation's response was that the rail option was not commercially viable. Hence an Act which was designed by its sponsor in all sincerity to ensure that railways gained a more appropriate share of the freight traffic served instead to accelerate the drift of consignments on to the road. It is also true that through the 1970s British Rail was showing less and less inclination to accept the smaller consignments of freight. The Beeching policies of railways concentrating on liner trains and merry-go-round traffic, rather than wagon load traffic, were continued long after Dr Beeching left the scene in 1965.

In commending her mammoth Transport Bill to the House of Commons on 20 December 1967, Barbara Castle contrasted the characteristics of freight and passenger transport. The former, she maintained, was 'an economic service to industry and must be organised on a national basis', whereas the latter was 'much more closely linked to local community life and had important social implications'. It was because of these features of passenger traffic that she decided not to recreate the British Transport Commission.[53] To organise public passenger transport services to meet social needs, the Act gave the Minister power to designate Passenger Transport Authorities, made up of representatives appointed by local authorities and by the Minister. Through their Passenger Transport Executives the PTAs could provide for the carriage of passengers by road, rail, or water (including Hovercraft). Local authority transport systems were to be transferred to the new PTA when the pending local government reorganisation, realised eventually under the Local Government Act 1972, had been carried through. Central government support for the transport services of the PTAs was provided in three principal ways. A 75 per cent grant was made available to enable conurbations to develop rapid transit systems, thus matching, for the first time, the 75 per cent grant available for road improvements. There were also bus replacement grants and a reduction in the duties on diesel oil used for public service vehicles. Although these improvements were slow to appear because of delays in local government reorganisation, by 1980 the transport services of the Clyde, Merseyside, the Tyne and Birmingham conurbations had been revitalised and there was an encouraging revival of public use of railway transport.

An outstanding feature of the Act was that, for the first time, the concept of a public service obligation was given material expression. In 1966 and 1967 the Ministry of Transport conducted surveys of the use of rail passenger services which did not cover their cost of operation, with a view to discovering which lines fulfilled a social need though not paying their way. Under section 39 of the Act grants were to be available for the provision of unremunerative services where this was found 'desirable for social and economic reasons'. This was a policy which saved the central Wales railway link to Aberystwyth – and many other rail lifelines – from extinction. Even so the new proposals did not, at first, gain universal approval in the Cabinet. On 8 July 1968, Roy Jenkins, Chancellor of the Exchequer, solemnly proposed the scrapping of the 'unremunerative lines' subsidy. It took some time before his suggestion was finally squashed.[54] For rural bus services a grant of up to £2 million was made available to those local authorities which replaced worn-out vehicles. It was by no means an adequate amount to stave off the sharp decline in rural bus services; but it was a step in the right direction. Revitalisation of the bus and coach services of the nation was not simply left to the PTAs. Part III of the Act set up the National Bus Company, which acquired the various road passenger transport undertakings previously under the umbrella of the Transport Holding Company: 25 per cent of approved capital expenditure of the new company was to be covered by a central government grant and it was declared to be the duty of the PTAs and the NBC to co-operate with each other in the reorganisation of the bus services within, and to and from, each area. For Scotland a separate organisation was created, the Scottish Transport Group, which included not only the principal bus companies, but also shipping packet services and travel and tourist agencies.

Parts of the Act released some transport undertakings from previously existing restraints on their activities. Out of 1·5 million commercial road vehicles, until 1968 subject to licensing, 900,000 of under 30-cwt unladen weight were to be freed from licensing control. The remainder would still require an operator's licence – what the Minister called the 'quality licence' – to continue in business. The railway unions greatly welcomed section 48, which conferred on all the boards power 'to manufacture for sale to outside persons anything which . . . can be advantageously so manufactured or . . . repaired'. This release from former restraints was long overdue.

Soon after the Act came into operation on 1 January 1969, the British Railways Board formed a subsidiary company, British Rail Engineering Ltd, with responsibility for the manufacturing side of the thirteen main railway workshops; a second subsidiary, BRE-Metro, a company linking the publicly owned railway workshops with some of the principal private manufacturers of railway equipment, whose specialised task is was to secure export orders, and a third, Transmark, an agency for developing overseas railway consultancy contracts. Business came slowly in the early 1970s but gathered momentum in the later years of the decade.

During his years of office as Senior Assistant General Secretary between 1969 and 1975, Sidney Weighell had special responsibility for railway workshop matters and became fully conversant not only with the problems, but also with the potentialities, of this part of the railway industry. Within two monhs of taking office as General Secretary in January 1975 he took the initiative in writing to the Secretary of State for Industry, Tony Benn, suggesting a meeting to discuss the development of exports of railway equipment. In the meantime the NUR produced a large-format, four-page printed leaflet, *A Market we Should be Glad to go to. It's worth £10,000 million,* in which the worldwide upsurge of interest in the expansion of national railways and conurbation rapid-transit systems was spotlighted, while regret was expressed that Britain's share of railway equipment exports was only 5 per cent of the total. The leaflet was sent to all MPs and to the Cabinet Ministers concerned, early in April 1975. Tony Benn was briefed on the subject by an NUR delegation on 15 May; but the highlight of the campaign to bring work to the railway workshops was reached at a meeting at Chequers, held on 3 December and attended by Peter Shore (who by then had succeeded Tony Benn as Secretary of State for Industry), and the representatives of BRB, the Railway Industries Association and the NUR. The Minister expressed surprise that it was the NUR, rather than private engineering firms or the BRB, that had taken the initiative in bringing the various parties together. He voiced his gratitude for the enterprise shown by the union. Sir Richard Marsh, Chairman of the British Railways Board, also acknowledged help from the NUR for sending him background material which had been useful in preparing his memorandum for the meeting. At the same time he quite justifiably impressed upon Peter Shore the importance of a *long-term* allocation of funds to British Railways to enable the Board to plan ahead and decide how much workshop capacity would be needed to meet domestic requirements and how much would be available to meet orders from outside the industry.

The upshot of this important meeting was the formation of British Railways Industries Export Group (BRIEG), representing BRE-Metro, Transmark and private companies in the Railway Industries Association, in April 1976. Overseas orders subsequently reached record levels. BRE-Metro secured export business worth nearly £50 million in 1978, while Transmark earnings rose from £2·9 million in 1977 to £4·5 million in 1978.

It had taken nearly a decade to demonstrate the value of Section 48 of Barbara Castle's Act; but there can be no doubt that the £115 million earned by BRE-Metro in export orders during 1968–78, to countries as far apart as Yugoslavia, Nigeria, Kenya, Tanzania, Bangladesh and Hong Kong, brought a new lease of life to railway workshops such as those at Ashford and Swindon.[55]

VI

The public resolution on transport policy carried unanimously at the AGM of the NUR at Scarborough on 12 July 1972 read:

That this AGM is agreed that a new statement on Transport policy is imperative if further contraction and consequent redundancies are to be prevented in the public rail sector.

We instruct our NEC to secure through our representatives on the TUC Transport Industries Committee a general policy statement on transport that will ensure a major and expanding role for the public rail sector.

This policy statement will be the basis for negotiating and enacting a new Railway Act immediately a Labour Government is returned.

In the meantime, however, the union had to live with a Conservative government, whose Minister of Transport Industries, Mr John Peyton, was preparing new legislation. The new Minister proved to have a greater understanding of the aspirations of the NUR and of the railway industry than most of his predecessors from the Conservative benches. He caused surprise by appointing Richard Marsh, at that time a member of the Labour Party, and ex-Labour Cabinet Minister, Chairman of the British Railways Board. Sidney Greene, therefore, took the bold step of inviting him to address the AGM at Exmouth on 17 July 1973. In the Minister's own words he was 'the first Tory lamb to enter this particular den'. He promised that in his Railways Bill, which he hoped to present to the Commons in the autumn, there would be 'no savage cuts in the system'.[56] However he was unable to get his Bill enacted before the Heath government fell in February 1974.

The Labour Minister of Transport, Fred Mulley, who succeeded him, adopted some of the proposals of the defunct Bill, including government financial support for railwaymen's pensions, in the new Railways Bill which he presented to the Commons on 21 June 1974. But the most important features of the new measure were the substitution of a block grant for the whole of the railway system for the 'unremunerative lines' grants given under section 39 of the Transport Act 1968 and the provision, under section 8, of grants to industrial and commercial firms for the construction of railway sidings, depots, access roads and equipment, to enable them to dispatch their freight through the railway system.

The decision in 1974 to substitute a block grant for the grants to individual lines, instituted five years earlier, reflected the British Railways Board's findings, published in its *Interim Rail Strategy* in June 1973, that no particular railway network size could be made financially viable. A railway system similar to the existing one was needed but with substantially increased capital investment, if the public-service obligation was to be met at all adequately. The significance of the change ushered in by the Railways Act 1974 was emphasised by the new chairman of the Board, Mr Peter Parker (later Sir Peter Parker), a few months later when questioned by Mr McNair Wilson, MP:

It has been said that Dr Beeching cut out quite a lot of secondary lines, in fact he cut out feeder lines into the main lines and thus, though he appeared to save money, in the end BR lost revenue?

Mr Parker: The importance of your point is what is the optimum size of the network system. Again if one looks at that, I think the philosophy has changed over the last decade. It is not felt that you could radically change the economics of the railways by continuing the Beeching thesis. That is not seen to be any longer a philosophy. There are areas where changes might take place because no network is immutable. Over the next 25 years it would be difficult to predict exactly what would happen. But the previous philosophy of hammering away at your various feeder lines until you were left with something called a viable railway seems a concept that has passed.[57]

The new chairman also used the changes brought by the 1974 Act to introduce more publicly acceptable concepts. He expressed a wish 'to change the language from dragging this ball and chain of "deficit" around and calling it a subsidy continually. We have a contract and we like to deliver on that contract'.[58]

In his contribution to the Railways Bill debate on 24 June 1974 Peter Snape, NUR-sponsored MP for West Bromwich, East, emphasised that the £5 million allocated for private railway siding grants – subsequently known as 'section 8 grants' – was a quite inadequate sum. He questioned how many minor roads, let alone major roads, £5 million would buy. Neil Carmichael, replying for the government, conceded that the sum mentioned was regarded only as a start. If the demand for more sidings warranted it, the sum allocated could be increased. In the event the response from industry was disappointingly slow. In the first four years of operation of the Act, to midsummer 1978, forty-one grants were made available at a cost to the government of £9·1 million and with an anticipated switch of freight from road to rail of 6 million tons.[59] Unfortunately, over the same four years, the number of private railway sidings closed was over three times the new sidings opened – with or without the help of the section 8 grants. A lot of the closures were of sidings long-since disused; but it was clear that getting freight back on to the rail, once it had left, was an uphill task.[60]

VII

The Labour Party's General Election manifesto, in October 1974, stated:

The energy crisis has underlined our objective to move as much traffic as possible from road to rail and to water; and to develop public transport to make us less dependent upon the private car.

The Secretary of State for the Environment, Anthony Crosland, in April 1976, instead of following the precedent set by Barbara Castle in publishing a large number of White Papers produced a large Green Paper in two volumes, bound in orange-coloured covers and entitled *Transport Policy: a Consultation Document*. In his Foreword to the document the Minister stated that the proposals it contained were the outcome of a comprehensive review of transport policy by his department, but that before the government proceeded to legislation it would welcome the forthright views of interested parties.

Despite the Labour Party's clear pledge in the manifesto, the authors of the Consultation Document described as a 'pipe-dream' the popular belief that a dramatic environmental gain would accrue if a large amount of long-distance freight traffic were switched from road to rail. They maintained that even if all freight movements of more than 100 miles were transferred to rail, total road traffic would be reduced by only 2–4 per cent.[61] They viewed with some alarm the rise in public transport subsidies from £300 million to £580 million over seven years and claimed that the richest 20 per cent of households accounted for nearly 50 per cent of total household expenditure on rail travel, thus conjuring up the image of the well-to-do Brighton commuter enjoying in comfort his subsidised rail journey to Victoria.[62] On the other hand, they recognised that there was a serious social problem of a substantial minority of the population which neither owns, nor has access to, private motor transport. It was conceded that in those country areas where public transport had been most extensively reduced the opportunity for mobility of people in the lower-income groups was lower than it had been for a generation or more.[63] It was also conceded that implementation of the Transport Act 1968 had not resulted in a shift of transport from road to rail; but though it was admitted that there was a case for considering the return of Freightliner Ltd and National Carriers Ltd to British Rail ownership, it was argued that, because of the national economic emergency, 'the upheaval of a major reorganisation' of freight services 'would not be appropriate'.[64] To placate the advocates of a return of the British Transport Commission – or some similar body – the authors of the document recommended the creation of a National Transport Council, 'a high level forum, with a minister as chairman on which all the main interests would be represented'.[65]

Many organisations, including the British Railways Board, the National Bus Company, socialist and environmentalist groups, and the trade unions concerned with transport, submitted commentaries on the Green Paper. The NUR's *A Policy for Transport* (52 pages, July 1976) was among the most substantial, carefully thought out and best documented. In answer to the Green Paper's 'pipe-dream' comment, it was stressed that what was important, if road congestion and accidents were to be reduced, was to get long-distance heavy goods vehicles off the road. The 2–4 per cent switch to rail which the Green Paper said would occur, if all road goods traffic being carried over 100 miles was transferred to rail, was expressed as a percentage of all road traffic, passenger as well as goods. The reduction in road goods traffic, if the transfer to rail was made, would be more like 25 per cent. At a time of growing public awareness of the need to conserve energy resources and to prevent further despoilation of the environment the NUR document stated succinctly the case for railways:

The railway system exists. Its development can be undertaken without the use of valuable farming land; electrification can improve the capacity of the line and enable the use of power generated from alternative fuel sources. Railways have a vastly superior safety record. They are efficient users of energy and have the ability to carry large numbers of passengers and large volumes of freight without imposing additional burdens on the community.

One result of the better organisation of the public transport and conservationist lobby – a development which will be discussed more fully in Chapter 12 – was that the government's White Paper, *Transport Policy* (Cmnd 6836), of June 1977 was more sympathetic to the claims of public transport services and less receptive to the demands of the road lobby than had been the case even a year earlier. Gone were the hints of government feather-bedding of wealthy commuters. In place of the Consultative Document's emphasis on the mounting cost of rail revenue support, the White Paper conceded that 'to maintain public transport will require a substantial and continuing commitment to financial support where the income from fares is not enough to ensure a reasonable level of services' (para. 14). Prominent in the 'Summary of Decisions' of the White Paper was the statement:

Expenditure in support of public transport and to moderate increases in fares will not be reduced, as had been planned, despite the declining share of public expenditure which can be devoted to transport. This will mean more support for buses, and less for road construction.

The grave deficiencies in the provision of public transport services in the rural areas were recognised. Emphasis was to be placed on local initiative and responsibility in transport planning and on a relaxation of public-service vehicle licensing laws to generate more flexibility in the provision of bus and minibus services. The government took a less interventionist stance on the problem of freight transport. The objective of policy was to secure 'a fair basis of competition between modes'. To make this possible, it was recognised that the largest lorries would have to be more heavily taxed until their contribution to Inland Revenue matched the cost of the damage they inflicted on the roads. The commitment to sustain a five-year rolling programme of investment for locomotives and air-braked wagons and the statement that 'any notion of imposing major cuts in the railway network' had been ruled out, were both reassuring. Unfortunately, the programme was never firmly established because of Treasury restraints in 1976.

The NUR head office research group, in a detailed commentary on the White Paper, published in July 1977, welcomed the conversion of Mr Rodgers to at least a part of the case being advocated by the BRB and the railway unions. On the other hand, it regretted the decision to cut the public-service obligation grant by £20 million by 1980, deplored the postponement of a decision about Freightliners and National Carriers and found it anomalous that much had been written about the need to conserve energy but that there had been no mention whatever of the case for further railway electrification.

The outstanding changes brought about through the introduction of the Transport Act of 2 August 1978 were the return of Freightliner Ltd to full British Railway Board ownership – since 1969 the BRB had held only a 49 per cent share in that undertaking, the balance being held by the NFC – the reduction of the National Freight Corporation's debt and the funding of its pension obligations; the increased provision for community bus services in the county areas; continuing support for railway passenger service; and the introduction of more stringent inspection and control of road goods vehicles.

The return of Freightliner to British Rail, under which it had

operated during 1965–8, was a carefully considered change and
by no means an act of doctrinal dogmatism. Under the Transport
Act 1968, section 1(a)ii, the National Freight Corporation had
an obligation to secure that freight went by rail whenever such a
mode was 'efficient and economic'. It was one thing to consider,
on its merits, the right mode of transport for each consignment
offered; it was quite another thing to send *all* traffic from a depot
by road. Mr Philip Whitehead, MP for Derby, North, shortly
afterwards to become an NUR-sponsored MP, told the House of
Commons on 23 January 1976 that both National Carriers Ltd
and Freightliners Ltd were deliberately turning from rail to road,
that the Bristol National Carriers Ltd depot was road-oriented,
as were the Freightliner terminals at Sheffield and Hull. The
Hull–Liverpool Freightliner services were exclusively carried out
by road.[66] The words of the National Freight Corporation's
Annual Report for 1972 read, in part, more like a publicity
handout of the Road Haulage Association than a survey of the
year's work of a public body which had been brought into
existence to integrate road and rail transport:

> 1972 was a year which marked a crescendo of shrill, and mainly
> ill-conceived, if understandable criticism of the road haulage
> industry, particularly directed against the large freight vehicle,
> and involving a sustained attack on many vital road investment
> programmes.
>   It is disturbing, therefore, to observe the 'lemming like'
> reaction of otherwise discerning people who, when faced with
> the difficult transport problems of congestion, pollution, noise,
> vibration, safety, investment and the survival of the city,
> assume that the answer lies in discriminating harshly against
> the road vehicle with the rider that traffic must be directed
> exclusively to rail.[67]

This was ignoring the fact that neither the British Railways
Board, nor the NUR, had ever claimed that *all* freight traffic
should be sent by rail.
   The case for an improvement in public passenger transport
services in the counties was overwhelming. Seventeen years before
the passing of William Rodgers's Act, the Jack Committee
Report of 1961 on Rural Bus Services noted that, in the context
of rapidly increasing private car ownership and decreasing bus
services, the hardship and inconvenience experienced by those
without the use of motor cars was undoubtedly increasing.[68] By
the late 1970s the situation was very much worse.

What was happening was that a major new underprivileged group was emerging in the community. Its members were to be found in urban areas as well as in the countryside. They were those whose mobility had been taken away in consequence of the decline in public transport services. The largest component of this underprivileged group was made up of the elderly. The predicament of some of them has been succinctly summarised in a recent study:

> What frequently happens is that an elderly couple in their sixties retire to a rural area with a car and the money to run it. Then inflation or the physical disability or death of the driver robs the couple, or the surviving member, of the use of the car. Quite quickly what was an attractive rural environment becomes a liability and the house-price gradient which originally attracted the couple from their high value urban or suburban home, now inhibits their return, or the return of the surviving member. A social problem ensues.[69]

It is not only the elderly who have been immobilised. All young people under 17 years of age· the large majority of married women wage-earners whose husbands use the family car during working hours; most of the low paid and the physically disabled have suffered severely from the decline in urban and rural bus services and the elimination of hundreds of branch line railways.

In 1975 80 per cent of the parish councils of Suffolk, questioned about local transport, found that there was 'an inadequate service which failed to meet the basic requirements of travel for shopping, visiting doctors and dentists and hospital visiting and failed lamentably with evening facilities for social and cultural activities outside the village'.[70] In a Commons debate on transport in rural areas held on 2 May 1977 Mr Caerwyn E. Roderick, MP for Brecon and Radnor, said that buses were 'almost non-existent' in the two counties he represented and Mr David Penhaligon, MP for Truro, found that octogenarians in his constituency felt that they had better transport facilities – by horse and cart – in their childhood than they did in their old-age.[71]

Under the 1968 Town and County Planning Act (as amended by the Town and Country Planning Act 1971 and the Local Government Act 1972) counties are entitled to claim central government financial support for their public transport services. The most important assistance is in the form of the Transport Supplementary Grant. Before 1979, however, it did depend very much on the initiative of the different county councils whether or not full advantage was taken of the opportunities for central government financial support for railway and bus services. In a large number of Tory-dominated shires councils were apparently indifferent to the needs of people without cars. In his contribution to the debate on 2 May 1977, William Rodgers, Minister of Transport, expressed concern that the National Bus Company was having to withdraw its services in many cases simply because county councils had refused to make available, to the company the revenue support the Minister had already allocated.[72] On 19 January 1978, in the second-reading debate on the Transport Bill, he repeated the charge. 'Some counties', he said, 'having been given grant explicitly to support public Transport, had not in fact paid it over.'[73] Later in the second-reading debate other members gave chapter and verse on the consequences of the Tory-dominated councils' failure to make full use of the resources available to them. Oxford and Suffolk county councils had refused to pass on any funds to the National Bus Company; Sussex asked for but 26 per cent of the sums considered necessary by the company and Kent applied for only 37 per cent of the total the four main bus operators of the county requested.[74] The result, according to Mr R. E. Bean, MP for Rochester and Chatham, was that the reduction in bus miles run in Kent was the largest of any county in Great Britain and that fare increases were at a rate well above the rise in the retail price index.[75] The Independent Commission on Transport found that in 1973 the county council of Lincoln, parts of Lindsey, refused to pay a subsidy of £33,000 towards the retention of thirteen bus services in the eastern part of the county, where as recently as 1971 substantial rail closures occurred. But the same county in 1971–2 spent £202,000 on subsidising car parking.[76]

William Rodgers attempted to overcome these severe short-comings in public transport provision in the counties by adopting a variety of measures included in clauses 1–7 of the Transport Act 1978. Under clause 1 it became the duty of each non-metropolitan county council in England and Wales, in consultation with public passenger-transport operators and district councils, to promote a co-ordinated and efficient system of public passenger transport to meet the county's needs. Under clause 2 they were required to prepare and publish, not later than 31 March 1979, a passenger-transport plan for the succeeding five years and to revise and republish it every twelve months. The details of the kind of information to be included in the plans were spelt out in the Act. They were to cover an estimate of public-transport needs and policies to be followed to meet them; the financial resources required and how they were to be met; a statement of how far earlier estimates had been realised; an account of the consultation that had been entered into before the plan was drafted; the agreements made between the county and the operators for the provision of financial support; and the travel concession schemes available within the county. Under clause 4 the vehicle licensing laws were changed to permit the traffic commissioners to grant road service licences to those willing to provide community bus services, using volunteer drivers and operating on a non-profit-making basis, the vehicles used being those adapted to carry at least eight and not more than sixteen passengers. Before they granted such licences the traffic commissioners had to satisfy themselves that there were no other public-transport facilities available to meet the needs of customers on the proposed route. Clause 5 legalised regular car-sharing for payment and public advertisement of non-profit-making social car schemes. All these proposals were designed to bring greater cost efficiency and flexibility into public road passenger transport. They were not intended to displace existing services of the National Bus Company or the services provided by British Rail, for both of which additional financial assistance was promised. Since the Minister was well aware of the failure on the part of many county councils to provide support for adequate public transport services, he sent them all a circular letter which emphasised what was required. The five-year transport plan was 'to identify the pattern of routes and the levels of service that the county council think needed, and indicate how the service will be provided.'

The NUR welcomed the Act; but Harry Cowans, one of its MPs, stressed the need for vigilance in its operation. He recognised that the aim was to establish passenger services where none existed. He appreciated the safeguards for existing bus operators, in that the traffic commissioners had to satisfy themselves that there were no other public transport facilities available before they granted licences for minibuses. But he feared that it would be relatively easy 'to make a situation fit that criterion by the running down of an existing service, by taking away a service that exists and making the situation fit the criterion'. He was concerned that those clauses in the Act should not be used as an excuse for closing further rural railway lines.[77] It seemed likely that the issue 'Can the bus replace the train?' would be a live one in the 1980s; and that warnings published by the Railway Invigoration Society that bus-substitution for railway services, such as those between Machynlleth and Pwllheli on the Cambrian coast, was no answer at all to customers needs, since – to give one example – the journey from Towyn to Barmouth by bus would take one hour and fifty minutes, whereas by train it took thirty-one minutes.[78]

Many aspects of transport policy were not covered in the 1978 Act. Despite the road-orientation of National Carriers Ltd – in contrast with the intentions expressed in the Transport Act of 1968 – no provision was made for the return of this subsidiary of the National Freight Corporation to British Rail. No mention was made of railway electrification. More important still was the absence of any firm commitment to provide railway investment adequate to match up to the desperate need of British Rail to replace equipment introduced in the 1950s. In his evidence to the Select Committee on Nationalised Industries in the autumn of 1976 Peter Parker urged the government 'to square up to the need for a national transport policy with stamina'. It was the manifest failure of governments over the preceding thirty years to take this requirement seriously which contributed to the decline in the labour force engaged in public transport[79] – the subject of investigation in Chapter 2.

CHAPTER 2

THE RAILWAY WORKFORCE

I

IN 1950 the British railway industry was highly labour-intensive; thirty years later it was very much less so. At mid-century the railways employed no less than 605,455 persons, a figure which did not include those working in hotels and catering services. Thirty years later the workforce had fallen to 182,031, a decline of 70 per cent. Despite this enormous rundown in the labour force, the passenger miles travelled in 1978 were only 5 per cent fewer than in 1950. The fall in ton-miles of freight carried was far more serious – in 1978 it was only 55 per cent of the total for 1950 – but it was substantially less than the fall in the numbers employed in the industry. Though there are pitfalls in attempting to give an exact measure of changes in productivity of the railway labour force, the above statistics provide indisputable evidence of an impressive improvement. The number employed at the end of each year are listed in Table 2.1.

The table reveals particularly sharp decreases in manpower in the years 1957–7, when there was a rapid replacement of steam by diesel locomotives, and 1961–4, when the Beeching closures of workshops and branch lines were carried out.

The level of employment in some of the principal workgroups in the railway service is shown in Figure 2.1, in which the clerical grades and the supervisory staff are shown separately, as well as being included in the more comprehensive grouping 'salaried staff'. In the case of the goods and cartage staff the comparison has to be made between 1950 and 1967, rather than 1978, since under the Transport Act 1968 most of the staff in this category were transferred to the National Freight Corporation. The 1978 figure for workshop staff includes both employees of British Rail Engineering Ltd in the larger workshops, and those employed by British Railways in smaller establishments.

The decline in staff numbers was steepest where the technological changes in the industry were most complete and far-reaching. The disappearance of the labour-intensive steam locomotive and its replacement by the labour-saving diesel, or still more labour-saving electric locomotive, contributed largely to the

Table 2.1   *British Railways: Staff at End of Year*

1950	605,455	1960	514,500	1970	273,063
1951	599,890	1961	500,434	1971	264,061
1952	601,381	1962	476,545	1972	256,007
1953	593,768	1963	464,286*	1973	250,083
1954	577,384	1964	422,167	1974	255,902
1955	563,040	1965	387,663	1975	251,627
1956	570,547	1966	360,696	1976	243,476
1957	573,499	1967	339,442	1977	240,073
1958	550,123	1968	317,478	1978	243,264
1959	518,863	1969	275,469†	1979	182,031‡

Notes:
   * Staff employed on ships and in harbours, hotels and catering are included in the figure for 1963 and subsequent years. There were 24,735 persons employed in these categories in 1963 and 20,960 in 1977.
   † At the end of 1968 24,690 staff were transferred to National Carriers Ltd and a further 1,519 to Freightliners Ltd. From 1 January 1969 these 26,209 former employees of British Railways or of the Transport Holding Company were part of the labour force of the National Freight Corporation.
   ‡ The 1979 figure includes 2,522 staff of Freightliner Ltd, from 1 January 1979 controlled by the British Railways Board. The figures do not include those employed in London transport.
Sources: British Transport Commission, *Annual Report and Accounts*, 1950–62; British Railways Board, *Annual Report and Accounts*, 1963–79; D. L. Munby and A. H. Watson, *Inland Transport Statistics; Great Britain, 1900–1970* (Oxford: Clarendon Press, 1978), pp. 49, 170. Also information kindly supplied by the Manpower Planning Officer, British Railways Board, 30 August 1979.

71·6 per cent fall in employment in the footplate grades, although branch line closure and the decline in freight traffic also played a part. Coming a close second to the footplate grades in the rate of decline in numbers were the signalmen, of whom 25,190 were employed in 1950 and only 7,961 in 1978, a decrease of 68·4 per cent. But whereas the fall in employment in footplatemen was most rapid in the late 1950s and the 1960s, reductions in the numbers of signalmen were more marked in the 1970s as the replacement of a large number of manually operated signal boxes by fewer, larger, power boxes gathered momentum. The introduction, first of punch-card machines and then of computers, into the head offices and regional offices of the railways, for operations such as accounting, wage and salary calculation and traffic censuses, greatly reduced the volume of routine work in administration, while the multiprinter ticket-issuing machines brought labour economies in the booking offices. Thus, the fall in numbers of

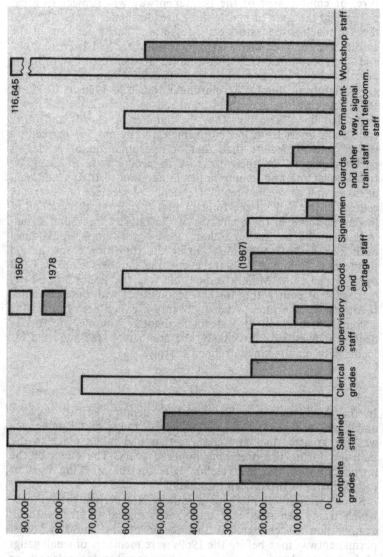

Figure 2.1 Railway staff by principal grades, 1950 and 1978

Sources: British Transport Commission, *Annual Census of Staff*, 1950; British Railways Board, *Census of Earnings*, October 1978

clerical staff of 68·2 per cent was only slightly less than the fall in numbers of signalmen. Not only the volume, but also the structure, of employment of the permanentway was subject to great changes in the span of nearly three decades under review. In 1960 the 374 machine-operators constituted less than 1 per cent of the workforce; eighteen years later their numbers had risen to 1,602 and their proportion of the total to 10 per cent. Within the permanentway category the signal and telecommunication staff grew slightly in numbers from under 10,000 in 1950 to 10,520 in 1978, marking the growth in overhead cable work on the newly electrified lines. The fact that the number of guards and other train staff, apart from locomotivemen, fell by only 47 per cent, a slower rate of decline than that of any other major grades, is partly explained by their increase in productivity in assuming ticket-collecting and issuing duties in addition to their traditional ones, as well as to the greater frequency of services on inter-city routes. In the light of the fundamental changes in the method of locomotion and in the character of the railway track and signalling, it might be assumed that railway workshops would have been kept exceptionally busy during the transition from the old to the new technology. In the event, the numbers employed fell by 51.3 per cent. Mainly responsible was the policy of railway management contracting for new locomotives with outside manufacturers. Furthermore, whereas twenty-five days are required for a complete overhaul of a steam locomotive, the electric variety needs but five days.[1] Inevitably, the number of staff required for locomotive maintenance declined sharply.

II

In the third quarter of the twentieth century British railways underwent a technical revolution whose range and significance was far greater than any changes that had taken place in the industry during the preceding hundred years. The effect of the introduction of the new technologies on the working lives of railwaymen has often been traumatic.

Since the first essential for a railway is a permanentway over which trains can pass with safety, it is logical to start with an examination of changes in this sector of the industry. Most permanentway men before the 1960s were members of small gangs of four men, led by a ganger, and responsible for a length or 'patch' of up to four miles of the track. They worked with almost the same equipment as had been used by lengthmen a century earlier – hammers, box spanners, fishbolt spanners, shovels, ballast forks, trenail cutters, clawbars, crowbars, barrows, the Abtus or other forms of riddles (for sifting the ballast) and track liners (for ensuring that the track is properly aligned). The work was physically exacting. Sidney Welborn, an experienced plate-layer and ganger, considered that, for the old methods of track maintenance, men with the constitution and stamina of trained athletes were required.[2] J. W. Stafford, who was a lengthman for thirty-three years before he was elected President of the NUR in 1954, asserted that it was management's view in the 1930s that the heavier the tool, the greater would be the output of work, and that this belief had not entirely died out in the 1950s. However, following the deliberations of a track tools sub-committee of the Railway Executive in 1954–5 there was a switch to lighter but still sturdy equipment.[3]

In the 1950s and 1960s many length gangs were merged to form larger 'section gangs' with responsibility for longer stretches of the track. They were often taken to the worksite on petrol-driven rolling stock. These larger gangs were needed for rail replacement and the ganger, often a man of strong and lively personality, was the 'conductor' of an operation which required the concentrated co-operative effort of as many as thirty men. At a late stage in the NUR Burns' Night celebrations in London, in January 1979, Sid Welborn, as his contribution to the evening's festivities, re-peated the words he had used to get the required response from his gang: 'Come on men. Close together now. All those who've got backs, get in the middle. Eyes down. Lifty, titty, titty, high!'

Increasingly from its first introduction as far back as 1932 what was known by platelayers as the 'whitewash train' was used by civil-engineering departments to indicate to gangs where there were defects in the track. The electric circuits in the special coaches were activated sharply or faintly according to whether the bogie of the coach had a bumpy or smooth ride. At the same time whitewash was splashed on to the track at points where the going was rough and the ballast or the rails needed attention. The apprehension felt by members of a gang at the approach of this mechanical aid to good track maintenance was expressed in verse by J. W. Stafford:

> The whitewash train! The whitewash train!
> Is running down our way again,
> And woe betide if joints are slack,
> Mayhap we all will get the sack,
> Our nerves are simply on the rack,
> We chant a sad refrain.

The whitewash train! The whitewash train!
We all have got it on our brain.
Inspectors warn us, 'Be prepared,'
The ganger he is badly scared,
Small wonder that he bawled and blared,
And shouted yet again.[4]

J. W. Stafford was writing about the original 'Hallade' recorder, which was in use for over thirty years until it was gradually replaced by a more sophisticated version from 1964 onwards. Then in 1978 came the Black Box, containing the most up-to-date electronic equipment which located and analysed faults in the track and rail bed with even greater accuracy and speed.[5]

In the autumn of 1951 an exhibition of permanentway mechanical equipment was staged at Marylebone station. The new machines were viewed with amazement and wonder by the members of the permanentway staff, who were quite unfamiliar with the vast majority of the exhibits. Demonstrations were staged of ballast-cleaning machines; ballast scarifiers; tamping machines, later known on the job as 'Waltzing Matildas' (for packing in the ballast); mobile cranes; pneumatic spike drivers; impact wrenches; track-slewing machines; motor scythes and hedge-trimmers; mobile weed-sprayers, and many other devices. The display revealed the potentialities for labour-saving in track-laying and maintenance rather than the then-existing practice of British Railways.

At an intermediate stage between the traditional method of track maintenance and the modern methods of the 1970s came the Kango gangs (so-called from the brandnames of the power tools they used) which, with the aid of power-driven wrenches and pneumatic jackhammers and the accompaniment of much noise and dust, performed in quick time the work formerly carried out by length gangs using the traditional handtools. Kango gangs experienced the worst of both worlds. The physical exertion needed was often greater than was the case with length gangs, since the heavy power-driven tools had to be manhandled often for long distance and over embankments and fences. At the same time, in consequence of the noisier nature of the job and the need to work to close time schedules, they were subject to as great mental strains as those experienced by operators manning the largest self-propelled machines.[6] The upkeep of the permanentway and its bridges, tunnels and earthworks, together with the signalling system, accounted for about 16·5 per cent of British Railways' working expenses in the mid-1960s.[7] This heavy cost of providing the railways' infrastructure was the spur to mechanisation. At this time the editor of the *Railway Review* observed that

> Huge maintenance machines are going into action all over Britain. They lift tons of rails and sleepers with ease, automatically levelling and making firm foundations and doing as much work in an hour as 100 men. There are machines which riddle the ballast at speeds unheard of only a few years ago.[8]

Outstanding among the innovations were machines for laying the railway track; ballast cleaning; tamping; aligning the rails, welding rails and digging trenches. In the early part of 1966 there were already twenty-seven huge tamping machines and twenty lining machines at work on different parts of the railway network, while eight automatic ballast cleaners, covering 300 yards in an hour's operation, were in use before the year's end.

One of the most labour-saving innovations was the welded rail, replacing the old sixty-foot rails which were jointed to each other by fishplates. The early experiments were with 300-ft lengths with which 300 miles of track had been laid by 31 December 1960. But before long 1,000-ft or 1,200-ft lengths were common. The pace of innovation was as brisk as the government's financial restraints on investment would allow. By the end of 1964 1,800 track miles, or 18·5 per cent of running lines, had been long-welded, and by 31 December 1979 9,527 miles of welded rails were in use.[9] Together with the welded rail came the prestressed concrete sleeper and spring metal tie (replacing the less durable and less stable wooden variety), both of which greatly reduced the costs of maintenance. Under the old system, with jointed rails, length gangs spent about half their working hours on joint maintenance, tightening and oiling fishbolts, attending to sleepers near the joints and hammering in the wooden ties. Under the new regime these tasks disappeared, even though in abnormal conditions, such as prevailed in the summer of 1976, new problems of buckling might arise. The upshot of all these remarkable changes was that substantial economies were effected in British Railways' maintenance costs. In the early 1970s £4,500 was needed to maintain each mile of track where the jointed rail was still in use, but £1,850 sufficed to maintain each mile of welded track.[10] There were also economies in railway operation. At a running speed of 50 mp.h. there was a saving in traction of 125 horsepower on hauling a train weighing 1,000 tons. At 75 m.p.h. the saving was 250 horse-power.[11]

The modern railway network of inter-city routes provided the

passenger with a smoother and faster ride and helped to reduce
BR's track-maintenance costs; but these were gains which were
paid for by a disruption of the work patterns and family and
social life of trackmen. Since the length of track which could be
relaid or maintained with the aid of the new machinery was far
greater than that normally looked after by the length gangs using
only handtools, the labour force was reorganised into mobile
gangs whose range of operations was up to twenty miles. Furthermore, the new machines were scarcely capable of neatly standing
aside on the approach of a train, as did the length gangs; in no
uncertain fashion they blocked the track on which they stood
and, when mobile cranes and ballast wagons were in use, even
caused the blockage of the neighbouring track as well. From the
management's viewpoint these were compelling reasons for concentrating the use of the machines and the mobile gangs at night
and at weekends when train timetables were lighter. It was a
change which disrupted the lifestyle of the trackman. It also
caused frustration to weekend travellers.

U. Bruce, secretary of the Willesden No. 1 branch of the NUR
which has over 200 trackmen members, came to London from the
West Indies in the mid-1950s when British Railways was desper-
ately short of staff. He has been employed on the permanentway
ever since. He recalled a fine spirit of comradeship in the length
gang he joined. The members of the four-man team got to know
each other and their families very well and stayed a long time in
the same job. They vied with other gangs to achieve the best-
maintained 'patch' on the line. They lived near their work. In
wet weather they took refuge in what was colloquially known as
'Fernando's Hideaway', the isolated trackside cabin. With the
advent of mobile gangs men were required to pass a test to work
with the new machines and this deterred a number of the older
hands from staying in the job. The new, larger groupings of men
lacked the old *ésprit de corps* and the turnover of labour was
alarmingly rapid. Of twenty men newly recruited at the beginning
of one week, half might remain to continue working in the week
that followed. The more impersonal nature of the job, the noise,
dust and vibration were all deterrents to continuity of employment.[12] Sid Welborn, a ganger from York, confirmed these impressions. In the early 1950s the men who worked on the track in
his district used to live in lineside cottages near their 'patch'
and their families formed close-knit communities. When mobile
gangs began to be formed in the following decade, the turnover of labour became far more rapid. It was not only that there
were objections to the unsocial hours worked on the track

machines, but also that Rowntrees and other firms in the area offered more congenial working conditions.[13] Harry Lofkin, a track machineman from Crewe No. 4 branch, also stressed the social consequences of mechanisation:

When the first track machines started on the permanentway most men were dedicated men of a high standard. Then as more machines were introduced the operators began to lose contact with other permanentway colleagues and began to believe they were an elitist group. The long travelling and heavy night-duty content began to change the operators both physically and temperamentally (most of the operators in the Crewe division have put on at least two stone and the saddest part is the number of marriage breakdowns that have occurred).[14]

When the International Transport Workers' Federation distributed a questionnaire among workers on the permanentway and invited comments, one respondent replied: 'One of the things I think you have missed is what the *wife* or family of a railwayman think about the railways. The social side of a track machine man is practically non-existent.'[15]

But the picture was not entirely bleak. A lot of track-maintenance work remained unmechanised. Sidings gangs and length gangs were still needed for stretches of the line near stations, junctions and points, and on the less-used branches of the railway network. In 1976 the ITF received comments such as 'Fresh air and freedom'; 'A good healthy open-air job'; and 'Friendship, teamwork' from men still employed in these locations. And some of those who worked on the new machines were more than contented. Their replies were exemplified by the comment of one of them: 'A new age in track maintenance and glad to be in the forefront of it.' A lot depended on age differences. The young, mechanically minded machine-operator, attracted by the extra money that rewarded the additional skill, and still without marriage ties, would find the job more appealing than would the older man with strong family attachments.

III

In 1950 the Railway's Executive's huge fleet of 19,790 steam locomotives completely dwarfed the 100 diesels and 17 electric locomotives in use on the rail network. (The 2,148 electric rail motor vehicles, employed mainly for Southern Region services, were in a class by themselves.) By 1977 steam had long since disappeared and the number of tractive units had been slimmed down to less than one-fifth of the figure a quarter of a century earlier. There were now 3,290 diesel and 320 electric locomotives, together with 76 power cars for the high-speed trains.[16] This was the revolution in methods of traction which was largely responsible for the 71·6 per cent drop in the number of staff employed in the locomotive department as shown in Figure 2.1.

With the passing of time it may easily be forgotten how labour-intensive the steam locomotive was. No one could question that two men – the driver and the fireman – were absolutely essential on the footplate. But behind them, and often unseen by the general public, was a small army of equally important supporting staff. The BTC's *Annual Census of Staff* for 1952 lists them. There were engine-cleaners and chargemen engine-cleaners; boiler-washers and chargemen boiler-washers; coalmen; fire-droppers; steamraisers; locomotive shunters; cranemen; shedmen; storekeepers; timekeepers; hydraulic and pumping-engine staff and the water-softening plant attendants. The size of this support army in 1950 was nearly 18,000 men and boys.

The career structure in the locomotive department in the age of steam began with the grade of engine-cleaner. Removing the mixture of grease and grime from the hundreds of moving parts of a large locomotive was a mammoth task, requiring the labour of a team of six or seven men and boys. The youngest cleaners were given the dirtiest job – that of cleaning the transmission lines and big-ends under the belly of the locomotive. The more experienced members of the team were given relatively more congenial tasks and the most senior were allocated the most sought-after job of cleaning the boiler. All the work was dirty; but those men and boys who had the dirtiest tasks were known by other railway staff as 'the Black Princes'.[17] The most unhealthy and dangerous work in the locomotive sheds was performed by the brick-arch attendant, who spent most of his working hours inside the locomotive firebox, scraping away the clinkers from the brick arch and the ends of the firetubes.

Having graduated in the locomotive shed as a cleaner and having risen to the grade of 'passed cleaner', the aspiring foot-plateman was allowed to take his turn as a fireman. Stoking the boiler of an express steam locomotive was one of the most physically exhausting jobs on the railway. On an uphill route or in conditions of contrary winds it could involve the shovelling of up to six tons of coal from the tender to the firebox in the course of one shift. Besides feeding the firebox, the fireman needed to break up the larger lumps of coal in the tender, the 'long toms', into the smaller sizes suitable for maintaining good combustion. It was generally only after many years of this back-breaking toil that the fireman had the opportunity to cross to the other side of the cabin and become a driver. Although the driver's job was not so exacting as that of his mate in the 'set' – the term used for a team of driver and fireman – he also needed to exert his strength as, for example, when he opened or closed the engine throttle. A good driver used his hearing as well as his sight. Without having to look at the gauge, he could tell by the sound made by the steam how fully the brake had been applied. For both men in the set the worries and tensions experienced in carrying hundreds of passengers safely to their destinations were to some extent relieved through the physical exertion required to control the engine.

By the late 1970s both the structure of employment in the locomotive department, and the character of footplatemen's work, had been completely transformed. The British Railways Board's Census of Earnings and Staff for 1977 makes no mention of boiler-washers, firedroppers, steamraisers, coalmen, hydraulic and pumping-engine staff or water-softening plant attendants. Through the disappearance of the steam locomotive and as a result of extended negotiations between management and unions culminating in the Pay and Efficiency agreements at Penzance and Windsor in 1968 and 1969 (discussed more fully in Chapter 5), there was a great simplification of the grade structure. In the locomotive department in 1977 those who remained were classified as traction trainees, drivers' assistants, relief drivers and relief drivers' assistants and drivers.

Relatively suddenly in the late 1950s and early 1960s thousands of drivers and firemen, many with practically a lifetime's experience with steam locomotives, had to adjust to the very different task of driving diesel or electric locomotives. Only three weeks were allowed for the training process; two weeks' instruction in the classroom and one week on the footplate. A leading driver who passed through this experience described the time allowed as 'ridiculously short'. There was a new kind of brake which did not hiss and give an aural indication of how effectively it had been applied. The driver had to watch the needle on the gauge. It was a foreign field to drivers familiar with the controls of the steam locomotive. Many drivers went home 'worried sick' about how they would manage.[18] The switch to driving diesel multiple units (DMUs) was easier. The brake was easier to manage, and for gathering momentum and controlling speed, it was somewhat like driving a motor car with gears. Many footplate-men, therefore, preferred to transfer to branch line working with DMUs rather than to undergo the terrors of manning the new powerful main line diesel locomotives.

The introduction of high-speed trains (Inter-City 125s) from 1976 onwards provided a much cleaner working environment for the footplateman. The physical strain, which was a marked feature of steam locomotive operation, largely disappeared. But higher speeds brought new strains of a mental and emotional character. Familiar landmarks succeeded one another in very quick succession and the driver had to maintain an unswerving attention to his job and keep a constant watch on the signals. It was a characteristic noted on other railway systems besides the British. An International Labour Organisation report in 1979 summed up the new working environment of the high-speed train driver with admirable succinctness:

> Although many automatic controls, both on the track, and in the cab, have been introduced in recent years, locomotive crew fatigue has not been greatly reduced. Although physical fatigue has been reduced by the introduction of the simplified diesel and electric traction units, there has been an increase in mental fatigue, induced by the greater amount of instrument data which the driver must process and by the increased stress due to greater operating speeds and heavier schedules.[19]

The NUR and ASLEF had a considerable say in the final design of the high-speed train. Demonstrations of a prototype and driver's cab mockup were arranged in Derby in the autumn of 1973 when the NUR representatives, chosen from the locomotive-men members of the EC, urged the construction of an enlarged screen, the placing of the driver's and assistant's seats side by side and the provision of better clothing lockers. They complained that there was too much noise and vibration in the driver's cab. In the guard's compartment they found excessive noise and draught and poor siting of the handbrake handle, intercommuni-cation equipment and speedometer. Numerous modifications of the original design were introduced as a result of the union's representations.[20]

A glance at photographs of nineteenth-century steam locomo-tives underlines, by the contrasts with modern times, the benefits brought by the exercise of union negotiating rights in the second half of the twentieth century. The earlier photographs show the driver and fireman on the footplate completely exposed to the elements. No thought appears to have been given to the health and comfort of those who drove the train.

The emergence of diesel and electric locomotives gave rise to the controversy over single-manning. Many critics assumed that, since a man was no longer required to feed a firebox with coal, all trains could be single-manned without any threat to the safety of passengers or staff. However, the problem is a little more complicated than the strident advocates of greater productivity have suggested. Moreover misleading comparisons have sometimes been made with manning policies on foreign railway systems. It has, for example, been suggested that the Dutch railways have a much higher proportion of single-manned trains than do the British, overlooking the fact that the average locomotive trip is much shorter in Holland than it is in Great Britain and that diesel multiple units figure much more prominently in Dutch than in British railways. If comparison is confined to the manning of DMUs, then the large majority of trains in both countries are single-manned. In 1977, 9·8 per cent of the British multiple-unit fleet was single-manned.[21]

Critics also tend to overlook the great increase in single-manning on British locomotives in the last quarter-century, largely through the implementation of two agreements reached between the NUR and ASLEF and British Railways in 1957 and 1965. The first of these, signed on 18 December 1957, when there were only seven diesel locomotives in service for other than shunting duties, became effective from 1 January 1958 and, therefore, applied to diesel train operation virtually from its inception. It provided that locomotives were to be single-manned wherever the driver's trip did not exceed 200 miles or his tour of duty six hours. There were important exceptions to this ruling. Double-manning was to apply between any two points where the scheduled non-stop distance was more than 100 miles, or the scheduled non-stop running time was more than two hours. At night-time, defined as between midnight and 6 a.m., locomotives were to be double-manned except in cases where trains were scheduled to finish between midnight and 1 a.m., or to start between 5 a.m. and 6 a.m. Where the train was steam-heated, a secondman was required to attend to the steam-heating apparatus. Finally, provision was made for a 'physical needs break' of thirty minutes between the third and fifth hours of duty on single-manned trains.[22]

By the mid-1960s steam locomotives had entirely disappeared, electrification was spreading and train speeds had been increased.

A new manning agreement, taking these developments into account, was therefore signed on 28 October 1965. The outstanding feature of the new agreement was that longer-distance single-manning was to be introduced. For express passenger, parcel and fish trains the limit was raised to 350 miles or six hours of duty; for stopping passenger trains the new limits were 250 miles or six hours of duty; in the case of express freight it was 250 miles or seven hours of duty, while for other through freight trains it was 200 miles or seven hours of duty; and for stopping freight trains there were the more modest limits of 100 miles and seven hours. It was agreed that trains should be double-manned where non-stop distance or running times were 175 miles or two-and-a-half hours in the case of express passenger, parcel or fish trains; 125 miles or three hours, in the case of express freight and 100 miles or three hours in the case of other through freight. The night-manning regulations remained unchanged for electric and diesel trains, except that for DMUs and EMUs single-manning was to be the rule for trains finishing their trips between midnight and 2 a.m. or commencing running between 4 a.m. and 6 a.m. It was noted by the parties to the agreement that a court of inquiry report, dated 22 September 1965, recommended, in its paragraph 102, that 'the final removal of restrictions on single-manning at night should follow in a year or two at most'.[23] In the event it was nearly three years before the change occurred. Under item 2 of the Pay and Efficiency (Stage I) Agreement for Footplate Staff between the British Railways Board, ASLEF and the NUR, signed on 29 August 1968, single-manning of locomotives was extended throughout the twenty-four hours of the day subject to the exceptions concerning distance run and hours of duty contained in the agreement of 1965.[24] There was a further extension of single-manning under an agreement reached by the same three parties on 13 October 1970, when the maximum distance for single-manning of Freightliner, express parcels and freight trains timed up to a maximum speed of 75 m.p.h. or over was raised from the 250 miles laid down in the 1965 agreement to 350 miles.

With the arrival of the high-speed train, single-manning was again the subject of prolonged discussions. In the course of 1972 prototype trains were ready for trial-runs, but ASLEF banned the manning of them unless it received from the BRB an assurance that in all cases the HSTs would be double-manned; that there should be higher pay for drivers when speeds in excess of 100 m.p.h. were scheduled; that the training schedule for drivers destined for the new trains should be agreed at a national level;

and that there should be substantial modification in the design of the driver's cab. The NUR representatives in the discussions wished the trials to proceed as soon as possible on the understanding that discussions on manning, pay, training and cab design would be continued. They were deeply concerned that delays in conducting the trials were holding up construction work on the new trains at Derby, Crewe, and elsewhere. Sidney Greene reported to the NUR AGM, in July 1973, that there had already been a considerable delay in the forward programming of the £60 million worth of new locomotives. However, the ban imposed by ASLEF on the movement of the high-speed train was lifted in the early summer of 1973 and the first Inter-City 125 services began to operate from Paddington to Bristol and Cardiff in 1976. The NUR's policy for the manning of high-speed trains was made clear by a unanimous decision of the EC, in August 1972, 'That in the interests of safety, the policy of the union is to be that all trains diagrammed to run at over 100 m.p.h. should be manned by at least two drivers and a guard'.[25] This also was the policy of ASLEF.

In 1971, when the daily number of drivers' turns of duty in excess of 350 miles was only twenty-three, management was not unduly concerned about the requirement of double-manning for distances of over 350 miles. But by 1977 there were 188 drivers' turns daily involving distances in excess of 350 miles. In 1976 the BRB reached a provisional agreement with the two railway unions concerned that there should be double-manning when high-speed trains were running at over 100 m.p.h. The longest round-trip – from London to Newcastle and back – was 536 miles, so that each driver would be required to drive 268 miles. The provisional agreement also limited the driving in terms of time, with an upper limit of six hours' driving in total and three hours' continuous. In the meantime, however, the 1973 ASLEF conference adopted a resolution that no driver should be required to exceed 350 miles in a day. The claim was discussed at meetings of the Railway Staff Joint Council at various times in 1974 and 1975 until it was rejected by the Railway Staff National Council (Locomotive Section) in February 1977. ASLEF's National Executive Committee therefore decided to refer the claim to the Railway Staff National Tribunal, the arbitration body set up under the Machinery of Negotiation Agreement of 28 May 1956.

The BRB's objection to a driving limit of 350 miles was that on trips such as that from London to York and back, a distance of 376 miles, it would be necessary, if the ASLEF claim was conceded, to make a hitherto unscheduled stop at an intermediate station, thus adding unnecessary time to the journey, 'blunting the

competitive edge of inter-city services and needlessly increasing
manning levels'. Lord McCarthy (the Chairman) and Messrs E.
Choppen (nominated by the BRB) and G. H. Doughty (for
ASLEF) delivered the RSNT's Decision No. 59 of 29 November
1978. They decided that where there was a need to operate trains
over distances in excess of 350 miles without a stop to change
drivers such trains would have to be provided with two fully
qualified men, with the drivers dividing the duties between themselves. Thus, on the trip from London to York and back, one of
the drivers would be at the controls on the outward run and the
other would take over for the return journey. Similarly, on the
418-mile return journey from London to Preston each of the two
men in the cabin would be driving for 209 miles.

Critics of railway management and the unions have maintained
that footplatemen's labour is 'unproductively' employed, that on
the London–Newcastle return trip, for example, each man does
only three hours thirteen minutes' actual driving within his turn
of duty. This is reckoning without making allowance for the
greater stress involved in driving at high speeds; and it is ignoring
the fact that during the part of the journey that a driver is not at
the controls, he is providing an additional check on the signals
and is available to discover the cause of any unusual noise
which would cause a driver alone in the cabin nagging doubts
as to whether a serious fault was developing in the locomotive.

The searchlight of criticism has been directed at the survival
of double-manning of locomotives in a minority of train services.
It has not often been directed at the productivity of the locomotive department as a whole. The steam locomotive rarely delivered tractive effort equal to as much as 5 per cent of the
energy contained in the fuel put into the firebox. By contrast, the
diesel engine can deliver 35–40 per cent of the energy it con-
sumes.[26] The advocates of single-manning tend to overlook the
fact that the man in the driver's seat of a diesel locomotive is in
control of a machine at least seven times as efficient in energy
terms as the steam locomotive and tend to ignore the enormous
labour-saving achieved through the elimination of thousands of
coalmen, steamraisers, firedroppers, cleaners and others needed to
prepare the steam locomotive for service. Electric locomotive
operation and maintenance is even more economical. Traction
costs are less than one-half and maintenance costs less than one-
eighth those of diesel locomotives. If, over the last quarter of a
century, the efficiency of the internal combustion engine had been
improved as dramatically as has the railway locomotive, the

motor industry would have been revolutionised and there would have been far less concern about an energy crisis.

It is true that from a purely technological point of view fully automatic train operation on selected routes was perfectly feasible, at least from the early 1970s. At an international trade union seminar held at Frankfurt-am-Main on 21–4 October 1974 German railwaymen delegates reported that 'automatically driven locomotives already exist and the Federal Railways intend to introduce them into service some time in the 1980s'. They went on to note that 'the driver will most probably be retained', not as a skilled craftsman, but 'to supervise the automatic driver'. On London Transport's Victoria Line, opened on 1 September 1968, the management decided to retain the driver, not because he was in any way needed to drive the train, but to reassure passengers. The same considerations must have been in the minds of the managers of Deutsches Bundesbahn.

One measure of passenger railway productivity is the ratio between the number of staff employed and the number of passenger miles travelled. The question whether the locomotive is single or double-manned is clearly an important element in determining whether the labour of the staff has a high or low productivity. But it is only one of the factors involved. If the cost of travel by train is high by comparison with that of private road transport because government support for the railway system is kept at a low level – as has been the case in Britain compared to other EEC countries – there will be more empty seats on the train and the driver's labour will be less productive than it would have been under a system of more competitive rail fares.

IV

Between 1950 and 1978 the number of signalmen on British Railways fell by 68·4 per cent at the same time as the route miles of railway in use declined by 43·9 per cent. More of the 8,350 route miles closed in those years were of branch lines where traffic was light. The lines which remained open were those on which the workload of the signalman had always been heaviest. Among the signalmen remaining in the service in 1978, there were very few that had time to grow hollyhocks in front of their signalboxes; in fact Victorian signalboxes were rapidly disappearing and with them the number of signalmen horticulturalists.

In the 1970s many long-service signalmen had experience of working in at least three different types of signalbox. They would

begin working life in the manually operated boxes before proceeding to power boxes, first of the one-control-switch (OCS)
variety and then to the push-button type. The signalman who had
to make the transition from the traditional mechanical system to
a modern electronically controlled one experienced as thorough
a change in working environment as did the steam locomotive
driver when switching first to diesel, and then to high-speed train
operation.

In the manually operated signalboxes the handlevers, controlling the points switches and the semaphore signals by means of a
network of lineside wire cables, are arranged in frames of various
sizes set into the floor of the cabin. The individual signalboxes are
linked to adjacent ones by aural and visual train indicators,
namely, simple bells and dials. Any additional information required is received by telephone. The nature of the mechanical
arrangements determined the architecture of the signalboxes. Any
additional levers required had to be installed at the same floor
level, within reach of the signalman, so that the building housing
the levers was extended horizontally, rather than vertically.
Working in such boxes can be physically exhausting as the movement of the levers requires both strength and dexterity. The
signalman has also to make the correct response to information
received. The job is a satisfying one, in that the signalman
has a wide range of vision of the track; from his box he can
see the passing of trains and even wave a greeting to the driver.
He can appreciate the usefulness of his work by seeing how
he has assisted the movement of passengers and freight trains.
The stresses of his job are relieved by the physical exertion
needed to move the levers. If he considers the cabin is too
stuffy, he can open one of the windows. He is largely his own
master.

The OCS type of power signalbox represented a more than
half-way transition from manual signal operating to full electronic
control. It came into use on many parts of the railway system,
including the Manchester area, in the early 1960s.[27] It incorpor-
ates electrical control of the track signal lights, electric pneumatic
control of points and electric track circuitry for carrying train
identification information. But each set of points and signals is
manually controlled by an individual switch and operates independently of other points and signals.

A further stage in the transition to full automation was reached
with the introduction of the push-button type of power signalbox,
the characteristics of which were described in 1977 by an International Transport Workers Federation research team:

The push button power box contains a more elaborate control mechanism which augments manual control over sets of switches with semi-automatic and automatic electrical systems. This makes it possible for the signalman to manipulate and control traffic over an expanded area of track. Simply by depressing a series of buttons on an illuminated control panel, multiple points and signals can be pre-set almost instantaneously. Often changes in points and signals are self correcting or contain an over-ride mechanism which may be activated for safety purposes. Consequently the push button box represents an extension of the co-ordinative route planning role of the signalman compared to older types of power boxes. The enlarged area of track covered means the push button power box develops the centralisation of signalling and track control more markedly than in earlier versions of power boxes.[28]

With the introduction of power boxes came the disappearance of semaphore signals and their replacement by the multiple-aspect colour-light variety. Under the new regime signals are brought closer and closer together until they are separated by scarcely more than half the distance required to stop the fastest train from its highest speed. Each signal shows a green, double yellow, single yellow, or red light according to the state of the line beyond. The driver of a fast train receives plenty of warning of a signal set against him; the signal preceding the red one shows a single yellow, and the one before that a double yellow light, so that he has two sections in which to bring his train to a stand. If three or more sections ahead are clear the signal will show green, enabling both high train speeds and less than five-minute train intervals to be maintained. These improvements made possible the fuller utilisation of the track and the achievement of faster train timings, but their introduction imposed new stresses on the driver and the signalman both of whom, within a given span of time, needed to assimilate a greater amount of information and to respond to this with appropriate action than had been the case with semaphore signals.[29]

When some of the first post-Second World War signalboxes were opened up, there were no special training facilities available to enable a man accustomed to the manually operated system to learn the principles and practices of the new one. C. Petty, a signalman of York No. 5 branch of the NUR, told delegates attending the AGM at Aberdeen in 1967 that sixteen years earlier when a new box was opened in his city, the 'bobbies' (as signalmen have been known from the times when they were also rail-

way policemen) were 'thrown in at the deep end and for years
had to struggle along teaching themselves'. What impressed some
of Mr Petty's contemporaries about the new working environment
was the reduced contact they had with the real world of railway
operation. Mr R. L. Tyler of Stafford, another signalman member of the 1967 AGM, pleaded that men of his grade should 'not
only be shown how to press the right buttons but should also be
allowed to go round the district so as to get to know it. Such
knowledge could not be obtained merely by looking at the diagrams because distances meant nothing'.[30]

Two circumstances were largely responsible for this divorce of
the signalman from the real situation on the tracks. First, the
compact, concrete structures of the 'power' signalboxes were
architectually in sharp contrast with their elongated 'mechanical'
predecessors. It was no longer an essential part of signalbox design that the signalman should have a view of the actual railway
network. When working in one of the new boxes, he lost the satisfaction of seeing directly the value of his contribution to traffic
movement. He also lost some of his responsibilities for the safety
of train operation. The manual-box signalman was required to
notify train control when a train passed his box without a tail-
lamp or with one or more passenger carriage doors open.
Secondly, the power signalbox controlled a much greater mileage
of track than did any one of the mechanical boxes it replaced. In
the early 1960s, when three power signalboxes, at Manchester
(Piccadilly), Wilmslow and Sandbach, displaced twenty-seven old
boxes on the thirty-one miles of route between Crewe and Manchester, the groups of men concentrated in the new boxes saw
the traffic situation only artificially, on panels. Between them the
men in the old boxes witnessed the actual movement of trains
along the entire route.

What worried signalmen was the pace and extent of innovation.
Whereas in the early 1960s the displacement of men resulting
from the introduction of one new power box was no more than
two dozen, later in the decade there were introduced in the newest
boxes miniaturised consoles covering as much as 150 miles of
track and displacing at one fell swoop up to 500 men formerly
employed in dozens of small manually operated boxes. The resignalling plan for the London Midland Region, in 1967, provided
for the replacement of 175 manually operated boxes by three
modern ones. It is through such far-reaching changes as these
that the number of signalboxes on British Railways was reduced
from about 10,000 in 1950 to 2,256 in 1979.[31]

In most manually operated boxes the signalman has some

moments of relaxation from working the levers, answering phone calls and transmitting messages. The critical difference for those who work in power boxes is that attentiveness and vigilance have to be continuous, because they have to receive a much greater volume of information – from telephones, teleprinters and computer terminals – than do those employed in the surviving manually operated boxes. In consequence the mental strain associated with the job is intensified at the same time as the physical strain is substantially lessened.

On the other hand staff who were left to operate the manual boxes took a rosier view of what life was like in the more modern onces. When W. Smithurst of Teeside, for example, began his shift one bitterly cold morning early in January 1970, his first job was to try and stop the wind whistling through a broken window. Then he tried, with numbed fingers, to light the oil lamp but gave up in despair and used the hand electric lamp instead. Between trains he managed to get his coal stove going and by 6.30 a.m. was able to dispense with his scarf and brew himself a cup of tea. Three hours later he felt warm enough to discard his overcoat. Shortly afterwards, while eating his sandwiches he glanced at a copy of the *Railway Review*, dated 2 January 1970, and saw a photograph of three immaculately dressed men in white shirts in the new Saltley power box. What he saw by no means made him contented with his lot.[32]

A further difference between the manually operated signalling era and the modern electronic one is that, in the old days, the signalman was much less subject to outside interference than is his latter-day successor. He frequently worked on his own and, provided he did his job competently, was largely immune from interference from any superior. Those working in power boxes are, however, subject to the control of a supervisor, often not promoted from the ranks of the signalmen but instead appointed from the lower ranks of management. It was a development which created some resentment and friction. In January 1977 the NUR EC resolved:

That from January 16, 1977, if any person is placed in charge of signalmen contrary to our policy (*vide* Decision No. 1279, September 1975) the signalmen involved are to immediately withdraw their labour.

In the event, strike action was avoided as the dispute was referred to the RSNT which, by Decision No. 48, resolved that there should be parity between signalmen and non-signalmen appointments to the rank of supervisor. This did not entirely settle the problem, since the wording of Decision No. 48 was vague in places and, in 1979, management was working on a policy of *interviewing* equal numbers of signalmen and non-signalmen, but not necessarily *appointing* the same number from each class.

Just as, from the purely technological point of view, the presence of a driver for the control of train movements is becoming superfluous, so the presence of lineside signals, whether of the semaphore or multiple-colour-light variety, could also well become unnecessary with the development of new technology. Under discussion between the British Railways Board and the unions in 1979 was the proposal to experiment with a direct locomotive to signalbox radio communication system. The electrified Kings Cross–Bedford suburban line was considered by the Board to be an ideal testing-ground for the new experiment.[33]

V

In 1952 the installation and maintenance of signal and telecommunication equipment on British Railways employed 9,596 men most of whom were concerned with handling mechanical rather than electrical devices. This preponderance of relatively simple manually operated equipment was reflected in the fact that more than two-thirds of the workforce were classed as either chief linemen, linemen, assistant lineman or labourers. In 1978 the grade of lineman had disappeared from the classification, though there were nearly 1,000 men doing linemen's work. The big change however was that there were by this time more than three times as many men dealing with electronic, as compared with mechanical, equipment.

The changes in methods of signalling outlined above enhanced the importance of good-quality telephonic communication between the ever-more widely separated signalboxes. Until the late 1950s railway telephone development tended to be localised. Individual exchanges were enlarged and re-equipped according to need, many with automatic calling between extensions. Between the exchanges, however, the trunk lines which were of the open-wire type, were frequently indifferent in quality and inadequate in number for the growing demand. There was consequently an increasing use of the public service. The introduction of British Railways' Modernisation Plan after 1955 presented an opportunity to make good these deficiencies and save the large sums being paid out for rented lines. Electrification and resignalling of the busier routes in any event necessitated cabling and the provision of telecommunication circuits for signalpost telephones, train describers, and so on. Thus, starting with communications between Leeds and York, direct trunk dialling by caller between all parts of the railway system was introduced. This entirely separate telephone network enables the train controllers to contact instantly their own operating staff. The switch panel on each controller's desk is his own exchange; he is independent of the 'outside' telephone network.

The spread of railway electrification – though nothing like as rapid as was merited in the national interest – gave rise to another telecommunication network linking the railway electrical control room with traffic control, the Central Electricity Generating Board, traction feeder stations, track sectioning cabins and lineside maintenance telephone points. Control is highly centralised. Thus, the whole of the London (Liverpool Street)–Enfield–Bishop's Stortford–Clacton–Southend alternating-current power distribution is controlled from Romford. Yet another development was the introduction of the Signal Transmitting, Receiving and Distribution System (STRAD), which made its first railway appearance at Crewe in 1960. This is a computer-type electronic memory which can handle multiple-route messages and sort out priorities when congestion of traffic has built up.[34]

The revolution in signalling technology had its repercussions on training and on the wages structure. In the early 1950s, when railway signalling was still largely mechanical in character, new recruits to the S and T grades had a mere fourteen days' training before being sent out to complete their practical education on the job. Two railway wagons were fitted out as classrooms and moved to a different location once a fortnight to provide the new railway staff of each neighbourhood with the necessary training. By the end of the 1970s there were eight separate courses of varying duration in permanently established training centres, such as Derby and Crewe. The NUR, from the mid-1950s, played a prominent part in establishing these more adequate arrangements for training staff.[35]

The highly skilled nature of the work of some men in the S and T grades and the frequent necessity for staff to work unsocial hours made the recruitment of staff in areas of high employment an acute difficulty. Thus, in the winter of 1971–2, there were severe staff shortages on the Southern Region.[36] In the following summer the National Conference of Permanentway, Signal and Telegraph, Overhead Traction and Canal Grades came to the conclusion that, 'due to the revolution in railway signalling in the past four years the 1968 S and T Classification Agreement no longer has any real substance and requires a drastic improvement'. It urged the EC to set up a consultative committee to make recommendations for the regrading of posts. It was a significant pointer to the rapidity of technological change that a complete restructuring of posts was considered necessary after the passage of only four years. Even under the 1968 agreement rates of pay of top-ranking S and T workers were equal to those of the highest-paid signalmen (at that time classified as Special, Class A) and above those of the highest-paid locomotivemen. In the reorganisation of the S and T grades, in 1972, the pay advantage over the locomotivemen was extended.

VI

In 1950 the Railway Executive possessed no less than 1,122,215 freight wagons with a carrying capacity, excluding brakevans, of 14,417,000 tons. The average wagon, therefore, had a capacity of under 12 tons. Eight years later the wagon fleet still exceeded a million units. Well-known components of the Beeching Plan (1963) included the drastic reduction in the number of small-capacity wagons, the playing down of small-consignment goods handling and the expansion of traffic carried in 'liner' and 'merry-go-round' freight trains. This was an aspect of the plan that was carried out with promptitude and thoroughness. The number of wagons in service was reduced by 24·9 per cent in just two years to the end of 1964, when the number remaining on the rails was down to 637,000. The policy of slimming down the size of the wagon fleet was continued by Dr Beeching's successors, so that at the end of 1979 its size had been reduced to 187,000 units with a carrying capacity of 3,863,533 tons. In short, the wagon fleet of 1978 was less than 14 per cent of that of 1950, but the average capacity per wagon, at 23 tons, had been nearly doubled over the same timespan. Simultaneously, there was a remarkable change in the character of the freight traffic. In 1967 69 per cent of rail freight moved in wagon loads and only 31 per cent in train loads. Ten years later the position was reversed; 80 per cent of freight moved in train loads and only 20 per cent in wagon loads.[37]

A large majority of the 17,592 railwaymen classified as shunters in 1952 were employed in unmechanised yards, and were engaged in the dangerous job of assembling or breaking up freight trains by connecting or disconnecting individual small-capacity wagons. These tasks were undertaken either with the aid of the shunting pole – a tool which had been in use for seventy years – or by means of fly shunting – the practice of the shunter coupling or uncoupling wagons while standing on the buffers, even when the freight train was in motion. The enormous drop in number of wagons in use; the increased capacity of those which remained; the growing number of liner and merry-go-round trains fitted with continuous brakes; the fall in the number of freight depots from over 6,000 in the pre-Beeching era to 475 in 1978; and the decline in the volume of freight traffic, all combined greatly to reduce the number of shunters employed. In fact, as part of the versatility arrangements in the pay and efficiency agreement of 1968, the grade of 'shunter' disappeared, being replaced by 'rail-man' or 'leading railman'.

Modern methods of wagon-handling have also, by greatly reducing the workload of shunting locomotives, lessened the demand for the labour of shunters. Humped marshalling yards began to be introduced in the 1950s. The trail-blazer and exemplar was the Thornton (Fife) marshalling yard, completed in 1956 at a cost of £1,300,000. Incoming trains to the yard are routed into one of six reception sidings at which they are 'cut', that is, sorted according to destination, and from which they are shunted over the hump into one of thirty-five sorting sidings. From information supplied to him the panel operator in the control tower is able to set the points which guide the 'cuts' into their correct sidings. Each wagon, as it descends the gradient, is accurately controlled in speed by two sets of automatically operated and automatically adjusted pneumatic rail brakes or retarders. Since the sorting of wagons in such yards as this accelerates their movement to their destinations, the shunters, who divide the train into cuts, are more productively employed. Many fewer shunters are needed per thousand freight miles of traffic than were needed under old methods of freight train operation and the work of those who remain is less dangerous.[38]

The most sophisticated of all innovations, which brought freight handling more completely into the age of electronics, was TOPS (Total Operations Processing System), pioneered on the Southern Pacific Railroad in the USA from 1968 and brought into use on British Railways between October 1973 and October 1975. In London, the control centre for TOPS, an IBM system 370/168 computer, is connected to each of 152 Area Freight Centres (AFCs) set up in the forty main marshalling yards and at principal freight depots. The computer stores information on the whereabouts of every wagon, whether loaded or empty, and its 'status', that is, whether it is in transit, in position with the customer, held for operational or commercial reasons, crippled, or stored. It can be used to instruct traffic controllers and train drivers on the best route available for the train to reach a given destination. It can also direct empty wagons to the nearest point where they can be usefully employed, thus minimising empty running. It does away with the necessity of labelling wagons. Clerical staff are employed for the bulk of the input and control work both in London and the AFCs. But there is still a need for the 'man on the ground' to check the accuracy of the data provided and to provide detailed basic information relating to freight train formations. Thus, the character of the work of the shunter has changed. It is no longer simply manual; he has now, in addition, to provide basic information for TOPS. It is an added responsibility which was the subject of discussion between the NUR and management, in 1974, and it led to an agreement that responsibility payments of £1·45 and £1·75, depending on grade, should be made to those involved.[39]

Before the Pay and Efficiency Agreement at Penzance, in 1968, there was a clear line of promotion for those aspiring to the rank of guard. By long tradition goods guards were recruited from the shunters, and passenger guards from the more experienced goods guards. There were also a few hundred travelling ticket collectors whose previous experience was often that of passenger guards. The rundown of freight traffic, the closure of branch lines, the locomotive single-manning agreement of 1965, and the increase in the proportion of freight trains fully fitted with continuous brakes, all served to reduce the number of guards employed by British Railways and to change radically the nature of guards' duties.

In 1968 69 per cent of all freight trans were either loose-coupled, or only partially fitted with continuous brakes, while 31 per cent were fully fitted throughout. Loose-coupled freight trains required a brakevan and a goods guard to help with the application of the brakes. On the growing proportion of freight trains which were fully fitted with continuous brakes the brake-van was unnecessary; in fact, this was an item of rolling stock which was less and less frequently seen on the railway network. Management's policy in the pay and efficiency discussions preceding the agreement of August 1968 was to hasten the demise of the brakevan and with it the goods guard, and where these were single-manned locomotives, to convert the goods guard into a 'secondman', who would occupy the rear cabin of the locomotive. To economise on manpower for passenger services the Penzance Agreement provided that the passenger guard should both assume new duties, and acquire a new name. Instead of being primarily responsible for the good order of the *train*, he would have a greater responsibility towards the *passengers* and have as one of his main duties checking, collecting and issuing passenger tickets. He would have the new name of conductor guard and would be paid additional money (originally 7s over and above the second-year guard's maximum of 313s per week). Simultaneously, the union agreed to the abolition of the grade of travelling ticket collector. On a large number of local trains the guard continued with his old responsibilities and had no ticket-collecting duties but the trend was towards ticket checking, collecting and, if necessary, issuance, on board the passenger train rather than at the platform barrier. To the passenger guard with long experience under the old system the switch to the role of conductor guard was often a difficult one. It involved communication with the travelling public not only on the occasion of ticket inspection, but also when making announcements over the intercom system. Some guards found this prospective change frightening and opted out of the promotion and the extra pay that went with the added responsibilities.

It was largely due to the NUR that the separate grades of goods guard and passenger guard disappeared from the terminology. The AGM at Penzance, in 1968, voted 'That there should be one grade of guard'.[40] However, at Llandudno a year later a majority of delegates accepted the BRB's recommendation for the appointment of conductor guards.[41] Over the period 1965–70 there was a good deal of discontent among guards over the question of payment in compensation for their contribution to increased productivity. Under the locomotive single-manning agreement of 28 October 1965 footplatemen were given additional weekly payments for accepting reduced manning levels. Guards felt that as members of train crews they should also participate in the sums made available for rewarding extra productivity. It was the NUR policy that all three members of the staff manning a train – the driver, the secondman and the guard – should benefit from the new manning agreement of 1965. However BR management was reluctant to give guards extra money unless they (the guards) were prepared to make their own separate contribution to increasing productivity. Among the changes BR suggested were the abolition of the brakevan on fully fitted trains and the acceptance by guards of some of the duties formerly undertaken by firemen, for example, the coupling and uncoupling of wagons and carriages.

While the long-drawn-out negotiations between the NUR and

BR were taking place, management in some of the regions was calling upon guards to do extra duties without extra payment. E. F. Judd of Feltham told the AGM at Plymouth, in July 1966, that on the Southern Region they were being required to undertake new tasks, such as ticket collecting at unmanned stations.[42] Matters came to a head early in 1967 when the union's executive instructed guards not to carry out any single-manning duties from 13 February of that year. The threat of non-co-operation was not, in fact, carried out, and the discussions with management continued.[43] Sidney Weighell told the AGM, in 1968, that for ten whole weeks the union's head office dealt with nothing but guards' matters until management eventually agreed to allow guards an extra half-hour's pay in exchange for productivity concessions, the principal one of which was the abolition of the brakevan on fully fitted trains.[44]

The number of railway staff employed in goods handling and cartage declined from 62,140 in 1950 to 24,017 in 1967, a drop of 61·4 per cent. The establishment of the National Freight Corporation under the terms of the Transport Act 1968 meant that many goods and cartage employees moved from the service of BR to the NFC and ceased to be included in censuses of railway staff. None the less the drop in numbers up to the end of 1967 was startling enough. The working lives of men and women in the important division of railway business were changed more by the decline in 'sundries', that is, small-consignment traffic, than by the introduction of new methods of goods handling. Jock Nicolson, who for most of his working life was employed at Camden goods depot, recalled that in the mid-1950s the platform bays were stacked so full of parcels that it was sometimes difficult for the drivers of electric trucks to weave their way through the mass of consignments without doing damage. A quarter of a century later the 'sundries' traffic was reduced to a trickle.[45] The explanation of this transformation lies partly in the growth of the liner train traffic, especially after the inauguration of the first Freightliner service – between London and Glasgow – in 1965. As late as 1967 only 31 per cent of freight traffic was sent in train loads; in 1977 it was 80 per cent. An increasing proportion of the remaining 20 per cent of freight was dispatched by Speedlink trains, which are timetabled in the same manner as passenger trains and on which regular customers can book space in advance and be sure of prompt delivery of their consignments.[46] The implications of these changes was that most goods traffic was handled in a small number of 'concentration depots', such as the one opened at Stoke-on-Trent in 1961. Here, the freight wagons are shunted into a large shed where their contents are offloaded on to conveyor-belts from which they are transferred via other conveyor belts to the bays at which lorries await orders for local distribution.[47] Where only small consignments are handled there is little justification for the installation of fork lifts, cranes, battery trucks and conveyor belts, but with the concentration of traffic all these innovations are economically justifiable. In 1978 the government showed its confidence in mechanical equipment by authorising an investment of £65 million on new equipment to be paid for from the national exchequer.

In the late 1970s the veteran railwayman whose career had been in cartage would have seen formidable changes. Thus Mr A. J. Toole, of Manchester No. 13 branch, started off driving a horse and cart before he learned to drive a Scammel three-wheeler. Thereafter, in succession, he drove 3 ton, 5 ton and 6–8 ton lorries before learning to manage a giant 32-tonner in the 1970s. In his early days he was involved in a great deal more man-handling of goods than was the case from the mid-1960s onwards, when the Joloda, manufactured in the British Railways' Earls-town works, eased the physical strain of his job when he was at an age most keenly to appreciate it.[48]

In 1952 porters formed the largest group within the more comprehensive category of 'traffic staff'. If porter-guards and porter-signalmen are included, there were 28,561 of them. Sixteen years later the last staff census – conducted before the Pay and Efficiency Agreement, of July 1968, absorbed the members of this grade into the all-embracing categories of railman, leading railman and senior railman – revealed that their numbers had fallen to only 11,306, a drop of 61 per cent. In a labour-intensive industry management found this the most obvious area in which to make economies. This impressive reduction in manpower was made possible partly through the disappearance, with railway modernisation, of some of the jobs formerly undertaken by porters, and partly through a decline in the standard of service offered to the travelling public. Platform sweeping, instead of being carried out by brush and manually operated barrow, was carried out more speedily by means of a machine powered by an electric motor; oil lamps, which took up much time and attention, gradually disappeared from use; the loading of freight became increasingly mechanised. At the same time 'weazling' – porters offering to carry passengers' luggage in the expectation of being tipped for their services – was rapidly becoming obsolete as lightweight trolleys were made available for customer use on station platforms.

To serve as a crossing keeper could be one of the loneliest jobs on the railway, since many of the level crossings were situated in the remoter parts of the countryside. However, with the closure of many branch lines before, as well as after, the Beeching Report of 1963, the number of manned level crossings declined. In 1952, 1,432 crossing keepers were employed and only 849 in 1968, the last year in which they were listed separately in staff returns. Since that date there has been a further shrinkage of numbers as more and more crossing gates are controlled electronically.

A familiar sight in the carriage depots of the 1950s and early 1960s were those known colloquially as 'pail hands' – the carriage cleaners, armed with water buckets and long-armed brushes. In the post-Beeching era they were a rapidly dwindling band as the cleaning of passenger coaches was increasingly mechanised. Early in 1961 at each of the two NE Region depots of South Gosforth and Heaton 200 electric and DMU (diesel multiple unit) coaches were being cleaned daily, unaided by the old-style carriage cleaner. By means of detergent sprays, large rotating nylon bristle brushes and water, applied at the rate of 120 gallons a minute, a rapid job was being done by a combination of electronic and mechanical devices. This pattern of development was before long being followed in other depots throughout the country.[49]

The technological revolution which transformed the working lives of railway conciliation staff, that is, those groups of grades concerned with the movement of traffic and the maintenance of the permanentway which came within the ambit of the first railway conciliation scheme in 1907, also greatly affected the numbers and working conditions of the clerical and supervisory staff. In 1952, the year in which the Railway Clerks' Association changed its name to the Transport Salaried Staffs' Association, there were nearly 74,000 men and women clerks in the service of British Railways; by 1978 fewer than one-third of that number remained. Only in the case of footplate staff was the drop in numbers employed so substantial.

For more than a century the Edmondson ticket machine, first patented in 1837, reigned supreme in British, and many overseas, booking offices. This small, sturdy and reliable desk-side device printed the date and serial number on printed cardboard tickets and served its purpose extremely well. It is still in use in many smaller booking offices. But for exceptionally busy stations there was a strong incentive to devise a machine that would print quickly a greater variety of station names than were available in the stacks of printed tickets the booking clerk normally had within easy reach. To meet this need a new Multiprinter machine was installed in the Paris Gare St Lazare in 1931 while, on this side of the Channel, the booking clerks at Liverpool Street station in London began issuing tickets with such a machine on 1 May 1935.[50] However, it was not until the late 1950s and the 1960s that the Multiprinter and Flexiprinter machines became more widely used in the main railway booking offices. When Cardiff (General) and Queen Street stations began using the Multiprinter Major, able to print up to 1,188 different names of stations and other information, in January 1959, it was the largest installation of its kind in Britain.[51] It reduced the demand for labour in both ticket printing and ticket issuing. As the use of machines like this spread through the regions, so the number of booking clerks declined.

From the point of view of the decline in demand for railway labour the spread of the computer into railway offices was far more important than the extended use of Multiprinter machines. Professor Rosenhead told a meeting of the mathematics section of the British Association, in 1953, that there were only about twenty electronic calculating machines in existence in Britain but that only ten of them were in working order. Five years later at the British Computer Exhibition in the autumn of 1958 thirteen different machines in commercial production were on display. By January 1959 the number of computers in use had risen to 120.

The Railway Executive was quick to seize the opportunity for labour-saving provided by the development of computers. In 1958 it hired a computer from J. Lyons & Co. for a few hours in order to determine the shortest distance by rail between all 4,000 local groups of freight terminals, a task which otherwise would have taken 250 manyears' working time. Later that year it brought its own machine for working out the weekly payrolls of 11,000 of its employees at Swindon. This was the first computer to be employed by any railway in Western Europe. By the end of 1959 the Executive had four other computers engaged in payroll calculations in other major rail centres. Since the machines were not fully occupied in preparing the payslips, they were also employed for stores accounting and stock control. Within a couple of years they were then used, first at York, for planning the design of electric circuits for a route-setting signalbox and for compiling railway timetables. Some mistakes were made. The scheme for computerised seat reservation was dropped when it was found that its cost was greater than the total of wages paid to the few railway clerks who had previously done the job. Through this miscalculation the Railway Executive learned the lesson that not many

passengers were in the habit of making sure in advance that they
would have a seat for their journey.[52] The availability of computers at British Rail headquarters made possible the agreement
between management and the unions, operative from 1 January
1965, for the deduction of union subscriptions through the paybills. The NUR agreed to pay the British Railways Board £22,500
annually for this service.

In the light of the fact that the volume of passenger traffic was
fairly well sustained through most of the 1970s, while at the same
time the number of specialised tickets increased, for example,
Awayday, weekend, student, senior citizen and family rail cards,
it might have been expected that administrative and clerical employment would have been maintained. That this was not the
case was largely due to the changes wrought by the electronics
revolution described above.

VII

It is dangerous to generalise about the changing character of employment in the railway workshops, since each establishment has
a separate history and tradition. Furthermore the Transport Act
of 1968 introduced a major change with the establishment of
British Rail Engineering Ltd as a separate undertaking to run the
main workshops, such as those at Derby, Crewe and Swindon,
while leaving the management of the remaining, generally smaller,
shops to British Rail. Nevertheless the switch from steam to diesel
and electric locomotion, which took place in the decade after the
introduction of the Railway Modernization Plan in 1955, brought
fundamental changes which affected all workshops. At the same
time there was a great improvement in labour–management relations; the 'atmosphere' of the workplace was completely altered.

It was a visit to the Litchurch Road works at Derby in the early
1920s that, more than any other single experience, converted the
celebrated Methodist preacher, Donald Soper, to socialism. The
noise, dirt, poor protection of the workforce from accidents and,
above all, the martinet-style discipline, created a lasting impression which remained vivid with him nearly sixty years later.[53]
Elder members of the carriage and wagon shop works committee
in 1979 confirmed these impressions. In the days before the
Second World War the manager's office was known as the 'Baron's
Fortress'. The foreman wore a bowler hat and other workmen
stood to attention when addressing him. For two clocking-on
offences a man was suspended and there was no listening to the

men's cases. The war was a big force for change, and in about 1952 consultation began to be effective. The experience in other major workshops was similar.[54]

The changes in the work pattern which came with the abandonment of steam locomotion in the 1960s were many and varied. Much of the earlier labour in the workshops was heavy and arduous. Muscular strength and stamina were required to hold down a job in the foundry or blacksmiths shop, or when a man was employed as a riveter or coppersmith. Most of the components for steam locomotives were made within the works. Men learned their particular manual skills gradually over a period as long as twenty years. With the disappearance of steam, much of the heavy work also disappeared. An increasing proportion of the labour force was employed fitting electrical, rather than mechanical, equipment. Riveting, blacksmithing and coppersmithing became obsolete. The forging department closed down at Derby in 1972, when the remaining work was concentrated at Shildon. At the same time foundries disappeared from all the works, except those at Swindon and Horwich. New assignments replaced those that had disappeared, though fulfilling them required less labour. Thus some men at Derby were engaged from 1968 onwards in fitting wagons with continuous brakes, while others were occupied in assembling the new containers for liner trains. In the carriage works the use of plastic rather than wood greatly reduced the demand for skilled carpenters, while at the same time posing the question of finding the appropriate grading for the less highly trained men who replaced them. The new passenger coaches for high-speed trains were much more sophisticated than their steam-age predecessors. Air conditioning, public address systems and automatically opening and closing corridor doors, which were unknown in the rolling stock of the 1950s, became standard for many coaches being built in the 1970s.[55]

Men employed in the railway workshops had particular cause to be angry with the Marples–Beeching policies of the early 1960s. In the days of the private railway companies the workshops competed for outside orders in the heavy-engineering field almost from their inception. In Chapter 1 reference was made to Marples's refusal, under the Transport Act 1962, to allow British Railway's workshops to accept orders from outside customers. At the same time the Beeching axe was wielded first against the workshops rather than the branch lines.[56] During the afternoon of Wednesday 29 August 1962 the men employed in the two Derby shops staged what was 'probably the biggest march of its kind' in the town in protest against the way their part of the railway industry was being treated. A member of the carriage and wagon works shop committee told the press that the demonstration was being held 'in collusion with the management'. The organisers were also supported by Mr George Brown, Labour MP for Belper, who joined the march and commented on its orderliness.[57]

VIII

Both the number and proportion of railway staff sustaining fatal accidents fell in the years following nationalisation. As the centralised accident-prevention service within British Rail was not established until 1965, it is difficult to give comparable figures for the period 1950–63. None the less the general downward trend in fatalities is made clear in Table 2.2.

For non-fatal accidents it would be misleading to juxtapose the pre- and post-1956 statistics, since during the earlier years there were varying definitions of what constituted 'reportable' accidents.

Table 2.2 *Fatal Accidents: Railway Staff*

Year	No. of Casualties	Rate per 1,000 Employees
1874	788	3·15
1899	531	0·96
1924	248	0·36
1949	209	0·32
1964	96	0·23
1965	105	0·27
1966	72	0·19
1967	77	0·21
1968	68	0·20
1969	73	0·25
1970	74	0·26
1971	59	0·21
1972	47	0·18
1973	36	0·14
1974	39	0·16
1975	44	0·17
1976	41	0·16
1977	36	0·15
1978	36	0·15

Source: Statement from D. F. Rugman, Safety and Welfare Officer, British Railways Board, 6 September 1979.

The figures for the years since 1965 reveal how difficult it has proved to make reductions in the non-fatal accident rate comparable to those for the number of fatalities, shown in Table 2.2. The British experience of a virtually static performance in respect of the numbers of all accidents per 1,000 employees was typical of most European railway systems in the 1970s. On the other hand, British Railways safety record compared well with that of the other fourteen countries sending returns to the UIC (International Union of Railways) in 1978. Whereas the British

Table 2.3   *Non-Fatal Accidents to Railway Staff Resulting in Absence of One Full Day or More*

Year	No. of Accidents	Rate per 1,000 Employees
1965	15,363	38·3
1966	13,298	35·5
1967	13,161	37·2
1968	11,944	36·1
1969	10,504	37·1
1970	9,919	36·1
1971	9,507	34·9
1972	8,950	34·4
1973	9,299	36·7
1974	8,866	35·4
1975	9,680	37·7
1976	9,413	37·8
1977	9,280	38·3
1978	9,084	37·7

Source: As for Table 2.2 above.

accident rate was 37·6 per 1,000, the average of all UIC countries was 53·2, and Britain was sixth best in the list of participating railways.[58] The achievement in respect of the reduction in the number of fatalities is not so impressive when compared with the record of other European railways. In 1978 British Railways stood ninth in the list of fifteen railway systems, that is, its fatality rate was above the average. The principal reason for this unsatisfactory state of affairs was the failure to make bigger reductions in the number of fatal accidents sustained by trackmen. Whereas before 1914 the most dangerous occupations on British railways were those of goods guards and shunters,[59] in the 1960s and 1970s trackmen had the unenviable distinction of

Table 2.4 *Fatalities per 1,000 Permanentway and S and T Staff,*
British Rail

Year	Staff	Killed	Rate per 1,000
1949	70,000	84	0·42
1954	64,000	57	0·36
1959	58,000	59	0·38
1964	47,000	40	0·28
1969	34,000	25	0·31
1974	32,000	14	0·19

Source: British Railways Board, *Safety in the Railway Industry* (1975).

having the highest fatality rate of any grade in the railway service. This was despite the fact that the fatality rate among trackmen showed a substantial decline in the postwar period (Table 2.3).

There were a number of reasons for continuing fatalities among trackmen. Electric and DMU locomotives make less noise in movement than do steam locomotives, thus reducing the aural warning to those working on the line. At the same time high-speed and electric trains have higher average speeds than did their steam-powered predecessors, thus giving the lookout man less time in which to spot an oncoming train and warn the gang to stand clear of the tracks. A further hazard is that Kango Kits, track-laying and tamping machines create a noisier environment than that normally experienced by gangs using handtools. In some areas the level of noise has increased for reasons unconnected with the railways, as where the railway tracks run parallel with a motorway or the site of noisy industrial premises. Strenuous efforts have been made by both management and unions to counter these new threats to safety. Permanentway men have been issued with improved standard 'vests' known colloquially as 'orange peel' and steps have been taken to improve the warning system. More than three years before the Health and Safety at Work Act 1975 came into operation on 1 October 1978, the BRB and NUR set up a joint working party on track safety. A new portable warning system, known as Yodalarm, was demonstrated at Marylebone in August 1975 and approved for experimental use. Early in 1978 there were 120 Yodalarm units in use and at its March meeting that year the executive of the NUR gave unanimous support for the speediest possible introduction of the system.[60]

When overhead electrification was extended in the 1960s and 1970s, the hazards of possible electrocution or severe burning were extended to a great number of staff. In the years when steam locomotion was being rapidly phased out the view of Brigadier C. A. Langley, Chief Inspecting Officer for Railways from the Ministry of Transport, was that the problem was largely a psychological one, especially with steam locomotivemen:

> They had been accustomed to examining their engines, climbing out of their cabs to clean windows and getting up into the tenders to trim coal. They did this at the most convenient places and frequently when they were stopped at signals awaiting clearance. The habit had been second nature to many and it was easy for them to forget the presence of newly energised overhead wires. Unfortunately there had been some accidents from this cause.

However, the management, with the full co-operation of the unions, conducted a comprehensive safety campaign, with warning notices placed on locomotives and in all positions where there was likely to be most risk to staff. In January 1960 a demonstration was staged at Colchester with the twofold object of assuring the staff that the new equipment was safe if working rules were obeyed, but highly dangerous if they were flouted. A locomotive, belching steam and smoke, was placed under a contact wire charged with 25,000 volts, with men on the footplate and others touching the locomotive. The wire was then lowered until there was a flashover, but it was shown that so long as men stayed within the locomotive or did not touch the wire they were safe. Then two dummies, one on the locomotive boiler and the other on the tender, were raised until they touched the overhead wires. The heads of both dummies were instantly burned off in a dazzling flash.[61]

The safety precautions proved largely effective. While two members of the railway staff attending to locomotives were killed by the overhead wires in 1959, three in 1960 and an average of two per year in 1961–5 inclusive, electrocution from the particular cause thereafter disappeared.[62] The accidents which continued were generally sustained by other railway staff, particularly trackmen, as when a man of this grade at Stafford in March 1973, contrary to regulations, raised a ladder against one of the overhead traction jibs to deal with a faulty light and grazed the traction wire with fatal consequences.[63]

An average of one member of the railway staff each year of the 1970s has been killed by the live rail on the electrified third-rail system which is largely confined to the Southern Region.

Most of the fatal and non-fatal accidents on this system were caused by trackmen stumbling or by other members of staff attempting to cross the lines and making misjudgements.[64] Thus, in August 1975, a young man who had not completed eight weeks' service with British Rail, at Horsley on the Southern Region, was electrocuted through slipping or tripping up when engaged in laying timber planks.[65] Miscellaneous shunting accidents, particularly those occurring when coupling or uncoupling wagons or passenger coaches, continued to bring their toll of loss of life and limb, though mercifully on a very much smaller scale than was the case before 1914.

Even allowing for a one-third reduction in the labour force during 1965–78, the figures for accidents caused by lifting, moving, or carrying materials, packages and all types of goods, suggest that the introduction of mechanical handling equipment, especially in parcels depots and in engineering departments, had a beneficial effect on the proportion of accidents to members of staff employed. The number of accidents in this category fell from 2,882 in 1965 to 1,415 in 1978, a more than 50 per cent reduction. The fourteen-year period for which statistics are available was one in which powered tools were rapidly replacing manually operated tools in railway workshops, in depots and on the permanentway. The total number of accidents with tools and portable equipment fell from 679 in 1965 to 478 in 1978, a 30 per cent drop, or a smaller decline than in the numbers of the workforce. This suggests that the introduction of powered tools entailed slightly greater risks than did the continued use of hand-tools.[66]

So far only what might be called the 'traditional' kinds of casualties – those involving physical injury or death – have been considered. However, a distinctive feature of developments in the last twenty years has been an increase in staff disability through the increasing stress and noise present in the work situation. Until the 1960s the presence of noise in the work situation was generally regarded as a part of the job. In the railway service boiler-making in the workshops was an outstanding example of this. Awareness of the damaging effects on health of an excessive level of noise and of the possibility of reducing the volume of noise in workplaces grew in the 1960s and 1970s. The Railway Executive and British Railways Board carried out workshop noise surveys in the early 1960s with advice from Professor Burns. Locomotive noise investigations, in 1964, led to extensive modifications in the Deltic-type diesel locomotives. NUR and ASLEF representatives participating in test-runs of high-speed trains urged the reduction of noise levels in the driver's cabin and, as a result of modifications subsequently introduced, the power unit of the HST is quieter than the cabins of other locomotives. In 1977 Sidney Weighell circularised branches of the NUR for suggestions on which parts of the industry were worst affected by noise and on what remedies were suggested. In December 1977 he wrote to the BRB for a report on positive steps being taken to reduce the noise problem.[87] The policy of the BRB from the mid-1960s was to issue Ferranti earmuffs to men working the tamping machines and to the engine test staff. Remedies are rarely complete, and this was as true of earmuffs as of other protective devices. Men who wore earmuffs while working on the track missed the opportunity of communicating with their workmates, even though this had been done in the past in an extremely noisy environment; they sensed a greater loneliness.[68]

Added stress accompanied employment in the most up-to-date console-type signalboxes and on the high-speed trains. In March 1978 the NUR executive instructed Sidney Weighell 'to seek from the BRB their views on the varying attitudes of regions towards causes of stress in signalboxes, and whether any overall policy is being applied to study such problems as workload, capacity and environmental stress'.[69] The problem was a real one. John Cogger, who was appointed to Euston signalbox in 1969, found that four years later, only one of the team had retired at 65 after completing the normal years of service and was, in 1978, still 'hale and hearty'. Two others had left before retirement age. One of these had dropped dead at home, aged 55, the other had left at the age of 63 through extreme nervous tension, and died shortly afterwards. NUR representatives on the Sectional Council fought for additional men to be appointed and the Divisional Manager, who was very concerned about the staff situation in the box, appointed three extra staff.[70] Close and constant watching of the illuminated panel in a power signalbox also imposed considerable strain on the eyesight. C. Petty, a signalman of York 5 branch, told his fellow delegates at the NUR's AGM at Aberdeen in July 1967 that in twelve years' working in the York box he had had his spectacles changed eight times. He worked no overtime since, after eight hours, he was 'all in'.[71]

Further evidence of the growth of stress (as well as of the easier accessibility of alcohol) was the growth in the number of disciplinary and accident cases whose immediate cause was the alcoholism of the member of staff concerned. In July 1977 the NUR AGM approved a Glasgow 5 branch resolution requesting the executive to assess the seriousness of the problem of alcoholism within the railway industry.[72] The EC subsequently found that during 1970–4 there were 798 disciplinary cases arising from this cause, while management estimated that each year some 17 per cent of accident cases had a similar explanation. At a meeting of the Joint Advisory Council on Welfare on 30 November 1977, Dave Bowman, for the NUR, urged that where alcoholism was seen to be the principal element in disciplinary cases something should be done beyond the mere punishment for a breach of the rules. Ill-health severance arrangements should be applied in these cases as in other cases of illness. The management representatives agreed to this suggestion.[73]

Another unpleasant development of the later 1970s was the increase in cases of vandalism and of assaults on railway staff. For drivers the greatest threat came from missiles thrown at the cab windscreens of passing trains from bridges crossing the railway. Both the NUR and ASELF wrote to the BRB, urging the installation of high-impact resistant glass screens in locomotive cabins. At a meeting of the Joint Safety Council, held on 12 October 1977, the management representatives reported that 86 per cent of the locomotives and 67 per cent of DMUs and EMUs had been refitted and that work on the remainder was in hand. The total cost of this operation was nearly half a million pounds.[74] On some regions, notably in the North East, two-way radio on trains was helping to check vandalism, but BR had inadequate funds to install the system generally.

The changes in size, structure and working conditions of the railway workforce, described above, meant that the organisations of the union, devised at a time when the industry was highly labour-intensive, was in need of substantial modification, if it was to be an appropriate instrument for dealing with the problems of the 1980s. The union's response to the challenge is the subject of Chapter 3.

CHAPTER 3

THE ORGANISATION OF THE UNION

I

A COMPARISON between the NUR's first *Rule Book*, issued in 1913, with that of August 1977 reveals little change in the basic structure of the union. In 1913 the new organisation reflected its leaders' strong attachment to the principles of industrial unionism and democratic control. It was emphasised that the NUR – widely acclaimed at its birth as the 'new model' union of the twentieth century – was designed to serve the interests of all railway staff. Rail transport has always depended on the combined effort of all grades for its successful operation. Each driver depends directly on railway workshop staff, trackmen and signalmen for the safe movement of his train. There would be no work for trackmen, signalmen and drivers, if clerical staff and conductor guards were not available to collect money from the railways' customers or to check that the services provided had been paid for. In every respect railway working is a co-operative enterprise. The logical deduction which follows from this fact is that a union representing all grades in the service makes more sense than a number of smaller unions limited to members of a particular grade or grades. These principles are as valid in the 1980s as they were in 1913, and this is the most important reason why the essential elements in the NUR constitution remained intact for over sixty years.

In 1980, as in 1913, the supreme governing body of the union was the Annual General Meeting of delegates elected by the single transferable vote system from geographically based groupings of branches. In 1913 sixty AGM delegates were regarded as an appropriate number to represent 170,000 members. In 1919, when membership had shot up to 480,000, it was decided to increase the number of delegates to eighty, a figure which remained unaltered until 1953, when the three seats until then occupied by representatives of branches in Ireland were abolished, thus reducing the number of delegates to seventy-seven. It is a tribute to the effectiveness of NUR organisation in Ireland that it was not until thirty years after the creation of the Irish Free State that the Irish branches decided to break away from the British parent body to form their separate union, NATE (National Association of Transport Employees). In the quarter of a century that has elapsed since the departure of the Irish delegates the size of the AGM has remained the same.

Under rule 2, section 4, the description of the powers of the Annual or Special General Meeting in the 1977 *Rule Book* is practically the same as that of 1913. In fact sub-sections (a)–(m) inclusive are identically worded in the two documents, except that by 1977 the term 'divisional officer' had been substituted for 'organiser' in sub-section (c), and a new clause had been added to sub-section (k). The overriding authority of the AGM or SGM is shown in its power to alter rules; remove from office any officer of the union; decide appeals made against the decisions of the EC; initiate movements and appoint sub-committees. Under sub-section (m) it is unequivocally stated that the AGM or SGM 'shall govern the Executive Committee'. Thus it is the membership, through delegates elected to one or other of the General Meetings, which is the ultimate arbiter in all matters of organisation and policy. The only significant proposal for alteration of the rules relating to the AGM was made by a special sub-committee of the EC in 1969, when it was suggested that the number of electorial districts – and hence delegates – should be reduced from seventy-seven to seventy. It was pointed out that, in 1919, each AGM delegate represented an average of 6,000 members, but that in 1969, he represented only 2,636. The members of the sub-committee were concerned lest the status of AGM delegates should be devalued. A growing number of seats were uncontested – as many as 36 per cent of them in 1965 – and it was hoped that a reduction in the number of constituents would increase the size of the individual electorates and improve the chances of elections being contested. However, the SGM held at Unity House in February 1970 was unconvinced by this argument and the proposed change was not adopted.[1]

II

From 1914 to the present the President of the union has been elected by the delegates on the last day of the AGM. Candidates, who must have a minimum of five years' membership of the union, are nominated by the branches and may serve for a maximum of three consecutive years, though being subject to re-election annually. In the succeeding years various attempts to alter the method of electing the President or to redefine his term of office were all defeated. Thus, a proposal put forward at the AGM in 1953 that the President be elected by the union's membership, instead of the AGM delegates, was rejected after T. Dudley, a timekeeper from Croydon, pointed out that the delegates saw the man at work but the mass of the membership did not. At the same meeting a proposal that the President should be elected for the full three-year term, without having to seek re-election, was defeated, despite Charles Evans's plea that the proposed change would make the President less subservient to the AGM during his second year in office.[2] From 1913 onwards the rules required the President to attend the annual congress of the TUC and from 1920 onwards the rule read 'He shall attend the Trades Union Congress and the Labour Party Conference'. However, for more than fifty years there was no requirement that the President should be an individual member of the Labour Party.

Inconsistencies in the union's rules were brought to light in 1957–8 when, following the death of Tom Hollywood, the President, in the same road accident which killed Jim Campbell, the General Secretary, Dundee and other branches nominated David Bowman, a Communist Party member and parliamentary candidate, for the Presidential vacancy. In a keenly contested election, fought by thirteen candidates in January 1958, David Bowman was narrowly defeated by Charles Evans, a compromise candidate of moderate views. Sidney Greene, who had just taken over the duties of General Secretary, accepted David Bowman's nomination because Communist Party members had stood for the Presidency in the past and he could find nothing in the rules which precluded their nomination. But he did so with reluctance and was relieved when Southend, Cricklewood No. 1 and Leeds No. 11 branches appealed to the EC on the ground that David Bowman's candidature was invalid, because rule 4, clause 4, stated that the President had to attend the Labour Party Conference. However, the EC at its March 1958 meeting, decided that there was nothing in rule 4 which precluded a member's candidature 'because of his political outlook'.[3] The matter did not rest there. The same branches which had unsuccessfully appealed to the EC tried again with the AGM in July and carried the day by 55–22 votes, overturning the executive's decision.[4] Nevertheless, the anomaly in the union's rules remained. Indeed, it was made more manifest when the Labour Party Conference, in 1962, made a new rule that 'Every delegate must be an individual member of the Labour Party'.

At the AGMs of 1961, 1964 and 1967, when according to rule, changes in the rules were possible, Dundee branch proposed an alteration in rule 4, clause 4, so that it should read (in part): 'The President shall attend, but not necessarily be a delegate to, the Labour Party Conference.' At the 1967 AGM F. Juett, an electrician from West Brompton, maintained: 'The whole situation is lopsided when we allow a man right the way through to aspire to being a member of a sectional council, a member of the EC, an organiser, but then, when he is in reach of the Marshal's baton, say "No".' However, on each of the three occasions the Dundee proposals were debated, delegates voted by large majorities against any change in the rules to make it easier for someone who was not an individual member of the Labour Party to become President of the union.[5]

In December 1968 Warrington District branch of the NUR nominated Harold Leigh, a goods guard of the London Midland Region who had served for three periods of three years each on the EC, as a candidate for the July 1969 election of a new President of the union for 1970. In June 1968 Leigh resigned his membership of the Communist Party and before his nomination papers were sent in he had paid two years' subscription to the treasurer of the Warrington branch of the Labour Party. Sidney Greene refused to accept the nomination as valid, since in earlier conversations he had heard Leigh pronounce himself a communist. He also informed the union branch secretary that membership of the Labour Party was not established until the management committee of the local Labour Party recommended an applicant's acceptance.[6] At the closing date for the receipt of nominations for President, Leigh had produced no clear evidence of his acceptance into membership of the local Labour Party branch and, therefore, his name was not included in the list of candidates. The Labour Party branch of the Islington, East, constituency, in which Leigh was residing while he was a member of the EC, did accept him as a member on 16 April 1969, three months before the elections for the presidency; but this was of little consolation to the would-be candidate, since the closing date for the receipt of nominations was 1 January of that year.[7] Harold Leigh then applied for an injunction to restrain the union from conducting the election of the President until his name had been included in the list of candidates and his election address had been circulated to the branches. In the case, *Harold Leigh* v. *The National Union of Railwaymen and Sidney F. Greene*, heard in the Chancery Division of the High Court of Justice on 17 July 1969 before Mr Justice Goff, judgement was given in favour of the plaintiff.

Mr Justice Goff maintained that there was nothing in the union's rules which stated that, at the time of nomination, a candidate for the presidency had to be a member of the Labour Party. Since the election did not take place until two or three months after the receipt of nominations, and since the successful candidate did not have to take office until a further six months had elapsed he had 'a considerable time in which to obtain the required qualification for attendance' at the Labour Party Conference. He considered, moreover, that 'the inability of the candidate at the moment of nomination, if elected, to perform his duties under rule 4, sub-rule 4 was a matter for the electors, not of his right to stand'. He, therefore, ordered the NUR and Sidney Greene to delay the election of the President until Leigh's name had been added to the list of candidates and his election address had been circulated to the branches, and he required the union to meet the costs of the case.[8]

Harold Leigh had won his right to be nominated and plaintiff's and defendant's costs, amounting to £3,076 13s 9d were met by the union. But it is doubtful whether these victories benefitted himself or his cause. The postponed election was conducted by postal ballot of AGM delegates in September 1969, and resulted in George W. Chambers, a locomotive driver of Nottingham Midland branch, being elected on the second count with 42 votes, compared with the 32 received by Ted Abraham, a signalman of Landore. Harold Leigh was out of the running, having received only 6 votes in the first count.[9] His prospects for future election to the presidency were bleak.

A further outcome resulting from Mr Justice Goff's injunction was that the General Secretary dispatched a circular letter to all branches on 17 October 1969, in which he concluded:

> It will be necessary for the rules of the union to be examined with a view to the Annual General Meeting deciding whether the rules should be amended to give legal effect to the wishes of the membership as laid down by AGM decision No. 146 1958 and Rule 4, Clause 4, which require the President of the Union to attend the Labour Party Conference as delegate.[10]

Although the SGM which met at Unity House during 17–20 February 1970, inclusive, to consider proposals for the reorganisation of the union, was productive more of lengthy speeches than significant agreed recommendations, two alterations to rule 4 were accepted by 51–24 votes. Clause 1 was amended to make it obligatory for candidates for the presidency to be individual members of the Labour Party *at the time of their nomination*, and clause 4 of the same rule made it obligatory for the President to attend the Labour Party Conference *as a delegate*. A minority recommendation that 'any member of the union should have the right to become President irrespective of any political affiliation' was defeated by 24–51 votes. These changes in rule were included in the new *Rule Book*, in 1971.[11]

In December 1969, when Dundee branch for the second time nominated David Bowman for President, the SGM had not met and rule 4 had not been altered. Sidney Greene was reluctant to accept the nomination, but he realised that, after the Leigh case, it would be difficult to prevent it. On 15 December 1969, to make sure, he wrote to the union's solicitors, Messrs. Pattinson and Brewer, asking for their opinion 'in the light of the judgment of Mr Justice Goff', whether or not 'he must accept as valid a nomination from our Dundee branch on behalf of Bro. D. Bowman, a known Communist Party member'. By return of post the solicitors advised the acceptance of the nomination. Sidney Greene followed this advice.[12] But in a covering letter sent to all branches with the candidates' names and circulars on 27 January the General Secretary wrote:

> Except in the case of Bro. D Bowman, Dundee Branch, it has been confirmed with the nominating branches that their candidate is at present an individual member of the Labour Party and qualified to carry out the duties of President as provided by rule 4, clause 4. Dundee branch, however, have failed to give a definite reply to a letter of 23 December 1969, which I sent to the five nominating branches asking to be informed if the branch nominee was an individual member of the Labour Party.

The letter did go on to quote from the judgement of Mr Justice Goff that 'the candidate had a considerable time in which to obtain the required qualifications for attendance at the Labour Party Conference', and that 'the inability of the candidate, at the moment of nomination if elected to perform his duties under Rule 4 sub-rule 4 was a matter for the electors, not of his right to stand'.[13]

Dundee branch complained that the General Secretary's circular contained misleading statements, prejudicial to their candidate, and appealed to the EC. The complaint was referred to the organisation sub-committee which noted that four of the candidates had given definite answers to the General Secretary's question about Labour Party membership but that David Bowman had replied by posing another question – 'If the General Secretary wishes me to give him an assurance that I accept the Judgement of Mr Justice Goff on Rule 4, then my answer is, as a law abiding citizen and a loyal NUR member, categorically "Yes".' The EC accepted its sub-committee report by 15–4 votes.[14] At the AGM at Inverness in July 1970 George Chambers, the sitting tenant, won handsomely on the first ballot, beating David Bowman by 50–9 votes.[15] The Dundee branch and the defeated candidate considered taking the General Secretary to court on account of the offending branch circular, and David Bowman was advised by D. N. Pritt, QC that, had he done so, he would have been almost certain to win. But he realised that, like Harold Leigh, he might gain a favourable court judgement but lose any prospect of becoming President, and so he held his hand. His success in the election for President at the AGM in 1974, after he had resigned his membership of the Communist Party and joined the Labour Party, would have been very unlikely had he resorted to law in 1970.

As might be expected the influence of the President on the conduct of the union's affairs depends very much on the character of the man. He is in charge for a maximum period of three years before he reverts to his employment in public transport or retires. Sitting beside him in the board room at Unity House or on the platform of the AGM are the General Secretary and his assistants with many more years of full-time employment in the union's business. It is his most important responsibility to ensure that the decisions of the AGM are implemented by the EC and by the full-time officers. He needs to be particularly well versed in the union's rules and in the rules of debate, if he is to ensure that the newly elected member of the EC or delegate to the AGM is not overawed by the greater experience and expertise of the full-time officers. The incident at Plymouth in 1971 when an over-sensitive AGM microphone broadcast an intended whisper from the General Secretary to the President: 'Shut that man up', and the President duly obliged by switching on the red light, was fortunately unique. Harold MacRitchie, who was President in the years 1972–4, inclusive, insisted on AGM delegates, particularly newcomers, having a chance to express their views fully, and David Bowman, who occupied the presidential chair during 1975–7, was widely respected as highly competent in office.[16]

III

The rules concerning the General Secretary of the NUR have altered very little over the last fifty years. For nomination to this office the candidate requires the support of at least ten branches, and he has to show continuous membership of the union for at least ten years. He is elected by the membership on the single transferable vote system. Once elected he stays in office subject to the will and pleasure of a majority of the members who, through their representatives at an AGM or SGM, have power to dismiss him or call upon him to resign. Since 1933 he has been precluded from being a member of Parliament.

It could be argued that the changes that have been made in rule 5 (which concerns the General Secretary) have meant a lessening of democracy within the union. The decision of the SGM, in February 1970, to substitute the block votes of branches for the individual votes of the members as the method to be followed in electing the General Secretary, was taken for reasons of administrative convenience rather than principle. The decision, by the same meeting, to make it the rule that the General Secretary should be an individual member of the Labour Party was consistent with what was to be required of the President, but it was limiting the tenure of office to members of one political party.[17]

Sidney Greene's seventeen-year tenure of office, from 1958 to 1975, was longer than that of any of his predecessors. His election, in the wake of the sudden death of Jim Campbell, was unopposed when 510 branches – well over one-third of the total – supported his nomination.[18] According to the *Rule Book*, his task was 'to discharge all duties assigned to him by the AGM and the EC'. He was well aware that by a strict interpretation of the union's constitution this was the case. In July 1967 he told the AGM at Aberdeen: 'It is not for me as General Secretary ever to criticise the AGM or say whether it was wise or not; I just get on and carry things out.'[19] However, he did not mention what he might quite properly do before an AGM or EC decision was taken. Unless he was unavoidably absent, he always had the last say – apart from the proposer of the motion – in all AGM debates on major issues of policy. At such times his influence was very great. It was, after all, an unequal contest. About one-third of the delegates on such occasions were attending their first AGM. There were always some very experienced representatives among the remaining two-thirds; but it would require exceptional authority and determination in a delegate to match the knowledge and experience of the General Secretary. Furthermore, just as a delegate was beginning to gain confidence through having become familiar with the major issues of policy, the rules of debate and the traditions of the AGM, he would be excluded by the rule which limited delegates' attendance to three successive years and precluded re-election until three further years had elapsed. Thus, although the rules might suggest that the General Secretary was the servant of the AGM, the reality was very different. It was only on very rare occasions that Sidney Greene's recommendations were brushed aside by delegates. If the rank and file showed deference to their General Secretary, they did so less frequently to his aides. One of the main tasks of the Assistant General Secretaries at the AGM was to defend earlier decisions of the officers and the EC against appeals from the branches. Delegates often considered on these occasions that, coming straight from the work situation, they knew as much about the matter under discussion as did the union's officers. Having accepted the General Secretary's lead on national issues, they were more ready to assert themselves on local concerns, especially as their constituents would be looking for evidence of their effectiveness as representatives of the branches.

The General Secretary was more evenly matched when he sat beside the President in the board room for meetings of the EC. It is true that at any one time eight of the twenty-four members of the executive would be serving their first year in a spell of office, but eight others would have had more than two years fulltime involvement in the union's affairs. There was also a nucleus of veterans with two, three, or even four, previous three-yearlong spells of office to their credit, acquiring in the process a profound knowledge of the union's affairs. By comparison with the members of the executive of ASLEF, who are allowed to serve continuously for an indefinite period, the NUR's executive is relatively less powerful. But it has been sufficiently equally matched to the General Secretary to 'send him to the cleaners' on occasion.[20]

Sidney Greene's interests were industrial rather than political. He was influential within the TUC, being its President in 1970 and chairman of its Economic Committee from 1968 to 1975 inclusive. He was at his best when negotiating improved wages and working conditions with members of the British Railways Board and in explaining and justifying to AGM delegates the settlement that had been reached. It was a remarkable Cockney astuteness and wit, rather than book-learning, which characterised his discussions with the Board. George Brassington, who worked with

him as Assistant General Secretary for twelve years, said that he
was 'a man with a memory like an elephant and a brain like
quicksilver'. Although he was cautious about committing himself
before he had obtained the consent of his executive, once he had
made a promise it was a matter of keenly felt honour for him to
keep it. That is why he was trusted by members of the Board,
even though at times they wished he had shown a greater bold-
ness. To reach an agreement he relied heavily on making personal contact, especially over lunch. He tried this method with
great success with John Peyton, Minister of Transport in the
years 1970–4.[21] He fought shy of any publicity. In moving a vote
of thanks to him (as President) at the conclusion of the 1970
TUC, Mr J. Torode, of the Labour and Industrial Correspondents
Group, recalled that on the first occasion that he (Torode) had
to contact Sidney Greene, he called him on the phone to ask
if he would speak with the labour correspondent of the
Financial Times. Sidney Greene answered: 'Who? No, sorry,
no. He don't live here. You must have got the wrong number.'
By 1970 relations between them had become much more
cordial. He now got an answer to his questions. It was 'No
comment'.[22]

In so far as Sidney Greene had a political standpoint it was
well to the right of the Labour Party. He had an intense dislike,
at times approaching the pathological, of all members of
the Communist Party. Although he gave loyal support to the
Labour Party, his interventions at its annual conferences were
less impressive than those of his predecessor, Jim Campbell,
or his successor, Sidney Weighell. During his period of office
as General Secretary he took less interest in the work of
the union's MPs than he did in the work of the Finance
Committee and the Trustees. He helped to ensure the strong
financial position of the NUR in the 1960s; but he allowed
the long-established meetings between the political sub-committee of the EC and the union's MPs to degenerate into purely
social occasions rather than opportunities for planning parliamentary strategy.

With Sidney Greene due to retire early in 1975, 169 branches
supported Northallerton branch in nominating as his successor
Sidney Weighell, the Senior Assistant General Secretary. The
election which followed was the first in which a new General
Secretary was chosen by the block vote of branches under the
single transferable vote system. In the event only one count was
needed as Sidney Weighell gained an overall majority. The result
of the ballot was as follows:

Sidney Weighell   85,553
Frank Cannon   34,855
Russel Tuck   29,476
Charles E. Turnock   10,190

The new General Secretary, who was born in 1922 and joined the union when he was 16 years of age, is a third-generation railwayman and a footplateman by grade. His father, Tommy Weighell, was a well-known figure at many AGMs. Sidney Weighell had been a delegate to four AGMs and eight SGMs, as well as a member of the EC (1953–4), before he was elected full-time organiser in June 1954. He took the next step up the ladder in 1965, when he was elected Assistant General Secretary, and he succeeded to the post of Senior Assistant General Secretary in 1969. In the six-year period which elapsed before he succeeded Sidney Greene, he gained a very wide experience since he frequently had to deputise for the General Secretary in negotiations with the Railway Board. His most important task in that period was in representing the union in the pay and efficiency discussions with the management.

There were remarkable contrasts in the style of leadership of Sidney Greene and Sidney Weighell. Whereas Sidney Greene was conservative and inclined to the view that if you waited patiently for long enough problems might well disappear, Sidney Weighell was an innovator and ardent reformer. He was overflowing with new ideas for reorganising the head office, revitalising the parliamentary activities of the union, restructuring the EC and developing educational work. He launched into these projects with sometimes impetuous enthusiasm. These characteristics earned him the nickname of the 'Yorkshire Terrier'. He was much more of a 'political animal' than was his predecessor and often intervened with constructive suggestions in the field of transport policy and railway administration.

IV

At its inception the NUR had four Assistant General Secretaries. Two of these had held such office under the old ASRS. The other two, Thomas Lowth, former General Secretary of the General Railway Workers' Union, and Samuel Chorlton, former General Secretary of the United Pointsmen's and Signalmen's Society, had been taken on board at the time of fusion in 1913. They had retired by 1920, when the *Rule Book* provided for the appointment of only one Assistant General Secretary. Between 1920 and

1931, however, the NUR had two General Secretaries: the Political General Secretary (J. H. Thomas), and the Industrial General Secretary (C. T. C. Cramp). The post of Parliamentary General Secretary disappeared with the disappearance of J. H. Thomas from the scene in 1931, and from that date until 1947 the union made do with one General Secretary and one Assistant General Secretary. The imminence of the Transport Act with its introduction of many new negotiating bodies, such as the Road Haulage Executive, prompted the amendment of the rules in 1947 to allow for the appointment of a second Assistant General Secretary. The introduction of new organisations such as the National Freight Corporation and National Carriers Ltd, under the Transport Act 1968, increased still further the work of the head-office staff and the full-time officers. The SGM, which met in Unity House in February 1970, had these changes in mind when it recommended that the amended rule 6 should make provision for the appointment of a third Assistant General Secretary. The same SGM, consistent with its requirement that both the President and the General Secretary should be individual members of the Labour Party, imposed the same obligation on all three of the Assistants.

It was characteristic of all those men who served as Assistant General Secretaries in the NUR in the 1960s and 1970s that, through economic necessity, their full-time education was cut short at an early age, but that their short formal education was greatly enriched through experience at work and in union organisation. Thus William Ballantine, who was elected Assistant General Secretary in October 1958 at the age of 53, started full-time work as a farm servant at the age of 12 but, even before that, worked on farms in the early mornings and late afternoons. He began his railway employment as an engine-cleaner at Carstairs Junction and worked his way up to become driver before leaving the railways to take up the post of full-time organiser for the NUR in 1946. George Brassington, who was elected Assistant General Secretary at the same time as William Ballantine, started work as an errand boy at the age of 13, earning 4s 6d in a working week of fifty-six hours. A year later he began his railway career as a horse delivery van parcels boy on the North Staffordshire Railway. Nevertheless, as one of the chief officers of the union for twelve years, he was highly esteemed as 'a man of tremendous strength of character and charm', widely read, eloquent and resourceful.[23] Russell Tuck, who was elected Assistant General Secretary in March 1970 and appointed Senior Assistant General Secretary five years later, entered the railway service at the age of

17. His education in economics, politics and union affairs began in the signalbox at Rhondda Cutting, near Pontypridd to which he resorted in off-duty hours. There he was greatly influenced by two of the signalmen, Dai Jones and Joe Champion, both of whom became Labour MPs, while Joe Champion was later elevated to the House of Lords. Frank Cannon, son of a Wigan coalminer and brother of Les Cannon of the EETU/PTU (Electricians Union) was elected Assistant General Secretary in November 1970, following the SGM decision earlier that year to increase the number of these appointments from two to three. He joined the railway as a junior porter and became a member of the NUR at the age of 17. He had a very varied experience as branch secretary and chairman, EC member, AGM delegate and grade conference secretary before being elected as organiser in 1959. Charles Turnock, who was elected Assistant General Secretary in 1975, augmented his short early education by attending many classes in economics and kindred subjects organised by the National Council of Labour Colleges. He had fifteen years' experience as an organiser before coming to Unity House.

In the second half of the twentieth century it was becoming clear that members of the NUR who aspired to positions of responsibility and authority needed to choose between a political and industrial career. Russell Tuck took the industrial option at an early age. Charles Turnock at first devoted more of his energies to politics. He was short-listed twice for selection as a Labour Party parliamentary candidate before his election as organiser. William Ballantine was the most left-wing in political outlook of the Assistant General Secretaries. In the 1930s and 1940s he was an ardent member of the ILP and served on its National Administrative Council. In the 1945 General Election he stood, unsuccessfully, as ILP parliamentary candidate in the Bradford, East, constituency against Labour and Conservative opposition. He retired in 1965, five years before the union required all its Assistant General Secretaries to be individual members of the Labour Party.

From 1970, when the numbers of the General Secretary's Assistants was increased to three, each man had clearly defined areas of responsibility. The Senior Assistant General Secretary dealt with all British Rail questions and with relations with the Labour Party. The next in line held responsibility for the union's education policy as well as for labour relations in the workshops, hotels and catering, docks, inland waterways and shipping. The third looked after all London Transport, National Carriers and Freightliner questions.

V

The full-time officers of the union most closely in touch with the membership were the organisers, in 1971 renamed divisional officers.[24] Throughout the period between 1947 and 1977 there were seventeen of them, each of whom was resident in the area for which he was responsible. In addition there was a head-office organiser responsible for co-ordinating the work of his colleagues and liable to be called upon to deputise for one of the assistant secretaries as occasion demanded. To qualify as organiser a candidate had to prove seven years' continuous membership of the union and to have the support of at least ten (after 1971, seven) branches. He had to pass a test in book-keeping and in the history and organisation of the union as well as being able to show competence in the writing of reports and in public speaking.[25] Before 1970, when a closed-shop agreement with British Rail came into operation, one of the tasks of the organisers was to help branch and district council officers with membership recruitment drives. Apart from the short period of operation of the Industrial Relations Act in 1972-4, such activity was thereafter unnecessary and other tasks such as attending medical appeal tribunals, MOT inquiries and inquests, and speaking at district council meetings, took up a larger proportion of the organisers' time.

The seventeen organisers in 1947 had between them responsibility for the welfare of 460,000 members. In 1972 the same number of divisional officers were concerned with a membership of less than 200,000. It by no means follows that the divisional officer of the 1970s had an easier life than did his predecessors. Protective legislation had increased, members were more conscious of their legal rights and the number of redundancy cases increased. In 1969 Organiser B. Entwistle, in charge of fifty-seven branches in the Manchester district, was concerned with forty-seven medical appeal tribunals and nineteen local appeal tribunals and attended eleven MOT inquiries and seven inquests.[26] Figure 3.1 shows there were great variations in the geographical areas and the membership for which organisers were responsible. Thus, in 1969, organiser J. Matheson's field of operations stretched from just north of Carlisle to Wick, and comprised the entire eastern half of Scotland; but the membership for which he was responsible was only 8,327. By contrast organiser A. Dodds's area, including the southern part of London with Kent and Sussex, was less than a quarter of the size of Matheson's but it contained more than twice as many members.

Figure 3.1 *Areas of divisional officers, January 1980*

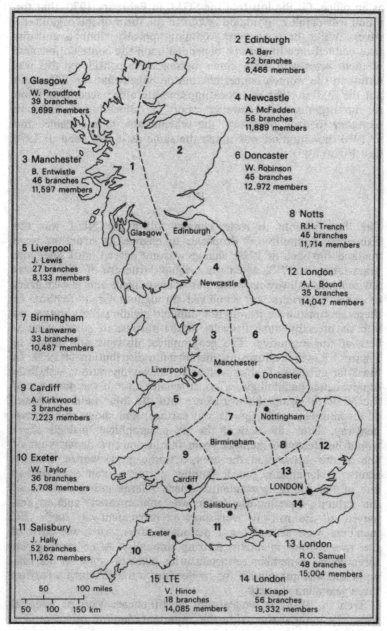

2 Edinburgh
A. Barr
22 branches
6,466 members

1 Glasgow
W. Proudfoot
39 branches
9,699 members

4 Newcastle
A. McFadden
56 branches
11,889 members

3 Manchester
B. Entwistle
46 branches
11,597 members

6 Doncaster
W. Robinson
45 branches
12,972 members

8 Notts
R.H. Trench
45 branches
11,714 members

5 Liverpool
J. Lewis
27 branches
8,133 members

12 London
A.L. Bound
35 branches
14,047 members

7 Birmingham
J. Lanwarne
33 branches
10,487 members

9 Cardiff
A. Kirkwood
3 branches
7,223 members

10 Exeter
W. Taylor
36 branches
5,708 members

13 London
R.O. Samuel
48 branches
15,004 members

11 Salisbury
J. Hally
52 branches
11,262 members

15 LTE
V. Hince
18 branches
14,085 members

14 London
J. Knapp
56 branches
19,332 members

50   100 miles
50   100   150 km

Organisers worked from their homes, using a spare bedroom as an office. G. Pimlott told the SGM, in February 1970, that the union was employing unpaid labour in the form of the organisers' wives. While the men were attending appeals, tribunals and district council meetings much depended upon the conscientiousness of their wives who took phone messages. He considered this was unfair to the women concerned and he hoped that the EC would put the matter right by allocating separate office accommodation to the organisers.[27] However, short of allocating a full-time secretary to each organiser, the scheme was impracticable, and in 1980 the situation was much the same as it had been in 1970 (see Figure 3.3).

VI

The 'last bastion' to resist change within the NUR was the Executive Committee.[28] Proposals to change its structure were made as far back as 1937; change was not agreed until forty-one years later. In 1913, when the original structure of the EC was devised, the railway network was near its peak and a vast army of railway workers was employed throughout Great Britain. In these circumstances it was not difficult dividing the country up into six broadly equal districts for the purpose of electing members of the executive. The geographical districts are shown in Figure 3.1, which illustrates membership distribution in 1979. In those far-off days of labour-intensive railway operation, with little sophisticated technology in use, it seemed fair to the pioneers of the NUR to group the workforce into the four main categories of locomotive, traffic, goods and cartage, and shops and permanentway. Thus, in each of the six geographical districts there would be elected a member from the locomotive department of one of the railways in the area; a traffic grade worker, for instance, a signalman, guard, shunter, porter; a man employed in one of the goods departments (where a large preponderance of the nation's merchandise traffic was concentrated) and an employee of the railway workshop or permanentway staffs. EC members were elected for a period of three years, one-third of the twenty-four members retiring annually. After serving for three years, a member returned to his place of work on the railways and was not eligible for re-election to the EC until a further three years had elapsed.

Even in 1913 the workgroup constituencies were of unequal sizes. By comparison with the representation of other grades,

locomotive and goods and cartage staff were over-represented on
the executive. The reasons for this imbalance were political. The
NUR was determined to forestall any suggestion, made by
ASLEF, that it did not cater adequately for the interests of footplatemen. To reassure ex-members of the General Railway
Workers' Union, many of whom belonged to the goods and
cartage grades, there was a somewhat generous allocation of
places to these workers on the EC.

More serious anomalies in the composition of the executive
became apparent in the interwar years. Before 1914 the NUR was
only weakly represented in the railway workshops. Hence the men
who worked on the permanentway or in signals and telecommunications, who were with the shopmen in one electoral group, could
be reasonably sure of representation on the EC. However, NUR
membership in the workshops doubled between 1914 and 1947,
largely as a result of C. T. C. Cramp's successful advocacy in the
arbitration court in 1922.[29] Thereafter it was frequently shopmen, elected by the large NUR membership in the big railway
workshops, rather than the permanentway men and S and T staff,
generally employed in smaller, more scattered groups, who secured
election to the executive. Thus, in 1937, the 50,000 members of
the NUR who belonged to the permanentway and S and T grades
had no direct representation on the executive.[30]

The pace of technological change on the railways quickened in
the third quarter of the twentieth century. Even in 1937 a delegate to the AGM referred to the growing importance of colour-
light signalling, automatic-exchange telephones and radio in railway communications, and stressed that this was altering the importance of the different grades.[31] From the mid-1950s onwards
the expansion of diesel and electric traction, the mechanisation
of track-laying and maintenance, the introduction of electronically controlled shunting, the spread of power signalling and the
use of the computers in many aspects of railway operation, rapidly
altered the structural composition of both the work force and the
membership of the NUR. These changes are summarised in
Figure 3.2. By the 1960s there were glaring contrasts between the
union's membership in the different grades and the composition
of the executive. In 1968 Sidney Greene pointed out that the
10,000 footplatemen and the 20,000 in the goods and cartage staff
each had as many representatives on the EC – six – as did the
80,000 members in the traffic grades and the 77,000 members
employed on the permanentway, the workshops and in
signals and telecommunications.[32] By 1978 the anomalies were
even more striking. The locomotive department membership had

Figure 3.2 *Size and composition of NUR membership by Executive Committee group categories, 1963, 1970 and 1978*

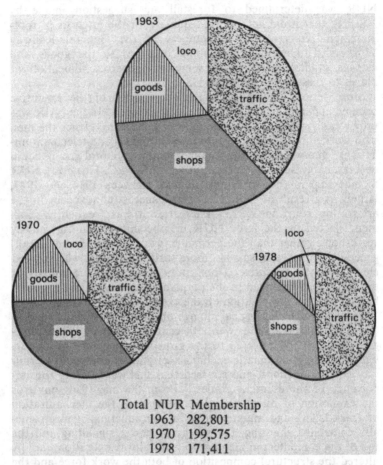

Total NUR Membership
1963 282,801
1970 199,575
1978 171,411

Note: Included in the electorate for the six traffic representatives were staff employed by British Transport Hotels, British Transport Docks Board, British Waterways Board, busmen and most London Transport employees, as well as those employed in a number of smaller undertakings such as the Caledonian Steam Packet. Included in the electorate for the six goods and cartage representatives were staff employed by National Carriers Ltd and Freightliners Ltd, as well as those employed by a number of smaller organisations. For a full breakdown of membership, see Table 3.1.

shrunk to only 3,057 (including those employed by the LTE), but this small group elected six full-time members of the executive, the same number of representatives as were elected by the 82,857 members in the traffic grades. The 17,946 members of the union in the 'goods and cartage' grouping elected six members of the executive, the same number as were elected by the 67,809 members in the 'shops and permanentway' groupings.[33]

Reform of the structure of the union's increasingly unrepresentative executive was considered by AGM delegates on seventeen separate occasions between 1937 and 1978; by SGM delegates in 1950, 1952 and 1970; by the executive itself and by subcommittees of representatives of both the AGM or SGM and the executive on numerous other occasions. The flood of words uttered on the subject was immense. The SGM at Unity House, in February 1970, spent four whole days debating the union's constitution; but it failed to agree to any one of the five different proposals offered for restructuring the executive.

The reasons for the long delay in carrying out essential reforms were diverse. In 1937 John Marchbank, the General Secretary, argued that there were far too many grades of staff in the railway service for each to claim the right of direct representation on the executive. Its members should have the ability to deal with the problem of *all* grades, since the NUR is an industrial union.[34] Whenever it was suggested that the representation of the locomotive grades should be reduced, there was always someone ready to follow the advice given by another General Secretary, John Benstead, to the AGM at Ayr in 1947, that such a change would 'make a present' to the rival ASLEF.[35] The frequent changes in the pattern of government control over the railways and other forms of inland transport in the thirty years following 1939 provided reformers within the union with powerful arguments to amend the union's constitution; but it also provided an excuse for the more conservatively minded to recommend delay until the full import of changes in transport policy had been appreciated. Thus, with the Attlee government's Transport Act on the horizon, H. W. Franklin endeavoured to persuade AGM delegates at Ayr in 1947, that the time was opportune to institute direct election of bus and hotel workers to the EC. John Benstead, in reply, urged caution. He questioned whether it was wise, at that stage, to rush through a reform, and argued 'it would be better to see how the new machine progresses' before they started tampering with their own machine.[36] However, by the summer of 1950 AGM delegates had had time to weigh up the implications of the Transport Act of 1947, and Jim Figgins, who had succeeded John Benstead as General Secretary in 1947, urged 'an immediate examination of the whole constitution' to be completed within a year.[37] At Hastings, in the following July, Jim

Figure 3.3   *Executive Committee districts, January 1980*

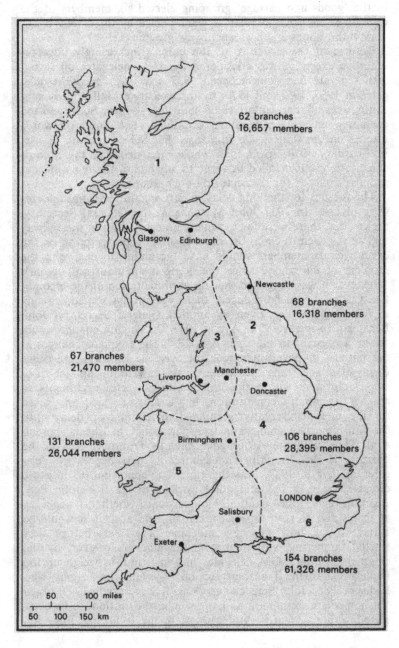

62 branches
16,657 members

1

Glasgow   Edinburgh

Newcastle

68 branches
16,318 members

2

3

67 branches
21,470 members

Liverpool   Manchester

Doncaster

4

131 branches
26,044 members

Birmingham

106 branches
28,395 members

5

LONDON

Salisbury

6

Exeter

154 branches
61,326 members

50   100 miles
50   100   150 km

Figgins declared that it was a matter of 'very great urgency indeed' that the AGM delegates should adopt an EC report which proposed to bring in representatives of bus, commercial road vehicle, hotel and dock workers on a completely overhauled executive structure. The rejection of this advice by the crushing margin of 78–2 votes was the most remarkable example of AGM delegates flouting the recommendation of the General Secretary.[38] By the time the question was considered again at an SGM, in August 1952, there had been a General Election and a change of government. It was known that the new Conservative administration planned the denationalisation of that part of the road haulage industry taken over by the BTC in 1948. Jim Figgins now argued that the union had 'missed the boat' by not acting promptly the year before. He supported the view of the EC that it would be unwise to reconstruct the organisation 'until they had a clearer view of the future of the industry'.[39] After a gap in time, during which little consideration was given to the reorganisation of the union, the problem was again tackled at the AGM in July 1964. Delegates considered a report from the executive which proposed an EC of twenty-two members with four districts of five representatives for the locomotive; traffic; goods and cartage; shops; and permanentway and E and T grades. On this occasion Sidney Greene argued that 1951–3 would have been better years in which to make the necessary changes. In 1963 the union lost 30,000 members because of the implementation of the Beeching Plan and there might be as many lost in 1964. The AGM delegates referred back to the executive the detailed thirty-nine-page printed report.[40] An important influence on the EC and the AGM, in 1967, was the imminence of Barbara Castle's Transport Act, which was placed on the statute book in the following year.

The principal reason why the alteration of the structure of the executive took so long to effect was the inbuilt resistance to change within the executive itself. Half its membership was from the over-represented locomotive and goods and cartage groups. Shopmen members were not always enthusiastic for change, since they thought that recognition of the right of permanentway men and the S and T grades to representation would quite possibly be at their (the shopmen's) expense. As early as July 1946 M. Hailes, a lineman from Newcastle upon Tyne, saw the big stumbling-block. 'I should hardly imagine,' he said, 'that the EC would recommend turning themselves out of some seats.'[41] Five years later, at Hastings, the same delegate caused loud laughter when he pointed out that 'everyone who has denounced sectionalism had spoken on behalf of his own section'.[42]

The way out of the impasse was also suggested at an early date. On 9 July 1951, J. J. Morris, an erector of Derby 3 branch, pleaded: 'Could we not have Mr G. D. H. Cole, or somebody like that, to advise us on the structure of our industrial union?'[43] A quarter of a century later, when delegate Morris's brief intervention had long since been forgotten, the idea was taken up. Only it had to be 'somebody like that', G. D. H. Cole having died in 1959. On the initiative of Sidney Weighell and Dave Shaw, a delegate from the Tyne Yard branch, the 1976 AGM was asked to authorise the EC to approach a university industrial relations faculty to produce proposals for the restructuring of the EC which would be acceptable to the union as a whole. In supporting the Tyne Yard branch resolution Sidney Weighell reminded delegates that it had been found in the past that there were 'so many vested interests that to try to placate them all was a sheer impossibility'. After a remarkably brief debate in which the only speaker, apart from the mover and seconder of the resolution and the General Secretary, was E. W. Bowers, a motor driver of Bethnal Green, the meeting gave unanimous endorsement of the proposal.[44]

The NUR already had its links with the Modern Records Centre of the University of Warwick, which had been granted safe keeping of the earliest records of the union and a representative sample of later documents. It was not surprising, therefore, that Sidney Weighell decided to ask the Industrial Relations Research Unit of the same university to undertake the task of reviewing the structure of the EC. A favourable reply was received and Professor J. England and Dr R. Price of the University of Warwick staff made a thorough inquiry and presented their report to the EC in March 1978. Meeting on 13 April the executive endorsed the General Secretary's proposal to present the report to that year's AGM for consideration.[45] In the meantime the sixteen-page printed *Report on the Structure and Composition of the National Executive Committee* was sent to every branch, so that AGM delegates could be properly briefed on the proposed changes.

In introducing the Report to the AGM delegates at Llandudno on 11 July 1978 Professor England said that he had been aware of 'a firm groundswell of opinion that something needed to be done'. Four major changes in the environment in which the union worked made the case for structural change in the executive imperative. First, the effects of successive governments' industrial and transport policies had been to transform the NUR from a single industry union to a multifirm union; secondly, the advent of the closed shop had changed the internal balance of membership, especially by bringing in a large group of hotel workers; thirdly, the volume of negotiations had greatly increased, with the result that members of the executive were not able to get so involved in them as they would have liked; and lastly, technical change had radically altered the number and type of grades and skills comprised within the membership. It was conceded by Professor England that on membership statistics alone there was no case for separate locomotive-grade representation on the EC. But he felt that there were strong grounds for continuing a degree of over-representation of the locomotive grades, because of continuing technological changes in locomotive design and the need for the union to keep a close watch on them; the separate sectional council for the men employed in this grade; their separate committee on the RSJC and the prominent part that locomotive-men had played in the history of the NUR. Also their continued presence on the EC would provide 'a basis for future developments in the structure of trade unionism'.

The principle which guided the Warwick proposals for the restructuring of the EC was the recognition of distinctive membership groupings in recognisable bargaining units. It was for the reason that staff in the white-collar grades were distributed over a large number of bargaining units – they were spread 'horizontally', whereas other sizable groups were concentrated 'vertically' – that it was decided not to recommend that white-collar workers should have an absolute right of representation on the executive. They were free, of course, to gain election in other constituencies.[46] The new structure for the EC recommended in the report was as shown in Table 3.1.

Table 3.1 *Proposed Executive Committee Composition*

Group	No. of EC Seats	No. of Members (December, 1977)	No. of Members per seat
*Locomotive	2	1,957	978
*Traffic	6	61,952	10,327
*Permanentway/S and T	3	19,226	6,408
*Shops	6	39,850	6,641
Buses	1	5,730	5,730
NCL/FL	3	12,816	4,272
LTE	2	14,065	7,033
Docks and shipping	1	6,544	6,544
BTH	2	9,524	4,762

*Excluding LTE membership.

For the purpose of electing members of the executive it was proposed to retain the six existing geographical areas, but to increase the number of departmental groupings from four to five. The new groups suggested were: (a) traffic and locomotive; (b) permanentway and S and T; (c) workshops; (d) road transport and London Transport; and (e) docks and hotels. The members of the EC were to be chosen triennally from each district or from combinations of districts in groups having less than six members. The transition from the old structure to the new would be gradually phased over the years 1979–82. A review of EC representation was recommended at six-yearly intervals.

A small group of AGM delegates wanted to refer back the report for consideration by a sub-committee comprising representatives of the AGM and the EC. Alun Rees, the President, was well aware that the same tactic had been adopted in a similar situation in the very same hall nine years before and that the result had been delay and frustration. He was determined that there would not be a repeat-performance in July 1978; the resolution to set up the sub-committee was not accepted. The dissident minority then proposed 'That the President leave the chair', a motion which was defeated by the decisive margin of 60–12 votes. The stalling-action had been nipped in the bud.

In moving the adoption of the report, Alan Kemp, a bus driver from Exeter, warned that the union would have to change, otherwise it would cease to exist. If the meeting accepted the report, it would then be possible for them to claim to all the main groups of members that they had a fair representation on the executive. Despite an appeal by Mrs J. Brightman, of March branch, the first woman delegate to an NUR AGM, that the proposals should be rejected as they failed to guarantee the right of representation of clerical and supervisory grades, the meeting approved the report and the consequential alteration to rules by 65–15 votes. It was a major turning-point in the union's history.[47]

In investigating the functioning of the union the Warwick team found that there was a gap between the 'shop floor' and the executive, and that 'the particular problems and viewpoints of the different grades and negotiating groups received only a muffled airing at levels below the EC'.[48] The occasions for these 'muffled airings' of grievances were the annual meetings of the union's fifteen grade conferences. The first of these, in the goods and cartage departments, had been authorised by the EC in August 1931.[49] In the following year approval was given to the holding of further conferences for workers in the permanentway and S and T; dock and marine; workshops and signals and shunting departments.[50] Conferences of locomotivemen and of miscellaneous grades were recognised in the following year.[51] From 1941 onwards EC members from the appropriate sub-committee began attending the grade conferences, but the AGM in 1952 restricted attendance to one EC member per conference.[52]

Until 1953 decisions reached at each grade conference were funnelled through a conference sub-committee which reported its recommendations direct to the national executive of the union. However, in September 1953, the EC adopted a recommendation that all minutes of national grade conferences be forwarded to the appropriate EC sub-committee for their consideration. It was also suggested that individual branches could write to the union's head office in support of grade conference decisions.[53] It was an unwise decision, since it led to an enormous increase in correspondence between branches and grade conference secretaries on the one side, and head office on the other. There were consequent delays in dealing with grievances. Mercifully, in December 1955, the EC rescinded its earlier decision. It now ruled that it was not necessary for branches to write in support of grade conference decisions, and the conference executives were requested to examine motions received from branches with a view to eliminating extraneous matters.[54] The decision helped to reduce the delays in dealing with the issues raised by grade conferences; but it did not entirely eliminate the rumblings of discontent from the rank and file, who were well aware that the conference lacked full official status (being not mentioned in the *Rule Book*) and knew that there was no guarantee that the recommendations they made would be adopted by the national executive.

The Warwick team's suggestion for dealing with the gap between branch opinion and the deliberations of the EC was to bring the national grade and group conferences formally within the *Rule Book*. It was proposed that these conferences be aligned as closely as possible to the new structure of the EC. A particular merit of the proposal was that the new executive groups which were relatively small in number, namely, the docks, buses, hotels and locomotive groups, would need the positive assistance and regular contact with shopfloor opinion which the conferences would provide. As the grade conferences were, strictly speaking, outside the remit of the Warwick team, it was suggested that the detailed implementation of the scheme should be left to the EC.[55]

On 26 September 1978 the General Secretary wrote to all branch, district council and grade conference secretaries, inviting their comments on the Warwick Report proposals for the future of grade conferences and consultative committees.[56] Eighty-eight

branches, six district councils and six grade conferences replied.
Taking into account the views they expressed the organisation
sub-committee presented a report to the executive on 18 April.
This was approved by the EC nine days later and by the AGM,
by the narrow majority of 40–37 votes in July 1979. Henceforward the grade conferences were to be included in the *Rule
Book*. Liaison committees of not more than six persons were to
be appointed by each conference to have an annual meeting with
appropriate members of the EC and national officers, and these
arrangements were to replace all existing consultative machinery.
Head office was to bear the cost. Whereas, hitherto, it was
optional for branches to affiliate to the grade conference, it was
now obligatory on any branch having members in a grade covered
by a national grades conference to affiliate to that conference in
respect of such members. Thus, it could no longer be pleaded
that the conferences were not fully representative. No major
changes in the structure of the conferences were initiated except
that it was felt justifiable to merge the carriage and wagon grades
with the miscellaneous passenger traffic grades. There was a departure from the Warwick Report recommendations, in so far as
it was thought to be wrong and impracticable to group into one
grades conference all the members who elect the traffic group
representatives on the EC. The outcome was that eleven grade
conferences were recognised for inclusion in the union's *Rule
Book*. These were for staff in goods and cartage; buses; hotels,
catering and ancillary trades; docks; marine, Sealink and inland
waterways; shops; signals; permanentway, S and T and overhead
traction; locomotive; miscellaneous carriage and wagon and
passenger traffic; and British Rail supervisory, clerical and other
salaried grades.[57]

<h2 style="text-align:center">VII</h2>

The point of contact between the rank and file and the union
has always been the local branch. There were 1,333 of these in
1962, the year before the publication of the Beeching Report.
The decline in railway employment and in union membership
shown in Figure 3.2 inevitably led to a sharp drop in the number
of NUR branches. In the winter of 1966–7 this fell to under 1,000
for the first time in nearly fifty years; by 1971 it was down to 741
and, at the end of 1979, it was 595.[58]

The drastic pruning of railway and bus services in many areas,
for instance, the Highlands of Scotland and Exmoor, was very

damaging to the survival of lively branch activity as it had been known in the fifty years before Beeching. Some members were virutally unable to attend branch meetings because the venue was too far distant. In December 1979 Mr W. G. Masson, secretary of the Inverness No. 1 branch, wrote that his members were working in locations as far apart as the Isle of Skye, eighty-four miles to the west; Golspie, fifty miles to the north; Forres, thirty miles to the east; and Dalwhinnie, thirty-six miles to the south. Despite the obstacles of distance, one member from time to time made the 100-mile round-trip by car from Tain to attend the branch meeting.

Most branches are multigrade in character; but throughout the districts there has been for many years a sprinkling of specialised ones, confined to a more limited range of grades. This specialisation is exemplified most thoroughly in the case of Hull, whose five branches are named: Hull, docks shop; Hull, docks conciliation; Hull, goods and cartage; Hull, rail; and Hull, locomotive. Particularly in the West Country, there are a number of branches confined to bus workers, as in the case of one of the two branches at Truro and also Newton Abbot, and in two out of three of the branches at Exeter. Newcastle upon Tyne, Darlington and other areas have branches confined to salaried staff. However, these are exceptions. The advantage of the more typical branch meeting is that staff employed in a wide variety of jobs can compare their problems and experiences in common service for a publicly owned transport undertaking.

A thorough reorganisation of the branches was needed in the wake of the rail closures of the 1960s. A conference of chairmen and secretaries of each of the twenty-six district councils was held at Unity House on 27–8 March 1962, when a considerable overlapping of branches and unnecessary duplication of office and organisational work, a legacy of the pre-1948 days of railway company railways, was revealed. In one town seven branch secretaries catered for 1,400 members, and in another there were fifteen branches sharing 3,000 members. At the other extreme, Euston and Earls Court branches had over 2,000 members each. The conference recommended that, in consultation with divisional organisers, the district councils should prepare a plan for the amalgamation of branches in the same depot or town where such mergers would make for more efficient organisation.[59] It was under this directive that the rationalisation of the pattern of branches took place after 1962. Sidney Greene told the AGM, in July 1967, that 413 branches had been closed during the preceding five years and fifty-five new ones opened, mostly as a result of the amalgamation of smaller branches. However, 163 of those which survived had less than fifty members each, while a further 209 had between fifty and 100.[60] Five years later the number of branches with a membership of less than fifty had declined to sixty-eight. The General Secretary complained that the much-needed regrouping was being hindered by 'parochial attitudes, local vested interests and personal antagonisms',[61] but there was an understandable reluctance to close down branches whose existence over many decades had helped to create a social life for the railwaymen of the district.

The individual member's links with the branch, and particularly with the branch officers, were reduced when agreement was reached with the employers in 1964 for the deduction of union membership subscriptions through the paybills.[62] Although this new procedure had long been advocated by the unions because of the difficulty, in a situation of a rapidly changing workforce, of recruiting the requisite number of dues collectors, in the eyes of the less dedicated member it tended to lessen the importance of the branch. Formerly, the brief, but regular, encounters between the dues collector and the rank and file were invaluable from the point of view of the branch officers keeping in touch with the personal problems of colleagues. Advice on members' rights, especially in fairly simple legal matters, was sought and given. However, after 1964 the member who had a grievance knew that he could raise it at the branch meeting, or he could phone the secretary.

VIII

The NUR has had women members' ever since 1915.[63] It is highly probable that the proportion which the female membership bore to the total was greatest in the two world wars; but the union's annual *Statement of Membership* had no separate classification of women members until 1951, so that it is only possible to give more precise statements of their numbers for the last three decades. The 12,173 women members in 1971 constituted only 2 per cent of the total membership. The proportion of women members rose to around 3·5 per cent in the early 1960s, but then sank to 2·6 per cent in 1968 and 2·4 per cent in 1975. Thereafter, largely through the operation of the closed-shop agreement for those employed in British Transport Hotels Ltd and in British Rail buffets and restaurants, the number of women members in the union rose from 7,366 in 1975 to 9,145 in 1978, when they accounted for 5·2 per cent of total membership. In 1979, when the union had 595 branches, only two of them, Newton Abbot, Bus, and Scunthorpe, had women secretaries. In more than a century no woman has ever been elected to the national executive, and it was not until 1978 that a woman was chosen as an AGM delegate. This last milestone was reached almost by accident. At a meeting of the March branch the chairman raised the question of the nomination of an AGM delegate. Mrs J. Brightman, a crossing-keeper of Middle Road Crossing, March, in an act of bravado, broke the silence by saying, 'I wouldn't mind going'. She was subsequently elected as group No. 34 representative at the AGM at Llandudno in July 1978.[64] These are prospects that with BR and LTE recruiting women for jobs, notably as passenger guards, hitherto regarded as male preserves, and with hotel workers gaining entitlement to direct representation on the EC, the male monopoly of the executive may be broken in the 1980s.

The reasons for women not being represented at the AGM or on the EC in proportion to their numerical strength in the union range from the prevalence of male chauvinism in some branches to the difficulty married women have of reconciling full participation in branch, district council and sectional council activities with their domestic responsibilities. In the past many railwaymen have considered that the appropriate sphere of activity for women was in the Railway Women's Guild, whose groups accepted responsibility for organising the social activities of branches and were foremost in fund-raising activities on behalf of railway orphans.

IX

In presenting the auditor's report to the AGM, in July 1978, Mr Brian Cotton declared that, from the viewpoint of its financial assets, the NUR was 'in the front-runners' among leading British trade unions. At that time the union's net assets amounted to £15·5 million. However, included in this total the valuation given to Unity House was £216,799, a figure based on a survey made in 1954. A more realistic price for the property would have been in excess of £1 million. The progress of the union's assets to this impressive figure is summarised in Figure 3.4. The benefits paid out to members are summarised in Table 3.2.

The outstanding influences on the financial policy of the union

Table 3.2 NUR Contributions and Benefits

Year	1961	1965	1967	1970	1972	1975	1979
Contribution	1s 3d plus 1d Political Fund	2s all-in contribution including 1s per quarter Political Fund	2s 6d all-in including 1s per quarter Political Fund	4s all-in including 1s per quarter Political Fund	20d all-in including 10p per quarter Political Fund	1 per cent of railman's basic rate, i.e. 26p	1 per cent of railman's basic rate, i.e. 49p
Accident benefit	10s per week for 10 weeks; 8s per week for further 10 weeks	£1 per week for 13 weeks	£1 per week for 20 weeks	24s per week for 20 weeks	£1·80 per week for 20 weeks	£2 per week for first 20 weeks	£4·90 per week up to 20 weeks
Death benefit (death through any cause prior to retirement)	£7 10s for 1 year's membership; £15 for 5 years' or more membership	£20 (if membership of 5 years)	£100 (if membership of 1 year)	£100 (if membership of 1 year)	£100 (if membership of 1 year)	£125 (if membership of 1 year)	£220 (if membership of 1 year)
Orphan	Eldest child 9s per week, others 5s	Eldest child 9s per week, others 5s	Eldest child 9s per week, others 8s	Eldest child 15s per week, others 8s	Eldest child £1 per week, 50p for others	£1 per week per child, except in case of only child paid £1·25 per week	£2 per week for each child under 18; £3 per week where bereft of both parents

Retirement	£1 per year for each year of membership up to 10 years; thereafter £1·10 per year to £70 max.	£85 max.	£85 max.	Benefit calculated according to years of membership	£1 per year for first 10 consecutive years' membership; £2 per year for each completed year thereafter	£2 per year for each year of membership after 1; 1·65 with £1 additional for each year of membership of old Disablement Fund
Out of work	24s per week	24s per week	24s per week	£1·20 per week for 1 year's membership for 10 weeks; if over 3 years' membership, £1·20 per week for 10 weeks plus 60p per week for further 10 weeks	£3 per week for 10 weeks. £1·50 per week for further 10 weeks where membership of 7 years or more	£3 for 10 weeks and if over 3 years' membership £1·50 for next 10 weeks
Strike (if official)	36s per week	£3 per week	£3 per week	£3 per week	£1 per weekday	£1 per weekday

Table 3.2 — continued

Year	1961	1965	1967	1970	1972	1975	1979
Sick Fund	Variable benefits according to age on joining Fund	Variable	Variable	Variable	Abolished, AGM 1971	—	—
Protection benefit	Grant not exceeding £100 or 15s per week for 1 year	Grant not exceeding £100 or 15s per week for 1 year	Grant not exceeding £100 or 15s per week for 1 year	Grant not exceeding £100 or 15s per week for 1 year	Grant not exceeding £100 or 75p per week for 1 year	Grant not exceeding £100 or 75p per week for 1 year	Declared obsolete, 1976 (EC 1053)
Suspension benefit	24s per week after 1 year's membership	24s per week after 1 year's membership	24s per week after 1 year's membership	Cancelled, replaced by out of work benefit	—	—	—
Donation benefit		15s per week for 10 weeks for 1 year's membership; 15s per week for 10 weeks plus 7s 6d per week for further 10 weeks if 3 year's membership	15s per week for 10 weeks for 1-year member; 15s per week for 10 weeks plus 7s 6d per week for further 10 weeks for 3 years' membership	Cancelled, replaced by out of work benefit (EC 45, 1969)	—	—	—

Figure 3.4 *Sixty-five years of growth*

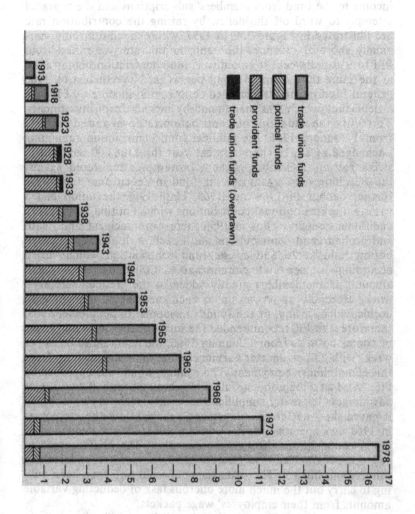

in the last thirty years have been the decline in membership which, in 1978, was well under half what it had been in 1949; the severe inflation in many years of the 1960s and 1970s; the constant tendency for contribution income to fall short of general fund expenditure and the changes in the relative yields on gilt-edged securities and investments in equities.

The tendency for general fund expenditure to outstrip the income to the fund from members' subscriptions and the repeated attempts to ward off the deficit by raising the contribution rate are illustrated in Figure 3.4. In 1957, with expenditure only marginally short of revenue, the contribution rate was raised from 8½d to 9½d per week, the political fund contribution being raised at the same time from ½d to 1d per week. Nevertheless by 1960 general fund payments exceeded contribution income by £79,000, a deficiency which was made good by income from investments. To rectify the situation the contribution rate was raised to 1s 3d from 1 January 1961, the political fund contribution remaining unchanged at 1d. In the very next year the £108,000 paid out in strike pay on 3 October, when a protest was registered against the Beeching cuts, again put the fund in deficit and there were further deficits in 1964 and 1965. Until 1965 the union had a variety of extra optional contributions which entitled members to additional benefits. Thus in 1959 there were accident and death and orphan fund contributions at 1d each, a disablement contribution fund at 2d and a sick fund contribution which varied according to personal circumstances. Collecting these small amounts from members greatly added to the branch secretary's work, especially as it was up to each member of the union to decide which, if any, of the funds to support. In September 1963, therefore, the EC recommended the introduction of an all-in rate of contribution as from 1 January 1965, the new rate to be 2s per week, with 1s per quarter earmarked for the political fund from this comprehensive payment. The change, which was approved by the AGM at Paignton, in July 1964, brought with it two major advantages. It greatly simplified the branch secretary's work and it paved the way for the agreement, reached with the employers in 1964 and operative from 1 January 1965, for the deduction of union contributions through the paybills.[65] The NUR agreed to pay the British Railways Board £22,500 a year for undertaking this responsibility.[66] The management would not have been willing to carry out the much more onerous task of deducting variable amounts from their employees' wage packets.

It became necessary to raise the all-in contribution rate to 2s 6d per week from 1 January 1969 and to 4s from 1 January 1970. The sum of 4s was chosen in preparation for decimalisation in the following year. Through the postwar years, the lowest-paid railwayman who was a member of the NUR was being called upon to pay a smaller proportion of his basic wage, in the form of union contribution, than was his counterpart of 1938. In that year the 5½d per week contribution was 1·1 per cent of the basic wage of 41s. The 4s contribution of 1970 was just under 1 per cent of the basic wage of £13.[67]

The AGM at Plymouth, in July 1974, agreed unanimously to a recommendation made by the EC that from the beginning of the following year the contribution should be fixed at 1 per cent of the railwayman's basic rate of pay. The executive had considered an alternative plan for making the contribution 1 per cent of each individual member's basic rate of pay, so that the higher-paid staff would be paying more to the union; but it rejected the proposal in favour of the simpler option of one rate for all members. The advantage of the new scheme was the greater certainty that general fund income would keep ahead of expenditure, and this would obviate previous practice of raising contributions on an *ad hoc* basis after a deficiency in the fund had appeared or was imminent. The NUR was a pioneer in introducing this new basis of calculating members' contributions just as it had been in the prompt introduction of a fully decimalised accounting system.[68]

Table 3.3   *Comparison of NUR's Assets with all Other Unions*[69]

	All Unions (%)	NUR (%)
British government securities	25·8	25·8
British municipal securities, including loans	27·7	32·2
Other investments, mainly dominion and colonial and public utilities	27·9	26·6
Mortgages	4·0	2·9
Land and buildings	5·8	3·6
Cash in hand and at banks	6·6	8·8
Other assets	2·2	0·1

Until 1960 the NUR, in common with other British trade unions, had placed its investments in gilt-edged securities bearing a fixed rate of interest. At the AGM of that year Desmond Hirshfield (later Lord Hirshfield), who had audited the union's accounts for the firm of Hesketh, Hardy, Hirshfield & Co. since 1940, compared the structure of the NUR's assets with that of all other unions registered with the Registrar of Friendly Societies (Table 3.3). Many of the NUR's gilt-edged investments had been made in the period of 'cheap money' during 1932–51, when Bank Rate stood at 2 per cent and the nominal yield of the securities was not more than 3 per cent. However, during the remarkable boom

in industrial production and employment in the 1950s and 1960s
the yield on ordinary shares (equities) was well above that of gilt-
edged securities and the selling price of the gilt-edged stock was
inconveniently low, especially when the rising trend of prices was
taken into account. Desmond Hirshfield's view, in 1959, was that
during the preceding decade 'foremost industrial equities had
proved more gilt-edged than government stocks'.[70]

In December 1959 the EC approved a finances of the union
sub-committee report, which endorsed the auditors' view that
part of the union's investments should be placed in equities. At
the AGM held in Torquay in the following July delegates accepted
the executive's recommendation by the overwhelming vote of
68–8 votes and carried unanimously the necessary alterations to
rule 8 which had hitherto limited the union's investments to gilt-
edged securities. These amendments to rule, permitting investments in equities, were passed in the knowledge that a recently
published White Paper, *Powers of Investment of Trustees in
Great Britain* (Cmnd 915), indicated the government's intention
to allow trustees to invest up to 50 per cent of the funds they
managed in equities.[71] In 1961 the Trustee Investments Act gave
effect to these intentions.

At Edinburgh, in July 1961, Desmond Hirshfield noted with
satisfaction that 'a portfolio of investments in forty companies
had been quietly built up'.[72] Four years later, at Hastings, he
urged that 'something like 75 per cent' of the union's funds
should be invested in equities. The purpose of the policy he advocated with so much enthusiasm was 'to protect the union's investments from being consumed by continued inflation'.[73] By 1972
the book value of the union's investments was about equally
divided between gilt-edged and equity investments, and by 1974,
the high-water-mark year of the new policy, the proportions were
40 per cent gilt-edged and 60 per cent equities.[74]

The beneficial effects of equity investment income on general
fund finances, particularly during 1965–71, is shown in Figure
3.5. Through the years 1965–9 inclusive, contribution income fell
short of general fund expenditure by many thousands of pounds,
and the deficiency was only made good by transferring income
gained from investments. Throughout most of these years also
the market value of the union's equity holdings rose impressively.
The auditors made much of these advantages arising from the
change in investment policy. In July 1965 Desmond Hirshfield, in
his report to the AGM delegates at Southport, expressed regret
that the change in direction had not taken place ten years
earlier.[75]

Figure 3.5 *NUR General Fund: income and expenditure, 1961–79*

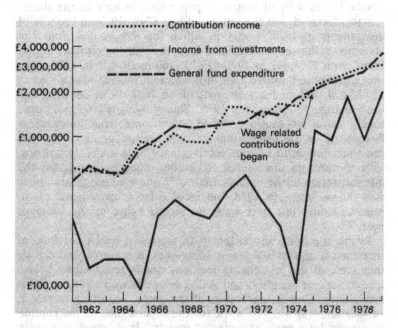

In the course of the 1960s neither Sidney Greene (who fully endorsed the plan for investment in equities), nor Desmond Hirshfield, gave any indication that there might be some pitfalls in the investment policies so enthusiastically adopted. The 1950s and 1960s were indeed decades of remarkable profitability for private industry and the temptation was to assume that this prosperity would continue into the foreseeable future. But the value and yield of equity holdings could plunge downward as well as rocket upwards. With escalation of oil prices from 1973 and severe industrial unrest in Britain in 1972 and 1974, the prospects for continued profitability of private enterprise looked decidedly less rosy.

In August 1974 the report to the EC of the directors of Unity House (Holdings) Ltd (the organisation which had recently taken over the job of managing the union's investments from the trustees) noted that 33 per cent had been wiped off the value of leading shares in the equity market in the past five months, the *Financial Times* index for share prices having fallen from 302·8 to just over 200 in that short span of time.[76] The market value of the union's investments fell by no less than £2,063,000 in the course of 1973, chiefly due to the decline in yields of ordinary shares.[77] This was, of course, a paper loss, so long as the shares remained unsold; but the union did lose £298,619 from the sale of investments in 1974, a year in which the *Report and Financial Statements* showed a decline in income from 'investment operations' from £554,841 in 1971 to £101,160 in 1974.[78] In 1975 there was a dramatic improvement in investment income which rose to £1,088,079; but in his statement of 18 June 1976, covering the year ending 31 December 1975, Sidney Weighell offered some timely words of caution: 'With the income from investments fluctuating to the extent that in 1974 the amount received was less than one tenth of that coming in 1975, it is clearly not possible to bank on this source of revenue when budgeting for the administration of the union's affairs.' [79] The wisdom of this advice was shown when, in 1978, the income from investments plummeted to only just over half the record figure of the previous year.[80]

In the late 1960s and in the 1970s the union held a portfolio of investments in over 100 major companies. It is scarcely surprising that some of the investment decisions were questioned by executive committee members and AGM delegates with strong socialist convictions. One of the objects of the union, according to rule 1, sub-section 4(a) was 'To work for the supersession of the capitalist system by a socialist order of society.' Investment in private enterprise as compared with that placed with Labour-controlled municipal corporations or with public utilities and state-owned enterprises was regarded as strengthening the capitalist system rather than superseding capitalism by socialism.

Following the auditors' report to the AGM at Penzance, on 8 July 1968, R. W. Kneller, a motor driver of Southampton No. 1 branch, said that as working people railwaymen 'had an interest in the provision of homes for working people' and he suggested the union should invest 'at far lower rates in local authority loans used to build homes'. G. Goddard, a passenger guard of Stockport No. 1 branch, questioned the wisdom of investing in Marks & Spencer, since he understood it was a non-union firm. The two delegates had certainly raised fundamental issues of policy and exposed the dilemma confronting those managing the NUR's funds. On the one hand, there was the practical necessity of giving the maximum financial backing to the union's activities; on the other, the organisation was committed to the political and social aims of transforming society. Sidney Greene, who replied to the arguments advanced by the delegates, made an unequivocal statement of his thinking on the question:

It is not our job in invest in local authorities at low interest rates but to invest the money of the union in the best possible way in order to obtain the best return on the money invested. Somebody mentioned Marks & Spencers. We put our money where we get the best return. Whether Marks & Spencers are a trade union firm or not I do not know, but they are one of the best growth firms in the country . . . We believe in socialism, but we have not yet got to it and have to live in the kind of situation which faces us today.[81]

During the afternoon of Thursday 1 October 1970 the Labour Party Conference at Blackpool debated composite resolution 23 which, *inter alia*, urged the government 'to curb further investment in South Africa, with particular reference to investment in the armaments industry'. The seventeen-man NUR delegation to the conference supported this resolution and joined in the applause given to Fenner Brockway who, on the occasion of his sixtieth appearance at a Labour Party Conference, urged trade unions 'to see that their funds were not invested in companies which are engaged in the partnership in apartheid in South Africa'.[82]

When the report of the union's trustees and finance committee was presented to the EC in December 1970 two executive members, Bob Kettle and Jack Hyland, moved the following amendment to the main resolution endorsing the sub-committee's proposals: 'That we note and adopt the Finance Committee report, and in view of the decision of the Labour Party Conference 1970, we closely review all future investments to make sure that we deal with no firms that have interests in South Africa.' With four EC members absent on union business, the amendment was defeated by 11–9 votes and the main resolution carried by the same margin reversed.[83] It was a decision which angered members of the Leeds 4 branch. At a meeting held in March 1971 they resolved that the question of investing funds in companies with South African interests should be resolved by the AGM.[84] An appeal against the EC decision was, therefore, placed before the seventy-seven delegates who met in the following July at Plymouth. Three other branches supported the Leeds 4 initiative. In moving the appeal W. R. Baxter, a motor driver from Leeds 2 branch, said that he had received a letter from the secretary of the Leeds 4 branch which concluded with the words, 'For ourselves we would rather be paupers than profiteers from slavery'. Another motor driver H. C. George of Feltham, warned delegates that they must not put themselves 'in a paradoxical position by giving verbal assent to the TUC and Labour Party resolutions on the one hand, and investing in South Africa on the other'. A loco driver from Glasgow, John Scanlan, pointed out that 'these investments enable the hierarchy to modernise their forces of retaliation against the struggles of the people'. In urging delegates to turn down the appeal, Sidney Greene, immediately challenged the critics of the finance committee 'to get up and tell us which ones they don't like. I want to say straight away that we have not got any'. Due to the 'barmy agitation' the union had, in the course of the previous year, sold its investment in Barclays' DC and O shares and made a £12,000 profit on the transaction. The appeal was, therefore, superfluous.

Both the General Secretary and the mover of the resolution were poorly briefed on this very important issue. W. R. Baxter was apparently unable to meet the General Secretary's challenge to the critics to name the investments they did not like, for he failed to exercise his right to reply. In fact at that time the NUR had investments with a total book value of £586,244, or approximately one-sixth of its total equity investment, in fourteen companies with major financial interests in South Africa. No doubt the investment of £46,597 in Chubb & Son was considered harmless (and safe) enough; but it was a different matter with the £107,812 invested in ICI, which had a 43 per cent interest in African Explosives and Chemical Industries Ltd, the largest industrial concern in South Africa and the one which manufactured the teargas used against the Soweto rioters in 1976; or the £28,136 invested in Plessey, a firm noted for its development of electronically controlled weapons; the £28,000 tied up in Rio Tinto Zinc, which provided some of the basic raw material for South African armaments; or the £13,274 worth of ordinary shares held in Westland Aircraft Ltd, whose Wasp helicopters were also engaged in quelling the Soweto riots.[85] By 1978 Unity House (Holdings) Ltd had disposed of shares in nine of the fourteen companies with large South African interests, but had increased its holdings in GKN, EMI, Plessey and Westland Aircraft. The union sold its investment in Rio Tinto Zinc in 1975, the year in which Sidney Weighell became General Secretary, and Sidney Greene, on relinquishing office, joined the company as a director.[86] The retail price index rose by nearly 19 per cent in 1974, reducing the purchasing power, or negotiating strength, of the union's investment assets to a broadly corresponding extent. It caused Mr B. J. P. Cotton (who in 1975, took over from Lord Hirshfield the job of presenting the union's accounts to the AGM) to suggest that the

THE ORGANISATION OF THE UNION

union's funds 'might be better utilized in providing greater services and benefits for members' than if they were left invested and falling in value with the impact of inflation.[87]

With hindsight over twenty years' history of the union's finances and the management of the general fund, it can be maintained that among the wisest recommendations that Sidney Greene gave to the numerous AGMs he so ably dominated was one, made in 1959, near the beginning of his term of office, and another offered in the year before his retirement. In 1959 he wrote: 'It is my considered opinion that there is only one sound financial policy for the union to pursue; to ensure that contribution income is adequate to meet the cost of running the union and in addition to make a current contribution to building up reserves.'[88] In the course of his last AGM, on 15 July 1974, he urged delegates at Plymouth to approve what he termed the 'final exercise' in the reform of general fund administration: the institution of a weekly contribution equal to 1 per cent of the railman's basic rate of pay. In giving unanimous approval to this recommendation delegates ensured a much more stable future for the finances of the general fund.[89] On assuming office early in 1975 Sidney Weighell initiated the moves for the purchase of two freehold properties. These were Old Bank House at Leighton Buzzard, to which the finance department was transferred, and Frant Place, set in forty-five acres of beautiful Weald countryside near Tunbridge Wells, which was quickly put to use to expand the education work of union members. The purchase price of Old Bank House was £79,560, and of Frant Place £125,326.[90]

X

Throughout more than a century the payment of provident benefits has been an important part of the union's service to its members. The contribution rates and the payment of benefits at different dates in the period since 1961 are summarised in Table 3.2. Following the passage of the National Insurance Act in 1948, sickness, accident and out-of-work benefit were less vitally important to members than they had been before the coming of the welfare state. Nevertheless, in 1970; provident payments amounted to nearly one-third of all general fund expenditure.

1975 marked the centenary of the union's organised help for railway orphans. In 1875 the ASRS contributed £500 to the Derby

Railway Orphanage. Since its foundation in 1880, the Orphan
Fund has been the source of assistance to more than 45,000 children. It might have been expected that with the halving of the
union's membership since 1960 the number of children for whom
claims could be made as a result of the death of one or both
parents would be reduced. Unfortunately, this has not been the
case. During 1961–65, inclusive, the average number of children
for whom orphan benefit was received each year was 1,755; in
1971–75, inclusive this number had risen to 1,817.[91] The activities
sponsored by the Railway Women's Guild, the branches of the
union and their special committees to raise money for the
Orphan Fund have provided the opportunity for continuing
voluntary effort and the maintenance of the social life of the
union.

The decision of the delegates at the AGM in Plymouth, in July
1971, to liquidate the Sick Fund was not taken lightly. In their
report to the AGM in 1970, the union's actuaries drew attention
to the complication that the thirty-six different rates of contribution to the fund would cause when decimalisation of the
currency took place in the following year. From British Rail there
was a firm refusal to deduct the varied Sick Fund contributions
through the paybills. Only 10 per cent of the membership sub-
scribed to the fund. Was it possible, the actuaries suggested, that
because of the advantage members were taking of the National
Health Service, the fund had outlived its usefulness? The delegates to the AGM at Inverness, in July 1970, decided to refer
the question of the continuance of the fund to the executive for
further consideration and report.[92] A special sub-committee of the
EC was set up in September 1970 and reported its findings to the
executive on 7 May in the following year.[93] In the meanwhile
Sidney Greene sent a circular letter to all branches on 1 January
1971, seeking the opinions of members on the future of the
fund.[94] Nearly half the 293 branch secretaries who replied to the
circular reported that their members agreed with the suggestion
that the fund had outlived its usefulness, whereas 38 per cent
wanted the fund continued; some wanted a uniform contribution
rate incorporated within the standard contribution and others
wanted a referendum of members. Finally, at Plymouth on 21
July 1971 there was a keen debate on the executive's proposal to
close the fund, with nineteen delegates speaking. Despite H.
Butler's telling the meeting that his Doncaster 3 branch had 850
subscribers to the fund, and A. M. Hutchins's opinion that closure
would be 'absolutely deplorable', the executive's recommendation
was adopted by the comfortable majority of 56–21 votes.[95] The

fund was closed from 1 September 1971, existing contributors being paid lump-sums in compensation.

Donation benefit and suspension benefit remained formal entitlements of members long after there was any need for their continuance. They were a relic of the days of martinet management of some of the pre-1921 railway companies. At the time of their abolition it was felt by the union's officers that their continued existence was an implied expression of doubt about the adequacy of the NUR as a guardian of the railwaymen's interests. In any case agreements such as those on the new machinery of negotiation in 1956, and the redundancy agreement of 1963, helped to render them obsolete.

XI

It is unusual for a trade union to process all the legal claims of its members through its own legal department rather than subcontracting this work to a firm of solicitors. The NUR's legal department has been in business throughout the entire history of the union and has won the great respect of the members through its achievements on their behalf. It is true that the department has enjoyed the advantage of a long-continued association with the firm of Pattison & Brewer, the union's solicitors since 1913, who have helped cases through the courts and have given legal advice.

Although the membership of the NUR fell from 335,000 in 1960 to 172,000 in 1978, the number of legal claims being dealt with by the seven or eight members of the legal department at Unity House did not decline proportionately. The average number of cases dealt with each week fell from 121 in 1960 to 75 in 1975; but thereafter it rose to 88 in 1978. There are three main reasons for this buoyancy in the figures. In the last two decades members have become more aware of the legal services on offer. 'Word gets around' about a successful compensation case more rapidly than hitherto. The union does not go quite so far as to encourage its members to have accidents, but it does give very effective publicity about the help it has been able to offer when they have occurred. Under the Workmen's Compensation Acts, which were operative until 1948, an injured wage- or salary-earner could be denied compensation if only 1 per cent contributory negligence could be proved by defending counsel. It was also true that the doctrine of common employment was invoked to deny an appellant full compensation in cases where it could be shown that the immediate responsibility for the accident lay with a foreman or manager 'in common employment' with the injured person, rather than with the ultimate employer. These stumbling-blocks to satisfaction of claims deterred many would-be claimants from approaching the union for support. However, these two obstacles disappeared with the passing of the National Insurance (Industrial Injuries) Act in 1948 and its successors. But it took some time before there was a general awareness of the changed situation in law. From 1975 onwards, at Frant Place, the union provided a more adequate training of its own members in safety and welfare matters.[96]

Although the number of cases dealt with each week by the union's legal department did not decrease as rapidly as did the membership, the number of fatal accident cases fell more than proportionately to both the numbers employed on the railways and the number enrolled in the union – evidence of safer working conditions. Between 1961 and 1965, inclusive, the department dealt with 419 fatal accident cases, or an average of nearly sixty-four a year. Ten years later, in 1971–5, inclusive, there were 181 such cases, or an average of just over thirty-six a year. In both periods the largest number of fatalities occurred on the per-manentway, where 136 men were killed in 1961–5 and 44 in 1971–5. The traffic grades, other than guards, produced the second largest number of deaths with 131 killed in 1961–5 and 53 in 1971–5. There was a steady flow of fatal accidents among both guards and shopmen. In the case of guards this fell from an average of 7·5 per year in the early 1960s to 4·2 per year ten years later, whereas an average of 8·2 shopmen sustained fatal accidents in the earlier period compared with 4·6 ten years later.[97] Working more closely with machinery all the time, the shopmen, whether employed in railway, National Carriers or docks workshops, were more prone to non-fatal accidents than any other grade of em-ployee in public transport. Nearly a quarter of all such cases arose in the workshops. In 1970, for example, there were 821 of them out of a total of 3,741 non-fatal accidents reported to the legal department.

In 1975–9, inclusive, the number of claims settled through the assistance of the NUR legal department averaged 1,102 a year. The trend in the number of settlements was upwards. The sums of money recovered for members rose from £1,135,598 in 1975 to £1,900,000 in 1979, an increase in the real, as well as in money, terms.[98] As might be expected, the compensation gained for members varied enormously, from the £100 secured for the London Transport booking clerk, who injured two fingers through a shutter falling on his right hand, to a record £50,000 obtained for a 50-year-old British Rail technician, who was thrown to the ground when a signal post broke.[99]

New sources of claims assumed prominence in the later 1970s. Although over 90 per cent of the legal cases arose from accidents at work, there was an alarming increase in the number of cases involving assault on union members and larceny of the employers' or their own property. Two-thirds of all instances of assault occurred within the Greater London area and half of these concerned staff employed in London Transport. The spread of one-man operation added to the danger of attacks on drivers. Soccer hooliganism became more widespread and serious. Apart from their damaging effects on the environment, beer cans featured prominently as causing accidents, for example, trackmen stumbling over them at night or being directly hit by cans thrown from railway carriage windows; as weapons of assault on staff and indirectly contributing to vandalism. In the later 1970s also there was a new awareness of the danger of industrially generated deafness. Probably because in earlier generations the prevalence of noise in the working environment was taken for granted, only spasmodic claims for compensation reached the legal department at Unity House. By 1979, however, there were over 800 claims receiving attention.[100] A large proportion of these cases arose in the workshops at Shildon, Doncaster and Crewe.

The dangers to health resulting from exposure to asbestos were more widely recognised in 1975, following the publication of a report called *Asbestos Kills*. A number of cases of men suffering from the effects of asbestos dust were reported to the NUR in the course of the following year. At Cowlais and Ashford workshops a programme of calling in all the railway carriage stock of the 1960s which had been soundproofed with asbestos was put in hand by British Rail. Then men who fitted the panels into the new carriages had worn their ordinary working overalls; those who extracted the same panels in the later 1970s looked more like spacemen than shopmen.[101] The effectiveness of the legal department's work was undoubtedly enhanced by the full co-operation of representatives from the British Railways Board, the forum for discussion of these questions being the Joint Staff Safety Committee of British Rail's Joint Advisory Council for Welfare.[102]

XII

The NUR branch secretary of the later 1970s could be excused for thinking he was in danger of becoming overwhelmed with an avalanche of paper. If his members worked for a variety of the transport undertakings in addition to British Rail, he would be receiving numerous branch circulars each week and bundles of the *Transport Review* fortnightly, with other separate bundles of seven different NUR *News Letters* at least once a month. By contrast, in the 1960s, there were but two main vehicles within the union for conveying information and discussing the significance of developments in transport. Branch circulars gave information of immediate importance to members, including details of wage settlements, arrangements for the election of the union's officers, and other matters requiring prompt attention. Although the *Railway Review* did publish the terms of wage settlements and other major agreements, it also constituted an open forum, in which through letters and articles the views of members were expressed. It also carried important statements of policy by Ministers of the Crown, MPs, the chairman of transport undertakings, reports of transport developments within the British Isles and overseas, and editorials.

The appearance of the *News Letters* was a belated outcome of the decision of the AGM in 1953 to establish a publicity department at head office, failing earlier attempts of the EC in 1951 and 1952 to make the *Railway Review* a more subordinate mouthpiece for the opinions and decisions of the executive committee.[103] The first two publicity officers followed a policy of preparing special pamphlets and leaflets dealing with important issues as they arose. But from 1970 the policy of their energetic and resourceful successor was to establish more regular publications to issue to members. It was stated in the first issue of the NUR *News Letter*, published in April 1970, that the intention was 'to present in a more handy form the sort of items which used to be published in the printed general circulars'. However, the new publication by no means superseded the traditional branch circulars. More specialised printed news letters followed, including *Shops News* (July 1970–); *Road Transport* (September 1970–); *BT Hotels* (March 1972–); *London Transport* (June 1972–); and *BT Docks Board* (May 1977–). The news letters, which were issued free of charge, were very popular with the staff, especially following new agreements reached with national management. They were also published so expeditiously that local hotel managers – to cite one example – would learn of new rates of pay and conditions of service from the news letter before they had official notification from BT Hotels Ltd in London.

The wide circulation of the new publicity material inadvertently gave encouragement to sectionalist tendencies within the union. Thus, the man who worked for Freightliners or National Carriers would take the Road Transport issue of the NUR *News Letter* but would be less enthusiastic about buying a copy of the *Railway Review*, in the mistaken belief that there was nothing in it for him. Public transport workers have many interests in common, as well as their own specialised interests, and the *Railway Review* throughout its century-long history – the first edition appeared on 16 July 1880 – has done the union invaluable service in emphasising the unity of interests of transport workers.

Through a combination of rapidly rising production costs, decreasing sales resulting from the sharp decline in the numbers employed in the railway industry and the competing attractions of the news letters, the circulation of *Railway Review* declined to uneconomic levels. The paper had to be subsidised from union funds. From the issue of 12 March 1976 its title was changed to *Transport Review*, in order to emphasise that the contents were by no means confined to railway matters. Unfortunately, the decline in circulation was not arrested.[104]

Delegates attending the AGM at Llandudno, in July 1978, had to consider an EC report on the *Transport Review*, which was reported to be costing the union £36,000 a year in subsidies. It was suggested that in future the paper should be issued fortnightly, instead of weekly and that delegates should decide whether the union should charge, say, 2p a copy, or issue the paper free to all members. In the discussion on resolution 35, John Scanlan, a driver of Glasgow No. 5 branch, maintained that social changes over the last two decades were largely responsible for the decline in circulation. Television had become a counter-attraction to the branch meeting; the uprooting of large industrial cities, including Glasgow, meant that many members lived farther away from their place of work and the venue of the branch meeting. Members now wanted 'instant trade unionism'. They also wanted 'instant industrial and political information at hand in the form of a free and regular trade union newspaper'. By the large majority of 63–12 votes delegates opted for the fortnightly issue of 25,000 copies to be sent free of charge to branches for distribution to members.[105] The change to the new system was made at the beginning of the new year. *Railway Review/Transport Review* had been published weekly – the only trade union weekly newspaper – for ninety-nine years. It was a great pity that it could not have continued on this basis to complete its century of production. Nevertheless it continued in its all-important role as a forum for information and discussion on trade union and

transport policy. Particularly for those branches with a widely
scattered membership, it remains one of the essential links between the union, the branch secretary and the membership.[106]

XIII

The writing of this volume of the union's history was begun in
1977 in Unity House, the same purpose-built head office which
had been opened by Sidney Webb on 17 September 1910; it was
completed three years later in a building on the opposite side of
Euston Road. On the site where Unity House once stood there
was an ugly gap in the building line. During the lunch-hour
breaks of the summer of 1980 members of the head-office staff
found an irresistible fascination in watching the huge mechanical
grabs and bulldozers eat away at the building in which they had
so recently spent their working lives. The change had been initiated by Sidney Weighell when, on 20 September 1976, he drew
the attention of the executive to the heavy running costs of
Unity House and the impracticability of its adaption to the work
requirements and changed environment of the last quarter of the
twentieth century. He was given authority that day to instruct a
reputable firm of architects and surveyors to undertake a
feasibility study to ensure the best utilisation of the Unity House
site. Carl Fisher & Partners, architects and planning consultants,
the firm chosen to make the study, presented a detailed report in
the spring of 1978. It revealed that the usable floor area formed
only about half the total area of the site, the remaining space
being occupied by long corridors and light-wells. It was a 'totally
uneconomical' use of a very valuable urban site. Refurbishing
within the shell of the old building, and demolishing the building
in two stages – with the staff squeezed together in half the old
building before crowding together again in the first half of the
new building to be built – were considered and ruled out as impracticable. Thus, with the professional assistance of J. W. Thorpe
of Savills as project manager and of the union's solicitors, Pattinson & Brewer, the freehold of Bentley House, 200 Euston Road,
former warehouse and showroom of the Cambridge University
Press, was acquired for £2,360,000 giving the union 35,930 square
feet of space to occupy, while the old Unity House was completely
demolished and a new building erected on the same site. On 25
October 1979 the redecoration and rewiring of Bentley House
was begun and the work was completed for the move across the
road during the last fortnight of March 1980. Demolition of the

old building began almost immediately. On the morning of 14 March, just before the move began, the Rt Hon. Michael Foot, MP and Len Murray, General Secretary of the TUC, were speakers at a short ceremony in Unity House to celebrate nearly seventy years of NUR endeavour since before the outbreak of the First World War. Michael Foot confessed that his wife, Jill Craigie, was appalled at the prospect of the demolition of a fine Edwardian building but he was sufficiently tactful not to say whether he agreed with her. However, he knew that it was planned to preserve the remarkable stained-glass window panels and other unique items from the old buildings and display them in the new office.

Big expenditures were involved. The estimated cost of demolition of the old buildings and construction of the new one was £6·7 million which, together with the purchase price of Bentley House, involved a total outlay in the order of £9·95 million. However, the new buildings would provide 60,000 square feet of office space of which the union would need to use only 25,000 square feet. The remaining 35,000 square feet of office space would be let to produce a large annual revenue, while the sale of the building temporarily occupied at 200 Euston Road was likely to produce at least £3 million. These were some of the reasons why Sidney Weighell assured AGM delegates at St Peter Port, Guernsey, on 30 June 1980 that the union 'could cope with this in the next three years quite easily'.[107]

CHAPTER 4

THE BEECHING ERA

I

THE fanfare of publicity which attended the publication of the Beeching Report – *The Reshaping of British Railways* – on 27 March 1963 tended to obscure the fact that what was being proposed was not the *initiation* of a policy of line closures combined with modernisation, but rather the intensification and speeding up of a process which had been continuing for many years. The erosion of services, closing of branch lines, and reduction in manpower had been proceeding steadily since nationalisation in 1948. From 1950 to 1962, inclusive, over 300 branch lines, involving 3,600 route miles, or some 19 per cent of the network, were closed to traffic.[1] In the Common's debate on the Beeching Report, E. Popplewell, the NUR-sponsored MP for Newcastle upon Tyne, West, informed the House that no less than 174,000 railway jobs had disappeared since 1948, underlying the heavy price paid by railwaymen through such slimming down of the railway system as had already taken place.[2] The Railway Modernisation Plan of 1955, which led to the rapid substitution of diesel for steam traction in the ensuing five years, was largely responsible for the loss of over 54,000 jobs in the two years of 1958–9.[3]

Nevertheless the campaign to make the railways pay their way commercially through the elimination of unremunerative services was stepped up following the Conservative victory in the General Election of October 1959 and the appointment of the successful road engineering contractor, Ernest Marples, as Minister of Transport in Harold Macmillan's new administration. The implication of the Guillebaud Report, which in 1960 largely supported the railwaymen's case for pay comparability and added at least £19 million to the BTC deficit, strengthened the government's resolve to overhaul the railway system. In his speech in the House of Commons endorsing the Guillebaud recommendations the Prime Minister warned:

The industry must be of a size and pattern suitable to modern conditions and prospects. In particular, the railway system must

be modelled to meet current needs and the modernisation plan
must be adapted to this new shape.[4]

Within a month of Mr Macmillan's statement the appointment of a
committee to examine the structure, finance and working of the
BTC was announced by Mr Marples. Its chairman was Sir Ivan
Stedeford, Director of Tube Investments, and its other members
included Mr H. A. Benson, a partner in Cooper Brothers, chartered
accountants, and Dr Richard Beeching, Technical Director of ICI.
Also included were representatives of the Treasury and the Ministry
of Transport. Despite protests from the opposition benches in the
Commons and the Lords, the Minister steadfastly declined to
appoint representatives of the railway unions or of the BTC to the
committee. He claimed that it would be wrong in principle to
include in it people who were themselves concerned. He even
rejected a suggestion by Lord Swinton, a Conservative peer, that
representatives of the Commission and the trade unions should
'sit in' with the committee, not as members but as observers.[5]

The report of the Stedeford Committee was never published.
Nevertheless it is fair to conclude that its appointment and activities
were in line with the government's objectives of scaling down the
operations of the railway system in order to achieve profitability,
and of using the services of Dr Beeching to achieve this aim. When
John Hay, the Parliamentary Secretary to the Ministry of Transport, spoke at the annual dinner of the Road Haulage Association
in May 1960, he said that the appointment of Dr Beeching and
his three associates on the Stedeford Committee would 'commend
itself' to those attending the dinner.[6] The committee's terms of
reference included the requirement to report on 'how best to give
effect to the government's intentions'. That these intentions included
a drastic reduction in the size of the railway network was made
clear by Mr Marples when he commended the Beeching Report to
the House of Commons on 29 April 1963. 'We have deliberately
worked towards this sort of plan for over three years', he said.[7]
More than two years earlier, on 15 March 1961, when announcing
Dr Beeching's appointment as chairman of the BTC, Marples
countered Opposition objections that the new chairman had little
experience of railways by pointing out that he had 'served his
apprenticeship' on the Stedeford Committee.[8]

When Dr Beeching's appointment was announced it was unfortunate that the main searchlight of criticism both in the press,
and in the House of Commons, was directed to the size of his
annual salary – £24,000, compared with the £10,000 of his predecessor, Sir Brian Robertson, rather than to the essential purpose

of his appointment. Although the reason offered by Mr Marples was that £24,000 was Dr Beeching's salary as a director of ICI, it was also the case that what was expected of the new chairman of the BTC was something very different in character from what had been required of his predecessors. Major surgery, rather than continuing administration, was the order of the day, and in the government's view such exceptional responsibilities commanded a higher reward. Neither Frank Moxley, the editor of *Railway Review*, nor Sidney Greene, was sidetracked into thinking that the salary question was the main point at issue. The editor regretted that the motive for the appointment had been lost sight of in the furore over the size of the salary. He felt sure that the Minister would be delighted by the media's response to the news. Sidney Greene saw the cuts coming, and saw that his main task would be 'to secure safeguards and assurances for the staff'.[9]

II

Most men who were holding high office in the union in 1978, and were also active in the union's affairs in 1963, felt that the campaign against the Beeching closures was ineffective and lacking in a strong, central direction.[10] It must be conceded that very few intended closures were stopped as a result of union pressure. It is, therefore, worth while examining the reasons for this lack of success.

At times in the nineteenth century railway-building had been on such a prodigal scale that there was an inevitable legacy of overcapacity. Through the reckless rivalry of the South Eastern and the London, Chatham and Dover Railways before 1899, most sizable towns in Kent had two railway stations where one would have served quite adequately. It would be easy enough to cite other examples of wasteful extravagance. It was never the official NUR policy to oppose *all* closures. Thus, the negotiating committee, in a report to the executive on 18 June 1962, admitted that industrial and population changes and modernisation of transport could create conditions in some areas where railways were no longer needed. When the Cheddington–Aylesbury line was closed on 31 January 1953, NUR members in the district made no large-scale clamour for its reprieve.[11] The Closure of Branch Lines subcommittee, established by the national executive in 1960, from time to time received frank admissions from branches that there was little point in opposing particular closures. On 30 August 1964 the secretary of the Ely branch wrote that 'in view of the sparse-

ness of trains and passengers' no worthwhile purpose would be
served in opposing the closure of the branch line to Newmarket.[12]
On 9 September 1961 Alderman J. Martin, secretary of the East
Anglian District Council, wrote to Sidney Greene that no sort of
case could be made for the retention of the Kelvedon–Tiptree
line.[13] But these were exceptions. Where major lines were concerned and where large regions were likely to be deprived of their
railways, the union opposed management's plans.

One consequence of the attenuated character of railway reorganisation was that proposals for the closure of lines and services,
with the attendant hardships to railway staff and railway users, hit
different parts of the country and different aspects of the industry
at different times. In this way Scotland was earlier affected than
the English Midlands and employment in railway workshops was
axed more thoroughly and at an earlier date than employment in
the traffic grades. With members in different parts of the country
feeling the pinch at different times, it was more of a problem for
the executive committee in Unity House to determine what was the
right psychological moment to launch a national campaign against
a one-sided axing of railway services. Paradoxically the only
instance of industrial action being taken was the one-day strike of
3 October 1962 in protest against workshops closures. This was
more than five months *before* the publication of the Beeching
Report.

It is very doubtful whether railways north and north-west of a
line drawn between Dundee and Greenock have been commercially
profitable, apart from the wartime emergency in 1939–45, at any
time during the last sixty years. In 1920 when Lloyd George's
coalition government was planning the grouping of the 120 prewar
companies into larger units, it was at first proposed that the railways of Scotland should unite to form one of the groups. This plan
was abandoned as a result of strong protests from Scottish MPs,
who maintained that, left to themselves, the Scottish railways would
not pay their way. The companies north of the border were therefore merged with either the London Midland and Scottish, or the
London and North Eastern – two of the four main line companies
brought into being after the passing of the Railways Act in 1921 –
on the assumption that these wealthier undertakings could 'carry',
that is, cross-subsidise, unremunerative Scottish lines.[14] It is not
surprising, therefore, that when successive Conservative governments after about 1953 began to examine critically the causes of the
growing deficits of the railways, the losses sustained on many
Scottish lines should have been noticed. As early as 12 May 1959
the Chief Commercial Manager, British Railways, Scottish Region,

announced his intention of closing passenger services from thirteen
stations and the reduction of freight facilities in the area Inverness–
Wick–Thurso, Mound–Dornoch and Ord–Portrose.[15]

By the late spring of 1961 the situation in Scotland was becoming
so serious that the Scottish District Councils Co-Ordinating Committee organised a joint weekend conference on 11–12 June 1961
in the Grand Hotel, Charing Cross, Glasgow. The large body of
railwaymen assembled urged the national executive of the NUR
'to seek the support of the TUC and the Labour Party in instituting
a nationwide campaign against the government's policy'.[16] It is clear
that one of the first decisions of Dr Beeching after his appointment
became effective on 1 June 1961 was to order a traffic survey of
Scottish railways to be conducted in the following August. It was
found that out of 2,750 daily train services in the region, something like 2,000 were running at a loss, and it was therefore proposed to withdraw 260 passenger train services, close seven branch
lines and curtail freight facilities in many areas to effect an economy
of approximately £450,000. The EC, meeting in October, instructed
Sidney Greene to take up the matter with the General Manager,
Scottish Region. The meeting took place on 19 October and, after
long discussions, it was agreed that the closures planned to take
effect from 6 November 1961 should be postponed until 'a later
date'.

Scottish railwaymen were well aware that this was only a
temporary reprieve. Branches and district councils of the NUR
and ASLEF, therefore, organised a lobby to Parliament on 8
March 1962. About a hundred men made the long journey south,
being joined by many other railwaymen from Lancashire, the North
East, Wales and London. They planned to call at union headquarters in Euston Road and Arkwright Road for moral support.
The NUR members in the party were sadly disappointed when all
attempts to see their union officers failed, despite appeals to the
President. Only two members of the executive committee, D. Bowman and E. Abraham, felt sufficiently strongly on the question to
quit the meeting of the committee in the board room at Unity
House as soon as they heard the skirl of the bagpipes outside, in
order to greet the Scottish and other deputations. The General
Secretary docked them an hour's pay for their pains! He maintained that the leaders of the deputation had not followed the
union's rules. This cold-shouldering by the union's officers was
bad enough, but the experience of the members of the ASLEF
lobbying party was far more shattering. On arriving at their union
headquarters in Arkwright Road they found that the officers and
staff had locked up the building for the day to make sure no

Plate 1 (a) Unity House, 1910–80.

(b) The new Unity House.

Plate 2 (a) Track maintenance old style.

(b) Look-out man.

Plate 3 New methods of track-laying.
(a) Duomatic '06 tamper.

(b) Laying welded rails.

Plate 4 (a) Steam locomotive – LMS 'Black Five' 4–6–0 in action.

(b) Inter-City 125 train.

Plate 5 (a) Footplate of steam locomotive – driver in control of Royal Scot 'Royal Ulster Rifleman'.

(b) Driving cab of Inter-City 125.

Plate 6 (a) Gantry signals, semaphore type, Heaton Norris Junction.

(b) Manually operated signals.

Plate 7 (a) Carlisle Station showing multiple aspect colour signalling.

(b) Interior of Warrington power signalbox.

Plate 8 Ais Gill signalbox.

Scottish deputation was received.[17] The Edinburgh and East of Scotland district council, contrasting the welcome given to the deputation at Westminster by Hugh Gaitskell and other MPs with the rebuff given them at Unity House, considered 'the attitude of the General Secretary, in the light of the serious situation arising from the policy of closures, to [have been] inimical to the best interests of the union and its members'. The aftermath came at the meeting of the EC, in December 1962, when a resolution was carried by 17–6 votes, instructing the General Secretary to ensure that 'when delegations are officially sent by branches and officers are available at head office, a hearing should be arranged for such delegations'.[18] Nevertheless, in the early months of 1962 it was obvious that whereas many Scottish members of the union considered that the whole future of the railways in Scotland was at stake, the union's officers did not, as yet, have the same sense of urgency about Dr Beeching's plans.

At the same time as the Scottish district councils were voicing their growing indignation at the truncation of their railway system, J. Lanwarne, the secretary of the West Midlands District Council bemoaned the deplorably low attendance of branch representatives at district council meetings. On no occasion in 1961 were more than 25 per cent of the branches represented. He attributed this shocking attendance record to the excessive amount of overtime, rest-day and Sunday working by members of the union.[19] But it also reveals an absence of serious concern about railway closures in that district. In the early 1960s less than 2 per cent of the workforce in the West Midlands were registered as unemployed. In the Scottish Highlands it was over 8 per cent.[20] With the situation so different in different parts of the country, it was to that extent less likely that a truly nationwide campaign against the Conservative government's transport policy would be mounted.

III

In 1948, at the peak of railway employment in the postwar period, over 78,000 men were employed in the twenty-nine workshops of the Railway Executive. The existence of so many workshops is explained by the historical development of railways in Britain before 1914 when all the larger companies, and some of the smaller ones as well, had workshops for the construction and repair of their own – and sometimes other companies' – locomotives and rolling stock. When the pre-1914 companies were merged into four large systems under the Railways Act 1921, they kept in being the large majority of the existing workshops. For more than a decade after nationalisation in 1947, there was plenty of work in the shops in making good war damage and losses, building the new standard steam locomotives and then, during 1955–61, building some of the diesel locomotives which replaced those powered by steam. However, the new diesel locomotives were more efficient than their steam predecessors. They required less hours of routine maintenance and, once teething-troubles were overcome, operated for a longer mileage before periodic overhaul. By the end of 1961 the majority of the new-generation locomotives had been built; there was a sharp tapering off in new construction and a decline in the amount of overhaul and repair work. The situation is summarised in Table 4.1. In the new situation of the early 1960s

Table 4.1 *Locomotives Owned by British Railways*

Stock at beginning of year	Steam	Diesel other than shunting	Diesel, shunting	Elec-tric	Others	Total
1957	17,527	7	600	71	2	18,207
1958	16,959	27	775	71	1	17,833
1959	16,108	109	1091	72	1	17,387
1960	14,457	426	1373	85	1	16,342
1961	13,276	847	1708	135	—	15,961
1962	11,691	1285	1894	158	—	15,028
1963	8,767		3683	175	—	12,626
1964	7,050		4060	194	—	11,304
1965	4,973		4462	198	—	9,633
1966	2,987		4811	277	—	8,075
1967	1,689		4962	340	—	6,991
1968	362		4742	341	—	5,445
1969	—		4326	329	—	4,655
1970	—		4183	328	—	4,511
1971	—		4126	323	—	4,449
1972	—		3756	318	—	4,074

Source: Information presented to Railway Staff National Tribunal, April 1974.

some 'railway' towns were in a highly vulnerable situation. In 1962 58 per cent of the insured male population of Horwich were employed in the railway workshops. In Crewe the corresponding figure was 34 per cent, and in Wolverton, 30 per cent.[21]

The first warning of future redundancies came with the publication of the Reappraisal of the Modernisation Plan in 1959.[22] A reduction by 11,000 in the railway workshops labour force was envisaged. Urgent discussions in the Railway Shopmen's National Council followed, resulting in a redundancy agreement for shopmen. The financial compensation offered those becoming redundant was based on length of service and varied in duration from thirteen weeks to twenty-six. Payments were based on two-thirds of standard time rate, less unemployment benefit.[23]

Throughout 1961 and 1962 railway workshop members of the NUR and the CSEU became increasingly alarmed as a growing volume of redundancies was announced by the BTC. In the northeast the closure of the Barnard Castle–Penrith line in the winter of 1960–61 aggravated the rundown of orders at the Darlington, North Road, works and caused rumours about redundancy to spread.[24] The staff at Horwich was subject to a nagging uncertainty about future job prospects as the number of locomotives under construction dwindled. At meetings with representatives of the BTC held in March and November 1961 Sidney Greene endeavoured to obtain a promise of 'no dismissals' for workshop staff similar to that given to traffic grades; but management replied that owing to the very substantial changes which were in the offing for the BR workshops, they could offer no such promise.[25] At a further meeting with representatives of the BTC on 15 January 1962, with Dr Beeching in the chair, Sidney Greene asked for 'hard and definite' information about job prospects in the workshops. Only three days later, at a meeting of the informal liaison committee on workshop matters, more precise details were offered by the management; but these brought no joy to the union side. No more new locomotives were to be built at Horwich after existing orders were completed. This would mean the loss of 180 jobs. For the whole of British Railways no more than 820 units of coaching stock would be required annually, though the rail workshops had the capacity for building 1,130, and some coaches were built by private firms. When current carriage orders were completed at Swindon by the end of 1963, no others would be built there and some 600 men of a total staff of 3,500 would be redundant. The prospects were even gloomier for those employed at the Eastleigh carriage and wagon works, where redundancies would total 850 in a staff of 1,750.[26] What added bitterness to the feelings of the shopmen was that over half the new locomotives were being built by private firms that were partly subsidised by the BTC. It was argued that the work could have gone to the railway workshops, if that subsidy money had been directed to the modernisation of equipment in them.[27]

At the AGM of the NUR at Margate, on 2 July 1962, W. Edgar,

a machinist from Stratford, maintained that railway workshops were being used as a proving-ground for private industry. The locomotives were manufactured by the private firms, tested out on the railways, and their faults corrected in the railway workshops until private industry was satisfied they could be manufactured for export. Meanwhile Ernest Marples maintained the ban on the BTC manufacturing locomotives or rolling stock for export.[28]

Matters came to a head at a meeting between management and the unions (NUR, CSEU and TSSA), chaired by Sir Steuart Mitchell, on 22 August 1962. In a comprehensive review of the situation the chairman stressed the excessive size of the rolling-stock fleet and the reduced maintenance requirements of diesel, as compared with steam locomotives. A much smaller locomotive, carriage and wagon fleet would be required in the future. He estimated the total staff requirements for the different railway work-shop departments (Table 4.2). Sir Steuart said that although the situation 'was unpleasant and undoubtedly distressing', it had to

Table 4.2 *Estimated Railway Workshop Staff Requirements*

	Existing (1962)	1963	1964	1965	1966	1967
Locomotive	28,042	24,800	21,500	19,200	18,850	17,900
Carriage	16,343	12,700	11,400	11,300	11,300	11,300
Wagon	11,940	9,200	8,000	7,900	7,800	7,800
Total	56,325	46,700	40,900	38,400	37,600	37,000

be faced. The views of the unions were invited and they would be taken into consideration before final decisions were taken.[29] When the two sides met again on 10 September 1962, the unions pressed for definite information to allay the dissatisfaction and uncertainty of their members and also said that they were not satisfied with the existing level of resettlement payments. Although Dr Beeching assured them that the Commission had a sub-committee whose special task it was to find additional orders for the railway workshops, he held out little hope for the reduction of work going to private firms which in many cases held manufacturing patents for component parts and entire proprietary designs.[30] Finally, at a further meeting held on 19 September a detailed statement of what was envisaged for all the railway workshops was presented to the unions by Dr Beeching. The emphasis in the statement was on concentration and specialisation. Some shops, such as those at Bromsgrove, Caerphilly, Darlington, Earlestown, Gorton, and Lancing, were to close down completely at various dates between December 1962 and December 1965; some were to merge their activities with those of other shops, as the St Rollox and Cowlais works in Glasgow were to do; others were to lose one or more of their departments, as Ashford was to cease locomotive-building. It was a shattering transformation and it was to be carried out in a very short span of time.[31]

In the meantime there were many indications that, although the shopmen were in the front line, the turn of other grades in the service to feel the effects of the closure policy would soon come. Indeed, by mid-April 1962 the union had already received notification of the intended closure of over ninety lines. On 7 May 1962, therefore, the EC requested its negotiating committee to present a full report on the most appropriate policies for the union to adopt to counter government plans for the railway industry. On 18 June, the executive, on the recommendation of this sub-committee, instructed the union's district councils to convene mass meetings, involving in their organisation ward, constituency and city Labour parties and trades councils. NUR local councillors were to be asked to co-operate, and a large-scale publicity campaign was to be launched through the columns of the *Railway Review* and through the printing of special leaflets. A circular letter enclosing a copy of the sub-committee report was sent to all branches and district councils on 19 June. In a further letter to the same destinations on 24 July Sidney Greene promised that the costs of organising the campaign would be met from the central funds of the union.[32]

By the end of December 1962 over half a million copies of a pocket-sized folder *Is this what you want?*, showing maps of the railway system in 1962 and as it would be if Dr Beeching's plans were carried out; over 380,000 *Save our Railways* leaflets and 65,000 folders *Facts and Figures* had been issued by the publicity department. Of a total of 189 meetings held, seventy-five had been organised by district councils and seventy-two had been addressed by the President or one or the other of the officers of the union. However, political involvement was not as great as might have been hoped, for only forty-two of the meetings were organised by local Labour parties. It may also be questioned whether a total expenditure on publicity and meetings of £7,547 1s 0d over six months was sufficient to have much public impact. It was certainly very small when compared with the union's total assets, as at 31 December 1962, of over £6·5 million.[33]

When the EC met early in September 1962, it considered demands for strike action from branches in Darlington, Derby and

Liverpool and from the Glasgow and West of Scotland and Swindon district councils. Liverpool and North Wales district council urged the summoning of a special general meeting of the union. The EC came to a unanimous decision to call a one-day strike for Wednesday 3 October 1962.[34] In a BBC television programme screened within forty-eight hours of the deadline for the start of the strike and whose audience-rating scarcely matched that of the Morecambe and Wise show, Ernest Marples asked Sidney Greene whether he would be willing to meet Dr Beeching again to discover whether the strike might yet be averted. Sidney Greene agreed and met the BTC chairman on 2 October, the NUR executive also being present. But as the outcome of their discussion was unsatisfactory from the union's point of view, it proved necessary to dispatch telegrams to all the union's 1,333 branches.[35]

In Sidney Greene's view the strike was a sober reminder of what the future might hold, if the government's 'ruthless policies' were pursued without proper regard and provision for the staff affected. He saw the one-day withdrawal of labour principally as a lever with which to obtain better redundancy payments for displaced railwaymen. A complete *volte face* in government policy was not envisaged. He praised the wonderful solidarity of the strikers, tens of thousands of whom had either refused to take their 10s (50p) strike benefit or else had given it back to the union funds.[36] Union members in branches in the South Wales district council determined that they were not going to put their feet up just because trains were not running on 3 October. They spent the day in door-to-door canvassing, explaining to the public the NUR's policy for transport and giving reasons for their opposition to the closure of workshops and stations.[37]

At the time of the strike some 10,000 applications for membership above the usual number at this time of year were received at head office. The executive committee had decided that any railway workers who joined the NUR on or before 30 September 1962 would be entitled to receive the 10s strike benefit. The extra influx included both former non-unionists and members of the ASLEF. The gains were not all permanent. The secretary of the Aberdeen No. 1 branch, for example, had 208 applications from members of ASLEF, but his colleague J. D. Burgoyne told the AGM in July 1963 that he was doubtful whether eight of them were still in the NUR. The one-day strike cost the union £107,922. This sum was in excess of the total amounts paid out by the NUR in strike benefits in the previous thirty years – a clear enough indication of the conciliatory policies pursued by the union over a long period of time.[38]

IV

That strike action by the railway unions was limited to the one-day stoppage on 3 October 1962 was largely due to Dr Beeching's willingness to lean over backwards to make concessions on redundancy payments, provided his main objective of a drastic slimming of the railway industry remained unimpaired, and to Sidney Greene's belief that the union's main objective in the negotiations was to obtain more generous terms of compensation for those members of staff who lost their jobs.

On 8 October, within a week of the strike, the EC met again and resolved to apply further pressure on the BTC in an attempt to exact better terms for redundant shopmen. It decided that, unless there were indications of a change of policy by the BTC, further industrial action would be taken. The negotiating sub-committee was asked to present a quick report with recommendations on the scope and length of the strike, the date of its commencement and the plans for co-operation with the other railway unions.[39] A full discussion with representatives of the other railway unions took place at Unity House on the following day. But when the NUR executive met on 16 October, it decided to defer a decision on strike action until after a planned meeting with the BTC two days later. At 222 Marylebone Road on 18 October Dr Beeching refused to budge on his plan to close workshops but did express a willingness to discuss such matters as the total number of redundancies needed and the amounts of compensation to be paid to men who were laid off. These concessions were enough to cause a split in the EC. Although ten out of its twenty-four members were for adhering to the decision to call another strike, the majority favoured further discussions with management.[40]

A number of meetings of the Railway Shopmen's National Council followed in November and December at which the employers' side made improved offers, in particular that no shopman should be discharged until 14 December 1962. Further talks were held early in January 1963 with the result that a comprehensive workshop staff redundancy agreement, operative from 15 June 1962, was reached in the Railway Shopmen's National Council on 17 January 1963.

The outstanding provisions of the new agreement were that at least six months' notice was to be given before a main works or a major activity at such a workplace closed down. Individual notice of dismissal would be at least six weeks for a member of staff with five years' or more service, and for older men an additional period of notice, up to eight weeks for a person over 55 years of age, would be given. For those discharged, a lump-sum payment equal to two-thirds of the standard weekly payment for each completed year of service was to be made. Thus, a skilled man with fifty years' service would receive £365, while an unskilled man with equally long service would get £305. There were to be additional weekly payments after discharge, for those still unemployed, equal to two-thirds of the standard weekly wage, less unemployment benefit, for a period of two weeks for every five years of completed service. Those over age 50 qualified for weekly payments for a further number of weeks (up to forty weeks in the case of some-one over 60 years of age). Reasonable time off (up to a total of three days) at time-work rates, plus free travel, was to be given to those looking for alternative employment.[41]

A defect of the agreement was that although workshop managements kept registers of employees who had left for other jobs within the railway industry, they kept no records of those who had been made redundant. At the AGM in Scarborough, on 10 July 1963, W. H. MacDonald, a welder from the Ashford works, reported that skilled fitters formerly employed in the works were pushing ice-cream carts round the town but that when management wanted to replace some skilled men who had left they had no means of tracing the whereabouts of former staff. The effect of the agreement on NUR influence in some parts of the country was devastating. In 1962 Lancing branch had over 800 members; following the closure of the works the branch had disappeared by the end of 1964. Nevertheless, as George Brassington, Assistant General Secretary, told the AGM delegates in July 1963, the redundancy agreement for workshop staff was 'in advance of anything in this country in any trade or industry'.[42]

Before the redundancy agreement for shopmen had been signed, a working party of representatives of management and trade unions had begun considering somewhat similar arrangements for conciliation staff. The signature of the agreement concerning shopmen on 17 January 1963 provided the foundation for advance in negotiations on behalf of other railwaymen. At a working party meeting on 29 January the British Railways Board Chief Industrial Relations Officer presented comprehensive proposals which, in respect of lump-sum payments, continued weekly payments when unemployed, time off for looking for alternative employment and personal notice of redundancy, were similar to the shopmen's agreement. In other respects there were improvements on the earlier arrangements. Members of the conciliation staff who were in the service on 1 January 1958 were assured against discharge, provided they were prepared to change their workplace if necessary. Those who were in receipt of continuing resettlement payments were to receive the same travelling facilities as active members of staff, and those who had left the service through redundancy, were entitled to the concessions on travel offered to staff who had retired normally. At its meeting on 8 February the EC gave its unanimous endorsement to these proposals which were backdated to 15 June 1962, in line with the provisions for shopmen. A similar agreement was reached in respect of workshop supervisors on 7 March 1963.[43] More compreshesive arrangements for salaried and supervisory staff were negotiated after the publication of the Beeching Report.

Although the British government was influenced by the legislation of a number of European states,[44] there is no doubt that the NUR's success in securing what were, by the standards of the time, generous redundancy compensation for railway employees, set an example which was later followed by other nationalised industries and private firms; and provided a yardstick against which the Minister of Labour could test the adequacy of the provisions regarding notice of dismissal in the Contracts of Employment Act (31 July 1963), and the sufficiency of compensation offered to redundant workers under the Redundancy Payments Act (5 August 1965). By the time the second law was passed arrangements for redundant railway employees seemed less remarkable; but the NUR was the trail-blazer in 1962 and 1963.

The fact that the union's negotiators had previously secured these important improvements in the entitlements of redundant railway workers softened the impact of the publication of the *Reshaping of British Railways* plan on 27 March 1963. Had members been suddenly thrown on the industrial scrapheap with little or no compensation and no assistance to tide them over the transition period to employment in other industries, they would have been more indignant and more responsive to the call for militant action in protest against government plans for transport.

Perhaps the most remarkable decision of the EC during the whole of the Beeching era was made at the regular quarterly meeting early in December 1962. It gave unanimous endorsement to the transport committee report, which concluded with the following expression of opinion:

There can be no doubt whatever that the campaign has been one of the most successful the union has ever undertaken, but we feel that the time has arrived for meetings at Executive Committee level to cease as from 31 December 1962. The campaign will, however, be continued on a local basis, and leaflets will be issued by head office. The whole question will be reviewed early in the New Year in the light of the circumstances then prevailing.[45]

At the AGM in Scarborough, on 4 July 1963, Sidney Greene defended the executive's decision to cease financial backing, from central funds, for the activity of branches and district councils on the ground that the attendance at meetings was beginning to taper off. However it was known that Dr Beeching's report was forthcoming, even though publication had been delayed beyond the originally anticipated date. The December executive decision meant that when the report *did* appear on 27 March 1963 the union was ill-prepared for the onslaught. The union sustained a substantial campaign against the workshop closures which attracted little attention in the national newspapers; its response to the publication of the Beeching Plan came after the psychological moment for catching public attention had passed.

The South Wales and Monmouth District Council was not content to ease up on the campaign after the executive's decision of December 1962. Pit closures as well as rail closures were threatening the livelihood of the workforce of the region and, therefore, joint meetings of miners and railwaymen were organised. The culmination of the campaign was a lobby of MPs at Westminster on 13 February 1963. The secretary of the district council wrote to all other district councils canvassing support. Hull and York, Darlington, Swindon, and Glasgow and South West Scotland District Councils, among others, sent representatives to the lobby. When Sidney Greene got to know of these activities, he wrote to the councils concerned informing them that, in accordance with EC Decision No. 2921 of December 1962, any expenditure which was incurred in connection with the lobbying campaign could not be a charge against branch or district council funds. This matter eventually came before the AGM in July 1963, when the appeal made by four district councils against the decision of the EC in March to refer the question of campaign expenses to the negotiating committee and to refuse the immediate granting of expenses, was upheld by 42–31 votes. H. B. Drury, dock checker of Hull, maintained that through the EC decision of December the campaign had been brought to an 'untimely end'. Henceforward branches and district councils could count on the support of central funds for their activities against the Beeching Plan. But this was more than three months after the plan had first seen the light of day and general public interest in the issues it raised had long since died down.[46]

V

The feature of the British Railways Board's *The Reshaping of British Railways* which attracted more attention in the press was the reduction proposed in passenger services. Of the 17,830 route miles in 1961, 5,000 miles and 2,363 stations (out of a total of 7,000) were to be closed. Although the report's statements about the future of freight services were less specific, the reduction of coal depots from 5,031 to 250 and of freight sundries depots from 900 to 100 was indicative of the drastic purging of small-scale mineral and sundries traffic which was envisaged. Although stopping train services were to be greatly reduced in number, it was planned to speed up and modernise the residue of the passenger train network which it was thought worth while retaining. On the freight side, the objective was to attract large-scale goods and mineral traffic back to the railways through the spread of liner and merry-go-round trains. From the union point of view, one of the most disturbing aspects of the report was the statement that staff reductions would be 'of a continuing nature with no precisely foreseeable end point'. Anything better calculated to depress the morale of railwaymen would be hard to imagine.[47]

The NUR executive received a copy of the reshaping plan on 26 March 1963 and immediately referred it to the negotiating committee for an early report. This was to hand when the executive next met on 3 April. On the grounds that the Beeching document was a political charter with the seal of the present government already appended, and that a public transport system based solely on profitability was the very opposite of the union's policy of public transport being predominantly a service to the community, the negotiating committee considered that complete rejection of the plan was the right response for the union to make. It recommended that the General Secretary should instruct all district councils to arrange mass public meetings, with the union's officers and EC men to be included among the speakers. A pamphlet should be prepared for mass distribution. Finally, the union's industrial strength should be used to protest against the proposals and the other railway unions were to be contacted in order to devise a common policy. The executive gave its unanimous endorsement to these proposals.[48]

At a joint meeting with the other rail unions on 8 April the representatives of the NUR, ASLEF and CSEU supported strike action. TSSA representatives did not. All were agreed that an approach should be made to the TUC general Council and the national executive of the Labour Party to organise a direct approach to the government. The following fortnight, during which public awareness of the severe consequences likely to follow from the Beeching proposals gradually faded, was largely occupied in meetings and discussions. On 18 April representatives of the railway unions met the finance and general purposes committee of the TUC and were informed that a meeting with the Minister of Transport was being arranged. On 23 April Mr Marples did discuss the plan with the TUC and railway union representatives, but he offered no concessions. The NUR executive met later the same day and decided by 16–8 votes to recommend a three-day strike on 14–16 May, inclusive, after rejecting by 17–7 votes an amendment in favour of a one-day strike on 16 May.[49] The negotiating committee then conferred once more with their opposite numbers of ASLEF and CSEU (The TSSA was not involved, having earlier decided against strike action). Although the CSEU indicated support for the NUR proposals, the ASLEF representatives said there were difficulties. The dates proposed for the strike occurred during the planned sitting of their Annual Assembly of Delegates. They were prepared to support any action to secure an improvement in the Beeching plan before embarking on a strike and they would consult their AAD. However, the NUR went ahead with its plans for the three-day strike confident that when the time came not only CSEU, but also ASLEF, would lend support.

Dr Beeching responded quickly. On 5 May he wrote to Sidney Greene, offering to meet representatives of the union. On the following day the executive agreed unanimously to accept the offer and the two sides met at 11 a.m. on 8 May, when a small sub-committee was set up to go into details. In the meantime the executive had agreed a six-point programme of demands to present to the Board. They were exclusively concerned with gaining better compensation for those likely to be affected by the implementation of the plan. The executive agreed that the negotiating committee should seek a general easing of the phasing of redundancies arising from workshop closures; that staff obliged to move to lower-grade jobs should be entitled to receive indefinitely the rate of pay they were getting before their move; that there should be no limitation on the time a man was given travelling facilities between the place at which he was made redundant and that to which he was transferred; that there should be an option of retirement for persons between 60 and 65 or with more than forty years' service, the persons thus qualified to receive the basic rate of wages until reaching the age of 65; that the lodging allowance of staff transferred on redundancy should be raised to £5 a week and that there should be an improvement in the resettlement payments. These points were discussed at meetings between representatives of the Board and the NUR on 8–9 May 1963 with a sufficiently promising outcome to persuade the executive, on 9 May, to cancel the order for the strike. At a further meeting on 13 May between the Board's representatives and those of ASLEF and the NUR the Board conceded two of the NUR's claims in full. These were concerning the pay of a transferred and downgraded member of staff and free travel to the new place of work. On lodging allowances they met the NUR half-way, agreeing to raise the amount from the existing 70s to 84s. For the over-60s made redundant the Board could not promise retention of previous rates of pay until the age of 65, but promised to shortly produce an alternative plan.[50]

The Railway Board's proposals for the over-60s came in the form of a letter to Sidney Greene on 18 June. A Welfare Fund, financed entirely by the Board, was to be set up for the purpose of making *ex gratia* payments to former members of staff over 60 years of age and with at least thirty years' service. This assistance was to be given after the cessation of continuing weekly payments under the redundancy arrangements and was to continue until the recipient reached the age of 65. The snag in the proposals was that there was to be no fixed scale of payment, each individual's case being considered on merits. But the NUR negotiators were unable to change the Board's policy in this respect.[51] All the same, the concessions which had been wrung from the Board, both shortly before and after the publication of the Beeching plan, added up to one of the most comprehensive and generous redundancy arrangements so far reached in British industry.

VI

The above record of negotiations, which took place in April, May and June 1963, make clear that the union's response to the publication of the Beeching plan was to seek an alleviation of its effects on the staff rather than to secure its rejection or substantial modification. The Board's willingness to soften the impact of redundancy is a part – but only a part – of the explanation of the executive's abandonment of the strike weapon on 9 May 1963. Views of union members on the proposed three-day strike were more mixed than they had been when there was overwhelming sup-

port for the one-day strike on 3 October 1962. While the minute
books of the Glasgow and South-West Scotland, Liverpool and
North Wales, Manchester and District, Darlington, and Swindon
district councils all reveal strong support for the three-day strike,
the Sheffield and Chesterfield District Council's resolution in support of strike action was only carried by 16–9 votes and the
Plymouth and West Midlands minute books are silent on the
subject. At a meeting of the Exeter No. 1 branch on 2 May
several speakers voiced opposition to industrial action, and claimed
that lack of support for this form of protest was widespread in the
whole area. At the AGM on 4 July 1963 a resolution in favour
of industrial action against the plan was eloquently supported by
two delegates from the Greater London area, but it was defeated
by 60–17 votes after Sidney Greene said that he had 'had more
letters against the three-day strike than [he] had received for a
very long time about any subject at all'. The tension of a keenly
contested debate was relieved by laughter after a delegate called
for a recount after the result of the rcorded vote was announced.[52]

The union's campaign against the Beeching Plan failed to achieve
a decisive political impact even in the higher echelons of the
Labour Party. The annual statement of accounts for 1963 reveal
that £11,672 18s 3d was spent in the course of the 'Future of
British Railways' campaign. This was a larger sum than had been
spent in 1962, but was less than half the £24,252 6s 2d spent on
celebrating the union's jubilee. A greater quantity of leaflets was
distributed after the publication of the *Reshaping of British
Railways* report than was the case after the announcement of the
workshop closures. The most popular, *The Mis-shaping of British
Railways – Retort*, made clear the vast areas of Britain which
would be denuded of railways if the report was implemented. But
it was a slim leaflet and not a substantial, closely argued publication detailing a positive alternative – the kind of case likely to
inform and educate influential opinion in the Labour Party. This
was no fault of the union's publicity officer, who was hard pressed
and completely lacking in the assistance of any research department at head office. By comparison, in 1976, the union's recently
established research department helped to prepare *Policy for
Transport*, a fifty-two page booklet produced in response to the
government's *Transport Policy: a Consultative Document*. The
authors of the booklet exposed the anti-rail bias of parts of the
government publication and could claim some credit for helping to
create a more sympathetic approach to railway transport in the
White Paper on transport policy in 1978.

Proof that the union's publicity on the Beeching Plan had failed

to have a truly decisive influence on the thinking of many leading
figures of the Labour Party was forthcoming after the party's
General Election victory in October 1964. Just over a year earlier
at the annual conference of the Labour Party held in Scarborough,
Sidney Greene moved a resolution on transport which included the
following sentence:

> Conference demands . . . that the government shall defer any
> action in regard to closures based on the Beeching proposals
> until a survey has been held into all forms of inland transport,
> and coastwise trading by British ships . . . and a national plan
> drawn up to enable transport to render full service to the nation.

The resolution was carried unanimously. In the party's General
Election manifesto *The New Britain*, published on 11 September
1964, a promise was made fully consistent with the above conference resolution:

> Labour will draw up a national plan for transport covering the
> national networks of road, rail and canal communications,
> properly co-ordinated with air, coastal shipping, and port ser-
> vices. The new regional authorities will be asked to draw up
> plans for their own areas. While these are being prepared major
> rail closures will be halted.

Nevertheless, under Labour Ministers of Transport in the two
Wilson administrations, between 1964 and 1970, a further 3,458
route miles of railway were closed.[53] During Tom Fraser's brief
tenure of office – just over one year – in the Ministry, major
closures of a large part of the old Great Central line and the
Somerset and Dorset line (Bristol–Bournemouth, 109 miles) were
carried out. The union's officers and its sponsored MPs, spurred on
by resolutions from the North London and other district councils,
expressed their grave disquiet at an interview with the Prime
Minister on 6 October 1965. They contrasted Labour's Election
promise with the performance of Tom Fraser in office. They complained that the policies of the preceding Tory administration had
continued practically unabated. These strong representations helped
to persuade Harold Wilson to replace Tom Fraser by Barbara
Castle in December 1965.[54]

When Dr Beeching's term of office expired, in December 1965,
Harold Wilson wished to reappoint him on the ground that time
was needed for the positive aspects of his plan, especially the
expansion of liner train traffic, to be developed. But when the

Prime Minister consulted some of his colleagues he found that the majority were opposed to Dr Beeching's reappointment. The significance of this incident is that their ground for holding this view was not disgust at his slashing of the railway system, but that they saw him as an enemy of road transport.[55] It was an episode which epitomises the failure of the NUR in the early 1960s to counter the influence of the road lobby. One influential member of the Cabinet who did not see railways as an essential service industry was Richard Crossman, who, in 1969, regarded the Central Wales line as 'a parody of a railway' for which there was 'an overwhelming case for closure'. He deplored the fact that, apart from Richard Marsh, the Minister of Transport, and Roy Jenkins (who both supported closure), it was mainly from fear of losing votes in the forthcoming Election that the rest of the Cabinet wished to keep the line open.[56]

The situation was very different in March 1979, when the British Railways Board planned the closure of an additional 700 route miles of railway. By this time the union had eleven sponsored MPs (compared with six in 1964), a research department, and a political liaison officer, who organised regular meetings between the union's leading officers and its MPs and the Minister of Transport. It had also helped to establish Transport 2000, an alliance of conservationist and pro-rail groups concerned to ensure a major role for railways in Britain's transport system. On this occasion the decision of William Rodgers, the Minister of Transport, to veto the Board's proposal was undoubtedly influenced by the more comprehensive briefing and political pressure the union had brought to bear over the previous two or three years.[57]

In the Beeching era the pro-rail lobby was in disarray. From 1867 to 1947 the Railway Companies' Association had, for the greater part of its existence, been the most powerful lobby in Parliament. Its decline in the interwar period, and disappearance with the passage of the Transport Act in 1947, created something of a vacuum which was filled by the emergence of the Road Haulage Association, the principal agency for advancing the interests of the road-construction firms, the road hauliers and motorists in Parliament. In the 1930s the Pedestrian Association was the most effective counterlobby to the road interests, but when this became a charity in 1952, it ceased its lobbying tactics.[58] A criticism of the NUR's leadership in the early 1960s is that it made no serious effort to bring together the disparate groups who were against rail closures, such as the Ramblers' Association and the Road and Rail Association. Such consolidation of effort was not begun until 1973 with the formation of Transport 2000. Although there was co-operation between the railway unions in the campaign, Glasgow and the West of Scotland district council, for example, sending a letter of thanks to ASLEF branches in the district which had supported the one-day strike on 3 October, and the Edinburgh and East of Scotland district council wholeheartedly supporting a meeting convened by ASLEF branches in Edinburgh, enlistment in the campaign rarely extended beyond local trade unions, Labour parties and trades councils.[59] It was an independent body, the Road and Rail Association, which sponsored a highly successful meeting against the Beeching cuts, chaired by Lord Stonham in Caxton Hall, London.[60] Lord Stonham was very active in speaking at meetings in all parts of the country in 1962 and 1963; but it was left entirely to the local initiative of NUR branches as to whether his services were invoked.

The union's Closure of Branch Lines sub-committee was not a very effective body. Roy Trench, a member of the EC during 1962–4, who served on the sub-committee, recalled that its members were sometimes confronted with a pile of papers up to a foot high and that a good deal of the work comprised 'rubber stamping' the closure proposals. Apart from what the local branches were able to supply, the sub-committee had little evidence to go on, there being no headquarters research team to provide factual information and suggest alternative solutions to outright closure. In these circumstances it depended a great deal on the zeal and initiative of branch and district council secretaries as to how far it proved possible to delay or stop the closure of lines and reduction of services.

The channels for opposition to rail closures in the localities were the Transport Users' Consultative Committees, which had been set up under the Transport Act 1947. The grounds for opposition had to be local ones, and it was necessary to prove that the closure of a railway would bring hardship to the local population through the unsatisfactory character of alternative bus services with the consequent delays in getting to work, visiting a hospital, and so on. The poor state of the roads was a further valid objection. In the first four years of its life the union's Closure of Branch Lines sub-committee and local branches and district councils were working at a disadvantage in that, until March 1964, working railwaymen and women were not allowed to sit on the TUCCs. The union was partly to blame for this situation. In December 1952 the West Midland district council expressed a desire to be represented on the local TUCC and asked Jim Figgins, the General Secretary, to take up the question with the Minister of Transport. Jim Figgins declined the request on the ground that the TUCCs were designed to protect the interests of the *users* of the railway rather than those of the railway workers. When the district council appealed against this decision, the executive gave unanimous endorsement to the General Secretary's ruling.[61] Nine years later, with concern about railway closures mounting, the AGM rescinded the executive's decision of December 1952 and demanded trade union representation on the TUCCs. However, it was not until March 1964 that this demand was conceded. The General Secretary informed branches and district councils immediately.[62]

In the meantime the Closure of Branch Lines sub-committee expressed its frustration and impotence in a report to the EC in May 1961. It commented on the absence of effective machinery to combat the proposals of the BTC, noted the inability of the union to nominate members of the TUCCs but felt most frustration from the fact that information about proposed closures came too late for effective countermeasures to be taken.[63] This last point was taken up by Sidney Greene at a meeting with representatives of the BTC at 222 Marylebone Road, London, on 8 June 1961. Although management claimed that existing arrangements for prior consultation with staff about projected changes were satisfactory, the chairman, A. R. Dunbar, promised that the points put forward by the union would be mentioned to regional managers.[64] It was subsequently arranged that where it was proposed to discontinue any railway passenger services from any station or on any line, the Board would have to give at least six weeks' notice of the intended closure by publishing this intention for two successive weeks in two local newspapers.[65] The TUCC had no power to delay or stop the closure of freight depots or freight services.

Despite the fact that as time passed the Closure of Branch Lines sub-committee had earlier warning of impending closures and more time to recommend countervailing measures, effective resistance still depended very much upon the branches of the union. Thus, in South Wales the district council used the large amount of information it received from branches to draft a memorandum in tabulated form to send to the major objectors to line closures to assist them in the meetings of the TUCCs.[66] The officers of the Eastern Region district council showed outstanding determination and initiative in mobilising the maximum local opposition to the wholesale railway closures contemplated by the Railways Board in their area. Through enlisting the support of the Peterborough city council and other local government bodies in areas likely to be affected by the rundown of the railways in East Anglia and the fenlands, they succeeded in delaying the carrying out of the Board's plans and completely stopped the proposed closure of the

Peterborough–Grimsby line.[67] In the South-West there was a prolonged and very determined struggle to keep open Meldon Quarry,
near Okehampton, high up on the northern edge of Dartmoor,
employing 130 men in the production of railway ballast and road
stone in an area where jobs were scarce. In 1965 British Rail
announced the intention of selling the quarry to British China Clay
(Quarries) Ltd. At first the argument used both by British Rail,
and by the Ministry of Transport, was that under section 14(1)(e)
of the Transport Act 1962, the Railway Board had complete freedom to dispose of any of its assets. The local NUR branch at
Okehampton and the district council were not deterred by this
seemingly conclusive answer. A Meldon Quarry Action Committee
was formed. It enlisted the support of all local MPs and parliamentary candidates (including John Pardoe and Dr David Owen).
Through Ernest Popplewell, MP and Devonshire members, it con-
trived an adjournment debate in the House of Commons on 26
May 1965; it persuaded Barbara Castle, Minister of Transport, to
write to the Regional Manager of British Rail; it held public
meetings and wrote numerous letters to all persons likely to be of
influence. Eventually the Prime Minister, Harold Wilson, was persuaded to give it his 'personal attention'. Both the Ministry and
British Rail eventually yielded. After various postponements of the
date of closure, final reprieve came towards the close of 1968.[68]

The above examples all illustrate how very much it was left to
the local initiative of branches and district councils to struggle for
the retention of railway services in their area. On transport policy,
apart from the important question of compensation to redundant
staff, a strong hand at the helm was sadly lacking. To the suggestion that in the Beeching era the leadership of the union left
the branches too much to themselves, Frank Cannon, Assistant
General Secretary, agreed that 'there was a great deal in it'.[69]

The absence of a decisive leadership sprang, at least in part,
from the character of the General Secretary. Sidney Greene was a
very able negotiator. He was most impressive in confrontations
with management on pay and conditions of service and in explaining to AGM delegates the nature of the deal that had been made
with the management. On at least one occasion his presentation of
the NUR case was so masterly that delegates asked that the speech
should be printed and circulated to branches. But he was cautious
and conservative, rather than adventurous and enterprising. He
shunned the limelight when the occasion demanded the maximum
of publicity for the union's alternative policy for transport. On 16
March 1962 D. H. Penman had written in a letter to the *Railway
Review*, 'We should all recognise that this is a fight railwaymen

cannot win on our own. The public should be roused to support us'. Sidney Greene was not the man for rousing public support. Where others might have seen opportunities, he advised circumspection. In September 1972 he declined an invitation to speak at a meeting in Brighton, pleading other commitments but adding that he did not favour the meeting 'because of the overriding interest in the Labour Party Conference' being held in the town at that time. He seemed to overlook the fact that the Tribune Group, the Labour Peace Fellowship and many other organisations found the conference an ideal occasion to hold evening meetings to put their case to the delegates. The Brighton NUR members went ahead with their meeting, presumably for this reason, despite the advice of the General Secretary.[70] David Bowman, who completed a total of nine years on the executive before serving as President during 1975–7 inclusive, considered that things would have been very different but for the car accident in Moscow in November 1957, which killed Jim Campbell, Sidney Greene's predecessor as General Secretary. With Campbell confronting Beeching, he claimed, 'there might well have been some blood-letting but no butchery'. From his experience as a member of the negotiating committee in 1962–3 he gained the strong impression that the General Secretary was not fighting all-out against the Beeching Plan, because he was led to believe that once the closure programme was completed the staff who remained to run a more efficient service would be a well-paid elite.[71]

Nevertheless, in the circumstances of the early 1960s the public would have taken a lot of persuading to demand a halt to the Marples–Beeching policies. With car ownership spreading rapidly, petrol selling at less than six shillings (30p) a gallon and blithe optimism that the era of cheap fuel would continue indefinitely, the growing body of motorists were not overconcerned at the disappearance of a large part of Britain's railway system. If the union had more success in resisting rail closures in the 1970s than it did in the 1960s, this was not only because it was better organised to meet the challenge, but also because the public had had its confidence shaken through the consequences of the Arab–Israel conflict of 1967 and of OPEC's determination to force up the price of oil.

VII

In April 1978 a veteran railwayman, Mr J. Holt, Secretary of the West Ham branch of the NUR, gave his assessment of the situation by saying, 'Most of the present-day difficulties spring from Beeching'.[72] It is an opinion widely held by those who were in the industry in the 1960s. He meant that during the Beeching regime the rundown of staff numbers, union membership and, most importantly, the morale of the workforce, was greatly accelerated. The number employed by British Railways, including those employed in the workshops, fell from 514,500 in 1960 to 273,000 in 1970. Over the same decade the membership of the NUR dropped from 333,844 to 193,924. Some of the long-established characteristics of railway employment virtually disappeared. Through the nineteenth century and, indeed, until the outbreak of the Second World War, a job on the railways was highly prized since it was a job for life, while many other employments were insecure. It was work which brought that sense of satisfaction which accompanies participation in an essential public service. There was a tradition of railway employment running in families. Second- and even third-generation railwaymen were numerous, and not rare exceptions, as in the case of the present General Secretary of the NUR. The rapid decline in the size of the railway workforce in the Beeching era destroyed much of the former sense of job security, and the emphasis on commercial viability rather than the maintenance of a public service, undermined the railwayman's sense of importance. With plenty of other work available – without the unsocial hours so often characteristic of railway employment – labour turnover greatly accelerated. Thousands of men and women did not stay in the job long enough for them to develop a sense of real involvement in the industry.

One of the finest traditions of the NUR was that many members of the union played an active part in the political life of their local community. An outstanding example of this was to be found in Wigan and district where, in 1962, twenty-nine NUR members were serving on local councils. After the Beeching closures, many towns had no railway service and therefore no railwaymen to act as JPs, serve on the local council, or play an active part in the affairs of the Labour Party. Mansfield in Nottinghamshire, though a large town of over 100,000 inhabitants, completely lost its railway service in 1964. The severe shrinkage of the railway network in the 1960s brought serious problems for union organisation. Many branches with a long tradition of vitality (as well as those who were more somnolent) had to close down. It was practically impossible for many members in Scotland and Wales to attend the meetings of their branches. Many members of the Inverness No. 1 branch, for example, would have had to travel over 100 miles there and back, if they wished to put in an attendance and had the time to do so.

It was only with the approach to stabilisation in the workforce, the impressive improvements in technology and the revival of rail passenger travel in the later 1970s that the severe damage done to Britain's public transport in the Beeching era was to some extent mitigated and a more hopeful phase of railway, and railway union, development began.

CHAPTER 5

PAY AND EFFICIENCY 1

I

IN a publicly owned industry like the railways, so-called
'industrial' issues, such as the progress of wage negotiations,
cannot be separated from the more obviously 'political' con-
troversies over government transport policy. Ultimately both these
important issues are political in character. The Attlee government's failure to accept the concept of public transport as a
service provided to meet the needs of the nation and its decision,
instead, expressed in the Transport Act of 1947, that 'taking one
year with another' the British Transport Commission was to pay
its way as a commercial concern, had important implications for
the Commission's staff. It followed that the level of wages and
the working conditions of those employed in public transport
were dependent on the profitability of the British Transport Commission's undertakings. Nevertheless, in the early 1950s the prospects seemed bright. In the first six years of the life of the
Commission, namely, 1948–53, a working surplus was earned,
and in 1951–3, inclusive, an overall surplus was achieved after
meeting 'central charges', the biggest element in which was the
interest charge on British Transport Commission stock – the compensation paid to the shareholders of the prenationalisation railway companies. It was the profits earned by British Road Services, the part of the road haulage industry owned by the BTC,
which were mainly responsible for improving the financial position of the Commission as a whole. BRS profits rose from £1·1
million in 1948 to £8·9 million in 1953 (with a setback to a £1·1
million loss in 1950).[1] It was reasonable to envisage that these
profits would rise still higher in subsequent years and that they
would enable the Commission to finance much-needed capital
improvements on the railways. On such foundations there could
have been constructed an integrated transport system, in which
each means of transport fulfilled the role for which it was
technically and economically best suited. A healthier industry of
this kind would have been better placed to pay its staff adequate
wages.

Political events determined otherwise. The Conservative Party's

General Election victory of 25 October 1951, resulted in a major change in transport policy. Under the Transport Act of 1953 arrangements were made for a transfer to private ownership of the majority of the vehicles owned by BRS. A specially created Road Haulage Disposal Board sold more than half the BRS's vehicles to private haulage firms at knockdown prices. This act of vandalism on the most profitable of the BTC's subsidiaries evoked strong protests from people of all political persuasions with the result that the government halted the sale of vehicles before the process was complete. The Road Haulage Disposal Board was abolished in the summer of 1956 and BRS was left with some 16,000 vehicles compared with the 41,000 it had owned in 1951.[2] But this concession to public opinion made little difference to the ultimate outcome. Once some of its most valuable assets had been grabbed for the benefit of the private road haulage industry, the prospects of the BTC's meeting the commercial requirements of the Transport Act of 1947 diminished rapidly. With the end of petrol rationing in 1950, full employment, and rising real wages and increasing car ownership, adversely affected the Commission's passenger receipts. By 1954 its overall finances were in the red to the tune of £11·9 million, and by 1957 it ceased to earn a working surplus before deduction of the central charges.[3]

II

Such was the background to the railway pay crisis of 1955. As far back as July 1953 the NUR put in a claim for a rise of 15 per cent in basic rates of pay. But over seventeen months of negotiations little progress was made in face of the 'repeated protestations by the Commission that they had already exceeded the limit of their financial resources'.[4] In October 1954, with great misgivings, a majority of the union's executive accepted the RSNT's very modest award of a rise of 4s a week on basic rates for all grades other than footplate staff. Members of the rank and file showed less hesitation in expressing their view about the award. A mass of protests from branches and district councils reached Jim Campbell, the General Secretary, and he felt obliged to summon the executive which, on 21 December 1954, decided to call a national strike from midnight of 9 January 1955. Within forty-eight hours of the strike decision Sir Walter Monckton, Minister of Labour, announced the appointment of a Court of Inquiry into the dispute, chaired by Sir John Cameron.[5] Its Interim Report, published on 3 January 1955, reproved the NUR executive for calling a strike after it had reached a settlement with the BTC but accepted the union's case for a substantial increase in wages. The members of the Court of Inquiry were unconvinced by the BTC's argument that 'they were not able to offer the wage rates they would have desired to offer because of the financial limits placed on their freedom by the terms of the Transport Act 1947'. They found it 'not only undesirable in this Nationalised Industry but . . . unsound in the light of the figures presented by the Commission'. The argument, they claimed, ought 'not to be repeated'. As they saw the 'core of the matter':

The Nation has provided by statute that there shall be a nationalised system of railway transport, which must therefore be regarded as a public utility of the first importance. Having willed the end the Nation must will the means.[6]

While the crisis was coming to a head the Ministry of Labour published figures which revealed that, at the end of 1954, whereas the average basic wage of all male employees was £9 17s 8d, that for railwaymen was only £7 6s 3d.[7] This disclosure helped the Court of Inquiry, in para. 60 of its Final Report, to concede that it was 'not to be expected that a rate of wages was to be established less than that being paid in a comparable industry'.

On 6 January 1955, in the knowledge that the government had announced its acceptance of the report, the NUR executive, by 20–3 votes decided to withdraw the strike notices. An improved settlement of the wages dispute was quickly arranged, to operate from 10 January. Not surprisingly, Jim Campbell expressed the 'deep satisfaction' of all railwaymen with the settlement. Two major principles had been established. The first was that the railways were accepted as 'an essential service' and that the men and women who ran them were entitled to 'a fair and adequate wage'.[8] The second was that the railway wages were to be comparable with those of outside industry. These two principles dominated the union's wage claims over the following ten years.

The establishment of principles was one thing, their implementation quite another. Throughout the wage negotiations of the later 1950s the BTC was hamstrung by its financial restraints. Thus, when the NUR put its case for 'a substantial increase' in wages and salaries to the RSNC on 24 January 1958, Sir John Benstead, for the Commission, said, 'I cannot make you any offer . . . the amount of money to be advanced to the Commission is strictly limited'.[9] This situation typified the wages impasse of the later 1950s. Furthermore, the Cameron Report's vague assertion that railway wages should be no lower than those paid in 'a comparable industry' left the door wide open to disagreement about which industries *were* comparable with public transport. When the above-mentioned wage claim came before the RSNT in March 1958, Sidney Greene, for the NUR, maintained that the basic rates of pay on the railways were lower than those of gas workers or county council roadmen, but Mr A. B. B. Valentine, for the Commission, countered by asserting that railwaymen's wages were comparable to those employed in electricity supply and road transport.[10]

III

When the 1958 wage dispute was finally settled in May 1958, with a 3 per cent increase in wages, Sir Brian Robertson, Chairman of the BTC, said that 'for the future health of the industry' he was prepared to discuss with the unions the setting up of an independent inquiry into the wages structure in the railway industry and the comparability of railway wages with the wages paid for similar work in other industries and services.[11]

As the three railway unions readily agreed to this proposal a Railway Pay Committee of Inquiry, under Professor C. W. Guillebaud, was appointed in November–December 1958. With the assistance of a team of ten investigating officers, it took the Committee seventeen months to complete its thorough investigation and publish its report. Comparison was made between basic rates of pay on the railway and the rates of pay ruling for similar-type jobs in building, civil engineering, electricity, gas, water, the National Health Service, local authorities in England and Wales, the government 'M' rate, municipal and company-owned passenger transport, engineering and road haulage. It was found that the median of railway pay was 10 per cent below that of the outside industries and services with which it was compared. But it was argued that the 'advantages' of work of the conciliation grades on the railways – for example, the granting of a limited number of free travel passes – outweighed the 'disadvantages', and to allow for this they deducted 2 per cent. Clerical and supervisory staff employment did not have so many advantages. Thus, their final conclusion was that railway rates of pay for conciliation staff needed to be advanced by 8 per cent and for clerical and supervisory staff by 10 per cent to bring them into line with rewards for similar work elsewhere. The Committee of Inquiry also recommended a major simplification in the number of different grades and rates of pay in the railway service. In place of the forty different rates of pay applicable to over 150 grades of railway conciliation staff, it urged a reorganisation into only twelve grades with a correspondingly drastic reduction in the number of different rates of pay.[12]

In a very significant speech in the House of Commons on 10 March 1960, Mr Harold Macmillan, the Prime Minister, said that 'the Government accepted the objective underlying the Report of the Guillebaud Committee that fair and reasonable wages should be paid to those engaged in the industry'.[13] In the opinion of Sir Brian Robertson, Chairman of the BTC, 'the value of the inquiry lay not only in relation to the claim being made in 1958–9 but also that future dealings of this sort would be more easy to grapple with'. The Guillebaud Report brought a measure of industrial peace to the railways. In the view of the NUR, at least for the next few years, wage negotiations were conducted 'in a completely different atmosphere'.[14] On only one occasion between 1960 and 1965 was it necessary to have recourse to the full negotiating machinery. The settlement arising from the report, negotiated during the first half of 1960, placed railway rates of pay on the median level in relation to the twelve industries or services with which railway pay was compared.

The ink was scarcely dry on this agreement before a worsening national balance of payments prompted the government to introduce a pay pause. This would have been bearable had the pause been applied with equal firmness to all types of income in all types of occupations. However, railway pay was more effectively restrained than was pay in the twelve industries listed in appendix 9 of the Guillebaud Report. From 31 March 1960 to 1 April 1962, when the next railway pay rise – a modest 3 per cent – was granted, pay in the twelve 'outside' occupations had risen by an average of over £1 per week and hours of work had been reduced from forty-four to forty-two, while the railway workers' hours still remained at forty-four.[15]

Because of the pay pause, the negotiations which resulted in a 3 per cent rise from 1 April 1962 were long drawn out and tedious. On 19 April 1961, the representatives of the three rail unions met and agreed to submit claims on the BTC. The NUR wanted 'a substantial increase'; ASLEF asked for a rise of 10 per cent; and TSSA demanded that 'parity with Guillebaud should not be lost'. The NUR's application was submitted to the BTC on 4 May 1961, two months after the government's wage pause had been announced. The Union had to wait until 4 August to put its claim before the RSNC – the next rung on the ladder of negotiations.

This meeting would normally have been followed by a further meeting of the same council at which the BTC would have given its reply; but on this occasion Mr Marples, the Minister of Transport, intervened. He wrote to Dr Beeching, Chairman of the BTC, asking him to refer the union's claim to arbitration. At its meeting on 24 January 1962 the EC, in a unanimous decision, 'emphatically protested at the Minister's blatant interference with the machinery of negotiation'.[16]

Meanwhile Dr Beeching had made an offer of 2·5 per cent, and at a meeting with the three railway unions on 31 January he increased this to 3 per cent. On the morning of 6 February the NUR executive in a unanimous decision declared the last offer unacceptable, and in the afternoon of the same day approached ASLEF and TSSA, who agreed to ask the Prime Minister, Mr Harold Macmillan, as a matter of urgency, to meet the representatives of the unions. Mr Macmillan agreed. At Number 10, Downing Street on 14 February, with the Chancellor of the Exchequer, the Minister of Labour, and Mr Marples also present, he was successful in persuading the union leaders to accept 3 per cent as an 'interim' settlement, effective (some railwaymen said, appropriately enough) from 1 April. It was suggested by the Ministers that later in the year, if the economy picked up, there would be an opportunity for further discussions. On the following morning the NUR executive endorsed the action of its negotiators by 14–10 votes, the minority favouring strike action.[17]

No one pretended that the 3 per cent restored railwaymen's wages to their relative position in the post-Guillebaud settlement. *The Times* assumed that 'Dr Beeching wanted to offer more than the Government thought suitable'. The *Daily Mirror* concurred. 'The Commission's new chairman', it believed, 'like Montgomery when he took over the desert campaign in World War II, wanted his troops wholeheartedly behind him.' In a front-page article in *Railway Review*, on 23 February 1962, Mr Greene defended the decision to accept the 3 per cent, since a strike would have been 'injurious to the industry'.[18] It was, he said, 'impossible to indulge in industrial warfare without suffering casualties'. He doubted whether all the union's members 'would have returned to railway employment after a strike'. Opinion at grass-roots level appears to have been more hostile to the settlement. For his issue of 23 February, the editor of *Railway Review* received fifteen letters criticising the executive's decision to accept, and none supporting its action. The rank and file were influenced by the fact that the cost of living had risen by 6·5 per cent over the past year and that the union had considered an 11 per cent rise was needed to conform to the Guillebaud formula. The Manchester district council of the NUR, after rejecting by 51–9 votes a proposal to approach the TUC with a view to calling a general strike, carried, by the same margin, a resolution in favour of a national railway strike to start on 4 March.[19]

On 18 June, following a joint meeting with representatives of the other rail unions, the executive of the NUR agreed that all three unions should make a simultaneous demand for the resumption of the pay claim discussions at the RSNC.[20] Dr Beeching, bearing in mind Mr Marples's interference in the negotiating procedures earlier in the year, thought it expedient to consult the Chancellor of the Exchequer and other Ministers before replying to the unions. He was advised not to make a settlement which would increase working costs by more than £10 million.[21] Thus, when the RSNC eventually met again on 5 November, after a delay of over four months, Dr Beeching's ability to make an adequate offer was circumscribed by the government's financial restraints as well as by the state of the Commission's finances. His offer of 5 per cent was rejected unanimously by the NUR executive that same day.[22] But at a meeting of the council two days later Dr Beeching, in raising his offer to 6 per cent, made it quite clear that no more money was available and the union's negotiating committee's recommendation to settle for this figure was endorsed unanimously the same day by the full executive.[23]

By November 1963 the rates of pay of railway staff had fallen some 13 per cent behind the Guillebaud appendix 9 median. Nevertheless, the Railways Board refused to offer any more than 6 per cent to the conciliation grades and 3 per cent to the salaried staff. At a meeting of the RSNC on 19 December Dr Beeching confessed that the backlog of wages, which, he accepted, did exist, 'could not be eliminated until the financial position of the Board had shown substantial improvements'. The NUR executive accepted the 6 per cent for the conciliation staff, later also extended to the workshop staff, as the best that could be obtained. The settlement had been achieved in the record time of two months through the Board's tactic of replying at a higher level to claims made at the lower end of the negotiating machinery. The award was effective from 23 December. TSSA, not satisfied with the 3 per cent offered to the clerks and other salaried grades, appealed to the RSNT, which awarded them 0·5 per cent more.[24]

By 6 July 1964, when the AGM of the NUR was in session at Paignton, there was widespread restlessness among the delegates about the government's policies of wage restraint. Under discussion was a resolution, moved by C. Bonnar, expressing rejection of 'all policies of wage restraint whether by government or by the employers with whom the NUR negotiates'. Despite Sidney Greene's passionate appeal to delegates to reject the resolution – 'Do we believe in a wages policy? Of course we do. We have been arguing in relation to Guillebaud that our rates of pay should be in line with those of other people in industry' – delegates carried the resolution by 69–7 votes.[25] It was unlikely in the light of this decision, that pay negotiations later that year would be concluded as speedily as were those of 1963. This proved to be the case. In October the Board offered 6 per cent to the conciliation grades, 5 per cent to the supervisory staff and 4 per cent to the clerical grades. The NUR executive turned down this offer and appealed to the RSNT for a ruling.[26] The Tribunal endorsed the Board's offer to the clerical and supervisory grades, but considered that the labour-market situation and the continuing upward trend in the cost of living warranted a rise of 9 per cent for the men and women in the conciliation grades.

IV

While the union's claims were under negotiation, the General Election in October 1964 had resulted in the formation of a Labour government under the premiership of Harold Wilson and the creation of the new Department of Economic Affairs. The emphasis of the Declaration of Intent on Productivity, Prices and Incomes which George Brown, head of DEA, persauded the leaders of the CBI and the unions to sign, along with government Ministers, on 16 December 1964, was on the importance of wage increases being matched by increases in productivity, so that British exports could be made more competitive.[27]

In the light of these developments at Westminster it is scarcely surprising that the RSNT award, announced in the same month as the Declaration of Intent, should include an appeal to the railway unions and to management for greater productivity:

> The Tribunal feels strongly that the future development of the railways depends on greater productivity and urges both sides to co-operate in achieving this, and by improvements in the efficient use of manpower and equipment. The Tribunal considers that this will call for even greater co-operation from the unions than has been given in the past and for reasonable safeguards against redundancy.

It was not a statement which cut much ice with the Board's industrial relations member, Charles McLeod, who considered it
'yet another of those high sounding but futile exhortations so
often used in many spheres'.[28] All the same, the statement was
the harbinger of the much more meaningful discussions of productivity as an outcome of the next round of pay claims.

Although as early as 8 April 1965 the executive of the NUR
accepted unanimously the recommendation of its negotiating committee that 'application be made to the BRB and other appropriate undertakings for an increase in pay', the negotiations on the
claim dragged on for nearly a year.[29] One difficulty was that
more was at stake than a simple claim for increases in rates of
pay. Also in the pipeline were demands for a reduction in the
standard weekly hours of work of wages staff from forty-two to
forty and of salaried staff from forty to thirty-eight; an increase
in holiday entitlement and a substantial improvement in the very
inadequate pension paid to wages staff.

Dr Beeching was very conscious of the fact that each item
conceded would add substantially to the Board's operating costs.
When he gave his considered reply to the unions' delegates on
20 August he reminded them that under the Transport Act of
1962 the losses which might be incurred by the railways over the
period 1963–7, inclusive, were not to exceed £450 million. He,
therefore, suggested the phased introduction of some part of the
improvements being demanded. On pay he proposed an increase
of 3 per cent for both conciliation and salaried staff operative
from the first full week in October 1965, with a further 3 per cent
payable a year later. The reduction in hours, he suggested, should
take effect from the first full week in April 1966. Annual paid
leave for those with ten years' or more service should be increased by one day in 1966. As for the Wages Grades Pension
Scheme, he could offer no more than the 'hope of making some
progress during the next year'.[30]

In September the executive decided to press the Board for an
improvement on its offer and opened discussions with the other
two rail unions for a common front on the issues at stake. When
the further meeting took place with the employers on 26 September, the NUR stressed that minimum-rated conciliation staff were
nearly 10 per cent below the Guillebaud median and that, even
on the Board's method of calculation, the lag was of 7·7 per cent.
If the Board's offer of 3 per cent were accepted, railwaymen
would be 'falling further behind than they were at the last pay
settlement'. Although ASLEF settled with the Board when the
wages offer was raised to 3·5 per cent, the NUR executive,

meeting on 5 October, decided by 15–9 votes to refer the claims to the RSNT.[31]

However, before the RSNT had time to meet, George Brown told the railwaymen at a meeting on 15 October 1965 that he had referred their case to the National Board for Prices and Incomes which he had set up earlier in 1965 under the chairmanship of Aubrey Jones, MP, a director of Guest, Keen & Nettlefolds and chairman of Staveley Industries. The purpose of establishing the Board was to make pay rises conditional on changes in the deployment of the workforce, so that productivity could be improved. It was to 'attack at the work place the old habits, inherited attitudes and institutional arrangements which had been won in the 'fifties and had placed labour in a commanding bargaining position'.[32]

The PIB's remit on 15 October was 'to examine the issues in dispute in the light of considerations set out in the White Paper on *Prices and Incomes Policy* (Cmnd. 2639), in particular para. 15, and to report back in eight weeks'. These terms of reference inevitably conditioned the character of the report, since para. 15 of the White Paper emphasised that making 'a direct contribution towards increasing productivity in the particular firm or industry' was the first and most important precondition for granting improvements in pay, though it was also conceded that where labour deployment was needed in the national interest or wages were too low to maintain a reasonable standard of living or they were 'seriously out of line' with the level of pay for similar work elsewhere, there would also be justification for granting improved rates of pay.

The report, which was published on 14 January 1966, in effect jettisoned the principles embodied in both the Cameron and the Guillebaud reports. To Aubrey Jones and his team from the Board, the prime consideration was that railway wages and salaries should be based neither on the ground of the nation's need for railways (Cameron), nor on comparability with wages in 'outside' industry (Guillebaud), but on productivity. In the government's White Paper on *Prices and Incomes Policy* it had been asserted that comparability in wage determination ought to be given 'less weight than hitherto'. The authors of the PIB report gave a more decisive twist to this thinking. In para. 22 they asserted that 'it was desirable for the railways and their workers to move away from a system of wage determination that relies almost exclusively on bringing up to date selected parts of the detailed comparisons with outside industries'. They claimed that because of occupational changes in outside industry and in the railway industry itself, such comparisons as had been made by Guillebaud were no longer valid. Nevertheless, they could not entirely avoid making comparisons with outside industry, since in para. 15 of the White Paper this was mentioned as one means of identifying the justice or otherwise of a particular wage claim. But what they did was to compare weekly *earnings* in outside industry with those of railway staff. Using this new yardstick they came to the conclusion that railway pay, with the exception of that of the clerical staff, 'did not require adjustment'. Hope for the future, in their view, lay in the establishment of pay and productivity councils, in which management and staff should negotiate productivity deals 'as a means of maintaining the earnings of railway workers'.

The NUR executive considered the report at a specially convened meeting on 19 January 1966. The resolution of rejection which was carried by 20–3 votes (with one member absent, sick) mentioned five principal reasons for this outspoken view. The claim for improved rates of pay was justified under para. 15 of the government's White Paper; the Guillebaud Report had been rejected; the nationally agreed rates of pay would be destroyed if the Board's report was adopted; the Board 'took into consideration earnings instead of rates of pay in an industry where overtime working is compulsory, but where a large section of the workers have no opportunity of working overtime' and the Board's conclusions regarding pension arrangements offered 'little prospect of improvement in the near future'. The resolution concluded with the decision to call a national railway strike from 14 February and to co-ordinate strike plans with ASLEF and TSSA.[33]

The union's case was presented in a forty-eight-page pamphlet *Railwaymen and the PIB*, in which it was maintained that the staff had already contributed greatly to improved productivity; para. 4 of the BRB's *Annual Report and Accounts* for 1964 was cited:

Total traffic, measured in passenger/ton miles, increased by 3·6 per cent compared with 1963, and manpower was reduced by 8·5 per cent. Roughly speaking therefore, productivity increased by about 13 per cent . . . Over the three years since the beginning of 1962, the total railway manpower has been reduced by 103,000 from 502,000 to 399,000. Since the total passenger miles of traffic hardly changed over the period, productivity may be deemed to have increased by rather more than 26 per cent.

What was regarded by the union as particularly misleading was the PIB's comparison between average earnings of railwaymen and those of workers in outside industry, without regard being paid to the number of hours worked. Ministry of Labour figures showed that in April 1965 the average of hours worked on the railways was 49·3 per week compared with an average of 46·7 in manufacturing industry and 47·5 in all industries. Thus the fact that thousands of signalmen, guards, drivers and many others were obliged to work on rest days, Sundays and overtime (often during unsocial hours), if the system was not to break down, was ignored in a crude comparison of gross weekly earnings of railwaymen with earnings in other industries.

Following the union's strike call, the new Chairman of the BRB, Stanley Raymond, invited representatives of the union to further discussions on 1–4 February, when the management improved its offer by proposing that the introduction of the shorter working week should be brought forward to 28 February and two days extra leave (instead of one) were to be available to all staff after five (rather than ten) years' service. In compliance with the recommendation of the PIB report, clerical staff were offered a further 1·5 per cent increase in their salaries. But the offer was conditional on progress being made on single-manning of locomotives during night hours and greater flexibility in the duties of guards and platform staff. The new offer included no improvement in the wages offered to conciliation staff and this fact undoubtedly influenced the NUR executive's unanimous decision, taken during the evening of 4 February, to turn down the proposals.[34]

With only four days to go before the start of the national railway strike, George Brown called the representatives of all the railway unions to a meeting with Barbara Castle and Ray Gunter (the Minister of Labour), over which he presided. Further minor concessions, including putting forward the date of the pay rises from 1 October to 1 September, were offered, but to no effect. The NUR executive, after rejecting by 18–5 votes a resolution calling off the strike, passed by a similar margin an amendment rejecting the new offer on the grounds that it did not maintain 'the standard of comparability reasonable with outside industries'.[35]

On the following morning, 11 February, George Brown tried again at a further meeting with the unions held at the DEA offices. He promised that the date of application for the rise in wages would be advanced still further to 28 February. Using all his persuasive powers, he very nearly succeeded in getting a

majority of the NUR EC on his side. There was no doubt that
the NUR executive was split. By 12–11 votes it turned down a
resolution to call off the strike, and by the same vote, reversed,
expressed willingness to continue negotiations but re-emphasised
the unsatisfactory nature of the offer.[36]

At this point Harold Wilson decided to intervene. At Number
10, Downing Street, at 6 p.m. the same day, he presided over a
meeting of the union representatives with George Brown, Barbara
Castle and Ray Gunter. Though he was of the opinion that 'the
underpaid railwaymen had a strong case', and that the PIB report was 'austere, almost unfeeling', and was 'applying the most
severe of norms', he was determined not to give in to the unions'
demands. He believed that 'to yield incontinently to strike threats
would mean the end of any meaningful prices and incomes
policy'.[37] It was no easy task to persuade the railwaymen to
change their minds. Recognising that it might take many hours
the Prime Minister asked the staff of the government Hospitality
Fund to prepare sandwiches and drinks. The refreshments they
provided were more appropriate for a garden party of delicate
convalescents than for sturdy railwaymen who had had little lunch
because of the day's almost continuous discussions. Emergency
measures had, therefore, to be taken to augment the meagre fare
provided. When Mrs Mary Wilson, the secretaries and the house-
keeper had made sandwiches, using all the remaining bread at
Number 10, Jim Callaghan's larder was raided through the ever-
open door linking the two houses, and the sleeping Chancellor
was relieved of his one remaining loaf. Meanwhile a journalist
friend, spotted waiting outside, was sent to the main line termini
all-night refreshment rooms to buy up their entire stock of
sausage rolls. All the stocks of whisky and beer and the cigars
'kept for visiting statesmen' were mobilised to help in 'lubricating
the machinery of industrial relations'.[38] It was just after midnight that the NUR's executive asked for a separate meeting
and were directed to the Cabinet Office. After 'what seemed an
age' to the waiting Cabinet Ministers, they returned with their
verdict. By 13–11 votes they had decided to accept the terms
offered and to call off the strike.[39]

How was it that in the early hours of 12 February the executive agreed to terms which 'varied by not a penny in amount nor
a day in terms of dating'[40] from those rejected less than twenty-
four hours earlier? The answer lies partly in the fact that the
railwaymen, not only in the executive, but also in the country,
were divided in their views. The members of the Cabinet were as
well aware as were the members of the executive that Sidney

Greene was 'passionately against' a strike.[41]The Eastern district council of the union criticised the leadership for press leaks which indicated divisions within the executive. Such reports were 'a source of manifestation of doubt amongst the members and should not have been published'.[42] This concern lest the strike was not 100 per cent effective influenced some of the members of the executive and helped tilt the balance in favour of caution. Then there was Barbara Castle's impassioned appeal. According to Harold Wilson, she spoke for twenty minutes, 'weaving a web of hope' with plans for higher productivity and higher wages. This was a cue that was taken up by the Prime Minister when he promised that, without delay, he would take the chair himself at the first of a series of meetings between management and unions in the railway industry to discuss ways of increasing productivity. Finally, Sidney Greene and some members of the executive were concerned not to 'rock the boat' of the Labour government, working with an extremely narrow majority in what could well be the run up to a General Election. Certainly, once the dispute was settled, the Prime Minister considered that 'the lines were cleared' for such an appeal to the country.[43]

V

On 10 March 1966, following the dissolution of Parliament, almost exactly a month after the crisis talks of 11–12 February and only three weeks before the General Election, Harold Wilson called another 6 p.m. meeting at Number 10, Downing Street, the refreshments this time having much less of a makeshift character. Barbara Castle, George Brown and Ray Gunter were again present, together with representatives of the BRB, the three railway unions and the CSEU. This meeting may be considered as the curtain-raiser to the pay and efficiency talks which extended over the following two and a half years. In his introductory speech the Prime Minister suggested that there were three major areas for future discussion; the wages structure, including the comparability of railway wages with wages in other industries; the linking up of pay with productivity; and possible changes in the negotiating machinery. These were, indeed, the principal subjects subsequently considered. Thereafter the major discussions, which did not begin until 10 May, were chaired by the Minister of Labour or his deputy, while more detailed problems were thrashed out at numerous meetings of a sub-group chaired by a senior officer of the Ministry of Labour, or at joint working parties of Board and union representatives. What were the objectives of the Board in these long-drawn-out talks? The Chairman, Harry Johnson, believed that recent technological changes had rendered the old wages structure obsolete. 'It was no good having a steam outlook with an electric and diesel railway', he said.[44] A prime consideration with many members of the Board was to reduce labour costs. Despite the remarkable streamlining of railway operation within recent years, these continued to account for 60–65 per cent of the Board's total annual expenditure.[45] To A. H. Nicholson, a Board member with large responsibilities on staffing matters, therefore, 'the underlying theme of the pay and efficiency talks was that ways should be found to produce monetary savings which would enable the Board to justify the introduction of a new pay structure'.[46]

Arnold Edmondson, who, as publicity and research officer of the NUR, sat in as observer at all the main sessions, recalls that Mr Len Neal (now Sir Len Neal), who was leading the management team in the pay and efficiency talks, brought 'a fresh approach to the problems of wage negotiations'. He refused to have the parties facing each other round a table as if their interests were diametrically opposed, but insisted that they sit round in a circle, since he regarded all those present as partners in a common enterprise.[47] His reputation as an authority on industrial relations preceded his arrival at the BRB, since he was the architect of the Fawley oil refinery productivity agreement of 1960. When asked what it was that made this important agreement possible his considered reply was 'the habit of discussion'. From experience and as a matter of faith, he believed in 'informal person-to-person consultation in large and unstinted quantities'. The consequences of this approach could be very important; 'This sort of habit of discussion make it terribly difficult for any agitator to argue convincingly that the only way to get action is to go on strike when the people he is talking to know differently from their own experience.'[48] When he came to the talks, therefore, it was not with the objective of achieving some short-term, patched-up compromise. On 11 December 1967, when he introduced the first of a number of booklets which the Board produced at different stages of the discussions, he stressed that the document was

not an attempt at a productivity bargain in the conventional sense . . . The railway approach was a joint approach . . . Because they are the result of a joint approach what emerges could be very much more enduring . . . This is a long-term study of the problems of the industry.

Sidney Greene found the informal approach of Len Neal 'a well-merited departure from the standard practice, permitting absolute freedom of expression and providing ample latitude for the development of ideas'. He conceded that the traditional relationships between grades would have to be changed and that the trade union would have to accept that 'something concrete' would have to be shown to set against the cost of improved grading. He urged that the reward for more flexible and productive employment of the staff should be better pay, particularly for the lowest-paid railwaymen.[49] He thought in terms of a large package-deal with the Board, which would bring a wide range of improvements to the staff in return for the abandonment of tradition job demarcations and gradings. In a letter written on 31 January 1968, to Charles McLeod of the BRB, he confided that the proposed changes were

> more likely to go through if tackled together, as far as possible, in one comprehensive settlement so that one factor may go towards balancing another. Either side may be prepared to accept something not entirely palatable to them if compensated for in another way.

It cannot be too much emphasised that the union team played a positive and constructive part in the pay and efficiency discussions. It was not content merely to respond to management's initiatives, it often took the initiative itself. Perhaps the best example of this was the presentation to the Board, in March 1967, of a twenty-one-page memorandum entitled *Railway Wages Structure, Pay and Productivity*, which made a thorough investigation into the workings of the bonus system, and the extent of overtime working and how it might be reduced.[50] Keith Mc-Dowall, industrial editor of the *Daily Mail* described the NUR proposals as 'Britain's biggest ever productivity deal which would pave the way to a completely new approach'.[51] When the memorandum was discussed at the next meeting of the sub-group at the Ministry of Labour, Len Neal congratulated the NUR on 'an extremely imaginative and comprehensive paper' which contained 'a good deal of sophistication and knowledge of the railway industry', while his colleague, L. W. Ibbotson, spoke of it as 'a most cheering document' which made a 'very useful contribution' to the progress of the talks.[52]

For at least two years rank and file railwaymen knew very little about the progress of the discussions. Although Arnold Edmondson typed out, in June 1967, a brief progress report headed

'Private and confidential, for information of EC members only', members of the executive only became involved from 15 January 1968, when discussions had passed the exploratory stage and the lines of the agreement were becoming clearer. It was not until 2 January 1968, when copies of the BRB booklets were sent with a circular letter from the General Secretary to the branch secretaries, that there was an opportunity for members of the union to be better informed. In his letter, Sidney Greene gave two reasons for the secrecy: the meetings had been conducted informally and the parties concerned were not, as yet, committed to any binding agreements, and it had been agreed between the Ministry of Labour, the Board and the unions that the arrangements should be kept confidential.[53] However, the AGM of the union was, as always, the final arbiter, and its members had ample time to discuss the final proposals of stage I of the pay and efficiency agreement at Penzance in July 1968.

The Guillebaud Report, in 1960, included a recommendation that the number of pay groups in the conciliation grades should be reduced to twelve. Progress was made along the lines suggested, but in 1966 when the pay and efficiency talks opened, there were still fourteen conciliation grades in the railway service. When the Board and the unions began their long task of restructuring the grades and rates of pay of the railway staff, they turned first to the group 'conciliation grades other than trainmen' (CONGOT), which included 77,000 out of the 127,000 persons in the conciliation grades as a whole. Within CONGOT they looked first at the 50,000 staff in groups 1–7, the lowest-paid categories, where it was generally agreed there was greatest scope for rationalisation.[54] The reason for leaving footplatemen out of consideration in the early months of the discussions was that at first ASLEF did not send representatives to the joint working parties as it was argued that the union was not in dispute with the BRB at the time of the crisis talks at Number 10, Downing Street, and that in any case it was not concerned with negotiations about the rates of pay and conditions of service of the lower-paid grades. ASLEF was, however, represented in the general discussions at the Ministry of Labour and in the sub-groups, and it participated in the working party talks from December 1967.

Following its census of the total railway staff in April 1967, the Board chose a sample of 150 representative goods and passenger stations with a total staff of some 3,000 persons to explore the possibility of merging the bottom seven grades in the pay scale into two, three or four 'versatility' grades. The Board's object of telescoping seven grades into a smaller number was to ensure that men and women were more fully employed during working hours; that they were employed in a more versatile fashion, giving more variety and interest to their work, and that machinery and equipment were more fully utilised.[55] In the meantime the union's research department drew up a proposal for two new versatility grades (to replace the seven in the old scale) which it felt was superior to the Board's scheme for three, because of its greater simplicity. However, agreement was eventually reached in principle to establish new grades of railman, leading railman and senior railman who would be responsible for the work done by the seven lowest grades.

That 'versatility' and 'flexibility' were to be the keywords of the new era was revealed in the list of duties that staff in the three new proposed grades would be called upon to perform. Thus under the heading of 'general labouring', the railman's duties could include sweeping up; loading, unloading and barrowing traffic; delivering messages; cleaning lavatories, messrooms, and so on; attending boilers; cleaning tubes and pumping equipment; cleaning drains; collecting and disposing of refuse; cleaning ashpits; clearing litter and weeds from the permanentway; cleaning retarders, oil points and crossings; crossing-keeping; lookout and hand-signalling duties; the issuing of stores, tools and clothing; the cleaning of rolling stock and other vehicles; cleaning, filling, trimming and replacing station and train oil lamps; the cleaning of electric light fittings and replacement of bulbs; and preparing brakevans. Under the general heading sub-clerical duties, the railman could be called upon to record the arrival and departure of staff; sort correspondence and documents; answer the telephone; dispatch correspondence; record drivers' tickets; assist in checking and recording goods in transit and store; and record train arrivals and departures. His platform duties could include attending trains; labelling and carrying luggage; the marshalling of barrows and trolleys; attendance at a carpark; the posting of bills and notices; the operation of mechanical sweepers, autotrucks and water bowsers; the filling of water tanks; the operation of lifts and hoists; giving assistance at ticket barriers as required and the whitening of platform edges. Finally, the railman's shed and yard duties could include the operation of carriage-washing machines; the collection, folding and distribution of wagon sheets, ropes and packing; the securing, sheeting and unsheeting of vehicles; the recording of crippled wagons; carrying out number-taking duties; and the operation of cranes. It would be a very versatile man, indeed, who carried out all these duties or even a sample of, say, one-third of the items listed!

The list of the leading railman's possible duties was nearly as long, though including a much larger clerical and administrative element. Thus, among many other things, he could be made responsible for preliminary paybill documentation; the maintenance of the ticket stock, stamps, stationery and stores; and the compilation of cash returns. His platform duties (to mention only a sample) could include the collection of tickets and excess fares; the collection of left and excess luggage charges; the announcement of the arrival and departure of trains. The leading railman's shed and yard duties were set out in a list of twenty-two items. The senior railman was to be responsible as 'a leader of men in the lower grades' for the proper performance of all the duties which railmen and leading railmen were expected to carry out.[56] Where it proved necessary to appoint a man to co-ordinate the activities of groups of men each of which might be led by a senior railman, a chargeman was to be appointed to do the work formerly undertaken by yard foremen and lower-paid supervisors.

Although the agreement on how this large section of the workforce was to be redeployed was reached relatively early on in the pay and efficiency discussions, the flesh and blood of improved pay scales had to be added at a later date, and the whole new scheme did not come into operation until 12 August 1968, following the Penzance Agreement of 5 July of that year.

When it came to a consideration of the staff in the upper half of the 127,000-strong CONGOT group, it was nothing like as easy to apply the principle of versatility as it was in the case of those in the lower-paid group. The men and women in the upper half included those working in signalling, goods handling, cartage, carriage- and wagon-examining, track-laying or maintenance, signal and telecommunications, overhead line maintenance, station and platform duties, including ticket-collecting, and railway dock duties. The Board divided these very diverse elements into two categories; those such as trackmen, ticket collectors and crane drivers, who worked alongside railmen, leading railmen, or senior railmen, or who were at least capable of a comparable degree of versatility, and the specialist staff, such as signalmen, carriage- and wagon-examiners, motor-drivers and technicians, who were grouped by degree of training and skill between pay groups 4–10. The fact that it was no easy task devising a productivity scheme for many workers in the skilled category, especially the signalmen, and that the total number of pay groups among *all* railwaymen was reduced from the post-Guillebaud fourteen to only ten, meant that anomalies were created, anomalies which had to be tackled in stage II of the pay and efficiency discussions.

Though there were problems in rationalising the CONGOT grades, these were not so formidable since only one union, the NUR, was involved. The regrouping of the train staff was a more difficult exercise since it involved the consent of ASLEF as well as the NUR. It was a delicate task to simplify train-manning without upsetting ASLEF through proposals to reduce the number of secondmen (firemen) in service or upsetting the NUR by hints that the guards, as secondmen, might be considered as being in the line of promotion to the grade of driver. On 15 December 1967, at the first joint working party meeting to be attended by representatives of ASLEF, Mr A. H. Nicholson, for the Board, proposed that the minimum staffing for every train should be two men. On a freight train the driver would be assisted by a trainman, who would combine the duties of goods guard and secondman. On a passenger train there would be a conductor, who would combine the duties of a passenger guard and a train ticket collector. At night or when trains were steam-heated, the train staff would be three, with a trainman assisting the driver. Trainmen would be concerned solely with operating the train and would be located either in the cab with the driver, or in the brakevan, according to the type of train. They would be recruited as traction trainees. Conductors, on the other hand, would collect, inspect and, where necessary, issue tickets, would protect the train, including its passengers and parcels, and dispatch trains from stations. Mr Griffiths, for ASLEF, had completely different proposals. They were that the grades of driver and secondman should continue, only with the new name of assistant driver to be given to the secondman. It was agreed that some freight trains should be worked without a guard. Recruitment to the grade of assistant driver should be from guards under 40 years of age, other railway staff under the age of 30 and men under 23 who would be directly recruited. Mr Nicholson thought very little of these proposals which he called 'a negation of versatility', since so-called non-progressive goods guards, namely those over 40 years of age, would not be allowed to undertake secondmen's duties and the best use would not be made of their experience.[57]

The Board took more notice of the NUR's comments on its proposals concerning train staff. The union favoured simplicity in pay scales and objected to the Board's proposed retention of separate, lower rates of pay for shunting drivers, since these numbered less than 1,000 men out of a total of 25,000 drivers. The union also found it 'absurd' that the Board should 'want to continue the archaic, time wasting and labour wasting practice of calculating higher grade terms for cleaners and firemen'.[58] The pay structure finally agreed, on 29 August 1968, was very like the simplified version advocated by the NUR in the earlier negotiations.[59] Many problems, including the conditions under which single-manning could be extended, were left to be dealt with in negotiations conducted in the early 1970s.

In the pay and efficiency discussions more time was spent in planning the restructuring of the clerical workforce than was devoted to any other group of railway employees. In an early and comprehensive memorandum (undated, but issued in the early summer of 1966) TSSA emphasised that 'a drastic change in the salary structure was urgently needed' to meet the requirements of the industry. The Board, the NUR and TSSA were all agreed that the survival of ten separate salary scales for clerical staff was anomalous and administratively wasteful of resources. By the end of the summer of 1968 they had brought the number down to five. Both the unions had campaigned for a long time for the abolition of the 'excluded grades' – a term used for female staff employed on machine, telephone and secretarial work, who did not receive equal pay with men doing the same type of work. By April 1967 they had persuaded the Board that the title 'excluded grades' was 'derogatory' and ought to be abandoned, with the staff concerned being brought into the general clerical structure.[60] However, at a very late stage, the Board tried to dodge meeting the full cost of the change by creating a new clerical assistant grade into which a large number of the younger or less well-qualified staff, including many women, were placed.[61]

There were many other serious problems of the clerical workforce which were dealt with in the discussions. Clerical workers had not shared in the 'productivity' benefits which had been achieved by many other groups, including drivers, guards and goods depot workers. Yet they maintained that their productivity had been increased with the introduction of new ticket-issuing machines, computers, and so on, and this was reflected in the decline of the clerical workforce from 61,000 in 1959 to 47,000 in 1966. However, the parties to the discussions agreed that the introduction of bonus schemes for clerks was impracticable and that the remedy lay in simplified and improved salary scales.[62] A further difficulty was that, in areas of full employment, traditional earnings differentials had been eroded or had entirely disappeared through the use of temporary expedients in the form of extra pay to attract the necessary number of recruits. Through the fact that railway clerical work was often less well paid than were comparable jobs in outside industry, the number of applications for railway appointments had declined and the quality of staff recruited had fallen. After many hours of frank discussion, it was generally agreed that the approach to a remedy for many of these problems lay in simpler and more clearly defined salary scales, with a larger proportion of the staff being placed in the better-paid scales; an improved training-scheme and the greater mobility of staff between jobs. Management put more emphasis on work-study projects but Mr Bothwell, for TSSA, preferred that the system of promotion by seniority and satisfactory service should not be unduly disturbed.

All parties were agreed on the great importance of the effective training, organisation and deployment of the supervisory staff. It was accepted as a cardinal principle 'that unless supervisors and above them, senior management, are selected, trained, organised and equipped for the demanding task of achieving greater efficiency, the efforts being focused on wages grades will lose the greater part of their effect'.[63] As a result of the spread of bonus schemes and productivity payments to men and women employed in the wages grades, it was sometimes the case that supervisors earned very little more, and sometimes even less, than those they supervised. To overcome this anomaly the members of the joint working party recommended that a curb should be placed on bonus schemes, while the salaries paid to supervisors should be raised to restore differentials. There were sometimes too many levels of supervision, and to remedy this situation, the Board proposed a reduction by 2,500 in the number of supervisors and the creation of 150 new clerical and 900 conciliation-grade appointments to take their place. The responsibilities of supervisors were to be more flexible and diverse. The principal disagreement between the NUR and the Board was with regard to the timing of the proposed reforms. The Board wanted piecemeal application after detailed job evaluation on a depot by depot basis. The union believed that such an approach would create anomalies in the period of transition and, therefore, it favoured a once for all exercise. In his lengthy branch circular of 15 March 1968 Mr Greene was pleased to report that the Board had accepted the union's view on this issue as well as adopting its proposals for reducing the number of supervisory grades from six to four, and for introducing a single rate of pay rather than a scale, for staff in each grade. By the time of the Penzance Agreement many problems remained to be solved, but Sidney Greene had every reason for asserting, in his branch circular, that 'the Board's offer in many ways met what the NUR had been seeking'.[64]

Throughout its history the NUR (and its predecessor the ASRS) had fought many campaigns for the reductions of the length of the working week. And yet in the 1960s the anomalous position arose that at the same time as the union was successful in its negotiations with management, in reducing 'normal' working hours from forty-four to forty-two in 1962, and from forty-two to forty in 1966, the actual average weekly hours worked by railway conciliation staff tended to rise, as is illustrated in Table 5.1.

Table 5.1 *Working Hours: Comparisons*

Railway Conciliation Grades			Rest of Industry			
Average weekly hours of male adults						
Date	Average hours	Nor-mal week	Average weekly over-time	Date	Average hours	Nor-mal week	Average weekly over-time
				Apr. 1963	46·9	42·0	4·9
Sept. 1963	46·5	42·0	4·5	Oct. 1963	47·6	42·0	5·6
Mar. 1964	48·1	42·0	6·1	Apr. 1964	47·8	41·9	5·9
Sept. 1964	47·9	42·0	5·9	Oct. 1964	47·7	41·9	5·8
Mar. 1965	49·3	42·0	7·3	Apr. 1965	47·5	41·2	6·3
Sept. 1965	48·5	42·0	6·5	Oct. 1965	47·0	40·7	6·3
Mar. 1966	48·6	40·0	8·6	Apr. 1966	46·4	40·3	6·1
Sept. 1966	50·1	40·0	10·1	Oct. 1966	46·0	40·3	5·7
Mar. 1967	48·2	40·0	8·2	Apr. 1967	46·1	40·2	5·9
Sept. 1967	47·9	40·0	7·9	Oct. 1967	46·2	40·2	6·0

Source: Joint Working Party Report, April, 1968.

Thus, it will be seen that overtime working on the railways was consistently higher than in outside industry, and that the trend was for the number of hours worked beyond the normal working week to increase. In April 1967 it was found that 32 per cent of overtime comprised Sunday duty; 20 per cent arose from staff working on their rest-days; a further 20 per cent was due to staff standing in for colleagues on leave, 7 per cent occurred from the incidence of sickness, while the remaining 21 per cent was explained by such causes as delays in filling vacancies or failure altogether to replace staff who had resigned or retired. A. H. Nicholson of the BRB considered that the deliberate creation of overtime by district managers to boost the earnings of poorly paid staff accounted for no more than 2 per cent of the total.[65]

At meetings of the sub-group and the joint working party Sidney Greene repeatedly asserted that there was no justification for most of the 5,800 planned redundancies the Board envisaged under the proposed versatility arrangements while overtime amounting to more than a normal extra day's work every week was being required of the staff, if the railway system was not to break down. He told a main group meeting at the Ministry of Labour, on 11 December 1967, that 'reduction in excessive overtime . . . without loss of earnings would enable many redundant staff to be absorbed without hardship'. In a lengthy letter to Sidney Greene, written seven days later, A. H. Nicholson of the Board, stressed that railway services had to be provided for twenty-four hours of each day, seven days a week, and that a large amount of overtime working was inevitable. But he also revealed that financial reasons were important in explaining why the Board felt unable to tackle the cancer of excessive overtime by retaining more staff in the service:

> In the case of timeworkers, the filling of a vacant post . . . produces a gross saving to the Board of outgoings on enhancements (i.e. overtime payment, P.S.B.) but, against this, has to be set the cost of employing a man, e.g. employer's contribution to National Health Insurance, Redundancy Levy, Pensions and liability to sick pay, and clothing.

Sidney Greene replied, on 20 December 1967, repeating the humanitarian reasons for reducing redundancies to the minimum and claiming that 'if overtime, including rest-day working, was considerably reduced, it would help to cushion some of the redundancy which would arise from the versatility aspects of pay and efficiency'. Len Neal, the Board's specialist on pay and efficiency, explained that it is 'general throughout all industries that it is often cheaper to incur the marginal increase in cost of increased overtime than to incur the permanent cost of employing more labour to cover peak periods and emergencies'.[66]

It was also a fact, at least for the 32,000 staff paid at the base rate of under £12 in 1967, that there was a strong incentive, especially for men with family commitments, to work a lot of overtime in order to make up a living wage. Paying a considerably enhanced basic wage would have contributed to a solution of the problem; but the financial straitjacketing under which the Board worked, and the requirement that all improvements in pay must be met by increased productivity, made it impossible to make any serious inroads into the problem. The Board, in its memoranda, and the joint working party reports, expressed the hope that the introduction of versatility would decrease the amount of overtime working needed, but the Penzance Pay and Efficiency Agreement, of July 1968, made no mention of the evil of systematic overtime working.

The failure to tackle the problem of excessive overtime working was a serious shortcoming of the Penzance Agreement. Outsiders were lured into the industry with the promise of high earnings, only to realise in no time at all, that to achieve the fabulous sums quoted, anything up to or even beyond, fifty hours a week had to be worked at all kinds of unsocial hours. Their stay in the industry was as short-lived as the illusion of easy money. With the rapid turnover of staff that resulted, both the level of skill and the morale of the staff declined. The result of the failure to grasp this nettle, when the big changes of the productivity agreement provided a favourable environment, was manifest even in 1978 when Sidney Weighell protested to the Board that at a time when there were 9,000 railway vacancies and over 1,300,000 unemployed persons in Britain railway staff were working an average of thirteen and a half hours' overtime per week[67]

The payment of productivity bonuses to railway workers had been increasing since locomotivemen's mileage allowances had been introduced in the early 1920s. But the number of these bonus deals increased greatly in the 1950s and 1960s. At first they were confined to footplate grades working passenger trains, but gradually they were extended to passenger guards and goods-handling staff on a district basis where, in a time of full employment, labour was scarce and extra inducements were deemed necessary to fill essential vacancies or expedite the movement of traffic. It was, however, a piecemeal development which created many anomalies. Thus from the same locomotive depot some drivers of passenger trains might be earning bonus payments, while drivers of freight trains were earning basic rates. Goods porters at main line termini might have bonus additions to their wages, whereas the goods porters in provincial stations, who worked equally hard unloading the same goods, did not qualify for the extra payments.

On 28 October 1965 the Board negotiated a single-manning agreement with the NUR and ASLEF under which the single-manning of trains was extended, *inter alia*, to the daytime running operation to express passenger or parcel trains running up to 350 miles or for up to six hours without a stop, and to stopping passenger trains or express freight trains with trips of less than

250 miles. The compensation given to drivers for abandoning double-manning were additional bonuses. But the agreement created new anomalies, in that many freight train drivers were not in a position to earn bonus payments. After a work to rule by ASLEF in January 1967 and an arbitration award by Mr Jack Scamp, the government's industrial 'trouble-shooter', peace was restored with a scheme (which was incorporated in the Penzance Agreement) for the payment of bonus to most freight train drivers. In the meantime guards working with the bonus-earning drivers grew increasingly discontented. They maintained that the operation of a train was a team job and that their responsibilities, especially the requirement that they should couple and uncouple trains, had increased with single-manning of locomotives. In support of the guards' claim on 4 April 1967, the NUR imposed a ban on guards undertaking secondman duties. After an inquiry conducted by Professor Robertson, many joint working party meetings and further meetings with the Minister of Labour and the Prime Minister, a formula was reached in which, in return for the union agreeing to the abolition of the brakevan on fully fitted trains and the drafting of more economical rosters, a bonus equal to thirty minutes' pay per trip was agreed for the guards.[68]

But the members benefitting from these concessions were a privileged few. Striking anomalies remained. In the early summer of 1967 Sidney Greene received a deputation of guards from King's Cross, who complained that there were 92 of their grade, the 'haves', who got good mileage payments, and 140, the 'have nots', who did not.[69] Some 37,000 staff, including signalmen, booking clerks, and crossing-keepers – to mention only three examples – did not qualify for bonus. After all, the signalman's *basic* wage was already calculated on a kind of bonus system. It was no use the booking clerk date-stamping more tickets, if no customers turned up to buy them; and the crossing-keeper would be scarcely helping the productivity of the industry or of the nation by opening and shutting the gates forty times a day, when the working timetable only required half that number.

It was not only the union's officers and many of the rank and file that saw the many drawbacks of the bonus system. The specialist on pay and efficiency on the Board, Len Neal, at an interview on 26 July 1978, said he found that 'railway pay was a wholly "unnatural" combination of small basic pay, supplemented by high overtime, mileage and bonus payments'. The consequence of this imbalance was that sick pay, holiday pay, overtime rates and, most importantly, pensions – all of which were calculated from the relatively low basic rates and not from

the substantially higher level of earnings – were all at unrealistic-
ally low levels and were a further source of discontent. Those not
privileged to be working under a bonus scheme felt that their low
basic wages were the result of too large a share of the Board's
revenue going on bonus payments, while the bonus-earners demanded that the sick, holiday, overtime and pension payments
should be based on average weekly earnings rather than basic
rates. No wonder that an AGM delegate, in 1966, spoke of the
'bitterness, misunderstanding and dissension' caused by the bonus
system, that another considered that 'allowing these ghastly
schemes ever to come on to the scene' was 'one of the greatest
mistakes' the NUR ever made, or that Sidney Weighell saw the
union 'riding on a tiger' when once it got involved with them.[70]

The policy of the NUR, determined at the historic Penzance
AGM in July 1968, and embodied in the Penzance Agreement,
was to freeze the bonus earnings at that time. Future bonus
earnings were to be calculated on the pre-Penzance rates of pay
and not on the basic rates achieved in subsequent agreements
with the Board. In future, whatever percentage rise in pay was
gained was spread equally on all basic rates. Thenceforward,
through this policy of consolidating bonus into basic pay, it was
no longer the case that the man who was on bonus was getting
twice the increase of the man who was not. The drift towards
ever-greater inequality in earnings within the industry was halted.
Reflecting on the matter three years later Sidney Weighell emphasised the principle of the decision:

> It was done as a deliberate policy, knowing that as a union
> based on the principle of industrial trade unionism, and repre-
> senting all grades of railwaymen, one cannot tolerate a situa-
> tion where men are going out with a pay packet twice as big as
> the chaps working alongside them sometimes in the same
> grade.[71]

In the pay and efficiency discussions no agreement was reached
on proposals for a revision of the negotiating machinery. The
initiative for the proposed changes came from the members of the
Board who saw the existing machinery, set up in 1955, as unduly
cumbersome and time-consuming. Whereas there was little complaint from the management side about the working of the local
departmental committees and the sectional councils – where local
and regional contacts were made – it was a different matter with
the national bodies, the Railway Staff Joint Council and the
Railway Staff National Council. Of the proceedings of these

bodies one Board member wrote that it was a 'common criticism by management that unions bring too many cases forward on the principle that it is permitted by the machinery and that there is no harm in making another attempt to secure a concession'. It was his opinion 'that the machinery had become clogged and inordinate delays occurred in settling individual grievances that should have been decided at an earlier stage'.[72] When Len Neal was asked why he was keen to change established procedures he replied:

> Well the machinery of negotiation is very elaborate and time-consuming and used to follow time-honoured practice of claim being made at the lowest level, to be rejected; presented three months later, at the next higher level, to be rejected; presented at the next higher level three months later again, to be rejected . . . Thus, time . . . in short term considerations, appeared to be with management, and my driver at the time, when I sought to short circuit that elaborate ritual said 'It's so different from when we used to get the beds out' I said 'What do you mean?' 'We used to do this and eventually got to the situation when the last stage of the negotiations was reached and the Board prepared for a siege and we were all instructed to go round collecting beds so that the railway management negotiators could stay up all night, night after night, for these various negotiations.'

Len Neal found frustration in the fact that in negotiations he headed a small team from the Board, including the chief financial officer, with wide powers to settle on the spot the principles of a new agreement on pay and conditions of service, while the NUR's negotiating committee had no such authority but had to report back to the full executive committee for its approval before returning to the negotiating table to reach a settlement.[73] What Len Neal found particularly frustrating was Sidney Greene's insistence that he must seek the views of his Executive Committee. This was a cause of delay and reflected 'a rather limited view of his responsibilities as a trade union leader'. His colleague, Charles McLeod, lamented that the executive 'decision is made by twenty-four men at least sixteen of whom have heard only at second hand the course of debate during discussions'.[74] What they both did not appreciate sufficiently was that the NUR executive, through the working of the very democratic constitution of the union, had to be sure it reflected, as accurately as possible, the majority view of its 200,000 members, while the Board was a small executive body with wide powers and, significantly, not directly respon-sible to a wider electorate. But, as Charles McLeod recognised, 'amendments to the machinery of negotiation would not remedy this situation'. It was 'for the unions to determine whether the interests of railwaymen were best served by the existing pro-cedures'. The verdict, so far, of the railwaymen is that at national level the existing machinery has served them well. Delays are admitted, but there is no desire to curtail the powers of the full Executive Committee and the AGM.

Management's ideas on reform were set out in memoranda presented for discussion in July 1966 and April 1967. It proposed that there should be a clearer definition of the functions of each body in the national negotiating machinery, so that issues con-cerning individuals or small groups should be settled at district council or sectional council level, while at the top of the RSNC should confine itself to items of major national importance. A Railway Council should be set up to take over the kind of work the British Railways Productivity Council had been undertaking since 1955, namely, the consideration of future developments in technology, organisation and welfare. The Board favoured greater flexibility in wage determination in the regions and, therefore, desired that sectional councils or even LDCs should have power to agree to local variations in wage rates.[75]

The unions were not greatly enamoured of any of these pro-posals. Mr Greene thought that when a satisfactory pay and grade structure had been established, the machinery of negotia-tion would no longer be overloaded with a large number of grading issues. Mr Griffiths, for ASLEF, agreed. He was of the opinion that 'with a few adjustments of a minor nature' the existing machinery would work well, provided the Board operated it in the right spirit. Mr Barratt, for the CSEU, thought it 'un-realistic' to suggest that 'negotiators of either unions or manage-ment could have authority vested in them to reach agreement without reference to their governing bodies'.[76] There was some-thing to be said, after all, for having time to think over the im-plication of the Board's proposals, especially when it is remem-bered that such proposals would have been discussed by members of the management meeting in the Railways Staff Conference before they were brought to the negotiating table.[77] On the other hand, the union leaders were in favour of reducing delays by cutting out the RSJC stage and proceeding direct to the RSNC where national wage negotiations were concerned. The members of the Board plugged away at their proposed reforms for many months without making headway. As late as 17 October 1967 Len

Neal confessed, 'There is no progress being made in the machinery of negotiation.' Eventually this whole area of debate was allowed to die a quiet death as the discussions switched to the central problems of productivity and the restructuring of the labour force.

VI

While the prolonged pay and efficiency discussions were taking place, railwaymen's pay was falling behind rates of pay in comparable occupations. Agreement had been reached for an increase of 3·5 per cent to operate from September 1966, but a government wage-freeze delayed its introduction until March 1967. Since the cost of living continued to rise and there seemed to be no immediate prospect of a satisfactory conclusion to the pay and efficiency talks, the NUR applied for a 'substantial increase' in wages and salaries later in 1967. The replies at RSJC and RSNC level were considered unsatisfactory, and a majority decision was taken at the quarterly meeting of the executive in March 1968 to appeal to the RSNT.[78] The Tribunal, in its Award No. 41 of 6 June 1968, recommended that a temporary supplement of 10s per week should be added to the weekly pay of those earning under 250s per week and a temporary supplement of 5s should be added to the pay of those earning between 254s and 268s per week, such increases to be absorbed into any pay awards arising from the conclusion of the pay and efficiency talks. By the narrow majority of 12–11 votes, with one member absent on union business, the executive decided at a meeting on 12 June to reject the Tribunal's award, because the improvements offered only covered some of the staff, and because it could not accept the principle that all pay increases should be linked to increased productivity. It therefore recommended that, as from Monday 24 June, at 00.01 hours, railway members including shopmen and London Transport workers, should work only a standard week and that no rest-days, no Sundays and no overtime should be worked. Members were also advised to 'work to rule'.[79]

In an endeavour to prevent the union's resort to industrial action Len Neal wrote to Sidney Greene, on 17 June, mentioning ten ways by which productivity could be increased, costs lowered and sums made available for 'some further improvements in rates of pay'. However, on 20 June the executive, by 16–8 votes, declined to call off the proposed industrial action and endorsed the principle laid down by the negotiating committee 'that general pay improvements should not be linked to productivity'.[80] It was indicative of the railways' dependence on overtime, Sunday and rest-day working by many thousands of the staff, that when members of the NUR began working only a 'normal', forty-hour week from 24 June 1968, the railway system, particularly in the south of England, was completely disrupted.

In its report No. 41 of 6 June 1966 the RSNT noted, of the pay and efficiency talks, that 'despite many meetings over a period of two years' much time was 'still being spent on skirmishing'. The discussions had been 'less than continuous' and they lacked 'an agreed view on the need to work against an agreed deadline for completion'. In the light of this distinguished tribunal's observations there is much truth in the comments, by the editor of *Railway Review*, 'No one knows how long the pay and productivity negotiations would have dragged on at the previous pace had it not been for the "shot in the arm" given to the proceedings by the work to rule decision of the EC a couple of weeks before the AGM'.[81] The chaos on the railway system after 24 June concentrated the minds of the members of the Board and the union's negotiators wonderfully; initiatives and decisions thereafter followed thick and fast.

On 1 July 1966, the opening day of the NUR AGM at Penzance, Sidney Greene received a telephone call from Len Neal, offering a 3 per cent increase to time-work railwaymen in addition to the improvements suggested in RSNT Award No. 41. Confirmation of this offer was received by letter the following day and the AGM suspended standing orders to discuss it. The argument continued long after 5.30 p.m., the normal closing time of the meeting, but eventually a resolution rejecting the Board's offer on the ground that it did not meet the claim for an increase for all the members, but expressing a willingness to continue negotiations, was carried by 61–15 votes. This further setback to their plans prompted the Board's negotiating team, Messrs. Neal, Bowick, Rusbridge and Wurr, to fly down to Penzance by helicopter on Thursday 4 July. Prolonged negotiations with the NUR negotiating team (which included three AGM delegates, Messrs. Arundel, Bonnar and Bowers) followed, and late on Friday 5 July, agreement between the two negotiating teams was reached on a six-point productivity deal for railway conciliation staff other than footplatemen. When all members of the AGM except six, who were against, had approved the proposed agreement Sidney Greene dispatched the following telegram to all branches: 'Agreement with BRB reached. Advise members resume normal working immediately. Circular will follow.' On

6 July Conference took the unprecedented step of meeting on a Saturday morning, when it gave unanimous approval to a productivity agreement for footplatemen negotiated between the BRB, NUR and ASLEF. The fact that on this occasion the decision was unanimous was not unrelated to the favourable impression Len Neal made on the delegates (and incidentally, the favourable impression they made on him), when he addressed the conference and answered questions after the vote was taken the previous evening.[82]

The essential elements of the two productivity agreements were that, with effect from 8 July 1968, 10s was added to the basic rates of pay of groups 1–5, inclusive, while 3 per cent was added to the basic rates of group 6 and upwards. The additional amounts were to be included for the calculation of enhancements, but not for bonus or mileage payments which were to be tied to the old rates of pay. There was to be an immediate return to work. The very necessary incentive, the previous absence of which the RSNT report No. 41 had regretted, was included in that a target date of 2 September was set for the conclusion of the pay and efficiency talks.

Following the Penzance Agreement the Board and the union took to heart the implied reproof of the RSNT that pay and efficiency discussions were 'less than continuous' and cooped themselves up for three weeks in the Board's Staff Training College at Windsor. No one could complain of a lack of productivity in their efforts. Before the deadline date of 2 September, they had put flesh and blood to the skeleton agreements of Penzance. Thus, on 14 August, they produced their plan for conciliation staff other than the footplate grades. As a result of the NUR's insistence on better rewards for the lowest paid, they raised the basic rate of pay for railmen to 260s a week, compared with the 240s first offered by the Board in earlier discussions, and the 250s offered earlier that year. With the introduction of the new versatility grades of railman, leading railman, senior railman and chargeman, no less than 170 former job titles disappeared. An extra three days' annual leave was given, but on condition that this part of the holiday quota was taken outside the summer-holiday months. Wherever possible the forty-hour week was to be divided into four ten-hour rosters. The new grade of guard replaced the old ones of goods guard, passenger guard and train ticket collector while, for inter-city trains, there was to be a new grade of conductor guard.

The agreement for footplate staff, reached on 29 August, provided for improved basic rates of pay, ranging from the 15-year-old cleaner's 117s a week to the driver's 379s. There were increased allowances to facilitate the transfer of surplus staff. opportunities for all-line promotion and a promise of a more extended use of single-manning.

The new pay structure for clerks, announced shortly afterwards, included five classes in place of the previous fourteen and provided for the staged elimination of the iniquitous excluded-grade category. In place of four different categories of supervisor, there was now a single-scale ranging from £1,100 to £1,520. Stationmasters and supervisors who came under these new arrangements were to be expected to undertake a wider range of responsibilities and unnecessary layers of supervision were to be eliminated. Traffic-control staff were placed on the same salary scale as supervisors except that the lowest grade, that of assistant controller paid £925 a year, came below the base of the supervisors' scale.

Very often when promises of greater productivity accompany wage settlements in industry, there is very little subsequent monitoring of the increased efficiency promised and any financial savings achieved. This was not the case with the railways. Immediately following the Windsor agreements staff consultation meetings, to explain the new staffing structure, ranges of responsibility, rates of pay and avenues of promotion, were held at all the main stations and depots in the country.[83] There was a quarterly detailed monitoring of the productivity savings planned and actually achieved. The changes took many months since reorganisation could not be achieved by a stroke of the pen. Where redundancies were involved, adequate notice had to be given to the staff involved and the possibilities of alternative employment examined. All the same, subsequent financial savings were achieved to help pay for the cost of the improved rates of pay, extended holidays, and so on, granted to the staff. Len Neal's assessment of the balance of gains and losses was: 'After one year of the agreements the chief financial officer was able to report that we had spent £19 million in extra remuneration to employees and saved, in the same twelve months, £18 million'.[84] The BRB, in September 1968, informed the unions that it hoped to save £20,700,000 by the exercise, nearly £10 million of the total coming from the CONGOT grades.[85] The Board's quarterly returns, reporting the monitoring of schemes, reveal the progress of the restructuring. Thus the return for footplate staff, dated 22 March 1969, shows that a reduction of 1,480 staff had been planned compared with the saving of 1,027 men actually achieved, while the planned monetary saving was £1,674,000 and that actually achieved was

£1,027,000, £630,000 of which arose from the displacement of 679 footplatemen through the extension of single-manning. About the same time the financial savings arising from the introduction of the new versatility grades amounted to 84 per cent of the planned reduction. In so far as there was a shortfall, this was mainly due to the failure to reduce overtime to the extent planned.[86] In sum, therefore, it may safely be said that the improvements in pay and holidays were very nearly, but not quite, paid for by staff reductions and the redeployment and more effective use of the railway labour that remained.

VII

The debate in the union on the merits and disadvantages of the pay and efficiency agreements of July and August 1968, was prolonged and sometimes heated. Understandably, the most consistent supporter of the decisions taken at Penzance and Windsor was Sidney Greene. Throughout the more than two years of discussions which had preceded the settlements, he gave primacy to the need to advance the rewards of the lower paid. The greatest merit of the agreements, therefore, was that they produced 'one of the biggest increases in rates of pay that the union had been able to negotiate'.[87] He claimed that 'by no other form of action' could such improvements have been achieved, since it was a fact that 'during the whole of the period when negotiations were taking place all unions were faced with a strict government prices and incomes directive'. Any increases granted had to be related to increases in productivity. It was also a fact of life that the finances of the Board were in deficit. He conceded that men and women in the skilled grades came off less well, being restricted to a 3 per cent increase in wages and salaries, but stressed that their claims would be given special attention in stage II discussions. He pointed out that the number of redundancies which would arise from the Penzance and Windsor agreements was less than had at first been anticipated. This was partly due to changes in government policy. Under the Transport Act 1968 the setting up of the separate Freightliner organisation precluded some of the telescoping of jobs originally planned on the traffic side. In the twelve months up to 31 March 1969 there were 11,628 redundancies, compared with 15,257 in the preceding twelve months. Thus, the rate of redundancy had actually declined under the productivity agreements. He saw some consolation in the way redundancy had been negotiated under the pay and efficiency discussions by comparison with the largely uncontrolled onset of dismissals in earlier years. He noted that

The only difference between the past and the present situation is that previously the staff reductions have taken place without much direct general return to the remaining staff in the way of wage improvements. There was no doubt at all that some staff redundancies were still inevitable, but this time the general monetary credit has gone to the whole of the railway staff.[88]

Talking with Len Neal after the stage I discussions had been completed Sidney Weighell said: 'If you had told me that we would have agreed to all these changes before the end of the century I would not have believed you.'

David Bowick, Chief Industrial Relations Officer of the BRB, knew that Sidney Greene was impressed with the results of the Penzance and Windsor agreements, and sought to exploit this fact to enhance the prospects of industrial peace on the railways. On 1 October he wrote to the General Secretary (with copies to Mr Griffiths of ASLEF and Mr Coldrick of TSSA) in the following terms:

Dear Mr. Greene,

Now that the first stage of the Pay and Productivity agreements have been concluded or are within sight of conclusion it is hoped that this will be a prelude to a period free from disputes or threat of industrial action which do so much harm to industry.

I am sure you share in the hope that the P. & E. agreements which have announced a definite step to a more suitable and just wages policy will lead to a desire on the part of all concerned to improve efficiency and generate a spirit of confidence in the industry.

Industrial disputes have undoubtedly influenced traffic away from railways in the past. The Board feel, therefore, that it would be of considerable advantage if, at this point in time, they and the trade unions were jointly to publicise their confidence the pay and efficiency agreement will bring to the railways a period of industrial stability. This could then be developed in commercial contacts.

If you agree with this proposal, I will draft a suitable statement for your consideration, which, when agreed, could be issued jointly.

Yours sincerely,
David Bowick

Sidney Greene, not the most venturesome of general secretaries, waited a week before replying in a letter of a kind likely to dampen the zeal of the most enthusiastic:

Dear Mr. Bowick,
   I am in receipt of your letter of 1 October 1968, and, while your idea might be well founded, as to whether this is the actual time to issue such a statement is a matter of opinion. You will no doubt have seen in the press varying expressions on the way the agreement has been received.
   In view of these circumstances it is questionable whether at this stage it would be wise to publicise such a statement which of itself might give rise to further criticism.
   I would have thought that the way in which the industry reacts to the settlement would be the better guide, and, given a period of industrial calm, that that would be a recommendation for the agreement.
                                          Yours sincerely,
                                          S. F. Greene [89]

The General Secretary had good reason for his caution. Piles of letters on his desk testified to the mixed reception given to the agreements. One included a resolution of the Plymouth District Council carried at a specially summoned meeting attended by thirty-three delegates:

Having listened to our NEC member, this Plymouth DC condemns the acceptance of an additional form of rostering, i.e. four x ten hours working week and calls for it to be rescinded. Stage two of the Pay and Efficiency agreement to be not agreed until a report has been given to a SGM.

G. Prior, in a letter to *Railway Review* reminded readers that a signalman's productivity 'depends on the work which comes to him' and that a booking clerk in a busy office 'cannot take on other work'. Some of the most vociferous protests in fact came from branches and DCs where the signalmen's influence was strongest. Thinking out a new pay structure for men in this grade was one of the thorniest problems on the agenda and it is not surprising that a thorough examination of this matter was deferred to the stage II discussions. Thus the signalmen, and many other skilled railway workers, had to be content, for the time being, with a mere 3 per cent rise (though many were able to take advantage of an improved classification of signalboxes).

Ill-considered application of 'versatility' and 'flexibility' could have serious consequences. W. H. Dobell, Secretary of the Clapham Junction and Waterloo branch of the NUR had strong views about this. A railman member of the staff at Clapham Junction sustained a fatal accident on 9 April 1969, when performing coupling duties. In his letter to the General Secretary, dated 19 July 1969, Dobell wrote:

> As regards the fatal accident, I consider that this may well become a greater problem as, under P. & E. a man, to obtain a higher grade award of leading or senior railman, is obliged in many cases to perform coupling and uncoupling duties; a duty that should be confined to a shunter with a rate of pay comparable with the risk involved, and not thrust upon men who are physically afraid of the risk.[90]

It is not suggested for a moment that the risk was widespread; but the case revealed that the limits of versatility would need to be borne seriously in mind.

The most substantial criticism to the productivity deal as a main avenue for improved wage settlements came from those who recalled the principles of the Cameron Report. Public transport, it was argued, ought to be a service available to the nation because it is basic to the nation's economic and social well-being. Since the nation needs a sound public transport system, it should pay a living wage to those who provide the service. Their pay should not depend on the possibility or otherwise of squeezing more productivity out of the industry; for the time could well come when the scope for increased productivity would be very limited. Sidney Greene hinted that he recognised the limitations of productivity deals as a permanent method of wage determination, when he admitted to the AGM delegates at Llandudno 'that at some time we shall reach the stage where productivity, in the sense that we understand it today, will run out'. However, he was also of the opinion that the opportunities for improved efficiency and better pay arising from it had not yet been exhausted and he looked forward to the stage II negotiations.[91]

CHAPTER 6

PAY AND EFFICIENCY II –
AND AFTER

———————————◆———————————

I

WHEN the first pay and efficiency agreements were signed at Windsor, in August 1968, both management and unions were conscious of the fact that what had been achieved was the completion of but one stage of what was bound to be a continuous process. For this reason a joint working party of management and union representatives was appointed to draft an agenda of outstanding problems and to make recommendations for their solution.

In the view of Arnold Edmondson, who was present throughout the discussions, the BRB initially listed 'everything that came to mind', 'scraping the barrel' for areas of possible productivity deals. When discussions with the unions began they suggested scrapping as 'non-starters', most of their original eighty items. Ironically, the NUR representatives would have been prepared to keep a larger number of these items on the agenda than were management.[1] By February 1969 the working party had agreed that the most important topics to include in the second pay and efficiency agreement should be recompensing those staff who had received a bare 3 per cent increase under the stage I pay and efficiency discussions; the establishment of a minimum wage for railwaymen of £15 a week; the rationalisation of the bonus-earnings situation so as to bridge the gap between bonus earners and non-bonus earners; the rationalisation of rest-day and overtime payments without reducing earnings; and the increase in the length of annual leave and in the payments made during the leave period.

After this substantial preliminary work, the pay and efficiency stage II discussions began in earnest when the leading negotiators, Messrs Neal, Bowick and Clemmett for BR, and Messrs Greene, Weighell and Brassington for the NUR, virtually incarcerated themselves in the BRBs training centre at the Grove, Watford, on 4 August 1969, and stayed there until the main features and many of the details of a settlement were agreed eleven days later. They often worked in the evening as well as during normal working

hours. Left-wing members of the NUR executive criticised the procedure, since it removed the union's officers from any control of
the EC in London, which was eventually presented with an entire
programme in the formulation of which it had played no immediate
part. At an early stage in the proceedings the BR representatives
chalked some basic figures on the blackboard:

	stage II	£ million
(1)	stage I anomalies (3 per cent)	0·6
(2)	general award (4 per cent)	4·25
(3)	consolidation of bonus £0·85,	
	say, £1·0 million equals 1 per cent	1·0
(4)	established status; management	
	will pay costs of benefits for	
	superannuation, sick pay, etc.	nil

£5·8, equals
5·25 per cent

This was what the BRB was stating that it was prepared to pay.
Thereafter the officers of the NUR tried their utmost to have the
total of £5·8 million pushed up – it was increased to £6·45 million
by the tenth day – and management constantly pressed the union to
consent to proposals for money-saving by means of greater productivity. The greater part of the eleven days of discussions, in fact,
was taken up by the NUR agreeing to various items of cost-saving,
including split turns, train preparation by carriage and wagon
examiners, a 'do-it-yourself' commitment for station staff, for
instance, railmen replacing broken panes of glass instead of the
work being done by a hired outside glazier, and many others.

Progress was made on most of the items given priority by the
working party before the Watford discussions began, and the
results were embodied in separate documents agreed for each of
the main grades for example: CONGOT: footplatemen; workshop
staff and clerical and supervisory staff in August and September
1969. Thus, annual leave of conciliation staff was increased to three
weeks after three years in the service; and 20 per cent of the difference between basic pay and average earnings over the past year
was paid, in addition to the basic rates, during the leave period.
For trackmen, large gang allowances were restored after being withdrawn under the stage I agreement. Clerical staff, in return for
greater mobility both within and between offices, were conceded
four weeks annual leave and in some cases were granted payment
for travelling time. For footplate grades, higher pay was awarded

to cleaners who had completed fifteen years' service in the line of promotion and the payment of freight bonuses were accelerated.

Looking at the two pay and efficiency agreements comprehensively it is worth stressing that, although the £15-a-week minimum wage was not achieved at that time, the basic pay of railmen – the lowest paid – was raised from the pre-Penzance 226s per week to 276s, a rise of 21·2 per cent in just over twelve months. The critics of the agreements argued that the gains received were paid for by the loss of jobs. But the decline of 11,626 in the BRB labour force in the twelve months ending 31 March 1969 was less than the 15,257 decline of the preceding twelve months. The much greater staff reductions of the Beeching era were introduced without any *quid pro quo* (apart from redundancy payments) being negotiated.

<h1 style="text-align:center">II</h1>

One very important item which did not appear on the working party's agenda, but which figures prominently in the pay and efficiency stage II documents signed in the summer of 1969, was the introduction of compulsory trade union membership. The relevant sentences in each of the agreements were:

> The Board and the Trade Unions accept that membership of a Trade Union, party to the Machinery of Negotiation, is in the best interests of employer/employee relationship.
>
> It is therefore agreed that membership of one of the Trade Unions party to the Machinery of Negotiation shall be a condition of employment to be effective from 1 January 1970. The detailed changes to give effect to this will be included in a further document.[2]

Although the agreement surprised many members of the general public, it came as a result of many years of agitation and patient negotiation. It should be seen as the culmination of a long campaign rather than as a 'bolt from the blue'. NUR adherence to the principle of the union shop predated the Second World War. Unsuccessful attempts were made at a Special General Meeting in London on 18 November 1935, and at the AGM in Plymouth on 14 July 1937, to commit the union to a policy of compulsory union membership in the railway service. The Darlington and District council resolution in 1935 was set aside when a motion that the previous question be put was carried by 49–22 votes.[3] At Plymouth a South Wales and Monmouth District resolution to instruct the executive 'to approach the railway companies and demand that membership of a trade union recognised by the TUC be a condition of service' was defeated by 57–23 votes after John Marchbank, the General Secretary, had asserted that 'where there is compulsory trade union membership there is compulsory employment', since 'a stoppage of work could not be associated with the union shop'. An amendment by Hither Green branch, moved by Sidney Greene, a porter from Paddington, that the names of all non-unionists be reported to the EC and notified to the railway companies by 15 November 1937, with the recommendation that all non-unionists be removed from the railway service by 22 December of the same year, under penalty of being boycotted by NUR members, did not have a seconder and was therefore dropped.[4] However, at Clacton-on-Sea on 11 July 1939 the feeling among AGM delegates was more militant than had been the case two years earlier.[5] The meeting approved by 52–28 votes a resolution moved by E. W. Perry, an engine driver from Plymouth, 'that the time had arrived when trade union membership should be a condition of service'. The EC was asked to take joint action with the other railway unions to secure this end, but to proceed on its own to negotiate with the railway companies if ASLEF and the RCA were not prepared to co-operate. The inquiries of the General Secretary, however, revealed that neither of the sectionalist unions was in favour of an approach to the railway companies with the object of negotiating a union shop agreement. Therefore the EC, at its March 1940 meeting, came to the unanimous decision that: 'No uniformity can be expected in the direction desired, and in view of all the circumstances, and the present abnormal situation, we recommend that this matter be allowed to remain in abeyance until after the end of the present war.'[6] When the war was drawing towards its close in January 1945, the NUR raised the subject again – but with no greater success than it had had five years earlier – at a meeting of the National Joint Council of the three railway trade unions. The relevant minute of the meeting read: 'This matter was discussed, but no agreement could be reached as the RCA and ASLEF were not prepared to support a policy of compulsory trade union membership under existing circumstances.'[7] Later that year the AGM of the NUR instructed the executive to raise the issue once more with the other unions; but at a meeting of the National Joint Council held on 7 December 1945 the RCA and ASLEF merely reiterated their previous statement.

The position throughout the years 1947–51 was that ASLEF adhered to its 'spheres of influence' policy – which was unacceptable to the NUR – and the RCA rejected compulsory trade union-ism and the railway companies. After 1 January 1948, the RE expressed regret at the failure of the unions to settle their differ-ences; rejected the principle of the union shop· but agreed to afford reasonable facilities for the display of union notices. In 1952 there were signs of a breakthrough when the RE announced its willingness to discuss the question of compulsory trade union membership once there was complete agreement between the three railway unions.[8] When new machinery of negotiation was estab-lished for railway staff in 1956, the BTC conceded the NUR demand that only members of unions that were parties to the agree-ment (that is, NUR, ASLEF and TSSA) would be eligible for membership of LDCs and sectional councils. But it was still not prepared to agree to the principle of the union shop.

In May 1959, in an endeavour to keep the 'pot on the boil', the NUR executive, by a majority of 19–5 votes, decided to advise members not to take part in consultation meetings with the BRB from 30 June 1959. Sir Brian Robertson, Chairman of the BTC, was informed of the decision.[9] The outcome of the union's action was a meeting between the representatives of the NUR and Sir Brian at which a statement of BTC policy was agreed:

The Chairman acknowledged the assistance and co-operation accorded by the trade unions. He also attaches great importance to being able, through the agreed machinery, to settle with the trade unions all matters which bear on the interests of the staff.

For these reasons he wishes to publicise the fact that it is the policy of the Commission to give all facilities and encourage-ment to the staff to join their appropriate trade union. Whilst it is a matter for each individual to decide, steps will be taken to ensure that the attention of all new entrants to the service is drawn to the desirability of trade union membership and to the facilities accorded to the staff through the recognised channels agreed with the trade unions for expressing their views on all matters affecting their employment and welfare.[10]

The impact of this important statement at local level was some-times decisive. As F. W. Flay, a senior checker of Bristol No. 3 branch, told AGM delegates at Aberdeen in July 1967: 'Whereas previously there was antagonism from local officers sometimes to our local people in their efforts to organise, they were now able to point to the document and say that the Chairman of the Commis-sion agrees that everyone should be a member of the union.'[11] A further step on the road to the union shop was the agreement for

the deduction of union subscriptions through the paybills (discussed more fully in Chapter 3) which came into operation from
1 January 1965 and was made possible by the computer revolution.
  The introduction of the new method of paying union subscriptions convinced Sidney Greene that there was less urgency in pressing for the union shop. At Stockport, in July 1965, when the
Dundee branch proposed 'that membership of a recognised trade
union should be a condition of service with the railway industry',
he claimed that the union was already reaching the objective 'by
another way, by the deduction of contributions through the paybill'. Although the new arrangements had been in operation less
than seven months, it was already the fact that 203,000 out of the
240,000 members working for BR were paying their subscriptions
that way. In any case, he assured delegates, management would
never agree to compulsory trade union membership. On this
occasion the General Secretary failed to win the day. The Dundee
resolution was carried by 70–4 votes.[12] The apprehension that
was felt by some union activists that the officers would 'do a
deal' with management on the union shop which would curtail the
NUR's freedom of action was expressed at the AGM at Plymouth,
in July 1966, in a Croydon 1 branch resolution, reaffirming the
policy of 100 per cent trade unionism but insisting that it should
be achieved 'on the union's terms and without conditions by the
management'. The delegates gave the proposition their unanimous
endorsement.[13]
  Sir Leonard Neal, the member of the BR Board principally
responsible for the pay and efficiency agreements, explained why in
1969 he eventually accepted the unions' case for compulsory trade
union membership:

  The unions, he said, were having to consider and eventually
  agree to proposals that had the effect of reducing their membership. It seemed unreasonable to put them in that situation where
  they were accepting a level of responsibility and showing great
  statesmanship that went far beyond the common experience of
  other industries and trade unions, without recognising their
  claim.[14]

There is, however, a more purely commercial explanation of the
Board's action. In the wider-ranging productivity talks which preceded the union shop agreement its representatives repeatedly
countered the union's claim for improved earnings by pointing to
the disruptive effects of unofficial strike action, particularly by
signalmen. Sidney Weighell's response to management was to argue

that the precondition for better work discipline was a watertight union shop agreement. The Board saw this as a convincing argument. In a later memorandum on the union membership agreements it gave pride of place to this aspect: 'The prime objects of the agreements was to enable the trade unions to have more control over their members in dealing with industrial action not officially supported by the union(s) concerned.' The Board also recognised that the greater the number of parties with which it had to negotiate wages and working conditions, the more difficult it would be to achieve trouble-free agreements. In the words of the memorandum:

> There were clear advantages to the British Railways Board as an employer in a large complex industry in having an organised structure for negotiating wages and conditions of service as it was impossible to negotiate with individuals or small groups. The Board's structure is based upon agreements with a small number of very strong unions.[15]

Nevertheless, the first BR detailed draft agreement, dated 26 September 1969 and sent to the unions by David Bowick, Executive Director, Personnel, at BR on 1 October 1969, contained a long list of categories of people who could be given exemption from trade union membership. It included senior officers; management staff; trainees under any of the Board's management training schemes; the British Transport police; staff engaged at any BRB department, division, subsidiary company, or local management area, where the level of membership was below 80 per cent of the total eligible staff employed; staff employed at any place where there was no LDC or shop committee; an existing employee who at 1 January 1970 was over 50 years of age and had been employed by the Board for twenty-five years; and finally, 'an existing employee with a conscientious objection to membership of a trade union and who, if required, is able to satisfy the Appeal Body . . . that his objection is reasonable'. However, following numerous discussions between the representatives of the Board and of the unions, the only groups who were allowed exemption from union membership were the Board's trainees; senior officers; management staff; BT police; and existing employees with a conscientious objection to joining a union. In the final draft precision was given to the term 'conscientious objection', the relevant clause 10(b) stating: 'It is agreed that "conscientious objection" is not confined to religious convictions, but will include staff seeking exemption on grounds of age, long service or political grounds.' Clause 7 of the final draft provided that a person granted exemption from union membership on conscientious grounds would be required to pay 'a sum to be agreed between the parties, but in any case not higher than the highest contribution of any trade union he may be eligible to join, to a Benevolent Fund operated by the BRB'.

From 1 January 1970, when the union shop agreement came into effect, non-unionists on the staff were required to enrol in one of the recognised trade unions by 31 March 1970. New entrants to the service of the Board were given twenty-one days in which to take similar action. A person who, during the three months' grace provided, wished to establish a claim for exemption from union membership, had first to submit the claim, with full supporting evidence, through his immediate supervisor to his local manager. The local manager and a trade union representative would then interview him/her and 'explain carefully the requirements of the agreement'. If the claimant adhered to his non-union stance, the case would then be considered at regional level by managers and union representatives. Finally, any employee who continued to claim exemption could apply to have his case considered by an appeals body comprising representatives drawn from a panel of members of the recognised trade unions and representatives of the BRB. The decision of the appeals body was 'final and binding on all parties and on the applicant'. If the non-unionist failed to convince the appeals body, he was liable to dismissal. Under clause 8: 'Any employee who is in breach of contract of employment by reason of non-compliance with this Agreement may be dismissed after adequate notice but not before 31 March 1970.'[16]

By 3 July 1970 the appeals body had notice of 245 claims for exemption from union membership (out of a total BRB staff – that is, exclusive of BTH and BREL employees – of 212,243). Eighty-five of the 245 came from the London Midland region, fifty-two from Eastern Region, forty from Southern Region, thirty from Western Region and fifteen from the Scottish Region. The largest group of claimants, 131 in number, came from the salaried grades. There were only two from the footplate grades, compared with sixty-nine from the other members of the conciliation staff. Research workers and P and T staff accounted for the remainder. Most claimed exemption on political grounds, namely, freedom of individual choice, with religious objections and age and length of service being the other principal reasons given for appeal. Fifteen signalmen claimed exemption on the ground of their membership of the Union of Railway Signalmen – a union not recognised by the BRB for purposes of collective bargaining.[17]

According to BRB records, in the period between 1 January 1970 and the coming into operation of the Industrial Relations Act on 29 February 1972, only twenty-three claims for exemption had been heard by the appeals body. Of these, five had their appeals allowed, seventeen were rejected and one claim was deferred. Of the seventeen staff whose claims for exemption were turned down, twelve subsequently joined a trade union. The remainder of the applications were awaiting consideration by the appeals body at the end of February 1972 when the union shop agreement became no longer enforceable. In the twenty-five months' duration of the agreement nine members of the BRB staff were dismissed for failure to comply with its terms.[18]

Those applicants who were able to quote from the Holy Bible in support of their stance against trade unionism were given exemption, if they were found to be church members. The railwayman who, in a letter to his superior, cited II Corinthians 6: 14–18, was typical of the religious objectors:

Be ye not unequally yoked together with unbelievers: for what fellowship hath righteousness with unrighteousness? and what communion hath light with darkness? And what concord hath Christ with Belial? Or what part hath he that believeth with an infidel? . . . Wherefore come out from among them and be ye separate, saith the Lord, and touch not the unclean thing.

He was granted exemption from union membership; as was a Christadelphian from Western Region, who submitted a lucidly written letter outlining the history of his church and explaining his reasons for not joining a union. Those nearing retirement were also excused, as were two members of the clerical staff at Marylebone.[19] On the other hand, those who simply asserted a citizen's basic right not to belong to a trade union were generally unsuccessful in their appeal unless they produced more substantial evidence than a bald assertion.

It proved impossible to secure union or closed-shop agreements with management in all the undertakings with which the NUR had negotiating rights before the Industrial Relations Act came into operation at the end of February 1972. Agreements similar to those reached with the BRB were concluded with National Carriers Ltd and Freightliners Ltd, to come into effect on 2 February 1971; but the managements of Thomas Cook & Sons (at that time a subsidiary of the BRB) and the Scottish Transport Group were adamant in resisting compulsory union membership.[20] The board of BTH claimed that, because of the high rate of labour turnover and the necessity of employing aliens with temporary work permits, it was unrealistic to think of employing only union members.[21] In the case of the BTDB, negotiations were overtaken by the passing of the Industrial Relations Act.[22]

Although the reintroduction of union shop agreements in 1975–6 came several years after the pay and efficiency stage II documents were signed in the summer of 1969, it is convenient to consider them here. With the passing of the Trade Union and Labour Relations Act 1974, the Industrial Relations Act 1971 was repealed and trade union and closed-shop membership agreements were again legal. Under schedule 1, para. 6(5) of the 1974 Act, it was provided that where there was a compulsory union membership agreement, an employee might be dismissed for refusing to join or remain a member of a trade union unless 'The employee genuinely objects on grounds of religious belief to being a member of any trade union whatsoever or on any reasonable grounds to being a member of a particular trade union.' Under the Trade Union and Labour Relations (Amendment) Act 1976, the words 'or on any reasonable grounds to being a member of a particular trade union' were struck out, leaving 'religious belief' as the sole legally recognised ground for claiming exemption from trade union membership where a closed-shop or union-shop agreement had been negotiated between the employer and the union or unions representing the employees. The BRB considered that by not defining in any way what constituted 'genuine religious belief', the two Acts 'created a difficult situation for employers with a union membership agreement'.[23] Thus when union and Board representatives met at the request of Sidney Greene, in the winter of 1974–5, to consider re-establishing the union shop agreement of 1969, the Board suggested that the acceptance of exemption on genuine religious grounds should apply 'only to those religious denominations which specifically proscribe their members from joining a trade union'.[24] Under the new agreement, which came into operation on 1 August 1975, serving employees were given until 31 October 1975 to join one of the recognised trade unions. New entrants, as in 1970, were given three weeks in which to do the same.[25] London Transport,[26] Freightliner Ltd, National Carriers Ltd,[27] Hovercraft Ltd[28] and even, this time round BTH[29] soon produced similar agreements.

An important feature in both the agreements was the clause, identical in the 1969 and 1975 agreements, in which the unions undertook to discourage unofficial industrial action by groups of their members:

In the event of any members of staff participating in any form of unconstitutional action, either by withdrawing their labour or otherwise designed to hamper the proper working of the railway in contravention of clause 17 of the Memorandum of Agreement on the Machinery of Negotiation for Railway Staff, dated 28 May 1956, the trade unions shall not afford them any support; shall use their best endeavours to induce them to conform to the Agreement and may consider taking disciplinary action in accordance with their respective trade union rule books.

The unions carried out the undertaking given in the above clause on a number of occasions in the late 1970s, but perhaps the most remarkable example of this kind of action was the NUR executive's disciplining of sixteen of its members employed in the Warrington power signalbox in November 1979. From August of the previous year the men concerned refused to 'stand in' for colleagues off sick or on annual leave and, in consequence, caused disruption in the main line rail services. They were dissatisfied with the classification given to their box and regarded themselves as underpaid by comparison with signalmen in certain other power boxes, for example, Euston. They were also impatient because of the slow progress of negotiations through the LDC and sectional council. The EC considered their case, in August 1978, and came to the unanimous decision to 'instruct the signalmen in Warrington power box to resume normal working immediately'. It also instructed Sectional Council 'C' to conduct an immediate inquiry into the working arrangements in the box.[30] In the first half of 1979 some progress was made in discussions between LDC and Sectional Council representatives in preparing the case for an upgrading of the box. Despite this, the signalmen continued their unofficial action, flouting repeated appeals from the General Secretary to resume normal working and to press their claim through the negotiating machinery. At last in November 1979 the sixteen men were called, two at a time, to Unity House, where members of the executive reminded them of the rules of the union and warned that they must return to work. In the meantime Sidney Weighell had gained an assurance from the BRB that if the men continued to defy their union executive's ruling, the Board would back up the EC by sacking the offending sixteen. The executive was unaware of this action by the General Secretary. Head office notified each man that he had a fortnight in which to comply, otherwise he would be expelled from the union. The men waited until the fourteenth day and then sent a telegram to Unity House, reporting that they were resuming normal working. Shortly afterwards the negotiations in Sectional Council 'C' resulted in the upgrading of the signalbox.[31]

The limitation, in the Trade Union and Labour Relations (Amendment) Act 1976, of the recognised grounds of objection to joining a trade union to religious conviction, and the provision in the new BR union shop agreement of 1975 that appeals should be finally settled at regional rather than national level, led to greater expedition in dealing with the cases and a larger number of dismissals from the service. By 15 November 1977 forty employees had been sacked from BR for refusing to join one of the recognised trade unions. A substantial proportion of the total dismissed were clerical officers from the Croydon area.[32] Advised and encouraged by the pressure group, the National Association for Freedom, three of the forty, Mr Iain Young, Mr Noel James and Mr Ronald Webster, appealed against BR's action in dismissing them to the European Commission of Human Rights. Their grounds for appeal was that their dismissal was in breach of the European Convention on Human Rights. The Commission, in a report published in June 1980, announced that it had decided, by a majority of 15–3 votes, that the dismissal of the three BR employees was in contravention of article 11 of the Convention, but it declined to give an opinion on closed shops in general.[33]

Conditions for non-unionists were greatly eased following the introduction of the Thatcher government's Employment Act in 1980. Its section 7 broadened the recognised basis of objection to union membership and made the establishment of a closed shop less likely by making it conditional on 80 per cent of the work group endorsing it in a ballot vote. The Act's new 'conscience clause' read :

> The dismissal of an employee . . . shall be regarded as unfair if he genuinely objects on grounds of conscience or other deeply held personal conviction to being a member of any trade union whatsoever or of a particular trade union.

The reporting of cases of the dismissal of non-unionist employees of BR in British newspapers has stressed the rights of individuals concerned not to belong to a trade union.[34] There has been a tendency to ignore the views of the large majority of railwaymen, who regularly pay their 60p or so a week trade union subscriptions and do not see why a handful of 'nons' should enjoy, free, the benefits of improved working conditions, better health and safety measures, longer periods of annual leave – not to mention improved rates of pay – negotiated by trade union officials on behalf of all staff.

One man by exercising his 'rights' can take away the rights of others. In a public transport undertaking a small group of individuals, acting irresponsibly, may impinge on the right of the travelling public to use a scheduled train service. The union shop agreement, while denying the right of individual employees – apart from those granted exemption under the appeals procedure – to be non-unionists, nevertheless helped to reduce the disruption of services by unofficial industrial action, as the Warrington signalbox case demonstrated. BR's view, given in a press statement on 15 July 1976, was that their admittedly severe interpretation of the union shop was justified by the need to ensure that trains faced the minimum of disruption. 'Above all we are seeking smooth industrial relations in this vital public service which is so vulnerable to industrial action', a spokesman said.[35] Nevertheless, in the light of the Employment Act 1980, some loosening of the rules for exemption from union membership seemed likely and one possibility, being canvassed by Eric Wigham, was to insist on union membership for new recruits and the continuation 'on the books' of those who are existing members, but to count on the passage of time for the eventual elimination of the very small number of non-unionists.[36] Some indication of the size of the problem was given by the BRB, which reported that in 1975 after three years in which railway workers were under no obligation to join one of the recognised trade unions, 96 per cent of them had, nevertheless, retained or taken up membership. Following the implementation of the 1975 agreement 99·84 per cent of the workforce was unionised.[37] Bearing in mind the rapid turnover of labour and the fact that many of the non-unionists (as shown by the appeals records) were older people there is reason to believe that, under the Wigham plan, it would have taken very few years to achieve an effective union shop.

III

Following the pay and efficiency stage I agreement of 14 August 1968, both the NUR and the BRB were agreed that a settlement of the complicated problem of signalmen's pay would have to be a top priority in future productivity discussions. On 20 January 1969 R. Clemmett, Chief Industrial Relations Officer of the BRB, wrote to Sidney Greene urging the setting up of a joint working party 'to look into ways of finding means to justify increased rates of pay for such staff'.[38] Since the NUR had already listed signal-men's pay as one of the major topics for future agreement the General Secretary readily agreed to Mr Clemmett's proposal. From the meetings of the working party, there eventually emerged the new classification scheme of 5 June 1972.

The reason for the importance attached to reaching agreement on a new basis for signalmen's rewards was the rapidity of tech-nological change in the 1960s and 1970s in this branch of the rail-way industry. For the best part of a century before the 1950s the technology of signalling had shown little fundamental change. It is true that in the 1930s power boxes – primitive in character by comparison with those of the 1970s were beginning to appear, but the semaphore signalling system was overwhelmingly predominant. Even so, the amount of work to be performed in manual signal-boxes varied enormously from the small branch line box with its handful of levers to the giants of the main line junctions. To meet this situation a marks system was devised, in 1922, under which the signalman was rewarded in proportion to the number of lever movements he executed and the number of messages he received or transmitted. The result of the introduction of the new system was that signalmen were the only major group of railway employees whose *basic wage* was determined by a kind of bonus system. Under this regime the signalman gained the strong conviction that, in contrast with the work situation of other railwaymen, he earned every penny he was paid. In the words of Sidney Greene: 'He could argue that he was only paid when he was actually moving a lever, pressing a button or opening or closing crossing gates. He was not paid for when he was sitting down.'[39] More than most rail-waymen, signalmen were 'work-study' conscious. Under the Rail-way Modernisation and Beeching plans of 1955 and 1963, the pace of substitution of manually operated signalboxes by power boxes quickened and posed new problems of how the signalman should be paid. In some instances a handful of men working in one of the latest power boxes were responsible for work formerly spread between more than a hundred manually operated boxes. Thus, the new Derby/Trent power box opened at the end of 1969 displaced 112 manually operated cabins.[40] With changes of such far-reaching significance it was inevitable both that the men man-ning the new boxes should demand higher pay for improved productivity and greater responsibility, and that those still left in one or other of the rapidly diminishing number of manually operated boxes should feel disgruntled because of their meagre chances of promotion and higher earnings.

Meanwhile successive annual national conferences of signalmen

pressed the EC to negotiate a new agreement which would take
into account the new situation brought about by the far-reaching
changes in railway signalling. The 1962 conference, for example,
wanted the union's executive to take 'the most militant action
possible' to have the negotiations on a new basis of awards
finalised.[41] After long negotiations agreement was reached on
November 1964 on a formula for the new power boxes which
awarded each cabin points based on the traffic handled and the
equipment it contained.[42] The new scheme came into operation
from 1 November 1965 but with backdating of enhanced payments
to 26 May 1964. Signalmen in power boxes with a points rating of
450 and over were given an extra 20s per week. Although the 1965
formula resulted in higher pay for signalmen working in power
boxes, its application by no means silenced the widespread discontent of men of this grade. One of the outstanding grievances
was that the earnings of men working in manually operated cabins
slipped well behind those of their colleagues who were reaping
some of the benefits of modernisation. Another grievance was that
although signalmen's *basic* rates compared favourably with those
of most railwaymen, they found that in order to achieve the level
of *earnings* of men paid productivity, incentive or mileage bonuses,
they had to put in a great deal of overtime and Sunday working.

The union first tried to resolve the problem of raising the earnings of men employed in manually operated cabins. At the 1969
AGM, dubbed by H. Garton, a signalman of March branch, as
'the Signalmen's AGM', Sidney Weighell described the frustrations
of the exercise:

We tramped this country looking at manual boxes to see whether
the power-work formula could be applied to them. We found
that it could not be. . . The two things (ie. power and manual
cabins P.S.B) are not comparable; they are like chalk and
cheese.[43]

In July 1971, when the joint working party had been hammering
away at the problems of signalmen's classification for more than
two years, Russell Tuck, Assistant General Secretary, again drew
attention to the difficulty of including power boxes and manual
boxes in the same classification scheme. After declaring that it
was 'one of the most difficult exercises that has ever been undertaken', he continued:

If you said to the committee: 'Draw up a nice classification
system and reward everybody according to the work done', we

could have found a system which would have given men in major power boxes something like £120 per week and the lads on the bottom something like 1s. a week – but that is how wide the difference is between the classifications as they exist at the present moment. . . . We have to try to get a formula to ensure that the people on the bottom are not too far away from the people at the top.[44]

In the meantime, in an endeavour to assuage some of the discontent of signalmen, it was agreed that additional allowances, on a percentage basis, should be given to power signalmen in line with general pay awards; that there should be meal breaks of twenty minutes between the third and the fifth hour of duty of signalmen in busy cabins and that relief signalmen should be given additional allowances where normal staff were entitled to receive them. These improvements were listed in the stage II agreement of 4 August 1969.

While the arduous task of working out a completely new classification scheme was being undertaken, an interim incentive bonus, ranging from 15s to 55s per week and depending on the traffic value and equipment value of each cabin was introduced in May 1970.[45]

The comprehensive new classification was introduced on 5 June 1972. This attempted what had previously been regarded as impossible – the introduction of a single classification scheme for manual and power boxes. The calculations were based on censuses of traffic taken during the second weeks of February and August of the preceding year. The rating of each cabin was determined by its traffic value and its equipment value. Thus one point was awarded for each through, stopping, starting or terminating train controlled by the box. There were considerably more variables determining the equipment value. They included automatic, semi-automatic, controlled, warning, calling-on and shunt-ahead signals, points and movable diamonds, block instruments, hotbox detectors, and many other items. The points for traffic and equipment for each cabin, whether manual or power operated, were then added up and the cabin given a rating according to the following scale:

classification	rating	weekly rate of pay
A	0–69	£22·95
B	70–174	£25·60
C	175–299	£28·35
D	300–549	£31·00
E	550 and over	£35·60

It was provided that a relief signalman would be paid the rate of pay associated with the cabin in which he did his spell of duty. Any signalman (or relief signalman) whose rate of pay would be otherwise reduced through the implementation of the new classification was to be allowed to retain his old rate of pay on a personal basis.[46]

If those who negotiated the new agreement at any time thought that it would assuage the discontents of signalmen, they were soon disillusioned. The National Signalmen's Conference, held at Southend on 16–17 September 1972, expressed 'extreme concern and dissatisfaction at the outcome of the new classification'.[47] At the following year's AGM at Exmouth, on 16 July 1973, G. H. Sharpe, a signalman from Loughborough, declared the new classification was 'one of the worst agreements this union has made on behalf of its members', while another signalman delegate, D. W. Green of Crewe, gave specific reasons for taking a similarly hostile view. 'Ninety-eight of the manual boxes in the London Midland Region were down in classification', he said. However, Russell Tuck, speaking from the platform, pointed out that only the gloomy side of the picture had been painted. He reminded delegates that some 4,000 signalmen, or somewhat more than half the number of men in the grade, had benefited from the reclassification.[48]

The difficulty with any points system is that it becomes out of date and creates anomalies almost as soon as it is negotiated. In the 1970s technological change was remarkably rapid. R. E. W. Greensmith, a S and T technician of Nottingham, reminded delegates at the AGM at Scarborough on 19 July 1972 that

> The revolution in signalling is almost beyond description . . . 3½ years ago Saltley, Derby and Trent were brought into operation as power signal boxes. At that time the equipment was absolutely revolutionary; but in 3½ years the advance has been such that it is now obsolete.

However hard the planners tried, the gap widened between the smaller manually operated cabins and the newest-design power cabins. The difficulty was, to some extent, met by lowering the points range in class A – the lowest-rated boxes, thus simultaneously keeping the men confined to these lowly outposts up to at least the basic rates of pay, while pushing many others into the higher-paid B and C categories. Thus, in a major revision exercise in 1974, the range of points in class A was lowered from 0–69 to 0–49 and, in 1980, it was lowered still further to 0–39. At the same time a few super cabins such as those at Motherwell, Glasgow and Trent were placed in a new category – F – where the rates of pay of signalmen were highest.[49] Nevertheless ludicrous anomalies remained. There were instances of signalmen in the same box doing the same work but receiving three different rates of pay – a result of reclassification and the 'retention of earnings' rule.

Technological changes in the motive power department and severe fluctuations and structural adjustments in the economy also affected adversely the smooth working of any classification based on the points system. Following the completion of the London–Glasgow electrification, Crewe signalbox was downgraded from class E to class D; the labour of the signalmen concerned had become more productive, yet their wage rates were reduced. The introduction of high-speed train services from, for example, Paddington and King's Cross, tended under the points system to downgrade their importance; since fewer shunting operations, and therefore less signal movements, were involved. Industrial recession, in 1979, affected adversely the coal traffic of an important marshalling yard such as Toton in Nottinghamshire, bringing down the classification of the signalbox.

Not surprisingly many of the more far-sighted signalmen were becoming disillusioned with the assessment of their work being based on the will-o'-the-wisp of a detailed points system. R. L. Tyler, of Stafford cabin, expressed this revulsion when he said: 'The sooner we get away from the idea of measuring our work the better.'[50] An alternative method being advocated in the later 1970s for determining the rewards of signalmen was the classification of signal cabins by the sectional councils with reference to broader considerations of the importance of each box to the railway system of the region. This is the method adopted on London Transport. If the railways were regarded, without reservation, as an essential public service, and financed accordingly, less time might be spent in a vain endeavour to discover a common classification between Victorian signal cabins and those of the microchip age and more on determining an enhanced wage level, reflecting the immense advance in productivity of signalmen's labour.

IV

For most years of the 1970s, the improvements in money earnings it was possible for the NUR to secure for its members were limited by the restraints of government incomes policies. In such years the union's efforts were directed at ensuring that maximum advantage was taken of new productivity deals to enhance earnings. At the same time opportunity was taken to raise the basic rates of the lowest paid when government incomes policies conceded that the low paid constituted 'a special case'. In 1970, however, the Heath government's policy as expounded by the Secretary of State for Employment, Mr Robert Carr, was that the rewards of labour were best determined by competition rather than by statutory control. Thus, the railway unions were free to make the best bargains they could with the BRB.

A feature of the pay settlements reached in the early 1970s was the progress made in consolidation of bonus earnings into the basic rates of pay. In the 1960s the introduction of many bonus schemes, for example, those for freight train crews; for passenger guards on trains where the footplate staff were entitled to mileage bonus; for certain categories of tasks performed by goods and cartage workers, greatly complicated the wages structure. Nevertheless, large numbers of staff remained outside the scope of these payments. In 1970 37,000 persons of a total conciliation staff of 89,490 were not entitled to any bonus earnings.[51] Inequalities in rewards inevitably increased. The pay structure became top heavy, with basic rates at a depressingly low level and the earnings of those 'on bonus' sometimes remarkably high. In that year, while thousands were taking home as little as £12·50 to £13·00 per week, others fortunate enough to pick up bonus earnings were being paid £40–£50 per week. Because so much of the revenue made available for wages and salaries was going in bonus payments, basic rates of pay were depressed. Moreover pensions and sick pay were calculated from the basic rates, not from average earnings, and thus a low base rate meant meagre pension and sick payments. The fact that in the same depot or station some workers' pay packets were swollen with bonuses, while others were not, led to jealousy and resentment. W. Smithurst, a signalman from Tyneside 2 branch, expressed a widespread feeling in the union when he told AGM delegates at Inverness, in July 1970, 'Let us give the men a decent standard of living within the forty hour week and we shall have better comradeship in the industry and better conditions'.[52] However, the desired changes had to be implemented slowly. It was not practicable to take bonuses away from those already entitled to them; but it was possible in future settlements to tip the balance in favour of the non-bonus earners.

This was done in the spring of 1970 when, following discussions at The Grove, Watford, agreement was reached on an 8 per cent increase for all members of the conciliation grades, effective from

4 May 1970 with a further 3 per cent paid from 3 August that year. But a third of the August increase, namely 10s, was in the form of consolidation of bonus into the basic wage.[53] The same policy was eventually embodied in the settlement reached in April 1971, though on this occasion the path to agreement was beset by a damaging work to rule by ASLEF members during 4–14 April and an evenly balanced vote between acceptance and work to rule in the NUR executive on 15 April. Since the rules of the NUR gave the President no casting vote, the branches were consulted by circular letter. As 125 of those replying favoured acceptance of the Board's offer, while only 40 were for rejection, the EC followed this majority verdict of the branches on 27 April and agreed to the proposed terms of settlement by 15–9 votes.[54] The increases eventually settled in May 1971 boosted the railman's basic rate from £15·20 to £17·20, 60p of the increase being consolidation; while the driver's basic rate rose from £26·60 to £30·45, £1·50 of which comprised consolidation of bonus.[55] The pay negotiations of 1972 were prolonged and embittered by the Heath government's invocation of the punitive clauses of the Industrial Relations Act 1971, examined in detail in Chapter 7.

An outcome of the 1972 pay negotiations which had an important impact on those of the following year was the agreement reached on 28 September 1972 to set up joint working parties of board and union representatives to examine the pay structure of (a) the footplate grades; (b) CONGOT; and (c) clerical and supervisory staff. A fourth working party to consider pay structure of workshop grades was established shortly afterwards. Differences between the unions made the achievement of a satisfactory pay settlement in 1973 exceptionally difficult. ASLEF wanted priority to be given to the restructuring of footplatemen's pay with the general pay settlement taking second place. It claimed extra rewards for men in the locomotive grades, because of the extra strains and responsibilities which accompanied the introduction of new technology. The NUR and TSSA, on the other hand, considered that the general pay settlement should take precedence and that the deliberations of the working parties should advance on a common front without any one group being given priority.

When talks on the drivers' restructuring claim broke down early in 1973, the ASLEF executive decided on 16 February to call a one-day strike on 28 February in support of its claim for a basic £40 a week and to follow an immediate policy of non-co-operation. In an effort to prevent the strike, further talks were held between the union side and the board on 23 and 26–7 February, when the Board made a final offer of £33·50 per week basic driver's pay, with mileage payments of 50p for every twenty-five miles over 149 miles. The offer was rejected by ASLEF which carried out its threat of a one-day strike on 28 February, causing a complete shut-down of services on BR and considerable disruption on London Transport. The next day the ASLEF executive voted for a further stoppage on 8 March and a ban on Sunday working. Meeting again on 13 March the executive called for a further one-day strike on 22 March and for a continuation of the ban on Sunday working. The BRB then took action to prevent the third complete shutdown by offering further talks, and on 16 March the ASLEF executive, by 5–4 votes, suspended both the strike action, and the work to rule and ban on Sunday working.

It was not until 18 April that the three railway unions accepted BRB's offer which was in line with government policy as laid down in *Controlling Inflation, the Second Stage* (Cmnd 5205, 17 January 1973), that is, £1 per week per head plus 4 per cent of the total paybill to be distributed to the members of the group. In the con-ciliation staff the railmen's rise was of 9 per cent, while the increase of most signalmen was in the 7–8 per cent range. The driver's rise in basic pay worked out at 7·3 per cent. Among the clerical staff the pay of the youngest clerical assistants was increased from £520 to £595 per year – a rise of 14·4 per cent – while the clerical officer, grade 2, in his fifth year, was awarded an increase of only 7·3 per cent. Another group benefiting from the agreement were BR's women employees. The Board sought to comply with the Equal Pay Act 1970, by reducing by one-third the differential between men's and women's rates for those engaged in similar work. This was an important step towards the achievement of equal rates of pay by 31 December 1975 as required under the Act.[56]

The 1974 pay settlement, like that of 1973, was reached against a background of government legislation placing restraints on the increase of wages and salaries. The Heath government's Phase 3 policy, which was intended to apply between 7 November 1973 'until the autumn of 1974', was set out in the *Consultative Document on the Price and Pay Code* (Cmnd 5444) of 8 October 1973. Annual pay increases were limited to *either* 7 per cent of basic rates, *or* up to an average of £2·25 a week for the group, with an individual maximum of £350 a year. As Sidney Greene stressed in June 1974, in his last report to an AGM, the Phase 3 counter-inflation policy was more flexible than that of Phase 2, and it therefore 'became imperative for the union to take steps to ensure that the maximum possible benefit was extracted from manage-ment' under the terms of the policy.[57] The greater flexibility of

Phase 3 lay in the provision that a further 1 per cent could be added to the basic rates of pay, if this was needed for 'the removal of anomalies'. Extra payment might also be made for increased productivity, the distortions caused by earlier pay standstills, for improving London allowances and for making progress towards equal pay for women.

The NUR's initial submission for a 'substantial increase' in rates of pay was based on conventional grounds. Reference was made to the pay of workers in comparable industries· the problems management was experiencing in recruiting essential staff because of the relative unattractivesness of railway wages; the continually rising cost of living and the need to improve railwaymen's living standards. The pay settlement, which was worked out at meetings of the RSJC and RSNC, in February and March 1974, added £2·05 to the weekly pay packets of those whose rates of pay were £27·65 or under, and 7 per cent, on average, to the weekly pay of those with over £27·65 per week. Most clerical officers' salaries were increased by £115 a year. The minimum earnings level was raised from £22·50 to £25 a week. Women's pay was increased by half the difference between men's and women's rates of pay for similar work, thus achieving the most substantial advance towards equal pay to that date. The Board agreed to implement the Phase 3 threshold clause. The 1 per cent flexibility allowance was used to increase the annual leave by two days within a ceiling of four weeks, and to increase holiday pay from basic rate plus 20 per cent of average weekly earnings to basic rate plus 33⅓ per cent of earnings. Unsocial-hours premia included 1¼-time for hours worked inside the standard week between 06.00 and 14.00 hours on Saturdays· 1½-time for overtime within these hours on Saturday and 1¾-time for rest-day time worked between these hours on Saturday; 1¼-time was to be paid for hours worked inside the standard week between 20·00 and 22·00 Mondays to Fridays, with 1½-time for overtime and 1¾-time for rest-day time worked within the same periods. The London Allowance for salaried staff was raised from £70 per annum to £95 per annum, while adult wages grade staff had their allowance increased from 90p per week to £1·20p. All these improvements were introduced on 29 April 1974.[58]

It is not difficult to see why the NUR accepted a settlement within the Stage 3 guidelines as it had done the 1973 agreement under Phase 2. At the AGM at Exmouth, in July 1973, resentment at the Heath government's policies of pay restraint was expressed in a public resolution on pay policy, which voiced 'a total opposition' to the policy of statutory restraint on wages and salaries. Conference carried this resolution by the handsome margin of 51–26 votes; but it defeated by 43–34 votes an amendment which coupled opposition to the Tory government's pay policy with opposition to 'any discussions between the TUC and the government which would limit free collective bargaining'. The rejection of this isolationist stand by a margin of 43–34 votes was largely due to the intervention of Sidney Greene, who said:

> In the first 25 or 30 or 50 years in the history of the trade union movement the whole object was the right to talk, the right to express ourselves, and now for some reason or other that I cannot understand in 1973 it is said to me 'Don't talk'. . . If we do not talk to them we do not influence them. . . Are we now not going to say anything to them and allow them to continue the restrictions without saying anything? Of course not. We have got to talk to them.[59]

By April 1974, when a decision had to be taken on the Board's offer made within the Heath government's Phase 3 limits, the third Wilson administration was installed. Ingrained loyalty to the Labour Party was an added reason for avoiding industrial trouble. In his report to the AGM in June 1974 Sidney Greene gave the 'NUR's determination to abide loyally by the TUC's social contract with the Labour Party' as one of two principal reasons why the executive gave unanimous endorsement to the Phase 3 settlement. The other reason was that the pay settlement of April 1974 was the result of a separate exercise from the pay structure review which was still in progress.

On 22 October 1973 the BR's draft reports of the joint working parties on the pay structures of the CONGOT and footplate grades were considered by the NUR's executive. The policy recommended by the union's negotiating committee and endorsed by the EC, with only one dissentient, was that all three working party reports should be considered collectively by the RSNC to ensure that future wages structures dovetailed into each other. The EC therefore waited until the third working party report – for the salaried and supervisory grades – appeared a month later before sending all three documents to the RSNC.[60] Trade union and BR representatives considered the three reports at meetings of the RSNC, held on 30 November and 10 December 1973, but made little progress, mainly because the second meeting took place against a background of industrial action by ASLEF in support of special responsibility allowances for drivers. At the invitation of the NUR, officers of the three trade unions, with members of their negotiating committees, met at Unity House on 21 January 1974 to try to reach agreement on policy for the next meeting of the RSNC; but a common approach proved impossible, partly because of differences between the NUR and ASLEF on the consolidation into the basic wage of drivers' mileage bonuses. On 11 February prospects looked brighter when ASLEF announced the suspension of its industrial action until 1 March. This persuaded the Board to resume discussions in the RSNC. However, at the meeting of the council on 20 February, ASLEF representatives announced their rejection of the entire pay restructuring proposals. BR then decided that there was no other course than to refer the dispute to the RSNT.[61]

The tribunal's Report No. 42, published on 24 July 1974, was hailed by ASLEF as 'a great victory' for sectionalist policy since the union's claim for special allowances for the extra responsibilities undertaken by footplatemen was met by the recommendation of a 10 per cent increase on basic rates. On the other hand, the tribunal rejected ASLEF's claim for mileage bonuses to be paid after 125 miles and went some way towards accepting the NUR case that all mileage bonuses should be consolidated. It ruled that the bonus should be paid only after 200 miles and that bonuses hitherto paid for distances under 200 miles should be consolidated into the basic rates. The tribunal accepted the NUR case that guards and conductor guards, as part of the train team, should also be granted additions to their basic rates of 7 per cent and 5 per cent, respectively. The recommendations for allowances for those working unsocial hours was in line with NUR policy. Additional payments were of 5·5 per cent, 7·5 per cent, or 10 per cent of basic rates according to the shift worked. For all conciliation staff other than trainmen, there was to be the total consolidation of all bonuses into basic rates with lump-sum payments being given in addition to the increases on the basic pay. The overall effect of the consolidation arrangements was to correct the imbalance of earnings between bonus and non-bonus workers in a manner which was of benefit to the vast majority of staff. The reform effectively ended the anomaly whereby staff in the same grade in different depots were receiving vastly different sums for time worked within the standard week largely because of the ad hoc development of bonus schemes.

V

After the return of a Labour government in February 1974, there was no question of a Phase 4 replacing the Phase 3 of the Heath administration. The Tories had been defeated on a programme which conceded that 'the case which the NUM has long presented is in the national interest' and one of the first priorities of the new Cabinet was to resolve the dispute in the coal industry, largely on the miners' terms. The General Election was fought on 28 February and a settlement of the miners' strike, costing more than double the maximum the Coal Board was previously prepared to offer, was reached on 6 March. The new government quickly carried out its pledge to abolish the Pay Board, the instrument through which its predecessor had vetted pay settlements under phases 2 and 3. Although it was argued the miners were 'a special case', the settlement of 6 March proved to be a harbinger of more generous wage agreements, since the negotiators were freed, at least for the time being, from any government-imposed pay restraints.[62] By November 1974 the average level of wage settlements stood 25 per cent higher than it had a year before. The reason why this happened was that the government persisted in its belief that wage demands would moderate as the implementation of its side of the social contract was felt at shopfloor level, while 'trade union leaders hoped that moderation would come of itself, and if it did not, that it would be engineered from within the trade union movement'.[63]

It would be unrealistic to imagine that delegates to the AGM of the NUR, in July 1974, would be immune from these influences. The wages resolution, which gained the unanimous support of the seventy-seven delegates, began by giving a nod in the direction of loyalty to the Labour government but continued by expressing the determination of railwaymen not to be left behind:

That this AGM, bearing in mind the need to give support to the policy measures of the Labour Government, nevertheless feels that as living standards were eroded because of the policies of the last government, our wage levels must be maintained.

We also consider that an important factor in the economy and productivity growth of the country is based on decent wage levels and living standards of working people being maintained. In order to meet this condition and protect the position of our members we instruct the NEC to make an immediate application for a substantial increase in salaries and wages on behalf of all staff for whom this union has negotiating rights.[64]

When the framers of the resolution included the words 'living standards were eroded' they were mindful of the fact that under phases 2 and 3 railwaymen's wage increases did not fully compensate for the rise in the cost of living. Retail prices were rising rapidly that summer and by December 1974 were 19 per cent above the level of December 1973. At the meeting of the RSNC on 14 February 1975 when the union presented its case for a substantial increase in the level of wages, it claimed that allowing for projected increases in retail prices up to July 1975, a rise of 27 per cent would be needed to restore the real wages of railwaymen to their level in 1972 – the last year in which rates of pay were determined under conditions of free collective bargaining.[65]

Although the three rail unions had been at loggerheads over the pay restructuring exercise, they worked closely together in pressing the BRB to make a generous settlement in 1975. As early as 5 November 1974 their representatives met at Unity House, where they agreed that each union would submit a claim for 'a substantial increase'. At further meetings on 1, 8 and 18 April they agreed to reject the Board's offer of 20 per cent and to demand that the cost of pay restructuring under RSNT Decision No. 42 should not be included in the cost of the 1975 pay settlement. At the next meeting of the RSNC, on 22 April, the Board faced with this common front of the unions raised its offer to 21·2 per cent. But when this was rejected, it referred the claim to the RSNT which in its Decision No. 45 of 29 May 1975 recommended that an increase of 27·5 per cent should be given. However, since the claim for 27 per cent had been submitted in February retail prices had soared further and other large groups of workers had been awarded very substantial wage and salary increases. These included a 32 per cent rise for 500,000 civil servants and a 31 per cent rise for 100,000 power workers. Thus, when the negotiating sub-committee of the NUR reported to the executive on 2 June, it recommended (by a majority) that the union should now press for a 30 per cent increase and that a national railway strike should be called from 00.01 hours on Monday 23 June if this demand was not conceded.[66] Meanwhile the two other railway unions, while having some reservations about RSNT Decision No. 45, were prepared to accept it.[67]

Nearly a fortnight passed of the three-week period before the strike was due to begin. Then on 14 June Sid Weighell informed the executive that Harold Wilson had asked to see him with the union's president, David Bowman, the previous evening and had told them that he would like to see the union's full executive at 8 p.m. the next day, 14 June. The decision to accept the invitation was unanimous and the traditional drinks and sandwiches were provided at Number 10, Downing Street that evening. In the discussions the railwaymen stressed their determination to achieve 'a just settlement', and Harold Wilson and his senior Cabinet Ministers emphasised the extreme gravity of the NUR's decision to strike. Back at Unity House on 16 June, the executive passed a conciliatory resolution:

> That having seriously considered what was said at No. 10 Downing Street by the Prime Minister and other senior Cabinet Ministers, we recognise the serious effects which would result from a rail strike. At the same time we would emphasise that the NUR claim is a just one. Further, we are prepared to negotiate at any time to see how our case can be met.[68]

Thereafter events moved quickly. On the morning of 17 June the General Secretary and President met Michael Foot and Tony Crosland, respectively Secretaries of State for Employment and for the Environment, and were asked whether the members of the EC would be willing to resume discussions with the Board. The executive gave its unanimous approval to the proposal later that day. Intensive negotiations with members of the Board were held at meetings of the RSNC from 18–20 June, inclusive, and resulted in a settlement which was to be applied in two stages. In the first stage, the increase of 27·5 per cent recommended in the RSNT Decision No. 45 was to apply from 28 April 1975, and this was to be followed by a second-stage increase of 2·5 per cent, making a total of 30 per cent, applicable from 4 August 1975. Temporary allowances, tapering from £1·30p to 5p, were to bring minimum basic rates to £36·00, on the understanding that these would be absorbed in the next pay award. The final stage in the progress of equal pay for women was to come on 29 December 1975 – two days within the limit imposed by the Equal Pay Act 1970. The executive has no hesitation in giving its unanimous approval of these arrangements, and in a further resolution voted its 'appreciation of the unstinted efforts of the head office staff' in helping the union's negotiators.[69]

The reason why the power workers and others got away with an award of over 30 per cent without needing to resort to arbitration, whereas the satisfaction of the NUR claim required both arbitration and the post-arbitration routine of beer and sandwiches at Number 10, Downing Street was partly a matter of timing. By the late spring of 1975 the Labour government, elected the previous year on a policy of opposition to statutory control of wages, was becoming alarmed at the size of wage settlements and was earnestly considering how they might be moderated. Likewise the TUC was discussing 'not *whether* but *how* incomes policy should be implemented'.[70]

On 1 July 1975 came the inevitable announcement by Denis Healey, Chancellor of the Exchequer, in the House of Commons, committing the government to holding the increase of wages and salaries during the next pay round to 10 per cent. The government White Paper, *The Attack on Inflation* (Cmnd 6151), followed ten days later. It included guidelines for pay settlements up to 1 August 1976, set out in an extract from the TUC document, *The Development of the Social Contract*. The proposal, originally put forward by Jack Jones, General Secretary of the TGWU, was that there should be a limit of a flat-rate £6 on pay increases in the twelve months from 1 August 1975 and that there should be no increases for those with incomes exceeding £8,500 a year. The BRB and the railway trade unions conformed to these new pay guidelines after sorting out the difficulty that settlement dates for pay increases under the 1975 pay agreements – 28 April and 4 August – did not correspond to the starting date (1 August) of the government's new pay policy. In the event the BRB agreed to pay the £6 increase from 28 April 1975, and this plan met the approval of the NUR and TSSA executives.[71] ASLEF had reservations; they wanted the 2·5 per cent increase introduced on 4 August 1975 carried through a full year and that this increase should form part of the basic rate for enhancement purposes. However, the RSNT, in its Decision No. 47, endorsed the BRB proposals, which had been accepted by the two other railway unions on the ground that the adoption of the ASLEF plan would lead to complications and anomalies.[72]

On 5 May 1976 agreement was reached between the government and the TUC on a second stage of the Social Contract, and on 16 June a special congress of the TUC held in London agreed by 9,262,000 to 531,000 votes the proposal that there should be a limit of 5 per cent in the increase on total earnings, with a cash minimum of £2·50 and an upper cash maximum of £4 a week, for the period 1 August 1976 to 31 July 1977. Twelve days before the date of the special congress, with the TUC General Council's report before it, the NUR executive was equally divided – 11–11 votes, with one member absent on union business and one on leave – between accepting or rejecting TUC policy.[73] Faced with this deadlock, Sidney Weighell proposed to the EC that, in accordance with rule, the matter should be decided at the forthcoming AGM and that, in the meantime, the union's delegation to the special TUC on 16 June should abstain from voting on the question of the renewal of the Social Contract. The executive agreed unanimously.[74]

On 14 July 1976 AGM delegates at Paignton had straightforward alternatives put before them. They could support *either* the resolution: 'That this AGM accepts the Social Contract 1976/77', moved by Tom Ham, a shopman of Derby 3 branch, *or* the amendment: 'That this AGM emphatically rejects the Social Contract', moved by C. C. Galvin, a clerical officer of Kings Cross. Tom Ham reminded delegates of the value of the understanding between the unions and the Labour government and pointed to the benefits brought to labour by such measures as the Trade Union and Labour Relations Act 1974 and the Employment Protection Act 1975. On the other hand, C. C. Galvin claimed that to continue to support existing policies which had the effect of keeping wage increases below the rise in the cost of living would alienate union leadership from the rank and file. He suggested cuts in arms expenditure and import controls as alternative policies. Sidney Weighell, in supporting the resolution, claimed that there was 'no credible alternative'. 'The Tories might give us free collective bargaining', he said, 'but they would also give us three million unemployed'. When a recorded vote was taken at the end of a lively debate the resolution was carried by the handsome margin of 54–22 votes, while the amendment was defeated by a similar margin.[75]

The pay settlement for 1977–8 was achieved with little difficulty, since both parties were committed to the government's Phase 2 guidelines. In December 1976 the NUR handed in to the BRB a formal claim for an increase in wages and salaries which was discussed at a meeting of the RSNC on 16 February 1977. BR agreed to pay 5 per cent on basic wages up to a maximum of weekly increase of £4 for any member of staff. These proposals were accepted unanimously by the executive at its meeting on 1 March. The union's claim for improved sickness and redundancy arrangements and for the reduction of the qualifying period of staff seeking to obtain established status was granted at a further RSNC meeting later that month.[76]

At Ayr, in July 1977, AGM delegates had the choice between supporting a March branch resolution

That this AGM recommends that there should be an orderly and gradual withdrawal from the Social Contract. We also realise that to carry on with a policy of incremental increases, non-enhanceable, will lead us nowhere, and so we instruct the NEC to a gradual free collective bargaining situation.

or of endorsing a Glasgow 5 resolution, which attempted to spell
out a constructive alternative:

That this AGM calls for the abolition of the Social Contract
and an alternative policy of economic growth. This can only be
achieved by
(1) Freezing prices, rents and fares (particularly to protect our
own industry).
(2) Raising wages, pensions and benefits.
(3) An increase in industrial investment in productivity sectors,
controlling imports and stopping the export of capital.
(4) Challenge the multi-nationals and sterling manipulators in
order to shift the balance of power to the working class.

Mr Hodgson, a guard from Peterborough, who moved the March
resolution, conceded that prices had run away from the level of
wages, but argued that the Social Contract had given 'a fair
measure of stability generally'. He pleaded with delegates 'not to
abandon the Labour government'. J. Scanlan, a driver from
Glasgow, moving the alternative resolution, denied that wage rises
were the main cause of the inflationary spiral. Real wages had
fallen and 'a further wages deal would inevitably mean another cut
in living standards creating political conditions for the certain
return of the Tories'. Russell Tuck, Senior Assistant General
Secretary, deputising for Sidney Weighell who was unwell, reminded delegates that on every previous occasion when there had
been a sudden lifting of restraints there were wage explosions, and
on this occasion 'an immediate return to free collective bargaining
would have appalling and immediate results on the economy leading to the downfall of the Labour government'. They should certainly demand 'direct action by the government on prices', but
since his firm priority was 'continued support for the Labour
government', he urged suport for the March resolution. Most
delegates agreed. The voting was: for, 45; against, 32, the Glasgow
resolution being defeated by 44–32.[77]
The same AGM was nevertheless aware of the necessity for
keeping up the pressure for improvements in money wages to
offset the ever-rising cost of living. Delegates therefore passed, by
the impressive majority of 75–2 votes, a Port Talbot No. 1 branch
resolution instructing the EC to submit an application for an increase in wages and salaries for all staff for whom the union had
neogtiating rights. On this occasion it was government guidelines
alone which put restraints on the negotiations over the next pay
settlement. At Blackpool, on 7 September 1977, the TUC had

approved a composite resolution in favour of 'an immediate return to free collective bargaining at the end of the second stage of the Social Contract'. The Callaghan government, therefore, went ahead with its own incomes policy. In its White Paper, *The Attack on Inflation after 31 July 1977* (Cmnd 6882), it stated that apart from self-financing productivity schemes, the general level of new settlements 'should be moderate enough to secure that the national earnings increase is no more than 10 per cent'. Both the BRB and the NUR were prepared to settle within these limits. At a meeting of the RSNC, on 14 April 1978, the BRB submitted the following proposals to apply for the twelve months from 24 April 1978 :

(1) to restore the basic rates of pay of August 1975;
(2) to increase these rates by 16 per cent;
(3) to withdraw the second earnings supplement;
(4) to maintain the first-stage non-enhanceable supplement of £6;
(5) to establish a minimum earnings level of £50 for staff aged 20 and over;
(6) to increase the London allowance by 10 per cent from £318 per annum to £350 per annum.

The offer was made on the understanding that there would be no improvement in sick pay, established status or pension arrangements in the twelve-month period. The executive gave unanimous approval to these proposals.[78]

On 13 July 1978 at Llandudno the supreme governing body of the NUR had its last opportunity to debate incomes policy before the defeat of Labour at the polls in May of the following year. The discussion centred round a resolution by Teesside No. 3 branch moved by T. H. Hartley, a track machineman of Northallerton :

That this AGM calls upon the trade union movement to enter into a continuing social contract with the Labour government, believing this is the way to a fairer society and real economic justice for our members.
These discussions with the Labour government should cover :
(1) Economic strategy, which will include incomes and investment, North Sea oil revenues, etc.
(2) Social services, including houses and hospitals.
(3) Education.
(4) Extension of public ownership.

In fact, all social and economic features which affect the everyday lives of the British people.

The opponents of the continuation of the Social Contract proposed an amendment to delete the words 'a continuing Social Contract' from the opening sentence of the resolution and to insert in their place the word 'discussions', and to delete the word 'incomes' from item 1. T. H. Hartley drew attention to the fact that under the Labour government's incomes policy the rate of inflation had been reduced; between May 1977 and May 1978 it had fallen to 7·7 per cent, with the result that under the previous pay award railwaymen had had an increase in their real wages. The result of the alternative policy would be that those 'with the strongest muscle' would come off best and 'those with the least bargaining power' would be left behind. F. J. Juett, in moving the amendment, reminded delegates that under rule 1, clause 4(a) the job of the union was 'to obtain and maintain' a decent wage for its members, but under a policy of support for the Social Contract real wages of railwaymen had fallen. Until prices and profits were controlled (as well as wages), there could be no just Social Contract.

Sidney Weighell, in a decisive intervention at the close of the debate, recalled the events of 1975 when the union won a two-stage settlement of 30 per cent – the highest rate of increase ever negotiated for railwaymen. Looking back from the perspective of three years later he could see 'just how quickly the benefits of that increase were eaten away'. In the end 'the combined effects of increased taxation, higher national insurance contributions and a rate of inflation which peaked at 27 per cent' actually meant that railwaymen were worse off by the time of the next pay settlement. He challenged the philosophy of those who wished to return to free collective bargaining:

I cannot see how members of the Labour Party who call themselves socialists can change their views when they come to the question of the determination of wages. They want a socialist planning to deal with the rest of our resources but they want a free for all market system about pay. I cannot reconcile these conflicting viewpoints. . . I think that all of us should reject this philosophy of the pig trough which advocates that those with the biggest snouts get the biggest share.

He was not advocating a policy simply of restraint on pay: collective bargaining, he maintained, should take the form of

mobilisation of the strength of 11,500,000 members of unions
affiliated to the TUC acting through the TUC bargaining with
the government of the day.
  We should be prepared to sit down with the Labour government to discuss a joint plan for the next twelve months. These
discussions should cover a whole range of economic decisions,
not only affecting pay, but investment, social services, unemployment – in fact the whole social and economic fabric of
national policy.

It had been a good debate, lasting throughout the morning session.
The rejection of the amendment, by 51–26 votes, and the approval
of the resolution for the continuation of a modified form of social
contract, by 50–27 votes, was a decisive victory for the platform
and especially significant when viewed against that summer's
strong upsurge of rank and file opinion in other unions against the
continuance of any form of wage restraint.[79]
  However, when it was the TUC's turn to debate the same broad
issues on 6 September that year, Sidney Weighell and the NUR
delegation were unsuccessful in gaining support for resolution 75,
calling for 'a new approach to pay within the framework of an
economic contract with the government', while composite resolution 12, expressing opposition 'to any form of restrictive government incomes policy', won the support of a clear majority of the
delegates.[80] The government, therefore, proceeded on its own in an
endeavour to implement the Phase 4 pay policy set out in the
White Paper, *Winning the Battle against Inflation* (Cmnd 7293),
which it published on 21 July 1978. A 5 per cent limit on earnings
with a continuation of the twelve-month rule between settlements
was decreed.
  Instructed by the AGM to submit a claim for 'a substantial
increase in salaries and wages', the NUR's officers presented such
a claim to a meeting of the RSNC on 7 November 1978. Detailed
submissions followed at another meeting of the Council on 20
January 1979. Both parties began negotiations with the assumption
of reaching a settlement within the government's guidelines; but
with the passing of time it became apparent that the Callaghan
5 per cent wage dam was not holding. Most notably the Ford
Motor Co. breached the pay defences with a 17 per cent settlement on 22 November, following a nine-week-long strike. Public-
sector workers were achieving wage advances nearer the 10 per
cent than the 5 per cent level. Furthermore, at a meeting of the
RSNC held on 21 February, the TSSA representatives drew attention to the fact that the retail price index had risen by 9·3 per cent

in the preceding twelve months. At this stage the NUR invited the other two rail unions to discussions on the pay bargaining. Agreement was reached on a policy to be adopted at the final stage of the negotiations.

Pay negotiations in the early weeks of 1979 were, however, bedevilled through differences of view between the unions on policies for rewarding extra responsibility and productivity. In the winter of 1977–8 some 1,600 guards who were being required to collect fares from passengers boarding trains at unmanned stations were refusing to carry out these new tasks until they were paid more money in compensation. To restore industrial peace and prevent further loss of revenue from fares, the NUR and the BRB reached agreement in January 1978 on a scale of extra payments for the men concerned, who formed only 8 per cent of the total number of guards employed by BR. But no sooner had this agreement been reached than the other railway unions demanded extra responsibility payments for drivers and for salaried staff. The RSNT, in its Award No. 60, defended the NUR–BRB agreement. Lord McCarthy, the tribunal chairman, and his two colleagues commented :

> We have observed the pay train guards at work and have been able to contrast what they do with what we know of the work of other guards. Our observations lead us to believe that the payment made under the new agreement can be regarded as compensation for additional responsibilities over and above those undertaken by the generality of guards.

It should be emphasised that the total number of BRB guards was 12,000, and that the tribunal was not in favour of extra payment being made to any but the 1,600 of them who had been given extra responsibilities. The claim made by the other unions was for extra payments to all those in the footplate and salaried grades. These broader claims the tribunal rejected :

> If we were to decide that a separate payment of a given size should be paid to footplate staff, the way would be open to further claims and counter claims on behalf of other occupational groups – many of whom might well argue that their contribution to productivity was at least as great as that of the footplate grades . . . a strong argument can be made out for regarding the contribution of the workforce to improved productivity in a way that facilitates a team approach.

The tribunal did, however, see the justification for extra payment being made to drivers of trains whose speeds exceeded 100 m.p.h. and it therefore recommended that these additional rewards should be made available. This recommendation was in line with NUR policy which was that all railwaymen who were called upon to perform extra duties should be given more pay. In the case of drivers the NUR asserted this warranted additional rewards for drivers of high-speed trains. The basis of the extra remuneration, however, should be train classification rather than grade classification.[81]

The RSNT Award No. 60 did not satisfy ASLEF demands for a 10 per cent productivity bonus for all footplate staff, 'in recognition of past acceptance of additional responsibility and changed methods of work'. Following unofficial action by Southern Region drivers, a series of official national one-day strikes by ASLEF members took place in mid-January 1979 until the NUR and ASLEF agreed to refer the claim to the RSNT. In its Decision No. 62 of April 1979 the tribunal rejected the claim for a 10 per cent bonus for all footplatemen, but agreed to a 'driver's responsibility allowance' expressed as 5 per cent of the driver's rate for the turn in question. The payment did not apply to drivers confined to shunting duties. There were many other outstanding issues, but the ground was now clear for the main pay settlement of 1979 to be concluded. The agreement with the BRB, backdated to 23 April 1979, gave 'new money' increase of over 9 per cent, plus 2 per cent, representing consolidation of the BR performance-linked productivity payment. A railman's basic rate rose from £44·70 to £48·95 per week. Drivers of trains received £2·50 in respect of the RSNT's 5 per cent award, bringing basic rates up to £78·20 a week. The top-class signalman received £88·85.

VI

By the time delegates assembled for the next AGM at Paignton at the end of June 1979, there had been a change of government, with Margaret Thatcher heading a team of mainly right-wing Ministers. The new administration completely rejected any idea of a social contract with labour or a national incomes policy. In its Election manifesto the Conservative Party declared that 'in the great public corporations pay bargaining should be governed, as in private ones, by what each can afford'. However, the new Secretary of State for Industry, Sir Keith Joseph, imposed severe financial restraints on public industries and wrote to inform the national industry chairmen that he expected them to bear these restraints in mind when they made their wage settlements.[82]

The AGM delegates at Paignton debated a resolution on national pay policy which had been drafted before the change in government. It could have been amended, but was left as originally drafted:

> That this AGM reiterates its policy as laid down in the 1978 AGM decision on item 10 and instructs the NEC to submit resolutions on these lines to both the TUC and the Labour Party Conference.

The debate revealed that there was some confusion as to what the resolution implied. Both the mover, D. Shepherd, a guard from Severn Tunnel Junction, and the seconder, K. Brining, a relief signalman of York No. 5 branch, suggested that an agreed incomes policy was negotiable with the Tory government. K. Brining said, 'What I am concerned about and what this resolution says, is that we must have a continuing dialogue with the government despite its political colour.' Sidney Weighell did not agree that this was what the resolution implied: 'You are not asking anything of the sort . . . talking to a Tory government.' He went on:

> Let it be clearly understood that when we talk about the merits or otherwise of the continuance of the social contract with the government that we are talking about a Labour government. That is what the resolution says. It says, go to the TUC and the Labour Party conference. What is that? It is part of our movement, is it not? For the benefit of those outside our movement who ask why no social contract with the Tory government, the answer is quite simple. We do not talk the same language, and I do not intend as part of this union to go to talk to the Tories about a social contract.

He said it was important to defend the railway industry and railwaymen against the Tory attack, but it 'was even more vital to prepare for the time when Labour is returned to power'. It was in this sense – that the Labour Party would have to make up its mind on an incomes policy – that the resolution was carried by 48–29 votes.[83]

That autumn, in the absence of a government incomes policy, higher wage settlements became the norm. In November the Ford Motor Co. offered its staff a twenty-one per cent rise; farmworkers accepted 19·5 per cent and the miners said 'Yes' to 20 per cent. It was in the light of these developments that the NUR lodged a claim for a rise of 20 per cent on basic wages, a reduction of the working week, longer holidays and extra payments for working unsocial hours. In the agreement reached at a meeting of the RSNC on 29 April 1980 the BRB conceded a 20 per cent rise on basic pay (effective from 5 May 1980) and a reduction in the working hours of wages staff from forty to thirty-nine, with effect from 1 November 1981. Salaried staff hours were to be reduced from thirty-eight to thirty-seven from the same date. In addition all railwaymen with two years' service were to be entitled to four weeks holiday with pay commencing with the 1981 leave period. At the AGM in St Peter Port, Guernsey, that July, Sidney Weighell explained how these improvements had been made possible. In response to a question in the House of Commons the Prime Minister, Margaret Thatcher, had said, 'I hope that the Railways Board will not bend to the demands of the NUR. We are not going to put up fares and freight charges in order to pay railmen if they get beyond the limit we think reasonable'. However that was reckoning without the dispute in the steel industry. The General Secretary was frank with delegates. 'The only reason we got 20 per cent', he said, 'was because of that thirteen weeks of the steel strike and they could not stand up to a railway strike.'[84] Whatever the reasons for the NUR's success, it did not result in the standard of living of railwaymen soaring to dizzy heights. As was the case with numerous previous pay negotiations, the union was involved in many hours of hard bargaining simply to try to avert a decline in the real incomes of its members. The 20 per cent settlement of the spring of 1980 looked a generous one, until it was compared with the 21 per cent rise in the retail price index since the previous pay settlement of April 1979.

CHAPTER 7

NEGOTIATING UNDER THE
INDUSTRIAL RELATIONS ACT, 1971-2

I

A PRIMARY objective of the ASRS before 1913 was to gain union recognition from the railway companies, and the establishment of a formal system of collective bargaining for determining the pay and conditions of service of all railway workers. Partial recognition of the unions by the railway companies came in 1914 with the setting up of the revised conciliation scheme and a more complete endorsement of the principle of collective bargaining in the form of a more comprehensive agreement followed in 1919. Part IV, para. 61, of the Railways Act 1921, gave statutory recognition to the Central and National Wages Boards, which were made up of an equal number of representatives of railway unions on the one side, and management on the other. The negotiating machinery for employees in the railway workshops came into operation in 1927. When the negotiating arrangements for conciliation staff were reviewed between 1933-5, the revision mainly took the form of changing the name of the 'Central Wages Board' to the 'Railway Staff National Council' and the 'National Wages Board' to the 'Railway Staff National Tribunal'; the essential function of each body remained virtually unchanged. The establishment of the Railway Staff Joint Council as a new preliminary negotiating stage in 1956 was primarily intended to syphon off the less important negotiations from the RSNC, which continued to deal with national claims made by the unions and management. By the mid-1960s, therefore, the negotiating machinery had stood the test of more than forty years and had made an important contribution to the industry's impressive record in industrial relations.

In January 1966 both the NUR and the BRB gave written evidence to the Donovan Commission on Trade Unions and Employers' Associations set up by the Wilson government in the previous year. Sidney Greene and Sir Stanley Raymond, Chairman of the British Railways Board, also gave oral evidence. Both organisations and their representatives were agreed that the machinery of negotiation for the determination of wages and conditions of service on the railways had worked well and they saw no good reason for altering its basic characteristics.

In its written evidence the union stated, in prosaic fashion, that the negotiating machinery in operation had proved to be 'adequate for settling any questions governing rates of pay and conditions of employment'.[1] The written evidence of the Railways Board was equally unequivocal. It found 'little wrong' with the machinery itself and considered that the framework, in its essentials established in 1919, had 'stood the test of time'. It maintained that the effectiveness of the machinery could be measured to some extent by the volume of industrial disputes on the railways. In the seventeen years 1948–65 there had been only two official strikes. The first of these, in 1955, affected only the members of ASLEF; the second was the one-day strike of 3 October 1962, called in protest against workshop and other closures. In the ten years, 1955–64, 1,323,772 man-days' work were lost through strikes on the railways, but 95 per cent of this loss was attributable to the two official strikes. The average annual loss in the other eight years was 7,000 man-days, which was extremely small when related to a labour force exceeding half a million persons over the greater part of the period. 'Railwaymen generally', the Board asserted, 'display a high standard of industrial discipline.'[2] Sir Stanley Raymond, in oral evidence, conceded that the unofficial striker was the problem:

But to take him to law, especially in our case where it would mean taking whole sections of staff to law, I do not think that is practicable. I think some other way of getting greater industrial discipline would have to be found. My own view is that it would have to be by agreement with the trade unions because one has to strengthen the position of unions in the matter.[3]

Although in the railway industry there was a measure of satisfaction about the past record of industrial relations, the situation was very different in a number of other sectors of the economy. As the country's balance of payments deteriorated in 1962–4, a deterioration for which the loss of working days through strikes was held partly to blame, increasing attention was focused on demarcation disputes and unofficial strikes in the engineering industry and particularly in motor-car manufacture. These circumstances led to Harold Wilson's decision to appoint the above-mentioned Donovan Commission in the hope that it would recommend reforms in labour law and industrial relations practice which would help to reduce the number of working days lost through strikes.

In the event both the Prime Minister and Barbara Castle, Secretary of State for Employment and Productivity, were disappointed with the findings of the Donovan Report, published in 1968. It stressed the merits of the voluntary system of industrial relations and rejected important proposals for compulsory 'cooling-off' periods and compulsory strike ballots. Nevertheless, there were increasingly strident demands, through the media, that the government should do something to curb the power of the unions. Disputes such as the seamen's strike of the summer of 1966 and the demarcation disputes in the Girling Brake factory in 1968, greatly influenced government thinking. Despite the Donovan Commission's reservations about increased legal intervention in industrial relations, Barbara Castle, opted for a policy of greater legislative control. Her plans, set forth in the White Paper, *In Place of Strife*, published in 1969, aroused intense controversy within the labour movement.

In the NUR rank and file opinion expressed by delegates to the AGM at Plymouth, on 7 July 1966, was overwhelmingly against any changes in the law of industrial relations. Delegates carried, by 60–6 votes, a resolution opposing 'legislation or any other measures which restricted the freedom of workers to withdraw their labour'.[4] On 17 February 1969, when the executive first considered *In Place of Strife*, two left-wing members, Bowman and Booth, supported a resolution of outright rejection of the White Paper on the grounds that the introduction of penal legislation would worsen labour relations. But by a 12–11 vote the majority favoured referring the document to the political sub-committee for a report to the regular March meeting of the EC. The sub-committee reported that there were some helpful proposals in the White Paper, including the right to trade union recognition by employers, the right of an employee to join a trade union and guarantees for protection against unfair dismissal. On the other hand, it declared its emphatic opposition to the proposed financial penalties on unions which refused to register with the Registrar of Trade Unions and Employers' Associations, as well as to the proposed compulsory 'cooling-off' periods in unconstitutional strikes and the Minister's power to order compulsory ballots before strikes were allowed to take place. Some members of the EC still wanted a blanket condemnation of the new proposals, but the report of the sub-committee was endorsed by 11–8 votes.[5]

By the time the delegates assembled for the AGM in Llandudno in the second week of July 1969, the Labour government's Industrial Relations Bill, which had incorporated many of the proposals in the earlier White Paper, had been abandoned. The revolt of the trade union group in the House of Commons was backed by a sufficient number of other Labour MPs to ensure that the Bill would not be passed. In substitution the government reached agreement with the TUC on *A Programme for Action* in which, *inter alia*, the TUC undertook to play a larger part in resolving jurisdictional disputes and in encouraging union mergers. Thus, the AGM public resolution pledging the union by all means in its power to oppose any legislation designed to restrict or interfere with the right to strike or impose conditions limiting the present rights of trade unions, lacked the degree of urgency it would otherwise have had. In the debate, Sidney Greene took the opportunity of commending to delegates the *Programme for Action* which, as a member of the General Council of the TUC, he had helped to draft. His recipe for improved industrial relations included greater consultation between management and workers – 'if a firm is going bankrupt there is consultation with the workers right away. Why should not all the books be put on the table if a company is doing well financially?' – and the closed shop as a means of achieving greater industrial discipline. In the latter context he had in mind the unofficial action of signalmen in the Sheffield, Doncaster and Tilbury districts, some of whom were members of the Union of Railway Signalmen. His comment that their action was not doing the image of the trade union movement any good was greeted with applause by the delegates.[6]

By July 1970 when the next AGM of the union met in Inverness, the Conservatives had returned to power under the leadership of Edward Heath. Through the 1950s Conservative Party leadership pursued a policy of 'non-interventionism' in industrial relations. In 1957 a Tory MP who demanded the appointment of a Royal Commission to inquire into the practices of the trade unions was rebuked by his Chief Whip, Edward Heath, and at the party conference in 1961 the platform put up a Tory trade unionist to denounce as 'shocking' a proposal for an inquiry into the unions, with legislation to follow on the basis of the inquiry's recommendations.[7] But by the mid-1960s the right wing of the party, which had long been pressing for legislative intervention to regulate industrial relations practices, had gained the ascendancy and the 1970 General Election campaign was fought – and won – on pledges to curb the power of the unions. It was claimed that the outgoing Labour administration had surrendered to the trade unions and that a firm hand was needed to deal with industrial unrest.

Such assertions cut no ice with NUR AGM delegates meeting in Inverness. A resolution, moved by Stan Mills of Croydon No. 1 branch, pledged the union's opposition to 'legislation designed to restrict or interfere with the right to strike or to impose limits on the rights of trade unions'. In his contribution to the debate Sidney Greene took a non-aggressive line. He assured delegates that he was prepared to talk to any government. 'I am not coming out of my corner fighting', he said. But to the members of the new Cabinet he warned: 'Life will be as difficult as you care to make it.' He foresaw immense difficulties, if an attempt was made to bring the law into industrial relations:

It is not legislation that we require . . . I would say to the government, for goodness sake, think again! This is not our method of running industrial relations in this country.[8]

C. F. Beer, for the Exeter Rail branch, thought that there might be a case for legislation to guarantee a worker's right, through a trade union, to negotiate conditions of employment. But his resolution was turned down by 69–8 votes after H. Keift, of Swansea, warned that if such a law was enacted the government would require, in return, its pound of flesh in the form of legally binding collective agreements.[9]

II

In December 1970 the Conservative government published its Industrial Relations Bill which, with some modifications, became law in August of the following year. It provided for the setting up of a National Industrial Relations Court which was given the authority, on request from the Secretary of State for Employment, to order 'cooling-off' periods and strike ballots and could impose fines for any of a long list of 'unfair industrial practices'. It banned the pre-entry closed shop and proposed, in substitution, the agency shop under which a union which had the majority of the workers in an establishment would be granted sole negotiating rights. Collective agreements were assumed to be legally binding unless both parties to an agreement specifically declared they were not so. Unions were invited to register with the Registrar of Trade Unions and Employers' Associations, if they did not wish to incur the financial penalties of non-registration; but the Registrar could order the amendment of their rules as a condition of a union's inclusion in his list. Among the rights guaranteed in the Bill was that of an individual to belong or not to belong to a trade union; his right to compensation in the case of unfair dismissal; and the right of a trade union having the majority support of the workforce in an establishment to receive recognition from an employer.

When the terms of the Industrial Relations Bill became known late in 1970, trade union reaction to the Heath government proposals took a variety of forms. Frank Chapple, of the Electrical, Electronic, Telecommunications and Plumbing Union, took the strict 'constitutionalist' view that since the Bill was being introduced by a democratically elected Parliament the way to remove tt, once it had been enacted, was through the ballot box in a General Election. On the other hand, some union leaders, such as Eddie Marsden, President of the Construction section of the AUEW, and many of the militant rank and file who organised themselves through the Liaison Committee for the Defence of Trade Unions, favoured the calling of a series of nationwide one-day strikes in an attempt to force the government to abandon its Bill. In between these two extremes stood the majority of members of the General Council of the TUC, who adopted a more liberally interpreted 'constitutionalist' view. By means of the dissemination of literature and the holding of mass meetings and demonstrations, the public would be informed of the reasons for trade unionists' opposition to the Bill and support for its outright rejection, or its substantial amendment, would be enlisted. But there was to be no resort to a general strike in an effort to destroy the Bill as it was argued that this would be counterproductive and would lead to a 'Who governs Britain?' appeal from the government to the electorate.[10]

NUR policy broadly corresponded with that of the majority of the TUC General Council of which Sidney Greene was Vice-Chairman. In order not to arouse anti-union hostility, the TUC arranged for the mass demonstration against the Bill to take place in London on a Sunday – 22 February 1971 – rather than on a working day.[11] The NUR executive decided unanimously to mobilise the union's full support for this form of protest and urged those branches possessing banners to bring them to the march. The occasion produced one of the most comprehensive displays of union banners seen in Britain since the Second World War.

In the Fairfield Halls, Croydon, on the morning of 18 March 1971 there assembled the first special congress of the TUC to be summoned since the time of the General Strike in 1926. Its purpose was to consider the strategy and tactics to be followed in the campaign against the forthcoming Industrial Relations Act. (The Bill was passing through its concluding stages when the Congress met and received royal assent in August.) Delegates gave their views on seven recommendations made by the General Council. These were that affiliated unions were 'strongly advised' not to register with the Registrar of Trade Unions; they were asked to support the General Council's appeal to the Labour Party for an 'explicit assurance' that the next Labour government would repeal the Industrial Relations Act; they were to take steps to ensure that collective agreements with employers were declared not legally binding; they would continue to observe the TUC's Bridlington 'no-poaching of members' agreement of 1939; their members were to refuse to take up appointments with any of the statutory bodies; such as the National Industrial Relations Court, set up under the Act; they were asked to endorse the General Council's offer of support for unions suffering penalties under the Act; and lastly to agree that 'Congress should concentrate its support behind the positive recommendations in this report and should preserve the unity of purpose that [had] hitherto characterised the campaign of opposition'.[12]

In the NUR executive seven members agreed with Sidney Greene in supporting all seven of the General Council's recommendations, but sixteen others, while endorsing items 1–6, found recommendation 7 weak and nebulous. They believed that industrial action would be necessary for trade unions to effectively demonstrate their opposition to the Act.[13] Thus when Sidney Greene spoke at the Croydon Congress, he explained that the union backed the TUC on items 1–6, but felt unable to support recommendation 7, since it wanted to keep its options open. In carrying out recommendation 1 against registration, and recommendation 4 on observing the Bridlington rules, it might be brought in conflict with the law, and industrial action might then be needed to defend members' interests.[14] Nevertheless, the NUR support for the General Council on the key issue of non-registration was of great importance as many unions, apprehensive about the loss of income-tax concessions on the earnings of their provident funds or fearful of the competition for members from rival unions which did decide to register, voted against the General Council's recommendation 1 which was carried by the relatively narrow margin of 5,055,000 votes to 4,284,000. The NUR delegation's vote helped to tip the balance in favour of the ultimate success of the whole campaign since, had recommendation 1 been rejected and had this been followed by a stampede to register, the opposition to the Act would have crumbled into ineffectiveness. The NUR was not alone in opposition to recommendation 7, the voting in this case being 5,366,000 in favour of the General Council's wording, and 3,992,000 against. Recommendations 2–6, inclusive, were carried without dissent.[15]

When the issue of registration as a trade union under the forthcoming Industrial Relations Act was debated at the AGM of the NUR on 14 July 1971, C. F. Robbins, a supervisor from Wolverhampton, warned that failure to register could involve the union in 'heavy fines on decisions taken, even by local representatives'. He advocated registration as a wise precaution. C. Wynd, a relief signalman from Perth, who moved a resolution from the Dundee branch opposing registration, admitted that non-registration would cost the union a lot of money – in his estimation £150,000 a year – largely through the loss of exemption from income tax and capital gains tax on provident fund investment income. But he believed that registration was the cornerstone of the Act and that if unions refused to register, as they were legally fully entitled to do, the new law would be largely ineffective. (This was, of course, also the view of Robert Carr, Secretary of State for Employment and Productivity, who told the members of the Industrial Society on 6 November 1970 that, if the unions were to refuse to co-operate at all, he would have to admit the Act 'would hardly be very effective'.)[16] The overwhelming majority of delegates felt that the right policy was not to register and they carried the Dundee resolution by 74–2 votes.[17] Mr Wynd had underestimated the annual cost to the union of a policy of non-registration. Sidney Greene informed the executive just over a year later than the true figure was £250,000.[18]

Non-registration also led to a change in the union rules. After taking legal advice, the executive decided to divide the union's assets into two categories, 'protected' and 'unprotected'. Under section 154(4) of the Industrial Relations Act the protected funds would be safe against judgements in civil courts proceedings, while the unprotected funds would be available to support industrial action. Once the division had been effected, the two funds were to be kept entirely separate. The executive agreed that a new rule 8A should be inserted in the rule book, establishing General, Orphan and Political protected funds.[19] The separation between the two types of fund came to an end with the repeal of the Industrial Relations Act in 1974.

In accordance with resolution 3 of the Croydon Congress of the TUC the executive of the NUR instructed the General

Secretary to ensure that each collective agreement to which the union was a party included a statement that it was not legally binding.[20] NUR negotiators had little difficulty in persuading all the employers with whom collective agreements were made to add a sentence stating that such agreements were not legally enforceable. In the case of British Rail, British Rail Engineering Ltd, British Rail Hovercraft and British Transport Hotels, the agreed wording was: 'This agreement does not in any way constitute a legally enforceable agreement between the parties.' But some of the employers with whom the union had dealings were not satisfied with such a *carte blanche* statement and wished to stress the moral obligation of both parties to adhere to the agreements reached. At the request of management, the negotiators in the National Council of the Omnibus Industry settled for a considerably more verbose statement:

> The parties hereto, being the employer and the organisation representing the employees, declare that they accept the agreement as binding in honour upon them, but that it is not a legal contract and does not create any obligation binding in law between them. Nevertheless, insofar as this agreement defines the terms now or in the future upon which employees shall be employed, such terms shall form part of the contract of employment of any individual employee.[21]

The Special Croydon Congress of the TUC had also advised trade unionists not to accept membership of the National Industrial Relations Court, the Commission on Industrial Relations, or Industrial Tribunals. Trade unions were expected not to recognise the NIRC, and therefore not to take part in any of its proceedings. In August 1971 the NUR executive loyally complied with these recommendations and Sidney Greene advised all branches by circular letter to adhere to the executive's decision.[22]

In so far as one of the objectives of the Heath government in passing the Industrial Relations Act was to do away with the closed shop, the change effected in the case of the railway industry was superficial rather than fundamental. Section 5 of the Act came into force on 29 February 1972, and made void any compulsory trade union membership agreements (except in the case of Equity and the National Union of Seamen). But on British Railways both management and unions were too keenly aware of the advantages of their closed-shop agreement, which had come into operation at the beginning of 1970, to have any enthusiasm for abandoning it. When the railway unions and the CSEU met representatives of the British Railways Board on 29 September 1971 to discuss the implications of the Act, the unions declared they were most anxious that the arrangements with regard to trade union membership on the railways should not be weakened. The Board representatives assured them that 'subject to observing legal requirements', they would continue to give every encouragement to staff to become trade union members and that they would continue to make facilities available for this.[23] The members of the London Transport Executive in the course of meetings with the trade unions early in 1972 gave an assurance that they would continue to foster a strong collective-bargaining machinery. Mr R. M. Robbins, of the LTE, who chaired the discussions, assured the unions that management would take the opportunity to explain to all new entrants to the service the advantages of union membership.[24] The chairmen of publicly owned transport undertakings were not alone in favouring the retention of the closed shop. They were supported in their view by the leaders of all nationalised industries and by the Engineering Employers' Federation.[25]

III

From August 1971 to February 1972 industrial relations in the railway industry had been largely immunised from the provisions of the Industrial Relations Act. During this period the intervention of the government and the implementation of the legal restraints embodied in the new legislation had largely been avoided. Thereafter events outside the industry, and the government's determination to apply the full rigors of the law to discipline the unions, combined to sour the traditionally friendly and conciliatory temper of collective bargaining on the railways.

It was the dispute in the coalmining industry, in the winter of 1971–2, which was a major influence in generating the crisis in industrial relations on the railways. There were some similarities in the situation of these two publicly owned industries in the 1950s and 1960s. Successive governments worked on the assumption that coal and railways were not as important to the economy as they had been earlier in the century and that there was no good reason why market forces should not be allowed to operate to diminish still further their role in the national economy. Pit closures and the mechanisation of coal-getting reduced the mining labour force by 400,000 between 1950 and 1970; line, station and depot closures, together with modernisation, reduced the railway labour force by 350,000 in the same period. In both cases adherence to the market system presented a choice between great insecurity and more rapid rates of redundancy, on the one hand, or the acceptance of a persistent relative decline in pay, on the other.[26] In the late 1960s the national executives of both the NUR and the NUM gave priority to raising the standard of living of the lowest paid of their members. In the case of the miners this was effected by reducing the bonus differentials earned by face workers in the most productive coalfields, such as Nottinghamshire and Kent, and by establishing, in stages, by June 1971 a simplified national day-wage structure. In the case of the railwaymen the same basic objective was achieved after 1968 by the gradual consolidation of bonus earnings into basic rates.

Fanning the discontent of the low paid in both industries was the erosion of the take-home pay, resulting from the failure of governments to raise income-tax thresholds to take account of inflation. In the period 1959–70 the proportion of the average manual worker's gross income taken by income tax and insurance contributions rose from slightly over 5 per cent to nearly 20 per cent, or by more than three times.[27] Those on lower earnings, in the 'poverty trap', felt the pinch most of all. These stark realities help to explain the militancy of both miners and railwaymen in support of their executives' stand for substantial wage improvements in 1971–2.

When the National Coal Board came nowhere near meeting the NUM's demand for £26 per week for surface workers, a minimum of £28 per week for underground workers and £35 per week for the most skilled men working under the power-loading agreement, the executive called for a ban on overtime working, to operate from 1 November 1971. Since this did not produce a satisfactory offer from the Board, a ballot of members held on 2 December, in which 84 per cent of members participated, resulted in a 59 per cent vote for strike action. The national coal strike began on 9 January and lasted until 28 February.

Initially the Heath government was confident that by standing firm on its 7–8 per cent pay norm – in contrast with the NUM's claim for increases varying upwards to 43 per cent – it would compel a climb down by the miners. Monty Meth in the *Daily Mail* saw 'clear evidence of the Government's determination to have a fight to a finish' and to show at the outset that Ministers meant business.[28] Four days earlier *The Times* reassured its readers that 'coal stocks away from the pits were large enough to last for weeks'.[29] Both Cabinet and the press made a gross miscalculation. They reckoned without the upsurge of solidarity with the miners shown by other trade unionists, and they failed to envisage the mobile deployment of pickets which enabled the NUM, backed by other worker's refusal to cross picket lines, to halt the movement of coal and coke to power stations and factories.

There was along tradition of solidarity between miners and railwaymen. Members of the ASRS refused to move coal when the miners were involved in their first nationwide stoppage in 1912. At the time of the General Strike in May 1926, the railways were brought to a standstill by NUR members striking in sympathy with the miners, who were locked out for refusing to accept savage wage cuts. Such co-operation was again manifested in the early weeks of 1972. In a branch circular issued by Sidney Greene, on 6 January, members of the NUR were advised against entering colliery precincts and warned not to do work normally performed by miners. No oil was to be carried into power stations where coal was the fuel normally used.[30] On 10 January, the day after the miners' strike began, the NUR executive carried unanimously the following resolution:

> That we declare our solidarity with the miners in their present struggle and decide to set up a special committee for the guidance of our members, the special sub-committee to consist of eight members of the negotiating committee.[31]

Support was not confined to pious resolutions passed in the board room at Unity House. Railwaymen were active in support of the miners in all the principal coalfields. In South Wales, for example, representatives of the NUR met with those of ASLEF, the NUS and TGWU on 14 January to plan a campaign of picketing and they joined with these and other trade unionists in a mass demonstration in Cardiff thirteen days later.[32] At the Trafalgar Square meeting following the miners' London march, Sidney Weighell, Assistant General Secretary, made the NUR's position abundantly clear. 'Mineworkers and railwaymen', he said,

> did not advocate public ownership for fifty years in order to be treated as second-class citizens. The call that must go out from this Square from the whole of the trade union movement is that we cannot allow the mineworkers of Great Britain to fail in this struggle. Their fight is our fight – their defeat would be our defeat.[33]

Following the Report of the Wilberforce inquiry into miners' pay, and subsequent negotiations, the miners returned to work on

28 February 1972. The settlement raised the weekly wages of surface workers by £5 to £23, while the pay of underground workers went up by £6 to £25 and that of men employed under the power-loading agreement by £4·50 to £34·50. The cost of the award was estimated at £100 million a year – four times the amount the Coal Board had originally declared to be available.[34]

IV

The outstanding success of the miners simultaneously raised the expectations of the railwaymen and lessened the ability of the Railways Board to meet them. After the severe defeat of his incomes policy at the end of February, Mr Heath still tried to cling to his 7–8 per cent norm on the grounds that the miners' settlement was 'unique to the miners'. A. Wolstenholm, a class-3 signalman of Leeds No. 4 branch of the NUR, could not accept this. In a letter to the *Observer* he pointed out that between fifty and sixty trains, with a cash value of hundreds of thousands of pounds – to say nothing of the lives of the passengers – passed his signalbox during each of his working shifts. His gross pay was £19·20 for a forty-hour week· but by working an eleven-hour Sunday shift he could push up his takehome pay to £23 per week. He ended his letter with a challenge: 'If this does not amount to a "special case" I do not know the meaning of the term.' But his basic wage was £2 above that of the lowest-paid BR staff, the railman.

No doubt Richard Marsh, Chairman of the Board, agreed with Mr Wolstenholm and would have been glad to increase his wages. But he was all too well aware that he was expected to run the railways as a commercial business and not primarily as a service to the traders and the public. Thus, when he met the leaders of the three railway unions at 222 Marylebone Road on 11 January 1972, he brought gloomy tidings. At the beginning of 1971 the Board had anticipated making a profit of £17 million; instead there had been a loss of £20 million. Coal and steel freight revenues were down by over £18 million compared with 1970, and the strikes of the Post Office and Ford workers early in the year had cost the railways £2·4 million. The dispute in the coalmining industry was losing the railways at least £2 million weekly.[35] Within the limits of the market system, the two sides were bound to reach an impasse on the question of railwaymen's pay. Sidney Greene summed up the situation admirably when he told AGM delegates at Scarborough later that year: 'If we were to base our

wages policy on the commercial structure of the railway industry
we would not be asking for any increase in wages at all.'[36]

Throughout the prolonged negotiations with the Board, and
with the Secretary of State for Employment, beginning with the
statement of the union's case before the RSNC (General) on 26
November 1971, and not ending until agreement was reached on
new scales of pay and conditions of service on 13 June 1972,
Sidney Greene and the executive showed considerable astuteness
in sticking relentlessly to the claim for a £20 basic minimum wage
for the lowest-paid staff in the service, the railmen. If it was right
to award a £5 rise to surface workers, the lowest paid in the
coalmining industry, bringing their basic wages up to £23, how
could it be deemed unreasonable for the NUR to ask for a rise
of £2·80 on the railman's basic wage of £17·20?

The union's leaders also acted wisely in working in close collaboration with ASLEF and TSSA at every important stage in the
negotiations. Apart from the exchange of correspondence, joint
meetings were held at Unity House on 8 November 1971, 15
February, 5 and 12 April and 9 May 1972, when a common
approach to the Board and to Mr Maurice Macmillan, Secretary
of State for Employment, was agreed.[37] The lasting impression of
those times on Mr Tom Ham, a member of the NUR executive
who addressed many meetings of railwaymen in the provinces,
was of the 'splendid unity of spirit' of the members of the three
railway trade unions.[38] When it was all over a meeting of the
Manchester District Council noted 'with some pride . . . the rail
unions together in our struggle', and expressed hopes that the
unity would continue in future years.[39] Unity in the campaign
was achieved despite the fact that the objectives of the TSSA and
ASLEF were different from those of the NUR. TSSA was aiming
for a 16–17 per cent rise for its membership, since the current
maximum salary for new clerical recruits to the railways was
£1,115, which compared unfavourably with the £1,359 paid those
in comparable positions in the mining industry and the £1,239
received by local government clerical workers as a starting maximum. ASLEF's main objective was the maintenance of the footplatemen's differentials. But the leaders of these two unions
appreciated that their chances of achieving their objectives would
depend on whether the NUR was successful in getting the £20 for
the railman, a figure which would be the foundation on which the
whole superstructure of other wages and salaries in the industry
would be based.[40]

One reason why the 1971–2 pay talks made heavy weather was
that the union leadership believed – rightly or wrongly – that they

were misled by Bert Farrimond, the newly appointed Board Member for Personnel. He had moved from Dunlops as recently as November 1971 – just as pay discussions were starting – to succeed Leonard Neal. At meetings held early in March 1972, when it became apparent that agreement was going to be very hard to achieve, Farrimond explicitly invited the unions to abandon the 'bargaining ritual' and instead to let him know what was the minimum for which they would settle. In the following few days the staff at Unity House, working overtime, redrafted the wage claim with this understanding in mind. They clipped £15 million from the lump-sum originally claimed in November 1971, but stuck to the minimum £20 claimed for railmen. A letter sent from Sidney Greene to R. Clemmett, Chief Industrial Relations Officer of the Board, on 15 March, reveals that he was under the impression that the schedules of proposed rates of pay enclosed constituted rock-bottom demands rather than inflated figures inserted with the intention of their becoming bargaining-counters. The General Secretary wrote: 'I cannot emphasise too strongly that these schedules represent an honest and realistic appraisal of what this union would regard as an acceptable minimum final settlement.'[41] But when the two sides met again on 20 March, it was clear that the cost of the NUR's minimum claim, £39·3 million, was more than the Board had government authority to spend. Because these demands were unacceptable to the government, Bert Farrimond's invitation to the unions to abandon the bargaining ritual and tell him precisely what they wanted was conveniently forgotten and the NUR's document was treated as a basis for negotiation. At the meetings on 20–21 March much discussion centred around how the cost of consolidation of bonus with basic rates should be financed. In the NUR's proposals the entire cost was to be met from the Board's day-to-day accounts. With this important element excluded from the global figure of the new pay award, the addition to British Rail's annual wages bill would be 11 per cent – a face-saving figure not so far different from the government's 7–8 per cent norm. However, the Board insisted that the whole of the cost of consolidation should be added to the cost of the new pay award, thus pushing the global increase up to 13·5 per cent – a figure too far above the government's norm to salvage any credibility for Mr Heath's incomes policy.

So far the negotiations had been conducted at RSJC and RSNC level. The machinery of negotiation provided that when there was a failure to agree at meetings of the RSNC, the parties in dispute should proceed to arbitration through the RSNT. There were two reasons why the unions declined to go to arbitration on this occasion. The NUR, which gave the lead from the union side at each stage of the negotiations, started off asking for a 16 per cent increase; it then submitted a document, including the claim for a £20 minimum for railmen, with other increases throughout the range of grades, at a cost of 14 per cent. Being then asked to state what was the minimum the members of the union were likely to accept, it produced a final document, with some proposals scaled down, so that the final increase would have been 13·5 per cent. As Sidney Greene made clear in discussions with Richard Marsh, you do not go to arbitration on the basis of a document which sets out your minimum requirements.

The second reason for the failure to resort to arbitration was that there was a substantial delay in the appointment of a successor to Professor Donald Robertson as chairman of the RSNT after his term of office expired in December 1971. The agreed first choice of both unions and Richard Marsh was Lord Donovan, but he died before being able to take up the post. The unions next suggested the left-wing Professor Bill Wedderburn of the LSE and, to their surprise, found Richard Marsh ready to endorse their proposal. But Wedderburn was in two minds about accepting the appointment and delayed giving a clear answer. In the meantime the government, through the Minister of Transport, John Peyton, made it clear that no more money would be forthcoming and Richard Marsh, no doubt foreseeing difficulties in appointing a man sympathetic to the railwaymen's case, withdrew his support from the nomination. Thus, the chairmanship of the RSNT was left vacant at a crucial time.[42]

Meanwhile the members of ASLEF in particular were in a restive mood. The union's executive met on 9 March, after two days in which the unions had inconclusive discussions with management, and agreed to call on the membership to stop work from 16 March. However, when Ray Buckton was shown a copy of the NUR's proposals two days before this deadline and noticed that a rise of nearly 20 per cent was proposed for footplatement, S and T grades, and top-class signalmen, he was pleasantly surprised and persuaded the executive to hold its hand. After two more days of discussions with the Board's representatives the executive voted 4–4, on 21 March, for immediate industrial action. A virtual shutdown of the railway system was only saved by the casting-vote of the moderate president, Les Felton. Ten days later, in a much more intransigent mood, the executive voted yet again, this time by a 6–2 margin in favour of some form of industrial action. It had been pushed forward by the militancy of

600 of its members at Stratford, who were already working to rule, and by reports that Southern Region footplatemen planned to follow suit from 10 April.

The unilateral action of the craft union was averted when the representatives of the three railway unions met at Unity House, on 5 April, and agreed to an NUR suggestion that before going 'over the brink' they should seek a meeting with Richard Marsh.[43] The British Rail chairman was still on holiday at his remote Pembrokeshire farmhouse which had no telephone link with the outside world. But he had made arrangements that, should he be urgently needed, a call could be put through to a nearby signal-box. The call was duly received. As there was not an over-abundance of trains on that part of the railway network the signalman found time to walk across the fields and deliver the message to his boss. On the following day Richard Marsh drove down to London to meet the representatives of the unions. The chairman played for time, while striving to keep the railwaymen's hopes alive. He said it would be arrogant of him to make any further offer without consulting the members of his Board. On the strength of the hopes raised, ASLEF's executive appealed to its Stratford depot members to resume normal working. When Marsh met the union's leaders again, on 11 April, he had already seen both John Peyton and Maurice Macmillan. He had nothing further to offer. 'There is no Father Christmas round the back to produce more money', he said. He turned down Sidney Greene's suggestion that they should make a joint approach to the government.

On previous occasions when such a sticking-point had been reached, it had become almost routine procedure for the union leaders to request a meeting with the Minister of Labour or even with the Prime Minister. When deadlock was reached in January 1955 the Minister of Labour, Walter Monckton, in discussions with the railwaymen, found a way out of the impasse. In February 1962 Prime Minister Harold Macmillan issued invitations to Number 10, Downing Street, and persuaded the unions' negotiating teams to accept an interim settlement. Harold Wilson carried out a similar exercise four years later. There was no repeat of this kind of performance in 1972. It was a feature of each of the earlier eleventh-hour discussions that both government and trade union leaders were willing to reach a compromise solution. In the spring of 1972 the Heath government, stung by its humiliating defeat at the hands of the miners and confident that it would have public support if it stood firm in resisting the railwaymen's claim, was in no mood for compromise. It believed that the credibility of its incomes policy would only be sustained, if the railwaymen were seen to have failed to achieve their objectives.

At Unity House on the morning of 12 April, within hours of the last abortive meeting with Richard Marsh, the NUR executive, with one dissentient, J. E. H. Wood, rejected the Board's offer of a global sum of £30 million, or 11 per cent on the paybill. It resolved that from a date to be agreed a work to rule, ban on overtime, rest-day and Sunday working should be recommended for adoption by the meeting of the three railway union representatives arranged for that afternoon. The larger meeting endorsed the NUR proposals and agreed that the industrial action should start at 00.01 hours on Monday, 17 April.[44]

Prompt action from Maurice Macmillan followed this clear cut decision from the three union's leadership. He invited them to meet him at his St James's Square office the following day, 13 April. When the railwaymen arrived, he asked whether they would settle for the £20 for the railman, without the consequential increases for the other grades – a proposal which he must have known would be turned down by both ASLEF and TSSA – or whether they would agree to a later starting-date for implementing the NUR programme. As neither of these proposals proved acceptable, the discussion ended without agreement. Back at Unity House on the following morning, the NUR executive reaffirmed, unanimously, its decision on industrial action.[45]

Maurice Macmillan tried again on the morning of 15 April, when he held a further brief discussion with the railwaymen's leaders before they were ushered into a nearby room where they met Richard Marsh. The chairman emphasised that what was needed was a new move to get them all 'off the hook'. Such a move was now possible, because more money had become available from the government. He, therefore, suggested the appointment of an independent chairman to hear the arguments of both sides and suggest an award. The public would regard whoever was appointed as an independent arbitrator; but it would be, in effect, a face-saving exercise. He suggested three possible candidates for this emergency job; Conrad Heron, who was a leading civil servant and at that time Vice-Chairman of the Commission for Industrial Relations; Richard O'Brien, a Midlands industrialist active in the CBI, and Alex Jarratt, managing director of the International Publishing Corporation. The union leaders took note of the names and agreed to return that afternoon with their answer.[46]

The impression gained by the NUR negotiators at this stage was that there were good prospects for a favourable settlement.

Robert Bonnar, of the Executive Committee, remarked confidently, 'It's in the bag'. Sidney Greene was, characteristically, more cautious; 'Things are looking a lot healthier', he told the waiting representatives of the press. It did not take the executives of TSSA or the NUR long to agree to the Marsh plan and to choose Alex Jarratt as the independent chairman. Their negotiating committees and officers quickly returned to 222 Marylebone Road to report their decision to Richard Marsh. The executive of ASLEF, on the other hand, took its time and was in any case more doubtful about accepting the plan. It did not meet until 3 p.m. and then only reached a decision two hours later. Once more, the casting-vote of the president tipped the balance. By 5–4 votes, they endorsed the Marsh proposals and the nomination of Alex Jarratt. Meanwhile the other railwaymen at the Board's headquarters were kicking their heels, awaiting the arrival of the footplatemen so that discussions could be resumed. When they were, there was a speedy acceptance of the appointment of Jarratt, but the ASLEF men persuaded Marsh to amend the terms of reference so that his award was declared 'not binding' on the parties to the dispute.

In the light of Richard Marsh's comments when he first proposed the appointment of an independent chairman, the NUR negotiators anticipated that the meetings chaired by Mr Jarratt on the following day, 16 April, would be brief and conclusive. They were to be disappointed. Contrary to their expectation, the Board's team, led by Bert Farrimond, strongly resisted the NUR's claim and the proceedings lasted through the day. Finally, having heard both sides of the argument, Jarratt called the two parties together just before 8 p.m. to hear his decision. The £20 basic rate for railmen, with the consequential increases for other grades would operate from 1 January 1973 (eight months later than the date expected). In the meantime there would be a 12 per cent increase in pay, starting from 1 May 1972. The total cost would be about £4·6 million more than the Board's earlier 'final' offer, but it fell short of the NUR's demands by £4 million. What the unions were being offered was the typical compromise solution of an arbitrator, not the face-saving formula which met their demands but saved the government from ignominy. The NUR leaders were 'in a cold fury', because they felt that Richard Marsh had lied to them.[47]

The NUR executive's decision was a foregone conclusion. In a unanimous vote it expressed 'extreme disappointment' at the Jarratt award and reaffirmed the resolutions of 12 and 13 April in favour of industrial action. As Sidney Greene left Unity House

with the members of the negotiating committee, he was sur-
rounded by BBC and press reporters. While making his way
through the mêlée he leaked the news of the executive's decision.
At the Board's headquarters, Marsh and Jarratt heard over the
radio the news of the rejection of their efforts. When Sidney
Greene arrived Jarratt rebuked him for the 'serious discourtesy'
of disclosing the executive's decision to the press and BBC before
reporting back at the Board's headquarters. Richard Marsh was
shocked and astounded at the union's decision. He spluttered out,
'This is a hold up'. He had taken the NUR's determined stand for
the £20 from 1 May as a persistent negotiating ploy. He completely misread the mood of the railwaymen. In this mood of
incredulity he reported the situation to Macmillan.

Despite the lateness of the hour, the Employment Secretary
summoned the three trade union leaders and their negotiating
committees to his office. Because the work to rule had begun at
a minute after midnight the three groups of railwaymen, coming
by taxis, were not assembled until 1 a.m. on 17 April. Everyone
was tired, but Macmillan was particularly tired and irascible. He
read a highly critical statement and grimly demanded of Greene,
Buckton and Coldrick an explanation of their behaviour. In
reasonable tones Sidney Greene explained that, if the lowest-paid
grades had to wait until 1 January for the £20 minimum, the value
of the increase would be largely eroded because of inflation.
Losing his temper, Macmillan replied that it appeared to him,
and it would appear to the public, that the unions were determined to get what they wanted regardless of the cost to the
economy and the inconvenience and irritation of commuters.
Then he stalked out of the room without even bidding the union
leaders goodnight.

The work to rule and ban on overtime, rest-day and Sunday
working was even more effective than the union had anticipated.
The current 280-page British Rail *Rule Book*, published in 1961,
was antiquated and under revision. It provided ample scope for
the delaying and cancellation of trains. Rule 20A, for example,
read: 'The cleaning, trimming and lighting of all lamps must be
carefully and regularly performed. Oil lamps must be taken to
the appointed place to be cleaned and trimmed.' But a main cause
of the many train cancellations was the fact that British Rail
was heavily dependent on key members of staff, such as drivers,
signalmen and guards, working many more than the forty hours
of the standard working week. In the 1960s the *average* railwayman worked between 48 and 50 hours a week.[48] It is not so surprising, then, that of the 535 trains scheduled to arrive at the

London termini between the hours of 7 and 10 on the morning of 17 April, only 147 completed the journey.[49] The breakdown in the other large centres of population was as serious.

Maurice Macmillan reported the facts of the breakdown of negotiations to a meeting of the Cabinet during the morning of Monday 17 July and received endorsement of his actions and approval for a policy of invoking the legal sanctions included in the Industrial Relations Act. During the preceding week Edward Heath had instructed Sir Geoffrey Howe, Attorney General, to discover whether it would be within the terms of the Act for the Secretary of State for Employment to ask the Industrial Relations Court to order a 'cooling-off' period on the railwaymen. He had come back with a positive assurance that such action would, indeed, be within the scope of the new law.

Macmillan played one more card before using what he expected to be the trump-card of the 'cooling-off' period and the compulsory ballot. He contacted Vic Feather, General Secretary of the TUC, who drove across in his maroon-coloured Rover car to St James's Square, followed by the sixteen members of the General Council. The eminent trade union leaders impressed on the Minister the dangers of invoking the sanction of the law in an attempt to resolve an industrial dispute and urged instead continuing discussions. Macmillan read this as an indication of the trade unionists' apprehension of what might happen if the Act was used, and concluded that they would be likely to do their utmost to dissuade the railwaymen from continuing industrial action. On returning to Congress House Vic Feather met the railwaymen's leaders, who were in an uncompromising mood after the fateful meeting in Marylebone Road. Nevertheless, he returned to St James's Square where it was agreed that the Finance and General Purposes Committee of the TUC should be invited to mediate in the dispute. There was one difficulty, Vic Feather explained. Three members of the committee: Jack Jones, of the TGWU, Alf Allen, of the Shopworkers, and the TUC chairman, George Smith, were attending the annual congress of the Scottish TUC. Macmillan, anxious to be seen to have done his utmost to resolve the dispute, offered to charter a government plane to fly the three men back to London from Glasgow. The offer was accepted and a meeting between the railway unions and the committee was arranged for the following afternoon.

A further meeting between Macmillan and the railway union leaders had been fixed for 8.30 on the morning of Tuesday 18 April. However, due to the late arrival of the NUR representatives, proceedings did not start until 9.15. Sidney Greene was unable to persuade two of the executive's negotiating committee, Bob Bonnar and Alex MacFadden, to accompany him. 'You go on your own if you want to Sid', Bonnar declared, 'but I'll not talk to him again.' There were further delays while the General Secretary located the President, Harold McRitchie, in his lodgings in Gower Street. When all three unions' representatives were at last assembled, Sidney Greene, already very rattled at being late and recalling with strong resentment the very offhand way in which the railwaymen had been treated on the last occasion they met the Minister, told Ray Buckton and Percy Coldrick that, contrary to precedent, he would not be standing up when Maurice Macmillan entered the room.[50] They replied that, in that case, they would also remain seated. The atmosphere of the short meeting which followed was chilly. The union leaders heard the Minister's request that they should agree to a voluntary ballot of their members on the Jarratt award and left the building unmoved.

That afternoon, in an earnest meeting lasting four hours, the members of the Finance and General Purposes Committee of the TUC heard the railwaymen's leaders put their case and expressed a particular dislike at the prospect of a ballot. With such an appeal to the workforce in prospect, they believed, negotiators would be in a fixed position when flexibility was most needed. Although they passed no formal resolution, it was clear that they favoured a resumption of negotiations between the three railway unions and the Board since the margin of difference between the two sides in the dispute seemed small. That evening Maurice Macmillan was disappointed with Vic Feather's report of the committee's proceedings earlier in the day. He felt that the time for stalling was past. Every day the railwaymen's work to rule continued the economy was being further disrupted. Nevertheless, Vic Feather's arguments about the pitfalls of a ballot carried conviction with many of the civil servants present and eventually the Minister was persuaded to drop the idea of balloting the railwaymen, at least for the time being.

V

On the morning of Wednesday 19 April Mr Macmillan reported the situation to the Cabinet and gained its endorsement of his proposal to apply to the Industrial Relations Court for a 'cooling-off' period of twenty-one days to be imposed on the railwaymen.[51]

At midday the request was sent to Sir John Donaldson, President of the Industrial Relations Court, at his Chancery Lane office. Donaldson acted with remarkable promptitude. He summoned the four other lawyers of the court to a hearing of the Minister's case at four o'clock that same afternoon. Meanwhile the secretary of the court notified Sidney Greene and the two other general secretaries of the hearing and invited them, or their deputies, to attend for the purpose of stating the union's case. In a unanimous decision, reached that afternoon, the NUR's executive expressed appreciation to the TUC for its efforts to resolve the dispute and indicated its willingness to resume negotiations with the Board on the basis of the Jarratt award. But in accordance with the previously declared policy of the union, it decided not to be represented at the hearing in the Industrial Relations Court. The TSSA and ASLEF executives made similar decisions. Just before the start of the court's proceedings Tom Ham and three other members of the EC of the NUR appeared at the entrance, seeking admission. They were informed by the usher that members of the general public were not being admitted. Only when they insisted that, as British citizens, they were entitled to attend as observers were chairs found for them. The impression they gained was that it was a 'lawyer's bonanza'.[52]

The decision of the court came as no surprise. Sir Geoffrey Howe, Attorney General, put the government's case for the 'cooling-off' period. The unions' case went by default. The court ordered a 'cooling-off' period but considered that fourteen days, rather than the twenty-one days requested by the government, would be adequate time for the two parties in the dispute to negotiate a settlement. Section 138 of the Industrial Relations Act required the Minister to show to the court that (a) a strike, or irregular industrial action short of a strike, had begun or was likely to begin (b) it would be conducive to a settlement of it by arbitration or conciliation if the industrial action were discontinued or deferred; and (c) the industrial action was likely to be among other things 'gravely injurious to the national economy'. It was not difficult to show that condition (c) had been met, since the railway services were breaking down; it did not seem unreasonable to assume that a 'cooling-off' period might provide the much-needed 'breathing-space for a settlement. But in the legal sense 'irregular industrial action' implied a breach of contract. Hitherto the compulsory working of rest days was not regarded by any major employer in Britain as part of the contract of employment. The court, however, accepted Sir Geoffrey Howe's contention that there was in every contract of employment an

implied obligation on the part of the worker to give 'faithful
service' to the employer. It therefore, ruled that

> The employee has an obligation to work reasonable overtime
> and rest days as required by the employer. If he is required
> to work a reasonable amount of overtime on a regular basis
> that becomes part of the employee's contract.

This was an interpretation which was challenged in the *Law
Society Gazette*:

> In theory it could bring the normal master–servant relationship
> enjoyed in industry closer to that obtaining in the armed forces
> in which a man's free time is dependent on the exigencies of
> the service, with the needs of the service being sole arbiter of
> how, when and if that free time is made available to him.[53]

Nevertheless the court found that the Secretary of State had
proved that all three preconditions for invoking the 'cooling-off'
period had been satisfied:

> Having considered these matters we are bound to say that in
> our judgment the Secretary of State has clearly been correctly
> advised as to the law and the industrial action which has taken
> place is in our judgment the plainest breach of contract.[54]

Late in the evening on Wednesday 19 April a messenger of the
Industrial Relations Court endeavoured to present to Brian
Williams, the night porter at Unity House, the 'cooling-off' order
addressed to Sir Sidney Greene. Williams refused to accept it.
The right person to receive the order, he maintained, was the
General Secretary himself, and he would not be available until
the following day. But Sir John Donaldson's emissary was persistent. Only when Williams threatened to summon the police,
did he abandon his attempt to hand over the order that night.
When he reappeared on the following morning, press photo-
graphers were there in strength to see him deliver the order to
the General Secretary.
    The leaders of all three of the railway unions obeyed the court
order that they should instruct their members to resume normal
working. Sidney Greene did this through a circular sent to each
of the union's 695 branches and 25 district councils, on 20 April.[55]

But in a further circular dispatched later the same day, it was pointed out that no court could order the union's members to ignore the safety regulations in British Rail's *Rule Book*, nor could a legal compulsion be placed on them to work overtime or on rest days.[56] The union had considered the implications of these circulars. If charged with contempt of court, it could quote the circular ordering members to end the work to rule; if charged on the second circular, it could claim that this was issued in clarification of the first.

On Friday 21 April railwaymen in all regions but Southern ceased the work to rule, but did not work any overtime. In consequence weekend services were still disrupted. On Southern Region the drivers, almost all of whom were members of ASLEF, continued the work to rule. David Binnie, the region's general manager, saw this as the last straw and ordered the display of notices at all the region's depots, warning that the unofficial action was to cease and that anyone who refused to work normally would be sent home. Faced with this challenge, the local ASLEF leaders warned that if Binnie carried out his threat there would be a general stoppage in the region. That this explosive situation did not reach flash-point was due to the prompt action of Macmillan advising Marsh to persuade David Binnie to withdraw his notices, and to the BR chairman's decision to act quickly on this advice. However, it was not until 6 p.m. on the evening of Tuesday 25 April that Maurice Macmillan felt justified in signing a certificate confirming that the court's order to the railwaymen to resume normal working had been carried out and that the 'cooling-off' period could therefore begin.

In the meantime the officers of the NUR considered challenging the National Industrial Relations Court's judgement in the Court of Appeal. But when Sidney Greene and Sidney Weighell discussed this proposal with Professor Bill Wedderburn on 25 April, he persuaded them to abandon it. He considered the union had weakened its case through not being represented at the NIRC hearing on 19 April.[57] The 'cooling-off' period did not achieve the objectives for which it was designed. In a circular letter sent to branches, on 9 May, Sidney Greene wrote:

> I would make it clear that the Board have just not been prepared to negotiate during the recent cooling off period. Indeed the only 'offer' made during this period viz: that paragraph 2 of the Jarratt statement should be implemented with effect from 5 June 1972, would have cost *less* than the total cost of the Jarratt award.[58]

In his report to the July 1972 AGM he wrote that the 'cooling-off' period was 'abortive', since only four hours of discussion with members of the Board took place in the fourteen days of its duration – a much lower level of negotiating activity than was the case before the order was imposed.

The outstanding reason for the failure to make significant headway during the fourteen days was that no more money was made available by the government. Maurice Macmillan and John Peyton were convinced that rank and file railwaymen would be glad to accept the increases already on offer in the Jarratt award and that they would bring pressure on their leaders to settle. Thus, there were only brief meetings between the representatives of the Board and the unions on 1, 2 and 4 May. There were no further discussions before 8 May, when the fourteen-day work to rule came to an end. All that BR management was able to do was to rejuggle the figures of the Jarratt award and hope that the unions would agree to their revised proposals. These were offered to the unions leaders in the afternoon of 10 May in the form of three alternatives. The first option was to apply the £20 minimum basic rate for railmen without the maintenance of differentials for the period 1 May–3 December 1972. This was seen by the suspicious union negotiators as an attempt to split the footplate grades from the traffic grades. The second option was to apply the £20 minimum basic wage without maintenance of differential from 5 June 1972. The third option was to apply the £20 minimum from 5 June, and to implement the minimum *earnings* level of £20·50 from 1 May. None of these proposals was acceptable to any of the three railway unions. The NUR turned them down, because their overall cost at £34·16 million was found to be £1·24 millions *less* than the cost of the Jarratt award which was £35·4 million.[59] The presence of Maurice Macmillan in the chair at the meeting on 10 May confirmed the union leaders' conviction that they were not really negotiating with the Board at all, but that they were up against the government's refusal to offer any more money than that provided under the Jarratt award. On 4 May the executives of the three unions met at Unity House and agreed unanimously to resume their work to rule and ban on overtime and rest-day working on 12 May.

VI

Before the Board and the unions had resumed discussions during the 'cooling-off' period, the Minister, with the co-operation of the

Board, was making preparations for a ballot of railwaymen. A list of all railway employees entitled to vote was compiled from the Board's computerised records and sent to the Commission on Industrial Relations from 24 April. On the morning of Thursday 11 May Maurice Macmillan gained the approval of the Cabinet for an application to be made to the National Industrial Relations Court for a compulsory strike ballot of the railway staff. The unions received an even-briefer warning of this second application to the court than they had of the earlier one – for the 'cooling-off' period – on 19 April. At 6 p.m. on 11 May a phone message was received at Unity House to the effect that the court would be meeting at 8.30 that evening to consider the request for a ballot. There was an occasion in 1813 when an Irish judge left Downpatrick Assize Court just in time to see one of the convicted prisoners hanged in the town.[60] The Heath government's rush for justice on 11 May 1972 could scarcely match the haste of the Irish court 159 years earlier, but it provoked disrespectful (and unprintable) comments from the union leaders and led one of the judges involved, Lord Justice Buckley, to regret, in more sedate language, that 'the case was conducted with an undesirable amount of expedition'.[61]

In deciding to make his second application to the court Maurice Macmillan was acting contrary to the advice given by Richard Marsh, Chairman of the Railways Board, who correctly forecast that the ballot would result in a vote of confidence in the union leaders. On 6 June 1972 at a meeting of the RSNC, held after the result of the ballot was known, Bert Farrimond, from the chair, assured the union leaders that it had not been the wish of the Board to have a ballot; this had been done on application made by the Secretary of State for Employment. The way in which the Board and the unions conducted their affairs was such that the Board had no reason to doubt that the unions had the confidence of the members they represented and this was confirmed by the ballot result. The trade union membership had a deep-seated loyalty to the unions, which was an honourable characteristic.[62] The minister and the other members of the Cabinet, however, were convinced they knew the mind of the rank and file railwaymen better than did the employers. They also expected an uncontested and expeditious hearing of the application for a ballot from the National Industrial Relations Court. In both of these expectations they miscalculated.

When the court assembled on the evening of 11 May, Bill Wedderburn was there to represent the NUR, Morris Finer, QC spoke for the TSSA and Peter Pain, QC for ASLEF. Speaking for the three of them, Morris Finer pointed out that they had been given inadequate time in which to prepare their briefs. Sir John Donaldson replied that, if the three general secretaries could persuade their executive committees to order a postponement of the industrial action due to start at midnight, he would postpone the court's hearing. But at that time of night the summoning of the three executives presented formidable difficulties, and Donaldson therefore agreed to delay the start of the hearing until 1.30 p.m. the following day, Friday 12 May. The appeal for the ballot was being made under section 141 of the Industrial Relations Act. This part of the Act was designed to apply in the case where a militant union leadership was determined on calling for industrial action against the clear wishes of the membership. The three counsel were naturally at pains to point out that the three general secretaries present had a reputation for moderation; it was a travesty of the truth to regard them as hotheads, egging on a reluctant rank and file. But, according to the Act, justification for the holding of the ballot depended on three conditions being satisfied. These were (a) that irregular industrial action was taking place; (b) that this action constituted a grave threat to the national economy; and (c) that the Secretary of State for Employment had reason for doubting whether the workers taking part in the industrial action were taking part willingly. Although there was disagreement on the question of whether a work to rule and abstention from rest-day and Sunday working was in breach of contract, there was no doubt about the harm being done to the economy. For the unions, all three of the counsel demanded to know upon what evidence the Secretary of State had reason to doubt that rank and file railway workers were in disagreement with the executives' decision to call for industrial action. But Sir John Donaldson, in his 3,500-word judgement, stressed that the Minister, by the terms of the Act, was not obliged to explain why he doubted the willingness of railway workers to follow the lead given by their officers. The union leaders might be 'honestly mistaken' in thinking that they reflected the opinions of the majority of their membership. He, therefore, found that the case for ordering the ballot had been made out.[63]

Immediately Sir John Donaldson had finished reading his judgement on the Saturday evening, Peter Pain stated that the unions would make an appeal. 'Of course', said Sir John briskly; they could do so immediately. Contingency plans had been made for just such a situation. He then telephoned Lord Denning, Master of the Rolls, who was standing by, and arrangements were made for the Court of Appeal to meet on the following afternoon. When the union's counsel expressed some amazement that for the very first time in history the Court of Appeal was to meet on a Sunday, Sir John replied that this was, after all, a national emergency. Lord Denning, for the Court of Appeal, in a hearing lasting four days (14–17 May) found no good grounds for overturning Sir John Donaldson's judgement. Arrangements for the ballot were to proceed. On the morning of 15 May Sidney Greene arranged for a telegram to be sent to all of the union's branch secretaries: 'In view of the Court Order normal working must be resumed forthwith. Circular will follow.' ASLEF and TSSA head offices sent out similar instructions. Industrial action was called off for the second time in the course of the dispute. On 16 May, while the Appeal Court was still sitting, a further telegram was dispatched to all NUR branches: 'Make immediate arrangements to call special meetings of branches, joint branches and DCs in connection with possible ballot. Circular to follow.'

The government was anxious for the ballot to be conducted with the minimum of delay, since it believed that it had the support of the public for its actions. In an opinion-poll conducted in May 81 per cent of those questioned favoured the holding of an obligatory secret ballot before any union resorted to industrial action, and 41 per cent believed that the government should get even tougher with the railwaymen.[64] Therefore ballot papers were dispatched to all British Rail staff on 19 May, the day on which Lord Denning officially informed Sir John Donaldson that the polling arrangements might proceed. The closing date for the receipt of ballot papers at the Commission on Industrial Relations was to be 26 May, and the counting of the ballot envelopes at the CIR was to take place during 24–26 May. Leonard Neal, Chairman of the Commission, turned down an appeal from the three trade union leaders to allow the full three weeks granted by the National Industrial Relations Court. But to give an opportunity for railway staff who were on holiday to take part in the ballot, arrangements were made for ballot papers to be available, on request, at local labour exchanges. Local union leaders were allowed to check the voting lists to ensure that all members entitled to vote were included.

In the brief time allowed before the receipt of the completed ballot papers an intense propaganda war was waged by the government, the BRB and the unions. Advertisements appeared in the press from the Commission (urging railway staff to vote); from the BRB (urging its employees to consider carefully, before voting, how much they would lose by resumed industrial action and how much was already available for them under the Jarratt

Vote for a
May Day Pay Date

A compulsory ballot has been granted on the request of the Government because they do not believe that N.U.R. members support their own Union's National Executive Committee. This is the real issue on which you are asked to vote.

Your Executive Committee believe that the Railways Board should be made to honour its undertaking to apply a pay settlement from May 1st.

GIVE YOUR VOTE

Abstention could mean a decision by a minority

Vote in support of your own National Executive Committee

Vote an overwhelming

YES

Published by the National Union of Railwaymen

award) and from the NUR (urging members to show loyalty to the union). The Commission ran into difficulties producing a colour television advertisement, urging railwaymen to vote. The actress secured to fill the role of a railwayman's daughter was found to have an unconvincing accent. She caused the Commission further embarrassment when she confessed to the *Daily Express* that it had been 'absolutely heavenly' living in her flat above Waterloo station during the work to rule. The final blow to the Commission's plans came when the Independent Television Authority pointed out that, under the provisions of the Television Act 1964, advertisements which had any relation to current industrial disputes were disallowed. By this time £2,000 had been spent.[65] The Board's principal effort was to send to all its staff a special issue of *Rail News*, including details of existing wage rates and those on offer. In some details the wages on offer were an improvement on the rates discussed at the last meeting with the unions on 10 May.

The wording of the ballot papers sent to all railway staff read: 'In the light of the BRB pay offer (about which you are being informed) do you wish to take part in further industrial action.' Beneath these words were two empty boxes, one marked 'Yes' and the other 'No'. Those voting were instructed to place a cross in one of the boxes. The NUR's reply to the Board was to issue hundreds of thousands of copies of four leaflets, the most effective of which is reproduced on p. 262. These were re-enforced by a steady stream of branch circulars, in which Sidney Greene wrote with warmth of feeling on the support he had received from branch secretaries and other members. On 17 May, for example, he wrote:

I have been re-enforced in my efforts during these difficult times by the volume of correspondence coming from branches in support of the stand which has been taken by the EC. The solidarity of the membership and their ready response to calls for action during the present period of crisis has served to confirm my belief in the unfailing loyalty of our members.[66]

At provincial railway centres and in London many meetings about the railway crisis were very well supported. About 500 railwaymen, members of the three trade unions, crowded into the Gateshead Town Hall on 14 May to attend a meeting called by the Newcastle District Council of the NUR. With understandable exaggeration, the secretary of the council reported that 'the roar of "Ayes" must have been heard all over Tyneside when the chairman, John Kay, called upon those present to support the decision of the three executives'. The importance of the 'loyalty to the union' aspect of the ballot campaign is perhaps best illustrated by what happened at a mass meeting called by the Manchester District Council a few days before the crucial vote took place. Fred McGrath, described by Peter Snape, MP (who was present at the meeting) as a 'pugnacious type of guy, as right-wing as they come, but . . . a likeable character', was there on the platform to put the national executive's point of view. After the chairman of the meeting had introduced him, the members of the large audience sat back expecting to be regaled with oratory about the iniquity of the government and the deviousness of the Board. Instead McGrath's speech was over almost before many realised it had begun. 'It's nice to be here', he said, 'Sid Greene has asked me to tell you to vote "Yes" in the ballot.' That was all.

The votes were counted in the Royal Horticultural Hall, Horseferry Road, London, on 28 May, the result being declared in the Industrial Relations Court on the following day. When members of the Unity House staff arrived at the count they discovered that the ballot envelopes were being opened individually by means of paper knives. They soon demonstrated the union's dedication to increased productivity by making available the letter-opening machine from the head-office goods department. The extent of the government's misreading of the mood of railwaymen was revealed on the following day when the result of the ballot was declared. In a heavy poll, with 87 per cent of those eligible voting, the proportion of Yes to No votes among ASLEF members was 21–1; among NUR members nearly 8–1 and among TSSA members nearly 2–1. The detailed results were as follows:

votes by persons stating themselves to be members of:	in favour of the question	against the question	abstaining
(a) ASLEF	23,436	1,043	108
(b) NUR	80,894	10,695	719
(c) TSSA	31,581	10,321	633
(d) More than one of the above unions	3,269	1,075	107
Total	139,180	23,134	1,567[67]

On 21 May, the same day on which the ballot papers were delivered to the homes of railway workers, the newspapers leaked the report of the Boyle Committee on the pay of chairmen of nationalised industries. In increase of £4,000 per year was recommended for the Chairman of British Rail. This may well have hardened railwaymen's determination to achieve the £20 minimum basic rate backdated to 1 May. The significance of the TSSA members' 2–1 vote in favour of further industrial action

can be better appreciated when it is remembered that this was the first occasion since 1926 that members of the union had taken part in any kind of industrial action.

VII

On 26 May, before the result of the ballot had been declared but when it was already suspected that a majority of the railway workers had voted 'Yes', the Prime Minister, Edward Heath, made a face-saving speech at Luton Hoo. While appearing to stand firm in resistance to the railwaymen's demands – 'if anyone imagines that they can, for political reasons, risk an easy fight with us they're coming to the wrong place' – he nevertheless hinted at the way in which a settlement would be reached. It would be through an increase in rail fares. From this point onwards he publicly washed his hands of the whole dispute and transferred the burden of reaching a settlement to the Railways Board.[68] Most of the railwaymen's leaders were also of the opinion that it was now up to the Railways Board to take the initiative for industrial peace. When the representatives of the three unions met at Unity House during the afternoon of Monday 5 June to determine a common policy for the resumed negotiations, men from the ASLEF executive wanted an immediate resumption of industrial action. Sidney Greene argued that the next move should come from the Railways Board and that an 'ominous silence' from the railwaymen's leaders would be as menacing as an open declaration of hostilities. Eventually it was agreed to await the initiative of the Board and, when the expected meeting came, to insist on the 1 May starting-date for the implementation of the Jarratt proposals.

An invitation from the Board duly arrived and a meeting was arranged for the afternoon of 6 June at 222 Marylebone Road. The union leaders arrived anticipating a new offer. Instead, Bert Farrimond stressed the serious state of the railway finances and pointed out that recent settlements for merchant seamen and workers at ICI and British Steel had given wage increases between 9·5 and 10·5 per cent. Sidney Greene stressed that it was the takehome pay that counted. A rise of 12·5 per cent on a low basic wage could mean a smaller money increase than one of 9·5 per cent on an above-average wage. The meeting then moved into Richard Marsh's room nearby. The Chairman asked the union leaders 'how to get over this wretched dispute. Surely it must be by some sort of compromise?' Since neither Ray Buckton nor

Percy Coldrick had anything to say at this point, Sidney Greene intervened with the only positive suggestion at the meeting. The Board had proposed a 5 June starting-date for the implementation of the Jarratt award; the staff, following the outcome of the ballot were expecting the pay rises to operate from 1 May. The cost of the difference between these two starting-dates was about one-half of 1 per cent on the total annual paybill. He proposed, therefore, that the improved rates should apply from 5 June but that the Board should give every member of staff a lump-sum equal to the extra amount that would have been received between 1 May and 4 June, inclusive. According to NUR head-office calculations, following this plan would save the Board £170,000 plus some administrative costs of calculating retrospective payments to 1 May.[69]

When the two parties reassembled the following day, Richard Marsh told the union leaders that the lump-sum proposal was not acceptable. The extra money was not available. The unions then decided to call the Chairman's bluff. At a further meeting at Unity House, on 9 June, they resolved to resume industrial action with effect from 00.01 hours on Wednesday 14 June. This gave plenty of time for further negotiations.[70] That same Friday afternoon the union leaders were summoned once more to the Board's headquarters. Richard Marsh, who was suffering from influenza, came straight from his sickbed to let it be known that he could now offer more money; but only in return for a promise that the unions would abandon the projected industrial action.

A settlement came at last after the weekend. On Monday 12 June a breakthrough was achieved when Bert Farrimond, for the Board, accepted in principle the NUR's proposal for lump-sum payments to be made in lieu of backdating the award to 1 May. There was still some hard bargaining. Two adjournments were needed before the Board was persuaded to raise its lump-sum offer to each member of staff from £5·50 to £12·50. There was also a 5p improvement on the basic rates offered by the Board during the run up to the ballot and some marginal advances in the pay of clerical workers. The award brought increases of 12·8 per cent for railmen; 12·2 per cent for other conciliation staff; 12·6 per cent for footplatemen and 12·5 per cent for the clerical and supervisory grades. Special working parties were to be set up, within the machinery of negotiation, to examine the wage structure of the footplate, conciliation and clerical and supervisory grades.[71]

One fortuitous circumstance greatly increased the pressure on British Rail management to make the new scales of pay operative from 1 May even though, as a matter of convenience, the increase for the first five weeks was paid in the form of a lump-sum. On 25 April Jim Mortimer, director of labour relations on London Transport, sent a letter to all 18,000 LT underground staff, promising them that the increases paid to main line staff would also be paid to them from 1 May 1972. At the time of dispatching the letter, he was unaware that there would be any hitch about the starting-date for the new pay scales on British Rail. It would have made for still more complications, if the two starting-dates had been different! On Tuesday 13 June the executive of the NUR came to the unanimous decision to accept the Board's latest offer and to call off the industrial action due to be resumed on the following day. It also expressed appreciation of the loyal support given by the membership and the head-office staff to the decisions of the executive during the difficult and protracted negotiations.[72] Similar decisions were made by the executives of ASLEF and TSSA. The long struggle was over.

VIII

The imposition of the 'cooling-off' period and the ballot in the railway dispute in April–May 1972 was the only occasion when government chose to use the emergency powers granted under section 138 and 141 of the Industrial Relations Act 1971. According to the consultation document which preceded the passing of the Act, the purpose of the new legislation was 'to improve industrial relations in Britain and to provide new ways of settling disputes and grievances'. The result of the application of the 'disciplinary' sections of the Act in the railwaymen's case were the opposite of what the government had intended. In the opinion of Sidney Greene, a man not prone to make extreme statements, the government's 'excessive zeal in applying the Industrial Relations Act left industrial relations on the railways worse than at any time since negotiating machinery was first introduced'.[73] Percy Coldrick, General Secretary of the TSSA, said that one indication of the poor state of industrial relations on the railways in the spring of 1972 was the fact that clerks and supervisors had taken industrial action for the first time since the General Strike forty-six years earlier.[74]

The miners played the biggest part in destroying the Heath government's incomes policy. The five dockers who, in July 1972, were imprisoned for defying the court's order to stop 'blacking' the Midland Cold Storage depot at Stratford, provided the Act's martyrs and helped to expose the limitations of the legal approach to improved industrial relations. But it was the railwaymen who did most to destroy the credibility of the Act and to lead the public to think that it was 'accident-prone'. It was not that the new legislation was badly worded or unclear. It worked perfectly well from the purely legal point of view. Though they did so with some reluctance, the unions co-operated in implementing the 'cooling-off' period. The rank and file voted in impressively large numbers in the ballot whose outcome was clear-cut. But the result was a demonstration of the inadequacy and inappropriateness of the Act's main instruments for industrial discipline. In the words of the *Sunday Times*, "the ballot which was intended to cool off the crisis only served to do the opposite'.[75]

It is clear that after the government had considered the full implications of its handling of the railway dispute and the dockers' case, important parts of the Industrial Relations Act were put in 'cold storage'. Within a year of the railwaymen's ballot Maurice Macmillan and Leonard Neal, Chairman of the Commission on Industrial Relations, were mulling over a 400-word memorandum drawn up in the Department of Employment, and containing a list of possible modifications of the Act. Changes in its provisions regarding registration of unions, tax exemptions on provident fund income, the closed shop, and many other aspects were being critically reassessed.[76] The action of an earlier generation of railwaymen had been largely instrumental in bringing into existence the Trade Disputes Act 1906 and the Trade Union Act 1913. In 1972 a later generation of railwaymen played a big part in undermining public confidence in the Industrial Relations Act 1971 and the government which introduced it.

CHAPTER 8

LONDON TRANSPORT

I

THE bus and underground railway services of the London area have been under some form of public ownership and control ever since the London Passenger Transport Board was brought into being on 1 July 1933 under the London Passenger Transport Act of that year. From 1 January 1948 the British Transport Commission became generally responsible for London transport under the Transport Act 1947, but its subsidiary, the London Transport Executive, which began functioning simultaneously with the Commission, inherited the responsibilities of the Board it susperseded. Like its predecessor it had the obligation to administer the bus and underground railway services 'as one undertaking', a requirement of significance to the NUR membership in the London Transport area; though the union's membership was confined to the railways, the prosperous functioning of the bus services was an important as that of the railways, since the revenues were placed in a common pool and the financial health of the whole undertaking was as essential for railwaymen as it was for busmen. In most years after 1962, however, train services produced a revenue surplus, while the buses were running at a loss. With the break up of the British Transport Commission under the Transport Act 1962, the independent London Transport Board (LTB) began operations on 1 January 1963. But again the change was of name rather than of function; the obligation remained to provide bus and rail services in an integrated system.

A radical reform of the structure of the London government came with the passing of the London Government Act, in 1963, which abolished the London County Council and established the Greater London Council, covering a much larger area. Soon afterwards the Transport (London) Act 1969 brought about 'the most far-reaching change since 1933'[1] for transport in the London area. The Act set up the London Transport Executive (LTE), a body corporate to take the place of the London Transport Board. Overall control of the new undertaking was given to the GLC, which had the duty of laying down 'principles' of transport operation and of giving 'general directions' to the new executive. One of the main changes involved was the transference of Country Bus services, which mainly operated outside the GLC boundaries, and the Green Line coaches, to a subsidiary company, the London Country Bus Services Ltd under the National Bus Company. In so far as the LTE was required 'to promote the provision of integrated, efficient and economic transport facilities and services for Greater London', its main responsibilities were similar to those of the LTB.[2] It is, however, arguable that placing the LTE under the general direction of the GLC caused London transport policy to be subjected to increased political interference with each major change in the fortunes of the two main political parties at County Hall. Thus the Conservatives' victory in May 1977 was quickly followed by the publication of London Transport – A New Look, which placed a much greater emphasis on the commercial viability of the Executive's undertakings than had been the case under the preceding Labour administration. In the Executive's Annual Report for 1979 Ralph Bennett, the Chairman, asserted that it had 'proved difficult to establish long-term policies and objectives for the future of public transport in London because of changes in political control and priorities'.[3]

II

Under whatever form of administrative direction London's transport services operated, the history of this great public utility over the last quarter of a century makes depressing reading – despite

Table 8.1 *London Transport, 1960–79*

Years (averages)	Passengers carried (million)				Passenger miles travelled (million)			
	Bus	Decline %	Under-ground railway	Decline %	Bus	Decline %	Under-ground railway	Decline %
1960–4	2,365		673		5,581		3,107	
1975–9	1,359	42·5	571	15·2	2,889	48·3	2,777	10·6

Source: London Transport Executive, *Annual Reports*, 1960–2; London Transport Board, *Annual Reports*, 1963–4; London Transport Executive, *Annual Reports*, 1975–9; D. L. Munby and A. H. Watson, *Inland Transport Statistics Great Britain, 1900–1970* (Oxford: Clarendon Press, 1978), tables C6.7 and C7, pp. 538, 543; GLC, *Transport Policies and Programmes, 1978–83* (London: GLC 1977), table 22, p. 94.

some important and valuable innovations such as the opening of
the Victoria Line from 1968 and the Jubilee Line nearly eleven
years later. The decline in the volume of passenger business is summarised in Table 8.1. Not included in the figures are the numbers
of commuters arriving at British Rail main line termini. These
fluctuated between 400,000 and 419,000 daily in the morning rush
hour. About 40 per cent of daily commuters by public transport
used this method of getting to work as compared with 60 per cent
entering central London by bus or tube train. The figures for
bus and tube passengers include those who made part of their
journey in BR trains. That the most serious decline in the public
transport sector was in the use of buses is shown more starkly in
Figure 8.1.

Part of the explanation for the fall in passenger journeys lies
in demographic changes in the second half of the twentieth century.
During the years 1951–79 the population of Greater London (the
GLC area) fell from over 8 million to under 7 million, or by
12·5 per cent, while in Inner London numbers fell from 3·3 million
to 2·4 million, or by 27 per cent. However, this outward movement
of people certainly provides no justification for the decline in bus
and tube travel shown in Figure 8.1. Many of those who had
moved out to Orpington, St Albans, Reading, or one or other of
the dozens of commuter centres surrounding the capital, still
worked in London and required to be carried by bus or underground train on the final stage of their journeys. Furthermore,
each year London attracted a huge influx of foreign visitors, growing from 6 million in 1972 to 7·8 million in 1977, and these were
among the most frequent users of public transport.[4]

A more important explanation of the decline in use of public
transport was the growth of car ownership and the increased use
of the family or business car to get to work, go shopping, call on
friends or visit the theatre. The number of private cars entering
London during the morning traffic peak (07.00–10.00 hours) rose
from 75,000 in 1962 to 129,800 in 1978. Between 1955 and 1965,
a crucial decade, when the economy of bus operation was undermined, the number of private cars heading for central London in
the morning peak rose by 28,800. These additional vehicles
occupied more than five times the amount of road space vacated
by the 1,900 fewer buses – partly driven off the road by traffic
congestion. Although, in 1965, peak-time buses represented less
than one-sixth of total traffic they carried 60 per cent of the passengers travelling by road, while private cars, taking up nearly
80 per cent of the traffic volume, carried only one-third of the road
passengers and only 15 per cent of all London commuters.[5] Traffic

Figure 8.1 *London Transport: passengers carried (millions annually)*

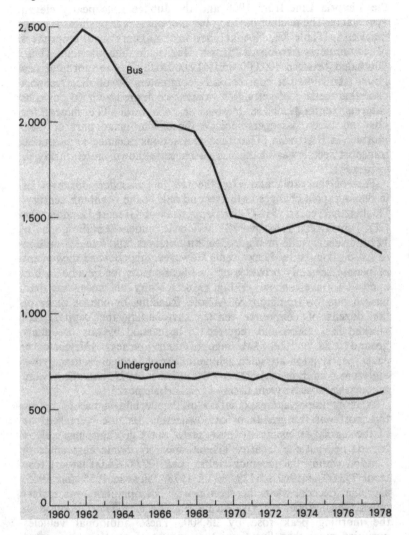

congestion prevented many buses from completing their scheduled runs and caused the cancellation of a number of services. In 1972, for example, nearly 3 million scheduled miles, or just over 1 per cent of the total, had to be cut because of delays resulting from traffic congestion.[6] The percentage may seem small, but for passengers on the routes affected it signified annoying delays and growing disillusionment with the performance of the bus services. The recurrence of bus service cancellations with varying degrees of severity each year plunged the bus operation side of the LTE's finances more and more into the red, with only the revenue surpluses of underground railway operations, for a time, redressing the balance.

Many more bus and train cancellations were caused by staff shortages. In some months of 1974, the grimmest year for public transport in postwar London, 15 per cent of the bus and 18 per cent of train services were cancelled, mainly for this reason. Obtaining an adequate supply of reliable labour was a serious problem for London Transport management throughout the three decades 1950–80. In these years the percentage of the workforce unemployed remained consistently lower in the Greater London area than the national average. Within the London area there were more job vacancies and lower levels of unemployment in the West and North, where many bus and train depots are located, than there were in eastern and southern boroughs such as Tower Hamlets and Southwark. The difficulty of recruiting sufficient staff in an environment of full employment was compounded by the reluctance of recruits to work the unsocial hours characteristic of railway and bus employment. Leaving a warm bed at 4 a.m. to start an early shift, or having to work on Saturday or Sunday afternoons instead of tending the garden or watching the TV, were characteristics of public transport employment which contributed most to the rapid turnover of labour and to bus and train cancellations. In 1955–6, 1964–6 and 1973–5 labour shortages reached crisis proportions. In 1964 there were over 70,000 unfilled vacancies in the London area, and in the years 1965–6 and 1973–5 the number of unfilled vacancies in the Greater London area was more than double the number of the unemployed.[7]

From the mid-1950s, for more than a decade, the labour shortage was eased, in part, by the recruitment of West Indians. By 1955 Barbados had such a surplus of labour that the island's government sent a Minister and a senior official to London to survey employment prospects. The Barbadians' visit coincided with a situation of acute shortage of underground station staff which compelled management to summon a special meeting of the staff side of Sectional Council 4 of the LTE in order to persuade the unions' representatives to accept the rest-day working of their members. For understandable reasons they failed to obtain a blanket endorsement of this proposal. However, in an endeavour to ease the situation, the officers of the NUR, in a meeting with management on 5 April 1955, agreed to recommend to the EC a scheme whereby staff would be assumed to be willing to work on rest days unless individuals notified manpower officers to the contrary. The executive endorsed this plan at its September meeting.[8] Nevertheless at the AGM held at Great Yarmouth in the following July, an appeal by New Cross and Covent Garden branches against the executive's decision was upheld in a unanimous vote.[9]

Frustrated in its attempts to pursuade staff to work longer hours to 'cover up' for those who had left the service, management met the Bardadian representatives in London and agreed with them to send a recruitment official and a medical officer to the island in the following year. Seventy stationmen and fifty men and twenty women bus conductors were immediately enrolled. Within the next decade up to 10,000 more followed. A free loan, made available by the British government to cover the cost of the fare from Barbados to the place of employment was repaid by the recipients in monthly instalments.[10] The sole reason for signing on the new recruits was to make good staff vacancies from a readily available supply of labour.[11] (British Railways was also short of staff. For some years before the new Euston station was opened in 1968 a recruitment office was housed in a prefabricated hut in Euston Square.)

Every effort was made to ensure that the West Indians settled in to their new environment with the minimum of difficulty. An *Information Booklet for Intending Emigrants to Britain*, giving tips about the British way of life, was issued in the West Indies. In view of the current fashion in Britain for men's suits to be dark, prospective emigrants from the Caribbean were warned against wearing the bright clothes they favoured at home lest they should become 'objects of curiosity' in England. In 1966 the London Transport Board included in its training programme for West Indian recruits a tape-recording of typical London Transport sounds such as the 'Min'er doors' heard from the platform staff in the underground. It was fortunate from the viewpoint of good race relations that advancement, at least in the operating department, went solely by seniority. It would be idle to deny that there were occasions of friction, or that some white staff tolerated rather than welcomed the newcomers. Small differences in social customs sometimes fostered resentment. It was traditional for the guard in a train 'set' to brew the tea for himself and the motorman when they reached the terminus at which they were entitled to a break. West Indians were accustomed to drinking Coca Cola and were sometimes reluctant to brew the expected pot of tea.

Management recruited coloured labour without first consulting the unions on their views. Though it was the policy to spread the new recruits thinly round the depots and stations, some NUR branch members became alarmed. In December 1959 Rickmansworth branch wrote to Sidney Greene, complaining about the LTE's method of recruitment of new staff. The EC decided to instruct the General Secretary to seek further information from the secretaries of all LTE sectional councils 'as to places abroad where labour is recruited, type of labour recruited and individual instances where labour is considered unsatisfactory'. The replies received were examined by the union's negotiating committee which reported back to the executive, in June 1960, as follows:

> We have considered the information submitted by our LTE Sectional Councils and are unable to find any adverse effects on our members. We therefore recommend that this matter should not be pursued.

The executive gave unanimous endorsement to this recommendation.[12]

Thereafter the NUR played an important part in fostering good race relations in the London area. More than a decade after many of the West Indians arrived in the capital, a social survey of the LTE workforce was conducted by a team headed by Dennis Brooks. When a lengthman member of the NUR was asked whether he had experienced hostility on the part of white staff to the employment of coloured workers he replied, 'Yes, there has been hostility, but on the transport you have so much backing from the union they can't do much'. Other respondents gave similar replies to the same question.[13]

However, it would be misleading to suggest that there were no problems arising from the employment of large numbers of coloured workers not only in the London area, but also in centres like the West Midlands and Bradford. Some NUR members in the 1960s and 1970s favoured government attempts to restrict entry of persons from the New Commonwealth. The union's AGM debated the issue on numerous occasions. At Margate, in July 1962, a resolution moved by Kentish Town No. 1 branch favouring legislation which restricted immigration was defeated by 69–4 votes after F. S. Mellors, a checker from Birmingham No. 5 branch, assured delegates that 'as soon as you forget they are coloured brothers and call them Brother Smith or Brother Jones you begin to make progress'.[14] Four years later, at Plymouth, delegates endorsed the Labour Party Conference decision of October 1965 accepting the 1962 Immigration Act and rejecting, by 49–25 votes a resolution moved by Stan Mills of Croydon No. 1 branch, opposing discriminatory controls 'in any shape or form'.[15] A Powellite resolution from Kentish Town No. 1 branch, moved at Llandudno in July 1969 was shelved when the proposal to pass to the next business was endorsed by 59–16 votes.[16] At Inverness in the following year a somewhat milder motion favouring restriction of entry of *all* immigrants, regardless of colour, was set aside by the same means by a vote of 45–22.[17]

In the middle and later 1970s the National Front stirred up racialist feelings in London and Midlands areas, prompting the North London District Council of the NUR to recommend an executive campaign to warn members of the dangers of the racist policies of the Front. In a letter to the Council, Sidney Greene agreed that the union had always opposed racial discrimination in any form, but considered that there were organisations, such as Liberation, which were better suited to conducting the campaign than was the NUR. The EC did not agree. With only two dissentients, it decided to circularise the district council's branches as suggested in the Council's original letter.[18] Matters came to a head in 1977–8, when a National Front Railwaymen's Association circulated its own *Newsletter* making scurrilous attacks on branch officers of both the NUR and ASLEF. The NUR's executive acted promptly, instructing the General Secretary to issue a branch circular reiterating the union's complete abhorrence of the anti-union, racist policies of the National Front. Sidney Weighell wrote to the branches at once and wrote a further circular on 7 April 1978, stressing that it was 'not the intention to expel members or get them sacked simply because they were misguided enough to become members of the National Front', but at the same time urging members to report any instance of branch officers abusing their official position in the union by promoting racism and anti-democratic policies.[19] After one of the best debates of the AGM at Llandudno in July 1978, during which Jock Nicolson showed the meeting some of the obnoxious literature of the National Front, a resolution condemning that organisation's activities and pledging the NUR's wholehearted opposition to all forms of racism was carried unanimously.[20] Thereafter there was a substantial decline in National Front activity on the railways.

If labour shortages were foremost among the problems faced by the LTB and LTE for many years, financial difficulties loomed large in the later 1970s. Enid Wistrich, a member of the Labour-controlled GLC of the mid-1970s who was responsible for the Council's transport policy, gave a considered view in 1978 that the chief obstacle to the successful achievement of an urban transport policy was 'the lack of adequate resources'.[21] In the case of London

this requirement that central and local government should face up
to the responsibility of providing adequate financial backing for
transport services was not consistently met.

Each year until 1965 public transport in London paid its way,
a bus strike in 1958 causing the only exception. But from 1965
onwards expenditure consistently exceeded the combined revenues
of train and bus fares. Nevertheless, Barbara Castle's 1968 White
Paper, *Transport in London*,[22] contained the proud boast that,
judged against transport undertakings in large cities abroad which
provided a similarly comprehensive range of activities, the LTB
had done well. So far it had needed no capital grants from outside
sources and its fares, though often criticised, were 'lower than in
many foreign undertakings'. Such confident assertions were no
longer possible a decade later. In 1979 with passenger journeys
by public transport lower than at any time since 1912, bus
journey times often slower than they were in the 1920s and fares
among the highest of any major city in Europe, London could no
longer boast about its public transport services.[23]

An *Evening News* survey, conducted early in 1977, described
Londoners as the 'New Poor of short-hop commuting', since they
paid more per mile travelling by bus or train than did their contemporaries in Paris, Moscow, Munich, Rome, Brussels and
Glasgow.[24] The reason for this depressing situation was principally
that 'lack of adequate resources' which Enid Wistrich rightly
emphasised. A British government Transport and Road Research
Laboratory report, published in March 1980, revealed that British
urban bus subsidies are among the lowest in Europe. In 1975 (the
latest year's figures in the study) subsidies accounted for only 29
per cent of operating costs, whereas in the Netherlands the comparable figure was 70 per cent; in Belgium 69 per cent, France 66
per cent, the USA 46 per cent and in Sweden and Australia 45
per cent.[25] The average figure understates the extent to which
Londoners were disadvantaged by comparison with their contemporaries in other large European cities. Labour Party policy
for Greater London transport announced in 1973 included 'a low
flat fare scheme leading to a free transport system which is our
long term aim'. For the following two years, with Labour in charge
at County Hall, fares were kept stable, while fare relief grants
were raised to over 30 per cent of expenditure (excluding depreciation and renewal provision). Under the pressures of Treasury
restraints, however, and with a Conservative administration taking
over in May 1977, fare relief was cut back to 18 per cent in
1977.[26] The results of the reduction in the real level of financial
support were swingeing fare increases in 1978 and 1979, a reduc-

tion of services and one of the most serious confrontations with the
union over pay since the Second World War, which brought
London to the brink of a public transport strike in June 1979. It
was not only in respect of revenue support that the LTE was
poorly served by comparison wtih other urban transport authorities.
Mr D. A. Quarmby, the member of the LTE Board responsible
for planning, told the Select Committee on Nationalised Industries
in February 1977 that the rate of investment in Parisian transport
improvements had been six or seven times as great as that for
London. Without a more substantial long-term backing from
government resources, the prospect for the LTE recapturing some
of the lost business of the 1970s was not bright.[27]

<h1 style="text-align:center">III</h1>

In contrast with what happened on British Railways, there was no
startling drop in employment in London Transport in the 1960s
and 1970s. The workforce fell from a total of 74,030 in 1964 to
60,449 in 1979, a decline of 12 per cent. But the earlier figure
includes more than 5,000 persons employed on London Country
and Green Line buses which, from 1 January 1970, were transferred from the control of the London Transport Executive to an
independent company. If these members of staff are deducted from
the 1964 total, then the decline in the number of staff employed
was only 11 per cent. The bus crews, with the inspectors who
checked their movements, formed the biggest contingent of the
LTE's workforce. In 1978, out of a total of 59,998 staff, 25,300
were engaged in bus operation, compared with the 11,800 needed
to run the underground services. Most of the remainder, some
21,000 men and women, were engaged in the engineering workshops, while a further 1,900 were occupied in general management.

As might be expected against a background of falling bus passenger traffic, the proportion of the total LTE workforce engaged
in bus operation fell from 47 per cent in 1969 to 42 per cent ten
years later, while the rail staff proportion rose from 18 per cent
to 20 per cent. At the same time those employed in the workshops
(for both bus and train engineering) increased from 32 per cent to
35 per cent of the total, while general management's share
remained steady at 3 per cent. There was little change in the
structure of the rail labour force. The number of motormen and
guards rose from 3,819 in 1969 to 3,975 in 1979, forming just over
one-third of the total, while over the same period of time those

employed in traffic control and station duties rose from 7,152 to 7,905.[28]

Bearing in mind the keen competition from ASLEF, TSSA and the engineering unions, the NUR kept up its membership very well on the railway side of the LTB/LTE undertakings, as is made clear in Table 8.2. Although ASLEF claimed that guards were in the line of promotion to motormen and ought therefore to be

Table 8.2 *NUR Membership: LTB 1963–9 and LTE 1970–79*

1963	11,346	1969	13,411	1975	14,119
1964	11,340	1970	13,664	1976	13,720
1965	11,471	1971	12,794	1977	13,298
1966	13,297	1972	12,796	1978	13,564
1967	13,887	1973	12,468	1979	14,513
1968	13,552	1974	13,207		

Source: Information supplied by Organisation Department, NUR.

recruited into its membership, most men working at the front or the rear of underground trains favoured the NUR. Of a total complement of 3,975 motormen and guards early in 1980, the NUR had recruited 2,537 and ASLEF 1,438. Over 3,000 station staff formed the largest component of the NUR's membership on the LTE; but there were also 1,870 of the union's members in the workshops, 1,580 among the signal engineers, 1,100 carriage and wagon examiners, 1,000 trackmen, 400 supervisors in the operating department, with the remainder of the membership made up from other supervisors, managers, booking clerks, and a large and varied range of other staff in advertising, station cleaning, canteen services, and so on. The large majority of the booking clerks and general management staff and office workers belonged to TSSA.

Part of the explanation for the NUR's increased membership lies in the introduction of the scheme for LTE deduction of union subscriptions from the paybills in 1965 and the arrangements for compulsory trade union membership operating from January 1970–28 February 1972, and since 1975. However, these developments only provided the *opportunity* for the NUR to acquire new members. That the members were actually recruited in the 1970s owed much to the appointment of James Knapp in June 1972 as the first full-time divisional officer solely responsible for the membership employed by the LTE and to Len Bound and Vernon Hince, his successors. In 1963 the 11,346 NUR members working for the LTB formed less than 4 per cent of the union's total membership; sixteen years later LTE members formed over 8 per cent of the total. It was this increase in the relative importance of London Transport workers in relation to overall membership which helped to persuade delegates attending the AGM at Llandudno, in July 1978, to accept the Warwick Report proposal allocating two seats on the executive to LTE members.

IV

Understandably in a period of continuing inflation, the main concern of the NUR representatives in the annual round of wage and salary negotiations was to ensure that the basic rates agreed at least kept pact with the rising cost of living. It was also a primary objective to secure for the workforce some of the benefits of increased productivity. The management side was very conscious of the fact that staff costs fluctuated between 74 and 76 per cent of the LTE's total expenditure, and that there was strong financial pressure to keep these to the minimum by the introduction of labour-saving innovations such as the one-man operation of trains and buses and the automation of signalling. On the other hand, there was an awareness that if the pay offered was below the 'going rate' for comparable jobs in the London area, the staff would not be forthcoming to man the offices, workshops, trains and buses. A further consideration was that many LTE staff at stations such as Watford and Wimbledon worked cheek by jowl alongside British Railways staff and that it was, therefore, politic to ensure that rates of pay of men and women doing similar work for these two transport undertakings were broadly comparable.

The machinery of negotiation for the LTE's railway operational and station staff is simpler than that for British Railways. The unions present claims at meetings with representatives of the management on the Railway Negotiating Committee (RNC). Generally there is agreement at this stage; but if this proves impossible, both sides put their case to the Wages Board, the arbitration panel comprising a chairman and two other members. One reason why there have been few appeals to the Wages Board is that ever since 1920 there has been an understanding between unions and management that wages and salaries for London Transport employees should broadly match those for comparative work on the main line railway companies or, after 1948, British Railways. Between 1953 and 1955 the LTE endeavoured to jettison this tradition in respect of the pay of motormen, the attempt being to fix the motorman's pay below that of the BR driver. In its historic

Decision No. 3 of 2 March 1955, the LT Wages Board, chaired by
Lord Terrington, ruled that:

> As regards the particular case of the motormen, to which all
> three parties directed the greater part of their evidence, the
> Wages Board are unable to find any ground for disturbing the
> relationship which has existed for some 35 years between the
> rates payable to this grade on the London Transport railways
> and on the main line railways.[29]

The decision had the effect of re-enforcing the tradition that pay
settlements for London Transport staff were not reached until after
negotiations for British Rail staff had been concluded. The tradition applied to major concessions of all kinds to railway staff.
Thus, following a RSNT award of mileage bonus payments to
guards on main line railways in June 1965, the LTB agreed to the
same payments being made to LT guards.[30] In his report to the
AGM in 1970 Sidney Greene wrote, 'The Pay and Efficiency Stage
II agreement gave members working in London Transport similar
increases to those on British Railways'.

With the establishment of the new LTE in 1970 management
suggested that there was a case for cutting the umbilical cord which
had linked the rates of pay of the two organisations for fifty
years. At a meeting of the RNC on 11 May 1971 the chairman,
Mr R. M. Robbins of the LTE, claimed that there were increasingly valid grounds for the establishment of a separate London
Transport pay structure at some time. Differences between the
duties performed by BR and LT staff in grades having the same
names were constantly being brought to his attention and he hoped
to establish a fully independent pay structure in the future.[31] To
this end job evaluation exercises which provoked a great deal of
discussion in the NUR executive and in the RNC were conducted
by management in 1971 and 1972.

Before these long-drawn-out exercises were completed, a manpower crisis on the buses and trains of the LTE in 1973–4 made
imperative substantial improvements in rates of pay and conditions of service of the Executive's staff. In the early 1970s Britain
experienced an industrial and commercial boom which peaked in
the period September 1972–September 1973 and was particularly
marked in the London area. During this critical year the number of
unemployed persons in London and the South East fell from
159,000 to 101,400, or from 2·1 per cent to 1·4 per cent of the
workforce, while the number of unfilled vacancies more than
doubled from 99,200 to 202,200. The boom was manifested most

strikingly in the rise in property values, a circumstance which adversely affected the LTE's recruitment efforts since potential recruits often found it impossible to obtain accommodation near the railway and bus depots at prices or rents they could afford. In its *Annual Report* for 1972 the LTE noted:

> The prices of houses in many parts of London are now such that they are beyond the means of many wage earners. It is not, therefore, possible for London Transport to recruit any significant number of men, particularly married men with families, from the provinces.

The LTE was aware of the need to improve the attractiveness of service with London Transport and that this principally implied a substantial rise in wages and salaries paid to those groups of the workforce where recruitment had fallen far short of establishment. In a letter to the unions on 9 January 1973 R. M. Robbins, for the Executive, submitted general proposals for a restructuring of pay and for improvements in working conditions. By the time the two sides got together at a meeting of the Railway Negotiating Committee, on 9 April, the Heath government's Phase 2 incomes policy was in operation, limiting pay increases to £1 per person per week plus 4 per cent of the current paybill to be shared between members of a given workgroup. But when the LTE proposed that the greater part of the 4 per cent should be allocated to those groups with the greatest labour shortages the TSSA representatives, in particular, were worried about the consequent disturbance of pay relativities. Furthermore, the new pay structure proposed by management meant a departure from the close link between BR and LTE rates of pay and the union negotiators were reluctant to abandon this sheet-anchor of policy until they had time to consider the implications further.[32]

Meanwhile the staffing situation worsened. In June 1973 a shortage of drivers and guards compelled the LTE to withdraw 8 per cent of its train services except on the Central and Victoria lines.[33] The average resignation rate for staff was double the rate of recruitment.[34] The NUR's branches in the London area were very worried. On 22 May Jock Nicolson, for the North West London District Council, wrote to Sidney Greene asking him to receive a deputation and also wrote to Sir Reginald Goodwin, leader of the GLC, asking that the crisis in London's transport services should be dealt with 'as a matter of urgency'. East Ham, Neasden and Earls Court branches also expressed their grave concern in letters to the General Secretary. Sidney Greene wrote to the GLC, on the

8 June and 18 July, stressing the seriousness of the problem.

These representations had the desired effect. On 3 July 1973 the LTE received a request from the GLC that it should submit for the Council's consideration a detailed and urgent review of London Transport's overall staff position indicating in particular (a) how bad the shortage is in the various departments of the Executive's work; (b) what additional steps the Executive are taking to improve the position; and (c) what are the ways in which, in the Executive's view, the council could give further help in this sphere.[35]

That the situation gave cause for alarm was revealed by Mr J. Cope, Chief Industrial Relations Officer of the LTE, in a letter to Sidney Greene dated 27 August 1973, in which he reported that the organisation was 566 persons, or 5·8 per cent, short of establishment, but that within the general total there was an unfilled vacancy rate of 7·8 per cent for guards, 17·6 per cent for railmen and 19·8 per cent for station foremen. Such general figures disguised the greater seriousness of the problem on particular lines. On 31 July the Secretary of the East Ham branch wrote to Sidney Greene that in the afternoon of 28 July only three trains were in service on the Bakerloo Line.[36] The LTE's response, which was largely the result of close and friendly liaison between its own board member, Jim Mortimer, and the NUR's Charlie Turnock,[37] was to present the unions with a nine-point plan on 31 July. These proposals included the improvement of earnings to a level sufficient to secure an adequate labour force; the enhancement of pensions to a level comparable with those in other public-sector employments; recognition by special premium payments for work done at socially inconvenient times; established staff status, namely, that given to salaried staff, to be given to all grades after five years' service; improved holiday entitlements; improved travel facilities for families of LT staff; an expansion of staff housing and mortgage arrangements; bonuses for staff finding recruits in areas of staff shortage; and greater flexibility in the use of labour, including the employment of women in grades until then restricted to men.[38] At the Railway Negotiating Committee meeting, on 1 August, it was agreed to refer these proposals for more detailed consideration by a joint working party. The NUR executive endorsed this action.[39]

In the meantime the LTE tried to increase the number of its bus services by lowering the qualifications needed for trainee-drivers; the proportion of applicants accepted for training rose from 33 per cent in 1970 to 42 per cent in 1973. The LTE also responded to

the GLC's offer to help.[40] Its *Annual Report* for 1974 noted that
400 council houses located near the depots had been made available to LTE staff and three-quarters of these homes were occupied
by bus or train crew members and their families by the end of
1975. In return the LTE offered the council land and air space
suitable for council house development in exchange for a corresponding number of council house nominations for its staff in
areas where access to housing was a vital factor in recruitment.
The Executive also took its own measures to improve housing
provision for its staff.

It was not until 18 August 1974, nearly a year after the LTE
had submitted its nine-point plan to the unions, that the plan was
brought into operation. The delay brought frustrations to both
commuters and staff, but is not difficult to explain. The joint
working party had a big task so that its report, giving flesh and
blood to the nine points of the plan, was not available until 11
December when the LTE and union representatives endorsed it
(with some union reservations on labour flexibility). On 8 January
the EC or the NUR both approved the report and the proposal
that it should be submitted to the government's Pay Board for
endorsement.[41] However, on 3 April 1974, the Pay Board turned
down the plan, because the proposal to raise LTE railmen's basic
pay from £22 to £26 per week exceeded the limits of the government's Phase 3 pay code restricting wage increases to £2·25 per
week or 7 per cent (whichever yardstick best suited the unions).
As the period of operation of the code was a year from October
1973, it was clear that emergency measures would have to be
taken if London transport services were not to suffer further
serious depletion. On 5 April, therefore, the EC of the NUR
instructed Sidney Greene to seek an urgent meeting with Michael
Foot, Minister of State for Employment in the recently established
Labour government. When the unions and the LTE put their
case at a meeting with Michael Foot on 1 May, he was impressed
by what he heard and subsequently wrote Sidney Greene conceding
that the case presented to him was 'an exceedingly strong one'. But
for the time being he was inhibited from action because of the
pay code.

Meanwhile the NUR's LTE branches and the members of the
executive became extremely restive. On 1 July at Unity House the
union's executive resolved that in view of the 'ever-worsening staff
position on the LTE', an immediate further meeting should be
sought with Michael Foot.[42] When he met the railwaymen four
days later, the Minister assured them that he recognised that their
case was of major importance. He hoped to be able to give a

more positive response to their demands 'within a short period of time'.[43] Just over a month later, on 7 August 1974, with rates of pay for British Rail staff settled after RSNT Award No. 43, and with the statutory limits on pay removed from 26 July, a lengthy meeting of the Railway Negotiating Committee agreed a modified version of the nine-point plan.[44]

The outstanding feature of the agreement, ratified by the EC on 8 August, was that the railman's rate of pay was raised from the £25·05 per week of the April 1974 Phase 3 award, to £28·35, and that there were upward adjustments to all the other wage and salary rates. Pay enhancements for staff working unsocial hours were substantially improved. Sunday working was to be paid at double-time rates instead of time-and-and-three-quarter rates; all the Saturday working rates were improved (to time-and-a-half for work between 00.00 hours and 18.00 hours and to time-and-two-thirds for work between 18.00 and 24.00 hours). Most rostered overtime duties and rest-day working were to be paid at double-time rates instead of time-and-a-half. All conciliation staff with at least five years' service were to receive established status, entitling them to improved pensions, holidays and sick-pay arrangements. All staff with more than one year's service were entitled to four weeks' holiday, which would be paid at the improved rate of basic pay plus one-fifth instead of basic plus one-eighth. Improved free-travel facilities were introduced for the members of the LTE and their families.[45] In the words of the LTE's *Annual Report* for 1974, this substantial package of improvements 'had a dramatic effect on recruitment' and wastage, especially in the key railway operating grades. In its report a year later the Executive noted with satisfaction that 'staff wastage was at a low rate' and that 'losses of scheduled mileage on buses and trains through staff shortages, which had reached levels of 15 and 18 per cent respectively in the worst period of 1974, were down to 6 and 2 per cent by the end of 1975'.

The hundreds of hours spent by Frank Cannon, Charlie Turnock and other NUR representatives in negotiations with the LTE, representations to the Pay Board, urgent appeals to Michael Foot and answering questions at branch and district council meetings were primarily aimed at improving the working conditions of those railway staff in the London area who over many months had borne the brunt of public criticism arising from the cancellation of train services. But the outcome of their labours was not only higher pay for the staff, but also the restoration of an essential public service.

The wage increases negotiated for London Transport workers in the years 1975–8 were in broad conformity with Phases 1–3 of the Labour government's Social Contract with the unions. Phase 4, which was intended to operate from 1 August 1978 to 31 July 1979, was explained in the government's White Paper, *Winning the Battle Against Inflation* (Cmnd 7293), published on 21 July 1978. Its leading feature was a proposed 5 per cent limit on earnings. But the government undoubtedly misjudged the groundswell of opinion against continued wage restraint (the increase in the retail price index between January 1977 and January 1978 was 9·9 per cent) and the 1978 TUC, despite an impassioned appeal from Sidney Weighell for the continuance of a carefully thought out incomes policy, opted for a return to free collective bargaining. Earlier the AGM of the NUR had instructed the EC to negotiate with the LTE for 'a substantial increase' in wages and salaries. The union's objective in the meetings of the RNC which began on 12 March 1979 was to restore and improve upon the living standards secured in 1975 – the last occasion on which there had been negotiations under 'normal' collective bargaining conditions. Since 1975 the retail price index had risen by 60·5 per cent, and the NUR research department calculated that rises of from 17 per cent for railmen to 25·3 per cent for top-grade supervisors were required to achieve comparability in real terms with the pay rates of 1975.

However, since 1975 important changes in the political complexion of the GLC and in the financial position of the LTE made it certain that a satisfactory wage settlement would be far more difficult to achieve. In December 1976 when Richard Brew, GLC Conservative opposition spokesman on transport, announced the changes his party would make if they won the May 1977 Election, he declared that the level of the council's support to London Transport was 'totally unacceptable'.[46] Following their Election victory, the Conservatives reduced the fares relief grant from £62,725,000 to £50,600,000 despite the prevailing high rate of inflation.[47] To make matters worse the LTE had budgeted for an increase in the wages bill of only 5 per cent in the anticipation that Jim Callaghan's 5 per cent limit would be acceptable by the TUC.[48]

These were among the reasons for the LTE responding to the unions' 1979 pay claim by a low offer of 6·5 per cent made at a meeting of the RNC on 30 March 1979. Mr Cameron, for the LTE, conceded that this figure was inadequate but pointed out that it was all the organisation could afford. When it was made abundantly clear to him that the offer was unacceptable, he and his colleagues had discussions with the GLC which refused to hand over any more money but authorised the use of funds from the

LTE's general reserves. On 20 April the Executive sent the unions details of a revised offer of 9 per cent plus other marginal improvements. But since this was well below the rise in the cost of living, the NUR executive, meeting on 18 May, unanimously rejected it as being 'totally inadequate'.[49] In an endeavour to find a way out of the impasse the union's representatives met the Chairman of the LTE, on 22 May, and met the representatives of the other unions at Unity House on the following day. The outcome was a further meeting of the RNC, on 31 May, when the wide gap between the unions' claim for 17 per cent and the Executive's final offer of 10·32 per cent on paybill costs was made manifest. Back at Unity House on 1 June, the EC of the NUR decided unanimously to call a strike of all its LTE members (including workshop grades) for Monday 18 June.[50] The EC, by no means anxious for a head-on confrontation, had left time for further negotiations and this time was profitably spent. Meetings of the parties in dispute were held at the London headquarters of the Advisory, Conciliation and Arbitration Service on 12 and 14 June, when it was agreed to refer the points at issue to an arbitration panel. On 15 June the EC agreed to postpone the strike action on the understanding that the arbitration would commence no later than 17 June and that the arbitrators would produce their award by 22 June.[51] The tribunal, comprising J. D. Hughes (nominated by the unions), E. C. Barber (nominated by the LTE), with I. Buchanan as the independent chairman, met on 17 and 19 June to hear the employer's and unions' arguments. Its award of an 11 per cent increase, plus the consolidation of the existing £2 supplement to wages and a consequential adjustment of differentials for the higher paid, though below the 17 per cent of the claim, satisfied the NUR which felt justified in standing firm for an improvement on the LTE's 'final' offer. The award was operative from 23 April 1979.[52]

In contrast with the uncomplicated machinery of negotiation for determining the pay and working conditions of train, platform, routine maintenance and administrative staff, the negotiation of wages and conditions of service of the railway workshop staff presented greater difficulties because engineering and administrative staff unions were involved besides the NUR and TSSA. At a meeting of union representatives, in April 1944, it was agreed to set up a joint committee of seven NUR and seven craft union representatives (later increased to nine from each group), to be known as the Joint Committee of Unions (JCU), to negotiate with management on behalf of London Transport workshop staff. The machinery of negotiation remained intact until a difference of opinion arose

between the NUR and the other unions on the method of applying
the government's pay guidelines effective from 1 August 1976.
Despite a reference of the dispute to ACAS on 3 December 1976,
it did not prove possible to reach an agreement. Hence in March
of the following year the EC of the NUR decided to withdraw from
the JCU, which it found no longer 'an effective and acceptable
negotiating body'.[53]

In the case it presented to the Buchanan arbitration panel on
17 June 1979 for parity in pay rises awarded to RNC-controlled
staff and the staff employed in the railway workshops, the NUR
made reference to the absence of any formal negotiating machinery
for the LTE workshop employees. The panel, in its award of 22
June, agreed that negotiations on workshop pay had been on an
ad hoc basis. It recognised the need to formalise railway workshop
negotiating procedures and suggested that the NUR should take
the lead in bringing the other unions together with the object of re-
establishing some formal negotiating machinery. This advice was
followed by the NUR, and discussions with the other parties concerned took place in the latter part of 1979.[54]

V

The tightening of the GLC purse-strings, the decline in passenger
traffic on both tubes and buses, and the worsening financial position
of the LTE in the later 1970s, combined to spotlight the importance
of increasing labour productivity. It is, however, a mistake to
imagine that it was only under the stress of financial crisis that
management and unions engaged in meaningful talks on increasing
the efficiency of the LTE's workforce. Labour-saving improvements were being introduced throughout the 1960s and 1970s. In
October 1971, for example, a new underfloor lathe, enabling the
machinery of the whole profile of the wheels of rolling stock to be
undertaken without the necessity of removing the wheels from the
vehicle, was brought into use at the Northfields depot of the Piccadilly Line.[55]

A few years later far more important labour-saving innovations
were effected in train operation and signalling. In the course of
1964 automatic train operation reached the stage of full-scale
trials in regular passenger services on the Hainault–Woodford
section of the Central Line, and as a result of the success of this
experiment it was decided to adopt the principle of automatic train
operation on the whole of the Victoria Line, the main part of
which was opened on 1 September 1968. The LTB considered

that the automatic operation of trains (employing a motorman to
open and close the doors, but no guards); the programme machine
signalling at seven interlocking machine rooms; the facilities for
communicating between the controlling staff, the station staff,
motormen and passengers and the automatic ticket-issuing system
represented 'as great an advance over its predecessors as an
electric railway represents over a steam railway'.[56]

The onset of automatic train operation posed the question of
the extent to which the man in the 'driving' cab should receive
extra payment, given his assumption of duties formerly undertaken
by the guard. The problem was first discussed at a meeting of the
RNC on 3 March 1964, when Mr Bull, for the LTB, proposed an
additional allowance of 48s per week above the wages received by
the motorman driving the non-automatic trains. The union representatives were not prepared to accept this offer and there were
two adjournments in the course of a long meeting. Eventually
the Board increased its offer to bring the automatic train operator's
wage up to 372s per week, on a par with the minimum rate paid
to supervisors, class I, but without supervisory status or conditions. These revised proposals received the unanimous endorsement
of the EC of the NUR and the other union executives.[57]

As the date of opening of the Victoria Line approached the
whole question of the automatic train operator's rate of pay again
came into the forefront of the discussions. At a meeting of the
RNC held on 29 November 1967 George Brassington, for the
NUR, claimed that since the Victoria Line would be 'a show-
piece' and its operation would produce a considerable saving in
staff such as trainmen and booking clerks, there was a strong case
for improving the rate of pay of the automatic train operator.
Mr Bull, for the LTE, asserted that it would be unwise to increase
still further the differential between the pay of the automatic train
operator and that of the motorman, but suggested that they should
set up a sub-committee to investigate the whole question of payments to Victoria Line staff. At its meeting in March 1968 the
NUR executive agreed to this proposal.[58] A report of the sub-
committee was available at the next meeting of the RNC, on 27
June 1968, but was not discussed as no ASLEF representatives
were in attendance.[59] When the RNC met again on 17 July, there
was deadlock as Mr Bull reported that the LTE considered that
it would be inequitable to increase the existing differential of 26s
per week above the motorman's rate.[60] It was not until 19 June
1969 that the problem was again raised at a meeting of the RNC,
when it was agreed to defer further consideration until after a
working party had been appointed and had reported.[61] Since

further meetings in the course of 1970 failed to result in agreement, the unions' claim was referred to the LT Wages Board, which in its Decision No. 7 of January 1971 ruled that automatic train operators' pay should be increased by 9s a week with effect from the first full pay period following 1 May 1970.[62] This ruling was accepted unanimously by the NUR executive in March 1971.[63] Under the new agreement the automatic train operator with a basic wage of £32·05 per week in 1971 was entitled to £4·65 per week more than the motorman, a sum which was only 21·7 per cent of the wage of the guard he displaced. Thus, the LTE saved well over three-quarters of the guard's wage when the switch to automatic train operation was made. By agreeing to these arrangements the unions had made a substantial contribution to increasing labour productivity.[64]

It is understandable, in the light of the operational economies achieved on the Victoria Line that the LTE was keen to extend one-man operation of trains on other lines of the underground system especially in the circumstances of the organisation's deteriorating financial position. Discussions on labour economies on the Hammersmith and Circle lines had taken place as far back as 9 October 1968 when, at a meeting of the RNC, the unions agreed in principle to one-man operation of trains on these lines; but implementation was impossible at that time, since the required new rolling stock was not available.[65] By 1976, however, the new rolling stock was available and at a meeting of the RNC held on 6 May 1977 the LTE endeavoured to get agreement with the unions on a rate of payment for the driver of one-man-operated trains. By this time the unemployment situation in the country was more serious than it had been ten years earlier, and the experience of operating the trains of the Victoria Line showed that the operator was subject to greater strains (including those arising from the fact that his entire shift was worked underground). Charlie Turnock therefore confessed that 'because of the general employment situation, the view appeared to be forming in the minds of the membership that they should have nothing to do with one-man operation.'[66] This view was reflected in a decision of the EC later that year that its members 'no longer wished to pursue one-man operation'.[67] In the meantime, in defiance of the wishes of the unions, the LTE referred the question of the rates of pay appropriate for one-man operation of trains to the Wages Board.

By the summer of 1979 the NUR executive thought better of the earlier opposition to the LTE's plans. In July it agreed to engage in discussions with management, and by 13 September a joint policy was agreed. One-man operation was to be introduced as soon as possible on the Circle and Hammersmith and City lines and was to be extended to the District and Metropolitan lines in due course. Furthermore, subject to any restraints being imposed by the Chief Inspecting Officer of Railways, one-man operation would be extended to the remainder of the underground system. In return a flat sum equal to the 7·5 per cent of the basic rate of pay was to be given to all staff employed in the traffic division of the Railway Operating Department. The driver was to be paid at the same rate as the automatic train operator. At the end of six months there was to be a review of the operation of the new system.[68] Undoubtedly, one of the main reasons why the EC was prepared to give such a wide acceptance of one-man operation of trains in 1979, whereas two years earlier it was rejected, was that extra money was offered by the LTE not only to the train operators, but to all operational staff.

VI

An aspect of working life on the London underground which caused the rank and file of the NUR to be hesitant about accepting one-man operation of trains was the increased incidence of violence and vandalism on the tubes – as on the buses. Since assaults were becoming more frequent, it was felt that there was safety in numbers, that two men on duty on a train were better than one. In an incident at Neasden tube station on the evening of 14 March 1980 when 200 youths devastated station property and injured twenty-five people, including a train driver, naturally attracted newspaper headlines. For many of the public this was the first indication they had had that violence and vandalism on the Underground was a serious evil. In fact, it was a persistent problem throughout the 1970s. In 1973 the union's LTE branches and the LTE sub-council of the North London District Council were so disturbed at the situation that they wrote to Sidney Greene demanding enclosed boxes for ticket collectors, improved telephone links with the police and other aids to improved security.[69] From that time onwards the *Railway Review*, the EC and the union's officers maintained a continuous campaign in favour of greater staff and passenger protection. The severity of the problem can be gauged from the figures of *reported* assaults (that is, generally those serious enough to involve bodily injury needing hospital treatment or a visit to a doctor) (Table 8.3).

The staff most vulnerable to attack were ticket collectors on late shifts and their most likely assailants were young people under

Table 8.3   *Assaults on LTE Staff, 1972–9*

1972	1973	1974	1975	1976	1977	1978	1979
280	200	190	270	214	240	300	369

Source: Home Office Working Conference on Violence on Public Transport, 6 May 1980; NUR file MLT/14/19.

the age of 25 (though older drunks were also a menace). In 1979 56 per cent of incidents occurred at ticket barriers, while a further 24 per cent happened on the station platforms. A typical incident was that reported at Clapham Common station, on 5 March 1973, when a woman ticket collector was felled to the ground by a punch in the face delivered by one of two young fare-dodgers. Nevertheless, no member of staff who had any sort of contact with the public was immune. During 1974–9 207 guards and 76 motormen or automatic train operators were assaulted and there were cases of booking clerks being injured through bricks or iron bars being thrown into their offices. (None the less the London Underground was a safer place in which to travel than was the Paris Metro or the New York Subway.) Outstanding among many interventions instigated by the NUR to try and improve the situation was the introduction of a resolution at the 1970 TUC, an interview with Reginald Maudling, Home Secretary, in the following year and an interview with William Whitelaw, Home Secretary, and Norman Fowler, Minister of Transport, on 2 October 1979, at which it was agreed that a working conference on violence in public transport should be arranged. In collaboration with the other railway unions the NUR prepared a detailed paper for discussion at the working conference held on 6 May 1980.

Meanwhile outbreaks of violence at Southgate, Finsbury Park and on the occasion of international football matches, besides the Neasden incident on 14 March 1980, were more than many LTE operational staff in the areas worst affected were prepared to tolerate. On the District and Central lines there were unofficial stoppages after 10 p.m. at weekends. Finally, the NUR executive called a one-day stoppage for Saturday 29 March and then instructed members that all LTE stations would close at 10 p.m. on Fridays and Saturdays on 18 and 19, 25 and 26 April to draw public attention to the urgent need for improved security on the Underground system. When there were indications from the Home Office that the allocation of police forces would be increased (there were only 175 British Transport Police available for service for the 280 stations of the LTE, whereas the New York Subway, with a system roughly comparable in extent, had 4,000 police), and when it became apparent that more money would be available for alarm systems, closed-circuit TV, and so on, the NUR EC called a halt to further strikes and the union played a useful part in the working conference. These security measures were undoubtedly necessary, but the lower figures for assaults in 1973 and 1974 when there was a GLC policy of static fares, suggest that a more fundamental reform would be a substantial improvement in government financial support – more in line with that made available to major cities overseas – to make possible a policy of stable fares. This would remove one of the main causes of public resentment and violence against LTE staff. But such changes in policy presuppose a recognition by the public and the government that efficient and inexpensive – or even 'free' – public transport services is a vital necessity for the social welfare and economic prosperity of the capital.

CHAPTER 9

THE NUR IN BUSES, DOCKS, HOTELS AND CATERING

I

T HE NUR has been involved in the organisation of bus workers for more than half a century. In case this involvement be considered an unjustified intrusion into territory generally occupied by other unions, it needs to be pointed out that some of the earliest motor bus services were established by railway companies as substitutes for railway branch line extensions. This was the case with the GWR, which inaugurated the first railway-owned motor bus service – in the Duchy of Cornwall – on 17 August 1903. Within a month of this pioneering venture the NER followed suit with a similar service in the East Riding of Yorkshire. However, these were small-scale experiments not widely followed before the First World War. But with the rapid increase in the number of motor lorries and independently owned motor bus services in the 1920s, pressure mounted in the board rooms of the four main line railway companies, established under the Railways Act of 1921, for a more systematic railway-company involvement in road transport. In 1928, therefore, each of these companies obtained an Act of Parliament, authorising investment in road-transport undertakings.

Charlie Cramp, the NUR's Industrial General Secretary, quickly grasped the significance of these changes in management policy and the opportunity they provided the NUR to extend its influence. In his report to the AGM in the early summer of 1928 he wrote:

> The future of railways and railwaymen will be profoundly affected by the progress of the measures now before Parliament by which the companies are seeking powers to use the public roads. . . It will be for the NUR to remove the stigma of sweated labour which has been the curse of a large number of men employed in road transport. . . We shall change our methods and enlarge our scope to meet it.

Within six months a specially summoned meeting of the EC, held

in Cardiff on 28 December 1928, learned that the Railway Staff
Conference, eight days earlier, had reached agreement on applying
to railway-company bus workers most of the conditions of service
previously negotiated for railwaymen.[1] The Executive felt fully
justified in organising the bus workers employed by the subsidiary companies of the railways. Rule 1, section 4(a) of the
union's current *Rule Book* read (in part): 'The objects of the
union shall be to secure the complete organisation of all workers
employed on or in connection with any railway in the UK or
Irish Free State.' It had no doubt that the busmen were employed
'in connection with' the railway companies. It was, nevertheless,
important to reach an understanding with the TGWU, which
organised bus workers in many parts of the country. To this end
numerous meetings were held between representatives of the two
unions over the period 1928–32, culminating in a formal agreement in June 1932, signed by Ernest Bevin (Secretary) and Herbert
Kershaw (Chairman), for the TGWU, and by Charlie Cramp
(Industrial General Secretary) and William Dobbie (President),
for the NUR. The policy agreed by the two parties was that the
TGWU recognised the NUR's claim to organise the employees of
eleven railway-controlled companies while, in return, the NUR
conceded the TGWU's right to develop its organisation of bus
staff in Scotland, London and in forty-nine major companies
operating in other parts of the country. With one important
exception, the eleven companies allocated to the NUR in 1932
covered the same territory as that covered by the union in 1980.
The original eleven companies were the Southern Vectis the Hants
and Dorset· Western National; Devon General· Mansfield and
District; Wilts and Dorset· Southern National; Lincolnshire Road
Car Co.; East Midlands Omnibus Co.; North West Road Car Co.;
and Western Welsh. In the case of United Automobile Services the
NUR was allocated its Northumberland territory, while the TGWU
was responsible for the remainder. The right of the NUR to
organise some of the depots of Ribble Motor Services was recognised, but the TGWU controlled most of them. The map of NBC
operating companies in 1979, in Figure 9.1, shows the companies
in which the NUR exercises organising rights. The one major
change in the division of responsibility came in 1971 when, as a
result of developments described below, Western Welsh territories
passed to the TGWU in return for the NUR assuming responsibility for the bus staff employed in Exeter.

Under the Transport Act 1947, ownership of the railway-
controlled omnibus companies passed to the British Transport
Commission, while their management was delegated to the Road

Figure 9.1 *National bus company operators with which NUR has negotiating rights*

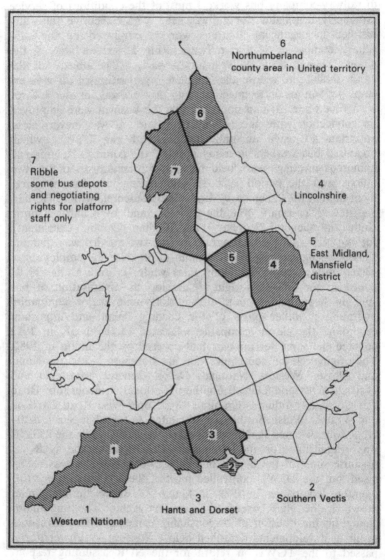

6
Northumberland
county area in United territory

7
Ribble
some bus depots
and negotiating
rights for platform
staff only

4
Lincolnshire

5
East Midland,
Mansfield
district

3
Hants and Dorset

2
Southern Vectis

1
Western National

Transport Executive. In 1949 the road passenger undertakings of the BTC were split from the road freight business and placed under the management of a new Road Passenger Executive. More

Plate 9 The General Secretary and Assistant General Secretaries – L. to R., Charles Turrock, AGS; Sidney Weighell, General Secretary; Russell Tuck, Senior AGS; Frank Cannon, AGS.

Plate 10 (a) Shunter with shunting pole.

(b) Millerhill marshalling yard showing control tower (centre right) and electronically controlled wagon retarders (centre).

Plate 11 (a) Goods handling, old style, Lime Street Station

(b) Mechanical goods handling – the 'Brute'.

Plate 12 Paddington booking office, old style.

Plate 13 (a) Modern booking office, Euston.

(b) Multi-printer ticket issuing and accounting machine.

(c) National Cash Register ticket machine.

Plate 14 (a) Old style locomotive maintenance.

(b) Driver of steam locomotive.

Plate 15 (a) Goods guard in brake van.

(b) Passenger guard.

Plate 16 Frant Place.

changes occurred at the beginning of 1963 when the Transport Holding Company, established by Ernest Marples under his Transport Act 1962, became responsible for the road passenger undertakings formerly controlled by the Road Passenger Executive. Finally, under Barbara Castle's Transport Act of 1968, the National Bus Company acquired all the publicly owned bus undertakings in England and Wales except the LTE and the municipally owned concerns.

Despite the name National Bus Company, wage and salary rates and working conditions in the industry lacked the degree of uniformity characteristic of railway employment. The pre-1969 bus companies still kept some of their separate identities. The bus or coach might be labelled 'National' but elsewhere on the bodywork it would carry a name such as 'Royal Blue' or 'Devon General', indicating its origins. The term 'old Spanish custom' was used to explain local bus agreements which, in part, ran counter to what had been settled on a national basis.[2] In 1974 responsibility for the express and coach tour business was transferred from the NBC to a new organisation, National Travel.

II

The decline in bus travel after 1960 was unmistakable. The total number of passenger journeys, excluding those in the London area, but including those made within the areas of the Passenger Transport Authorities, the NBC, the Scottish Bus Group and the local authorities, fell from 10,931 million in 1960 to 6,003 million in 1978, a decline of nearly 45 per cent. For the companies which in 1969 merged into the NBC, the reduction in the number of journeys made was from 3,233 million to 1,825 million over the same span of time, a fall slightly less than the national average.[3] The principal reason for the industry's reduced contribution to road passenger travel was the rapid increase in the use of privately owned road passenger vehicles which grew in number from 5·5 million in 1960 to 14 million in 1979. A further cause of the decline in bus usage was the virtual disappearance of Saturday working in offices and factories and the increased reliance on the TV for entertainment. However, it would be quite wrong to conclude that bus services were no longer needed. In 1978 over a half of the households of Britain north of a line drawn from the Humber to the Mersey were without private motor transport.[4] The growth in private car ownership increased the mobility of millions of more fortunately placed members of society; simultaneously it was indirectly respon-

sible for the decrease in mobility of millions of others less fortunately placed. Inevitably the decline in road public passenger
transport was accompanied by a decrease in employment in the
industry. In 1960, exclusive of private bus concerns and the LTB,
the industry had nearly 216,000 employees. A decade later the
workforce had fallen by nearly one-fifth to 176,000. In the NBC
companies jobs disappeared at a faster rate than the national
average. There were 87,614 staff on their books in 1965, and only
63,649 in 1978.[5]

Through the 1960s and 1970s between one-eighth and one-
twelfth of the NBC's workforce were members of the NUR
although, as shown above, the union recruited in a minority of the
NBC companies. NUR bus membership in the two years 1962
and 1978 is summarised in Table 9.1. Most of the NUR's members

Table 9.1 *NUR Bus Membership*

	1962	1978
Bristol Omnibus Co.	—	26
Devon General	931	828
East Midland	794	749
Greenslades Tours	—	75
Hants and Dorset	2,150	2,020
Lincolnshire Road Car Co.	1,217	752
Mansfield District Traction	452	264
National Travel Co.	—	88
Red and White	—	1
Ribble Motor Services	461	230
Southern Vectis	452	300
Southern and Western National	2,744	1,542
South Wales Transport	—	7
Terranean's	—	3
United Auto Services	1,661	1,100
Western Welsh	1,039	22
Totals	11,901	8,007

Source: Movements Department, NUR.

came from the platform staff, that is, the drivers and conductors;
but in 1962 the total included 716 men and women from the
clerical and supervisory staffs. Both the AUEW and the NUR
compete for membership among the labour force in engineering
maintenance.

Collective bargaining has been a feature of municipal bus management since at least 1919, when the National Joint Industrial Council (NJIC) was set up to regulate the wages and conditions of tramway workers. In subsequent years, as buses replaced trams, the same machinery of negotiation was used for determining the terms of employment of bus workers. The bus and coach operators which served longer routes, mainly outside municipal boundaries, had no national agreements until 14 June 1940 when the representatives of forty-three of the larger companies reached an agreement with the unions involved, the TGWU, NUR and GMWU, to establish the National Council for the Omnibus Industry (NCOI). Unions and management were equally represented on this new negotiating body, whose overall size and structure of union representation varied over time. In 1978 there were twenty representatives each of the employers and the unions, with the union panel divided on the basis of fifteen TGWU, three NUR, one GMWU and one craft union.[6] Although the three NUR representatives have always been very much of a minority on the Council, this has not deterred them from taking the initiative on a number of important issues. The viewpoint expressed by NUR leaders was that members of a minority group (such as the busmen) got good value from their membership, since the union 'leant over backwards' to show that it had not forgotten their interests.[7] The representatives of the NUR on the NCOL brought their experience of pay negotiations in parallel or complementary organisations, such as National Carriers, to the discussions of the Council.

The one big change in the division of the field of organisation between the NUR and the TGWU came in June 1971, when the NUR agreed to relinquish its responsibility for organising the platform staff of the Western Welsh Omnibus Co. in return for the TGWU's yielding to the NUR the right to organise the staff of Exeter City Bus Services, from that date merged with the Devon General Omnibus Co. The change came about as a result of a dispute between the EC and national officers of the NUR on the one hand, and the members of its Bridgend No. 2 (Bus) branch on the other. The exceptionally stable employment situation in the bus depot generated a remarkable continuity of branch membership whose loyalty to the branch officers was strengthened at the focal point of branch activity, the bus depot canteen where 'Ossie' Evans, the secretary, collected members' dues. The two main policy developments in 1968–9, the proposed one-man operation (OMO) of buses and the introduction of an urban bonus scheme were the immediate occasion for a large majority of members of the branch leaving the NUR; but a further underlying cause of the erosion of loyalty to the national organisation was the strong sense of local patriotism and a resentment at being 'steam-rollered' by the national officers into the acceptance of unpalatable facts and new methods of operation.[8] Sidney Greene, Russell Tuck and organiser J. Kirkwood (who negotiated directly with the branch) found inconsistencies in Ossie Evans's behaviour. As secretary of the NUR Busworkers' National Conference, in 1966, he had advocated management deduction of union contributions through the paybills. As one of the NUR representatives on the NCOI at its meeting on 19 April 1968 he had been a party to the unanimous decision of the Council to approve an urban bonus scheme. On the other hand, at a further meeting on 3 May 1968 he strenuously opposed an OMO bonus scheme, which was nevertheless agreed by a narrow majority.[9] Early in 1969, consistent with EC and NUR Busworkers' National Conference policy, organiser A. Kirkwood signed an agreement with the General Manager of the Western Welsh Omnibus Co. for the deduction of union subscriptions through the paybills from 23 February 1969. But when Kirkwood attended a special meeting of the branch on 28 January 1969, a majority of the members present followed Ossie Evans's advice to reject the agreement the organiser had signed. In a letter to Sidney Greene dated 26 October 1968 Evans had warned that the Bridgend No. 2 members were 'disenchanted with the NUR on the question of urban bonus payments and single-manning agreements'. On 22 February 1968 Evans wrote again, informing the General Secretary that members of the branch had instructed him to make arrangements for them to leave the NUR. Every effort was made to prevent the breakaway. The chairman and secretary of the branch were invited to Unity House to discuss their grievances with members of the organisation sub-committee. Circulars were sent to all branch members at Bridgend and A. Kirkwood was active in the area. Between thirty and forty of the 300 busmen concerned remained loyal to the NUR. Most of the remainder formed the Bridgend Busworkers' Association, which survived until its members joined the TGWU in 1971.

The agreement with the TGWU recognised the right of NUR members at Bridgend and TGWU members at Exeter to retain their membership – and their branches – even though all the Western Welsh staff were urged to join the TGWU and the Exeter staff the NUR. The arrangement was justified on the grounds of preserving the individual's liberty; but it created problems. Competition for members was keen. Allan Kemp, an NUR busmen's leader in the area, recalls an episode which occurred in the Exeter depot in 1971:

I had been informed by management that they had taken on a Mr Jenkins, so on the Monday morning that he was due to start I set out in search of him. On entering the canteen I saw a strange face. The man was sitting at a table drinking tea. He was wearing a blue dust jacket and had a cash bag slung round his neck. 'Are you Mr Jenkins?' I asked him. On being told that that was his name, I launched into my usual speech about why he should join the NUR, outlining the benefits of such membership. He remarked, 'That's all very well but I'm not going to join'. I returned to the attack and finished with the words 'Anyone who comes on these premises joins the NUR' and with the same thrust the forms under his nose. He uttered a deep sigh and began to fill them in. 'I've heard of closed shops', he said, 'but this is ridiculous; I only came in here to deliver the milk!' I signed the correct Mr Jenkins later in the day.[10]

III

Improvements in bus workers' wages and conditions of service came slowly in the course of the 1960s and 1970s. The most striking improvements were in the length of the working day. Under the terms of an NCOI agreement dated 9 May 1960, the working week was reduced from forty-four hours to forty-two from 8 August of that year. Five years later a committee of inquiry under the chairmanship of Sir Roy Wilson, QC recommended the introduction of the forty-hour week, a proposal which was implemented in April 1966. On the other hand, enhancement payments to busmen for overtime, Sunday late-night/early-morning and Bank Holiday working were less generous than those made to railwaymen. The Robertson Award of May 1961 recommended the payment of time-and-a-quarter rates for Saturday-afternoon working with improved allowances for early starting and late finishing of weekday shifts and double-time for all public holidays.[11] Sidney Greene described the March 1970 settlement of the NCOI as a 'landmark for busmen', since for the first time, parity in the pay of municipal and NBC busmen was achieved.[12]

On 26 June 1967 the trade union side of the NCOI presented an agreed programme of improvements for consideration and action by the management panel. This was the Busman's Charter. The programme included (a) a minimum wage of £15 a week; (b) the forty-hour week to be worked in five days; (c) Sunday working to be outside the guaranteed week; (d) the introduction of an adequate pension scheme; (e) the abolition of spreadover duties and the two-hour flexibility clause; (f) the limitation of overtime (currently an average of thirteen extra hours were being worked on top of the standard forty-hour week); (g) three weeks' annual holiday with payment based on average earnings; (h) compulsory trade union membership; (i) a redundancy agreement; (j) the limitation of continuous driving to four and a half hours; and (k) the launching of a campaign for the government to buy substantial holdings in private bus companies.[13] Inflation made the first of these demands the easiest to achieve. By 1971 drivers' basic wages had risen to £16·75 per week.[14] Management's reaction to the other claims was that improvements in productivity were a precondition for their fulfilment.

When management raised the subject of productivity, it was mainly thinking of the single-manning of buses. Bill Leeming, a veteran Plymouth busman, who served on the EC of the NUR from 1976–8 recalled that this item had been on the agenda of wage negotiations before the Second World War. In the late 1930s the driver of a single-manned bus received 1d (old pence) an hour bonus for taking over the work of the conductor.[15] In the 1950s and 1960s the standard of living rose and an ever-increasing number of households had access to motor vehicles, more and more rural bus services ran at a loss. Although there was a degree of cross-subsidisation from the still-profitable urban services, there was no central government subsidy until 1969. At a meeting of the NCOI held on 9 May 1960, therefore, the management side argued that the alternatives were the withdrawal of services and licences, with the consequent loss of jobs, or a substantial extension of single-manning. Since management produced the books to show that some country services were losing money, the trade union side was induced at this meeting to agree to an OMO driver being paid 15 per cent above the basic rate for undertaking the extra responsibilities involved.[16] It was not until 3 May 1968 at a meeting of the NCOI that the enhancements were extended to include 25 per cent for an urban decker, and 20 per cent for an urban saloon or rural decker.

It may be questioned why trade union leaders accepted with apparent readiness bus drivers being given such a small share of savings arising from OMO. The answer lies partly in the fact that single-manning came in gradually. At first its introduction was confined to links between isolated villages. Union leaders took the view that it was better to accept the change to OMO where it seemed unavoidable, thus retaining employment for one busman, than to face outright closure of a service with the loss of two jobs.

At the time of the May 1960 agreement no one foresaw the rapid spread of OMO caused by the decline in passenger carrying brought on by extended car ownership. A further reason for union leaders' acceptance of low levels of OMO bonus was that the meagre rewards offered would dampen drivers' enthusiasm for the change and, thus, preserve jobs in the industry.[17] In the event, as a result of commercial pressures, single-manning spread, despite the small financial inducement offered drivers. On NBC vehicles mileage OMO increased from 25 per cent to 78·4 per cent in 1969–78.[18]

The spread of single-manning convinced the unions of the need to press for a more comprehensive and generous agreement with the management, and at meetings of the NCOI held on 5 July and 15 August 1972 a new formula was accepted for distributing the savings effected by OMO. Each one-man bus unit was assumed to be saving £300 a year through dispensing with the conductor. Half this figure, that is, £150 per unit, would then be converted to an hourly rate and added to the current 15, 20 or 25 per cent OMO bonus. The new plan came into operation on 1 October 1972. Although it brought platform staff more of the savings arising from single-manning, its drawback was that the hourly rate added for OMO applied only to the basic rate of pay and the standard working week. A driver of a single-manned bus got no OMO hourly-rate bonus payments for overtime working or for any other of the working hours which brought him pay enhancements. A new agreement, signed at a meeting of the NCOI on 29 February 1980, removed this limitation. Henceforward the OMO hourly pay bonus was added to the overtime and other enhancement rates. Furthermore, as an incentive to staff to convert their depots as nearly as possible to 100 per cent single-manning, a twenty-stage hourly bonus rate was introduced. Thus, a depot 50 per cent of whose buses were single-manned came in stage 10 at which the driver would qualify for a 10·33p per hour bonus. Where a depot was 100 per cent single-manned, the drivers would be at stage 20 and would be entitled to the 31p per hour (maximum) bonus. Since, in the settlement reached in the NCOI on 4 April 1979, it had been agreed that the whole of the savings accruing from OMO would go to the staff, it could be said that there had been a major advance in rewards for higher productivity in the two decades following the first agreement in 1960.

In the view of long-service busmen one of the best things to come out of the nationalisation of a big section of the bus industry was an industrial retirement-pension scheme. Some of the companies in the British Electric Traction and Tilling group of the Transport Holding Co. (1963–8) had pension and sick-pay schemes, though these were generally poorly structured and financed. As late as 1976 three-fifths of all bus companies had no sick-pay or pension provisions. (However, the structure of the industry was one of over 5,001 small companies and under fifty large ones.)[19] On 28 November 1962 the trade union panel of the NCOI submitted a detailed case for a national bus workers' pension scheme, but this was rejected by the employers at a subsequent meeting on 29 January 1963. It was not until April 1974 that a more comprehensive scheme for the constituent companies of the NCOI was at last introduced. There were two main aspects of the scheme; a lump-sum death grant of one-half annual earnings of men and women dying before reaching retirement age (65 and 60) and a lump-sum and pension for employees reaching retirement age. The pre-retirement age death grant to next of kin was paid for entirely by the employers; the scheme for the post-retirement grant and pension were contributory by both parties. A man or woman retiring with ten years' contributions and with earnings in his final year at work of £4,000 was entitled to a pension of £436·96 plus a lump-sum of £207·98.[20] If a widow outlived him after his retirement, she would be entitled to three-eighths of his pension. From 1 April 1979 the real terms of the pension scheme were substantially improved with, for example, a lump-sum of one year's earnings paid to the next of kin of the worker who died before retirement age and the widow of the retired busman receiving one-half, instead of three-eighths of her dead husband's pension.[21]

In both 1959 and 1964 the trade union panel of the NCOI proposed a sick-pay scheme for employees. On both occasions the employers rejected the proposals on the ground that 'a payment in respect of sickness should be a national responsibility'.[22] However, in the following year both sides of the industry agreed to accept the provisions of the Wilson Report on pay and working conditions in bus operation, including the recommendations that a sick-pay scheme should be introduced. The proposals, which were brought into effect on 1 January 1966, were not generous. The weekly payment was £4 for platform staff and £4 0s 6d for workshop staff. For those with less than ten years' continuous service, the maximum period of benefit was six weeks. Those completing twenty years or more in the industry were entitled to eighteen weeks' benefit.[23] Inflation quickly eroded the real value of the payments. Not surprisingly the NUR National Busworkers' Annual Conference, in 1970, declared that 'the amount of money paid to members off sick is nothing but a farce'.[24] In September

1974 agreement was reached on the NCOI for an improved scheme to come into operation in the following month.[25]

Progress in workers' participation in management was patchy and slow in the bus industry. Discussions with the staff about any proposed innovations were rare. In their absence ludicrous mistakes were sometimes made. Thus, in 1974 management ordered standard summer-issue uniforms for all platform staff without consulting those who would be called upon to wear them. Allan Kemp recalls the ridicule and merriment that followed:

It was a masterpiece, in that it had no side pockets, just two pockets on the chest. When staff had loaded up with timetables, farecharts, cigarettes, etc., they looked like statuesque ladies, while the female staff lost sight of their feet.

Protests were registered at the next meeting of the NCOI and the NUR's executive minutes for March 1975 laconically summarised the aftermath: 'NBC have replied stating that modifications have been made in the design specification for uniforms under the 1975 contract, in particular the design of the shirt which has been much improved.'

IV

In the same way that the pre-nationalisation railway companies had interests in bus operation, so they were also involved in dock operation. The London and North Eastern Railway Company, for example, had substantial capital investment in dock installations in Hull, the Hartlepools and elsewhere, assets it had inherited from its predecessor the North Eastern Railway.[26] By the same logic that led the NUR to organise the men employed in railway-controlled bus companies, the union recruited members in railway-owned docks. So successful was the early NUR in its recruitment drives that it aroused the concern of the Dock, Wharf, Riverside and General Workers' Union (a forerunner of the TGWU) which was losing out in the struggle for members in some ports. In March 1914, therefore, the DWRGWU proposed an amalgamation with the NUR. A meeting of the two unions' executives was held, but nothing came of the merger. However, in April of the same year the two parties met again in Liverpool and agreed to a 'no poaching' proposal submitted by the Parliamentary Committee of the TUC. Both unions accepted a formula 'that any men starting work on the docks shall become members of the union governing the particular class of work they are employed on'. This meant that where the railway company was the employer, as in the case of the cranemen employed on Cardiff docks, the NUR was the appropriate union for new recruits to join, but that those working for the independent dock companies and for semi-public bodies, such as the Port of London Authority, would be expected to join the dockers' union.[27]

From nationalisation in 1948 until 31 December 1962 the staff of the former railway-owned docks were employed by the Docks and Inland Waterways Executive of the BTC. Under the Transport Act 1962, the assets and staff of the Executive were transferred to the independent, publicly owned British Transport Docks Board (BTD) as from 1 January 1963. Throughout these years the employees of the Executive and of the BTD constituted a relatively small proportion of the nation's dock labour force. In 1970, for example, the 11,341 employees of the Board formed 11 per cent of the total employed in and around British docks and harbours. In consequence of the growth of containerisation and mechanical handling, the total number of dock workers fell sharply in the 1960s and 1970s. However, the Board's docks generally proved more prosperous than those managed by its competitors and thus the numbers it employed rose slightly, rather than fell, despite its active policy of modernisation. Hence its proportion of the total workforce increased substantially to nearly 17 per cent in 1976.[28] In addition to its regular staff BTD hired other dock workers through dock labour contractors. The number of these engaged fluctuated substantially according to the state of the nation's coastwise and overseas trade and ranged from a low of 2,263 in 1962 to a high of 5,069 in 1978. A map showing BTD dock locations in 1963 includes a greater number of ports than was the case in 1979. The establishment of new estuarial port authorities, such as the Forth Port Authority, in the later 1960s, took some of the smaller ports such as Methil, Burntisland and Grangemouth, out of the BTD's jurisdiction. In the later 1970s the ports remaining under the Board's administration included Hull, Goole, Grimsby and Immingham, King's Lynn, Southampton, Plymouth, Newport, Cardiff, Barry, Port Talbot, Swansea, Garston, Fleetwood, Barrow, Silloth, Ayr and Troon. Measured by the strength of the labour force, Hull and Southampton outclassed the remainder. In 1979 they employed 57 per cent of the Board's workers, largely because of their prominence in both passenger and container traffic. Nationally about half the Board's staff were described as 'operational', that is, engaged in moving the traffic;

rather more than a quarter were engaged in maintenance, while most of the remainder came under the classification 'administrative, technical and clerical'. The major structural change after 1963 was in the reduction of maintenance or workshop staff from 4,583 in 1963 to 3,139 in 1968 (after which the Board's reports did not provide statistics on the structure of the workforce).

At the end of December 1978 the NUR had 2,846 members who were employed by the BTD. To them may be added an interesting miscellany of other members who nevertheless had the common characteristic that they all depended on water transport for their livelihood. Closest to the BTD group were those who had formerly worked for the Board but were currently employed by the Forth Ports authority (127); the Port of Tyne Authority (161), and the Tees and Hartlepools Port Authority (176). From the pre-1914 days when the Caledonian Railway ran its own steamships, the NUR had established a foothold among its staff. In 1979 the independently managed Caledonian Steam Packet Co. provided the union with a further 238 members. A further 65 were employed by the Manchester Ship Canal, while 77 more were scattered up and down the country in the service of the British Waterways Board. Finally, came 47 Humber pilots, 39 working for Harwich Transport Ltd; 35 in the pay of International Cold Storage and 12 employees of the Yarmouth Harbour Commission. With this varied group added to those employed by BTD and NUR's 'water transport' membership amounted to 3,823 or 2·2 per cent of the total union strength at the end of 1979.

From the viewpoint of achieving satisfactory wage settlements for the labour force, there is a world of difference between negotiating against a background of financial stringency – as has often been the case with BR – and bargaining in an industry experiencing healthy growth and financial solvency–the situation with BTD. Measured by the volume of traffic entering and clearing its ports, its share of the nation's total port traffic, and by its profitability, the BTD's performance as a major public transport enterprise was impressive. The volume of traffic passing through its ports grew from an average of 52·6 million tons (53·4 million tonnes equivalent) in 1963–7 to an average of 78·6 million tonnes in 1975–9, an increase of 47 per cent. Despite relinquishing control of a number of small ports to newly created estuarial authorities, BTD's share of the nation's port traffic grew. Thus, between 1970 and 1974 its share of the volume of imports rose from 20 to 24 per cent and of exports from 17 to 24 per cent.[29]

One of the advantages arising from the fact that BTD's revenues exceeded expenditure, including interest charges and allowances for depreciation, was referred to by the Chairman, Sir Humphrey Browne, CBE, in the annual *Report and Accounts* for 1978 :

> The Board's positive cash flow permits rapid and positive response to investment opportunities for customer demand projects and provides for needs for essential renewals. The pace of investment is quickening.

V

At the end of the 1970s, the wages paid many NUR members employed by BTD compared favourably with those of railmen. That this was the case was partly due to the dock industry's comparative freedom from the severe financial restraints which so frequently plagued wage negotiations with BR; but it was also due to the influence of the Devlin Report of 1965. For centuries before the passing of the Docks and Harbours Act 1966, and the amendment to the Dock Workers (Regulation of Employment) Order 1947, in the same year (which implemented Devlin's findings) the unskilled work in British dockyards was carried out by casual labour which, at least until the 1920s, was very poorly paid. In these circumstances the regular staff employed in the railway-owned docks enjoyed better conditions of employment than did the casual labourers employed by the dock companies. However, from 18 September 1967 when the Devlin recommendations were put into effect and the dock labour force was decasualised, the boot was on the other foot. Each registered dock worker became a permanent employee of a licensed dock employer and, in return for accepting greater job flexibility and equipment modernisation, was assured more regular work and substantially improved conditions of employment. It was then the case that the operational staff of BTD found their wage rates and conditions of service inferior to those of the registered dock workers. It was a situation which could scarcely be sustained in a financially solvent industry. It was a fact of life that BTD employed registered dock workers as well as its own staff in most of its ports. The NUR, therefore, used the enhanced status and pay of the registered dock workers as a lever with which to secure parity in rewards for its members.

From the date of the implementation of the Devlin Report, in September 1967, one advantage the registered dock workers had over the NUR operational grades was the receipt of £2 weekly as a modernisation payment applicable where the particular dock labour force agreed to the ending of restrictive practices. The NUR immediately pressed for the modernisation payment to be given to its members who worked on the BTD docks. To this management replied that, while it had no objection to discussing the improved productivity of dock workers, it could not agree to opening discussions directly on the question of extending the modernisation payment to NUR members. The frontal approach having failed, the union then tried and was eventually successful with the indirect approaches of job evaluation and management–worker consultation. The initiative on job evaluation came from the Board which paid for the services of a specialist firm, Urwick, Orr & Partners, to conduct the exercise; but the union negoiators had no hesitation in entering into both job evaluation and productivity discussions.[30] Both sides were encouraged to bring these talks to a successful conclusion by 'the state of unrest among NUR dock staff membership arising from the effects of decasualisation'.[31] At Southampton, in October 1967, discontent was expressed by an unofficial ban on overtime and weekend working by NUR members, a protest which was only brought to an end following a visit from AGS Sidney Weighell, the union's president, Frank Lane, the area organiser and members of the negotiating committee.[32] Early in the following year, as the Board seemed to be dragging its feet on the question of pay comparability with registered dock labour, the NUR executive decided to call a strike of its BTD members from 00.01 hours on Monday 8 April 1968. This decision served to give urgency and renewed purpose to the discussions. On 23 March the Board offered negotiations on an interim payment pending the finalisation of the productivity discussions and the strike was called off.[33]

By the early summer of 1969, following the completion of the job-evaluation exercise and 'intense negotiations', agreement was reached on a new pay structure for the operational staff. With effect from 19 May 1969 the number of basic wage rates was reduced to five in a valuable exercise of simplification.[34] But still the rates of pay and conditions of service of NUR operational staff remained inferior to those of registered dock workers. The next stage in the campaign for parity was the setting up of a BTD–NUR working party, which reported in 1974. The NUR accepted this report as a basis for parity negotiations. What Sidney Greene described as 'a notable breakthrough' with an agreement for the reduction of overtime and the elimination of all locally agreed allowances, was achieved in 1975. There was little progress in the next three years, because of the limitations imposed by government pay policy and the Board's concern not to undermine its competitiveness with other dock undertakings; but a step further forward towards parity was achieved in the course of the pay negotiations in 1978 when the union gained an additional two days' leave for all manual staff to bring them into line with the annual-leave arrangements for registered dock workers. In October 1978 a comprehensive agreement for manual grades' pay parity with registered dock workers was reached and given effect as from 1 August 1978. The object of the exercise was to maintain the national rate of pay for manual grades staff while raising the wages of workers in group 5 – the top pay group of the BTD operating class – to a level equal to the mean of the Southampton and Hull weekly rates for registered dock workers.[35] The effect of the change was to raise the basic rates of pay of the manual grades' group 5 workers to £77·55 in 1979, while under the terms of the 1980 pay award the lowest basic rate – for those included in group 1 of the manual grades – was £80 per week. Manual-grade workers for BTD were, as a result of these improvements, receiving substantially higher wages than those paid to railmen working for the BRB. Thus, in 1979 the lowest-paid manual-grade worker of the BTD was paid a basic wage of £61·15, compared with the £51·25 basic wage of the railman.[36]

The condition BTD laid down for conceding manual staffs' pay parity with registered dock workers was that they should accept the principles of flexibility, interchangeability and mobility. Thus they would be required to assist in the upkeep of the dock estates, so that port operations could continue without interruption and men employed on floating craft would be expected to help with the general upkeep of the vessel. The staff were also expected to agree to shift and overtime working, while union officials undertook to do their utmost to prevent industrial disputes arising or, when they could not be prevented, to resolve them as quickly as possible.

The acceptance of revised methods of working was no new departure for NUR members in the docks. What contributed greatly to the achievement of pay parity with registered dock workers was the wide measure of understanding and co-operation between management and the labour force in this sector of public transport. Assistant General Secretary Charlie Turnock summarised the viewpoint of the NUR, when he told a gathering of managers and staff employed in the industry in the spring of 1978 that the union's activities were 'not confined to getting whatever it could from the BTD but were also designed to strengthen the industry, because a prosperous dock industry means stable and secure employment'.[37]

A spirit of confidence and co-operation was fostered in the

meetings of the British Transport Docks Consultative Council established, following joint consultations between unions and management, in October 1963. The Council consisted of twenty members; ten chosen from the Board and ten from the five unions with negotiating rights in the industry, each union selecting two representatives. The objectives of the Council were defined as follows:

(a) To consider and discuss matters concerning the Board and its employees.
(b) To enable the Board to impart information on
    (i) traffic trends in the ports;
    (ii) proposed developments;
    (iii) the plans and policies of the Board.
(c) To enable the staff organisations to raise matters about which they may wish to receive or impart information.
(d) To consider and discuss matters of local and national economic interest affecting the ports under the control of the Board.
(e) To discuss such other matters as may be considered appropriate for joint consultation.[38]

Although the Council only met twice a year, its terms of reference were not mere window-dressing. Supervisor grade 2 dock foreman Ron Thompson, a representative of the NUR on numerous dock bodies, confirmed that the Joint Consultative Committees set up simultaneously in the larger ports, or in groupings of smaller ports, were very effective vehicles for discussion and greater understanding. Chairmanship of these Committees rotated between representatives of the unions and of management and any member of staff was free to question the port manager or his colleagues.[39]

A further vehicle for co-operation between staff and management was the Modernisation Committee, set up in 1965 following the publication of the Devlin Report. This comprised three representatives each of employers and unions with an independent chairman and three independent members.[40] The unions found it easier to accept such proposals as were contained in the Board's publication, of June 1967, *Containerisation: the Key to Low Cost Transport*, because, as the annual statistics of the number of staff employed suggest, there was no serious problem of redundancy in the BTD's domain. By contrast, contemporaneously, there were wholesale redundancies from BRB, with consequent serious effects on staff morale. It is true that there was a change in the Board's formal policy in May 1974, when its members refused to endorse a 'no redundancies' understanding reached five years earlier. It was, nevertheless, the fact that natural wastage took care of such changes in staffing as occurred in the later 1970s.

Sick-pay and pension arrangements were the subject of numerous meetings between management and unions, resulting in steady improvements in staff welfare provisions. A new, non-contributory, sick-pay scheme was introduced for the manual grades on 1 January 1966. This was revised in 1968 and commended by Sidney Greene as 'a great improvement on its predecessor'.[41] The revised scheme entitled a member to ten weeks' sick-pay on completion of twelve months' service and to eighteen weeks' benefit if in the service over ten years. Pension schemes for both manual and salaried grades were greatly improved in the course of the 1970s. Under a contributory pension scheme for salaried staff introduced in 1970, those serving forty years with BTD were entitled to a pension equal to two-thirds of their salary.[42] In 1974 an existing manual-grades scheme was modified by the reduction of the averaging period for the calculation of pension from three years to one year.[43] In 1977 a completely new scheme was introduced with more generous lump-sum and weekly pension payments.[44] All these changes combined to make service with BTD more attractive and to develop the sense of common endeavour in the undertaking.

The BTD alone among the major publicly owned transport undertakings has not made membership of a recognised trade union a condition of employment. The failure to establish a union shop was in the last resort due to differences between the trade unions involved, although reluctance on the part of the Board to concede the union shop was the principal obstacle to an agreement before 1976. The fact that so many unions were involved did not make the achievement of a union shop any easier. In 1975, of the 6,798 BTD staff, other than registered dock workers, the NUR had the lion's share with 3,018 members. A further 1,389 belonged to TSSA and 650 to the TGWU. There were 299 members of the Electrical, Electronic, Telecommunications and Plumbing Union and 232 in the AUEW. But there were also considerably smaller groups including 100 members in the NUGMW, 73 in the Union of Construction, Allied Trades and Technicians and 47 in the Amalgamated Society of Boilermakers, Shipwrights, Blacksmiths and Structural Workers. The TGWU's principal strength was among the registered dock workers, where it had in membership the large majority of the 5,058 employed by the Board.[45]

The NUR's endeavour to secure a union shop agreement involving its dock members began before the formation of the BTD, in 1963, and involved the most prolonged and frustrating campaign in which the union was engaged in the course of two decades of its recent history. The weighty file on the subject at Unity House opens with a resolution, proposed by the Barrow-in-Furness No. 2 branch, and carried unanimously by the NUR dock and marine grades annual conference on 29 April 1961, that the national executive 'should press with every vigour for the principle of the closed shop to be obtained for staff employed in docks'.[46] Sidney Greene soon discovered that the view of F. J. Morris, first Staff Officer of BTD, was hostile to any form of closed shop in the industry though favourable to the maintenance of collective bargaining. In a letter to the General Secretary, dated 9 January 1964, he wrote:

> Whilst the Board attaches great importance to negotiating machinery whereby all questions affecting the interests of the staff are discussed and settled with the trade union representatives and are prepared to give all facilities and encouragement to join their appropriate trade union they are unable to agree that trade union membership should be a condition of service.
>
> The Board are prepared to draw the attention of the present staff and all new entrants to the service to the desirability of trade union membership and to the facilities which are offered to staff through the recognised channels for expressing their views on matters affecting their employment and welfare.

Mr Morris's successor at BTD, K. W. B. Domony, who was the Board's officer responsible for industrial relations during the years 1965–77 inclusive, was every bit as reluctant to concede any form of closed shop. The union's largely fruitless discussions with BTD continued throughout the later 1960s. The EC reached the conclusion that the only hope for progress on the docks front would be after concessions had been made on the railways. Thus, following BRB's dispatch of a letter to all its staff explaining the advantages of trade union membership, Sidney Greene wrote to Mr Domony on 2 July 1968, enclosing a copy of the BRB letter and requesting that BTD should follow suit. A reply was received three weeks later, declining the suggestion. However, following the signature of the union shop agreement for the railways in the autumn of 1969, the BTD's stance weakened. Sidney Greene wrote again to its industrial relations officer on 9 October 1969, and received a reply on 6 January 1970 which included the following statement:

For your information I confirm that, following the recent discussions with your representatives and representatives of other trade unions involved, and in the light of anticipated government legislation, it is agreed in principle that trade union membership will be a future condition of employment within the BTDB for Manual, Clerical Technical and Supervisory grades.

In a further letter sent to the unions eight days later a draft agreement was promised. When no such document was received from the Board after eight months, Sidney Greene wrote again on 21 September 1970, requesting to see it. Mr Domony replied on 2 October, citing press reports of the dismissal of a clerk at Paddington for declining to join a union and inquiring whether the NUR anticipated similar dismissals of dock staff once a union shop agreement became operative. No document was enclosed. Sidney Greene wrote again on 30 October 1970 and 20 January 1971. To the last letter Mr Domony replied on 2 February 1971, suggesting the question be deferred in the light of the Heath government's Industrial Relations Bill (which ruled out closed shops). When, in conformity with an EC resolution, Sidney Greene continued to press the Board on the question, Mr Domony wrote a long letter of 28 July 1971, quoting chapter and verse from the Act and pointing out that there was the additional difficulty that NALGO, the TGWU, and 'various craft unions' were claiming representation in the negotiating machinery for supervisory staff. There was, clearly, little chance of any progress in the campaign until the Industrial Relations Act was repealed.

However, with the passage of the Trade Union and Labour Relations Act 1974, by the incoming Labour government the 1971 Act was repealed and there were no longer any legal obstacles to any form of a closed shop agreement. But when Sidney Greene approached Mr Domony, he was met by further stalling. Eventually, the Managing Director of BTD met the union officers and negotiating committee on 6 April 1976 to inform them 'that as a matter of deep principle he was against any form of compulsion whatsoever', though he would, as before, only negotiate with recognised trade unions.

The EC's response to that statement was to instruct dock members to refuse to work all overtime from 00.01 hours on Monday 10 May 1976.[47] In coming to this decision, it must be admitted that for once the executive was out of touch with the views of the union's dock members Secretaries of NUR dock branches wrote to Sidney Weighell, making it clear that members felt that the union had not got its priorities right. There was much stronger feeling on the loss of overtime earnings resulting from the 1975 pay settlement and the Board's refusal to make the annual leave allowance up to four weeks, than there was on the closed-shop issue. The employees in the docks were a close-knit community, and they felt that even if the Board did not capitulate on the closed shop the situation *de facto* would be much the same as if a formal agreement was in existence. To the credit of the executive it quickly changed its policy to take account of rank and file opinion. It linked the claim for four weeks' leave and improved overtime payments with the original demand on the closed shop.[48]

The imposition of the overtime ban from 10 May was sufficient to expedite a settlement. In a letter to Sidney Weighell written on 14 May Mr Domony wrote that the Board conceded the four weeks' annual leave, the principle that overtime should be calculated on the basic rate of pay and the principle that all new entrants to the BTD should be trade union members with effect from 1 September 1976. On the same day in which the letter was received telegrams were sent to the union's dock branches, bearing the words 'BTDB overtime ban lifted immediately. Details later'.

Within two months a draft union shop agreement was drawn up after consultation with all the unions involved in the negotiating machinery. To date (July 1980), it has not been implemented. The sole reason for the absence of a union shop more than four years after the Board had overcome its earlier reluctance to such a procedure was disagreement between the unions. The TGWU would not sign the draft agreement unless and until it was conceded a share in negotiating rights for the supervisory grades. Both the NUR and TSSA were opposed to increasing the number of unions involved in those negotiations since, apart from Hull and Southampton where TGWU did have a preponderance of members, but where pay was settled by local negotiations, the TGWU had only 73 supervisor members in the BTD docks compared with TSSA's 190 and the NUR's 188. Although the TGWU referred the dispute to ACAS and Ken Graham, Assistant General Secretary of the TUC, attempted mediation, no compromise solution could be discovered.

It would be wrong to end an account of labour relations in BTD without re-emphasising the fact that, in 1980, conditions in respect of real wages, annual leave, sick-pay, pensions and welfare services were vastly improved by comparison with 1963, the year in which the Board came into being. The NUR as the union with the largest number of members among BTD staff (apart from the registered dock workers it employed) played the greatest part, from the employees' side, in bringing about these improvements.

VI

In his address to the delegates attending the first national conference of NUR members of the railway catering grades, held at the Royal Hotel, Upper Woburn Place, London, on 23 June 1945, General Secretary John Benstead declared: 'catering is as much an integral part of railway working as is the running of trains and the operation of signalboxes'. It is for this reason that throughout its history the NUR has sought to organise men and women employed in station restaurants, train restaurant cars and buffets and railway hotels.

The union's records show that there was a world of difference between recognising the necessity of 100 per cent organisation of workers in these occupations and achieving the objective sought. Catering is a service industry without long traditions of trade unionism. Traditionally, it has employed a large proportion of both women and part-time workers. The rapidity of turnover and often wide dispersal of the labour force present formidable obstacles to the union organiser. Not surprisingly, then, through most of the twentieth century, only a minority of railway catering and hotel workers were trade unionists. These are some of the reasons why the main line railway companies of the interwar years did not see fit to recognise the NUR as representing the interests of men and women in these grades until 28 September 1937 – more than two decades after the union achieved recognition as representing the conciliation staff. A further indication of the backwardness of organisation in this area of railway operations was that it took until 3 June 1940 for the union to persuade the companies to accept the principle of a basic minimum wage for all catering and hotel staff.

During the Second World War, Parliament recognised that Britain would have a balance of payments problem in the postwar period. It is clear from the tenor of debates in the House of Commons on 25 and 31 March and 1 and 6 April 1943 that one of the principal reasons for the passing of the Catering Wages Act, in June of that year, was a lively concern to attract more overseas visitors – and hence foreign exchange – to Britain by improving the quality of food and service in restaurants and hotels. This implied raising the qualifications and living standards of the industry's workforce. The Act set up a Catering Wages Commission, with power to enforce minimum wages and conditions of health and welfare. Its powers were exercised mainly indirectly through the Minister of Labour and National Service, establishing Wages Boards, the principal ones of which were those for Licensed Non-Residential Establishments (22 March 1945) and for Licensed Residential Establishments (17 December 1945).

Although these measures helped to bring about improved working conditions in thousands of catering establishments, it was not long before the NUR began to regard them as impediments to its aim of raising conditions of employment of its catering and hotel staff to the levels secured for other railway staff. The difficulty was that the Wages Boards, which were large and cumbersome bodies on which no less than ten trade unions were represented – besides many representatives of the employers-tended to establish a lowest common denominator of wages and working conditions, well below those being claimed for catering and hotel staff linked with the railway service. By 1961 the NUR executive was on record as favouring the union's withdrawal from the catering wages boards which were seen, alongside the existence of part-time and women's employment, living in and 'personal' rates of pay, as serious obstacles to advance.[49] A front-page article which appeared in the *Railway Review* in the summer of 1962 – nearly two decades after the passing of the Catering Wages Act – revealed the survival of conditions of employment almost Victorian in character:

> The rates of pay and conditions of service of the staff working in railway refreshment rooms are a shocking indictment of management . . . It is regrettable that this is also a sad reflection on our organisation . . . The courtesy, tact and diplomacy afforded by these girls make them worthwhile ambassadors of our industry, even with the most awkward of customers. How does a benevolent management repay such sterling qualities? A 48 hour week; no enhancements for shift working, Saturday afternoons, nights or Sunday working, the last named of which was granted to railway staff in 1919. All for the handsome sum of between £6 and £7 per week, less deductions for food taken on duty or full board and lodging.[50]

VII

When the railways were nationalised in 1948, the BTC, through the Hotels Executive, had responsibility for 44 hotels and 400 railway station restaurants or buffets, besides restaurant-car and buffet services on trains. The reduction in the railway network in the years which followed was accompanied by a decline in the number of railway hotels to 29 and of station catering establishments to 195 by the end of 1979. The total number of full-time staff employed fell from nearly 16,000 in 1961 to 11,000 in 1979, a drop of 30 per cent. In 1961 6,690 or 42 per cent of the workforce, were employed in the hotels; 4,645 or 29 per cent in station restaurants and buffets and 2,235 or 14 per cent provided food and drinks on trains. The balance were employed at headquarters or in providing common services. By 1979 the pattern was changed, with relatively less concentration on station services and relatively more on the provision of train buffet facilities. At the close of that year the hotels employed 3,570 full-timers, or 38 per cent of the total BTH workforce; the station refreshment services engaged 2,502, now only 23 per cent of the total, while there were 2,323 or 21 per cent (compared with 14 per cent nineteen years earlier) employed on the trains.[51]

Throughout the entire period from 1961–79 the hotels made a profit each year, the most successful results being achieved in the boom year 1972. The station catering services also more than covered their expenses through the two decades. The restaurant cars and train buffets consistently made losses. A new brandname for the train refreshment services, Travellers Fare, in place of British Rail Catering, was introduced in 1973, in an endeavour to attract more custom; but thereafter losses increased rather than diminished. Nevertheless, management's policy was to regard the losses incurred in this department as the price to be paid for attracting more passengers.

The reduction in the numbers of staff by nearly a third in twenty years owed little to any dramatic improvements in productivity. Simultaneously with the pay and efficiency exercises carried out in relation to the main railway staff, British Transport Hotels (BTH), the organisation which replaced the Hotels Executive in 1963, conducted investigations into the running of twelve of its hotels and an unspecified sample of its station catering establishments; but Mr R. W. Shaw, the organisation's labour relations officer, informed the union representatives at a meeting on 1 June 1970 'that there was very little scope for improving productivity'.[52] Thus, as far as BTH was concerned any improvements in wages and working conditions had to come through making the service attractive to customers and ensuring that prices charged at least kept pace with the increase in the Retail Price Index.

VIII

The outstanding characteristics of the NUR's negotiations with
BTH on wages and salaries in the 1960s and 1970s were the
union's attempt to raise pay rates until they become comparable
with those of the railway conciliation and salaried staff and
management's insistence that its staff were employed in *catering*
and should, therefore, be subject to the conditions of employment
prevalent in that industry. For as long as it could, management
took refuge behind the awards of the Wages Councils for the
catering industry, maintaining that as the NUR was represented
on these councils it must expect to be guided by the awards they
issued. Thus, in March 1963 Mr Hole, the management spokesman,
turned down an NUR application for an increase in the minimum
rates of pay for BTH staff by pointing out that

It had been the practice over the years, when negotiating rates
of pay, to have regard to movements within the hotel and
catering trades and generally to relate improvements to the
statutory orders. It was essential to keep in mind the rates
of pay and conditions of work in comparable establishments.[53]

A few months later, when a further union application was being
considered, Assistant General Secretary, Bill Ballantine, pointed
out that the rate of pay for those employed in the railway hotel
'other male worker' grades was 165s minimum for a forty-eight-
hour week, subject to compulsory deductions for national insurance
and BTC male wages grade pension contributions. Hence, a man
employed in this category had a take-home pay little better than
the 153s paid in unemployment benefit to a man with a wife and
three children. Mr Hole expressed sympathy, but emphasised the
necessity to have regard to the rates of pay and conditions of
service in the hotel and catering industries as it was in this market
that labour was obtained and the company had to compete.[54]
In June 1964 BTH rejected the union's claim that the rates of
pay of main line canteen staff should be raised by 6 per cent, to
match the increase granted by the BRB to conciliation staff from
23 December 1963, on the ground that canteen staff pay should
be in accordance with the provisions of the Industrial and Staff
Canteens Undertakings Wages Council.[55]

There were powerful reasons for the NUR's application to the
Minister of Labour, in 1964, for the union's withdrawal from the
Wages Boards and the Industrial and Staff Canteens Wages
Council. The Minister of Labour promptly appointed a Committee

of Inquiry, which heard the unions' and the employers' arguments, and in the following year, recommended that NUR members should be withdrawn from the scope of the Licensed Residential Establishment and Licensed Restaurant Wages Boards. The Minister agreed to this recommendation which came into effect on 1 July 1965.[56] Through further representations made by the union and the approval given by the Minister in 1971, staff in station kiosks were withdrawn from the scope of the Retail Newsagents, Tobacco and Confectionary Wages Council and laundry staff from the scope of the Laundry Wages Council.[57]

The NUR's National Conference of BTH Catering and Ancillary Grades greatly welcomed these changes. Resolution 14 of its Blackpool conference, on 15 May 1965, read:

> Now that this union has thrown off the shackles of the LRE and LR Wages Councils this conference of hotel and catering grades calls upon our NEC to negotiate with British Transport Hotels Ltd with a view to securing comparable rates of pay and conditions of service for all hotel and catering workers to bring them in line with other grades in railway employment.

'Throwing off the shackles' did make possible some significant improvements in conditions of service of BTH staff. In 1966 prolonged negotiations with management resulted in the concession of payment to hotel and station catering staff at time-and-a-quarter rates for work performed after 2 p.m. on Saturdays and for all time worked on Sundays. In 1966 also an additional three days' annual leave after ten years' service was obtained for hotel refreshment-room staff, salaried staff paid by analogy with railway salaried staff, restaurant-car and depot wages staff and restaurant-car inspectors.[58] But the campaign to achieve some degree of comparability between the rates of pay and conditions of service was a long-drawn-out and difficult one. It was often impossible to find work in the main railway service which was similar in character to that of many hotel and catering employees. A new obstacle arose after the conclusion of the railway pay and efficiency agreements in 1969 and 1970, one of the principal features of which was the consolidation of bonuses into the basic rates of pay. When the union's negotiators met the BTH representatives to negotiate improved rates of pay on 11 May 1971, Mr R. W. Shaw pointed out that

> a severe problem existed in attempting to reach a similar agreement for restaurant car staff to that concluded for railway staff

because of the extent of consolidation of bonus payments contained in the railway settlement. No restaurant car staff were in receipt of bonus payments and the extent to which the payroll cost for this section of the staff could be increased was limited.[59]

In the protracted discussions, punctuated by several adjournments, which followed this depressing statement, management was persuaded to increase its original offer of 8·75 per cent on paybill costs to 9·66 per cent; but, for the reasons given by Mr Shaw, these advances were less than had been obtained under the pay and efficiency deals for the main railway staff.

However, persistent negotiations, particularly those conducted at top level between representatives of the board of BTH and union officers, resulted in steady gains in conditions of service, so that by the end of the 1970s refreshment-car travelling depot wages staff and hotel wages staff were entitled to three weeks and two days' paid leave after one year's service, the third week to be taken at a mutually convenient time outside the seasonal peak period at the depot or hotel concerned. Hours of work were reduced from forty-four to forty-two per week for wages staff in restaurant cars and depots and forty-two to forty for salaried staff, both with effect from 1 January 1962. They were again reduced for the same grades of staff by a further two hours in 1966. For hotel and station refreshment-room catering staff reduction of hours to forty per week was not conceded by BTH until 27 December 1971, but this important concession did mean that staff working in railway hotels and refreshment rooms were privileged by comparison with the majority of employees in the catering industry.

IX

When comparison is made between the strength of the trade union movement among employees of BTD and BTH, the paradox becomes apparent that throughout the third quarter of the twentieth century dock workers were well organised, while hotel and catering staff were not. None the less, a union shop agreement for all employees of BTH became effective from 31 December 1976, whereas, as we have seen, BTD staff entered the 1980s without any such arrangement. The paradox needs explanation.

In the late 1950s and in the 1960s recruiting initiatives to enrol members in the hotel and catering grades came from the branch

activists, rather than from the organisers or members of the EC.
Employees in these grades were not directly represented on the
executive until 1979, when the Warwick Report reforms began
to be implemented. Hence the state of organisation of hotel and
catering workers in any district depended to a large extent on the
willingness of existing members in these grades to give up their
rest days to canvassing for new recruits to the union. Thus,
members of Manchester No. 13 branch enrolled restaurant-car
staff, who were based on the London Road station, while their
contemporaries in Manchester No. 2 took over responsibility for
Manchester Central crews and the employees of the Midland
Hotel.[60]

An issue which generated militancy and a sense of solidarity
among the restaurant-car staff was the BTC plan, advanced in
1959, to extend Pullman-car services on some of the main routes
from London to the industrial cities of Lancashire and Yorkshire.
The AGM held at Blackpool, in July 1959, carried unanimously
the following composite resolution:

> This AGM expresses concern at reports that under the
> Modernisation Plan a number of trains will be replaced by
> trains with Pullman service and staffed by Pullman Car staff.
> We demand from the BTC that any new Pullman trains operat-
> ing on British Railways shall be operated by the BTC and
> manned by BTC staff, and further we instruct the Executive
> Committee to work for the abolition of Pullman Car services
> operating on British Railways and their assimilation into the
> Hotels and Catering Services of British Transport.[61]

The first time the newly constructed assembly hall in the basement
of Unity House was used, was to accommodate an 'unofficial'
meeting of restaurant car workers held on 11 October 1959. After
a 'long and heated' discussion, the meeting resolved that if the
BTC attempted to add a single new Pullman service, *all* Pullman
cars would be declared black and would be neither handled nor
serviced.[62] The reason for the strong feelings of those attending
the meeting was that conditions of employment under the Pullman
Company (the majority of whose capital was held by the BTC)
were inferior to those in other restaurant cars. A fifty-two-hour
week still applied at a time when conciliation grades were on
forty-four hours, and men resented being required to 'sleep rough'
in the Pullman cars drawn up in railway sidings. The policy of
the EC, on the other hand, was to negotiate with the company

with a view to achieving parity in conditions of service between Pullman and other restaurant-car workers. When it discovered that the company was prepared to substitute an eighty-eight hour fortnight for the fifty-two-hour week and to make other concessions, it resolved that if the company agreed to assimilate the working conditions of its staff to those of other restaurant-car workers, it would withdraw its opposition to the extension of Pullman Car services, thus reversing its own Decision No. 1735 of September 1959 and the AGM Decision No. 96(d).[63] This backsliding was regarded as the last straw by militant restaurant-car workers. In the fourth week of October 1959 they began an unofficial strike, which prompted Sidney Greene to send a circular letter on 28 October to all branches involved, pleading that 'no useful purpose' would be served by the continuance of the unofficial action.[64] When the strikers showed themselves to be in no hurry to resume normal working, a special meeting of the executive was summoned for 2 November. It invited elected representatives of the restaurant-car workers to a meeting two days later and reiterated the General Secretary's appeal for a resumption of normal working.[65] The meeting between the executive and the rank and file was a success. Twenty-three out of twenty-six men invited attended and agreed to recommend a resumption of normal working in return for an undertaking from the EC that it would hold a further special meeting of its members to give urgent consideration to the important issues raised by the strikers.[66]

The militants had won a notable victory. As a result of their protest, the working conditions of Pullman Car workers were placed on a par with those of other restaurant-car workers. The members of the EC rightly considered they had carried out a useful negotiating role. Above all, the rank and file employees saw that the union had been instrumental in securing significant improvements in their conditions of employment.

This demonstration of the union's value, together with the example provided by the strong unionisation of footplatemen and guards manning the same trains, helped to ensure the relatively high degree of organisation of restaurant-car workers during the 1960s and 1970s. When NUR branches were asked to submit to head office a return of all their BTH members in 1971, it was revealed that the union had 1,874 restaurant-car members, or some 82 per cent of those employed in this grade. The union's foothold in the station buffets, kiosks and restaurants was weaker. It had 1,766 members, or about 54 per cent of those employed in these establishments. Its foothold was weakest in the hotels where the 2,103 members constituted no more than 47 per cent of the workforce.

From the earliest weeks of the existence of BTH the NUR endeavoured to secure a union shop agreement, being backed in this endeavour by the TSSA. It was an uphill task. Before 1970 management relied on two main arguments to rebuff the union's claim. These were that there was no closed-shop agreement for BR staff and that, in any case, the majority of BTH employees were not union members. When the union shop agreement came into force for BR employees on 1 January 1970, it was no longer possible for the board of BTH to maintain its first argument; the union shop was conceded with respect to restaurant-car staff and to salaried staff paid by analogy with BR salaried staff. But at a meeting with union representatives in St Pancras Chambers, on 9 November 1970, Mr R. W. Shaw, for the BTH, said that it would be impracticable to operate a union shop agreement in hotels and refreshment rooms, because of the severe difficulties which were being experienced in recruitment. The company had to compete within the industry where wages and conditions of employment were often inferior to those in BTH establishments. He also repeated the argument that most of the staff were not trade unionists and that it would, therefore, be unfair to impose trade unionism on large numbers of them. The unions challenged his figures of membership, pointing out that he was counting only those members who were having their subscriptions deducted through the paybills and ignoring others who continued to pay through the union branches. They challenged him to discuss the question again as soon as they could bring clear proof that more than 50 per cent of the staff were organised; but he would make no promises.[67]

What helped to overcome management's resistance was evidence presented by the unions early in 1972 that they had a majority of hotel staff in membership.[68] Much wider use was also being made by hotel workers of the machinery of negotiation – a development given favourable comment by Sidney Greene in June 1972.[69] Most important, the TGWU and NUGMW were bestirring themselves. Towards the close of 1973 their officers agreed on a territorial division of spheres of influence in a new recruitment drive to enlist members in the hotel and catering trades.[70] They had good reason for this new move since, with the decline in manufacturing employment, their membership in this sector of the economy was falling, while it was well known that the large majority of employees in hotels and catering – the biggest single source of employment outside of engineering – were as yet unorganised. In the view of one experienced NUR hotel representative, the BTH industrial relations officer, F. G. Hole, preferred to negotiate with the NUR's 'kid-gloved' Sidney Greene, George Brassington and Russell Tuck rather than with any representatives the TGWU and NUGMU were likely to present to management.[71]

Thus it was, in August 1976, that an agreement for a union shop for all salaried and wages staff of the BTH employed in hotels, station catering units, laundries and central cellars was signed by representatives of the unions and of management. All members of staff who had not joined one of the recognised trade unions – NUR and TSSA and some craft unions – by 1 October 1976 were to do so by 31 December of that year. There were the usual arrangements for exemption on the ground of strongly held religious convictions.[72] It would be a big mistake to assume that the signing of this agreement solved all remaining problems. As Sidney Weighell commented in his report to the AGM in June 1977, 'it cannot be expected that the catering industry will be dragged into the twentieth century without a struggle'. In December 1979 the NUGMW had but 30,000 and the TGWU only 12,000 members out of a total workforce of at least 800,000 employed in hotels and catering.[73] The fact that the industry as a whole was so poorly organised constituted a continuing threat to the standard of living of the privileged 9,000 BTH employees organised by the NUR.

CHAPTER 10

CONDITIONS OF SERVICE

I

THE view of the nineteenth-century railway companies was that 'all of a man's time waking or sleeping, belongs to the employer'.[1] In December 1871 a passenger guard, having completed eighteen hours of continuous duty, was nevertheless ordered to take a train from Leeds to London. In desperation he asked his superintendent how many hours he was expected to work. He received the reply, 'That's our business. You've got 24 hours in a day like every other man and they are all ours if we want you to work them'.[2] After 1884 most railwaymen had the vote, giving them some say in how the government of the country should be run. In 1900, for the first time, a working railwayman was elected to the House of Commons. But these indications of the extension of political rights only served to point the contrast with the situation in the railway industry, where employees had no control over their conditions of employment. Not surprisingly, as the nineteenth century drew to its close, an increasing number of railwaymen were challenging the companies' claim to exercise a complete dominance over their working lives.

When the delegates attending the AGM of the ASRS at Newport, Monmouth, in October 1894, resolved 'That we consider every effort should be made to get the railways nationalised', they were expressing their belief that under a publicly owned industry they would have a greater chance of exercising control over their hours of duty and working conditions. They would no longer be at the beck and call of the railway companies.[3] When J. E. Williams, General Secretary of ASRS, joined Will Thorne, MP and A G. Walkden, of the Railway Clerks' Association, in a deputation to Herbert Asquith, the Prime Minister, early in 1912, to advocate public ownership of the railways, he told the Prime Minister that 'railway workers, the trading public and the community generally would get fairer treatment under a public authority than under the companies'. 'At present', he said, 'the railway workers simply could not get their case before the companies.'[4]

Two years later the delegates attending the AGM of the recently formed NUR had no doubt that workers' participation in management was the cornerstone of the arch of the welfare of railwaymen. They were unanimous in asserting that

No system of state ownership of the railways will be acceptable to organised railwaymen which does not guarantee to them their full political and social rights, allow them a due measure of control and responsibility in the safe and efficient working of the railway system, and assure them a fair and equitable participation in the increased benefits likely to accrue from a more economical and scientific administration.[5]

When the future organisation of the railways was under discussion in Parliament and in the Cabinet in the years 1919–21, a government White Paper conceded that 'the time had arrived when the workers, both official and manual workers, should have some voice in the management'. The leaders of the NUR were at first greatly interested. But by April 1921, when it became clear that all that was being offered was four railwaymen directorships out of a total of twenty-one, and that the four would not be union nominees but men chosen directly from the workforce, the proposal was seen as a trap to lure railwaymen from their allegiance to the unions towards identification with management, rather than as a first step on the road to workers' control of the industry. The EC finally rejected the government's plan on 29 April 1921.[6]

In the interwar years, following the Mond–Turner conversations of 1928, the concept of joint consultation in industry for a time replaced that of workers' control. However, with the return of a Labour government in July 1945, pledged to a policy of public ownership of the principal means of transport, there was intense discussion on the role of the workers in the management of the nationalised industry. The AGM of the NUR, meeting at Morecambe on July 1946, welcomed the contemplated legislation for the public ownership of transport but went on to demand that

In any scheme affecting nationalisation, provision shall be made for the establishment of national, local and area boards of management with representatives of His Majesty's Government and transport workers constituting the personnel. We are definitely of the opinion that an efficient transport system is an imperative necessity for the restoration of Britain's economic life and that workers' participation in management is an indispensable condition of this.[7]

By the time the next AGM assembled at Ayr a year later the Attlee government's Transport Bill had been published. The unease which was felt by many members of the union about the Bill's clauses concerning management was expressed in a resolution from the Eastern District Council:

> This AGM of the NUR, having examined the contemplated National Transport Bill now before Parliament, regrets HM Government have not seen fit to incorporate within the proposed scheme workers' representation by statutory right upon the proposed national, area and local boards.
>
> Having regard to AGM decision 17 of 1946, we reiterate our previous views and emphasise that in our opinion the full benefits of a nationalised transport system will not be conveyed to the community without the cultivation of the knowledge, goodwill and experience of the workers in the industry being sought and the opportunity given for them to obtain a voice in the highest managerial offices.

Although some delegates were worried lest union nominees placed on boards of directors would experience a divided loyalty, the resolution was carried by the large margin of 47–16 votes.[8]

A year later still, when the AGM met at Wallasey, the Bill had become law. Although John Benstead, General Secretary of the NUR, had been appointed Vice-Chairman of the British Transport Commission, the union's views on worker participation had largely been ignored. In a lengthy public resolution members reiterated the views expressed at the two previous AGMs and went on to instruct the EC to seek an interview with the Minister of Transport with the object of persuading him 'to meet the desires of the membership and the needs of the industry'.[9]

On 28 September 1948 Alfred Barnes, the Minister of Transport, met a delegation from the NUR headed by the recently elected General Secretary, Jim Figgins. After the usual exchange of pleasantries the Minister declared that the union's proposals for greater worker participation on the boards of the BTC and Railway Executive were 'an impracticable way of dealing with the problem'. Transport was an essential service to the community and *all* interests were included. If you admitted one section to special interests or representation, you would be 'sunk' by other similar demands John Benstead had been chosen to be Vice-Chairman of the BTC not because he was General Secretary of the NUR, but 'because of his inherent qualities'. The men appointed to serve on the BTC and the various executives were

chosen 'because of their qualifications'. Jim Figgins pleaded with
the Minister, arguing: 'If there were to be success under nationalisation there must be encouragement for those engaged in the industry to take a keener and more responsible interest in it, and to
produce that situation consultation must be replaced by a
machinery where the men could share in making decisions.' It was
not the case that the union's officers were asking for lucrative
jobs. But it was true that within the ranks of railwaymen there
was 'the experience and the capacity from which could be drawn
the appropriate people'. He claimed that the NUR should be
allowed to put forward a panel from which the Minister could
make the appointments. While he conceded that the men already
appointed were, no doubt, persons of great distinction, they had
been brought up in 'an atmosphere belonging to the past'. Men
were needed 'whose outlook was in keeping with nationalisation.
The workers would then have confidence in them'. It was all to
no avail. The Minister's mind had been made up and Jim Figgins's
eloquence fell on deaf ears.[10]

This rebuff did not deter the delegates at the AGM at Brighton,
in July 1949, from returning to the subject. They were fortified in
their belief in the need for workers' participation by the decision
of the annual conference of the Labour Party in May of the
previous year that 'The principle of workers' participation through
their trade unions in the direction and management of nationalised
industry at all levels should be firmly adopted in practice'.[11] By a
majority of 72-3 votes the AGM delegates instructed the EC to
work for 50 per cent trade union representation on the national
and regional boards of nationalised industries.[12] A year later
delegates assembling at Morecambe were vaguer in their demands
on the executive, which was instructed to take steps to secure
'greater participation' by workers in the management of the railway industry.[13] However, at least this was better than the somewhat contradictory instructions approved in 1952 when the executive was charged with 'drawing up a scheme for workers' control
which gives us a greater part in the function of management'.[14]

In 1953 the NUR made a different approach in order to try
and secure the same objective. At the annual congress of the TUC
that year the union's delegates proposed that 50 per cent of the
management of the nationalised industries should come from the
trade union movement. It was not a very successful venture. A
number of other trade unions, notably the National Union of
Mineworkers, were opposed to their members' appointment to
seats on boards of directors. With this 'great gulf of disagreement'

between the leaders of powerful unions it is not surprising that the boards of nationalised industries contained very few trade unionists.[15]

Meanwhile some progress was made in joint consultation between the two 'sides' of the publicly owned transport sector. In December 1948 there was set up the British Transport Joint Consultative Council, comprising representatives of both management and trade unions. Its terms of reference were

> to provide by regular meetings opportunity for the exchange of information and views upon matters of common interest in relation to Inland Transport and the activities of the BTC and its various undertakings, not being questions of wages or conditions of service or otherwise coming within the scope of the established machinery of negotiation or matters dealt with or to be dealt with by any statutory committee.[16]

Though by no means the complete answer to the union's demands, the Council did have its uses. For example the 1948 AGM passed a resolution urging the government to make more steel available for the development of the railway industry, as a result of which a NUR delegation waited on the Minister of Transport. At a later stage the question was considered, at the request of the NUR, by the BTJCC, and as a result, future representations made to the Minister were made in the name of the Council and with the joint backing of the BTC and the unions.

At the lower levels in the management of the industry there was consultation on regional issues in the sectional councils, of which there were four in each of the five railway regions, and at local level in the local departmental committees (LDCs), of which there are 1,600, based on a minimum of thirty-five staff for each LDC. A political sub-committee report to the NUR executive, in 1953, indicated some of the snags of consultation at sectional council level. It claimed that the joint consultative machinery had been brought into disrepute 'by reason of policy decisions at higher level, fettering the management at a lower level'. It found that while some LDCs functioned smoothly, in others there was a practice of confronting the staff with a *fait accompli* while at the same time giving lip-service to joint consultation.[17]

Such frustrating experiences became more common as the number of railway closures and staff redundancies increased in the Beeching era. Once more the subject of workers' control figured largely on AGM agendas. It was discussed in 1963 and from 1965-7, inclusive. The 1963 resolution favouring participation by the workers in the management of the nationalised industries 'at all levels' was carried unanimously as were similar resolutions in 1965 and 1966. In 1967 there were two doubters, who voted against. On that occasion R. L. Taylor, a signalman from Stafford No. 1 branch recalled an experience which helped to convert him from a policy of worker participation in management. When electrification of the Euston–Crewe route was undertaken, it involved the raising of the level of certain bridges. At one point on the route the surveyor told him that he had a plan for a bridge, but when he (Taylor) saw the plan, he told the surveyor it was faulty. The surveyor said that the engineers had drawn up the plan, so that it must be right. Two months later the surveyor returned with a new plan for the same bridge, confessing 'You were right, it was too low'. But when Taylor saw the new plan, he could see that it contained another mistake. Although the surveyor found it hard to believe him, the signalman was proved right a second time. Taylor's somewhat sweeping statement to the AGM delegates was: 'The management completely ignore us when we want to assist them. They do not appreciate that we have outside (i.e. on the spot) knowledge and that we are railwaymen and proud of our industry.'[18]

In 1967, at the instigation of the NUR, the TUC nationalised industries sub-committee met Barbara Castle, the Minister of Transport, in an endeavour to persuade her to add a clause to her Transport Bill authorising union participation in decision-making at all levels in the nationalised transport undertakings However, there was a division of opinion among union leaders being interviewed by the Minister. The NUR was committed to worker participation at all levels, while other unions felt that the all important objective was 'workers on the board', with less emphasis being placed on employee representation at lower levels of management. Consequently, the passing of the Transport Act in 1968 brought no significant advances in industrial democracy. However, the Minister promised to initiate a special study of the transport industry in order to discover the views of its rank and file workers. When Richard Marsh succeeded Barbara Castle, in April 1968, he wrote to the heads of the public transport undertakings and to the general secretaries of the unions informing them that he had asked the Tavistock Institute of Human Relations to carry out an invesigation of the opinions of the railway staff. All the parties concerned, including the NUR, promised the fullest co-operation. On 22 January 1970 Sidney Greene notified all branch secretaries about the project and urged their support.[19] During 3–27 February 1970 the Tavistock Institute field workers interviewed railway staff at Ipswich, Euston, Ashford, Newport (Monmouth), Maesglas, Birmingham (New Street), York and Glasgow (Queen Street) to determine what would be the most appropriate items to include in the questionaire.[20] The main investigation took place between 22 June and 25 July 1970, when 2,042 members of staff from all five railway regions and from headquarters offices at Waterloo, Cardiff, Liverpool and Manchester were interviewed and answers to the issues raised in the questionnaire were provided. The remit of the investigating team was 'to carry out an investigation into the attitudes of BR employees towards various possibilities for increased participation in decision making and to report to the steering group on its findings'.

One of the key questions asked was: 'Thinking about the work the Board does, should representatives of the men take more part in this work?' Of the sample 78·9 per cent answered 'Yes', compared with 16·8 per cent who thought 'No'. However, answers to a follow-up question 'How do you think they should take part?' revealed that staff were primarily concerned to have representatives on the Board in order to improve communications between management and workers rather than that they should be involved in decision-making; 31·49 per cent felt they should take part by making direct representation to the Board, and a further 30·43 per cent looked primarily to receiving more information from it; 27·33 per cent thought that the greater involvement should be expressed by railway workers 'acting in an advisory capacity'. Only 145 opinions (from the 2,042 in the sample) made any reference to being involved in decision-making on the Board. But the overwhelming majority wanted to be better informed on future plans. In the words of the Tavistock Report, 'Railwaymen would appear to favour hearing about things "from the horse's mouth".' It was also emphasised 'that communication "face to face" from those who know the facts to the representatives of the staff can have an almost magical effect on a hostile situation'. There could be no mistaking railway workers' desire to be kept informed of management's plans; 93·7 per cent of those who did not normally hear of such plans wanted to be told about them and wanted an opportunity to discuss them. The minority of the staff – 17 per cent – who did not favour greater participation of workers in railway management gave a variety of reasons for thinking as they did. Just over half of them considered that workers did not have the necessary training for the increased responsibilities which they would incur; more than a quarter thought that it was 'management's job to manage'; others said that greater worker participation would lead to quarrels and delays in reaching decisions.

The investigating team reported very favourably on the quality of the staff representatives on LDCs and sectional councils. They found that there was

> ample evidence to suggest that BR employees select representatives who tend in general to have the characteristics necessary to make participative schemes work in practice . . .
>
> Those who hold representative office do reflect those characteristics which are immediately relevant to effective participation; representatives and union officials tend to have a sense of responsibility, to have authority, a positive attitude to information and a constructive view of innovation, change and the various forms of participation.

When the report reached the steering-group, which comprised the representatives of the BR Board, the railway trade unions and the Minister of Transport, Richard Marsh, made it clear that the government had now completed its part of the exercise and that thenceforward it was up to the Board and the trade unions, in the light of the report, to decide to what extent they should make provision for increased worker participation in decision-making.[21]

There was no rush to make innovations. On 10 July 1973 there was carried at the AGM of the NUR the, by now, familiar resolution calling for greater staff involvement in decision-making. G. Hodgson, a conductor guard of Leeds No. 12 branch moved

> That this AGM considers that the railway trade unions ought to be represented on the British Railways Board. We instruct the NEC to pass this view through all appropriate channels. The railway industry is the ideal organisation for full workers' participation at all levels, with representatives taking part in policy and management decisions.

In the meanwhile developments elsewhere in Europe encouraged the advocates of greater industrial democracy in Britain. In 1973 a union-based worker-director system which provided for two worker appointments per board of six to eight directors was established in Sweden. In the EEC a Green Paper, entitled *Employee Participation and Company Structure*, was published in 1975. It envisaged a standard two-tier company structure to be a common feature in all member countries. Worker directors constituting not more than one-third of the total, and shopfloor rather than union-based, would be elected to the upper-tier board. By the end of 1976 eight European countries had schemes of one kind or another which provided for the representation of employees on company boards.[22]

In its manifesto for the October 1974 General Election the Labour Party gave a commitment to 'a radical extension of industrial democracy' in both private and public sectors, and to amending the Companies Act and the statutory basis of the nationalised industries accordingly. In the same year the TUC published a policy document, called *Industrial Democracy*, which had been approved by Congress in the previous September. It advocated a 50 per cent representation of trade union nominees on single-tier boards of directors. There were deep divisions within the Labour Cabinet and between trade union leaders on the merits of the policy advocated in the document. For this reason the government played for time. No new legislation was drafted. However, the success of Giles Radice, MP, in introducing his Industrial Democracy Bill, under the ten-minute rule, on 15 January 1975, and his good fortune in getting the Bill past the second-reading stage, forced the government's hand. As an alternative to adopting the Radice Bill and modifying it in committee it appointed a committee of inquiry under the chairmanship of Lord Bullock to consider how the extension of industrial democracy could best be achieved.[23]

While the Bullock Committee was hearing evidence and considering what means increased worker participation might be introduced, principally in private companies, government Ministers with responsibilities for the nationalised industries conducted their own inquiries. On 19 July 1976 Sidney Weighell, speaking in support of a Bletchley branch resolution on workers' control, informed AGM delegates of the contents of a questionnaire he had received from Peter Shore, Secretary of State for the Environment, and of the answers he had submitted to the Minister. It was the fullest exposition of NUR policy so far given by any one of the union's officers. He said that the NUR wanted the railway unions to appoint half the members of the BR Board, the number each union appointed being proportional to its membership. The union did not favour the two-tier system in which a supervisory board, with a minority of worker directors, discussed broad issues of policy and an executive board, without union representation, gave practical application to the general directives it received from the 'top tier'. There was no objection in principle to consumer representation on the board, but there might be practical difficulties in their selection. To the question: 'How should decisions be taken if opinions were equally divided?', Sidney Weighell replied: 'The idea is to obtain a consensus about particular policies . . . only in extreme cases should there be any need to resort to voting.' When asked 'Should worker directors have the same responsibilities as other board members, that is, to account to the Minister for the running of the industry; or do you think they should be responsible primarily to the employees?', the General Secretary replied: 'We take the view that generally speaking they should be bound by the Board decisions and should support such decisions when they believe in them, because we believe there has to be a proper dialogue established within the board between all the different interests involved.' The union wanted worker participation at all levels of decision-making through the industry, not merely on the BR Board and the boards of the other transport undertakings in which it had members. It is significant that after this detailed statement, which embodied past decisions on union policy, the AGM delegates voted unanimously for the Bletchley branch resolution.[24]

On 10 January 1977 Sidney Weighell expounded NUR policy to a more diverse audience when he spoke at a meeting of the Chartered Institute of Transport. He again stressed the comprehensiveness of the union's aims regarding worker participation:

We do not believe that the appointment of worker representatives to the boards of industry will bring industrial democracy. The view of the NUR is that there must be worker participation at all levels eventually leading to worker participation at Board level.

Eighteen months later, at Llandudno, the General Secretary struck a more pessimistic note. He confessed that the NUR's objective of full participation was a 'long way off'. The stalemate was caused by the fact that each of the three main railway unions had a different policy regarding participation at the lower levels of organisation within the industry. He summed up ASLEF's view as 'Until we've destroyed the capitalist system we don't want to participate'. It was clear that progress towards industrial democracy depended upon a major improvement in inter-union relationships. In the light of these circumstances Sidney Weighell suggested to the BRB that in those grades for which the NUR has exclusive negotiating rights, it would proceed alone in a policy of 'transferring consultative procedure into the negotiating machinery'. He saw that this approach to the problem involved taking risks:

We could have 75 per cent of the railways and railmen through
LDCs and Sectional Councils participating and we would have
one group, the trainmen's council, having nothing to do with
it. It has enormous risks because you will be blamed . . . If you
pick it up alone, and there are unions in your industry that will
not have anything to do with it, they will exploit the situation.

He also expressed doubts about the policy of appointing worker
directors. 'The more I look at it, the less I like it', he said. There
would be problems about 'how the cake was to be shared' between
investment and wages. Taking part in board meetings would also
be time consuming. 'How do general secretaries of big unions
devote the time to look after an organisation of this size and sit
on the board participating in management? It is an enormous
responsibility.' [25]

In default of agreement between the railway unions, the BRB
took the lead in providing opportunities for consultation between
management and union representatives. For most of the period
following the passing of the Transport Act 1947 there was provision for formal top-level discussion between the two sides in the
industry. As we have seen, the British Transport Joint Consultative Council provided the forum for such discussions from 1949
until its demise, in 1962, under the Transport Act earlier that
year. However, consultation was still possible at the meetings of
the British Railways Productivity Council from its foundation
in 1955 until 1967, when it was agreed to wind it up since many
of the items it had dealt with were being covered by *ad hoc* meetings between management and unions. For the ensuing seven
years the need for continuous contact at top level was met by
less formal meetings between board members and the general
secretaries and presidents of the trade unions. By 1974, with
Britain a member of the EEC, and a government committed to
a policy of industrial democracy, the situation had changed. There
was now a consensus favouring the re-establishment of a more
formal consultative machinery.

On 4 July 1974, at a meeting between management and trade
unions called to discuss the implications of the Railways Bill
then before Parliament, it was agreed that a new body should be
set up. Management subsequently prepared and circulated a proposed constitution for a British Railways Joint Consultative Council (BRJCC). On 2 August 1974 representatives of ASLEF, the
NUR, TSSA, the CSEU and the British Transport Officers' Guild
met Richard Marsh, the Chairman, and seven other members of
BRB, at 222 Marylebone Road, and after discussion, approved the

constitution and aims of the Council. The objective agreed was

> To provide by regular quarterly meetings, an opportunity for discussion at national level between BRB and the trade unions, of consultative matters relating to all the activities and interests of the BRB.

The subjects for discussion at subsequent meetings were wide-ranging. At the meeting held on 10 December 1976, for example, they included the government's Consultative Document on Transport Policy; the one-man operation of trains; the BREL export position; bus and rail integration; Speedlink operation and disciplinary cases arising from the consumption of alcohol. The meetings were consultative; no executive decisions were made. This was demonstrated at the meeting held on 15 September 1976, when the NUR advanced a proposal for a 10 per cent reduction in passenger fares. The BRB countered by outlining the new passenger-traffic marketing initiatives – senior-citizen railcards, student railcards, children's flat-rate fares when accompanying adults, and so on – which it had taken. Its representatives declared that they would not accept the union's proposals.

One of the main reasons for the BRB's concern to establish new avenues for consultation with the trade unions was the need to increase productivity, an objective all the more compelling because of the financial straitjacket within which the Board had to conduct its operations. It was management policy to encourage the railway worker to feel that he was a 'stakeholder' in the enterprise, a development more likely to occur if he was better informed about future plans and the reasons for their adoption.[26] In 1974 the BRB set up a management productivity steering-group, under the chairmanship of Mr D. Bowick, to identify and quantify opportunities for improving productivity and to work out a strategy for their implementation. At subsequent meetings of the BRJCC the unions were invited to participate in the work of the steering-group. The response of the NUR and TSSA was positive. At its meeting on 26 January 1976 the executive of the NUR came to the unanimous decision 'to join the Productivity Steering Group, subject to our representatives adhering to previous decisions on the size, shape and manpower requirements for BRB, our representatives to be the President, General Secretary and two members of the EC'.[27]

In 1978 the BRB took another initiative in forming a British Railways Council, chaired by Sir Peter Parker, and including other members of the Board and the presidents and general secretaries of the trade unions. It was empowered to discuss such topics as 'planning, marketing, financial information, public affairs and special projects'. BRB clearly hoped that the Council would be seen as an alternative to the appointment of worker directors. Its statement on its role read:

> The Council is an innovation which on the one hand avoids some of the self contradictions of Board membership of trade unions; on the other hand it exposes those issues on which common sense and commitment are vital.[28]

When the BRB mentioned 'the self-contradictions of Board membership by trade unions', it feared that worker directors would be mandated by the unions they represented – a state of affairs which it regarded as inadmissible under existing law. In its statement *General Management View on Industrial Relations* it quoted para. 25 of the Labour government's White Paper of May 1978 on *Industrial Democracy*: 'Company Law prohibits the mandating of a director to vote in a particular way.' (More than two years earlier Sidney Weighell had made it clear to AGM delegates meeting at Paignton that worker directors would not be mandated, that the 'idea was to obtain a consensus'. However, it was obvious that the BRB still had doubts that the proposals would be workable.) As a complement to its Railway Council, the Board established Regional Advisory Councils which would be charged with the responsibility of promoting the Board's business, securing traffic, and so on. Sidney Weighell advised AGM delegates at Llandudno on 11 July 1978 to co-operate with the Board's schemes even though they were 'not a solution, or even going half way, to what we have in mind'. The delegates endorsed his recommendation by the overwhelming majority of 64–4 votes.[29]

At Swansea in June 1914 the AGM delegates who carried unanimously the pioneering resolution in favour of workers' participation in management would have been incredulous had they been told that their objective would still not be attained sixty-six years later. However, had any of them survived that long span of years they would have been gratified to learn of the much greater degree of consultation between management and unions which had been established by the end of the 1970s.

II

Many of the Victorian railway companies recognised that a worker's estimation of the value of his job would be determined

not only by the wages he was paid, but also by the way he was
treated in sickness, in disability following an accident, or on retirement. The larger companies therefore established provident
or friendly societies, partly from motives of genuine benevolence,
but partly also to secure the loyalty of their staff. Dr P. Kingsford listed nearly fifty such societies functioning in 1870, which
paid some or all of the following: sickness benefit; death benefit
to a railwayman's next of kin; superannuation payments; and
either lump-sum, or weekly, payments on behalf of widows and
orphans. The oldest society was the Great Western Provident,
established in 1838, membership of which was compulsory to all
traffic grades. In return for contributions varying between 8d
and 1s 4d per week, the member was entitled to sickness benefit
of between 12s and 20s a week; superannuation of between 4s
and 10s a week; while his widow received a lump-sum of between
£3 10s and £6, a widow's pension of 4s a week and an allowance
of up to 1s a week for her children. This was, by the standards
of the age, a remarkably comprehensive, and even generous,
scheme. It was not matched by any other railway company.
Most of the schemes run by the larger railways provided benefits
for a select few of their staff. Thus the London, Brighton and
South Coast Railway Benevolent Fund, founded in 1852, gave
pensions to 'deserving men', but in 1872 was paying weekly sums
to only twenty-three of its former staff. Clearly, the company
put a very high rating on the term 'deserving'. More common was
the practice of paying men a lump-sum on retirement. Thus in
1914 the Midland Railway paid £20 to traffic grades, goods and
shed staff and permanentway and signals and telegraph labourers,
while enginemen, carriage and wagon examiners and road motor
staff received £40 after fifty years' service.[30]

Most of the larger railway companies continued to pay the
salaries of their clerks for at least the first month of sickness. By
1870 four companies, namely, the MR, LNWR, LSWR, and
GWR, provided their clerical staff with retirement pensions which
increased with the number of years' contributions and were based
on a percentage of average salary, and gave a lump-sum to the
next of kin where death occurred before retirement age. The
general picture was one of very patchy provision for a railwayman's security, the situation being summarised by Dr Kingsford:

The general effect was as follows: temporary disability, whether
through accident or sickness – for many men about half pay;
permanent disability – usually only a small sum and when
possible alternative employment; death – small pensions for

dependants for a few and a sum to pay for burial for the majority; old age – small pensions or gratuities for comparatively few, and for the majority their savings, their children's support or the poor law.

The Railways Act 1921, which merged more than 120 railway companies into the four familiar to the interwar railway traveller, also safeguarded the old pension and lump-sum entitlements for those who had been in the service before 19 August 1916. These rights continued to be safeguarded under the Transport Act 1947 and subsequent transport legislation affecting railway operations. However, from 8 July 1954, when the first British Railways pension scheme came into operation, members of the old company schemes sometimes found their payments wholly or partially offset against their total pension entitlements.

III

For more than six years following nationalisation British Railways had no pension scheme for its employees. When the unions met members of the Railway Executive on 13 September 1948, they urged that this obvious gap in the provision of satisfactory conditions of service should be filled as soon as possible. It was an anomaly that was again discussed at a meeting between railway union representatives and members of the Railway Executive on 5 January 1949, when the chairman, Mr W. P. Allen, announced that the BTC had asked the Minister of Transport to issue regulations under section 98 of the Transport Act 1947, closing the four main line railway companies' superannuation funds to any new entrants as from 6 April 1949. He added that it was proposed to establish, from the same date, a provisional superannuation scheme for all BTC staff who would contribute 5 per cent of their weekly pay to its financing. He could give no further details. Meanwhile members of the Manchester No. 12 branch of the NUR felt that it was high time that 'pensions of all on retirement from the industry through age or ill health' were provided by the BTC. They resolved that the executive 'should formulate as soon as possible a positive policy for the membership' on this and other important issues. Jim Figgins, the General Secretary, wrote to the branch in reply that pensions, pay and workers' participation were all being dealt with in discussions with the RE. The EC endorsed his action. This did not satisfy the branch which appealed to the AGM at Brighton, in July 1949, and carried the day by 52–18 votes.[31] However, attempts made by the General Secretary in the latter part of 1949 to persuade the RE to give more details of the Commission's scheme proved fruitless.[32] When the matter was eventually considered, at a meeting of the Railway Staff Conference on 7 February 1950, Mr Allen, for the RE, pleaded 'the very unsatisfactory financial position of the railways' as reason why management felt 'unable to carry the matter further', at least for the time being.[33] For this reason no progress was possible during the remainder of that year.

However, in 1949–50 the TUC put pressure on the Attlee government to view more favourably the establishment of special pension schemes in the nationalised industries. Its economic committee met the Lord President of the Council and Ministers responsible for the state-owned industries several times in 1950 with the result that, although the government was by no means enthusiastic, its resistance to the idea of negotiations between the boards of nationalised industries and the unions on the subject of pensions was weakened.[34] Consequently, when Lord Hurcomb, Chairman of the BTC, met the union delegates on 2 February 1951, he referred to the discussions between the TUC and government Ministers and declared that 'the Commission was empowered to consider, along with the representatives of the unions, the establishment of a pension scheme for wages grades'.[35] Though progress in the discussions was still very slow, at least the log-jam had been broken.

At Scarborough, in July 1952, the delegates to the AGM added their voices to the demand for adequate pensions for railwaymen. They carried unanimously the composite resolution:

That this Annual General Meeting instructs the National Executive Committee immediately to advise the British Transport Commission of our grave dissatisfaction at the long overdue introduction of an adequate pension scheme for all workers in our industry, and decides to press strongly for such a scheme to commence not later than 1 January 1953.[36]

The pension scheme which emerged as the outcome of the negotiations conducted between 1951–3 was patiently explained by Jim Campbell, the newly elected General Secretary, in a masterly exposition to delegates attending a Special General Meeting held in the Victoria Halls, Bloomsbury Square, London, on 13 and 14 October 1953. Arguments which he advanced in support of the proposals were that they embraced all male wages staff, including workshop grades – which for the most part had received a raw deal under the old railway company's provisions. It was also proposed to make payments to those obliged to retire early on account of ill-health and to pay lump-sum death grants to next of kin of men who died in the service of the BTC before reaching normal retirement age. The General Secretary conceded that the minimum pension at 9s 9d a week – at a time when the state retirement pension stood at 32s 6d for a single person and 54s for a married couple – was by no means generous, but explained that it meagreness was in part explained by the cost of meeting the NUR's demand that men nearing retirement should be entitled to benefits. It was also inevitable – in the light of the financial situation of the BTC – that the scheme would be a contributory one. But contributions at 1s 8d to 2s 5d under scheme A, and 8d to 11d under scheme B, were not excessive.

Under questioning, the General Secretary admitted that there was no provision for old railwaymen already retired. He also conceded that it was a very serious weakness that women were not included. He said: 'We were of the opinion that certain female grades ought to join the scheme and we pressed it very strongly with the Commission.' The BTC was unyielding. It brought out the traditional arguments against giving women equal conditions of employment to those offered to men. It considered:

Female employment on the railways was of a transitional character. Young females come into the service but do not look upon the railways as a career. They are more concerned about marriage. Some women employees are already married and consider their domestic responsibilities to be more important.

The delegates were aware that there were many shortcomings in what was being offered. But they considered that the BTC pension scheme could be regarded as a beginning. By subsequent union pressure, there would have to be improvements. By the large majority of 69–8 votes, but without much evidence of enthusiasm, they endorsed the proposed scheme which came into operation on 8 July 1954.[37]

If the delegates attending the SGM in October 1953 had been told that fourteen years would pass before any alteration in the provision of pensions for wages-grade railwaymen would be possible, no doubt many more would have held out for better terms there and then and would have voted against what was being offered. For more than ten years after the introduction of the 1954 scheme, management found a variety of excuses for inaction. Thus, in response to an NUR demand, made early in 1958, that something should be done to provide pensions for ex-railwaymen who had retired too early to benefit under the 1954 scheme, the BTC replied that the issue had been 'greatly complicated by the change in legislation affecting state pension arrangements' and that in these circumstances it was not possible to give the union a positive reply.[38]

As the years passed with no prospect of any improvement in the pension arrangements the weekly payments made to many railway pensioners became increasingly derisory. In January 1961 A. Agram, of Hove, wrote:

After 46 years of loyal service to British Railways I have now reached retirement. The reward for this loyalty is a pension of 11s 6d per week, which will provide me with 1 cwt of coal. For this noble sum I have been paying 3s 4d per week for 5 years.[39]

Six months later the editor of *Railway Review* wrote:

One man told us this week that he had served the railways for over 50 years. His pension was 12s 6d a week. Some get less. If working half a century on the railway is rewarded so parsimoniously, appeals for a revival of smouldering pride ought to be spurned with disgust.[40]

AGM delegates expressed their opinons clearly enough and often enough to leave management in no doubt of the strength of rank and file feeling about the inadequacies of the 1954 scheme. In 1960 they instructed the union's executive to take steps to bring about its improvement.[41] In 1962 they wanted urgent action to ensure that the 10,000 or more railwaywomen were given entitlement to pensions on retirement.[42] However, both the EC and the General Secretary were met with determined stonewalling from the secretary of the Male Wages Grade Pension Central Committee. In December 1962 he wrote to Sidney Greene, expressing regret that he was 'not yet in a position to convene a meeting'. In May 1963, following the receipt of further letters from the union, he wrote that he would convene a meeting of the Central Committee 'as soon as he was in a position to do so'. But in December 1963, and March, May and December 1964, all that Sidney Greene was able to report to the executive was that he was 'continuing to press for an early meeting'. At the end of 1964 the executive showed signs of losing patience. It was unanimously resolved that Sidney Greene should write to Dr Beeching drawing his attention to the fact that 'the secretary of the pension scheme was deliberately flouting the requests of the union for a meeting of the central committee to discuss the matter' and conveying to him their 'disgust at the secretary's continued inaction'.[43] The executive was prompted to take this more decisive step by what delegates had said at the union's AGM that July when they debated the following composite resolution:

> That this AGM expresses its complete disgust with the present pension arrangements for its wages grade members.
>
> We demand that the NEC take immediately the necessary steps to bring about a considerable improvement in the pension arrangements to provide not less than half pay for its male and female members on retirement, excluding any state pension payments and affording the opportunity to be contracted out of the Government (graduated) pension scheme.

R. Taylor, a checker from Kings Cross, who moved the resolution, said: 'We have to do forty years' service in order to draw 30s. That would still not stop our members from having to go to national assistance.' J. J. Carty, a clerk from Derby No. 6 branch, the seconder, said that the women workers of BR were known as 'the Legion of the Lost' since they were the only employees without any pension rights, and P. Donohoe, a technician from Croydon, declared that 'the time has come when paying compliments is out of date, and we should give them the money'.[44] When Sidney Greene in December 1964 followed the executive's instructions and wrote to Dr Beeching, the BR chairman at first followed the stalling-tactics of the secretary of the pensions scheme. On 22 January 1965, he replied that pensions for women could not be included as an item on the agenda of the committee.[45] The union's executive refused to accept this excuse. They instructed Sidney Greene to quote para. 46 of the existing pension scheme regulations which gave 'ample scope' for a discussion of the question. By June 1965 the executive learned that Dr Beeching had changed his mind and three months later they learned that a meeting of the pensions committee, with the item of pensions for women on the agenda, was at last to be held on 8 October 1965.[46] The new pension scheme for railway wages-grade staff which came into operation in 1967, after more than a year's discussion between the representatives of management and the unions, included women employees for the first time. Membership was compulsory for all new entrants to the industry aged

21 and over. It was designed, in the case of someone with forty years of service, to make up the income of the pensioner when the flat-rate state retirement pension and the graduated state pension were added, to two-thirds of the average rate of pay over the last three years of service. Thus a 65-year-old shunter, in 1967, earning a basic wage of £13 3s 0d would be entitled on retirement to the flat-rate state pension of £4 0s 0d, to a graduated state pension of approximately £1 7s 0d and to a railway pension, under the new scheme, of £3 8s 4d, making a total pension income of £8 15s 4d – considerably better than would have been his situation under the 1954 pension scheme when his total pension income (from the three sources) would have been less than 40 per cent of his basic wage just before retirement. The contribution of 6s 1d per week from each member of the scheme was matched by an equal contribution from BR and was funded; and the unions had equal membership with the Board on the management committee of the fund. The NUR representatives in the negotiations leading up to the establishment of the scheme secured improved back service credit arrangements (that is, seven years); improved death benefits and the inclusion of a rule under which the worker's contributions to the fund were excused during periods of certified sickness.[47] Similar schemes were introduced in respect of workers employed by the LTE and the BTDB.

In 1966 the Prices and Incomes Board Report No. 8 *Pay and Conditions of Service of British Railways Staff* (para. 37) noted the contrast between the inadequate total pension income of the wages grades under the 1954 scheme of railway pensions and the far more generous provision for the salaried grades. Most of these members of staff were covered under superannuation schemes established by the four main line railway companies in the interwar period, though some were provided for by even earlier schemes initiated before 1914. The PIB noted that these superannuation schemes, which paid both a capital sum and an annuity, brought annual benefits (including the annuity value of the capital sum) equal to between 40–45 per cent of earnings in the year before retirement. When the state flat-rate and graduated pension were added, the total income would be about 75 per cent of retirement earnings.

In the course of 1970 working parties comprising representatives of both management and unions agreed improvements in both the BR and BTDB salaried grades superannuation schemes. The outstanding improvement was the annual revaluation in accordance with the provisions of the Pension (Increase) Acts.[48] There was still plenty of scope for improvements in all the pension schemes. In 1971 Sidney Greene requested that both BR and the BTDB should ask their actuaries to report on the cost of introducing eight new features, including the reduction of the minimum pension age to 62; the calculation of the final average pay to be based on two rather than three years' service; the provision of a lump-sum benefit on retirement; the payment of post-retirement increases in pensions which would be wholly financed by the boards; improved ill-health provisions; provision for a deferred or immediate pension after age 55; automatic provision for widows and children; the abolition of the waiting period before entry into the pension scheme; and a reduction of the qualification period for a pension from ten to five years.[49] The replies received from the actuaries in response to this request provided the NUR with the detailed factual information needed in subsequent union negotiations with management and led to the introduction of many of the eight improvements in the middle and later 1970s.

The Penzance No. 1 branch gave priority to one improvement suggested in a resolution to the AGM at Llandudno, in July 1969, the resolution being amended in the light of others from Swansea No. 1 and Leeds No. 10 branches:

That this AGM believes that after 40 years' service with appropriate bodies with which we have membership and the age 60 being reached, optional retirement with full pension rights or resettlement arrangements be allowed.

Sidney Greene warned delegates that 'in many places it is not possible to get sufficient men, and many railwaymen go on to 70'. Though he was sympathetic to the proposal, he did not think that management would take kindly to it. Consequently opinion among the delegates was divided, the vote being 44 in favour of the resolution to 29 against.[50] When the union's representatives argued the case for retirement at 60 with representatives of BR at a meeting of 222 Marylebone Road, on 3 February, and quoted the police and Post Office experience in support of the claim, the response of management was as Sidney Greene had predicted. They pointed out that retirement at 60 was very exceptional and that the adoption of the proposal would add 20 per cent to the cost of the provision of pensions. Furthermore, 'the majority of fund members would find it difficult financially to retire until they reached age 65 and were able to draw the state pension.'[51]

However, remarkable improvements in the wages-grade pension scheme were hammered out in a series of meetings of the joint working party in 1972–3. The outcome was the much more attractive pension scheme which was put into operation from 1 July 1974. What helped to make the transformation possible was the acute labour shortage in many parts of the railway system (as well as in London Transport) and the urgent need to make the railway service more attractive. Under the new scheme the period of membership before a member becomes eligible for pension benefits was reduced from ten to five years; the calculation of the pension was based on the standard rate of pay in the final year of employment; the minimum age at which a male member could receive his pension was reduced from 65 to 62 (for women it was 60); the opportunity was provided for members retiring from the service on the ground of ill-health, at or above age 55 (men) and 50 (women) to take a reduced immediate pension actuarially equivalent to the deferred pension; the opportunity was provided for members to commute at retirement up to a quarter of their pension for a lump-sum; post-retirement increases in pensions to be made annually in line with the Pension Increase Acts; there were improved ill-health pension benefits and lump-sum death benefits; on the death in service of a married man with the minimum five years' membership, his wife would be entitled to half the man's pension rate, and if he had children of school age, the eldest would be entitled to one-quarter and the second child to one-eighth the pension rate.

The introduction of these more generous payments was made possible mainly through increased contributions. (However, under the Railways Act 1974, capital assistance from government funds was provided to make good the massive book-deficits of the old railway-company pension schemes of which many railway workers were still members. The deficits had arisen from the fact that railway-company managements had not invested staff contributions in the normal way, but had instead used them to make investments in their own businesses.) Under the 1974 pension arrangements the joint contribution rate was increased from 13 per cent of net pay to 23·33 per cent split between the Board and the member on a 60–40 basis. Thus, the member paid 9·33 per cent of his or her net pay and the Board added 14 per cent.[52]

Within a short time of completing the negotiations for the staff of BR in 1974, the NUR had negotiated broadly similar schemes for the employees of London Transport, the British Transport Docks Board, British Transport Hotels Ltd and the National Freight Corporation.[53] The general effect of the changes instituted in 1974 was to place wages grades in a similar position in respect of pension contributions and benefits as the salaried staff. They reflected the movement towards equalisation of conditions of service – other than pay – of all the wages and salaried staff of BR and its subsidiary organisations.

A motion tabled by Mr Timothy Short, a clerical officer at York, at a meeting of the BR Superannuation Fund members in June 1976, that BR should cease to invest in works of art, drew the attention of the media to the fact that the contributions to the fund from the 77,000 members of the salaried staff were being invested in this way, while the contributions of the wages grades to their separate fund were invested more traditionally in equities and gilt-edged securities. At the end of 1975 the salaried staff Superannuation Fund trustees owned 300 works of art – including furniture and ceramics as well as paintings – to the value of £3·46 million, located in numerous galleries and private residences in various parts of the world. However, the trade union nominees who were represented equally with management on the fund's committee were satisfied that the investment policy of BR's broker was a sound one. Mr Short's resolution was rejected by a comfortable majority.[54]

IV

Traditionally the clerical and supervisory grades enjoyed more generous sick-pay conditions, a shorter working week and longer holidays than did the men and women employed in the wages grades. However, in the course of the 1970s rank and file opinion in the NUR moved strongly in favour of the levelling up of the working conditions of the wages grades to those of the salaried staff. The mood of the decade was captured by Southend branch in its resolution to the AGM, in July 1971:

That apart from acceptance of differences in rates of pay, it is considered that the time has arrived when equal conditions could and should be conceded to all staff employed in the railway industry.

P. A. Lindsay, the mover, wanted the NUR 'to have on record a policy of trying to equal up all the conditions, except rates of pay, based on technical experience and qualification'. The resolution was carried with no dissentients.[55] At the same AGM an even more radical and wide-ranging, but clumsily worded, resolution was moved by R. F. Herbert, a relief signalman from Neasden No. 3 branch:

That this AGM instructs the NEC to negotiate for parity of conditions for all staff (below management range) represented by the NUR. This means in terms that, where the best conditions possible which are agreed for one section of grades can be extended to all parties represented by the NUR, then the NEC should take immediate steps to formulate common conditions for the entire membership of our industrial organisation.

In urging delegates to reject what he obviously regarded as a utopian resolution, Sidney Greene expressed a wish 'that they had taken the typewriter away from that lad at Willesden No. 4', who was responsible not only for this, but for six other resolutions on the agenda! The main reason for the General Secretary's ridicule was the differing conditions of operation and financial strength of such organisations as the National Bus Company, Freightliners Ltd and the Manchester Ship Canal in which the NUR had membership. In the event the mover and seconder were the only delegates to vote for the resolution.[56]

The situation throughout the 1960s and 1970s was that the NUR had a long list of demands for improvement in the conditions of service, originating from resolutions passed at AGMs and transmitted to the executive for negotiation. The simultaneous implementation of them all would have cost BR much more than the funds it had available, especially when it is remembered that claims, such as those for longer holidays, competed with those for improved rates of pay for a share of scarce resources. Because this was the case, unions and management in the early 1970s set up a 'rolling programme' of claims, which it was hoped would gradually be met in the course of the decade. In 1972 items in the programme included four weeks' leave for BR staff; additional bank-holiday leave on Christmas Day in Scotland and New Year's Day in England and Wales; the five-day week for BR staff; the shorter working week; an improved BR wages-grade sick-pay scheme; improved rates of payment during annual leave of conciliation and salaried staff; the introduction of an incremental scale for clerical officers, grade 2; and the spread of established status to a wider range of staff.[57] The extent to which differences in the conditions of service of salaried and wages grades were narrowed in the decades before 1980 can be illustrated with reference to minimum hours of duty, holiday entitlements and sickness payments. Although the trend was for wages-grades' conditions of service to approximate more closely to those of the salaried staff, in 1980 BR employees in the salaried and supervisory grades still enjoyed advantages not available to their wage-earning contemporaries in the railway service. The same situation prevailed in the subsidiary companies of BR.

In 1947 a Court of Inquiry chaired by Mr G. W. Guillebaud considered that it was 'impossible to justify a forty-eight-hour week against the march of events' and ruled that for the conciliation grades the working week should be reduced to forty-four hours from 24 June 1947. The hours of the salaried staff were reduced to forty-two per week from the same date.[58] The forty-eight-hour week had been operative for more than a quarter of a century, and the reduction in working hours introduced in 1947 was the most substantial ever introduced at one time. The next improvement came into effect on January 1962 when under RSNT Award 25 the hours of work of the wages grades were reduced to forty-two per week, while consequent upon further netgotiations between the unions and management, the hours of work of men and women in the salaried grades were reduced to forty from the same date. After the short space of four years the working week was again reduced, to forty hours for the wages grades and thirty-eight for salaried staff from 16 and 28 February 1966, respectively.[59] These changes made possible for the first time for many wages staff a much prized five-day week. As part of the pay settlement reached in April 1980, it was agreed that the basic working week for conciliation staff would be reduced to thirty-nine hours and for salaried and supervisory staff to thirty-seven hours from November 1981.

It would be wrong to conclude that once a reduction in the standard working week had been agreed, actual working hours fell correspondingly. Because of severe labour shortages in key grades, such as those of signalmen and guards, the working of substantial hours of overtime was commonplace as shown in Table 5.1. Thus, in 1965 railwaymen were working an *average* of six hours' overtime weekly. Bearing in mind that many thousands employed in the industry worked only the standard hours, the extra hours worked in those grades where there were staff shortages were well above the average.

V

Before 1950 most members of the salaried staff, as well as many men and women in the conciliation grades, were given some protection against loss of earnings during periods of sickness through their membership of railway-company provident societies. From 1948 all were given more comprehensive coverage under the National Health Scheme. During the first two-and-a-quarter years of its existence the BTC made no special arrangements for the insurance of the health of its employees; but from 1 April 1950 all new entrants into the salaried grades who were away from work sick were entitled to receive full pay for the first thirteen weeks of their illness to be followed, in necessary, with a further thirteen weeks on half-pay.[60] It was an arangement which predated by more than six years the first sick-pay scheme for wages-grade staff, which came into operation on 1 December 1956. The payments made to sick members of the wages grades under this latter scheme took the form of a flat weekly sum unrelated to wage rates or earnings, but increasing with length of service. Those with up to ten years' continuous service were entitled to 30s sick-pay for up to six weeks in any one year; staff who had completed ten, but not fifteen years, of service received the same weekly payment for up to nine weeks and those with fifteen or more years' continuous service were entitled to 40s a week for up to twelve weeks in any one year. Women in the railway service were apparently not allowed to be ill up to 25 years of age, and they were required to complete at least five years' continuous working before being entitled to 30s a week for up to six weeks in any one year. With over ten years' continuous service, women's entitlements were similar to men's.[61]

New schemes for both salaried and wages grades were introduced in April 1965; but although the improvements in the wages-grades scheme marked a greater advance on previous conditions than did the new proposals for salaried staff, the salary-earners were still privileged by comparison. Under their scheme there were two stages of sickness benefit; the 'normal', during which benefits equalled basic salary less National Health insurance contribution, and the 'reduced', in which benefits amounted to half-salary less National Health insurance contribution. With between six months and a year of service, a member was entitled to six weeks on 'normal' followed by an equal period on 'reduced' benefit. With longer service, the duration of benefits increased until with over ten years service, a member was entitled to the maximum of twenty-six weeks on 'normal' and twenty-six weeks on 'reduced' benefit in one year. The wages-grades scheme, by contrast, provided only a 'normal' benefit of three-quarters of basic wage, less National Insurance contribution, for a period of seven weeks only, to staff with up to ten years' service; of ten weeks in the case of a member with between ten and fifteen years' service; of thirteen weeks for those with fifteen to twenty years' service; and of eighteen weeks for those whose period of service exceeded twenty years.[62]

Under the latest arrangements which came into operation in 1979, salaried-staff 'normal' and 'reduced-rate' sickness benefits were calculated by the same rules as had applied from 1965; but a sick person was entitled to the maximum benefit of twenty-six weeks on 'normal' and twenty-six weeks on 'reduced rate' after only five years' continuous service instead of after ten years as previously. By contrast sick people in the wages grades were still only entitled to a maximum of three-quarters of basic pay, less National Health insurance contributions, but they were entitled to receive these payments after a shorter period of service and for a longer period of time. Thus under the 1979 scheme the maximum duration of benefit was twenty-six weeks after five years' service, compared with the eighteen weeks maximum attainable after twenty years under the earlier scheme.[63] Manifestly the salaried and supervisory grades were better shielded against the misfortune of sickness than were the men and women in the conciliation grades. It was a state of affairs which led the AGM, in July 1979, to pass the following resolution in a unanimous vote:

> That this AGM requests the NEC to negotiate with the BRB for the implementation of a fully Salaried Sick Pay Scheme for all wages grade staff in line with that scheme negotiated by the union on behalf of wages grade staff employed by National Carriers.[64]

VI

After 1945 conciliation staff were nearly, but not quite, as well off in respect of annual-leave entitlements as were the clerical and supervisory staff. By an agreement reached between the four main line railway companies and the unions on 17 August 1945, junior and lower-grade clerks together with supervisors, stationmasters and controllers in class 5 with less than ten years' service, were allowed twelve days' annual leave with pay. The more senior of the clerical and supervisory staff, with more than ten years' service, got fifteen days, and those in the special class, eighteen. It was in the extra days that were granted according to length of service that the white-collar staff were privileged by comparison with men and women in the wages grades. By another agreement, in August 1945, all conciliation staff with a minimum of twelve months' service were entitled to twelve days' holiday with pay. As far as was practicable these days were to be given 'in two

consecutive weeks during the customary staff holiday season'.[65]
In January 1958 the NUR pressed for the annual-leave period to
be extended, so that it stretched from the second Monday in May
to the Saturday nearest to the 30 September. This demand was
rejected by management, which nevertheless conceded that 'where
by local arrangement, the overall annual leave period could be
reduced without incurring additional cost, no objection would be
raised'.[66] Staff in both major categories had to wait twenty years
before there were any improvement in the annual-leave allocations.
On 16 July 1965 the RSNT, in its Award No. 39, ruled that salaried
staff under 21 years of age with a minimum of twelve months'
continuous service were to be allowed two weeks' holiday; staff in
class 4, and women on scales 'A' and 'B' over the age of 21 with
less than ten years' service, were awarded two weeks and two
days; most of those with over ten years' service were entitled to
three weeks, while staff in the special class were allowed three
weeks and three days. The concession made to conciliation grades
a few months later was that staff who had completed ten years'
service were entitled to an additional three days' holiday.[67]

By 1974 the need to attract and retain staff in the service at a
time of railway labour shortages helped to bring about marked
improvements in holiday entitlements. Clerical officers in grades
1 and 2 were allowed three weeks and two days' holiday after a
years' continuous service and four weeks after only one year in
service, but received no extra entitlement after ten years of
service. Entitlements of supervisory and traffic-control staff were
along the same lines with a maximum allowance of four weeks'
holiday.[68] In the meantime all staff in the conciliation grades with
the minimum year's service had been granted three weeks and
two days' holiday, two of the weeks to be taken during the
customary holiday period and the remainder outside the peak
period. A further concession to both salaried and conciliation
staff was that pay during annual leave was to be at the rate of
basic pay plus $33\frac{1}{3}$ per cent of the difference between average
weekly basic pay and average weekly earnings during the fiscal
year preceding the date of leave.[69] Finally, in the spring of 1978
management accepted 'in principle' RSNT Award No. 56, giving
two extra days' holiday for conciliation staff 'as a move towards
harmonisation between salaried and wages staff conditions'.[70]

In the course of the prolonged pay and efficiency discussions of
1968–9 the representatives of the BR Board expressed a willingness to raise the status and privileges of conciliation-grade staff
to those of the salaried staff. The cost of equating conditions of
service of the two major groups would have been too prohibitive

to introduce in one fell swoop; but union and management representatives agreed on a declaration of intent, which was included
in the pay and efficiency stage II agreement signed on 22 August
1969:

> We will, in addition, develop an examination of staff differen-
> tials between salaried and wages staff. These may have been
> appropriate in the previous national social pattern but now
> look obsolescent, if not obsolete. But social attitudes take a
> long time to form and are slow to change, therefore progress
> towards future common conditions of employment will be de-
> liberately phased over a period of time to match the pace at
> which social thinking moves.

Viewing the progress of the project over a period of ten years
one is forced to the conclusion that it was financial restraints,
rather than the slow advance of social attitudes, which were the
major obstacle to its fuller implementation.

Initially 'established status' – the means by which this great
social change was to be effected – was granted to well-paid and
experienced staff such as signalmen in class A, special class relief
signalmen, S and T technicians and drivers with a minimum of
twenty-five years' service. Staff who were given established status
were to be paid on an annual salaried basis including, where
appropriate, a London allowance. They continued to receive
wages-staff conditions, except that they were to be regarded as
salaried staff for the purposes of sick-pay and superannuation.
Because of the limited scope of established status, a large minority
of delegates attending the AGM in July 1970 felt that a privileged
group was being created within the industry and that this development was contrary to the spirit of industrial unionism. They took
an 'all or none' attitude. Mr F. J. Hardy, a motordriver, therefore moved a Willesden No. 4 branch resolution:

> That having regard to the fact that some signalmen, S and T
> grades and footplate drivers with 25 years' service in August
> 1970 are recognised in a category of their own amongst wages
> grades for additional privileged conditions, it is the contention
> of this AGM that we as an organisation stamp out this con-
> servative attitude and instruct our NEC to ensure that before
> the 1971 AGM all wages staff with 10 years' service are brought
> into line for Established Status conditions.

The mover stressed that the NUR was an industrial union. 'The last situation we want to be faced with', he said, 'is one of segregation among our members.' G. R. T. Gilbody, a guard from Southport who supported him, warned that 'up to the introduction of stage 2 pay and efficiency agreement we had the utmost co-operation among all grades. But now the differentials can only lead to one end; no more co-operation and a build up of animosity between grades'. But Sidney Weighell assured delegates that the objective was 'to transfer wages grades over to salaried conditions'. This could not be done in one fell swoop since the cost would be prohibitive; but at least they could make a move in that direction. At the end of a keen debate, the delegates, by a majority of 39–31 votes endorsed the General Secretary's view that it was unrealistic to expect all wages-grade staff to be given established status within twelve months.[71] The sceptical view was expressed by Bill Fordham, a guard from March, during another debate at the same AGM:

I would suggest to you that the offer of established status to some of the staff was only a sop. It has not altered the type of work they do. Signalmen still work in signalboxes; drivers still drive engines. It would probably be true to say that some members have, in becoming established status staff, also become the owners of somewhat larger heads.

There was no disagreement about the desirability of improving the conditions of service of the men and women in the conciliation grades. But the fate of the 'established status' scheme epitomised the dependence of management and unions on the state of the economy and the attitude of government towards the claims of public transport. The financial crisis of 1975–6, and the deep industrial depression from 1979, resulted in such severe government financial restraints that the prospects of further progress in the 1980s towards equalisation of conditions of service between the two main groups of employees were extremely bleak.

CHAPTER 11

INTER-UNION RELATIONS

———◆———

I

CHARLIE CRAMP, who played a leading role in the creation of the NUR in 1913, had a clear vision of the scope and purpose of the new organisation. He believed that the union should recruit into membership all those who were either directly or indirectly employed by the British railways. When the discussions on the fusion of forces took place between representatives of the railway unions in 1911–12, he brushed aside suggestions by J. E. Williams, General Secretary of the ASRS, that the new union should not cater for shopmen and refused to accept the view of the Assistant General Secretary of the ASRS, J. H. Thomas, MP that it would be inappropriate for it to recruit clerks and supervisors.[1] When the merger of the ASRS, UPSS and GRWU was completed, the rules of the NUR reflected the industrial unionist beliefs of those who had played a dominant part in bringing it to life. Rule 1, clause 4(a) read:

The objects of the union shall be to secure the complete organisation of all workers employed on or in connection with any railway in the United Kingdom.

Subsequent amendments to the rule were designed to take account of the organisation of the railways and ancillary organisations following nationalisation in 1948. They extended, rather than limited, the scope of union recruitment as revealed in the 1977 *Rule Book* version of clause 4:

The object of the union shall be to secure the complete organisation of all workers employed by any board, company or authority in connection with railways and other transport and ancillary undertakings thereto in the United Kingdom.

With these objectives so unequivocally stated, it is scarcely surprising that on no less than eighteen occasions during 1918–80 the NUR made approaches to the two unions which did not join the merger in 1913, ASLEF and the RCA/TSSA, for discussions on a possible amalgamation or federation.[2] Nor was it only the NUR which took the initiative. In May 1917 the AGM of the RCA instructed the union's executive to open negotiations for a merger with the NUR. Though the subsequent discussions proved fruitless (partly through the unimaginative outlook of some of the NUR negotiators), the passing of the AGM resolution reflected an important groundswell of opinion in favour of greater trade union unity.[3] Coming down to more recent times, in the summer of 1971 the AGM of TSSA voted in favour of establishing 'a joint trade union committee of national officers and executive committee members to meet a minimum of twice yearly.'[4] In May 1967 Sir Stanley Raymond, Chairman of British Rail, addressed the AGM of TSSA, urging the creation of 'a federation of railway unions, followed, perhaps, by a federation of transport unions'.[5] Nevertheless, moves towards the achievement of closer unity between railway unions were generally started by the NUR. The character of the approach to the other unions varied, but the outcome was uniformly unfavourable to the cause of industrial unionism.

In December 1951, for example, the NUR executive instructed the General Secretary to inquire of the RCA and ASLEF whether they were willing to enter into discussions with the NUR 'with a view to the formation of one union for all railwaymen'.[6] A meeting of the three parties was held at Unity House on 20 February 1952, but proved fruitless because the two sectionalist unions were only prepared to discuss an arrangement for spheres of influence, whereas the NUR's objective was an amalgamation.[7] In 1964 the AGM on the initiative of the Feltham branch agreed, with only one delegate dissenting, to instruct the EC 'to approach the other railway unions, on a friendly basis, to discuss the early unifying of the railway unions'. The General Secretary and the members of the executive having burnt their fingers on this issue before, were in no hurry to act on the AGM's instructions. The matter was referred to the trade union structure and function sub-committee which, in its report back to the EC in December that year, advised delay until the TUC report on union structure was published. In consequence no approach was made to the other unions.[8] At the AGM, in July 1966, a further attempt was made to get negotiations restarted. Glasgow No. 24 branch wanted 'an approach to be made to the other two unions . . . for amalgamation, having in mind the reduction in the number of railway employees due to modernisation'. This time most delegates were sceptical and Sidney Greene suggested that the time was inopportune for a new approach. Thus, the resolution to proceed to next business was carried by 48–8 votes.[9] A year later the General Secretary reported to the AGM that in the past few months ASLEF had issued 'scurrilous literature attacking the NUR', from which he concluded that there was no concern shown 'even to maintain existing relationships between the two unions'.[10]

By 1969 the Beeching cuts had caused big reductions in railway employment, affecting particularly adversely ASLEF membership figures and casting doubt on that organisation's future viability. To try and recoup losses, a sustained effort was therefore made by the sectionalist union to recruit guards and platform staff employed by the LTE on the questionable ground that these grades were in 'the line of promotion' to motormen. According to E. E. Barker, a leading railman of Holborn NUR branch, members of NUR and ASLEF had 'almost come to blows' in trying to attract new members on the Underground. At the AGM, in July 1969, the Willesden No. 4 branch considered that the best approach towards the objective of industrial unionism was to start with ASLEF. It moved that the executive should correspond with ASLEF with a view to the merger of both unions, and suggested that an equal number of representatives of each of the two unions should be appointed to a sub-committee to work out the details. Despite Sidney Greene's warning that there was no enthusiasm for such a move on the other side and that the NUR delegation would be engaged in 'a fool's errand', the mover of the resolution recalled Bruce and the spider and thirty-nine out of the seventy-five delegates voting thought it was worth while having another try.[11] On 10 September 1969 Sidney Greene wrote to Albert Griffiths, General Secretary of ASLEF, enclosing a copy of the AGM resolution with the comment: 'I shall be obliged to have your views on the suggested merger.' On 22 September Albert Griffiths replied with equal succinctness: 'This Society does not wish to participate in the proposed amalgamation.'[12]

By the summer of 1971, with two recent pay and efficiency agreements reducing the number of railway jobs and requiring greater 'versatility' of those who remained in the service, the traditional boundary-lines between grades had been subjected to rapid change. The prospects for closer unity between the railway workers seemed brighter than had been the case for some years. Thus at the AGM, in July 1971, Sidney Greene felt able to give cautious support to a Brighton branch resolution which called upon the three railway trade unions 'to set up a co-ordinated body to present a united front on behalf of the members' they represented. The General Secretary, in the course of the debate, mentioned that he had received a letter from his opposite number in TSSA, recommending the establishment of a joint trade union committee of national officers and executive members. The AGM delegates, therefore, carried the Brighton resolution by an impressive majority of 73–4 votes.[13] A month later the EC noted that the TSSA invitation was in line with the AGM decision and, therefore, accepted the invitation to attempt a co-ordination of the future relationships between the three railway unions. Despite this promising start, there was no further progress. In December 1971 the EC noted that 'the matter had been listed for discussion at the next meeting of the three railway trade unions' and that arrangements were being made accordingly. But in both March and August 1972 the EC minutes merely recorded, 'This case awaits the meeting of the three railway trade unions'.[14]

In the meantime delegates at the AGM, in July 1972, reiterated the demand of the previous AGM that efforts to secure a closer working together of the railway trade unions should be continued as a matter of urgency. By 68–6 votes, delegates carried a Glasgow No. 6 branch resolution that the EC should 'set up a permanent working party or sub-committee to examine in detail, with a view to early implementation, the forms of federation or alliances that are possible with other unions with a similar interest'.[15] In August the executive followed this up by referring the proposal to its organisation sub-committee for examination and report,[16] and on 11 October, heartened by the success of the co-operation of the three unions in the recent wage negotiations with the BRB, it endorsed the sub-committee's recommendation 'that an early meeting be sought with ASLEF and TSSA with a view to either amalgamation or federation or some other form of alliance'.[17] However, in December the all-too-familiar and depressing statement, 'This case awaits the meeting of the three railway trade unions', appeared once more in the EC minutes.[18] The fact of the matter was that the executive of ASLEF had second-thoughts on the wage settlement with BRB, and concluded that because of what it saw as slow progress in the deliberations of the footplate-grades working party (set up as part of the wage settlement with BRB), it would organise a ban on rest-day working, unrostered overtime and Sunday working, and stage a series of one-day strikes. The ASLEF strikes early in 1973 afflicted the Western Region on 5 February; the Eastern Region on 12 February; the Southern Region on 14 February; and the London Midland Region on 19 February.[19] These actions soured relationships with the other two unions and held back for nearly a year any progress in negotiations on closer working. Nevertheless, it was recognised that there were advantages in the unions' officers and representatives meeting together before confronting management. Early in 1974, therefore, a meeting of the three parties took place, when it was agreed that each union should consider the suggestion that a small sub-committee of representatives of each union should be set up to make recommendations for a common union policy in negotiations with the BRB.[20] However, the other two unions soon destroyed any hopes ardent industrial unionists in the NUR may have had that the joint consultations would lead on to discussions on amalgamation or federation. At the end of August 1974 Sidney Greene informed the executive that ASLEF was not prepared to discuss an amalgamation or federation, though it was willing to continue participating in the joint trade union meetings to 'present united policies on matters of common interest'. TSSA expressed a similar view. The NUR's executive could merely 'take note' of the other unions' standpoint.[21]

When David Bowman began his term of office as President of the NUR in January 1975, and Sidney Weighell took up his appointment as General Secretary in the following April, each had hopes that, as experienced footplatemen, they might be able to establish a closer understanding between the NUR and ASLEF. In January 1976 informal discussions took place between the presidents and general secretaries of all three of the railway unions on an NUR proposition to set up a working party to examine closer liaison between the unions and the establishment of a federation at an early date.[22] On 12 March, however, the EC of the NUR learned that ASLEF was not interested in considering either federation, or amalgamation, but that it was 'desirous of improving relations between the three unions'. TSSA, on the other hand, agreed to take part in the proposed working party.[23] Unfortunately, no further progress was made. In August the NUR executive was informed that arrangements for the working party meeting were in hand, but four months later it was informed that 'owing to un-foreseen circumstances' the meeting arranged for September had to be cancelled.[24]

II

One of the circumstances which prevented further progress in the talks was the row over the poaching of NUR members by TSSA and ASLEF. As long ago as 1939, in its Bridlington Recommenda-tions, the TUC had tried to reduce the likelihood of inter-union

disputes of this kind. It was laid down as a general principle that
no person

> who is or has recently been a member of any trade union should
> be accepted into membership in another without inquiry of the
> present or former union which would be under obligation to
> reply within 14 days, stating (a) whether the applicant has
> tendered his/her resignation; (b) whether he/she is clear on the
> books; (c) whether he/she is under discipline or penalty and (d)
> whether there are any other reasons why the applicant should
> not be accepted.

It was also laid down that under no circumstances should a union
accept members from any other union which is engaged in a trade
dispute.[25] In 1939 all three railway unions accepted the terms of
the Bridlington Recommendations.

Adherence to the Bridlington principles did not preclude unions
making separate arrangements with other unions, regulating the
transfer of members. The 1955 edition of the NUR's *The Branch
Officer* includes a list of forty-four unions with which the NUR
had signed transfer agreements. On 7 October 1952 one such agreement was signed at Unity House, following a meeting between Jim
Campbell, General Secretary of the NUR, and G. M. G. Morris,
General Secretary of TSSA. Its terms, which were less stringent
than the Bridlington Recommendations and reflected a conciliatory
spirit on the part of both parties, were as follows:

1 Neither organisation should accept a member of the other
  organisation without enquiry being made to the headquarters
  of the parent organisation to ascertain that there were no objections to the man transferring his membership.
2 The organisation receiving the application for membership
  should allow the 'Parent' organisation reasonable time to contact the applicant with a view to persuading him to retain his
  original membership, and should inform the branch concerned
  that this is being done and that the applicant should be advised
  to continue to pay his contributions to the 'Parent' organisation
  until his application for transfer has been approved. It is understood that the applicant will be seen by the representative of
  the parent organisation with the minimum of delay.
3 Objections to the acceptance of an applicant should not be
  pressed by the 'Parent' organisation to the point of making the
  man become a non-unionist in order to join the other organisation as such. This, of course, is not to apply in cases where

the member is (a) under discipline (b) engaged in a trade dispute or (c) in arrears in contributions i.e. cases covered by
Clause 4 of the Bridlington Recommendations.
4 Whilst the intention is to conform to the spirit of the TUC
   Bridlington Recommendations the obligation under the latter
   for a union to reply within 14 days is not to apply.[26]

Although the 1952 agreement was sometimes under strain, as in
October 1962 at the time of the strike protest over the Beeching
closures, it worked reasonably smoothly for more than twenty
years. In the later 1970s however, the drift of membership of
supervisory grades to TSSA and ASLEF was accelerated and
caused considerable concern in the NUR. On 11 September 1976
the union's national conference of clerical and supervisory grades
carried unanimously the following resolution:

> That this conference is deeply concerned with the continuing
> drift of existing and recently recruited members of grades
> covered by this conference to the TSSA and the ASLEF. We
> request the NEC to examine as a matter of urgency the reasons
> that brought about this serious state of affairs, and to take
> remedial action.[27]

In fact from October 1975 head office abandoned its somewhat
lenient attitude towards NUR members switching allegiance to the
other railway unions. On the ground that members of the clerical
and supervisory and footplate grades were adequately catered for
by the NUR, through its grade conferences and EC and AGM
representation, most applications for transfer to TSSA or ASLEF
were resisted, though in a majority of cases they could not be
stopped.
  Matters came to a head with TSSA when that organisation
refused Sidney Weighell's request that it should advise the persons
concerned to cancel their membership of TSSA and resume their
membership of the NUR. Sidney Weighell wrote again with a
warning that, if he did not get a satisfactory reply, he would have
to refer the matter to the TUC disputes sub-committee. Tom
Jenkins, General Secretary of TSSA, then replied that his executive
regarded as unacceptable the NUR's objections to transfers 'solely
on the grounds that it could represent the individuals concerned'.
This stung the NUR's executive into instructing Sidney Weighell
to refer all outstanding cases between the NUR and TSSA to the
TUC disputes sub-committee.[28] On 18 January 1978 E. A. G.
Spanswick of the General Council chaired a meeting of the disputes

sub-committee which heard the NUR's request that 299 persons, formerly its members, should be advised to resume membership, and that in return, any members who had switched to the NUR from TSSA should be advised to resume their original membership. TSSA's representatives said that they must consult their executive before giving a reply. The meeting then stood adjourned pending further separate discussions between the disputants. As these informal talks produced no agreement, the two parties were summoned before the disputes sub-committee on 12 June 1978 to hear its ruling that the 299 persons whose membership was in dispute should return to the NUR. In the meantime the two unions agreed that with effect from 18 January 1978 the Bridlington Recommendations should apply in the case of future applications for transfers of membership.[29]

The logical next step was to try and stop ASLEF 'poaching' NUR members. In his *Report* to the AGM, in June 1978, Sidney Weighell wrote:

We have now turned our attention to the jungle which surrounds relations between the NUR and ASLEF. For as long as most of us remember the ASLEF have poached our members without any recourse to the Bridlington principles and protests from the NUR have mostly been greeted with a stony silence.

We have decided to document all instances where the ASLEF have taken NUR members into membership without recourse to Bridlington.

By 22 September that year 109 instances of this kind had been listed at Unity House.[30] But since no promise could be exacted from ASLEF that it would discontinue trying to recruit NUR members, Sidney Weighell wrote to Ray Buckton on 20 June 1978, informing him that the NUR had decided to take ASLEF to the TUC disputes sub-committee.[31] This action raised the hackles of the ASLEF executive and, on 26 July 1978, Ray Buckton wrote to Sidney Weighell that it had decided that it would 'forthwith cease to participate in the trade union membership agreement which was reached between the unions the BRB and LT respectively until such time as the subject matter is resolved'. The ASLEF decision distressed Mr J. Cope, the Chief Industrial Relations Officer of LT, who wrote to Ray Buckton on 24 August reminding him that, under clause 6 of the trade union membership agreement, six months' notice was required for its termination and expressed the hope that during that period the problem would be resolved. When Sidney Weighell wrote to Len Murray, General Secretary of the

TUC, on 20 September informing him that the NUR was in dispute with ASLEF and asking for the quarrel to be referred to the disputes sub-committee, he mentioned in justification for the request, that NUR members had 'been subjected to a great deal of local pressure' to join the other union.

When the representatives of the two unions appeared before the disputes sub-committee of the TUC at Congress House on 17 November 1978, a temporary peace formula was agreed for submission to the two union executives. The NUR complaint would be held in abeyance while discussions between the officers continued; both parties agreed to give strict adherence to the Bridlington principles and a further meeting of the two unions would be held under the auspices of the TUC in January 1979 to report progress. The NUR executive considered the formula at its December 1978 meeting and Assistant General Secretary Charlie Turnock wrote to the TUC accepting it. ASLEF was somewhat slower in complying. Although the TUC's Assistant General Secretary wrote to Charlie Turnock on 11 January that ASLEF had also accepted the formula, NUR District Officer McFadden informed Albert Dudley, head of the Organisation Department at Unity House, that Norman Pinches, ASLEF organiser, had told him that he had received no new instructions and that he was recruiting members on the same basis as previously. On 2 February 1979, however, ASLEF sent circular 31/1979 to its branches, advising compliance with the TUC formula. Further discussions and exchanges of correspondence took place through the spring and summer of that year until Sidney Weighell advanced a radically new proposal for trying to solve a problem which had persisted through at least two generations of railwaymen. But to understand the new turn of events, it is necessary to examine more fully the reasons for the failure of all previous attempts at reconciliation.

III

For at least forty years after the establishment of the ASLEF in 1880, a majority of footplatemen who were trade unionists belonged to the ASRS or, after 1913, the NUR. In 1904 ASLEF membership was 11,500, while the footplate-grade members of the ASRS numbered 18,546.[32] The ASLEF membership figure of 30,000 for 1913 looks impressive until compared with the railways total footplate-grades staff of 94,099 men and boys, most of whom still preferred to belong to the NUR, an industrial union, rather than the craft-oriented ASLEF.[33]

Events of the First World War had an enormous influence on subsequent relationships between the two unions. Before the war the basic wage of a porter was a meagre 18s per week, while the express driver's rate was a relatively affluent 48s, a sum 2⅔ greater than the porter's. This huge differential may be explained with reference to market forces; but it was unjustifiable on moral or social grounds. In the emergency of rapid wartime inflation eight separate flat-rate war bonuses, totalling 33s per week were awarded to all adult employees of the railway (with lesser amounts paid to the under 18-year-olds). At the war's end, therefore, the porter's rate had risen to 51s or by 183·3 per cent, while the express driver's pay was up to 73s, a rise of only 82·5 per cent. More significantly the express driver's pay was now less than 1½ times that of the porter, compared with 2⅔ times in prewar days.³⁴ The erosion of differentials between the pay of skilled and unskilled workers during the war years was a *national* experience, affecting all trades. It was justifiable on social grounds. But this did not prevent ASLEF leaders blaming the NUR for the decline in status of its members, in so far as this was measured by the size of the pay-packet, and making the claim that a sectionalist union could best serve the interests of footplatemen. Exploiting the footplatemen's resentment at the relative decline in their earnings compared with those of other grades, in the early 1920s, for the first time, ASLEF succeeded in recruiting a majority of the staff in the footplate grades. Its success was most marked on the GWR and in the more rural areas of the SR and LNER. In the more industrialised parts of England and Wales and Scotland, where traditions of trade union solidarity were older-established, the NUR had preponderance. By 1924 ASLEF membership reached 59,000, while the NUR's stood around 25,000.

Another major influence preventing amalgamation or federation of the two unions was the bitterness and resentment which followed strikes called by ASLEF, the three outstanding examples of which were those of 19–29 January 1924, 28 May–13 June 1955 and the one-day regional strikes of February 1973. The fact that in each case NUR footplate members – as well as other grades – were instructed to work normally (though not to undertake work which would have been done by the striking footplatemen) placed them in an extremely difficult position where there was an agonising conflict between loyalty to the NUR and a staunch trade unionist's dislike of crossing picket lines. At the same time ASLEF members were bitterly resentful at being 'betrayed' by NUR colleagues in the same depot. Memories died hard. At the outbreak of the Second World War there were still cases of men in the same depot who would not speak to each other because of what happened in the strike over fifteen years earlier. Even more remarkably, a quarter of a century after the seventeen-day ASLEF strike of 1955, two delegates at the NUR's AGM in Guernsey, in July 1980, spoke of the lasting damage the dispute had brought to personal relationships. P. Wigley, from Shildon No. 2 branch said: 'Even to this day, twenty-five years later, we have what were lifelong friends before the strike pass each other in the street, members of the same family not speaking to each other.' G. G. T. Wakenshaw, a locomotive driver from Normanton, said: 'I went to work for seventeen weary, hard days in 1955, and believe you me, I have suffered since. . . There are people in my area who do not talk to me after twenty-five years because I went to work.'[35]

In depots where they formed a small minority of the footplate staff and most of their kind were members of ASLEF, only the staunchest of NUR loyalists could stand up to this kind of ostracism. It was during ASLEF strikes and in their aftermath that a lot of NUR members were lost to the rival organisation. An indication of what happened to NUR footplatemen members at Plaistow in East London during the 1955 strike was given in a letter from A. McAulay, Secretary of Plaistow No. 2 branch, dated 23 June 1955, to Jim Campbell, the General Secretary:

> Some of the branches loco members were on their way to work but were stopped by a very strong picket force, some of them from other depots, and, as you know, told a pack of lies and paid their shilling and became members of ASLEF. Now the point is that the members who were loyal to the NUR are now paying the price as we are now banned from sick clubs, social events, etc. And some of them were trying to treat us like dirt and I had to go to the local management and police on behalf of some of my members.

Mr McAulay's branch of the NUR lost twenty-two of its sixty-two footplatemen members as a result of the strike. From returns sent in by 599 branches with footplatemen members six weeks after the dispute was settled, it is clear that nearly a 1,000 members were lost in less than two months. The twenty-four NUR branches with the largest number of footplatemen members lost 1,940 members of all grades, most of whom must have been locomotivemen, in the year to 31 December 1955.[36]

The fact that sectionalist strikes, such as those of 1924 and 1955, were as much against the NUR as against management, and that they resulted both in a substantial accession of members to ASLEF and a legacy of bitterness at the local level, made it immeasurably more difficult for the unions to achieve a harmonious working agreement, let alone fusion or federation.

The industrial experience of long-serving members of the NUR, particularly those who secured election to the EC or the AGM, reinforced their conviction that it was the combined strength of an all-grades industrial union that had been instrumental in securing enhanced earnings and improved working conditions for railwaymen. When they thought of closer working with colleagues in other railway unions, it was in terms of opening up for them the benefits of industrial unionism. But Sidney Weighell reminded delegates at the AGM, in July 1980, that 'they are as adamant in ASLEF about their philosophy as you are'.[37] The craft union 'obduracy', which the General Secretary recalled was evident on repeated occasions in the second half of the twentieth century. At the 1957 TUC, for example, Albert Hallworth, General Secretary of ASLEF, denounced Jim Campbell's resolution favouring a reconstruction of the trade union movement as a demand that the TUC should 'put up a formula for fusion'. 'My members would not accept it', he said.[38] The fundamental reason for ASLEF rejecting all attempts at federation or amalgamation was that its entire *raison d'être* was to organise workers on a craft basis.

The leaders of TSSA, though inclined to be more favourable to the idea of federation than were their counterparts in ASLEF – as their actions in 1971–2 and 1979 demonstrated – nevertheless justified the existence of their union on the ground that members of the clerical and supervisory grades would benefit more by belonging to a specialist union than they would as part of a much larger organisation embracing many grades in the railway service. When D. A. Mackenzie, TSSA General Secretary, was asked by Russell Kerr, MP, Chairman of the Select Committee on Nationalised Industries (sub-committee A), in 1967: 'Do you believe that a case exists for a single national union to cover all railway workers or, for that matter, all transport workers?', he replied:

So far, as far as we are concerned, my organisation has always resisted this in two senses. One is, perhaps, that we are specialists in salaried staff matters. I think if one union had been necessary they would not have joined us or the ASLEF. The other thing is that we have some affinity with salaried workers generally in the country. Therefore we think it right that we should remain an entity within the railway industry.[39]

As has been shown above, membership transfers were the most important cause of friction between the NUR and TSSA. The transfer agreement between the two unions which lasted during the years 1952–78 gave time for NUR organisers and branch secretaries to contact members who had made application to switch to TSSA and to discover their reasons for wanting to make the change. Promotion from a work situation, in which the majority of colleagues were members of the NUR, to one in which the TSSA had a strong preponderance, was one reason. A NUR branch officer in 1960 reported of one lapsed member: 'All his fellow clerks are members of TSSA.' In another case a branch secretary commented: 'Being made supervisory grade foreman I am afraid has gone to his head.' At least until the 1970s clerks and supervisors had a strong antipathy to striking, under any circumstances, and gave this as a reason for leaving the NUR and joining TSSA. Early in 1960 the NUR issued strike notices to take effect from 15 February, and later that year it called for a strike to begin on 17 October. In both cases the strike action was averted. But the threat of the strike caused the number of applications to transfer to TSSA for the months February–April 1960 to exceed the average of previous years by 550.[40] Sidney Greene gave another reason for salaried staff leaving the NUR when there was any likelihood of industrial action:

It is unfortunate that on each occasion the NUR appeared likely to become involved in industrial action some of our salaried staff members suddenly decide they should be in membership with TSSA. A few of these members take the greatly mistaken view that to remain in the NUR with the possibility of being called out on strike will prejudice their prospects of further promotion; this despite the fact that some of our most capable branch officers are salaried staff members.[41]

Another reason for Sidney Weighell's decision to attempt, in 1979–80, a completely new approach to the problem of closer working between the railway unions was the failure of earlier efforts by the NUR to achieve reform via the TUC. In September 1942 at the TUC Congress, F. J. Burrows, President of the NUR, moved:

This Congress calls upon the General Council to make a complete examination of the following two points, and to report their views and recommendations to the next Annual Meeting:
(a) To report upon the present structure of affiliated unions in order to determine (1) where competition and overlapping exist; (2) where such structure is uneconomic; and (3) where policy is diverse within an industry.

(b) To report upon the advisability of altering the constitution of unions where it can be shown that their present basis of improving the conditions of employment of their members is ineffective from the point of view of general progress both now and in a visualised Socialist Economy.

The General Council, dominated by representatives of either craft or general unions, put up the formidable Sir Walter Citrine, General Secretary of the TUC, to demolish the proposal. He declared that 'it started from a false premise that it was possible to plan the future of trade unionism in this country, and secondly, that having made their plan, they could get their organisations to conform to that plan'. In the face of this opposition it is surprising that, on a card vote, the NUR resolution gained as many as 2,153,000 votes to the majority vote of 3,085,000.[42]

Jim Campbell tried again for the NUR in 1957. At that year's Congress he moved:

This Congress welcomes the statements of prominent trade union leaders stressing the need for a reconstruction of the trade union movement. It believes that much can be done to improve our trade union structure to the great benefit of the membership. Congress therefore instructs the General Council to conduct a survey and make recommendations to the 1958 Congress designed to assist in any re-organisation necessary. Further, Congress realises that in any such contemplated reconstruction the interests of trade union officers and staffs should be protected.[43]

This time the climate of opinion in Congress was less favourable to the industrial unionist point of view than it had been fifteen years earlier. In the interim the Organising Committee of the TUC produced a series of reports in 1945–6 under the general title of *Trade Union Structure and Closer Unity*. The recommendations for railway labour were that there should be a loose federation of the unions with separate 'spheres of influence' for the NUR, ASLEF and RCA. The two sectionalist unions accepted the report but John Benstead, General Secretary of the NUR, speaking against it at the 1945 TUC, declared it 'totally unsatisfactory'.[44] In 1957, therefore, both W. J. P. Webber of TSSA and A. Hallsworth of ASLEF smelt a rat They saw Jim Campbell's resolution as an attempt to overturn the TUC policy of 1945 in favour of the different policy of industrial unionism and, helped by Sir Vincent Tewson, the General Secretary of the TUC, they secured its rejection on a show of hands.

In 1962 the new General Secretary of the TUC, George Wood-cock, was more sympathetic to the ideas of industrial unionism than his predecessors had been and thus when Ron Smith, of the Union of Post Office Workers, moved a resolution instructing the General Secretary 'to examine and report to the 1963 Congress on the possibility of re-organising the structure of both the TUC and the British trade union movement with a view to making it better fitted to meet modern industrial conditions', he supported it and helped to secure its adoption by Congress.[45] On 23 May 1963 the General Council followed up the decision of the previous year's Congress by writing to all affiliated unions inviting their comments and suggestions.[46] The NUR, in reply, maintained that 'the first step to be taken to improve the situation would be the formation of one union for railwaymen, keeping in mind the broader picture of one union for all transport workers'.[47] The TUC followed up its initiative of 1963 by planning a series of ten conferences of unions in the main trade groups with its Finance and General Purposes Committee. One of these, involving the NUR and ASLEF, was arranged for 17 March 1964, but was cancelled after George Woodcock received a letter from ASLEF declining the invitation.[48] Thus at least as far as railway workers were concerned, another attempt at rationalising the trade union structure came to nothing.

IV

By the late 1970s, therefore, Sidney Weighell was all too well aware of the repeated failures, extending over more than half a century, of the various initiatives taken by the NUR, both through direct approaches to the other unions and through the TUC, to achieve the aim of one union for all railway workers. His concern to attempt a new kind of approach is understandable. The first indication that he was seeking to break the deadlock by advancing a proposal, unprecedented in the long history of the NUR, came during an informal meeting with ASLEF leaders at Congress House on 12 June 1979. He asked Ray Buckton, General Secretary of ASLEF, whether his union would be willing to relinquish its right to organise employees of London Transport in return for the NUR ceasing to recruit footplatemen employed by British Rail. Ray Buckton expressed an interest but warned that he would need to seek the views of his executive. When they met again at the same venue two months later, Ray Buckton reported his executive's opposition to the proposal but their willingness to agree to limit

ASLEF recruitment on the LT to guards and motormen. Sidney Weighell, replying, doubted whether the NUR executive would give its consent. The NUR General Secretary outlined his proposals in a letter to Len Murray, General Secretary of the TUC, written on 26 September 1979. He claimed that if it was adopted it would lead to 'the substitution of competitive effort by co-ordinated effort in organisation in depots, stations and offices'. The 1,800 NUR members who were in the footplate line of promotion about matched in number ASLEF membership working for LT. It was also proposed to establish a Joint Trade Union Committee comprising representatives of all three railway unions and meeting every three months, the chairmanship to alternate as frequently.[49] In trying to advance his plan Sidney Weighell encountered a succession of obstacles. At a meeting held in Congress House on 25 October the ASLEF representatives refused to relinquish its right to organise staff on LT. Then at a meeting of the NUR executive, on 1 November, a resolution empowering the negotiating subcommittee to continue discussions at the TUC was defeated by 12–9 votes, while an amendment totally rejecting any agreement with ASLEF on spheres of influence was carried by 11–10 votes.[50] The final blow came at the AGM at St Peter Port, on 2 July 1980: P. Wrigley, a shopman from Shildon No. 2 branch, moved

> That this AGM re-affirms the principles which guided our fore-fathers to build this trade union on Industrial Trade Unionism. Further we declare our main organisational objective to be 'the complete organisation of all workers employed by any board, company or authority in connection with the railways and other transport undertakings in the UK'.

In the debate which followed it soon became clear that clause 4 of the union's rule 1 – part of which was incorporated in the resolution – is as sacred to many active members of the NUR as is clause 4 of the Constitution of the Labour Party to dedicated socialists within that organisation. All eleven speakers from the floor of the hall supported the resolution. C. Moriarty, a charge-man from Landore, expressed the widespread disquiet at the General Secretary's plan when he claimed that, if it was accepted, it would lead 'to the break up of the NUR' – a similar view to that of E. P. Loughran, a guard from Teesside, who said, 'Either the NUR is an industrial union or it is not. There is no middle path which we can tread'. Sidney Weighell, from the platform, gave an impassioned defence of his initiative. He pointed out that, although members of the NUR had talked about one union for railwaymen ever since 1913, they had 'not moved an inch' in that direction. He stressed the importance of the proposed Railway Trade Union Council

> with a constitution drawn up by the TUC, tight, tough, that nobody can renege on; it is the federal arrangement which this union will be committed to see that it works; and in five years we could possibly move to one union for all railwaymen.

He warned that, failing the adoption of his plan, ASLEF might go somewhere else, it being publicly known that they were having talks with the TGWU. But despite his appeal to delegates 'not to throw out the baby with the bathwater', the voting reflected widespread apprehension about his proposals. The resolution was carried decisively, by 61–12 votes, with four delegates abstaining.[51] In the light of this vote and ASLEF's refusal to budge on the question of its LT membership, in July 1980 the prospects of achieving one union for all railwaymen looked as dismal as that month's weather.

V

If sectional unionism was still very much alive among footplatemen and the clerical and supervisory grades at the end of the 1970s, it had just disappeared from the ranks of signalmen after a long and tenuous existence. The Union of Railway Signalmen (URS) was launched in 1924 with the aid of a 'loan' of £3,000 from ASLEF; it disappeared from the scene only in 1979. The union was never affiliated either to the TUC, or the Labour Party.[52] Its motto was 'Safe Passage for the Railway Traveller'. The highest membership figure claimed by the URS was in 1950 when it stood at 8,333 organised in 180 branches. Apart from 1973–4, the decline was continuous thereafter. In any case, the union's membership claims were highly dubious. The annual income to the general fund, given in returns to the Registrar General of Trade Unions and Employers' Associations, was never as large as it should have been, given the membership figure stated and the known weekly subscription rates. This was a feature of the URS which, naturally enough, formed a part of the NUR's long continued propaganda attack on the organisation. In 1951, for example, an NUR leaflet pointed out:

> A full year's General Fund and Superannuation Fund contribution at 10d a week is £2 3s and 4d, and on their own calcula-

tion of membership the total General Fund income should be
£17,190 6s 8d The actual sum shown on the balance sheet is
£8,511 6s 2d. This represents a full paying membership of only
3,844 members as against the average of 8,317 claimed.[53]

If we assume the URS claimed membership figure is correct, this
still only represents 32 per cent of the signalmen employed in
1951. If, as is more realistic, we assume 3,844 members, then the
percentage falls to only fifteen. In 1960 there was a claimed
membership of 3,690 organised in eighty-seven branches, and in
1970, 2,705 in sixteen branches. When the union shop agreement
came into operation from I January 1970, the URS suffered, since
the NUR, with the overwhelming majority of signalmen in its
membership, had sole negotiating rights with the employers for
this grade of staff. Unless they could prove strong conscientious
grounds for a non-unionist stance, all signalmen were obliged to
belong to the NUR, though there was nothing to stop their
simultaneous membership of the URS. By 1973, therefore, membership of the URS had slumped to 150. The banning of the closed
shop under the Industrial Relations Act 1971, and the unofficial
strikes of signalmen in December 1974, brought about a temporary revival; the returns for 31 December 1974 showed a membership of 220 (but a footnote revealed that half the total had enrolled during the December strikes). In 1975 the reintroduction
of the union shop agreement helps to explain the fall in membership to seventy. Only eighteen members were reported at the end
of 1976 and just eight a year later, when income from members'
subscriptions was down to 44·20 and income from investments
amounted to 27p. The last return received by the Registrar
General was for 31 December 1978, when the union reported four
members. It can safely be said that the URS died in May 1979
with the death of Charles Holloway, of Kensal Rise, London, its
secretary and chief sustainer for over ten years.

Considering the guerilla war which had been conducted between the NUR and the URS for more than half a century, the
sequel was ironic. Early in June 1979 a temporary exchange operator at Unity House, Mike Crawshaw, who was known by his
colleagues as 'Cowboy Joe' because of the high-heeled, hob-nailed
boots and jeans which he wore, and who was quite unaware of
union battles of the past, received a telephone call from the Co-
operative Bank: £6·60 was held in account for an organisation
known as the Union of Railway Signalmen. Now that Mr Holloway, its secretary, had died, what should they do about it? 'Send
it here, to the office manager', Crawshaw replied without a

moment's hesitation. Albert Dudley, head of the organisation department who dealt with the cheque, though tempted to spend the money on celebrating the demise of a rival organisation, acted, as always, with the strictest rectitude, and arranged for the £6·60 to be sent to one of the URS former auditors.

It is important to explain what kept the URS alive for so long before it faded away in the late 1970s. When the organisation was founded in 1924, there must have been many hundreds of signalmen who had been members of the sectionalist United Pointsmen's and Signalmen's Society (UPSS) before it merged with the ASRS and General Railway Workers' Union in 1913. In their younger years they had been nourished on the idea that a specialist craft union would best suit their interests, so that when a new union appeared making the same sort of claims as did the UPSS, they gave it a sympathetic hearing. The NUR reacted too slowly to counter these influences. The rank and file National Signalmen's Movement which organised NUR members in the years 1918–24 was never given official recognition, and it was not until 1932 that the first National Signalmen's Conference was organised with the blessing of the union hierarchy. More importantly, as has been shown in Chapter 1, far-reaching changes in the technology of signalling were taking place in the 1930s and again in the years after 1950. Discontent with the marks system, established in 1922, and under which a signalman's pay was determined by the number of lever movements he made and telephone or telegraph messages he received or sent during a working shift, was a reason for many men being disenchanted with the NUR. As the technology of signalling changed, so the number of anomalies multiplied. This was made clear in a leaflet issued by the URS in the late 1940s; under the heading 'Abolish the Marks System', it was pointed out that

> This ever increasing tendency towards a complete change in the signalling system, whereby lever movements are considerably reduced, but the mental work of the men considerably increased, makes it more necessary to change ideas and reconsider our values.

The URS proposed substitute for the marks system was a higher basic rate with local committees to make necessary social variations of pay according to the density of the traffic. Ignoring the fact that the large majority of signalmen were in the NUR, and that they were well represented in its executive committee and at its AGM, the URS claimed that only signalmen could deal with problems of signalmen's wages and conditions.

Discontent among signalmen erupted again in the late 1960s and early 1970s. As has been shown in Chapter 5, since it was very difficult, in the short run, to increase a signalman's productivity, his workload being determined by conditions beyond his control, no major revision of the wage structure of men in this grade was included in the agreement on pay and efficiency reached at Penzance in the summer of 1968. As an interim measure, pending a more thorough reassessment of signalmen's pay, a modest 3 per cent was added to each wage packet and some signalboxes were given an improved classification.

These circumstances provided Charles Holloway, URS General Secretary, with a golden opportunity to exploit signalmen's discontent. In a leaflet which revealed his gift for choosing the colourful metaphor rather than his abilities as a trade unionist, he wrote:

Acknowledge now that you have once again been thwarted in your attempts to get your rightful dues. The years roll by, the tides come in and go out. You are still the pebble on the beach awaiting the next tide to push you here, there and everywhere else. As though completely lost.

The answer to your complete deliverance is up to you and you alone. Act now. Join the URS.[54]

There were spasmodic strikes by a small minority of signalmen in July 1968, causing Sidney Greene to send a circular to all NUR branches notifying them of a unanimous resolution of the AGM, urging all strikers to return to work in the knowledge that problems would be dealt with under stage II of the pay and efficiency discussions.[55] Later that year the General Secretary received warnings of continuing discontent. T. H. Taylor, secretary of the NUR branch at Barnehurst in Kent, wrote on 2 September:

The URS which I had thought was DEAD in this area has again raised its ugly head. The recent agreement on wages has not helped the position. Signalmen are furious and are saying the NUR has let them down . . . The URS are really living this up. To them it is a gift.

H. W. Burgess, secretary of the North Midlands District Council of the NUR, wrote to Sidney Greene on 31 October 1968: 'My members are certain that unless there is something tangible for them in Phase II . . . there will be wholesale resignations from our union.'[56]

In the next few months the negotiating strength of the NUR
did secure something very tangible for signalmen. Following the
stage II pay and efficiency agreement, men in this grade secured
rises of between 44 and 50 per cent in the period 1 January 1970–
31 December 1972, bringing the class A/1 signalman's wage up
from £23·95 to £35·60 a week and raising the class 3 signalman's
pay from £15·40 to £22·15. In addition, under the 1972 classification exercise more than 5,000 signalmen gained additional pay
through the upgrading of their signalboxes.[57] It was these very
substantial gains secured by long and patient negotiations between
representatives of the NUR and BR, rather than the union shop
agreement – which did not preclude any signalman from holding
joint membership of the NUR and URS if he thought that a craft
union for signalmen was in his best interests – which caused the
slump in URS membership from the 2,918 claimed for 1970 to
150 claimed for 1973.

In the period December 1974–February 1975 there were further
unofficial one-day strikes involving up to 650 signalmen mainly
from the London Midland and Eastern regions. This action which
was backed neither by the NUR, nor by Charles Holloway of the
URS, was led by David Theedon, an Essex signalman and sprang
from dissatisfaction with the findings of an Independent Tribunal
on the Railway Pay Structure, which reported earlier in 1974.[58]
For more than a fortnight Russell Tuck, Senior Assistant General
Secretary, and his colleagues toured the trouble spots, exhorting
signalmen to work normally. Success came at the end of February
1975. It was the last industrial action in which members of the
URS were involved.

Very often it was through the initiatives of branch and district
council secretaries that the claims of craft unionists were dis-
credited and the merits of industrial unionism explained. A
Liverpool and North Wales District Council pamphlet *Our
Answer to the URS*, first published in 1949, may be cited as an
example:

> Though circumstances may have made you a signalman, you
> are first of all a railwayman, employed on the British Railways;
> secondly, that as a railwayman your service is bound up with
> that of other railwaymen. So mutually dependent are you on
> each other that affairs cannot be viewed from a personal stand-
> point alone. Wherever other railwaymen may be they are de-
> pendent upon your membership, just as you in turn have to
> rely upon the membership of men elsewhere, and of other
> grades, for your economic and industrial safety.

A URS pamphlet stated the basic approach made by the union, 'We affirm that what is good for the footplatemen, the clerks and the supervisors must be good for signalmen'.[59]

Through the years subsequent to its publication in 1938 most locomotivemen were members of ASLEF, which played a major part in negotiating their wages and conditions. The large majority of signalmen belonged to the NUR, which enjoyed the sole bargaining rights for staff in this grade. But by the 1970s signalmen were among the best-paid employees of the railways, and top-ranking men of the grade earned higher wages than top-ranking locomotive drivers who had been at the head of the railway wages league until the later 1960s. Clearly, the signalmen had not done too badly as members of an industrial union, and this was undoubtedly the most important reason for the failure of the URS to recruit more than a small fraction of this grade and the main reason also for the disappearance of the union in 1979.

The most extreme example of sectionalist organisation among railway employees was the brief-lived Federation of Power Signalmen, set up by the same Charles Holloway who later served as General Secretary of the URS. The Federation issued its first circular in January 1945, in which it claimed to be 'the power-signal operatives' organisation'. At a meeting held in London on 15 February that year the aims of the new union were stated to be 'improving the wages and conditions of cabin inspectors, regulators, signalmen and relief signalmen engaged in power-operated signal boxes'. Although by April that year a membership of 'over 60' was claimed, the large majority of signalmen were even more doubtful about the value of this elitist organisation than they were of the URS. When a much-publicised 'mass meeting' was held at the Memorial Hall, London, on 30 January only thirty of the 1,500 power-box signalmen of the London area bothered to turn up. Not surprisingly, Charles Holloway's venture fizzled out within five months of its launching.[60]

CHAPTER 12

THE NUR AND POLITICS

I

ACTIVE members of the NUR and of its predecessor, the ASRS, have always been keenly aware of the importance of railwaymen's interests being represented in Parliament. The major part played by the ASRS in helping to create the Parliamentary Labour Party is well known. On 6 March 1899 the union's executive committee endorsed a resolution of the Doncaster branch calling upon the Parliamentary Committee of the TUC 'to summon a special congress of representatives of co-operative, socialist, trade union and other working class organisations for the purpose of securing the return of an increased number of Labour members of Parliament'. The same resolution moved by James Holmes, an ASRS delegate, was approved by the TUC, meeting in Plymouth early in September that year. When the special congress, called for in the resolution, was held in the Farringdon Hall, London, on 27–8 February 1900, ASRS representatives, including Richard Bell, the union's General Secretary, and George Wardle, editor of *Railway Review*, played a prominent part in the establishment of the Labour Representation Committee (LRC), the forerunner of the Parliamentary Labour Party.

Only seven months after the creation of the new organisation the country was plunged into a General Election. There was precious little time in which to select, and prepare support for, LRC candidates, only two of which, Richard Bell and Keir Hardie, were elected. The success of the ASRS General Secretary, at Derby, owed a great deal to the political consciousness of many of the 609 members in the two large branches in the town, helped as they were by the services of the union's four organisers, mobilised specially for the occasion.

The lessons of this campaign were not forgotten. By the time of the next General Election, in January 1906, two other ASRS nominees, Walter Hudson in Newcastle upon Tyne and George Wardle in Stockport were well entrenched in their adopted constituencies. In Newcastle the union had over 1,300 members, besides elected local councillors and many representatives on the trades council. The union's membership in Stockport was only a third of that of Newcastle, but it was well represented on the local council and trades council. Both candidates secured election to Parliament to join the re-elected Richard Bell on the benches of the Commons.

It was local influences of the kind that were present in Derby, Stockport and Newcastle in the pioneering days that ensured continuous ASRS/NUR representation in Parliament throughout the period 1900–80, with the sole exception of the four-and-a-half years following the serious decimation of the Parliamentary Labour Party in the General Election of 27 October 1931. In July 1945, when a record number of fifteen members of the NUR were elected to the House of Commons, the union had 1,487 branches (apart from those in Ireland) and a total membership of 400,639 in Britain. The NUR was an important political force both nationally through its MPs, and locally through its members' presence on city, borough and county councils and on selection committees of constituency Labour Parties. In the 1960s, however, with the acceleration of rail closures, redundancy, the drop in the number of branches and the decline in attendance at both branch and public meetings consequent upon the spread of television, the grass-roots influence of the union in the constituencies was on the wane.

In view of the reduction in railway employment and the consequent fall in NUR membership, it was all the more important that the union's maximum political influence should be mobilised. This implied ensuring that the greatest possible proportion of members paid the political levy and that branches of the union affiliated to local constituency Labour parties. The rail closure and redundancy aspects of the Beeching regime in the first half of the 1960s caused some demoralisation of the labour force, which found reflection in an increasing number of members' 'contracting out' of payment of the political levy. Between 1960 and 1962 the proportion of members contracting out grew from 13·9 per cent to 19·7 per cent. This alerted Sidney Greene and the union's executive to launch a campaign through the district councils and organisers to check and reverse the fall in members' contributions to the political fund. These efforts bore fruit. At the end of 1963 the proportion of members 'contracting out' had fallen to 14·4 per cent, and by 1970 had fallen still further to 3·7 per cent. The situation through the 1970s was much more gratifying to the leadership than it had been in the 1960s; the proportion of members 'contracting out' only rarely rose above 5 per cent and was generally well below that figure.[1]

Another facet of the individual member's involvement in politics was the *amount* of his political contribution. From 1957 to 1965 this was at the rate of 4s 4d per annum. It is indicative of the comparatively easy-going attitude of the leadership to the union's political role in the 1960s that, in 1965, the levy was then reduced to 4s per annum, at which rate it stayed until 1 July 1972 when it was doubled to 40p a year. What prompted the EC to make the recommendation for the increase was the effect of inflation on the diverse items of expenditure from the Political Fund including the affiliation fees to the Labour Party; the grants to constituencies represented by NUR MPs; the allowances to those MPs towards their parliamentary and constituency expenses; the payment of part of the salaries of the union's officers and staff; the payment to the Electoral Reform Society for conducting ballots on behalf of the union; besides many smaller items, such as the cost of printing. In supporting the resolution for the increase in the political levy Sidney Greene assured delegates attending the AGM at Scarborough, in July 1972, that there would be no increase in the individual members' all-in contribution to the union. The money for the increased political levy would come from the General Fund. He was completely frank with the delegates when he commented:

> If I were to say, 'All right we are going to increase the contributions of the union by 20p a year purely for the Political Fund', that would cause a hell of a row, out of all proportion to what is involved; and I think, therefore, this is the best way of doing it in the circumstances.

The delegates gave unanimous endorsement to the change.[2]

By 1976 Labour Party affiliation fees, which in 1972 were at the rate of 10p per member per year, had been more than doubled to 21p. In addition (as explained more fully below) four more MPs had been attached to the NUR group in the Commons, making a further claim on the union's Political Fund. For these reasons the EC, on the advice of its political sub-committee, recommended an increase in the political levy of members of the union to 60p a year. The proposal was approved by the AGM in July of that year with only one dissentient.[3]

A further weakness in the union's political armour was the failure of many of its branches to affiliate to their local constituency Labour Party. At the end of 1974 173 of the union's 660 branches had not affiliated to any constituency Labour Party. It was not always easy for branch officers to change the situation.

The decline in both railway employment and the number of NUR branches meant that in areas, such as East Anglia and the Highlands of Scotland where the railway network was thin on the ground, the members of a single branch could come from as many as half a dozen or more constituencies. Should the branches affiliate to all the CLPs or only to one? These stumbling-blocks did not deter Sidney Weighell from his energetic campaign to ensure that every branch had secured its affiliation. Already by 31 December 1975 the number of branches still not affiliated had fallen to 138; but the disturbing fact was that this group represented approximately a quarter of the total.[4]

In June 1976 the EC's political sub-committee, which included as members both Sidney Weighell and Dave Bowman, the President, reported that the union's rules were silent on the subject of branch affiliations to CLPs. It recommended that affiliation should be made mandatory by altering rule 16, clause 7. It pointed out that 'the difficult task of obtaining selection for an NUR nominee was virtually impossible without grass roots support'. The proposed alteration to the rule was seen as 'a further step in improving the union's political organisation and representation'. The members of the EC and the delegates at the AGM in July that year agreed. Both groups gave unanimous endorsement to the proposal.[5]

II

By 1975 NUR representation in Parliament rested on insecure foundations. Six of the union's sponsored candidates secured election in February 1974 and were re-elected in October that year. But under rule 16, clause 10, NUR MPs were not allowed to stand for re-election after reaching the age of 65. (It was this rule which obliged one of the union's ablest and most distinguished MPs, J. B. Hynd, MP for Sheffield, Attercliffe, to stand down before the General Election of 1970.) If the October 1974 Parliament survived to a full five-year term, then three of the NUR MPs would be obliged to retire at its end with very little prospect of being succeeded by other members of the union. In Carlisle, for example, where Ron Lewis was elected as an NUR-sponsored candidate on 15 October 1964, the subsequent rationalisation of the railway services in and around the city and the re-organisation of the NUR branches in the area altered the political balance of power in the constituency. There was only a very slim chance of another NUR nominee being chosen following the enforced retirement of the sitting member.

These circumstances prompted the members of the Derby No. 3 branch to pass the following resolution for consideration by the union's executive at its meeting in March 1975:

> This branch calls on the National Executive Committee to examine every aspect of the union's political activities, with a view to increasing our representation in the House of Commons. Such examination to take into account the way we select our candidates and the possibility of sponsoring selected nominees other than those on List 'B' of the Labour Party. Further, to consider the sponsorship of existing MPs who represent 'railway' constituencies, i.e. York, Crewe, Swindon, Derby, etc.

The resolution from Derby provided the political sub-committee of the EC with the opportunity to prepare a report on this important question. Its members concluded that changes in the method of selecting the union's parliamentary candidates were imperative. The existing arrangement was that the union selected nominees for vacant seats from its members on the Labour Party's List 'B' of parliamentary candidates. This comprised people nominated by any constituency party or affiliated organisation. But having names on this list does not involve the nominating body in any responsibility for sponsorship. The sub-committee recommended that the EC should select candidates from List 'B' to place on the Labour Party's List 'A', containing possible parliamentary candidates whom trade unions and other affiliated organisations are willing to sponsor. In making this recommendation the sub-committee was merely proposing that NUR practise should be brought into line with that of other large trade unions. In its other major recommendation, however, it was proposing a complete break with tradition. It advocated forming 'a supplementary list of suitable candidates among people on List "B" and from existing MPs in appropriate constituencies who would be people considered to have a special knowledge of industrial problems and of transport'. When such persons were selected, it would be on the understanding that they became members of the NUR group in the House of Commons. Furthermore, to give the union time to reconstruct its arrangements for parliamentary representation, it was proposed to rescind the 'retirement at 65' rule for its MPs.

With executive endorsement this report was presented to the AGM at St Helier, Jersey, on 15 July 1975. In recommending its adoption Sidney Weighell warned that unless the delegates approved the changes proposed the union would be 'left at the start-

ing gate', with its parliamentary representation halved after the
next General Election. The meeting had no hesitation in giving
unanimous endorsement to the proposed changes in procedure
and rules.[6] The political sub-committee wasted no time in implementing the decision of the AGM. By the December meeting of
the executive Messrs R. Faulkner, A. Garner, B Jones and A. W.
Kemp had been transferred from the Labour Party's List 'B' to
its List 'A' and four sitting MPs, Messrs R. Cook (Edinburgh,
Central), Tam Dalyell (West Lothian), M. O'Halloran (Islington,
North), and P. Whitehead (Derby, North) had been given provisional approval for inclusion on the union's supplementary list.
It was the original intention to limit the number of sitting MPs
on the supplementary list to three, but the four interviewed impressed the sub-committee so favourably that it was decided to
recommend the adoption of them all. At its December 1975
statutory meeting the executive gave unanimous support to the
sub-committee's proposals.[7] In July 1977 Sid Weighell was pleased
to report to the AGM that the union's representation in the
House of Commons had been increased to eleven, the six NUR
MPs elected in 1974 having been joined by the four adopted MPs
and by Harry Cowans, the NUR-sponsored candidate who won a
by-election in the Labour seat of Newcastle, Central, in 1976. (The
union also had four representatives in the House of Lords including two of the NUR's former member in the Commons – Lords
Champion and Popplewell – Lord Heycock, made a peer by virtue
of his services to local government in South Wales and Lord
Greene, whose elevation to the peerage was announced just before his retirement as General Secretary early in 1975.) The beneficial effects of the new policies were revealed in the General
Election of May 1979, when twelve of the NUR-sponsored candidates were successful and only one, R. O. Faulkner at Hudders-
field, West, was defeated.

III

It was one thing to have a sufficient number of able MPs, it was
quite another to have an effective NUR team in the House of
Commons. Before the introduction of radical changes in the
years 1975–7, the NUR parliamentary group was lacking in
purposeful direction and concerted effort. The union's MPs made
often well-informed intervention in crucial debates on transport
policy, and they were effective in voicing the union's discontent
in 1965 with the failure of the Wilson government and of its first

Minister of Transport, Tom Fraser, MP, in particular, to fulfil electoral promises regarding the halting of rail closures. They played a major part, along with other members of the Labour Party's transport group in the House of Commons in securing Tom Fraser's dismissal.[8] Some of them, including Ron Lewis, were exceptionally effective constituency representatives. But they scarcely worked as a team and they lacked an adequate backing in research. Meetings with the members of the political sub-committee of the executive were infrequent and social, rather than political, in character. Sidney Weighell said that the sub-committee 'ambled along every six months and had a lunch and talk'.[9] Dave Bowman recalled that the first time, as a member of the political sub-committee, he met the MPs he was impressed by the conviviality of the gathering but then began to wonder when the business of the day would start. Eventually he had the temerity to ask for a copy of the agenda – a request that was met by looks of blank amazement. He then felt it pointless to mention the minutes of the last meeting.[10]

An important step taken to give the parliamentary group a more effective political impact was the appointment of Keith Hill as Political Liaison Officer in July 1976. On 3 June of that year the political sub-committee received a request from Peter Snape, MP, secretary of the NUR panel of MPs, for 'specialised assistance to enable the enlarged group to work as a more effective and cohesive force'. The sub-committee recommendation that such assistance should be provided was endorsed by the EC on 8 June, with only one dissentient. Keith Hill, described to AGM delegates by Sidney Weighell as 'a highly political animal', is a graduate of the University of Oxford, who was previously employed for three years as lecturer in politics at the University of Strathclyde and for two-and-a-half years as research officer in the International Department of the Labour Party at Transport House. Just over three years after the appointment had been made, Peter Snape described the work of the Political Liaison Officer as of 'immeasurable value' to the parliamentary group.[11]

Among Keith Hill's many activities were the drafting of House of Commons questions to the Secretary of State for Transport and to junior Ministers; the provision of research backing for MP's speeches; the briefing of the General Secretary on political issues; the preparation of proposed amendments to transport Bills and MP's briefings on them; attendance at Standing Committees of the House to provide on-the-spot assistance to members of the group; the organisation of meetings with members of the BRB and with the board members of other public transport bodies;

preparation of newspaper articles and letters and the organisation of a political course at Frant Place, Tunbridge Wells (the NUR education centre) for potential parliamentary candidates.[12]

Sidney Greene's approach to many of the union's political problems was that of personal contact, that is, lunches and informal discussions, with the Secretary of State for Transport or one of his junior Ministers. He achieved greatest success with these tactics in the case of John Peyton, Edward Heath's Secretary of State for Transport, 1970–74, whom he even persuaded to address the union's AGM at Exmouth in July 1973. However, by 1976 not only had Sidney Greene left office, but the political situation at Westminster was vastly different. A Labour government with a precarious majority had taken the place of the Heath administration. In these changed circumstances a well-organised group of eleven NUR MPs was in a favourable position to influence transport policy by *collective* action, since without its support, the government's majority would have been in jeopardy.

The chief characteristics of the new, collective, working of the group were the holding of meetings on a regular, monthly, basis instead of spasmodically and for *ad hoc* reasons, as previously; more frequent meetings with the General Secretary and the other members of the union's political sub-committee and the increasingly formal quality of those meetings; MP's attendance since November 1979 at meetings of NUR district councils and railwaymen's places of work, including Swindon and London Bridge, to keep them in better touch with rank and file opinion; liaison, hitherto very tenuous, with members of the British Railways Board, including its Chairman, Sir Peter Parker, to plan joint action on transport issues and meetings with the Secretary of State for Transport to ensure continuing support for the public sector and to counter the influence of the road lobby. The meetings with members of the British Railways Board were valuable in that, before being prodded by the NUR, the members of the Board had shown some reluctance to get engaged in any actions which might be regarded as political. However, Sir Peter Parker was enthusiastic since he was impressed by the business-like attitude of the NUR MPs and the General Secretary. The meeting in one of the committee rooms of the House of Commons on 14 February 1979, for example, hammered out a common approach on issues such as the Channel Tunnel, railway electrification and section 8 grants for factory sidings under the Railways Act 1974.[13]

In November 1977 William Rodgers, Secretary of State for

Transport, expressed the view privately to Peter Snape, MP that the NUR group of MPs was 'the most effective trade union group in the House of Commons'.[14] There can be little doubt about his reasons for reaching that conclusion. On the occasions when he met the members of the group, he was impressed by their grasp of the facts and by their persistence in pressing their arguments. At a meeting held on 22 April the MPs immediately put the Minister on the defensive. They warned him that if the policies of higher rail fares, reduced subsidies on some services and possible further rail closures, referred to in the Consultation Document of 1976, were to appear in the forthcoming White Paper on transport policy, he would meet 'the strongest opposition in the House of Commons'. When the Minister asked that the discussion should concentrate on the post-1981 period as 'financial restraints were strong to that date', the MPs stressed that to hold back investment in the late 1970s would undermine the future of the industry since 'the infrastructure would have been irreparably damaged by that date'.[15]

The Minister was also bound to note the unprecedented number of questions on transport matters put by NUR MPs at Question Time in the House of Commons. From mid-1976 up to the end of 1978, NUR MPs put down over 300 Written and Oral Questions on transport matters. In the same period, the NUR MPs were regularly succeeding at Transport Oral Questions in making at least half a dozen interventions on behalf of the union despite the intense competition among MPs 'to catch the Speaker's eye' on such occasions. There was an effective division of labour among NUR MPs in the asking of questions and in speeches on transport questions. Gordon Bagier and Peter Snape, chairman and secretary of the NUR Group, concerned themselves with the main railway business; Donald Anderson and Ron Lewis concentrated on rural rail services; Robin Cook specialised on issues relating to the NFC and the British Rail subsidiary businesses; Phillip Whitehead and Tam Dalyell, a member of the original Labour delegation to the European Assembly, kept up the pressure for the Channel Tunnel; Harry Cowans dealt with rail electrification; Frank Dobson, who represented Holborn and St Pancras, made the problems of London Transport his responsibility.

The Parliamentary Group's sustained efforts bore some fruit. The White Paper, *Transport Policy* (Cmnd 6836), which appeared in June 1977, contained no reference to further rail closures. While the Consultative Document bemoaned 'indiscriminate subsidies which tend to benefit the better-off rather than the poor'

(p. 84), the White Paper envisaged the switching of resources from the national road programme to the budget for local transport. It is noteworthy that during the remaining period of the Callaghan administration and in the early months of the Thatcher government, plans for railway investment escaped relatively unscathed (though total allocation of funds for this purpose was still grossly inadequate) compared with the more severe reductions in other sectors of public expenditure. Furthermore, the case made for the return of Freightliner Ltd to British Rail was recognised when Bill Rodgers announced his decision to transfer to the British Railways Board the NFC's controlling interest in Freightliners Ltd in the course of the debate on transport policy on 21 November 1977.

The first fifteen months in the life of Mrs Thatcher's Conservative government were arguably the busiest in the history of any NUR parliamentary group. The focus of attention was Norman Fowler's Transport Bill, enacted in July 1980. In July 1979 the MPs invited the Secretary of State to a special meeting at which the considered objections to his proposals to denationalise the NFC, allow private bus operators to cream off the most profitable of the bus routes and withdraw government support from BR and NFC pension funds were voiced in no uncertain terms. Discussions were arranged with the TGWU parliamentary group, the NBC and BR, to sound out opinion and ensure concerted opposition to the Bill. In the Standing Committee on Transport, Harry Cowans and Frank Dobson, armed with excellent briefs by the research department at Unity House, supplied *all* Labour MPs on the committee with information and arguments. Frank Dobson was present for 109 hours and Harry Cowans for 104 hours of the 110 hours in which the committee were in session.[16] In the course of the progress of the Bill the union's MPs tabled dozens of amendments and secured concessions from the Minister in respect of NBC and BR pension funds and the NBC's right to have the Minister reconsider the role of free-enterprise bus operators in the event of the government's new policies proving detrimental to passenger interests.

Indirect proof of the value of the appointment of the union's Political Liaison Officer and the revitalisation of the work of the parliamentary group which followed came with the decision of the executive of the 2-million-strong TGWU, on 8 December 1978, to follow the NUR's example. It was reported that 'special machinery' would be set up 'to enable the union to meet its sponsored MPs at monthly intervals rather than just once a year'. Meetings were to be arranged regularly for union research

representatives and executive officers with an *ad hoc* committee to
be elected by the union's twenty-six sponsored MPs. Furthermore,
Moss Evans, the TGWU General Secretary, revealed that the
union was 'to appoint one of its staff with a special responsibility
for supplying MPs with details of union policy on issues affecting its
members as they arose in Parliament'. The appointment of Jenny
Pardington as TGWU Political Liaison Officer followed in the
autumn of 1979.[17]

IV

Following the defeat of the Labour Party in the general election
of 9 May 1979 and the post mortem on that defeat at the party's
annual conference in October that year, the NUR was in the
forefront of the trade union campaign to establish a Commission
of Inquiry into the organisation of the party. Among the key
issues to be examined were the election of the party leader, the
responsibility for producing General Election manifestos, the reselection of parliamentary candidates and the reorganisation of
the party's finances. As he made clear in his *Political Report to
the AGM in 1980* – from 1978 these had been printed separately
from the General Secretary's main report, in itself an indication
of the importance given to political issues – Sidney Weighell felt
that the NUR had as strong a claim as any union to make recommendations for the reform of the Labour Party. It was affiliated nationally to the extent of 100 per cent of its membership;
its rules required all branches to affiliate to constituency parties
and it had the largest number of sponsored MPs in proportion to
its membership of any trade union. The union made the maximum
contribution permitted under the Hasting Agreement to the constituency Labour parties, where it had sponsored the candidate.

The NUR's contribution to the debate on the reform of the
Labour Party took the form of a printed folder, entitled *Towards
a New Compact for Labour*, which appeared in April 1980. The
processes through which the annual conferences reached decisions were criticised as inadequate, in that composite resolutions
'were hastily scrambled together and then disposed of in ludic-
rously short debates'. It was, therefore, proposed that in future
Conference should devote a full-day's debate to each of two major
policy areas to be chosen by the national executive committee
(NEC) of the party. Regional conferences would be required to
devote a day to debating these policies, and would have the power
to submit amendments to the NEC which would take them into

THE NUR AND POLITICS

account when preparing a final statement for presentation to the
annual conference.

Regarding the composition of the NEC, the main criticism
made in the union's statement was that there was a 'total absence
of genuine grass-roots representatives' and that the Parliamentary
Labour Party was represented by only two persons – the leader
and the deputy leader. To remedy these defects it was proposed
that one representative should be elected from each of the eleven
regional conferences of the Labour Party and that a new Parliamentary Labour Party section of seven members should be
included in the NEC, which would be reconstituted as follows:

section	number
Trade unions	12
CLPS	11
PLP	7
Young Socialists	1
Socialist societies	1
Women's sections	1
Councillors	1
Treasurer	1

Provided that these changes were made in the structure of the
NEC, the union was prepared to accept the 1979 Labour Party
annual conference decision that the NEC alone, after the widest
possible consultation with all sections of the movement, should
take the final decision on the contents of the General Election
manifesto. The union also supported the policy of reselection of
Labour MPs in circumstances where 'that confidence which ought
to exist between the MP and the majority of the party breaks
down'. On the other hand, the view of the majority of the Parliamentary Labour Party that the party leader should be elected by
the party's MPs, rather than by a wider constituency, was supported on the ground that the more limited body would be more
familiar with a candidate's qualities as a Minister and as a parlia-
mentarian.

Sidney Weighell and the members of the NUR political and
finance sub-committees felt particularly strongly the urgent necessity of putting the Labour Party's finances on a sounder footing.
Since in proportion to its membership, the union paid more into
the funds of the Labour Party than did any other union, there
was naturally a concern that the party's resources should be de-
ployed to the best advantage. *Towards a New Compact for Labour*
advocated the creation of a new, full-time post of Labour Party

Financial Secretary, to be filled by a professionally qualified person enjoying a status of that of the National Agent. It was suggested that organisations affiliated to the Labour Party should be obliged to pay in full the maximum amounts set out in the Hastings Agreement in respect of sponsored candidates and MPs. In addition, the union supported the decision of the Labour Party annual conference, in 1977, in favour of state financing for political parties.

V

In its campaign against the Beeching cuts in 1962–3 the NUR endeavoured to enlist the support of local authorities, trades councils and other interested parties. At the time environmentalist groups were less influential than they were a decade later. Partly for this reason, support for the campaign often proved disappointing. Furthermore, Sidney Greene was a man who concentrated on doing a first-class job in negotiating improved wages and working conditions for the union's members rather than involving himself in the politics of transport. The union had plenty to say on questions of transport policy in the 1960s; but for the most part it acted in isolation. It was to the credit of Sidney Greene that when public disquiet about the relative neglect of the nation's railways began to mount in the early 1970s, he allowed his senior assistant, Sidney Weighell, full scope to organise a new, more comprehensive, movement for the revitalisation of the railway system.

Transport 2000, which was established on 6 December 1972, was largely the brainchild of Sidney Weighell. Within the Labour movement earlier that year he prepared the ground for its launching by moving an NUR resolution at the Brighton TUC on 8 September in favour of 'an integrated socialist transport policy which would ensure a larger and expanding role for the railways'.[18] He followed this up, on 4 October, in Blackpool by moving a similar resolution at the annual conference of the Labour Party when delegates entering the conference hall were met by a line of six uniformed railwaymen handing out free copies of a special issue of *Railway Review*. At both gatherings the resolutions were ably seconded by Ray Buckton, General Secretary of ASLEF, and were supported by an overwhelming majority of the delegates on a show of hands.[19]

At its meeting on 10 October the NUR EC gave unanimous support to a report from its transport policy sub-committee,

whose chairman was Sid Weighell. Among other measures recommended for adoption was 'exploring the possibility of setting
up a pressure group with railway trade unions, the BRB, the
Railway Industries Association, the National Council for Inland
Transport, the Pedestrians Association for Road Safety, the
Transport Reform Group and the Save our Services (SOS) campaign'.[20] Meanwhile, Frank Moxley, editor of *Railway Review*,
gave prominence to a letter received from Brian Rome, of Bristol,
who read the special issue of 29 September with great interest, but
urged that the NUR's aims could best be achieved only if the
union and BRB 'combined their efforts with the efforts of other
bodies seeking similar solutions to transport problems'.[21]

Back from the Labour Party conference, Sidney Weighell
carried out the policy approved by the EC and sent letters to the
general secretaries of the other railway trade unions and to the
secretaries of environmentalist and other bodies thought likely
to support a campaign for the railways, inviting them to send
delegates to an exploratory meeting at Unity House on 13 November 1972. The response was heartening. Representatives of over
twenty organisations, including the Civic Trust, the Conservation
Society, the Commitment Group, the All-Change Group, Friends
of the Earth, the National Council for Inland Transport, the
Railway Industries Association, the Ramblers Association, the
Scottish Association for Public Transport, the Save our Services
(SOS) Campaign, ASLEF, TSSA, and the NUR, were present at
the meeting. The agreed statement issued at the end of proceedings read as follows:

This meeting believes that railways have a major contribution
to make in protecting the environment and improving the
quality of life in Britain and calls upon the government to
ensure that:
1 Before any more large scale road investment programmes
   are initiated full consideration should be given to the extent
   to which the nation's future transport needs can be more
   economically met in other ways, e.g. by the fuller use of
   railway facilities.
2 Consideration is given to diverting from roads freight traffic
   which could equally well travel by other modes of transport.
3 Local planning authorities should be advised that when considering applications for large scale new industrial developments they should take into account that such developments are well served by rail as well as road. If the site is in

an area where railway lines have been closed the BRB should be consulted about re-opening them.

This meeting also believes that the time is ripe for a fresh look at the state of or transport system with a view to greater emphasis being placed on the need to preserve our environment and calls for a halt to the piecemeal planning of the transport system of this country.

At the foundation meeting of Transport 2000, held in the Assembly Hall at Unity House on 6 December 1972, the name of the new organisation was agreed, an executive committee and working group were elected and officers were appointed. Sidney Weighell was the obvious choice for secretary, while the chairman chosen was Dr Leonard Taitz of the Conservation Society. An annual affiliation fee of £5 per organisation was approved while the unions, in addition, paid larger contributions to fund a part-time co-ordinator of activities. The first 'Operations Manager' of Transport 2000 was Mike Harris, who also worked for the Railway Industries Association and was allowed to use the Association's office at 9 Catherine Place, London, SW1 for the work of the new organisation. This was an arrangement which worked very well until April 1977, when Mike Harris was appointed editor of *Railway World*. Transport 2000 then had to find a new office and a new Operations Manager. Laurie Harries of the NUR head-office staff acted as Acting Operations Manager until 28 September, when Mick Hamer moved from Friends of the Earth to become the director, using accommodation provided by Earth Resources Research Ltd, at 40 James Street, London, W1.

Following the establishment of the new organisation a series of public meetings was arranged in London and the provinces, the object being to attract maximum support, from persons of all political parties, for an enhanced role for railways in the transport system. George Thomas, MP, who later became Speaker of the House of Commons, was among the speakers who addressed a meeting of some 500 people in Cathays Park, Cardiff, on 6 January 1973. Three days later at a meeting held in Congress House, London, Jim Callaghan pointed to the absurdity of the government spending £300 million on aeronautical research, while only allocating £3·5 million for research on railway development. Addressing an audience of 450 at the AEU Hall, Holloway Circus, Birmingham, on 2 March, Angus Maude, MP (Conservative) maintained that 'the ordinary citizen is suffering as a result of the overemphasis on road transport'. Both Dr David Owen, MP (Labour), and John Pardoe, MP (Liberal) were speakers at

the meeting in the Plymouth Guildhall, on 3 February, attended
by more than 300 persons. The best-attended meeting, with over
600 people present, was held at the Central Hall, Westminster on
15 March, when Harold Wilson, MP, and Hugh Dykes, Conservative MP for Harrow, East, were among the speakers.[22]

What helped to give a sense of urgency to the new movement
was the publication in the *Sunday Times*, of 8 October 1972, of
secret Department of Transport Industry plans for the further
axing of the railway network. While the disclosures did not come
as a surprise to the leaders of the NUR who were aware that for
some years blueprints for further rail closures were among the
policy options kept available in a strongly road-oriented department, the disclosure helped to alert the public to the threats of
further destruction to one of the nation's vital assets. The successful Transport 2000 campaign made it less likely that the rail-
closure option would be adopted by government. By the later
1970s Transport 2000 had established itself more firmly as a body
in its own right. In 1977 it received financial backing from the
BRB which contributed £5,000, to add to the £4,000 voted by the
NUR, and the £1,500 of ASLEF and £1,250 of TSSA, sums which
made possible the employment of Mick Hamer as director and ensured the publication of a stream of booklets and pamphlets including *An Electrifying Case* (1974), *British Rail, 1975–2000*
(1975), *A Load on your Mind* (1978), and many others.

When the research department was established as a part of the
reorganisation of the administration at Unity House, in 1975, its
purpose was stated to be the briefing of the union's officers presenting claims for improvements in wages and working conditions.
It was not long, however, before the small group of seven persons (including a filing clerk and typist) was also engaged in preparing substantial publications on aspects of transport policy. In
addition to the substantial commentaries on the Consultation
Document (Green Paper) of 1976 and the White Paper on transport policy, mentioned in Chapter 1, the group prepared submissions to the Secretary of State for Transport for the Railway
Electrification Review, *Railway Electrification, 1978*, and a statement of the case against relaxation of the law concerning heavy
lorries submitted to the Layfield Committee of Inquiry on that
subject in 1979. The leading members of the research group
helped to co-ordinate the activities of the union's officers and the
parliamentary group, in that they helped the former with material
on transport policy, and discussed with the latter through the
political liaison officer, those issues most worth raising at Question Time or in debates in the House of Commons.[23]

In meetings of the executive committee and at AGMs the members of the NUR took a stance on national issues of major political importance. The decisions reached on these occasions then influenced the deliberations of both the TUC and the Labour Party. The problems discussed were so wide-ranging that it is only possible to consider here some of those which promoted the keenest debate. It was not always possible, by glancing through the agenda of the AGM, to predict which items would provoke the strongest feelings among the delegates. In the summer of 1979, for example, in the context of national controversy between the advocates of free collective bargaining and the proponents of an incomes policy, it might have been expected that item 19: 'Continuing Social Contract and economic strategy' would have produced the bitterest controversy; while item 12; 'State death grants' would have been dealt with quickly and unobtrusively. Delegates determined otherwise. Although ten of the seventy-seven present took part, the debate on incomes policy was a low-key affair with no great heat generated. On the other hand, the Earls Court branch resolution:

> That this AGM instructs the NEC to press the government for an increase in the state death grant to raise it to at least £200 and that, to prevent in the future the distress that the miserly grant of £30 causes, the grant should be reviewed annually.

gave rise to some of the most eloquent and impassioned speaking of the entire fortnight's deliberations. Tom Nolan, a technician of Earls Court branch, who moved the resolution, contrasted the £30 of the state grant with the £180 cost of a simple funeral and the £170 involved in the case of a cremation. He continued:

> The low level of death grant is something which worries many elderly people a great deal. They scrimp and save while trying to manage on their pension so as to provide a decent burial for themselves without being a burden on the shoulders of their relatives. We must admit that amongst elderly people a pauper's funeral is regarded as a final degradation. I am a local councillor and have seen some people going without food that they should have eaten; they were saving up to die.

The speaker put his case so eloquently that it was highly probable that, after the formal seconding, the motion would have been put to the vote and carried without more ado. However, Rees Taylor, a signalman of Stafford branch, came to the rostrum and raised a discordant note by suggesting that too much importance had been attached to funerals and to elaborate gravestones in particular. 'When I pass away', he said, 'the doctors at the hospital can take any spare part they want off me. There will be one or two that will be of no use to anyone at my age. They can put the rest into a plastic bag, haul it up to the crematorium, pitch it on the fire and Bob's your uncle, that's it.' This was enough to provoke six other delegates, each recalling poignant case histories, to speak in support of the Earls Court motion. Russell Tuck, from the platform, wound up proceedings by giving the motion official support and by mentioning that the union's death grant to next of kin of members was being raised from £200 to £210 that year. Overwhelmed, Rees Tyler called out, 'Mr President, I have had my arm twisted.' When the show of hands was taken, he helped to make the vote unanimous.[24]

Issues such as this only occasionally found a place on the agenda either of the EC, or the AGM. By contrast the question of whether Britain should join, or, after 1973, should leave, the Common Market (EEC) was more frequently a subject of debate. In 1962, with Harold Macmillan's Conservative government in power, and the conditions required for Britain's entry into the Common Market still uncertain, delegates to the AGM at Margate debated, as a public resolution, the Croydon No. 1 branch recommendation against entry. In a long speech Sidney Greene argued that it was foolish to come to a decision until the public knew what the terms of entry were. He maintained that if, following Britain's membership, the Channel Tunnel was built, it could do the union 'a power of good', since the standing of some of the railwaymen in some of the Common Market countries was higher than it was in Britain. However, most delegates agreed with the veteran Stanley Vincent of Southampton, who argued that the campaign for entry was 'an organised attempt on the part of capitalism to divide the east from the west' and they carried the Croydon resolution by 45–30 votes.[25]

General de Gaulle's veto in 1963 killed, for the time being, any prospect of Britain's entry into the Common Market. However, in the General Election campaign of 1966 Harold Wilson promised to seek admission to the community, provided the conditions of entry were favourable to Britain's interests. At the AGM of the NUR in Aberdeen, in July 1967, therefore, with a Labour government in power, the arguments for membership of the EEC were seen in a more favourable light than had been the case five years earlier. Even so, the resolution from the Liskeard branch was circumspectly worded:

That this AGM welcomes the inquiries the government is making in reference to Britain's entry into the Common Market, and in seeking the necessary safeguards in respect of the Commonwealth and our partners in EFTA.

Although L. Carey, of Norwich No. 1 branch, warned that Britain's true potential for expansion as an industrial nation lay with the underdeveloped areas rather than with Europe, the majority of the speakers felt that there was a case for 'trying again' and the resolution was carried by 54–24 votes.[26]

When AGM delegates assembled at Inverness in July 1970 the political environment had changed yet again, with Edward Heath, an enthusiastic 'European', heading a Conservative administration bent on securing Britain's admission to the EEC. On this occasion the resolution before the delegates was more decisively worded:

That this AGM is of the opinion that the alleged advantages of Britain's entry into the EEC will be outweighed by the disadvantages so far as the British people are concerned.

We therefore instruct the NEC to inform the government that the NUR is opposed to entry.

A. Williamson, a guard from Dundee, moving the Croydon No. 1 branch resolution, said that entry into the Common Market would lead to a deterioration in British living standards as illustrated by the fact that the price of butter in Britain was 3s 4d a pound, while in the EEC countries it was equivalent to 7s 5d. But after a speech by Sidney Greene, in which he argued that if Britain gained admission, she would have the advantage of access to a bigger market, the delegates turned down the motion by 51–25 votes.[27] A year later, at Plymouth, opinion was more evenly divided as doubts increased about the possible consequences of British membership of the EEC. There were many more speakers against than there were in favour of joining. However, in a long speech in which he again referred to the potential advantages of the Channel Tunnel and also stressed that the trade unions in Europe would welcome Britain's membership, Sidney Greene succeeded in tipping the balance in favour of the pro-Marketeers, who defeated an anti-Market resolution by 40–36 votes.[28] By the summer of 1972 the Heath government had negotiated Britain's entry into the EEC – to take effect on 1 January 1973. The Preston No. 1 branch resolution, before the AGM delegates at Scarborough, followed the official Labour Party line that the terms secured by the Prime Minister were unsatisfactory, and that when a Labour

government was elected, it should renegotiate with EEC members
'to obtain a better deal for the working people of this country'.
This time the hard-line anti-Marketeers spoke against the motion
on the ground expressed by C. F. Robbins, a depot supervisor
from Wolverhampton, that 'anyone who thought the terms could
be renegotiated was living in cloud-cuckoo land'. Nevertheless,
after a long speech from Sidney Greene in favour of the resolution,
it was carried by 45–32 votes.[29] At Exeter in July 1973, in the last
AGM debate during the Heath era, delegates were offered the
proposal that the government should be urged, within the community, 'to negotiate some of the benefits of EEC membership as
promised in the pre-entry propaganda, such as higher wages and
salaries, better pensions and longer holidays'. Only the hard-line
anti-Marketeers opposed this resolution which was carried by
58–17 votes.[30]

The Labour Party General Election manifestos of February and
October 1974 included promises that the terms of British membership of the EEC would be renegotiated to secure major changes
in the Common Agricultural Policy, the financing of the community budget, and to make many other changes. When sufficient
progress had been made in the drafting of a new compact between
the British government and the community, a national referendum
would be held to determine whether Britain should, or should not,
stay in the EEC. In March 1975, at a conference in Dublin, Jim
Callaghan secured an agreement which Harold Wilson and a
majority of members of the Cabinet considered went far enough
to meet the party's election pledges. The renegotiated terms were
carried through the Commons only through the backing of the
Conservative opposition, 145 Labour MPs, including seven Cabinet
Ministers and thirty-one junior Ministers, voting against.[31]

Sidney Weighell, who became General Secretary in April
1975, was a strong advocate of British membership of the Common Market. In October 1972 he headed an NUR delegation
to Brussels to participate in discussions on the Commission's
transport policy. On 4 December the delegation reported to the
EC that it considered it 'vital' that the voice of British railwaymen
should be heard in Brussels, since 'the NUR's transport policy
was identical to that of other railway unions in EEC countries'.
The EC endorsed this view.[32] However, when the Common Market
issue was in the forefront of discussions, in April 1975, the new
General Secretary was aware that opinion in the executive was
sharply divided. He therefore invited a prominent anti-Marketeer,
Tony Benn, and an equally distinguished pro-Marketeer, Shirley
Williams, to address its members before they decided which way

the union's representatives should be mandated to vote at the special Labour Party conference on the issue on 26 April. The timing of the speeches was of some significance. Tony Benn was at Unity House on the morning of Tuesday 8 April, when he spoke for about an hour and answered questions. Shirley Williams's visit was on the afternoon of Thursday 10 April, immediately before the executive voted. With the experience of five years to give hindsight, it can be seen that Tony Benn was right in describing the Common Agricultural Policy as 'a high food-tax policy' and in claiming that Britain was paying 'well over the odds' for its membership. Nevertheless, at the time, Shirley Williams proved more convincing to her audience. She was careful to avoid 'extreme' statements. 'It was not a black-and-white issue', she said. She showed cleverness in pointing out that railwaymen in the Community were entitled to better pensions than were their counterparts in Britain. It was difficult at that point in time to disprove her claim that, as a result of Jim Callaghan's negotiations, the British contribution to the Community budget would be fair and 'related to our ability to pay'.[33] Even so, more than a third of the executive remained unconvinced. By 14–9 votes, with one member absent, it was agreed that the renegotiated terms 'met to a great extent' the terms of the AGM Decision No. 20 of July 1972 and those of the Labour Party's Election manifesto. Because both the membership of the union and the members of the executive were deeply divided on the whole question the EC, by a a unanimous vote, went on to recognise that the forthcoming (5 June) referendum allowed 'every individual NUR member to express his own point of view'.[34]

An attempt by the AGM, in July 1975, to overturn the EC's pro-Market decision was defeated by a 54–17 vote in favour of 'proceeding to next business'.[35] Three years later a Chalk Farm–Camden branch resolution to instruct the EC to campaign for withdrawal from the EEC was rejected by 45–29 votes. But in 1979, with the new Prime Minister, Mrs Thatcher, complaining forcefully about the injustice of Britain's excessive contribution to the Community budget, public opinion was more keenly aware of the disadvantages of Britain's membership. At Paignton, on 26 July, the AGM approved by a narrow margin of 39–35 votes a Sheffield City branch resolution instructing the EC to campaign in the Labour Party and the TUC for Britain's withdrawal from the Common Market.[37] It would be safe to surmise that that was not the end of the story.

The threat to civilisation posed by the arms race and the spread of nuclear weapons was the subject of debate at most AGMs in the period 1960–80. For most of the time there was a sharp

division of opinion between the unilateralists and the advocates
of disarmament by international agreement. The split was manifested in July 1960, when delegates approved, by the narrow
margin of 39–38 votes, a public resolution demanding the withdrawal of US forces and the removal of nuclear weapons from
Britain.[38] In 1963 and 1964, however, resolutions favouring the
rejection of any policy based on nuclear weapons were rejected
after interventions by Sidney Greene, who claimed that the
unilateralists 'split the union from top to bottom'.[39] When G.
Perkins, a permanentway inspector of Croydon No. 1 branch,
moved 'the unilateral renunciation of nuclear weapons by Britain'
at Southport, in July 1965, and asserted that it was 'criminal
folly to continue to spend more than £2,000 million a year mainly
on weapons which cannot do anything to defend the British people
in the event of attack', Sidney Greene again took a major part
in the debate. He said:

> The fact remains that there are two sections of the world, the
> Communist bloc and the Western bloc, and that we are a
> member of NATO and come under the NATO banner, and
> therefore we agree with the Americans in maintaining nuclear
> weapons . . . If we unilaterally renounce nuclear weapons it
> will also mean leaving NATO and to do that would be to turn
> the world upside down.

On this occasion the Croydon resolution only attracted 24 votes,
while forty delegates took the advice of the General Secretary and
rejected a policy of unilateral nuclear disarmament.[40] A year later,
at Plymouth, Stan Mills, another member of the Croydon branch,
tried again with a similar resolution which was again opposed by
Sidney Greene. The General Secretary again carried the day, but
by the narrower margin of 42–34 votes.[41]

In 1967 and 1968 the unilateralists concentrated on opposition
to the Polaris nuclear submarine and cited the Labour Party's
1964 General Election manifesto which declared 'we are not
prepared any longer to waste the country's resources on endless
duplication of strategic nuclear weapons'. On these occasions
Sidney Greene's interventions were to no avail and the nuclear
disarmers won majority support: 38–24 votes in 1967, and by
38–33 in 1968.[42] In 1969 the pendulum of opinion swung the
other way again when the East Ham branch resolution 'for a
substantial cut in the defence budget, with the first priority given
to the scrapping of nuclear submarines' was defeated by the substantial margin of 55–19 votes. The same branch tried again in

the following year, when it mustered more support but was nevertheless outvoted 49–28.[43] During 1971 and 1973 inclusive, disarmament was not the subject of a debate at the AGMs, which were preoccupied with issues such as the industrial relations policy of the Heath government.

In 1974 it was the Truro branch which directed delegates' attention once more to the problem of disarmament. Its resolution asked for a 50 per cent cut in military expenditure, but made no specific reference to nuclear weapons. Attending his last AGM, Sidney Greene, in a speech consistent with all his many utterances on the subject, said that he supported agreed plans for disarmament but feared that a sudden halving of arms expenditure 'would bring more problems initially than any government could handle'. The Truro motion was then defeated by 39–26 votes.[44] In 1975, as was the case in 1967 and 1968, the disarmers used the latest Labour Party General Election manifesto to back their case. The Glasgow No. 6 branch simply called upon the EC to urge the government 'to honour its election manifesto pledge to drastically reduce expenditure on arms'. Sidney Weighell, attending his first AGM as General Secretary, had helped to draft the election manifesto and, thus, found it entirely consistent to give his blessing to the Glasgow resolution which delegates then carried by a vote of 56–15.[45] There was no further debate on disarmament until 1979 when another Glasgow branch, No. 14, urged that the government should make 'a real and genuine attempt for peace and disarmament by curbing its defence estimates' and that 'at the next UN special session on disarmament it should announce that as a first step it intended to phase out its nuclear weapons'. Once more the drafters of the resolution had taken care to make it consistent with the General Election manifesto. Senior Assistant General Secretary, Russell Tuck, from the platform, pointed out to delegates that this was the case when he gave broad support to the proposition before the meeting which delegates approved by the decisive margin of 52–21 votes.[46]

By June 1980 when delegates assembled for the next AGM at St Peter's Port, Geurnsey, the cold war had been intensified. The government of Margaret Thatcher was committed to an increase, in real terms, in military expenditure, to the replacement of the Polaris submarine, and to the siting of American Cruise missiles in Britain. The Earls Court branch resolution, debated on the first day of the AGM was strongly, but carefully, worded:

That this AGM is resolutely opposed to any replacement for the Polaris submarine and is disturbed at the lack of progress

towards disarmament and a secure peace. It calls for
(1) a stronger campaign by the TUC and the Labour Party to counter cold-war propaganda;
(2) dissociation by the British government from the warmongers who attacked the Salt 2 agreement;
(3) no British involvement in NATO plans to modernise tactical nuclear weapons in Europe. Instead Britain should join those European NATO countries which have refused to have such weapons on their soil and should press for NATO–Warsaw Pact negotiations to eliminate nuclear weapons and to seek agreement for a gradual reduction in all armaments.

Tom Nolan, a technician of Earls Court branch, in proposing the motion declared that the country was in danger 'precisely because of our nuclear bases'. Britain had more of them per square mile than any other place on earth. There were no opposing speakers. Sidney Weighell from the platform gave wholehearted support to the resolution. He declared:

We are opposed as much to the new generation of tactical nuclear weapons as we are to the new generation of strategic nuclear weapons. We believe in particular that the development of the Cruise missile in Western Europe constitutes an encouragement of the arms race between East and West . . . We support the Labour Party's longstanding demand for the removal of all nuclear bases from the UK and we extend that demand to Western Europe . . . In stating this opposition we proclaim our refusal to contemplate the use of these disgusting weapons.

On a show of hands the resolution was carried unanimously.[47]

It was not, of course, a unilateralist motion as some of the earlier AGM resolutions had been; but it advocated a complete reversal of the Thatcher government's policies of confrontation and the competitive building up of weapons of terror. In his contribution to the debate, P. Devitt, a guard from Glasgow No. 5 branch, put very clearly the alternatives facing mankind in the 1980s:

We must think of all humanity first and the resolving of differences in political beliefs at a more civilised level than the military minds and the Maggie Thatchers of this world can ever think of . . . Unless there is a conscious world effort to divert the wealth of the developed countries into sane, progressive paths, such as raising the living standards of the poor Third World countries we shall embark on a war that nobody can win.

On 30 June 1980 the supreme governing body of the NUR, by backing the initiative of the Earls Court branch, made a contribution to peace-making which did it credit.

CHAPTER 13

THE NUR AND EDUCATION

THE trend in trade union education altered with the takeover of the National Council of Labour Colleges by the TUC under a rationalisation scheme initiated by the NUR at the 1957 TUC at Blackpool. As in the previous half-century, the NUR was taking the lead, pioneering as the union had done in the earlier part of the century when the foundations of trade union education – independent of state provision and sponsorship – were laid, through the Labour College and later the NCLC. But what the NUR intended at Blackpool through rationalisation of trade union educational facilities was, in the view of some closely involved, not fulfilled. In the two decades that followed there was a loss of the drive which had sustained the trade union rank and file in educational terms. But there was work of a more orthodox kind going on – more of this later. The objective of rationalisation was highlighted in the resolution, moved by the NUR President, Tom Hollywood, which was remitted to the General Council of the TUC. The first sentence clearly indicated the direction desired at that time:

Congress approves the emphasis which is being laid upon improved working-class education, realising that only by a thorough understanding of the social sciences, new techniques and economic factors can the workers hope to achieve full emancipation.

The transfer was complicated. There were many disputes between the TUC and the NCLC negotiators. It was not completed until 1964. The leaders of the NCLC, particularly the General Secretary, Jim Millar, charged that the TUC failed to maintain the strong educational groundwork developed over many years by local Labour colleges, and through the highly effective postal-courses department. It was felt that the enthusiasm of a large number of voluntary tutors and activists in working-class education was dissipated. The result seemed to be that much of the basic educational work among the rank and file trade union membership was lost or seriously weakened. This depressing and pessimistic view was held by many NUR activists, who had from the beginning formed the backbone of the Labour college movement.

However, there was a growing realisation that with wider opportunities for individuals in state education and in higher education, evening classes provided by local authorities, the broadening of TUC activity in the field of practical training and the fundamental changes in communications brought about by the spread of television and radio, working-class education and the needs of trade unionists were changing. In addition, particularly in the 1970s, labour and social legislative provisions relating directly to the work of the trade unions required educational changes to fit the activists in the movement for new tasks within a radically different social and economic environment. The Employment Protection Act 1975, giving time off, resulted in an expansion of trade union training. For instance, in 1977–8 some 27,878 students attended TUC courses. By 1978–9 the figures had risen to 43,670 – an increase of 50 per cent.

For the NUR there were other problems, which needed matching educational and training facilities. With the Tory break-up of integrated publicly owned transport, the union was faced with new sectional structures, managements and procedures. Active members, who were expected to deal with and to negotiate on new functions and strange situations with different levels and types of management, some with varying and non-traditional objectives and constitutions, were called upon to exercise skills that needed to be learned. A vast amount of fresh information on machinery and policies had to be absorbed, if the representatives were to carry out their jobs efficiently and effectively. Competence as officials became a new aim, whereas in the past trade union education had concentrated more on social and economic theories, history and ideas on systems. These demands were made against a background of social and economic flux in Britain, with management techniques, industrial relations, productivity, trade union rights and functions and political instability thrusting forward for widespread discussion.

All these changes were reflected in the attitude of the NUR to education. A start was made through weekend schools organised by NUR district councils. A series of summer courses were centrally organised and tutored by appointees from the National Executive Committee. The future Assistant General Secretary, Russell Tuck, was one of these tutors. The courses were designed to equip new secretaries and representatives with the basic knowledge of the machinery and procedures within which they had to operate. The quality of the organisation and conduct of the district council schools was not uniformly of a standard which in the long run was thought the best the union could provide. A major weakness was that there was at that time an absence of clarity on subject-matter and the method of teaching, from the centre of the organisation. With some exceptions, it was considered that educationally the value to the union and its future was not as serious and effective as it might be.

If there was blame, it was not deserved by or apportioned to those involved, but more to the lack of point and direction. The union had not made up its mind what education was for, and how it related to the progress of the organisation in terms of efficiency and positive direction. It is necessary to stress that this widely held view existed among those who had been brought along educationally with the bias towards what was then called independent working-class education on basic economic and social subjects. All the same, the NUR was not entirely dormant. According to the Donovan Commission report in 1968, the NUR had the best record on ensuring its representatives were trained better than they had been – 69 per cent had been through a practical course, compared with 40 per cent in the TGWU, 22 per cent in the GMWU, 29 per cent in the ETU and 23 per cent in the AEU. But there was a feeling that much more attention and resources should be devoted to education in the new circumstances. The idea of a central residential education centre, though not new in view of the ASRS–NUR involvement in the highly significant Central Labour College, was again revived, particularly under the thrust of the newly elected Sid Weighell as General Secretary of the union. Eventually, in 1976, Frant Place, a large country house in its own spacious grounds near Tunbridge Wells, was bought and adopted as an education centre. It was officially opened on 30 April 1977 by the then Prime Minister, the Rt Hon. James Callaghan, MP.

The Prime Minister described Frant Place as 'this magnificent education centre', and stressed the great importance of working-class education. He recalled and recognised the great contribution the NUR, and its forerunner the ASRS, had made in this sphere since the beginning of the century:

This educational centre, in its own beautiful surroundings, once the home of a millionaire, will now be used to train trade union members in present-day industrial relations, including the recent Labour government's Health and Safety Act which is vital to the railway industry. And why not. As a former South Wales miners' union leader said – 'there's nothing too good for the workers'.

National president Dave Bowman recalled the fine history of the union in trade union education and added that 'the Manchester District Council and the Sheffield and Chesterfield District Council asked that the union set up its own residential college. While it has taken thirty years to come about it is now here and it is fitting that this magnificent building should be opened by the Prime Minister.' The General Secretary, in an article in the *Railway Review* at that time, said that 'with the opening of Frant the education sub-committee set out to reorganise the education facilities offered by the union'. But he stressed that 'no one is suggesting that Frant is the "be all and end all" of the NUR education programme'. He emphasised the value of the new tutors' training. A great step forward had been made:

It will help to make sure that the NUR remains the best and only union for railwaymen and all other grades who look to us to maintain their standard of living in this highly competitive society we live in.

In his report to the AGM, in 1977, the General Secretary said that 'for years we have been plodding along appointing tutors to take one-day and weekend schools without any thought being given to equipping them to do the job we want them to do or even of identifying what we wanted them to teach and why. At that AGM in Ayr, the Assistant General Secretary, Frank Cannon, reviewed policy and created much enthusiasm for the new direction the NUR was taking in education. But in a debate there were different assessments from delegates of the value of district council schools. At that early date, however, policies had still to evolve at Frant and elsewhere.

Schools were run for branch secretaries and for representatives. But one of the urgent needs was to set out to recruit and train a new generation of tutors. Candidates from within the membership were carefully selected for training. Expert guidance was provided by an experienced tutor from the British Railways Board. Valuable foundation-building work was also done by some of the union's own divisional officers and from head-office staff. In his report, the General Secretary pointed out these tutors would not only be provided with training, but with the backup apparatus and materials vital for teaching, in such a way that students would be interested and encouraged to think for themselves on the topics being taught.

Development at Frant Place followed. Classroom accommodation was enlarged and, in the autumn of 1979, a specialist education officer was appointed. Ben Stoneham, after taking a degree in economics at Cambridge, did research at Oxford University on the Labour government's prices and incomes policy in 1964–70; he also worked for the Coal Board including a spell as private secretary to the Board chairman, Sir Derek Ezra, and as a deputy section head in the industrial relations' department. Mr Stoneham had considerable experience in lecturing, and with the WEA, and was active as a member of APEX. He contested the Saffron Walden parliamentary by-election for Labour in 1977 and 1979.

The NUR had by that time expanded the range of sponsorship of candidates for Parliament, and for a group of MPs. The crisis in the railway industry, with threats of further closures, and the need for the political views of the union to find stronger voice in Parliament, made it desirable not only to enlarge the group, but to ensure that suitable members of the union could be selected and supported as parliamentary prospective candidates. The selection and training of suitable members became part of the work at Frant Place. Initial selection courses and more intensive follow-up courses were organised with the assistance of the union's political liaison officer, Keith Hill, and members of the group of NUR-sponsored MPs.

At the same time, legislative changes, particularly the Employment Protection Act 1975 and legislation on health and safety, presented a challenge in educational terms. For the first time it was laid down that employee representatives and trade union officials should be released with pay by an employer for industrial relations training. Some training schemes were run by the TUC. The NUR education sub-committee, at the end of 1979, reported that

LDC courses on the machinery of negotiation and health and safety courses for safety representatives are run under the auspices of the TUC on a ten-week day-release basis. These courses were run throughout the country with divisional officers nominating the members to attend. The British Railways Board have agreed to pay meal allowances to students attending these courses. A total of 1,083 members attended both these courses during the year. This compared with 461 in the previous year.

The NUR's own educational schemes began to be shaped to cater for these developments. In the early period after Frant was opened the courses for representatives were fairly elementary. Later, progress was made in providing more advanced courses. It was felt, however, that the training of younger members not yet serving as representatives was also necessary. The report for 1979–80 to the NEC said that general representatives' courses should continue throughout 1980 with specialised courses for staff employed by the various companies with whom the union had negotiating rights. This was a new development, to have joint courses on industrial relations subjects with the British Railways Board and other undertakings. NUR tutors taught in BR schools and BR tutors took courses at Frant. In 1980, a total of thirty-four joint courses were organised, more than half at Frant, with the others held at the BRB training school at Darlington. Courses were also started with British Transport Hotels, some at Frant, others at the company's hotels. Similar joint courses with Freightliners were developed. In 1980, discussions were in progress with National Carriers, London Transport, British Transport Docks Board, BREL workshops and the National Bus Company.

Because of the lack of direction and positive shape of the education and methods and quality of teaching in the union during the rather fallow period after the war years, and the hiatus which followed the disappearance of the NCLC, some of the educational activity organised by district councils lost point and drive. A remedy had to be found as part of the general educational provision of the union. With the appointment of a full-time education officer a start was made to produce course material on general and specialist subjects, such as accident prevention and the auditing of branch accounts, as well as negotiation and disciplinary procedures and branch administration. There was also a feeling in branches and district councils that pensions, redundancy and re-settlement, promotion and transfer arrangements needed to be more closely studied and training given in these topics. Progress in the expansion of these subjects depended upon the preparedness of the union in tutor training. It was not enough that the material and experience of the teachers matched the requirements; the ability to impart it and to provide guidance and scope and method were just as important. The constant aim of the new look in NUR education was to ensure that as far as possible members became more thoroughly informed and practised in the arts of discussion and negotiation.

There was, however, a lack of what might be called serious study of social and economic theory. The work of the NCLC in this field equipped many thousands of activists in the Labour movement, including the leadership and full-time officers in the NUR.

Most of them attended day and weekend schools, heard branch lectures by visiting tutors and studied with the NCLC's very successful postal-courses department. Some acted as voluntary tutors and class organisers. The NUR's participation in the college movement is well-known and probably the most intensive of any trade union in the country. Indeed, the NUR with the South Wales miners was a leader in independent working-class education. Jim Millar, general secretary of the NCLC, proudly records the fact that it was James Robertson, a railway signalman and keen socialist and member of the ASRS who persuaded him during Millar's visits to a quiet signalbox on the line between Edinburgh and Peebles – about the need for independent working-class education. The drive for education for socialist change had inspired earlier generations, and *Railway Review* played a leading part as a forum for discussion of ideas on the subject. Rationalisation of trade union education – proposed by the NUR – was not intended to stop or hamper the development. On the contrary, as has been stressed, it was meant to help in a thorough understanding of social sciences, new techniques and economic factors without which the workers could not hope to 'achieve full emancipation'.

At the time of the takeover by the TUC, the NCLC's work was thriving with over 12,000 class students, 10,000 students at day and weekend schools, nearly 600 at summer schools, with thousands of trade unionists attending branch lectures. There were seventy-six postal courses available, and during the last year, 1963, more than 21,200 were studying postal courses. Extensive work had also been organised by the WEA and the WETUC. But the NUR had not officially participated in this activity, although individual members no doubt attended classes and schools run by the WEA and WETUC. When the NCLC was wound up, the gap in basic subject education was not filled by the TUC. Those NUR members who had been absorbed in the activities of the NCLC suffered the loss of these facilities. Individuals, of course, found their own way into various channels for trade union education, including those run by the London School of Economics and other establishments, such as the Polytechnic of Central London and the Middlesex Polytechnic.

It has always to be stressed that there had been for many years different approaches to trade union education. The NCLC believed there was a bias in the teaching of subjects like economics, history and sociology, and the working class had its biases which had to be catered for. Others did not acknowledge this, and proposed that the aim was objectivity. There were still more who equated trade union education with simple practical training.

In the initial years, the ASRS–NUR sided in the main with the case for independent working-class education, which is one reason why the union gave such powerful support to the Labour College and the NCLC.

In the new era, begun by the acquisition of Frant Place, the urgent need was to work up tutor training and to make up for the past neglect in practical training of secretaries and representatives. Nevertheless, useful work was started in lectures on the history of the union and the theoretical justification for industrial unionism. Political ideas and the history and development of the Labour movement, in which the ASRS–NUR played a significant role, were discussed within the context of the early courses. The objective was to get the centre working and to use it as fully as possible for the union's purposes. Towards the end of 1980 it was clear that this was being achieved, particularly with the improved lecture facilities. Education in the NUR has a developing role. Frant Place will play its part. But there is no doubt that education for members will be seen in the wider context of the whole union and the movement as they face the challenges of the last two decades of the twentieth century.

APPENDIX A

THE MACHINERY OF NEGOTIATION

MACHINERY OF NEGOTIATION: RAILWAY CONCILIATION STAFF

The following are the various stages of the negotiating machinery through which applications are considered:

(a) *Matters Arising from Conditions of Service*

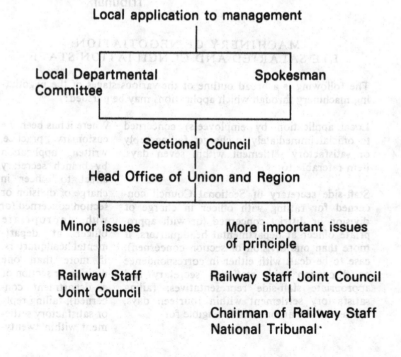

(b) *Proposals to Vary National Agreements*

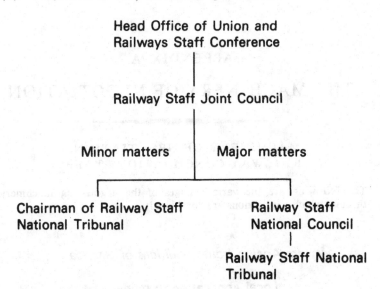

Head Office of Union and
Railways Staff Conference

Railway Staff Joint Council

Minor matters   Major matters

Chairman of Railway Staff   Railway Staff
National Tribunal   National Council

Railway Staff National
Tribunal

MACHINERY OF NEGOTIATION:
LTE SALARIED AND CONCILIATION STAFF

The following is a broad outline of the various stages of the negotiating machinery through which applications may be pursued:

Local application by employee(s) concerned to official immediately in charge; failing reply or satisfactory settlement within seven days, item referable to

Staff-side secretary of Sectional Council concerned for raising with officer in charge of division or district concerned (or with appropriate officer at departmental headquarters, if more than one division or section concerned); case to be dealt with either in correspondence or discussion with staff-side secretary and appropriate staff-side representatives; failing satisfactory settlement within fourteen days, matter will be automatically eligible for

Where it has been the customary practice, written application by branch secretary direct to officer in charge of division or section concerned (or with appropriate officer at departmental headquarters, if more than one division or section of a department concerned); failing reply or satisfactory settlement within twenty-

one days, automati-
cally eligible for
agenda of

Sectional Council concerned; failing satisfactory
settlement after discussion at two or more meetings,
matter may be discussed between staff representatives
concerned and officer appointed to deal with such
matters at second stage; still failing agreement,
matter may be referred for

Discussion between headquarters officers of trade
union(s) concerned and the chief officer; minor
matters shall not be carried beyond this stage, but
matters other than those of minor character may
be referred to

LTE Railway Negotiating Committee; in the event
of failure to agree, matters may be referred to

London Transport Wages
Board

MACHINERY OF NEGOTIATION:
NATIONAL CARRIERS, OPERATING AND OTHER
WAGES GRADES, AND ENGINEERING, MAIN-
TENANCE AND REPAIR GRADES

The following is a broad outline of the various stages of the negotiating machinery through which applications may be pursued:

Written application to the individual's
immediate supervisor

Local representative or local committee

Regional Company Committee

Group Joint Negotiating Committee

National Joint Negotiating Committee

Independent arbitration

Note that individual claims would not normally be eligible for discussion at JNC level unless a matter of principle which applied
nationally was involved.

MACHINERY OF NEGOTIATION:
RAILWAY WORKSHOP STAFF

The following, in outline, are the stages in which applications are considered:

Shop, Works or Departmental Line Committee
|
National Railway Shopmen's Council
|
Arbitration reference to Industrial Court

MACHINERY OF NEGOTIATION:
HOTELS STAFF, STATION CATERING STAFF OR ANCILLARY ESTABLISHMENTS

The following are the various stages through which applications are pursued:

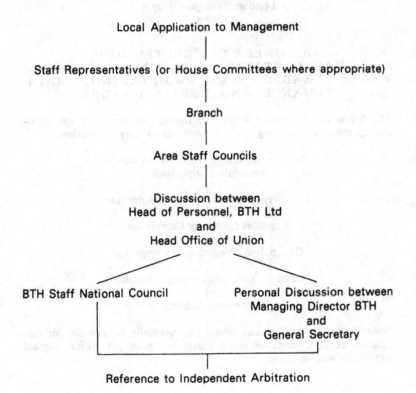

Refreshment Car, Travelling and Depot Wages Staff

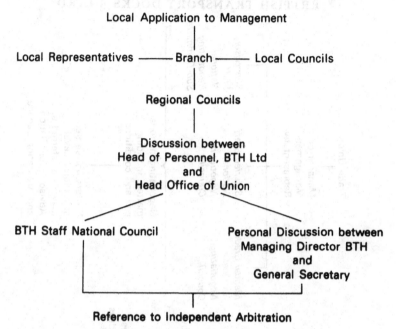

Local Application to Management

Local Representatives ——— Branch ——— Local Councils

Regional Councils

Discussion between
Head of Personnel, BTH Ltd
and
Head Office of Union

BTH Staff National Council

Personal Discussion between
Managing Director BTH
and
General Secretary

Reference to Independent Arbitration

MACHINERY OF NEGOTIATION:
BRITISH TRANSPORT DOCKS BOARD

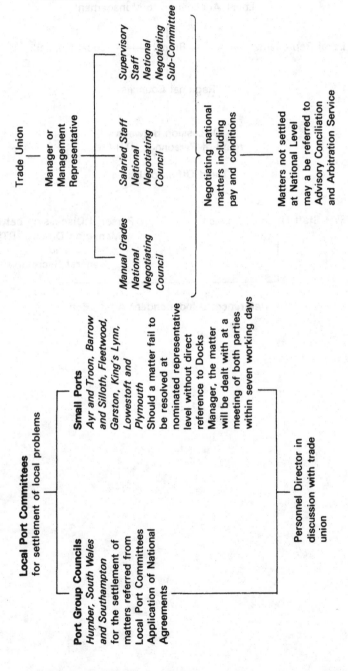

APPENDIX B

DISTRIBUTION OF MEMBERSHIP BY EMPLOYER CODES AS AT 16 DECEMBER 1978

Accident only			59
Provident Fund only			89
NUR			167
Bateman's Catering			34
British Railways Board			
Unspecified	265		
Locomotive	1,877		
Traffic	58,841		
Permanentway and S and T	26,521	87,504	
Shopmen			
Unspecified	3,482		
Category 1	1,991		
Category 2	3,740		
Category 3	3,421		
Category 4	6,433		
Apprentices	613		
Junior Shopmen	—		
Foremen	9		
Labourers	—	19,689	107,193
BREL			13,916
SISD			2,377
British Transport Advertising			7
BTDB			2,846
BT hotels			9,031
British Waterways Board			77
Busmen			
Bristol Omnibus Co.	26		
Devon General	828		
East Midlands Motoring	749		
Greenslades Tours	75		
Grenville Motors Ltd	—		
Hants and Dorset	2,020		

Lincolnshire Road Car Co.	752	
Mansfield District Traction	264	
National Travel Co.	88	
Red and White	1	
Ribble Motor Services	230	
Southern Vectis	300	
Southern and Western National	1,542	
South Wales Transport	7	
Terraneau's Coaches	3	
United Auto Services	1,100	
Wallace Arnold Tours	—	
William Gash & Son	—	
Western Welsh	22	8,007

City Link Transport		39
Caledonian Steam Packet		238
Dart Valley Railway		7
English Clays Clavering		6
Express Cleaners Co.		32
Express Link Ltd		5
Fashion Flow		424
Festiniog Railway Co.		45
Forth Ports Authority		127
Freightliners		1,256
Harwich Transport Ltd		39
Highway Link Transport		8
Humber Pilots		47
International Cold Storage		35

London Transport		
Unspecified	45	
Traffic	8,390	
Shops, Permanentway and S and T	5,630	14,065

Manchester International Freight Terminal		11
Manchester Ship Canal		65
Midland Catering Co.		38
National Carriers Ltd		10,700
National Coal Board		5
Port of Tyne Authority		161
Strathclyde Regional Council		7
Tees and Hartlepools Port Authority		176
Thomas Cook Ltd		1
Transfesa Terminals Ltd		55
Transtec International		13
Yarmouth Harbour Commission		12
		170,420

NOTES

CHAPTER 1

1 Glover K. F. and Miller D. N., 'The outlines of the road goods transport industry', *Journal of the Royal Statistical Society*, vol. 17, 1954, pp. 297–330.
2 Munby, D. L. and Watson, A. H., *Inland Transport Statistics: Great Britain, 1900–1970* (Oxford: Oxford University Press, 1978), tables A18, p. 104, and B7, p. 311.
3 Department of Environment, *Passenger Transport in Great Britain, 1971* (London: HMSO, 1973), p. 2.
4 Department of Transport, *Transport Statistics: Great Britain, 1968–1978* (London: HMSO, 1979), pp. 28 and 8.
5 *Jane's World Railways*, annually
   Observer, 21 March 1977, letter from Roger Calvert.
6 British Road Federation, *Basic Road Statistics*, 1979, p. 29.
7 Department of the Environment, *Transport Statistics: Great Britain, 1964–1974* (London: HMSO, 1976), p. 178; *Transport Statistics: Great Britain, 1968–1978* (London: HMSO, 1979), p. 157.
8 Quoted by Barraclough G., 'The great world crisis', *New York Review of Books*, 23 January 1975, p. 22.
9 Figures cited by Richard Hope in the *Guardian*, 27 September 1977.
10 *Sunday Times*, 7 January 1968.
11 Hamer, M., *Wheels Within Wheels* (London: Friends of the Earth, 1974), p. 42; the estimate is based on the Civil List.
12 Jenkins, G., *The Ministry of Transport and Civil Aviation* (London: Allen & Unwin, 1959), pp. 199, 218–19.
13 *Hansard*, vol. 859, col. 556, 4 July 1973.
14 *Guardian*, 3 November 1978.
15 Hamer, M., *Wheels Within Wheels*, chapter 4; Finer, S. E., 'Transport interests and the roads lobby', *Political Quarterly*, vol. 29, January–March, 1958, p. 47.
16 *Financial Times*, 12 October 1977.
17 *Drive*, no. 1, Spring, 1967; *Drive*, no. 6, Summer, 1968.
18 Gwilliam, K. M., *Transport and Public Policy* (London: Allen & Unwin, 1964), p. 169.
19 British Road Federation, *Basic Road Statistics*, 1967.
20 *Financial Times*, 12 May 1977.
21 *Hansard*, vol. 932, col. 560, 26 May 1977.
22 *New Society*, 17 March 1977.
23 *Daily Telegraph*, 18 February 1976.
24 Reprinted in the Labour Party's *The National Planning of Transport* (November, 1932).
25 Select Committee on Transport, *Report*, 1918 House of Commons 130/136; *The Co-ordination and Development of Transport*, Final Report of the Royal Commission on Transport, Cmnd 3751 (1930); Davies, E., *Nationalisation of Transport*, Labour Discussion Series No. 10 (January, 1947).

26 Some of the details of the following account are taken from the transcript of an interview between Mr D. Robertson, one-time officer of the Railway Clerks' Association and subsequently Director of Establishment, British Transport Commission, and Dr M. Bonavia. I am grateful to both Dr Bonavia and Mr Robertson for permission to quote from this document.

27 Cited by G. R. Strauss in the second-reading debate on the Bill, *Hansard*, vol. 431, col. 1973, 18 December 1946.

28 Morrison, H., *An Autobiography* (London: Odhams Press, 1960), p. 259.

29 *Hansard*, vol. 329 cols 492, 518, 17 November 1937.

30 *Hansard*, vol. 431, col. 1623, 16 December 1946.

31 I am indebted to Dr M. Bonavia for recalling this development.

32 Bonavia, M. R., *The Organisation of British Railways* (Shepperton: Allan, 1971), p. 52.

33 Pryke, R. W. S., *Public Enterprise in Practice* (London: MacGibbon & Kee, 1971), p. 42.

34 TUC, *Public Ownership: an Interim Report*, presented to 85th TUC, Douglas, Isle of Man, September 1953, p. 10; J. Elliot, 'An act of stewardship', *Journal of the Institute of Transport*, vol. 25, no. 7, November, 1953, p. 245.

35 British Transport Commission, *Annual Reports and Accounts*, 1948–52.

36 *The Economist*, 10 May 1952, p. 349.

37 EC 1286, May, 1952.

38 EC, 12 July 1952, p. 65, General Secretary's 'write-up' for discussion on Transport Bill.

39 *Modern Transport*, 10 May 1962.

40 Quick Smith, G. W., 'British road services in the competitive era', *British Transport Review*, vol. 4, no. 2, August, 1956.

41 Letter to *The Times*, 23 April 1952.

42 By a decision of the Prime Minister, *Hansard*, vol. 619, cols 650–1, 10 March 1960.

43 Select Committee on Nationalised Industries, *Railways, Minutes of Evidence*, 1960, appendix 250.

44 *Hansard*, vol. 690, cols 90–91, 26 February 1964.

45 AGM Margate, 2 July 1962, verbatim report.

46 *The Times*, 17 February 1965.

47 *Hansard*, vol. 676, col. 963, 30 April 1963.

48 Ministry of Transport, *Carriers Licensing*, 1965, p. 45.

49 Munby, D. L. and Watson, A. H., *Inland Transport Statistics: Great Britain, 1900–1970*, op. cit., table A22, p. 118.

50 Ibid., table A1, p. 21.

51 Bonavia, M. R., *The Organisation of British Railways*, op. cit., p. 128.

52 Notes of a meeting of NUR with the Minister of Transport and representatives of the three railway unions, 8 June 1966.

53 *Hansard*, vol. 756, cols 1282–3, 20 December 1967.

54 Crossman, R., *The Diaries of a Cabinet Minister*, Vol. 3 (London: Hamish Hamilton/Jonathan Cape, 1975), p. 124.

55 NUR file GS/610, 'The railway industries exports, British Railways Board', *Report and Accounts*, 1969–78, inclusive.

56 NUR AGM, Exmouth, 17 July 1973, verbatim report.

57 *Select Committee on Nationalised Industries* (sub-committee A), 19

October 1976, Q373.
58 ibid., 15 February 1977, Q887.
59 British Rail, *Facts and Figures*, 1978 edn, p. 25.
60 *Hansard*, vol. 959, col. 787, December, 1978.
61 *Transport Policy: a Consultation Document*, Vol. 1 (1976), p. 14.
62 ibid., p. 20.
63 ibid., p. 12.
64 ibid., pp. 64–5.
65 ibid., p. 90.
66 *Hansard*, vol. 903, col. 1690, 23 January 1976.
67 National Freight Corporation, *Annual Report and Accounts*, 1972, p. 31.
68 HMSO, *Rural Bus Services*, Report (1961), p. 10.
69 Moseley, M. J., *Accessibility: the Rural Challenge* (London: Methuen, 1979), p. 46.
70 Standing Conference of Rural Community Councils, *The Decline of Rural Services* (London: National Council of Social Service, 1978), p. 30.
71 *Hansard*, vol, 931, cols 61, 66, 2 May 1977.
72 ibid., col. 54, 2 May 1977.
73 *Hansard*, vol. 952, col. 696, 19 January 1978.
74 ibid., cols 768, 802. A full statement on transport supplementary grants was given by the Minister of Transport in reply to a parliamentary question on 14 January 1977, see *Hansard*, vol. 903, cols 621–2, 14 January 1977.
75 *Hansard*, vol. 942, col. 768, 19 January 1978.
76 Independent Commission on Transport, *Changing Directions* (London: Coronet Books/Hodder Paperbacks, 1974), p. 206.
77 *Hansard*, vol. 942, col. 755, 19 January 1978.
78 Railway Invigoration Society, *Can Bus Replace Train?* (London: Railway Invigoration Society, 1977), p. 15.
79 Select Committee on Nationalised Industries (sub-committee A), 19 October 1976, Q347.

CHAPTER 2

1 Inland Transport Committee, International Labour Organisation, *Social Consequences of Changing Methods and Techniques in Railways and Road Transport* (Geneva: International Labour Office, 1961), p. 19.
2 Interview with S. Welborn, EC member, 5 February 1979.
3 J. W. Stafford, *We See Ourselves: a realistic picture of Permanent Way Staff employed on British Railways* (London: Railway Review, 1954), p. 11.
4 ibid, p. 17.
5 Information kindly supplied by Graham Bryant, Civil Engineering Department, British Railways, 29 February 1980; see also *New Scientist*, vol. 77, no. 1093, 9 March 1978, p. 659.
6 International Transport Workers' Federation, *We don't hate technology, but . . .* (London: The Federation, 1977), pp. 40, 44, 65.
7 G. Freeman Allen, *British Rail After Beeching* (London: Ian Allan, 1966), p. 362.

8 *Railway Review*, 4 March 1966.
9 G. F. Allen, *British Rail After Beeching*, op. cit., p. 365; *Transport Age*, vol. 4, no. 25, April, 1963, p. 11; *New Scientist*, vol. 8, no. 213, 15 December 1960, p. 1577.
10 R. W. S. Pryke, 'Rail transport', in 26th Round Table on Transport Economics Report, *Effect of Productivity and Technological Progress on Transport Workers* (1975), p. 47.
11 Allen, op. cit., p. 366.
12 Interview, 22 May 1978.
13 Interview, 5 February 1979.
14 Letter to the author, 21 July 1979.
15 ITF, *We don't hate technology, but . . .*, op. cit., p. 176.
16 British Transport Commission, *Annual Report*, 1950, p. 333; British Railways Board, *Annual Report*, 1977, p. 66.
17 Many of the details in the following account of the locomotive grades in the age of steam are taken from Frank McKenna's *A Glossary of Railwaymen's Talk* (Oxford: History Workshop, Ruskin College, 1970).
18 Interview with David Bowman, 23 October 1979.
19 ILO Inland Transport Committee Report III, *Working Conditions in Rail Transport* (Geneva. ILO, 1979), p. 52.
20 EC 3016 and 3245, December 1973.
21 Letter from Sir Peter Parker, published in the *Daily Telegraph*, 23 April 1977.
22 *Memorandum of Agreement in regard to manning of diesel or electric locomotives and multiple unit trams*, BTC, NUR and ASLEF, 18 December 1957.
23 *Memorandum of Agreement on Single Manning*: BRB, ASLEF and NUR, 28 October 1965.
24 Industrial Relations Department, British Railways Board Pay and Efficiency (Footplate Staff), August 1968.
25 EC 1801, August 1972.
26 F. Cottrell, *Technological Change and Labour in the Railroad Industry* (Lexington, Mass.: D. C. Heath, 1970), p. 11.
27 ITF, *We don't hate technology, but . . .*, pp. 35–8.
28 ibid., p. 35.
29 *Transport Age*, vol. 3, no. 18, July, 1961, p. 8.
30 NUR AGM, Aberdeen, 7 July 1967, verbatim report, debate on item 57.
31 *Transport Salaried Staff Journal*, July, 1967; information kindly supplied by British Railways Board Personnel Department, July, 1979.
32 Letter to *Railway Review*, 23 January 1970.
33 Memorandum from the Personnel Department, British Railways Board, 20 August 1979.
34 British Transport Commission, vol. 3, no. 20, January, 1962, pp. 34–9.
35 Interview with Mr Peter A. Lindsay, EC member, NUR, 31 January 1979.
36 EC 3436, December, 1972.
37 British Railways, *Yearbook, 1965*, p. 15; British Railways Board, *Annual Report and Accounts*, 1977, pp. 24, 66.
38 *Transport Age*, April, 1957, pp. 3–6.
39 Information kindly supplied by British Railways Board Personnel Department, August 1979; NUR General Secretary's report to the AGM, 1972, p. 17.

40 NUR AGM, Penzance, July 1968, item 103.
41 NUR AGM, Llandudno, July 1969, verbatim report, debate on item 97.
42 NUR AGM, Plymouth, 11 July 1966, verbatim report, debate on item 95.
43 NUR AGM, Aberdeen, 10 July 1967, verbatim report, speech of A. Williams in debate on item 91(a).
44 NUR AGM, Penzance, 5 July 1968, verbatim report, debate on item 110.
45 Interview, 20 December 1978.
46 'The Story of Freight', *Transport Review*, 23 March 1979.
47 *Transport Age*, vol. 3, no. 19, October, 1961.
48 Interview, 28 November 1978.
49 *Transport Age*, vol. 3, no. 17, April, 1961, p. 33.
50 *Railway Gazette*, vol. 104, no. 1, 6 January 1956, pp. 17–19.
51 *Transport Age*, vol. 2, no. 8, January, 1959.
52 G. H. Hinds, 'Computers in transport', *Engineering*, vol. 188, no. 4874, 18 September 1959, pp. 229–33; 'Compiling railway timetables by computer', *New Scientist*, vol. 8, no. 195, 11 August 1960, pp. 396–8; Brigadier Hinds was electronics advisory officer of the British Transport Commission.
53 Interview.
54 Interview with members of works committee, Derby carriage works, 19 January 1979.
55 This paragraph is based on helpful discussions with Mr Tom Ham, a workshops representative on the NUR EC on 23 January 1979. I am also indebted for information about Crewe works provided by Mr Moss, an NUR EC member from Crewe's No. 5 branch.
56 F. Cottrell, *Technological Change and Labour in the Railroad Industry* (Lexington, Mass.: D. C. Heath, 1970), p. 55; L. Cook, *Railway Workshops: the Problems of Contraction* (Cambridge: Cambridge University Press, 1964), *passim*.
57 *Derby Daily Telegraph* and *Derby Evening Telegraph*, both of 28 August 1962.
58 Report of UIC Staff Committee, kindly supplied by D. F. Rugman, Safety and Welfare Officer, British Railways Board, 17 August 1979.
59 See P. S. Bagwell, *The Railwaymen*, Vol. 1 (London: Allen & Unwin, 1963), pp. 94–106.
60 EC 350, March 1978.
61 British Railways Electrification Conference, *Proceedings*, London (1960), p. 57.
62 Department of Transport, *Railways Accidents, Report to the Secretary of State for Transport on the Safety Record of the Railways of Great Britain during the year 1975* (London: HMSO, 1976), appendix X.
63 British Railways Board, *Report on Personnel Accident at Stafford*, 1 March 1973.
64 Department of Transport, op cit., appendix X.
65 British Railways Board, *Report on Personnel Accident at Horsley*, 14 August 1975.
66 Information kindly supplied by D. F. Rugman, BRB, 17 August 1979.
67 EC 346, March 1978.
68 Information kindly supplied by M. J. Moss of NUR Crewe No. 5 branch.

69 EC 121, March 1978.
70 Interview with John Cogger, 10 May 1978.
71 NUR AGM, Aberdeen, 7 July 1967, verbatim report, debate on item 57.
72 NUR AGM, Ayr, July 1977, resolution 150.
73 EC, March 1978, appendix M2, minute 976.
74 EC, March 1978, appendix M1, minute 37.

CHAPTER 3

1   SGM, London, 17 February 1970, 4th report, presented by T. Hodgson.
2   AGM, Paignton, 11 July 1953, verbatim report.
3   EC 84, March 1958.
4   AGM, Exmouth, July 1958, decision on item 146.
5   AGM decision 173(2) of 1961; 128(1) of 1964; and 132(1) of 1967.
6   Letters from S. Greene to Warrington District branch secretary, 6 and 15 January 1969, in NUR file 0/23/8. As subsequent events were to demonstrate, the General Secretary had not got it quite right. The final say on Leigh's application for membership rested with the Warrington Trades and Labour Council, which declined to accept him.
7   Branch circular 0/3235/16411, 17 October 1969.
8   Transcript of Judgement, in NUR file 0/23/8.
9   EC, December 1969, appendix D11.
10 Branch circular 0/3235/16411, 17 October 1969.
11 Agenda and decisions of the SGM, 17–20 February 1970, pp. 23–4, EC 681, March 1970.
12 Letters in NUR file 0/23/8.
13 Branch circular 0/3262/16541, 27 January 1970.
14 EC 719, March 1970; and EC 1370, June 1970.
15 Agenda and decisions of the AGM, Inverness, July 1970, p. 114.
16 Interview with John Cogger, who was a delegate to the Plymouth AGM in 1971 and a member of the EC between 1974–6.
17 SGM, London, 17–20 February 1970, items 5(r) and (s), EC 383 and 384, March 1970.
18 EC 133, March 1958.
19 AGM, Aberdeen, 6 July 1967, verbatim report, p. 4.
20 The expression was used by David Bowman, who served as an EC member in the years 1953–4, 1955–7, 1961–3 and 1967–9, and between 1975–7 presided over its affairs.
21 Speech at AGM, Llandudno, 18 July 1969.
22 I am grateful to Mr W. Little, for many years secretary to Sidney Greene, and to Mr A. Edmondson, who as a member of the head-office staff was present during many important wage negotiations, for information on which this account of the General Secretary is based.
23 Report of 102nd Annual Trades Union Congress, 1970, p. 738.
24 Railway Review, 17 and 24 October 1958; AGM, Llandudno, 18 July 1969, verbatim report, tribute to George Brassington from F. O'Garr, metal machinist, Eastleigh No. 2 branch.
25 NUR Rules, rule 8, various years.
26 NUR file 0/12/1; information and comments received from organisers in reply to questionnaire sent to them by General Secretary, November 1969.

27 SGM, London, 20 February 1970, debate on the 23rd report.
28 The expression was used by Sidney Weighell on 11 July 1978; AGM, Llandudno, 1978, verbatim report.
29 P. S. Bagwell, *The Railwaymen*, Vol. 1 (London: Allen & Unwin, pp. 425–9; AGM, Ayr, 14 July 1947, verbatim report, debate on item 150.
30 AGM, Plymouth, 15 July 1937, debate on item 121, speech of A. E. Russell.
31 ibid., speech of M. Hailes.
32 AGM, Penzance, 11 July 1968, verbatim report, debate on item 159.
33 AGM, Llandudno, 11 July 1978, verbatim report, debate on item 211, speech of Sidney Weighell.
34 AGM, Plymouth, 15 July 1937, verbatim report, debate on item 121.
35 AGM, Ayr, 14 July 1947, verbatim report, debate on item 150.
36 ibid.
37 SGM, 16 August 1950, verbatim report, debate on item 212.
38 AGM, Hastings, 9 July 1951, verbatim report, debate on item 199(b).
39 SGM, St. Pancras Town Hall, 2 August 1952, verbatim report, debate on item 170.
40 AGM, Paignton, July 1964, verbatim report, debate on item 126; NUR, *Reorganisation and Reconstitution of the Union*, report of the National Executive Committee to the AGM, 1964.
41 AGM, Morecambe, 12 July 1946, verbatim report, debate on item 134(c).
42 AGM, Hastings, 9 July 1951, verbatim report, debate on item 199(b).
43 ibid.
44 AGM, Paignton, 22 July 1976, verbatim report, debate on item 177.
45 EC 548, 13 April 1978.
46 AGM, Llandudno, 11 July 1978, verbatim report, speech of Professor J. England.
47 Agenda and decisions, AGM 1978, pp. 74–5; and verbatim report, debate on item 211.
48 NUR, *A Report on the Structure and Composition of the National Executive Committee* (Warwick Report), May 1978, para. 21.
49 EC 1145, 1931.
50 EC 296, 657, 759, 1054 and 1459, 1932.
51 EC 730 and 731, March 1932, upheld by AGM, Folkestone, June 1932, item 43.
52 Agenda and decisions, AGM, Scarborough, July 1952, item 154(a).
53 EC 2191, September 1953.
54 EC 2710, December 1955.
55 Warwick Report, paras 38–41.
56 Branch circular 0/4407/21423, 26 September 1978.
57 EC 665, 27 April 1979; AGM, Paignton, July 1979, item 180.
58 *Railway Review*, 5 July 1968; NUR, *Address Book*, various dates; Branch circular 0/4540/21802, 2 October 1979.
59 EC 1690, June 1962; and EC 2825, September 1962; Branch circular 0/2407/13441, 10 January 1963.
60 AGM, Aberdeen, 13 July 1967, verbatim report, debate on item 123.
61 *NUR General Secretary's Report to the AGM*, 1972, p. 35.
62 *NUR General Secretary's Report to the AGM*, 1965, p. 9.
63 Bagwell, *The Railwaymen*, Vol. 1, op. cit., p. 357.
64 Interview with Mrs J. Brightman, 10 July 1978.

65 EC 2573, September 1963; AGM, Paignton, July 1964, item 114; Branch circular F526/13815, 14 January 1964.
66 AGM, Llandudno, 14 July 1969, verbatim report, debate on item 160, speech of Sidney Greene.
67 ibid.
68 AGM, Plymouth, July 1974, agenda and decisions, p. 75, speech of Lord Hirshfield for the union's accountants.
69 AGM Agenda and decisions, 1960, p. 93.
70 AGM Agenda and decisions, 1959, p. 99.
71 EC 3788, December 1959; AGM Agenda and decisions, 1960, item 128.
72 AGM Agenda and decisions, 1961, p. 92.
73 AGM, Southport, 5 July 1965, verbatim report, p. 63.
74 EC, August 1972, p. 452; Report of the Directors of Unity House (Holdings) Ltd; AGM Agenda and decisions, 1974, report presented by Lord Hirshfield, pp. 72–7.
75 AGM, Southport, 5 July 1965, verbatim report, p. 63.
76 EC, August 1974, p. 428.
77 AGM Agenda and decisions, 1974, pp. 72–7.
78 NUR, *Report and Financial Statement*, 1974, p. 23.
79 NUR *Report and Financial Statement*, 1975, p. 4.
80 NUR *Report and Financial Statement*, 1978, p. 10.
81 AGM, Penzance, 8 July 196, verbatim report, discussion following the report of the auditor, Lord Hirshfield.
82 Report of the 69th Annual Conference of the Labour Party, 1970, pp. 247–52; EC, December 1970, pp. 42–4, Report of Labour Party Conference delegates.
83 EC 3499, December 1970.
84 *Railway Review*, 2 April 1971, branch reports.
85 AGM, Plymouth, 21 July 1971, verbatim report, debate on item 167; NUR, *Report and Financial Statement*, 1970, table of Equity investments, pp. 32–4; Counter Information Services, *Black South Africa Cape Argus Explodes* (1969), pp. 49–52. The other firms with large South African interests in which the NUR owned shares were Dunlop (£41,281), Thorn Electrical (£31,416), British Leyland (£40,131), EMI (£23,212), GEC (Marconi) (£76,256), Tube Investments (£32,425), Courtaulds (£27,678), British Oxygen Co. (£22,688), GKN (£54,627), and Rio Tinto Zinc (£53,715).
86 NUR, *Report and Financial Statement*, 1975 and 1976; *Who's Who* entry, Lord Greene of Harrow Weald.
87 AGM Agenda and decisions, 1975.
88 NUR, *Report and Financial Statement*, 1959, report of General Secretary, p. 3.
89 AGM, Plymouth, 15 July 1974, verbatim report, debate on item 164.
90 NUR, *Report and Financial Statement*, 1975, p. 17.
91 NUR Orphan Fund Annual Reports, 1960–75.
92 AGM, Inverness, July 1970, item 169(a).
93 EC 2535, September 1970; EC 942 7 May 1971.
94 Branch circular F593/1707, 1 January 1971.
95 AGM, Plymouth, 21 July 1971, verbatim report, debate on item 164.
96 Thanks are due to Mr M. Rowlinson, interviewed on 27 November 1979 on the work of the NUR legal department.
97 NUR EC Minutes, quarterly or triennial summary of fatal and non-fatal accident cases in period since 1960.

98   NUR, *General Secretary's Report on Legal Services,* 1975–9, inclusive.
99   ibid., 1979 and 1975 reports, respectively.
100 'Industrial Deafness', *General Secretary's Report on Legal Services,* 1979, p. 6.
101 Interview with Mr M. Rowlinson, 27 November 1979.
102 The meeting on 17 October 1973, for example, considered the effectiveness of new earmuffs devised by the Research Department of British Rail, EC, March 1974, appendix M4.
103 AGM, Paignton, July 1953, item 8(a).
104 EC 105, 23 January 1976.
105 AGM, Llandudno, 19 July 1978, verbatim report, debate on item 35.
106 A letter kindly sent by Mr W. G. Masson, of Inverness No. 1 branch, on 3 December 1979 emphasised this point.
107 EC 1799, 20 September 1976; EC 480, 7 April 1978; EC 715, 11 May 1978; EC 924, 23 June 1978; 24 August 1978, appendix A13; EC 1761, 4 October 1979; EC 2381, 13 December 1979; *General Secretary's Report to the AGM,* 1980, NUR, Unity House Souvenir, March 1980.

CHAPTER 4

1   EC, September 1962, Negotiating Committee Report.
2   *Hansard,* vol. 676, no. 103, col. 951, 30 April 1963.
3   British Transport Commission Annual Report, 1959.
4   *Hansard,* 5th series, vol. 619, col. 643, 10 March 1960.
5   *Hansard,* 5th series, vol. 620, col. 1319, 30 March 1960.
    Hansard (Lords), vol. 222, cols 745–6, 6 April 1960.
6   Cited in speech by Mr John Hynd, NUR-sponsored MP for Sheffield, Attercliffe, *Hansard,* vol. 676, no. 122, col. 768, 29 April 1963.
7   *Hansard,* vol. 676, no. 102, col. 722, 29 April 1963.
8   *Hansard,* 5th series, vol. 636, col. 1404, 15 March 1961.
9   *Railway Review,* 24 March 1961.
10 Among those who expressed this view in interviews with the author in 1978 were Alun Rees, the President; David Bowman, President, 1975–7; Russell Tuck, Senior Assistant General Secretary since 1975; Frank Cannon, Assistant General Secretary since 1971; and veteran executive committee members G. Coles, J. Nicolson, O. Conheeney, G. Sharratt, and others.
11 A. E. Grigg, *In Railway Service: the History of the Bletchley Branch of the NUR* (published by the branch in 1972), p. 164.
12 Eastern District Council minutes. 31 August 1964.
13 File MM7/49/1/2.
14 Philip S. Bagwell, *The Transport Revolution from 1770* (London: Batsford, 1974), p. 247.
15 File MM7/49/1/119.
16 Scottish DC's co-ordinating committee minutes, June 1961.
17 *Railway Review.* 16 March 1962; EC 1962, September 1962; letter from D. Bowman, 26 April 1979.
18 Edinburgh and East of Scotland DC, minutes, 17 April 1962; EC 1962, December 1962.
19 West Midlands DC annual reports. 1961 and 1962.
20 *Hansard.* vol. 676, no. 102, Cols 69–73, 29 April 1963.

21 Dorothy Wedderburn, *Redundancy and the Railwaymen* (Cambridge: Cambridge University Press, 1965), p. 24.
22 Cmnd 813 (London: HMSO, 1959).
23 EC, September 1959, appendix S16.
24 Darlington DC, AGM, 28 January 1961, minutes.
25 EC, March 1961, appendix M6; EC, March 1962, appendix M16.
26 EC, March 1962, appendix M17.
27 Negotiating and Shops sub-committee report to the EC, 11 April 1962.
28 NUR, AGM, verbatim report, 2 July 1962, p. 166.
29 EC, December 1962, appendix D5.
30 EC, December 1962, appendix D6.
31 EC, September 1962, appendix S44.
32 EC, 1787, June 1962, MM7/45/2/2540 and 0/2368/13237.
33 EC, December 1962, p. 42.
34 EC, 1966, September 1962. In his briefing to the executive the General Secretary had not mentioned all communications in favour of strike action that he had received. At its meeting on 29 July 1962, for example, the Manchester and District council demanded that the EC should call a national token strike. Other district councils, including the North of Scotland DC, expressed readiness to support such industrial action as the EC deemed appropriate.
35 EC 2861 and 2862, 20 October 1962.
36 AGM, verbatim report, 4 July 1963, p. 40.
37 Interview with Gordon Coles, 6 June 1968.
38 AGM, verbatim report, 4 July 1963, p. 40.
39 EC 2864, 9 October 1962.
40 EC 2880, 16 October; and EC 2883, 18 October 1962.
41 EC, March 1963, appendix M18; Wedderburn, *Redundancy and the Railwaymen*, op. cit., appendi 1, p. 189.
42 AGM, verbatim report, 10 July 1963, pp. 76, 73.
43 EC 100, 8 February 1963, appendix D26; EC 267, March 1963, appendix M43; and June 1963. appendix J3.
44 Article: 'Redundancy Abroad'. *Ministry of Labour Gazette*, April, 1963.
45 EC 2921, 3 December 1962.
46 EC 864, March 1963; AGM, 4 July 1963. item 146, verbatim report, p. 4/81.
47 British Railways Board, *The Reshaping of British Railways* (London: HMSO, 1963), p. 51.
48 EC 870, 26 March; and EC 873, 3 April 1963.
49 EC 881, 18 April; and EC 884, 23 April 1963.
50 EC 936–49, pp. 31–6. 4–13 May 1963; and EC. June 1963, appendices J21–3.
51 EC 1620, 25 June 1963.
52 DC minute books. Exeter No. 1 branch minute book, 2 May 1963; AGM, 4 July 1963, verbatim report, p. 32 *et seq.*
53 EC, March 1970, p. 35, parliamentary report.
54 NUR, Notes for meeting with Prime Minister. 3 p.m., 6 October 1965, EC 967, June 1965; interview with Ron Lewis, MP secretary of the NUR parliamentary group at the time.
55 Harold Wilson, *The Labour Government, 1964–70* (Harmondsworth: Penguin, 1974), p. 240.
56 Richard Crossman, *The Diaries of a Cabinet Minister*, Vol. 3 (London:

Hamish Hamilton/Jonathan Cape, 1975), p. 603.
57 *Financial Times*, 29 March 1979.
58 Interview with Mick Hamer, Transport 2000, 2 October 1978.
59 Glasgow and West of Scotland DC, minute of meeting held on 7 October 1962; Edinburgh and East of Scotland DC, minute of special meeting, 21 April 1963.
60 *Railway Review*, 13 April 1962.
61 EC 2474, December 1952.
62 Item 84(c), AGM, July 1961.
63 *Railway Review*, 12 May 1961.
64 EC, September 1961, appendix S54.
65 NUR Branch circular M5561/13613, 11 June 1963.
66 *Railway Review*, 1 March 1963.
67 Eastern District Council, minutes, 2 March, 1 June, 31 August and 23 November 1964; 15 February 1965; this was a closure which on the recommendation of the TUCC was stopped by Tom Fraser.
68 Letter from Mr T. J. W. Head, secretary of Okehampton branch, NUR; many thanks are also due to Mr Head for the loan of all the papers in the case.
69 Interview, 16 August 1968.
70 Southern DC, minutes, 9 September 1962.
71 Interview, 2 December 1977.
72 Interview, 17 April 1978.

CHAPTER 5

1 National Board for Prices and Incomes, Report No. 162, *Costs Charges and Productivity of National Freight Corporation*, appendix A, Cmnd 4569 (1971).
2 ibid.
3 British Transport Commission, *Annual Report and Accounts*, 1948–62.
4 Published in *Railway Review*, 3 December, 1954.
5 Jim Campbell's evidence to the Cameron Court of Inquiry, *Railway Review*, 7 January 1955.
6 *Interim Report of a Court of Inquiry into a dispute between the BTC and the NUR* (Cameron Report), Cmnd 9352 (1958).
7 *Railway Review*, 3 December 1954.
8 *Railway Review*, 14 January 1955.
9 EC minutes, March 1958, pp. 25–6.
10 *Railway Review*, 24 January 1958, and 21 March 1958.
11 NUR, *Railwaymen and the PIB* (1966), p. 6.
12 Special Joint Committee on Machinery of Negotiation for Railway Staff, Report of the Railway Pay Committee of Inquiry, 2 March 1960.
13 *Hansard*, 10 March 1960.
14 NUR, *Railwaymen and the PIB*, p. 10.
15 NUR, *Railwaymen and the PIB*, p. 11.
16 EC 87, 24 January 1962.
17 EC 103, 15 February 1962.
18 Quoted in *Railway Review*, 2 February 1962.
19 Manchester DC, 11 February 1962.
20 EC 1788, 18 June 1962.

21 McLeod, C., *All Change* (London: Gower Press, 1970), p. 119; Charles McLeod was the member of the Board responsible for industrial relations.
22 EC 2893, 5 November 1962.
23 EC 2895, 7 November 1962.
24 McLeod, *All Change*, op. cit., p. 120.
25 NUR, AGM, 6 July 1964, verbatim report, item 14, p. 67.
26 EC 2920, 21 October 1964.
27 Wilson, H. *The Labour Government 1946–70* (Harmondsworth: Penguin, 1974), p. 97.
28 McLeod, op. cit., p. 125.
29 EC 885, 8 April 1965.
30 EC, minutes, 24 August 1965, pp. 30–3.
31 EC 2885, 5 October 1965.
32 Widgery, D., *The Left in Britain, 1950–1965* (Harmondsworth: Penguin, 1976), p. 246; EC special meeting, 15 October 1965.
33 EC 11, 19 January 1966.
34 EC 30, 4 February 1966.
35 EC 32, 10 February 1966.
36 EC 35, 11 February 1966.
37 Wilson, H., *The Labour Government, 1964–70*, op. cit., p. 259.
38 ibid., p. 274.
39 EC 36, 11–12 February 1966.
40 Wilson, *The Labour Government*, op. cit., p. 274.
41 Crossman, *The Diaries of a Cabinet Minister*, Vol. 1: Minister of Housing, 1964–6 (London: Hamish Hamilton/Jonathan Cape, 1975), p. 451.
42 Eastern DC, 28 February 1966.
43 Wilson, op. cit., p. 274.
44 PE, Main Group meeting, 11 December 1967.
45 Sidney Greene speaking at the NUR AGM, Scarborough, 14 July 1972, estimated wages and salaries formed 65 to 70 per cent of total costs but a lower estimate was given in the union's paper RPE(S) 22 of 24 April 1967.
46 Joint Working Party, 15 December 1967.
47 Interview with Arnold Edmondson, 19 September 1977.
48 Flanders, A., *The Fawley Productivity Agreements* (1964), pp. 36–7.
49 NUR General Secretary's report to the AGM, June 1967, pp. 10–11.
50 RPE (S), 22 March 1967.
51 *Daily Mail*, 24 April 1967.
52 Meeting of the sub-group, 21 March 1967.
53 NUR Branch circular M6900/15571, 2 June 1969.
54 RPE (S), 13 October 1966.
55 RPE (S), 4 July 1966.
56 Details of duties taken from BRB's green booklet, *Pay and Efficiency* (August 1968), appendix D: 'Multiplicity of Duties'.
57 Minutes of Joint Working Party, BRB, NUR and ASLEF, 15 December 1967.
58 NUR Notes of meeting at Ministry of Labour on 19 July 1966.
59 Agreement between BRB, ASLEF and the NUR, 29 August, 1968.
60 Report of Joint Working Party, Clerical Grades, RPE(S), 27 April 1967.
61 NUR Branch circular M6949/13644, 15 March 1968.

62 Revision of Clerical Pay Structure, RPE(S), 15 October 1966.
63 Report No. 2, Working Party D: supervisory structure, April 1967.
64 NUR Branch circular M6949/13644, 15 March 1968.
65 Letter from A. H. Nicholson, Director of Industrial Relations, BRB, to Sidney Greene, 18 December 1967.
66 Interview with Sir Leonard Neal, 26 July 1978.
67 *Transport Review*, 22 September 1978.
68 McCleod, op. cit., pp. 78–86.
69 NUR, AGM, verbatim report, 6 July 1967, debate on item 33.
70 H. Garton, speaking to resolution 103, 7 July 1966; A Wolstenholme, speaking to resolution 37, 7 July 1970.
71 NUR, AGM, verbatim report, 13 July 1971, debate on item 42.
72 McCleod, op. cit., p. 18.
73 Interview with Sir Leonard Neal, 26 July 1978.
74 McCleod, p. 34.
75 ibid., p. 25.
76 Minutes of eighth meeting at the Ministry of Labour, 2 May 1967.
77 McCleod, p. 38.
78 EC 84, 4 March 1968.
79 EC 1426, 12 June 1968.
80 EC, 19 June 1968, pp. 14–15, 20 June resolution 1434.
81 Editorial, *Railway Review*, 25 August 1968.
82 NUR Agenda and decisions of AGM, 1968, pp. 30–35; *Railway Review*, 5 and 12 July 1968; interview with Sir Leonard Neal, 26 July 1978; NUR Branch circular M7045/15785, 6 July 1968; interview with Mr G. Sharratt, EC member.
83 See, for example, British Railways Civil Engineering Department, Memorandum of staff consultation meetings held at Taunton, 10 September 1968; Gloucester, 11 September 1968; Bristol, 11 September 1968; and Plymouth, 17 September 1968.
84 Interview with Sir Leonard Neal, 26 July 1978.
85 Letter from BRB to trade union secretaries, 23 September 1968.
86 Minutes of a meeting between the BRB and the railway unions, 30 April 1969.
87 NUR, AGM, Llandudno, 8 July 1969, verbatim report, debate on item 50.
88 General Secretary's report to the AGM, July 1969.
89 Letters contained in file, 'Revision of the wages structure 4' at Unity House.
90 *Railway Review*, 19 July 1969.
91 NUR, AGM, Llandudno, 8 July 1969, verbatim report, debate on item 50.

CHAPTER 6

1 Interview with Arnold Edmondson, 12 May 1978; see also twenty-three-page typescript of notes of pay and efficiency stage II discussions, the chief source of information for the first section of this chapter.
2 British Railways Board, *Pay and Efficiency (Stage II)*, Conciliation Staff other than footplate staff; agreement between BRB and NUR, August 1969, p. 3.
3 NUR SGM, London, 18 November 1935, verbatim report, debate on

item 22.

4   NUR AGM, Plymouth, 14 July 1937, verbatim report, debate on item 85.

5   NUR AGM, Clacton-on-Sea, 11 July 1939, verbatim report, debate on item 66.

6   EC 553, March 1940.

7   NUR file 0/4/2.

8   EC 1140, June 1952, discussing report of the NUR negotiating committee.

9   EC 1036, May 1959.

10 EC 2837, 1 October 1959.

11 NUR, AGM, Aberdeen, 7 July 1967, verbatim report, debate on item 55.

12 NUR AGM, Stockport, 12 July 1965, verbatim report, debate on items 30 and 30(b).

13 NUR AGM, Plymouth, 7 July 1966, verbatim report, debate on item 53.

14 Interview with Sir Leonard Neal, 26 July 1978.

15 BRB Personnel Department, *History of BRB trade union membership agreements*, Memorandum 82-4-127(IR/G).

16 EC, December 1969, pp. 27, 65–9, and decision 2542; NUR Branch circular MM7/22/3/239A, 5 January 1970.

17 NUR file 0/4/1/1970; notes of an informal meeting of the appeals body held on 3 July 1970.

18 BRB Memorandum 82-4-127(IR/G).

19 NUR file 0/4/1, 1970.

20 EC 29, 2 February 1971; EC 30, 2 February 1971; EC 974, March 1971.

21 NUR Branch circular M7822/16715, 8 May 1970.

22 EC 750, March 1971.

23 BRB Memorandum 82-4-127(IR/G).

24 EC 1004, 2 July 1975.

25 EC September 1975, appendix A39.

26 EC 829, 11 April 1975.

27 EC 967, 27 May 1976.

28 EC 1063, 1 August 1975.

29 EC 722, 8 April 1976.

30 EC 1064, August 1978.

31 Interview with Sidney Weighell, 31 October 1980; EC 1742, 28 September 1979; and EC 2150, 22 November 1979.

32 *Hansard*, 5th Series, vol. 939, col. 272, 15 November 1977.

33 Income Data Services, brief 183, June 1980.

34 For example, Robert Moss's article, 'Non-unionists have the right to work', *Daily Telegraph*, 27 May 1976.

35 *Daily Telegraph*, 16 July 1976.

36 E. Wigham, 'Making the closed shop an acceptable and invigorating part of industrial life', *The Times*, 4 June 1976.

37 BRB Memorandum 82-4-127(IR/G).

38 NUR file, Pay and Efficiency stage II.

39 Interview, 13 June 1978.

40 NUR Branch circular M7243/16052, 7 February 1969.

41 National Conference of Signalmen, 15 September 1962, EC, December 1962, appendix D12.

42 Railway Staff Joint Council (Traffic Section), 26 May 1964, minute T743; and EC, September 1964, appendix S8; EC 2826, 24 November 1964.

43 NUR AGM, Llandudno, 15 July 1969, verbatim report, debate on item 120.

44 NUR AGM, Plymouth, 19 July 1971, verbatim report, debate on item 130.

45 NUR Branch circular M7838/16738, 21 May 1970.

46 EC August 1972, appendix A46.

47 EC December 1972, appendix D30.

48 NUR AGM, Exmouth, 16 July 1973, verbatim report, debate on item 108.

49 Interview with John Cogger, signalman and EC member, 17 November 1980.

50 NUR AGM, Llandudno, 19 July 1969, verbatim report, debate on item 120.

51 Statement by Sidney Greene, NUR AGM, Inverness, 8 July 1970, verbatim report, debate on item 38.

52 Statements by S. R. Mills and W. Smithurst made in the same debate, n. 51.

53 EC 724, 19 March 1970.

54 EC 909, 15 April 1971; and EC 913, 27 April 1971.

55 EC August 1971, appendix A9.

56 EC 1154, 18 April 1973 and appendix A11.

57 *General Secretary's Report to the AGM*, June 1974, p. 14.

58 EC 895, 18 April 1974 and appendix M42.

59 NUR AGM, Exmouth, 10 July 1973, verbatim report, debate on item 181.

60 EC 2564 and EC 2569, and appendices D16, D17 and D28, December 1973.

61 EC 103, March 1974.

62 NUR, *Pay Structure Review BRB Staff*, 17 September 1974.

63 D. Coates, *Labour in Power* (1980), p. 60.

64 NUR AGM, Plymouth, July 1974, resolution 176.

65 EC, March 1975, appendix M40.

66 EC 199, 25 March 1975; EC 842, 23 April 1975; EC 903, 30 May 1975; and EC 904(a), 2 June 1975.

67 EC 982, 12 June 1975.

68 EC 985, 16 June 1975.

69 EC 988 and EC 989, 20 June 1975.

70 Coates, *Labour in Power*, op. cit., p. 64.

71 EC 79, 5 May 1976.

72 RSNT Decision No. 47, in EC, August 1976, appendix A62.

73 EC 999, 4 June 1976.

74 EC 1050, 8 June 1976.

75 NUR AGM, Paignton, 14 July 1976, verbatim report, debate on item 27B.

76 EC 243, 1 March 1977; and EC 561, 24 March 1977.

77 NUR AGM, Ayr, 13 July 1977, verbatim report, debate on items 7 and 19.

78 EC 554, 14 April 1978.

79 NUR AGM, Llandudno, 13 July 1978, verbatim report, debate on items 10 and 10(a).

434   NOTES TO CHAPTER SEVEN

80 Report of 110th Annual TUC, 1978, pp. 549–54, 678, 687.
81 RSNT Decision No. 60, 1978, *NUR News*, no. 99, November, 1978; and *NUR News*, no. 101, November, 1978; letter from S. Weighell, 'Behind the rail dispute', *Guardian*, 24 January 1979.
82 *Hansard*, vol. 973, no. 64, col. 891–2, 12 November 1979.
83 NUR AGM, Paignton, 26 June 1979, verbatim report, debate on item 18.
84 NUR AGM, St Peter Port, Guernsey, 1 July 1980, verbatim report, debate on item 14.

CHAPTER 7

1 *Royal Commission on Trade Unions and Employers Associations*, Minutes of Evidence 17, 18 January 1966, s. 43.
2 ibid., Minutes of Evidence 14, s. 24 and s. 32.
3 ibid., Answer to question 2129.
4 NUR AGM, 7 July 1966, item 17.
5 EC 23, 17 February 1969; and EC 54, March 1969.
6 NUR AGM, 9 July 1969, verbatim report, p. 19.
7 Michael Moran, *The Politics of Industrial Relations* (London: Macmillan, 1977), p. 16.
8 NUR AGM, 7 July 1970, verbatim report, item 16.
9 ibid., item 16.
10 Moran, op. cit., pp. 111–17.
11 EC 3, 5 January 1971.
12 *The Industrial Relations Bill: Report of the Special TUC* (London: TUC, 1971), pp. 40–42.
13 EC 63, March 1971.
14 *The Industrial Relations Bill: Report of the Special TUC* (1971), p. 75.
15 ibid.
16 *The Times*, 7 November 1970.
17 NUR AGM, 14 July 1971, verbatim report, item 26.
18 EC, August 1972, p. 134.
19 EC 98, March 1972.
20 EC 1002, August 1971.
21 EC, December 1971, appendix D58.
22 EC 1003, August 1971.
23 EC, December 1971, appendix D58.
24 EC 443, March 1972.
25 *Financial Times*, 27 October 1970; *The Times*, 11 January 1971.
26 John Hughes and Roy Moore, *A Special Case* (Harmondsworth; Penguin, 1972), ch. 1 and p. 155.
27 H. A. Turner and F. Wilkinson, 'Real net incomes and the wage explosion', *New Society*, 25 February 1971.
28 *Daily Mail*, 10 January 1972.
29 *The Times*, 6 January 1972.
30 Branch circular M8455/17643, 6 January 1972.
31 Branch circular M8465/17652, 11 January 1972.
32 'The story of the miners strike', *Labour Research*, vol. 61, no. 4, April, 1972.
33 *Railway Review*, 18 February 1972.
34 Huges and Moore, *A Special Case*, op. cit., p. 139.

35   EC, March 1972, appendix M20.
36   NUR AGM, 11 July 1972, verbatim report.
37   EC, August 1972, pp. 3, 6, 29.
38   Interview, 31 January 1979.
39   Manchester District Council, minutes 18, June 1972.
40   Except where otherwise specified with reference to NUR records,
     many of the details of the following account are taken from a type-
     script on the working of the Industrial Relations Act prepared by
     Mr Bryn Jones of the *Daily Mirror.* I am most grateful to Mr Jones
     for generously allowing me to use the information contained in his
     account.
41   NUR file M7/3651, 'Wages 1972'.
42   EC, August 1972, appendix A38; and EC December 1972, appendix
     D16.
43   EC, August 1972, p. 4.
44   EC 1017 and 1021, 12 April 1972.
45   EC 1055, 15 April 1972.
46   EC 1057, 15 April 1972.
47   Jones's typescript, op. cit., ch. 5, p. 75.
48   Joint Working Party Report, 1968.
49   *The Times,* 18 April 1972.
50   Interview with William North, of the NUR head-office staff, who
     accompanied the union's negotiating party on 18 April 1972.
51   EC 1061, 19 April 1972.
52   Interview with Mr Tom Ham, 31 January 1979.
53   *Law Society Gazette,* 26 April 1972; see also O. H. Parsons, 'Unions
     and the NIRC', *Labour Research,* vol. 61, no. 6, June, 1972; and the
     same author's 'Breaches of contract', *Labour Research,* vol. 61, no. 7,
     July, 1972.
54   *The Times,* 20 April 1972 (law report).
55   Branch circular M8582/17814, 20 April 1972.
56   Branch circular M8581/17812, 20 April 1972.
57   NUR file MM7/3651.
58   Branch circular M8603/17837, 9 May 1972.
59   EC, August 1972, p. 32; Branch circular M8606/17841, 12 May 1972.
60   Vincent Hanna, in *Sunday Times,* 21 May 1972.
61   NUR file MM7/3651, containing verbatim reports of NIRC and
     Court of Appeal hearings.
62   EC, December 1972, appendix D58.
63   NUR file MM7/3651.
64   *Daily Mail,* 15 May 1972.
65   Jones's typescript, op. cit., ch. 7, p. 24.
66   Branch circular M8616/17853, 17 May 1972.
67   *Railway Review,* 26 May 1972.
68   EC, August 1972, p. 32.
69   Minute 539 RSNC, 7 June 1972.
70   EC 1148, 9 June 1972.
71   Minute 540, RSNC, 12 June 1972.
72   EC 1202, 13 June 1972.
73   NUR General Secretary's report to the AGM, June 1972.
74   Minute 537 of meeting of RSNC held on 1, 2 and 4 May 1972.
75   *Sunday Times,* 4 June 1972.
76   *The Times* (Labour correspondent), 7 June 1973.

CHAPTER 8

1   D. L. Munby and A. H. Watson, *Inland Transport Statistics: Great Britain, 1900–1970* (Oxford: Clarendon Press, 1978), p. 464.

2   E. Wistrich, 'Transport in Greater London', *Political Quarterly*, vol. 49, no. 1, January–March, 1978, pp. 1–12.

3   London Transport Executive, *Annual Report*, 1979, p. 4.

4   Greater London Council, *London Facts and Figures*, 1973 and 1978 editions.

5   London Transport Board, *Annual Report*, 1965, p. 23; London Transport Executive, *Annual Report*, 1978, p. 9.

6   London Transport Executive, *Annual Report*, 1972, p. 17.

7   NUR EC, March 1964, report of Railway Negotiating Committee/ London Transport Board. Greater London Council, *London Facts and Figures*, 1978, figure 15; see also T. C. Barker and M. Robbins, *A History of London Transport*, Vol. 2 (London: Allen & Unwin. 1974), pp. 352–3.

8   EC 1585, September 1955.

9   AGM, Great Yarmouth, July 1956, item 108.

10   D. Brooks, *Race and Labour in London Transport* (London: OUP, 1975), pp. 256–7.

11   Interview with Mr R. M. Robbins, London Transport Executive, 12 September 1979.

12   EC 1179, June 1960.

13   D. Brooks, *Race and Labour in London Transport*, op. cit., p. 299.

14   AGM, Margate, 5 July 1962, verbatim report, debate on item 55.

15   AGM, Plymouth, 4 July 1966, verbatim report, debate on item 14.

16   AGM, Llandudno, 7 July 1969, verbatim report, debate on item 24.

17   AGM, Inverness, 6 July 1970, verbatim report. debate on item 23.

18   EC 2230, December 1974.

19   National Front Railwaymen's Association *Newsletter*, Jannary, 1978; EC 474. 31 March 1978; NUR Branch circular GS/21158, 7 April 1978.

20   AGM, Llandudno, July 1978, verbatim report, debate on item 28.

21   E. Wistrich, op. cit., p. 12.

22   *Transport in London*, Cmnd 3686 (London: HMSO, 1967–8).

23   Munby and Watson, op. cit., table C6.4, p. 537; LTE *Annual Report and Accounts*, 1979, p. 21.

24   *Evening News* (London), 12 January 1977.

25   P. H. Bly, F. V. Webster and S. Pounds, *Subsidisation of Urban Public Transport*, Transport and Road Research Laboratory Supplementary Report No. 541 (1980), p. 17.

26   LTE, *Annual Report and Accounts*, 1977, p. 4.

27   Select Committee on Nationalised Industries (sub-committee A), 3 February 1977, answer to Q773.

28   London Transport Board, *Annual Report and Accounts*, 1964–9; London Transport Executive, *Annual Report and Accounts*, 1970–79.

29   EC, September 1968, appendix S35; and EC, March 1970, appendix M24.

30   London Transport Board, *Annual Report and Accounts*, 1965, p. 28.

31   EC, December 1971, appendix D7.

32   EC, August 1973, appendix A55, A57 and A58, reporting meetings of the Railway Negotiating Committee.

33 NUR file MLT/209.
34 *The Times*, 2 June 1973.
35 LTE, *Annual Report and Accounts*, 1973, p. 25.
36 NUR file MLT/209.
37 Information kindly provided by Len Bound, NUR organiser in charge of LT matters in the mid-1970s, in an interview on 12 October 1979.
38 EC, March 1974, appendix M3.
39 EC 1715, August 1973.
40 J. W. Smith, *Labour Supply and Employment Duration in London Transport*, London School of Economics, Greater London Papers No. 15, 1976, table 8, p. 3.
41 EC 3 and appendix M3, March 1974.
42 EC 988, 1 July 1974.
43 EC 1014, 8 August 1974.
44 EC, December 1974, appendix D27.
45 EC 1014, 8 August 1974 and appendix A87; NUR LTE Branches circular M9559/19110, 9 August 1974.
46 *The Times*, 13 December 1976.
47 LTE, *Annual Report and Accounts*, 1978, p. 27.
48 LTE, *Annual Report and Accounts*, 1979.
49 EC 707, 18 May 1979.
50 EC 834, 1 June 1979.
51 EC 928, 15 June 1979.
52 NUR LTE Branch circular M11193/21697, 22 June 1979.
53 NUR case submitted to the LTE, 17 June 1979; EC 467, March 1977.
54 NUR LTE Branch circular M11193/21697, 22 June 1979; information kindly provided by Messrs B. Kew and S. Ellis, NUR Head-Office staff.
55 *Railway Review*, 20 October 1961.
56 London Transport Board, *Annual Report and Accounts*, 1964, p. 1; and 1965, p. 1.
57 EC 1117, 4 May 1964, appendix J12.
58 EC 250, March 1968, appendix M22.
59 EC, September 1968, appendix S37.
60 EC, December 1968, appendix D7.
61 EC, December 1969, appendix D39.
62 EC, 7 March 1971.
63 EC 328, March 1971.
64 London Transport, *NUR News*, 2 July 1972.
65 EC, December 1968, appendix D38.
66 EC, December 1977, appendix D43.
67 EC 2015, 11 November 1977.
68 NUR LTE Branches circular M11236/21790, 13 September 1979.
69 Report of open meeting of North London District Council, *Railway Review*, 1 June 1973.

CHAPTER 9

1 EC 938, 28 December 1928.
2 NCOI Minutes of the 143rd meeting, 13 December 1965.
3 D. L. Munby and A. H. Watson, *Inland Transport Statistics: Great Britain, 1900–1970* (Oxford: Clarendon Press, 1978), table 86, p. 306;

HMSO, *Transport Statistics Great Britain 1968–1978* (1978), table 60, p. 79.
4 British Road Federation, *Basic Road Statistics*, 1971 and 1979; HMSO, *Transport Statistics: Great Britain, 1968–1978*, table 59c, p. 77.
5 HMSO, *Transport Statistics: Great Britain, 1968–1978*, table 68, p. 86.
6 ACAS Report No. 16, *Industrial Relations in the Coaching Industry* (1978), p. 37.
7 J. Hemingway, *Conflict and Democracy* (Oxford: Clarendon Press, 1978), p. 92.
8 This account of the Bridgend dispute is based on an interview kindly given by Russell Tuck, Senior Assistant General Secretary, NUR, on Hemingway's *Conflict and Democracy* and on NUR EC minutes.
9 EC, September 1968, appendix S23.
10 Letter from Allan Kemp, 1 May 1978.
11 National Board for Prices and Incomes Report No. 50, *Productivity Agreements in the Bus Industry* (Cmnd 3498) (1967).
12 NUR, *General Secretary's Report to the AGM* (1970), p. 29.
13 EC 1494, 14 May 1967.
14 ACAS, *Industrial Relations in the Coaching Industry*, table 3, p. 141.
15 Interview, 14 December 1978.
16 EC, September 1960, appendix S5, p. A41.
17 Letter from Allan Kemp, 6 June 1979.
18 NBC Annual report, 1978, p. 14.
19 ACAS, *Industrial Relations in the Coaching Industry*, p. 58, and appendix 2, tables 8 and 9.
20 EC, March 1974, appendix M19.
21 *NUR News*, Road transport, no. 39, March 1979.
22 NCOI Minutes of meeting, held 14 December 1964.
23 EC, March 1966, appendix M25.
24 EC, August 1970, appendix S42.
25 EC, December 1974, appendix D47.
26 R. J. Irving, *The North Eastern Railway Company, 1870–1914* (Leicester: Leicester University Press, 1976), pp. 169–71.
27 EC, March 1914, p. 179; and special EC meetings, 22 April and 6 July 1914.
28 HMSO, *Transport Statistics: Great Britain, 1968–1978* (1979), table 171, p. 166; BTD Annual report and accounts.
29 British Transport Docks Board (BTD), *Report and Accounts*, 1974, p. 14.
30 EC 3135, December 1968; and EC 585, March 1969.
31 EC 3535, December 1967.
32 EC 2841 and 2842, December 1967.
33 EC 798, March 1968.
34 NUR, *General Secretary's Report to the AGM*, 1969, pp. 33–4.
35 EC 1759, December 1978 and appendix D23.
36 Information kindly provided by Ron Thompson, NUR EC member, representing dock workers in an interview on 12 June 1980.
37 *NUR News*, BT Docks Board, no. 13, May 1978.
38 NUR Dock branches circular M5623/13730, 1 October 1963.
39 Interview, 12 June 1980.
40 BTD Report and accounts, 1965, p. 4.
41 NUR, *General Secretary's Report to the AGM*, 1968, p. 25.
42 EC, June 1970, appendix J22.

43 EC, March 1974, appendix M1.
44 *NUR News*, BTD no. 4, August, 1977.
45 Information kindly supplied by Mr A. Douglas, BTD, in letters dated 10 and 11 July 1980; also information kindly supplied by E. Laws, NUR head-office staff.
46 NUR file 0/4/13 from which the information which follows is also obtained.
47 EC 790, August 1976.
48 EC 823, August 1976.
49 EC 3415, December 1961.
50 'Slave girls of the refreshment rooms', *Railway Review*, 15 June 1962.
51 Statistics taken from British Transport Commission, *Annual Report and Accounts*, 1961; British Railways Board, *Annual Report and Accounts*, 1963–79; and a statement kindly supplied by Alan Craig, NUR head-office staff.
52 EC, September 1970, appendix S49.
53 EC, March 1963, appendix M46.
54 EC, September 1963, appendix S54.
55 EC, September 1964, appendix 527.
56 NUR, *General Secretary's Report to the AGM*, 1965, p. 22.
57 NUR, *General Secretary's Report to the AGM*, 1971, p. 31.
58 NUR, *General Secretary's Report to the AGM*, 1966, p. 23.
59 EC, August 1971, appendix A33.
60 Information kindly provided by Jack Hyland in an interview on 14 January 1980.
61 AGM, Blackpool, July, 1959, resolution 96D.
62 *Railway Review*, 16 October 1959.
63 EC, 2842, 16 October 1959.
64 NUR Branch circular, M4405/11998, 28 October 1959.
65 NUR Branch circular, MM4414/12004, 2 November 1959; EC 2848, 2 November 1959.
66 NUR Branch circular, M4418/12009, 6 November 1959.
67 EC, December 1970, appendix D37.
68 EC, March 1970, p. 300.
69 *General Secretary's Report to the AGM*, 1972, p. 31.
70 *Labour Research*, December, 1973, p. 263.
71 Interview with John Rennie, 23 January 1980.
72 NUR Branch circular MS2/H/3195, 21 September 1976.
73 L. Dronfield and P. Soto, *Hardship Hotel* (London: Counter Information Services, 1980), p. 31.

CHAPTER 10

1 F. McKenna, *The Railway Workers, 1940–1970* (London: Faber, 1980), p. 250.
2 James Greenwood, article in *Daily Telegraph*, 19 December 1971.
3 ASRS AGM, 2 October 1894, item 42, p. 5.
4 ASRS, *General Secretary's Report to the AGM*, 1912, p. 25.
5 NUR AGM, Swansea, 15 June 1914, item 10.
6 For a fuller examination of the events of 1919–21, see P. S. Bagwell, *The Railwaymen*, Vol. 1 (1963), pp. 408–12.
7 NUR AGM, Morecambe, July 1946, item 17.
8 NUR AGM, Ayr, July 1946, verbatim report, debate on item 24.

9 NUR AGM, Wallasey, July 1948, item 212.
10 *Notes of statement by Mr A. Barnes, MP, Minister of Transport, to deputation from union regarding AGM resolution on nationalised transport, 28 September 1948*, NUR file GS/610/2.
11 Labour Party, Report of 47th Annual Conference, May 1948, p. 167.
12 NUR AGM, Brighton, July 1949, item 16.
13 NUR AGM, Morecambe, July 1950, item 231.
14 NUR AGM, Scarborough, July 1952, item 197.
15 The expression was Sidney Greene's; AGM Stockport, 5 July 1965; verbatim report, debate on item 13.
16 BTC, *Annual Report*, 1948.
17 NUR file GS/610/10, Workers' control in the transport industry.
18 NUR AGM, Aberdeen, 6 July 1967, verbatim report, debate on item 28.
19 NUR Branch circular 16557, 22 January 1970; NUR AGM, Plymouth, 15 July 1971, verbatim report, debate on item 84, speech of Sidney Weighell.
20 The account which follows is based on E. L. Hilgendorf and B. L. Irving, *Worker Participation in Management: a study of the attitudes of British Railways' employees* (London: Tavistock Institute of Human Relations, 1970).
21 EC 1197, August 1971.
22 J. Elliott, *Conflict or Co-operation? The growth of Industrial Democracy* (London: Kegan Page, 1978), pp. 135–6 and 224–5.
23 G. Radice, *The Industrial Democrats* (London. Allen & Unwin, 1978), provides essential background reading.
24 NUR AGM, Paignton, 19 July 1976, verbatim report, debate on item 19.
25 NUR AGM, Llandudno, 11 July 1978, verbatim report, debate on item 24(a).
26 Typed statement, 'General management view of industrial relations in BR' (1979), supplied by Mr R. H. Wilcox of BRB.
27 EC 98, 26 January 1976.
28 Typed statement, British Rail, 'Worker participation', 1979, supplied by Mr R. H. Wilcox of BRB.
29 NUR AGM, Llandudno, 11 July 1978, verbatim report, debate on item 24(a).
30 P. W. Kingsford, *Victorian Railwaymen* (London: Frank Cass, 1970), pp. 148–69 and appendix 1: 'Railway Companies Friendly Societies in 1871.
31 EC, March 1949, appendix G and 1142, May 1949.
32 EC 2236, September 1948; and EC 3166, December 1949.
33 EC, March 1950, appendix M36.
34 TUC, September 1950, pp. 238–40.
35 EC 133, March 1951.
36 NUR AGM, Scarborough, July 1952, p. 44.
37 NUR SGM, London 13–14 October 1953, verbatim report, BTC (Male Wages Grades) Pension Scheme; rules updated, April 1976, BR 6908. A full statement of the pension scheme is also to be found in EC, March 1953, appendix M10.
38 EC 176, March 1958.
39 *Railway Review*, 27 January 1961.
40 *Railway Review*, 16 June 1961.

41 NUR AGM, 12 July 1960, verbatim report, debate on item 90(a), p. 90.
42 NUR AGM, 9 July 1962, verbatim report, item 87 (agreed unanimously without debate), p. 87.
43 EC 1143, May 1963; EC 426, March 1964; EC 1195, May 1964; and EC 3226, December 1964.
44 NUR AGM, Paignton, 14 July 1964, verbatim report, debate on composite resolution 78–82(b).
45 EC 334, March 1965.
46 EC 1566, June; and EC 2751, September 1965.
47 EC 1580, June 1966 and appendix J18; *General Secretary's Report to the AGM*, June 1967, p. 22.
48 EC 621, March 1970 and appendix M33.
49 *General Secretary's Report to the AGM*, 1971, p. 30.
50 NUR AGM, Llandudno, 11 July 1969, verbatim report, debate on item 79(a) and (b).
51 EC, March 1970, appendix M23.
52 EC, August 1974, appendix A16; and EC 955, 15 May 1974.
53 NUR, *Conditions of Service*, separately issued for LT, BTH, BTDB and NFC.
54 *Financial Times*, 8 June 1976.
55 NUR AGM, Plymouth, 13 July 1971, verbatim report, debate on item 74.
56 ibid., debate on item 75.
57 EC, August 1972, p. 193.
58 Cmnd 7161 (1947).
59 RSJC minute G103; RSNC minute 445.
60 RE letter, dated 20 March 1950.
61 NUR, *The Sick Pay Scheme* (1956).
62 NUR, *Conditions of Service of BRB Salaried Staff; Conditions of Service of Conciliation Staff, 1967*.
63 NUR, *Conciliation Staff Conditions of Service*, 1979, pp. 126–32.
64 NUR AGM, Paignton, 26 June 1979, verbatim report, debate on item 39.
65 NUR, *Rates of Pay and Conditions of Service of Salaried and Conciliation Staff*, 1952 edn, pp. 313, 266.
66 ibid, July 1962 edn, p. 200.
67 RSJC G103, 16 February 1966.
68 RSNC minute 559, 26 March 1974.
69 Pay and Efficiency stage II Agreement, 22 August 1969.
70 EC, August 1979, appendix A9.
71 NUR AGM, Inverness, 8 July 1970, verbatim report, debate on item 77.

CHAPTER 11

1 P. S. Bagwell, *The Railwaymen*, Vol. 1 (London: Allen & Unwin, 1963), pp. 325–35.
2 AGM, St Peter Port, 2 July 1980, verbatim report, debate on item 227, speech of Sidney Weighell.
3 Bagwell, *The Railwaymen*, Vol. 1, op. cit., pp. 362–4.
4 NUR EC, August 1971, p. 466.
5 *Financial Times*, 18 May 1967.

6   EC 3733, December 1951.

7   EC 1049, March 1952.

8   EC 3756, December 1964.

9   AGM, Plymouth, 14 July 1966, verbatim report, debate on item 141.

10   *General Secretary's Report to the AGM*, June 1967, p. 9.

11   AGM, Llandudno, 18 July 1969, verbatim report, debate on item 173.

12   EC 1507, 19 August 1969; EC 3163, December 1969 and file 0/5/1.

13   AGM, Plymouth, 13 July 1971, verbatim report, debate on item 76.

14   EC 2222, August 1971; EC 3338, December 1971; EC 998, March 1972; and EC 2433, August 1972.

15   AGM, Scarborough, 21 July 1972, verbatim report, debate on item 161.

16   EC 2418, August 1972.

17   EC 3636, 11 October 1972.

18   EC 2433, December 1972.

19   Information kindly supplied by Mike Evans, research department, NUR, and by head office of ASLEF, 9 Arkwright Road, London, NW3; see also B. Murphy and A. Field, *ASLEF, 1880–1980* (London: ASLEF, 1980), p. 58.

20   EC 7, 8 January 1974.

21   EC 2099, August 1974.

22   EC 147, 23 January 1976.

23   EC 639, 12 March 1976.

24   EC 2499, December 1976.

25   For the full terms of the Recommendations, see *TUC Annual Report, 1939*, pp. 103–11.

26   EC, December 1952, appendix D2.

27   EC, March 1977, appendix M5.

28   EC 138, March 1977.

29   EC, March 1978, appendix M22; and August 1978, appendix A68.

30   Head-office note appended to a memorandum for a meeting of London Transport's Railway Negotiating Committee, 22 September 1978.

31   This, and the following, information is contained in NUR file 0/6/3A.

32   Bagwell, Vol. 1, op. cit., p. 310.

33   B. Murphy and A. Field, *ASLEF, 1880–1980* (1980), p. 25; D. L. Munby and A. H. Watson, *Inland Transport Statistics: Great Britain, 1900–1970* (Oxford: Clarendon Press, 1978), p. 46.

34   *The Railwaymen*, Vol. 1, op. cit., p. 349.

35   AGM, St Peter Port, 2 July 1980, verbatim report, debate on item 227.

36   Letter and the replies to the questionnaire in NUR box files, labelled 'ASLEF Strike Questionnaire'.

37   AGM, St Peter Port, 2 July 1980, verbatim report, debate on item 227.

38   *TUC Report, 1957*, p. 336.

39   *Select Committee on Nationalised Industries, Sub-Committee A*, 27 July 1976, Q300.

40   Notes for a meeting between NUR and TSSA, 29 March 1961, at Walkden House.

41   *General Secretary's Report to the AGM*, June 1966, p. 10.

42   *TUC Report*, 1942, pp. 161–8.

43   *TUC Report*, 1957, pp. 331–8.

44   *TUC Report*, 1945, pp. 234–5.

45   *TUC Report*, 1962, pp. 294–9.

46   *TUC Report*, 1963, p. 124.

47   EC 2633, 20 September 1963.

48 EC 890, March 1964.
49 NUR file 0/6/3A.
50 EC 1935, 1 November 1979.
51 AGM, St Peter Port, 2 July 1980, verbatim report, debate on item 227.
52 For a fuller account of the origins of the URS, see Bagwell, *The Railwaymen*, Vol. 1, op. cit., pp. 439–40.
53 NUR files 0/4/9 0/4/10.
54 Leaflet contained in NUR box file, 'Propaganda literature, other unions', this file is now housed at the Modern Records Centre, University of Warwick.
55 NUR Branch circular M7490/16268, 10 July 1968.
56 Box file, 'Propaganda literature'.
57 NUR printed leaflet for signalmen, December 1972.
58 *Daily Telegraph*, 3 February 1972.
59 *Signalmen*, eight-page pamphlet, in NUR file 4/1/10.
60 NUR file 0/4/10, 'Organisation of signalmen'.

CHAPTER 12

1 Figures of General Fund and Political Fund members taken from NUR's annual *Statement of Membership*.
2 EC 2314, December 1971; AGM, Scarborough, 11 July 1972, verbatim report, debate on item 28.
3 EC 280, March 1976; AGM, Paignton, 20 July 1976, verbatim report, debate on item 33(a).
4 AGM, Paignton, 13 July 1976, verbatim report, debate on item 10, speech of Sidney Weighell.
5 EC 1048, 8 June 1976; AGM, Paignton, 13 July 1976, verbatim report, debate on item 33(b).
6 EC 863, 6 May 1975; AGM, St Helier, 15 July 1975, verbatim report, debate on item 37.
7 EC 2107, December 1975.
8 Interview with Ron Lewis, MP, 16 November 1978.
9 AGM, Paignton, 13 July 1976, verbatim report, debate on item 10.
10 Interview, 23 October 1979.
11 Interview, 26 September 1979.
12 Political Liaison Officer's Report, 1976–7.
13 Interview with Keith Hill, 15 March 1979.
14 Letter from Peter Snape, MP, to Sidney Weighell, 7 December 1977.
15 Report of meeting with Secretary of State for Transport, 22 April 1977, Political Liaison Officer's file.
16 Peter Snape. MP, report to the AGM, July 1980, printed in *Transport Review*. 18 July 1980; interview with Keith Hill, 22 August 1980.
17 *Financial Times*. 9 December 1978; Keith Hill, interview, 22 August 1980.
18 Report of the 104th TUC, Brighton. 1972. p. 529.
19 *Railway Review*, 13 October 1972.
20 EC 2474. 10 October 1972.
21 *Railway Review*, 20 October 1972.
22 Reports of meetings in *Railway Review*. various dates 19 January–23 March 1973.
23 Interview with Mike Evans, principal administrative officer in charge

of research group, Unity House, 29 August 1980.

24 AGM, Paignton, 25 June 1979, verbatim report, debate on item 11.
25 AGM, Margate, 4 July 1962, verbatim report, debate on item 157.
26 AGM, Aberdeen, 5 July 1967, verbatim report, debate on item 17.
27 AGM, Inverness, 8 July 1970, verbatim report, debate on item 12.
28 AGM, Plymouth, 14 July 1971, verbatim report, debate on item 22.
29 AGM, Scarborough, 10 July 1972, verbatim report, debate on item 20.
30 AGM, Exeter, 9 July 1973, verbatim report, debate on item 23.
31 D. Coates, *Labour in Power* (London: Longman, 1980), p. 231.
32 EC 2541, 4 December 1972.
33 *Railway Review*, 18 April 1975.
34 EC 822 and 823, 10 April 1975.
35 AGM, St Helier, 15 July 1975, verbatim report, debate on item 25.
36 AGM, Llandudno, 11 July 1978, verbatim report, debate on item 19.
37 AGM, Paignton, 26 June 1979, verbatim report, debate on item 16.
38 AGM, Torquay, 5 July 1960, verbatim report, debate on item 165.
39 AGM, Scarborough, 4 July 1963, verbatim report, debate on item 24;
   AGM, Paignton, 8 July 1964, verbatim report, debate on items 7,
   8 and 9.
40 AGM, Southport, 5 July 1965, verbatim report, debate on item 8.
41 AGM, Plymouth, 4 July 1966, verbatim report, debate on item 7.
42 AGM, Aberdeen, 5 July 1967, verbatim report, debate on item 10;
   AGM, Penzance, 8 July 1968, verbatim report on item 7.
43 AGM, Llandudno, 8 July 1969, verbatim report, debate on item 7;
   AGM, Inverness, 6 July 1970, verbatim report, debate on item 24.
44 AGM, Plymouth, 8 July 1974, verbatim report, debate on item 10.
45 AGM, St Helier, 14 July 1975, verbatim report, debate on item 7.
46 AGM, Paignton, 26 June 1979, verbatim report, debate on item 13.
47 AGM, St Peter Port, 30 June 1980, verbatim report, debate on item 8.

BIBLIOGRAPHY

STATUTES

Railways Act 1921, 11 & 12 Geo. V, c. 58.
Transport Act 1947, 10 & 11 Geo. VI, c. 49.
Transport Act 1953, 1 & 2 Eliz. II, c. 13.
Transport Act 1962, 10 & 11 Eliz. II, c. 46.
Transport Act 1968, 16 & 17 Eliz. II, c. 73.
Railways Act 1974, 22 & 23 Eliz. II, c. 48.
Transport Act 1978, 26 & 27 Eliz. II, c. 55.
Transport Act 1980, 28 & 29 Eliz. II, c. 34.

ROYAL COMMISSION

Royal Commission on Trade Unions and Employers' Associations: Minutes of Evidence and Report, 1966–8.

SELECT COMMITTEES

Report from the Select Committee on Nationalised Industries: British Railways, House of Commons Paper, No. 254 (1960).
First Report of the Select Committee on Nationalised Industries: the Role of British Rail in Public Transport (London: HMSO, 1977).

OTHER OFFICIAL PUBLICATIONS

Railways Re-organisation Scheme (Cmnd 9191, 1954).
BTC, *Proposals for the Railways* (Cmnd 9880, 1956).
Re-appraisal of the Plan for the Modernisation and Re-equipment of British Railways (Cmnd 813, 1959).
Re-organisation of the Nationalised Transport Undertakings (Cmnd 1248, 1960).
Rural Bus Services, Report (London: HMSO, 1961).
Report of the Committee of Inquiry into the Major Ports of Great Britain (Cmnd 1824, 1962).
The Transport Needs of Great Britain in the next Twenty Years (London: HMSO, 1963).
Ministry of Transport, *Report of a Committee on Carriers Licensing* (London: HMSO, 1965).
National Ports Council, *Port Development: an Interim Plan* (London: HMSO, 1965).
Transport Policy (Cmnd 3057, 1966).
Railway Policy (Cmnd 3439, 1967).

The Transport of Freight (Cmnd 3470, 1967).
Public Transport and Traffic (Cmnd 3481, 1967).
Ministry of Transport, *British Railways: Network for Development* (London: HMSO, 1967).
Department of the Environment, *Passenger Transport in Great Britain, 1971* (London: HMSO, 1973).
Department of the Environment, *The Channel Tunnel* (Cmnd 5430, 1973).
BRB, *Review of Railway Policy: Summary of Report to Government* (1973).
Department of Transport, *Transport Policy: a Consultation Document* (London: HMSO, 1976).
Transport Policy (Cmnd 6836, 1977).
Department of Transport/BRB, *Review of Main Line Electrification* (London: HMSO, 1979).
ACAS, *Industrial Relations in the Coaching Industry*, Report No. 16 (London: ACAS, 1978).

STATISTICAL SOURCES

Munby, D. L. and Watson, A. H., *Inland Transport Statistics: Great Britain, 1900-1970* (Oxford: Clarendon Press, 1978).
Department of the Environment, *Transport Statistics: Great Britain, 1964-1974* (London: HMSO, 1976).
Department of the Environment, *Transport Statistics: Great Britain, 1968-1978* (London: HMSO, 1979).
Central Statistical Office, *Social Trends*, No. 10 (London: HMSO, 1980).
British Road Federation, *Basic Road Statistics* (London: British Road Federation, 1980).

SECONDARY AUTHORITIES

Aldcroft, D. H., *British Railways in Transition* (London: Macmillan, 1968).
Aldcroft, D. H., *British Transport since 1914* (Newton Abbot: David & Charles, 1975).
Allen, W. F., *British Railways after Beeching* (London: Ian Allan, 1966).
ASLEF, *Transport for the Nation* (London: ASLEF, 1976).
Bagwell, P. S., *The Railwaymen*, Vol. 1 (London: Allen & Unwin, 1963).
Bagwell, P. S., *The Transport Revolution* (London: Batsford, 1974).
Barker, T. C. and Robbins, M., *A History of London Transport, Vol. 2: The Twentieth Century to 1970* (London: Allen & Unwin, 1974).
Barker, T. C. and Savage, C. I., *An Economic History of Transport in Britain*, 3rd rev. edn (London: Hutchinson, 1974).

447

Bly, P. H., Webster, F. E. and Pounds, S., *Subsidisation of Urban Public Transport* (Crowthorne: Transport and Road Research Laboratory, 1980).

Bonavia, M. R., *The Organisation of British Railways* (London: Ian Allan, 1971).

Bonavia, M. R., *The Four Great Railways* (Newton Abbot: David & Charles, 1980).

Coates, D., *Labour in Power* (London: Longman, 1980).

Cottrell, R., *Technological Change and Labour in the Railroad Industry* (Lexington, Mass.: D. C. Heath, 1970).

Deakin, B. M. and Seward, T., *Productivity in Transport: a Study of Employment, Capital, Output, Productivity and Technical Change* (London: OUP, 1969).

Elliott, J., *Conflict or Co-operation: the growth of industrial democracy* (London: Kogan Page, 1978).

Foster, C. D., *The Transport Problem* (London: Blackie, 1963).

GLC, Transport Facts and Figures (London: GLC, 1973).

GLC, *London Rail Study*, 2 parts (London: GLC, 1974).

Grigg, A. E., *In Railway Service: the History of the Bletchley Branch of the NUR* (Bletchley: NUR Bletchley Branch, 1971).

Gwilliam, K. M., *Transport and Public Policy* (London: Allen & Unwin, 1964).

Hamer, M., *Wheels within Wheels* (London: Transport 2000, 1974).

Hamer, M., *A Load on Your Mind* (London: Transport 2000, 1978).

Hammond, R., *Modern Methods of Railway Operation* (London: Muller, 1968).

Hemmingway, J., *Conflict and Democracy* (Oxford: OUP, 1978).

Hilgendorf, E. L. and Irving, B. L., *Worker Participation in Management* (London: Tavistock Institute of Human Relations, 1970).

Hillman, M., Henderson, I. and Whalley, A., *Personal Mobility and Transport Policy* (London: PEP, 1973).

Hillman, M. and Whalley, A., *The Social Consequences of Rail Closures* (London: Policy Studies Institute, 1980).

Hughes, J. and Moore, R., *A Special Case* (Harmondsworth: Penguin, 1972).

ILO, Inland Transport Committee, *General Report* (Geneva: ILO, 1979).

ILO, Inland Transport Committee, *Vocational Training and Retraining of Railwaymen* (Geneva: ILO, 1979).

ILO, Inland Transport Committee, *Working Conditions in Rail Transport* (Geneva: ILO, 1979).

Independent Commission on Transport, *Changing Directions* (London: Hodder Paperbacks, 1974).

International Labour Organisation (ILO), Inland Transport Committee, *Social Consequences of Changing Methods and Techniques in Railway and Road Transport* (Geneva: ILO, 1961).

International Transport Workers' Federation (ITWF), *Manning of Locomotives and Trains* (London: ITWF, 1968).

ITWF, *We don't hate Technology, but* . . . (London: ITWF, 1977).

Kingsford, P. W., *Victorian Railwaymen* (London: Frank Cass, 1970).

McKenna, F., *A Glossary of Railwaymen's Talk* (Oxford: History Workshop, 1970).

McKenna, F., *The Railway Workers, 1840–1970* (London: Faber, 1980).

McLeod, C., *All Change* (London: Gower Press, 1970).

Martin, D. E. and Rubinstein, D., *Ideology and the Labour Movement* (London: Croom Helm, 1979).

Moran, M., *The Politics of Industrial Relations* (London: Macmillan, 1977).

Moseley, M. J., *Accessibility: the Rural Challenge* (London: Methuen, 1979).

Muller, W. D., *The Kept Men* (Hassocks: Harvester Press, 1977).

Murphy, B. and Field, A., *ASLEF, 1880–1980* (London: ASLEF, 1980).

NUR, *Planning Transport for You* (London: NUR, 1959).

NUR, *Railwaymen and the PIB* (London: NUR, 1966).

NUR, *A Policy for Transport* (London: NUR, 1976).

NUR, *Railway Electrification* (London: NUR, 1978).

Pearson, A. J., *Railways and the Nation* (London: Allen & Unwin, 1964).

Plowden, W., *The Motor Car and Politics, 1896–1970* (London: The Bodley Head, 1971).

Pollins, H., *British Railways: an Industrial History* (Newton Abbot: David & Charles, 1971).

Pryke, R., *Public Enterprise in Practice* (London: MacGibbon & Kee, 1971).

Pryke, R. and Dodgson, J., *The Rail Problem* (London: Martin Robertson, 1975).

Radice, G., *The Industrial Democrats* (London: Allen & Unwin, 1978).

Railway Invigoration Society, *Can Buses replace Trains?* (London: The Society, 1977).

Rolt, L. T. C., *Red for Danger* (London: Pan Books, 1960).

Rubinstein, D. and Speakman, C., *Leisure, Transport and the Countryside* (London: Fabian Society, 1969).

Smith, J. W., *Labour Supply and Employment Duration in London Transport*, London School of Economics, Greater London Paper No. 15, 1976.

Thomson, J. M., *Great Cities and their Traffic* (Harmondsworth: Penguin, 1977).

Wardroper, J., *Juggernaut* (London: Temple Smith, 1981).

Wedderburn, D., *Redundancy and the Railwaymen* (London: CUP, 1975).

Wilson, H., *The Labour Government, 1964–1970* (Harmondsworth: Penguin, 1974).

INDEX